INTRODUCTION TO THE
HISTORY OF RELIGIONS

INTRODUCTION TO THE
HISTORY OF RELIGIONS

BY

CRAWFORD HOWELL TOY

LATE PROFESSOR IN HARVARD UNIVERSITY

AMS PRESS
NEW YORK

Reprinted from the edition of 1913, Boston
First AMS EDITION published 1970
Manufactured in the United States of America

International Standard Book Number: 0-404-06498-1
Library of Congress Number: 76-126655

AMS PRESS INC.
NEW YORK, N. Y. 10003.

PREFACE

The object of this volume is to describe the principal customs and ideas that underlie all public religion; the details are selected from a large mass of material, which is increasing in bulk year by year. References to the higher religions are introduced for the purpose of illustrating lines of progress.

The analytic table of contents and the index are meant to supplement each other, the one giving the outline of the discussion, the other giving the more important particulars; the two together will facilitate the consultation of the book. In the selected list of works of reference the titles are arranged, as far as possible, in chronological order, so as to indicate in a general way the progress of investigation in the subjects mentioned.

C. H. T.

CAMBRIDGE, MASSACHUSETTS

CONTENTS

(The Arabic figures in the chapter summaries refer to paragraphs) .

ix

INTRODUCTION TO THE
HISTORY OF RELIGIONS

CHAPTER I

NATURE OF RELIGION

1. It appears probable that primitive men endowed with their own qualities every seemingly active object in the world. Experience forced them to take note of the relations of all objects to themselves and to one another. The knowledge of the sequences of phenomena, so far as the latter are not regarded as acting intentionally on him, constitutes man's science and philosophy; so far as they are held to act on him intentionally, the knowledge of them constitutes his theory of religion, and his sense of relation with them is his religious sentiment. Science and religion are coeval in man's history, and both are independently continuous and progressive. At first science is in the background because most objects, since they are believed to be alive and active, are naturally supposed by man to affect him purposely; it grows slowly, keeping pace with observation, and constantly abstracting phenomena from the domain of religion.[1] Religion is man's attitude toward the universe regarded as a social and ethical force; it is the sense of social solidarity with objects regarded as Powers, and the institution of social relations with them.

2. These Powers are thought of in general as mysterious, and as mightier than ordinary living men.[2] Ordinarily the feeling toward them on man's part is one of dependence — he is conscious of his

---

[1] That is, phenomena regarded as special acts of a superhuman Power; in the larger conception of religion all phenomena are at once natural and divine acts.

[2] In early religion they are usually ghosts, beasts, plants, or inanimate objects; rarely living men. Cf. Marett's remarks on pre-animistic religion in his *Threshold of Religion*.

inferiority. In some forms of philosophic thought the man regards himself as part of the one universal personal Power, or as part of the impersonal Whole, and his attitude toward the Power or the Whole is like that of a member of a composite political body toward the whole body; such a position is possible, however, only in a period of very advanced culture.

3. There being no records of initial humanity, it is hardly possible for us to know certainly what the earliest men's feeling was toward the animate and inanimate forces around them. Not improbably it was simply fear, the result of ignorance of their nature and absence of social relations with them. But in the human communities known to us, even the lowest, the relations with extrahuman beings appear to be in general of a mixed nature, sometimes friendly, sometimes unfriendly, but neither pure love nor pure hatred. So refined a feeling as love for a deity is not found among savages. As religion springs from the human demand for safety and happiness as the gift of the extrahuman Powers, hostility to them has been generally felt to be opposed to common sense.[1] Coercion there has been, as in magical procedures, or to bring a stubborn deity to terms; and occasional antagonism (for example, toward foreign gods); but not hatred proper as a dogma, except in the great ethical religions toward evil spirits, and in certain elaborate philosophic systems — as, for example, in the Gnostic conception of an imperfect Demiurge, or in the assumption of an original blind Chance or blind Will whose products and laws are regarded as not entitled to respect and obedience.

4. Instead of complete friendliness and unfriendliness in early tribes we find more commonly between the two a middle ground of self-regarding equipoise. The savage, the half-civilized man, and the peasant often deal with superhuman Powers in a purely selfish commercial spirit, courting or neglecting them as they seem likely

---

[1] Appeal to the Powers carries with it a certain sense of oneness with them, in which we may reasonably recognize the germ of the idea of union with God, which is the highest form of religion. This idea is not consciously held by the savage — it takes shape only in highly developed thought (Plato, the New Testament, Christian and other mysticism). If the impulse to religion be thought to be love of life (so Leuba, in the *Monist*, July, 1901), this is substantially desire for safety and happiness.

to be useful or not. The Central Australian (who may be credited with a dim sense of the superhuman) conducts his ceremonies, intended to insure a supply of food, apparently without the slightest emotion of any sort except the desire for gain.[1] The Italian peasant, who has vowed a wax candle to a saint in return for a favor to be shown, does not scruple to cheat the saint, after the latter has performed his part of the agreement, by offering tallow instead of wax, if he thinks he can do so with impunity. A recusant deity is sometimes neglected or even kicked by way of punishment or to force him to give the desired aid, and a god or a saint is valued and sought after in proportion to his supposed ability to be useful.

5. And this naïvely utilitarian point of view is by no means confined to the lowest forms of religion; in the Old Testament, for example, the appeal to Yahveh is generally based on his assumed power to bestow temporal blessings,[2] and this is a widespread attitude at the present day in religious communities, where salvation is commonly the end had in view by the worshiper. Love toward the deity simply on account of his personal moral character, without regard to the benefit (namely happiness) to be got from him, is found, if found at all, only in highly cultivated natures, and is rare in these. And, in truth, it is difficult if not impossible to justify religion except on the ground that it brings satisfaction (that is, happiness through and in perfection of nature) in the broadest and highest sense of that term, for otherwise it could not be regarded as a good thing.

6. On the other hand, fear of the superhuman Power is a common feeling, recognizable everywhere, at all times, and in all stages of social and intellectual development. By many it is regarded as the original and essential attitude of the religious mind.[3] To this view it is sometimes objected that religion could never have arisen from fear — that religion, as a cult, of necessity involves amicable relations between man and the deity. The objection, however, is based on an arbitrary and incorrect definition of religion; it is quite conceivable that man might cultivate the deity through fear of the

---

[1] Spencer and Gillen, *Native Tribes of Central Australia*, p. 170.

[2] Gen. xxviii, 20–22; Hos. ii; Ezek. xxxvi; and the Psalter passim.

[3] The classic expression of this view is given by Statius (*Th.* 3, 661): *primus in orbe deos fecit timor.* Cf. L. Marillier, in *International Monthly*, ii (1900), 362 ff.

latter's displeasure, and that an elaborate system of ceremonies and beliefs might arise from the desire to avert his anger. Such a conception — which is certainly not a lofty one — is not unnatural in the presence of a great Power whose dispositions and purposes are not well understood ; numerous examples of such an attitude might be cited from various religions, savage and civilized.

7. But, on historical grounds, as in the examples given above, it seems better to say that the earliest known attitude of man toward the superhuman Power is one of interested observation and fluid emotion — the feeling is determined by experience of phenomena. The man is pleased, displeased and afraid, suspicious or careless, according as he sees things to be helpful, harmful, doubtful, or resultless. In process of time, by observation and reflection, he succeeds in tabulating phenomena, and more or less definitely fixing his emotional attitude toward their assumed cause. A tradition is gradually established, and men are trained from infancy to welcome certain things, to fear others, and to accept certain others as meaningless ; from time to time strange things will appear, and these will be treated according to established principles or will remain mysterious. A germinal conception of natural law will arise from the observation of periodically occurring phenomena (such as the rising and setting of the sun, periodic rains, tides) and familiar facts of everyday life, as, for example, the habits of men and other animals. Everything outside this sphere will be ascribed to extrahuman agency — so sickness, death, and sometimes birth.[1]

8. The history of religion, which is a part of the history of thought, necessarily shows, as is observed above, a constant enlargement of the domain of natural law, and a consequent contraction of the direct action of the supernatural, though this does not always or generally lessen the conviction that the Supernatural Power, acting through natural law, controls all things. In this process, also, the conception of the attitude of the Supernatural Power is more or less definitely fixed ; a formulation of signs is accomplished, whereby it is known whether the deity, at particular moments, is pleased or

[1] For numerous examples of the belief in supernatural birth see E. S. Hartland, *Primitive Paternity*.

displeased, and whether a given deity is generally friendly or hostile. This method of determining the attitude of the deity continued into late stages of social life, and still exists even in professedly Christian communities.[1]

9. As the basis of the religious feeling we must suppose a sense and conception of an extrahuman Something, the cause of things not otherwise understood. All things were supposed to have life, and therefore to be loci of force; man's sense of social relation with this force constituted his religion. This sense was at first doubtless vague, ill-defined, or undefined, and in this form it is now found in certain tribes.[2] Gradually, as the processes of human life and of the external world become better known, and the vastness of the extrahuman control becomes evident, the Something is conceived of as great, then as indefinitely great, and finally, under the guidance of philosophic thought, as infinite. Thus the sense of the infinite may be said to be present in man's mind in germinal form at the beginning of truly human life, though it does not attain full shape, is not formulated, and is not effective, till the period of philosophic culture is reached.[3]

10. As far as our present knowledge goes, religion appears to be universal among men. There is no community of which we can say with certainty that it is without religion. There are some doubtful cases — for example, certain Australian tribes reported on by Spencer and Gillen, among whom it is difficult to discover any definite religious feeling: they offer no sacrifices or petitions, and appear to recognize no personal relations with any supernatural Power, beyond the belief that the spirits of the dead are active in their

---

[1] Modern civilized nations, after victories in war, commonly assume that God has thus pronounced in favor of the justice and right of their side, and sing Te Deums.

[2] This vagueness reappears in some systems of late philosophic speculation. On the question whether a sense of the divine exists anterior to conscious experience cf. Marett, *Threshold of Religion.*

[3] This is only a particular application of the general assumption that all human powers exist in germ in the lowest human forms. Discussions of the sense of the infinite are found in the *Gifford Lectures* of F. Max Müller and Tiele, and in Jastrow's *Study of Religion.* But early man thinks only of the particular objects with which he comes into contact; the later belief in an Infinite is a product of experience and reflection.

midst, causing sickness, death, and birth; nor is there any sign that they have lost earlier more definite beliefs.[1] Yet they have solemn ceremonies in which human blood plays a great part, and these may have reference to the intervention of supernatural beings, the term "supernatural" being taken as expressing any mysterious fact lying outside of the common course of things. A mysterious being called Twan is spoken of in initiation ceremonies, chiefly, it seems, to frighten or train the boys. Is there an indication that the tribal leaders have risen above the popular belief in such a being? Experience shows that it is difficult for civilized men to get at the religious ideas of savages; and it is possible, in spite of the careful investigations thus far made, that the last word on Central Australian beliefs has not yet been spoken. A similar reserve must be exercised in regard to reports of certain other tribes, whose ceremonies and institutions have appeared to some European and American observers to be without a religious element.[2]

11. There is at present no satisfactory historical evidence (whatever psychological ground there may be, or whatever deduction from the theory of evolution may seem necessary) of the existence of a subreligious stage of human life — a stage in which there is only a vague sense of some extrahuman power affecting man's interests, without definition of the power, and without attempt to enter into social relations with it.[3]

12. True, in the great mass of existing savage humanity we find social and religious customs so definite that we are forced to suppose a long preceding period of development. It has even been

[1] Cf. *Année sociologique*, iii (1898–1899), 205 ff.

[2] On the Fuegians cf. R. Fitzroy, in *Voyages of the Adventure and the Beagle*, ii (1831–1836), 179 ff.; on the African Pygmies, A. de Quatrefages, *The Pygmies* (Eng. tr., 1895), p. 124 ff.; W. Schmidt, *Pygmäenvölker*, p. 231 ff.; on Ceylon, T. H. Parker, *Ancient Ceylon*, iv; and on the Guaranis and Tapuyas (Botocudos) of Brazil, Waitz-Gerland, *Anthropologie*, iii, 418, and the references in Hastings, *Encyclopædia of Religion and Ethics*, ii, 837 f. The Fuegians are said to stand in awe of a "black man" who, they believe, lives in the forest and punishes bad actions. On the people of New Guinea see C. G. Seligmann, *The Melanesians of British New Guinea*, chaps. 16, 25, 48, 55.

[3] Such relations exist between men and the vague force variously called mana, manitu, wakonda; but the conception of this force is scientific rather than religious, though it is brought into connection with religious ideas and usages.

held that traces of religious conceptions are discernible in the first surviving records of "prehistoric" man, the contemporary of the cave bear — a period separated from the earliest clear historical records by many millenniums;[1] but, though the existence of such conceptions is by no means improbable, the alleged traces are too dim to build a theory on. The supposition of a continuous religious development from the earliest times is in accord with all that we know of human history, but, until more facts come to light, it will be prudent to reserve opinion as to the character of prehistoric religion.[2]

13. In general, religious development goes hand in hand with social organization. Those groups which, like the Rock Veddas of Ceylon (described by Sarasin) and the Yahgans of Tierra del Fuego (described by Hyades and Deniker), have scarcely any clan organization, have also scarcely any religion. In most of the lowest communities known to us we find well-constituted clans and tribes, with strict (and usually complicated) laws of relationship and marriage, and a somewhat developed form of religion.[8] Here again it is evident that we see in the world only the later stages of a long social process; the antecedent history of this process belongs to sociological science, and does not concern us here ;[4] its later history is inseparably connected with the development of religion.

[1] The evidence is summed up in G. d'Alviella's *Hibbert Lectures*. Cf. Brinton, *Religion of Primitive Peoples*, p. 30 ff.

[2] The question whether the religious sense exists in the lower animals is discussed by Darwin, *Descent of Man* (1871), p. 65 ff., 101 f., and others. The question is similar to that respecting conscience; in both cases there is in beasts a germ that appears never to grow beyond a certain point. On the genesis of the moral sense see (besides the works of Aristotle, Spinoza, Kant, and their successors) G. H. Palmer, *The Field of Ethics*; L. T. Hobhouse, *Morals in Evolution*; E. Westermarck, *Origin and Development of the Moral Ideas*. In regard to religious feeling we observe in certain animals, especially in the domesticated dog, an attitude of dependence and devotion toward the master as a superior Power that is similar to the attitude of man toward a deity, only with more affection and self-surrender. But in the animal, so far as we can judge, the intellectual and ethical conceptions do not come to their full rights — there is no idea of a Power possessing moral qualities and controlling all phenomena. The beast, therefore, is not religious in the proper sense of the term. But between the beast and the first man the difference may have been not great.

[8] The Central Australians, however, have an elaborate marriage law with the simplest political organization and the minimum of religion.

[4] Cf. L. M. Keasbey, in *International Monthly*, i (1900), 355 ff.; I. King, *The Development of Religion*, Introduction.

14. It is in this social process that science, philosophy, art, and ethics are constructed, and these, though distinct from the religious sentiment, always blend with it into a unity of life. Religion proper is simply an attitude toward a Power; the nature and activity of the Power and the mode of approaching it are constructed by man's observation and reflection. The analysis of the external world and of man's body and mind, the discovery of natural laws, the history of the internal and external careers of the human race — this is the affair of science and philosophy; rules of conduct, individual and communal, grow up through men's association with one another in society, their basis being certain primary instincts of self-assertion and sympathy; art is the product of the universal sense of beauty. All these lines of growth stand side by side and coalesce in unitary human life.

15. The external history of religion is the history of the process by which the religious sentiment has attached itself to the various conceptions formed by man's experience: ritual is the religious application of the code of social manners; the gods reflect human character; churches follow the methods of social organization; monotheism springs from the sense of the physical and moral unity of the world. Ideas concerning the nature and functions of the deity, the nature of the soul and of conscience, and future life are all products of scientific thought and might exist if religion did not exist, that is, if men did not recognize any practical relations between themselves and the deity. But, as a matter of fact, the religious sentiment, coexisting with these ideas, has always entered into alliance with them, creating nothing, but appropriating everything. Supernatural sanctions and emotional coloring are products of general experience and feeling. The intellectual and ethical content of religion varies with the intellectual and ethical culture of its adherents; we may speak properly of the philosophy and morals, not of a religion, but of the people who profess it.

16. The internal history of religion is the history of individual religious emotional experience (a phenomenon that hardly appears at all in the records of early life), and becomes especially interesting only in periods of advanced culture. It is true that this experience is based on the whole reflective life of man, whose beginnings go back to the earliest times. Aspirations and ideals, connected especially with man's religious life, spring from the long line of experiences with which men have always been struggling. The central fact of the higher religious experience is communion and union with the deity, and the roots of this conception are found in all the religious ideas and usages that have been formulated and practiced in human history. The study of such ideas and practices is thus important for the understanding of the later more refined spiritual life, as in turn this latter throws light on its crude predecessors. It is no disparagement to the higher forms of thought that they have grown from feeble beginnings, and it does not detract from the historical value of primitive life that we must decline to credit it with depth and refinement. Every phase and every stadium of human experience has its value, and the higher stages must be estimated by what they are in themselves. In the history of religion the outward and the inward elements have stood side by side in a unitary experience. But, though the deeper feeling is necessarily more or less closely connected with the external history, it is an independent fact requiring a separate treatment, and will be only occasionally referred to in the present volume.

CHAPTER II

THE SOUL

17. The doctrine of the soul is so interwoven with the history of religious beliefs that a brief statement of its early forms will be appropriate before we enter on the consideration of religious institutions and ideas.[1]

1. NATURE OF THE SOUL

18. The belief in an interior something in man, different from the body, appears to be practically universal in early human history; the ideas concerning the nature of the soul have changed from time to time, but no tribe of men has yet been found in which it is certain that there is no belief in its existence. The Central Australians, religiously one of the least-developed communities known, believe in ghosts, and a ghost presupposes some sort of substance different from the ordinary body. Of some tribes, as the Pygmies of Central Africa and the Fuegians, we have no exact information on this point. But in all cases in which there is information traces of a belief in a soul are found. We are not concerned here with philosophic views, like that of Buddhism and many modern psychologists, that do not admit the existence of the soul as a separate entity. The proofs of the universality of the belief in a soul are scattered through all books that deal with man's religious constitution and history.[2]

19. For the basis of a universal fact of human experience we naturally seek a universal or essential element of human thought. In this case we must assume a natural or instinctive conviction of the existence of an internal life or being — a consciousness (at first

---

1 *Cf.* Tylor, *Primitive Culture*, chap. xi f.

2 Beasts, plants, and what we call inanimate objects, also are held, in early stages of civilization, to have souls — a natural inference from the belief that these last are alive and that all things have a nature like that of man.

doubtless dim and vague) of something diverse and separate from the visible physical being, a sense of mental activity in thought, feeling, and will.

20. It is not surprising that we do not meet with the expression of such a consciousness among savages: partly, as is well known, they are like children, intellectually incapable of formulating their instinctive beliefs (and they have, consequently, no word to express such a formulation); partly, they are not disposed to speak frankly on subjects that they regard as sacred or mysterious. Attempts at formulation follow the lines of culture, and it is not till a comparatively late stage that they reach definite shape.

21. The interior being, whose existence was vaguely felt, was recognized by early man in many common experiences. Certain phenomena were observed that seemed to be universal accompaniments of life, and these, by a strictly scientific method of procedure, were referred to an inward living thing. It was hardly possible for early observers not to notice that when the breath ceased the life ceased; hence many peoples have regarded the breath as the life, and as the form of the interior being, and in many languages the words for 'soul' and 'spirit' are derived from the word for 'breath'.[1] The breath and therefore the soul of a dying man might be received (inhaled) by any person present; it was sometimes obligatory on a son to receive his father's last breath — he thereby acquired the father's qualities.[2]

22. Another accompaniment of the body that attracted the attention of early men was the shadow, for which the science of that day, unacquainted with optical laws, could account only on the supposition that it was a double of the man, another self, a something belonging in the same general category with the breath-soul, though usually distinguished from it.[3] The shadow was

---

[1] So Semitic *nafs* 'soul,' *ruḥ* 'spirit'; Sanskrit *ātman* 'soul,' 'self'; Greek *psyche*, *pneuma*; Latin *anima*, *spiritus*; possibly English *ghost* (properly *gost* 'spirit'); and so in many low tribes. See Tylor, *Primitive Culture*, i, 432 f.; O. Schrader, in Hastings, *Encyclopædia of Religion and Ethics*, ii, 15.

[2] The expression ' to receive the last breath ' (*Æneid*, iv, 684 f.), used by us to represent the last pious duty paid to a dying man, was thus originally understood in a strictly literal sense.   [3] So the Delaware Indians (Brinton, *The Lenâpé*, p. 67).

regarded as a sort of independent objective being, which might be seized and destroyed, for example, by a crocodile, as the man passed along a river bank; yet, as it was the man, its destruction involved the man's death.[1] The soul, regarded as a shadow, could not cast a shadow. Similarly one's reflection in water was regarded as a double of him.[2]

23. Blood was known by observation in very early times to be intimately connected with life, acquired the mystery and sacredness that attached to life, and has played a great part in religious ceremonies.[3] As soul is life, a close relation between blood and soul appears in the thought of lower and higher peoples, though the relation is not always the same as that described above. The blood is sometimes said to be the soul,[4] sometimes the soul is supposed to be in the blood as it is in the hair or any other part of the body. Blood could not be regarded as the soul in the same sense in which the breath, for example, was the soul — if the breath departed the man's life departed, but one could lose much blood without injury to vital power. It is not to be expected that the relation between the two should be precisely defined in the early stages of society. If Homer at one time speaks of the soul passing away through a wound and at another time of the blood so passing (death being the result),[5] this variation must not be pressed into a statement of the exact identity of blood and soul. By the Californian Maidu the soul is spoken of as a ' heart ', apparently by reason of the connection of the heart with the blood and the life.[6] There is to be recognized, then, a vague identification of ' soul ' and ' blood '; but in

[1] Cf. the name ' shade ' (Greeks, Redmen, and others) for the denizens of the Underworld.

[2] Photographs are now looked on by some half-civilized peoples with suspicion and fear as separate personalities that may be operated on by magical methods. A similar feeling exists in regard to the name of a man or a god — it is held to be somehow identical with the person, and for this reason is often concealed from outsiders.

[3] Cf. Tylor, *Primitive Culture*, ii, 402; Frazer, *Golden Bough*, 1st ed., i, 178 f.; article " Blood " in Hastings, *Encyclopædia of Religion and Ethics*.

[4] So in the Old Testament, in the later ritual codes: Deut. xii, 23; Lev. xvii, 14; Gen. ix, 4; and so Ps. lxxii, 14; cf. Koran, xcvi, 2 (man created of blood).

[5] *Iliad*, xiv, 518; xvii, 86; cf. W. R. Smith, *Religion of the Semites*, 2d ed., p. 40 n. (Arabic expression: " Life flows on the spear-point ").

[6] R. B. Dixon, *The Northern Maidu*, p. 259.

common usage the two terms are somewhat differently employed — 'soul' is the vital entity, the man's personality, 'blood' is the representative of life, especially on its social side (kinsmen are of "one blood," but not of "one soul")[1] and in offerings to the deity. Early man seems, in fact, to have distinguished between life and soul.[2]

. **24.** As the soul was conceived of as an independent being, it was natural that it should be held to have a form like that of the external body — it could not be thought of otherwise.[3] This opinion was doubtless confirmed in the savage mind by such experiences as dreams, visions, hallucinations, and illusions, and by such phenomena as shadows and reflections. The dreamer believed that he had been far away during the night, hunting or fighting, and yet the testimony of his comrades convinced him that his body had not left its place; the logical conclusion was that his inner self had been wandering, and this self, as it seemed to him, had walked, eaten, hurled the spear, done all that the ordinary corporeal man would do. In dreams he saw and conversed with his friends or his enemies, all in corporeal form, yet all of them asleep in their several places; their souls also, he concluded, were wandering. Even in his waking hours, in the gloom of evening or on some wide gleaming plain, he saw, as he thought, shadowy shapes of persons who were dead or far away, and heard mysterious voices and other sounds, which he would naturally refer to the inner self of the absent living or the dead. Reproductions of himself and others appeared on land and in water. All such experiences would go to convince him that there were doubles of himself and of others, and that these were corporeal — only dim, ethereal, with powers greater than those of the ordinary external body.

25. While the soul of the living man was most commonly conceived of as a sublimated replica of the ordinary body, it was also

---

[1] So friendly (fraternal) compacts between individuals are sealed by exchange of blood, whereby the parties to the covenant become one ; many examples are given in H. C. Trumbull's *Blood-Covenant*, 2d ed.

[2] In many languages (Semitic, Sanskrit, Greek, Latin, English, German, etc.) the word for 'soul' is used in the sense of 'person' or 'self.' But the conception of "life" was in early times broader than that of "person" or that of "soul."

[3] An incorporeal or immaterial soul has never been conceivable.

supposed in some cases to take the form of some animal — an opinion that may have arisen as regards any particular animal from its appearance at a time when the soul was supposed to be absent from the body,[1] and is to be referred ultimately to the belief in the identity of nature of animals and man. The souls of the dead also were sometimes supposed to take the shape of animals, or to take up their abode in animals[2] or in trees (as in Egypt): such animals (tigers, for example) were commonly dangerous, and this theory of incarnation is an expression of the widely diffused belief in the dangerous character of the souls of the dead. In later, cultivated times the bird became a favorite symbol of the soul — perhaps from its swift and easy flight through the air.[3]

26. Savage science, though it generally identified the soul with the breath, and regarded it as a separate interior form, seems not to have attempted to define its precise locus, posture, and extension within the body — the early man was content to regard it as a vague homunculus. The whole body was looked on as the seat of life, and was sometimes eaten in order to acquire its qualities, especially the quality of courage.[4] Life was supposed to reside in the bones as the solid part of the body, and these were preserved

---

[1] For old-German examples see Saussaye, *Religion of the Teutons*, p. 297; for Guiana, E. F. im Thurn, in *Journal of the Anthropological Institute*, xi, 368; compare the belief in the hidden soul, spoken of below, and article "Animals" in Hastings, *Encyclopædia of Religion and Ethics*.

[2] So the bush-soul or beast-soul among the Ewe-speaking peoples of West Africa (A. B. Ellis, *The Ewe-speaking Peoples*, p. 103) and in Calabar (Kingsley, *West African Studies*). Spirits (Castrén, *Finnische Mythologie*, p. 186) and demons (as in witchcraft trials) sometimes take the form of beasts. For American Indian examples see Brinton, *Myths of the New World*, p. 294.

[3] See the Egyptian representations of the soul as bird (Ohnefalsch-Richter, *Kypros, the Bible and Homer*, pl. cvi, 2; cix, 4, etc.); Maspero, *Dawn of Civilization*, p. 183, compare p. 109. Other examples are given by H. Spencer, *Principles of Sociology*, i, 355 ff.; N. W. Thomas, in Hastings, *Encyclopædia of Religion and Ethics*, i, 488. On *siren* and *ker* as forms of the soul see Miss Harrison, *Prolegomena to the Study of Greek Religion*, pp. 139, 197–217. Cf. Hadrian's address to the soul:

> Animula vagula blandula
> Hospes comesque corporis
> Quae nunc abibis in loca
> Pallidula rigida nudula
> Nec ut soles dabis jocos?

[4] The body is spoken of as the person, for example, in *Iliad*, i, 4; Ps. xvi, 9.

as the basis of a future life.[1] But even in early stages of culture
we find a tendency to specialize — courage, for example, was assigned particularly to the head and the heart, which were accounted
the most desirable parts of a dead enemy.[2] These organs were
selected probably on account of their prominence — the heart also
because it was the receptacle of the blood. The soul was located
by the Indians of Guiana in the pupil of the eye.[3]

27. Gradually a more precise localization of qualities was made
by the Semites, Greeks, Romans, and other peoples. These, for
reasons not clearly known to us, assigned the principal emotional
faculties to the most prominent organs of the trunk of the body.
The Semites placed thought and courage in the heart and the liver,
anger in the liver (the bile), love and grief in the bowels, voluntary
power in the kidneys.[4] The Greeks and Romans were less definite: to the heart, the diaphragm, and the liver (the upper half of
the trunk) the Greeks assigned thought, courage, emotion;[5] the
Romans placed thought and courage in the heart, and the affections in the liver. Among these organs special prominence came
to be given to the heart and the liver as seats of mental faculties.[6]

28. It is not clear how early the brain was supposed to be connected with the mind. Alcmæon of Crotona (5th cent. B.C.), who,
according to Diogenes Laertius, wrote chiefly on medical subjects,
is credited with the view that the brain was the constructor of
thought.[7] Plato suggests that the brain may be the seat of perception and then of memory and reflection, and calls the head the
most divine part of man.[8] Cicero reports that some persons looked
on some part of the cerebrum as the chief seat of the mind.[9]

---

1 Hence various means of preserving the body by mummification, and the fear of
mutilation.

2 On the cult of skulls in the Torres Straits and Borneo see Haddon, *Head-
hunters*, chap. xxiv. 3 J. H. Bernan, *British Guiana*, p. 134.

4 See Old Testament passim, and lexicons of the various Semitic languages.

5 An elaborate account of the loci of qualities is given by Plato in the *Timæus*,
69 ff.

6 On the importance attached to the liver as the seat of life see Jastrow, *Aspects
of Religious Belief and Practice in Babylonia and Assyria*, p. 149 ff.

7 Diels, *Fragmente der Vorsokratiker*, 2d ed., i, 101 f., quoted in Hastings, *Encyclopædia of Religion and Ethics*, article " Brain and Mind."

8 *Phædo*, 96 B; *Timæus*, 44. 9 *Tusc. Disp.* i, 9, 19; cf. Plautus, *Aulul.* ii, 1, 30.

In the Semitic languages the first occurrence of a term for 'brain' is in the Arabic.[1] Some American tribes are said to regard the brain as the seat of the mind.[2] The scientific Greek view appears to have been connected with medical research, but the process by which it was reached has not been recorded. The Arabic conception of the brain was probably borrowed from the Greeks.

29. The soul as an independent personality was supposed to leave the body at times, and its departure entailed various consequences — in general the result was the withdrawal of the man's ordinary powers to a greater or less extent, according to the duration of the soul's absence. The consequences might be sleep, trance, swoon, coma, death; the precise nature of the effect was determined by the man's subsequent condition — he would wake from sleep, or return to his ordinary state from a trance, or come to himself from a swoon, or lie permanently motionless in death. When he seemed to be dead there was often doubt as to his real condition — the escaped soul might seek its old abode (as in the case of the vampire, for instance), and means were sometimes taken to prevent its return.[8]

30. The obvious difference in serious results between sleep and other cessations of the ordinary consciousness and activity led among some tribes to the supposition of a special dream-soul that could leave the body without injury to the man. It was believed by certain Greenlanders [4] that a man going on a journey might leave his soul behind. It was a not uncommon opinion that souls might be taken out for a while, with friendly intent, to guard them during a period of danger (so in Celebes when a family moves into a new house). In Greenland, according to Cranz, a damaged soul might be repaired. Or the soul might be removed with evil intent by magic art — the result would be sickness or swoon; it was then incumbent on the sufferer or his friends to discover the hostile magician and counteract his work by stronger magic, or force him

---

1 Arabic *dimāg* appears to mean 'marrow,' but how early it was employed for 'brain' is uncertain.
2 Waitz, *Anthropologie*, iii, 225 ; cf. Roger Williams, *Language of America*, p. 86.
3 *Journal of the American Oriental Society*, iv (the Karens).
4 Cranz, *Greenland* (Eng. tr.), i, 184.

to restore the soul.[1] On the other hand, the soul of a dead man might be so recalled that the man would live again, the usual agency being a god, a magician, or a prophet.

31. It has been and is a widespread opinion in low tribes that the life of a person is bound up with that of an animal or plant, or with the preservation of something closely connected with the person. This opinion springs from the conviction of the intimate vital relation between men and their surroundings. From the combination of these beliefs with the view referred to above [2] that a man's soul might dwell in a beast or a plant, the idea of the hidden soul, common in folk-lore, may have arisen [3] — the idea that one might conceal his soul in some unsuspected place and then would be free from fear of death so long as his soul remained undisturbed.[4] These folk-tales are products of the popular imagination based on materials such as those described above. From the early point of view there was no reason why the vital soul, an independent entity, should not lead a locally separate life.

2. ORIGIN OF THE SOUL

32. Theories of a special origination of the soul belong only to the more advanced cults. In early stages of culture the soul is taken as a natural part of the human constitution, and though it is regarded as in a sort an independent entity, the analysis of the man is not carried so far as to raise the question of separate beginnings of the two constituents of the personality, except as this is partially involved in the hypothesis of reincarnation. The child is born into the world equipped with all the capacities of man, and further investigation as to how these capacities originally came is not made.

33. It was, however, thought necessary to account for the appearance of man (a clan or tribe) on earth, and his creation was generally ascribed to a supernatural being. Every tribe has its

---

[1] Examples in Frazer, *Golden Bough*, chap. ii.   [2] § 25.

[3] For folk-tales of the hidden 'external' soul see Frazer, *Golden Bough*, 2d ed., iii, 389 ff.

[4] The coyote (in *Navaho Legends*, by W. Matthews, p. 91) kept his vital soul in the tip of his nose and in the end of his tail.

history of man's creation — the variety in the anthropogonic myths is endless, the diversities depending on the differences of general culture and of surroundings ; but the essential point is the same in all · some god or other supernatural Power fashioned human creatures of different sex, whether with well-considered aim or by caprice is not said.

34. The first pair is thus accounted for in a simple and generally satisfactory manner. But the fact of the perpetuation of the tribe or the race appears to have offered serious difficulties to the savage mind. Some tribes are reported to be ignorant of the natural cause of birth. Some Melanesian women believe that the origin or beginning of a child is a plant (coconut or other), and that the child will be the *nunu* (something like an echo) of that thing or of a dead person (this is not the transition of a soul — the child takes the place of the dead person). In Mota there is a similar belief.[1] The Central Australians, it is said, think that the birth of a child is due to the entrance of a spirit into the body of a woman[2] — every child is thus the reincarnation of some ancient person (an "ancestor"), and the particular person is identified by the sacred object (stone or tree, or other object) near which the woman is when she first becomes aware of the child within her ; every such object (and there are many of them near any village) represents some spirit whose name is known to the old men of the tribe, and this name is given the child.[3]

35. Similar theories of birth are found among the Eskimo[4] and the Khonds,[5] in Melanesia,[6] in West Africa,[7] and elsewhere.[8] Such

1 *Journal of the Anthropological Institute*, xviii, 310.
2 Spencer and Gillen, *Native Tribes of Central Australia*, p. 124. Andrew Lang (in *Anthropological Essays presented to E. B. Tylor*) holds that this Australian view comes not from ignorance but from the desire to assign a worthy origin to man in distinction from the lower animals. Some tribes in North Queensland think that the latter have not souls, and are born by sexual union, but the human soul, they say, can come only from a spiritual being. Decision on this question must await further information.
3 Spencer and Gillen, loc. cit.   4 *Journal of American Folklore*, xvii, 4.
5 Hopkins, *Religions of India*, p. 530 (the child is the returned soul of an ancestor).
6 Codrington, *Melanesians*, p. 154 (a spirit child enters a woman); cf. *Journal of the American Oriental Society*, viii, 297 (the Nusairi), and Lyde, in Curtiss, *Primitive Semitic Religion To-day*, p. 115 ; Hartland, *Primitive Paternity*, i, 50, and chap. 3 passim.
7 A. B. Ellis, *The Ewe-speaking Peoples*, p. 15 ; *The Tshi-speaking Peoples*, p. 18.
8 For the belief that the soul of the child comes from the shades see *Journal of American Folklore*, xiv, 83. Further, Tylor, *Primitive Culture*, chap. xii ; Lang, in article cited above ; Frazer, *Totemism and Exogamy*, ii. 96.

views thus appear to have been widely diffused, and are in fact a natural product of early biological science. They embody the earliest known form of the doctrine of reincarnation, which is so important in the Buddhistic dogma.[1] With it must be connected the fact that among many peoples (savage, half-civilized, and civilized) birth was intimately connected with supernatural beings, whence the origin of numerous usages : the precautions taken to guard the woman before delivery, the lustrations after the birth, the couvade, the dread of menstrual and seminal discharges, and further, customs relating to the arrival of boys and girls at the age of puberty.

36. At a later stage of culture the creation of the soul was distinguished from that of the body, and was generally regarded as a special act of the deity : the Hebrews conceived that the body was fashioned out of dust, and that the breath of life was breathed into it by God, so that man became a " living soul "[2]; Plato at one time[3] thought that the soul of the world was created by God, out of certain elements, before the body, and was made prior to it in origin and excellence so that it should be its ruler, and that afterwards he placed separate souls in the various separate bodies ; the immortal gods, says Cicero, have placed souls (*animos*) in human bodies, and the human soul has been plucked (*decerptus*) from the divine mind.[4]

37. In the early Christian centuries the question of how the soul came into the body was an intensely practical one — it was closely connected with the question of man's inherent sinfulness and his capacity for redemption. Tertullian's theory of the natural propagation of souls (traducianism), which involved the inheritance of a sinful nature, was succeeded on the one hand by the theory of preëxistence (adopted by Origen from Plato), and on the other hand by the view that every soul was an immediate creation of

---

[1] Possibly a survival of the theory is to be recognized in the custom, prevalent among some peoples, of naming a male child after his grandfather; examples are given in Gray, *Hebrew Proper Names*, p. 2 f. All such theories appear to rest on a dim conception of the vital solidarity of the tribe or clan — the vital force is held to be transmissible ; cf. the idea of *mana*, a force inherent in things.

[2] Gen. ii, 7 ; cf. Ezek. xxxvii, 10. [3] *Timaeus*, 34 f.

[4] *De Sen.* 21, 77 ; *Tusc. Disp.* v, 13, 38.

God (creationism, held by Jerome and others), these both assuming the natural goodness or untainted character of the soul at the birth of the human being.

38. The mysterious character of death, the final departure of the soul from the body, called forth in savage communities feelings of awe and dread. As death, in the savage view, was due to the intervention of a supernatural agency, the dead body and everything connected with it partook of the sacredness that attached to the supernatural.[1] Hence, probably, many of the customs relating to the treatment of corpses — taboos that survived into comparatively late times.[2] The Old Testament ritual term ' unclean ' is used of corpses and other things that it was unlawful to touch, things taboo, and in this sense is equivalent to ' sacred.'[3]

3. Polypsychism

39. In the preceding section only the general fact of the existence of the soul is considered. We find, however, a widespread belief among savage and half-civilized peoples that every human body is inhabited by several souls (two or more).[4] Thus, the Fijians, the Algonkins, and the Karens recognize two souls; the Malagasy, the Dahomi, and the Ashanti three; the Congoans three or four, the Chinese three, the Dakotas four, the Malays (of the peninsula) seven; and this list is not exhaustive.[5] To these various souls different procedures and functions are assigned.

1 The term ' sacred ' in early thought has no ethical significance; it involves only the idea that an object is imbued with some superhuman quality, and is therefore dangerous and not to be touched.

2 On modes of burial, see article " Funérailles " in La Grande Encyclopédie. Other considerations, however (hygienic, for example), may have had influence on the treatment of corpses.

3 In the Talmud the books of the Sacred Scriptures are said to " defile the hands," that is, they are taboo (Yadaim, Mishna, 3, 5).

4 The lower animals also are sometimes credited with more than one soul: so the bear among the Sioux (Charlevoix, Nouvelle France, vi, 28; Schoolcraft, Indian Tribes of the United States, iii, 229).

5 Williams, Fiji, i, 241; Tylor, Primitive Culture, i, 434, cf. Brinton, The Lenâpé, p. 69; Cross, in Journal of the American Oriental Society, iv, 310 (Karens); W. Ellis, Madagascar, i, 393; A. B. Ellis, The Ewe-speaking Peoples, p. 114, and The Tshi-speaking Peoples, p. 149 ff.; Kingsley, West African Studies, p. 200 ff.; Skeat, Malay Magic, p. 50.

40. In general, as to place and function during the man's life, the following classes of souls are distinguished: the vital soul, or the principle of life, whose departure leaves the man insensible or dead (Malagasy *aina*, Karen *kalah*, Ewe 'ghost-soul'); the dream-soul, which wanders while the man is asleep (probably a universal conception in early stages of culture); the shadow-soul, which accompanies him by day (also, probably, universal); the reflection-soul (similar to the preceding); the beast-soul, or bush-soul, incarnate in a beast (among the Congoans, the Ewe, the Tshi, the Khonds), with which may be compared the Egyptian view that revenant souls and Underworld shadows may assume the form of animals, and the Hindu metempsychosis. A particular responsible moral soul is also reported (among the Karens),[1] but it is doubtful whether this is native; and still more doubtful are the Karen ' reason ' (*tsö*) and the Khond beatified soul.[2]

41. In regard to procedure after the man's death, it is generally held in early stages of culture that one soul stays with the body, or at the tomb, or in the village, or becomes air, while another departs to the land of the dead (Fijians, Algonkins, and others), or is reborn (Khonds), and in some cases a soul is said to vanish.[8]

42. It is obvious that there was great flexibility and indefiniteness in early theories of the soul. The savage mind, feeling its way among its varied experiences, was disposed to imagine a separate interior substance to account for anything that seemed to be a separate and valuable manifestation of the man's personality. The number of souls varies with the number of phenomena that it was thought necessary to recognize as peculiar, and the lines of demarcation between different souls are not always strictly drawn. As to the manner of the souls' indwelling in the body, and as to their relations one to another, savages have nothing definite to say, or, at least, have said nothing. In general our information regarding savage psychical theories is meager ; it is not unlikely that with fuller acquaintance the details given above would have to be modified, though the general fact of polypsychism would doubtless remain.

---

[1] *Journal of the American Oriental Society*, iv, 310.
[2] Cf. Hopkins, *Religions of India*, p. 530.   [8] See below, § 46 ff.

43. In the higher ancient religions there are only more or less obscure indications of an earlier polypsychic system. The Egyptian distinction between soul (*bai*), shadow (*haibet*), and double (*ka*) appears to involve such a system; but the Egyptologists of the present day are not agreed as to the precise interpretation of these terms.[1] The Semitic terms *nafs* and *ruḥ* (commonly rendered 'soul' and 'spirit' respectively) are of similar origin, both meaning 'wind,' 'breath'; in the literature they are sometimes used in the same sense, sometimes differentiated. The 'soul' is the seat of life, appetite, feeling, thought—when it leaves the body the man swoons or dies; it alone is used as a synonym of personality (a 'soul' often means simply a 'person'). 'Spirit,' while it sometimes signifies the whole nature, is also employed (like English 'spirit') to express the tone of mind, especially courage, vigor. But, so far as the conception of an interior being is concerned, the two terms are substantially identical in the Semitic languages as known to us.[2] And though, as is noted above, 'spirit' is not used for the human personality, it alone is the term in Hebrew for a class of subordinate supernatural beings standing in close relations with the deity.[3] Greek literature seems to know only one personal soul (*psyche*, with which *pneuma* is often identical in meaning); a quality of nature (as in Semitic *ruḥ*) is sometimes expressed by *pneuma* ('spirit').[4] The *thymos* appears in Homer to be merely a function of the *psyche*,[5] in any case it does not represent a separate personality alongside of the *psyche*, and the same thing is true of the *daimon*. Similarly, in Latin, *animus* and

---

[1] See Maspero (1897), *Dawn of Civilization*, p. 108 f.; W. M. Müller in *Encyclopædia Biblica*, article "Egypt"; Petrie, *Religion and Conscience in Ancient Egypt*, pp. 30 ff., 48 ff.; Breasted, *History of Egypt*, p. 63 f.; Erman, *Handbook of Egyptian Religion*, pp. 86 f., 108; Wiedemann, *Religion of the Ancient Egyptians*, p. 234 ff.

[2] R. H. Charles in his *Eschatology, Hebrew, Jewish, and Christian*, p. 153, holds that the Hebrews made a distinction between soul and spirit (the former being "living" only when the latter is present), and that the recognition of this distinction is necessary for the understanding of the Old Testament conception of immortality. His discussion is valuable if not convincing.   [3] 1 Kings xxii, 21 f.

[4] For the New Testament usage see 1 Cor. vi, 17: 2 Cor. iv, 21: xii, 18; Luke ix, 53 (in some MSS.): Rev. xix, 10; John vi, 63. Cf. Grimm, *Greek-English Lexicon of the New Testament*, ed. J. H. Thayer, s. vv. *pneuma* and *psyche*.

[5] Cf. Rohde, *Psyche*, 3d ed., i, 45 n.; ii, 141, n. 2.

anima are substantially synonyms [1]— *animus* sometimes expressing tone of mind — and *spiritus* is equivalent to *ruḥ* and *pneuma* ; the individual *genius*, with its feminine representative the *juno*, is a complicated and obscure figure, but it cannot be regarded as a separate soul.[2]

44. This variety of terms in the more advanced religions may point to an early polypsychic conception. The tendency was, with the progress of culture, to modify or efface this sort of conception.[3] From a belief in a number of entities in the human interior being men passed to a recognition of different sides or aspects of the inward life, and finally to the distinct conception of the oneness of the soul. The movement toward psychic unity may be compared with the movement toward monotheism by the unification of the phenomena of the external world.

4. FUTURE OF THE SOUL

45. Savage philosophy, recognizing the dual nature of man, regarded death as due to the departure of the soul from the body. The cessation of breathing at death was matter of common observation, and the obvious inference was that the breath, the vital soul, had left the body. Reflection on this fact naturally led to the question, Whither has the soul gone ?

46. *Death of the soul.* The general belief has always been that the soul survived the man's death.[4] There are, however, exceptions; the continued existence of the soul was not an absolutely established article in the savage creed. According to the reports of travelers, it would seem that among some tribes there was disbelief or doubt on this point. A West African native expressed his belief

---

1 In philosophical thought the two are sometimes distinguished : the *anima* is the principle of life, and the *animus* of thinking mind (Lucretius, iii, 94–141).

2 A curious resemblance to the cult of the 'genius' is found in the Ewe (Dahomi) custom of consecrating a man's birthday to his "indwelling spirit" (A. B. Ellis, *The Ewe-speaking Peoples*, p. 105). Compare Horace's designation of the genius as 'naturae deus humanae' (*Ep.* ii, 2, 188), and Servius on Verg., *Georg.* i, 302.

3 So in Plato and Aristotle, and in Brahmanism.

4 The evidence for this belief is found in hundreds of books that record observations of savage ideas, and it is unnecessary to cite particular examples.

in the form of the general proposition, "The dead must die"; that is, apparently, the dead man must submit to the universal law to which the living are subject.[1] In another African community some held and others denied that a spirit could be killed, and one man was certain that spirits lived long, but was not certain whether they ever died.[2] Differences of opinion in regard to the fact of immortality are said to exist in Banks Islands.[3] The Eskimos are reported as holding that the soul may be destroyed, and then, however, repaired.[4]

47. It thus appears that even among low tribes there is speculation on the question of the continuance of existence after earthly death; there is admission of ignorance. We have, however, examples of a definite belief in annihilation. In some cases, when the theory of several souls is held,[5] one of these souls is supposed to become extinct at death: this is the case with the Malagasy *saina*, and the 'beast-soul' among the Ewe, Tshi, and Congoans; but such a soul represents only a part of the man, and its disappearance does not signify the extinction of the man's personality.

48. Complete extinction of the soul and the personality, in the case of certain persons, is found among the Fijians: in the long and difficult way to the Underworld, bachelors (as a rule), untattooed women, false boasters, and those men who failed to overcome in combat the " slayer of souls " (the god Sama) are killed and eaten.[6] Something like this is reported of the Hervey Islands,[7] New Zealand,[8] the Hawaiians,[9] and other tribes. Among the wild tribes of India, the Khonds and the Oraons, or Dhangars, hold to annihilation of the soul in certain cases.[10] Miss Kingsley reports a specially interesting view in Congo to the effect that souls die when the family dies out.[11] The ground of this sense of the solidarity of the living

---

1 Ellis, *The Ewe-speaking Peoples*, p. 108. Cf. Hinde, *The Last of the Masai*, p. 99.
2 D. Macdonald, *Africana*, i, 58 f.
3 *Journal of the Anthropological Institute*, x, 283; cf. Codrington, *Melanesians*, p. 277.   4 Rink, *Tales of the Eskimo*, p. 36.   5 See above, § 41.
6 Thomas Williams, *Fiji*, i, 244. Cf. W. Ellis, *Polynesian Researches*, i, 303.
7 Gill, *Myths and Songs from the South Pacific*, p. 160.
8 *Journal of the Anthropological Institute*, xix, 118 f.
9 Jarves, *History of the Sandwich Islands*, p. 42. Cf. Tylor, *Primitive Culture*, 2d ed., ii, 22 f., and Codrington, *The Melanesians*, p. 256 ff.
10 Hopkins, *Religions of India*, p. 530 f.   11 Kingsley, *Travels*, p. 444.

and the dead is not clear; the most obvious explanation is that the latter get their sustenance from the offerings of the former, and perhaps from their prayers; such prayers, according to W. Ellis,[1] are made in Polynesia. This belief appears also in some advanced peoples: so the Egyptians,[2] and apparently the Hindus.[8]

49. In these cases no explanation is offered of how a soul can die. Earthly death is the separation of the soul from the body, and by analogy the death of a soul should involve a disruption of constituents, but the savage imagination appears to have passed lightly over this point: when a soul is eaten, it is destroyed as the human body is destroyed when it is eaten; if it is drowned or clubbed, it dies as a man does under similar treatment. The soul is conceived of as an independent personality, with a corporeal form and mental powers; the psychic body, it would seem, is endowed with power of thought.[4]

50. This vagueness of conception enables us to understand how savage logic reaches the conclusion that the soul may be mortal: all the possibilities of the earthly person are transferred to it. In regard to the occasion of its death, it is sometimes represented as punishment for violation of tribal customs (as in Fiji), sometimes as the natural fate of inferior classes of persons (as among the Tongans, who are said to believe that only chiefs live after death),[5] sometimes as a simple destruction by human agency.

51. In the popular faith of the Semitic, Egyptian, Chinese, and Indo-European peoples there is no sign of an extinction of the personality after earthly death. The Babylonian dead all go to the vast and gloomy Underworld (Aralu), where their food is dust, and whence there is no return.[6] The Old-Hebrew 'soul' (*nephesh*) continues to exist in Sheol. True, its life is a colorless one, without achievement, without hope, and without religious worship; yet it

---

[1] *Polynesian Researches*, p. 218.

[2] Maspero, *Dawn of Civilization*, pp. 112, 185.

[3] *Taittiriya Brahmana*, 3, 11, 8, 5; *Çatapatha Brahmana*, 12, 9, 3, 12. Cf. Bloomfield, *Religion of the Veda*, p. 253.

[4] The same remark holds of later conceptions of the departed soul and of deities.

[5] Mariner, *Tonga*, pp. 328, 343. Gods also die, as in the Egyptian religious creed (Maspero, *Dawn of Civilization*, p. 111), in Greek myths and folk-beliefs (the grave of Zeus, etc.), and in the Norse myth of the combat of the gods with the giants.

[6] Jastrow, *Religion of Babylonia and Assyria*, chap. xxv.

has the marks of personality.[1] The fortunes of the spirit (*ruḥ*), when it denotes not merely a quality of character but an entity, are identical with those of the 'soul.'[2] In India, belief in life after death has always been held by the masses, and philosophic systems conceive of absorption, not of extinction proper. Zoroastrianism had, and has, a well-developed doctrine of immortality, and the Egyptian conception of the future was equally elaborate. In China the cult of ancestors does not admit belief in annihilation.[3] No theory of annihilation is found in connection with the Greek and Latin 'soul' and 'spirit' (*psyche, pneuma; animus, anima, spiritus*); the *thymos* is not a separate entity, but only an expression of the 'soul';[4] and the Greek *daimon* and the Latin *genius* are too vague to come into consideration in this connection.[5]

52. Omitting the purely philosophical views of the nature and destiny of the soul (absorption into the Supreme God, or the Universal Force, is to be distinguished from annihilation), and the belief of certain Christian sects in the future annihilation of the wicked (based probably on a misunderstanding of certain Biblical passages[6]), it may be said that the rôle of the theory of extinction of the soul in the general development of religion has been an insignificant one. Beginning among the lowest tribes as an expression of belief in the universality of mortality, it assumed a punitive character in the higher savage creed, and was gradually abandoned by the religions of civilized peoples.

53. The belief in the continued existence of the soul, on the other hand, has maintained itself from the earliest known times to

---

[1] 1 Sam. xxvii, 11 f.; Ezek. xxxii, 17 f.; Isa. xiv, 9 f. Eccl. iii, 19 f., ix, 5, 6, 10, which are sometimes cited in support of the opposite opinion, belong not to the Jewish popular belief, but to a late academic system which is colored by Greek skeptical philosophy. All other late Jewish books (Apocrypha, New Testament, Talmud) assume the continued existence of the soul in the other world.   [2] See above, § 43.

[3] Hopkins, *Religions of India*, pp. 130, 143 ff., 396; Rhys Davids, *Buddhism*, p. 111 ff.; Spiegel, *Eranische Alterthumskunde*, ii, 161 ff.; Wiedemann, *Egyptian Doctrine of Immortality*; De Groot, *Religion of the Chinese*, chap. iii.

[4] On the Homeric usage see Rohde, *Psyche*, as cited above, § 43.

[5] Several early Christian writers (Tatian, *Address to the Greeks*, 13; Justin, *Trypho*, cap. vi) held that souls are naturally mortal, but these views did not affect the general Christian position.

[6] Such as Ezek. xviii, 4. This view appears in *Clementine Homilies*, vii, 1.

the present. The inquiry into the grounds of this survival belongs to the history of the doctrine of immortality, and will not be pursued here in detail.[1] Doubtless it has been the increasing sense of the dignity of human nature, the conviction of the close connection of human life with the divine, and the demand for a compensation for the sufferings of the present (together with the instinctive desire for continued existence) that has led men to retain faith in the continued life of the soul. Modern beliefs in ghosts and in spiritualistic phenomena testify to the persistence of this article of faith.

54. *Abode of the surviving soul.*[2] Opinions regarding the destiny of the surviving soul have changed from time to time in accordance with topographical conditions and with changes in intellectual and moral culture. There is no place or thing on or under or above the ground that has not been regarded, at some time and by some communities, as its abode. The selection of the particular thing or place has been determined by local conditions — by what was supposed to be observation of facts, or by what was conceived to be appropriate. The obscurity of the subject has allowed free play to savage imagination. The paucity of data makes it impossible to give a complete statement of the views that have been held, or to arrange such as are known in accurate chronological order; but the principal opinions may be mentioned, following in a general way the order of refinement.[3]

55. 1. One of the earliest (and also one of the most persistent) views of the future of souls is that they are reborn or reincarnated as human beings, or as beasts or plants or inanimate things. It was not unnatural that, when a new human being came into the world, it should be regarded as the reproduction of a former human being, especially if the physiological conditions of birth were not understood;[4] the basis of the belief may have been the general similarity between human forms, and, in some cases, the special similarity between the infant or the adult and some deceased person.

---

[1] Cf. W. R. Alger, *Critical History of the Doctrine of a Future Life*; Harvard Ingersoll Lectures on " The Immortality of Man."

[2] Cf. H. Spencer, *Principles of Sociology*, i, chap. xv ; article " Blest, abode of the," in Hastings, *Encyclopædia of Religion and Ethics*.

[3] Cf. Tylor, *Primitive Culture*, chap. xii f.

[4] Cf. Hartland, *Primitive Paternity*, i, 254, and chap. iii.

An extension of the sphere of reincarnation would also naturally arise from the recognized kinship between man and other things, animate or inanimate.

56. Examples of these views are found in many parts of the world. Tylor[1] and Marillier[2] have collected instances of such beliefs among savage tribes in the Americas, Africa, Asia, and Oceania, as well as in higher religions (Brahmanism, Buddhism, Plato, Mani, the Jewish Kabbala, Swedenborg).[3] Other instances of belief in rebirth in human beings or in animals are found among the ancient Germans,[4] the people of Calabar,[5] the Torres Straits islanders,[6] the Central Australians,[7] and the Yorubans.[8]

57. There is an obvious relation between the belief in reincarnation in animal form and the worship of animals;[9] both rest on the assumption of substantial identity of nature between man and other beings, an assumption which seems to be universal in early stages of culture, and is not without support in modern philosophic thought.[10] Ancient belief included gods in this circle of kinship — a view that appears in Brahmanism and the later Buddhism.

58. The higher forms of the theory introduced a moral element into the process of reincarnation — the soul ascends or descends in the scale of being according to the moral character or illumination of its life on earth.[11] Thus it is given a practical bearing on every-day life — a result that is in accordance with all religious history,

[1] In *Primitive Culture*, chap. xii.   [2] In *La survivance de l'âme*, passim.

[3] See also the discussion of the subject in Alger, op. cit. (in § 53), p. 62 f. This work contains a bibliography of the future state (by Ezra Abbot) substantially complete up to the year 1862.   [4] Cf. Saussaye, *Religion of the Teutons*, p. 295 f.

[5] M. Kingsley, *Studies*, p. 122; *Travels*, p. 445.

[6] Haddon, *Head-hunters*, p. 179 ff.

[7] Spencer and Gillen, *Native Tribes of Central Australia*, Index, s.v. *Alcheringa*; id., *Northern Tribes of Central Australia*, p. 271.   [8] A. B. Ellis, *Yoruba*, p. 128.

[9] Cf. especially the Central Australian conception.

[10] It is involved in all monistic systems. It appears also to be silently made in the Old Testament: the lower animals, like man, are vivified by the "breath of God" (Ps. civ, 29, 30; cf. Gen. ii, 7; vii, 22), and are destroyed in the flood because of the wickedness of man (Gen. vi, 5-7); cf. also Rom. viii, 22.

[11] So in the Upanishads (but not in the poetic Veda); see Hopkins, *Religions of India*, p. 227; Bloomfield, *Religion of the Veda*, p. 257. Tylor (*Primitive Culture*, ii, 18) points out that in this conception we have a suggestion of the theory of development in organic life.

in which we find that religious faith always appropriates and utilizes the ethical ideas of its time.

59. At the present day the interest in the hypothesis of reincarnation springs from its supposed connection with the doctrine of immortality. Brahmanists and Buddhists maintain that it is the only sure basis for this doctrine; but this view appears not to have met with wide acceptance.

60. 2. An all but universal belief among lower tribes is that departed souls remain near their earthly abodes, haunting the neighborhood of the body or the grave or the village.[1] It is apparently assumed that a soul is more at home in places which it knew in its previous life, and this assumption is confirmed by sights and sounds, chiefly during the night, that are interpreted as the forms and utterances of wandering souls.

61. Generally no occupation is assigned to these ghosts, except that it is sometimes supposed that they seek food and warmth:[2] scraps of food are left on the ground for them, and persons sitting around a fire at night are afraid to venture into the dark places beyond lest they meet them.[3] For it is a common belief that such souls are dangerous, having both the power and the will to inflict injury.[4] It is easy to see why they should be supposed to possess extraordinary powers.[5] The belief in their maliciousness may have come naturally from the social conditions of the place and time: in savage communities a man who is stronger than his fellows is likely to treat them as his savage instincts prompt, to seize their property or kill them; and departed souls would naturally be credited with similar dispositions.

62. It is also true that the mysterious is often dreadful; even now in civilized lands there is a general fear of a 'ghost.' Precautions are taken by savages to drive or keep the soul away: the

---

[1] So the Central Australians (Spencer and Gillen, *Native Tribes of Central Australia*, p. 514), the Californian Maidu (Dixon, *The Northern Maidu*, p. 246). Cf. the cases in which precautions are taken against a ghost's entering its old earthly abode.
[2] *Rig-Veda*, 15. [3] Spencer and Gillen, loc. cit. and p. 516 f.
[4] Probably the Greek *ker* ($\kappa\acute{\eta}\rho$) and the Teutonic 'nightmare,' French *cauchemar* (*mara*, an incubus, or succuba), belong in this class of malefic ghosts.
[5] See below, § 92.

doors of houses are closed, and noises are made. On the other hand, ghosts, as members of the family or the clan, are often regarded as friendly.[1] Even during a man's lifetime his soul may be a sort of guide and protector — may attain, in fact, the rank of a deity ;[2] and after death it may become, as ancestor, the object of a regular cult.

63. Fear of ghosts has, perhaps, suggested certain methods of disposing of the dead body, as by interring or exposing it at a distance from the village, or burning it or throwing it into the water ; other considerations, however, as is suggested above,[3] may determine, in whole or in part, these methods of dealing with the body.

64. 3. It may be considered an advance in the organization of the future life when the soul is supposed to go to some distant place on the earth or in the sea or in the sky.[4] This is an attempt to separate the spheres of the living and the dead, and thus at once to define the functions of the dead and relieve the living from the fear of them. The land of the dead is sometimes vaguely spoken of as lying on earth, far off in some direction not precisely defined — east, west, north, or south — in accordance with traditions whose origin is lost in the obscurity of the past.

65. Possibly in some cases it is the traditional original home of the tribe ;[5] more often, it would seem, some local or astronomical fact has given the suggestion of the place ; one Egyptian view was that the western desert (a wide mysterious region) was the abode of the departed ; it was a widespread belief that the dead went to where the sun disappeared beneath the horizon.[6] Tribes living near the sea or a river often place the other world beyond the sea or the river,[7] and a ferryman is sometimes imagined who sets souls

---

[1] Steinmetz, *Ethnologische Studien zur ersten Entwicklung der Strafe*, i, 141 ff.

[2] For West Africa see above, § 43, n. 2 ; for the Norse *fylgja* ('follower') cf. Saussaye, *Religion of the Teutons*, p. 292 ff.   [3] § 38, n. 2.

[4] A transitional stage is marked by the theory, in a polypsychic system, that one soul remains near the body while another goes to the distant land.

[5] So, perhaps, among the eastern Polynesians (W. Ellis, *Polynesian Researches*, i, 303) and the Navahos (Matthews, *Navaho Legends*, p. 38).

[6] Maspero, *Dawn of Civilization*, chap. iii, 183 ff. ; Teit, *Thompson River Indians*, p. 85 ; Rink, *Tales of the Eskimo*, p. 40.

[7] *Odyssey*, xi (by the encircling Okeanos) ; Williams, *Fiji*, p. 192 ; Brinton, *Myths of the New World*, p. 288 f. ; Saussaye, *Religion of the Teutons*, p. 290 ; *Rig-Veda*, x, 63, 10 ; ix, 41, 2.

over the water.[1] Mountains also are regarded as abodes of the dead.[2] It is not unnatural that the abodes of departed souls should be placed in the sky, whose height and brightness, with its crowd of luminous bodies, made it an object of wonder and awe, and caused it to be regarded as the dwelling place of the happy gods, with whom deserving men would naturally be. Sometimes the expanse of the upper air was regarded as the home of souls (as in Samoa), sometimes a heavenly body — the sun (in India), or the moon (in the Bowditch Islands), or the stars.[3] The schemes being vague, several of these conceptions may exist side by side at the same place and time.

66. The occupations of the dead in these regions are held usually to be the same as those of the living; no other view is possible in early stages of social life. Generally all the apparatus of earthly life (food, utensils, weapons) is placed on the grave or with the body, and wives and slaves are slain to be the companions of the deceased.

67. 4. A more decided separation between the living and the dead is made in the conception of the underground world as the abode of the latter. It was, however, only at a late period that this conception was carried far enough to make the separation effective. Among the Central Australians there were folk-stories of early men who traveled under the ground, but this is represented as merely an extraordinary way of getting from one place to another on the surface of the earth. Some North American tribes tell of an underground world inhabited by the ants and by beings similar to man, but those who live up on the earth are seen there only by accident, as when some hero dares the descent.[4] The conception of a real subterranean or submarine hades is found, however,

---

[1] Breasted, *History of Egypt*, p. 65; Charon; Saussaye, op. cit., p. 290; Rohde, *Psyche*, 3d ed., i, 306. For the story given by Procopius (*De Bell. Goth.* iv, 20) see Tylor, *Primitive Culture*, ii, 64 f.   [2] Saussaye, op. cit., p. 291.

[3] *Rig-Veda*, x, 154, 4, 5; Lister in *Journal of the Anthropological Institute*, xxi, 51 (moon). Cf. Breasted, *History of Egypt*, p. 64; Hopkins, *Religions of India*, pp. 129, 206; Brinton, *Myths of the New World*, p. 284 ff.; Müller, *Amerikanische Urreligionen*, i, 288 ff.; Saussaye, op. cit., p. 291; Spencer, *Principles of Sociology*, i, 232 f.

[4] Matthews, *Navaho Legends*, p. 185 f.; Teit, *Thompson River Indians*, p. 78.

among many savage and barbarous peoples, as the Samoans, the inhabitants of New Guinea, the Zulus, the Navahos, the Eskimo, the Kafirs of the Hindu Kush, and others.[1]

68. These pictures of the future world are crude, and usually stand side by side with others; they are experiments in eschatology. But the constructive imagination moved more and more toward an organized underground hades as the sole abode of the dead — the place to which all the dead go. Such a hades is found among the civilized peoples of antiquity, Egyptians, Semites, Hindus, Greeks, and Romans, and, in more recent times, among the Teutons (Scandinavians). The suggestion for this position may have come from the grave (though it does not appear that the grave was regarded as the permanent abode of the dead), and from caverns that seemed to lead down into the bowels of the earth. The descent of souls into a subterranean world offered no difficulties to early imagination: ghosts, like the Australian ancestors, could move freely where living men could not go; where there was no cavern like that by which Æneas passed below,[2] they could pass through the ground.

69. A lower region offered a wide land for the departed, with the possibility of organization of íts denizens. Ghosts gradually lost their importance as a factor in everyday life; sights and sounds that had been referred to wandering souls came to be explained by natural laws. Wider geographical knowledge made it difficult to assign the ghosts a mundane home, and led to their relegation to the submundane region. Further, the establishment of great nations familiarized men with the idea that every large community should have its own domain. The gods were gradually massed, first in the sky, the ocean, and hades, and then in heaven. For the dead the first organization (if that term may be allowed) was in hades; the separation into heaven and hell came later. A specific divine head of the Underworld is found in Egypt, Babylonia and Assyria, India,

---

[1] Turner, *Samoa*, p. 257; Lawes (on New Guinea), in *Journal of the Anthropological Institute*, viii, 371; Callaway, *Zulu Nursery Tales*, p. 316; Matthews, *Navaho Legends*, p. 215; Rink, *Tales of the Eskimo*, p. 37; Sir G. S. Robertson, *The Kafirs of the Hindu-Kush*, p. 380 f.   [2] *Æneid*, vi.

Greece, Rome, but not in Israel. Such a definite system of government could exist only when something approaching a pantheon had been established; the Babylonians, for example, whose pantheon was vague, had also a vague god of hades.

70. Theories of the occupations of the dead varied in the early civilized stage, before the rise of the idea of ethical retribution in the other life. In the absence of earthly relations, imagination could conceive of nothing for them to do, and hence an ardent desire for the continuance of earthly life.[1] For the Hebrews the Underworld was without pursuits; the shades sat motionless, in the dress and according to the rank of the upper world, without emotions or aims (except a sparkle of malicious satisfaction when some great man came down from earth), and without religious worship.[2] A similar view was held by the Greeks and the Romans. Certain Egyptian documents speak of mundane occupations for the dead, but these documents belong to a comparatively late stage of culture, and what the earlier view was we do not know.[3] Of Hindu ideas, also, on this point we have only relatively late notices.

71. 5. A radical transformation in the conception of the state of the dead was effected by the introduction of the idea of moral retribution into the life of the Underworld.[4] The basis of the movement was the natural conception of life as determined by ethical considerations, but the process of transformation has extended over thousands of years and has hardly yet reached its completion. In the lowest eschatological systems known to us there is no marked difference in the status of departed souls; so among the Central Australians, the tribes of New Guinea and the Torres Straits islands, the Zulus, the Malagasy, the West African peoples, and some North American tribes.[5]

---

[1] *Odyssey*, xi, 489; Isa. xxxviii, 10 ff.; Prov. iii, 16, etc.
[2] 1 Sam. xxviii, 14; Ezek. xxxii, 19–32; Isa. xiv, 9–15; xxxviii, 18. For the early Babylonian conception of the Underworld see the *Descent of Ishtar* (in Jastrow, *Religion of Babylonia and Assyria*, chap. xxv); S. H. Langdon, "Babylonian Eschatology," in *Essays in Modern Theology and Related Subjects* (the C. A. Briggs Memorial). [3] Breasted, *History of Egypt*, p. 175. [4] Cf. Tylor, *Primitive Culture*, ii, 83 ff.
[5] Spencer and Gillen, *Native Tribes of Central Australia*; Callaway, *Amazulus*, pp. 12, 151 f.; W. Ellis, *Madagascar*, i, 393 (cf. J. Sibree, *Madagascar*, p. 312); A. B. Ellis, *The Ewe*, p. 107 f., and *The Tshi*, p. 156 ff.; M. Kingsley, *Travels*, pp. 461, 480; R. B. Dixon, *The Shasta*, p. 469.

72. The earliest grounds of distinction are ritualistic and social; these occur among the higher savages and survive in some civilized peoples. The Fijians assign punishment in the other world to bachelors, men unaccompanied by their wives and children, cowards, and untattooed women.[1] Where circumcision was a tribal mark, the uncircumcised, as having no social status, were consigned to inferior places in hades: so among the Hebrews.[2] The omission of proper funeral ceremonies was held in like manner to entail deprivation of privilege in hades: the shade had an undesirable place below, as among the Babylonians and the Hebrews,[3] or was unable to enter the abode of the dead, and wandered forlorn on the earth or on the border of the Underworld, as was the Greek belief.[4] Exposure of the corpse to beasts and birds, making funeral ceremonies impossible, was regarded as a terrible misfortune for the dead.[5]

73. Such of these beliefs as relate to violations of ritual appear to spring from the view that the tribal customs are sacred, and from the consequent distinction between tribesmen and foreigners. All persons without the tribal mark were shut out from the privileges of the tribe, were outlaws in this world and the next; and those whose bodies were not properly disposed of lost the support of the tribal deities or of the subterranean Powers.[6] It was also held that the body retained the form in which it went down to hades;[7] hence the widespread dread of mutilation, as among the Chinese still. On the other hand the brave were rewarded.[8]

74. Sometimes earthly rank determines future conditions — a natural corollary to what is stated above (§ 72 f.). A distinction is made between nobles and common people in the Bowditch Islands.[9] The members of the Fijian Areoi Society are held to enjoy special privileges in the other world.[10] The belief in the Marquesas Islands is that the sky is for high gods and nobles.[11] According to John Smith,

---

1 Williams, *Fiji*, p. 194.   2 Ezek. xxxii, 23, 27 ; Isa. xiv, 15.
3 Jastrow, op. cit., p. 601 ; Ezek. xxxii.   4 *Iliad*, xxiii, 71.
5 Jastrow, op. cit., p. 602 ; *Iliad*, i, 3 ff. ; 2 Sam. xxi, 10 ; Prov. xxx, 17.
6 Hence special desire for sons, who were the natural persons to perform funeral rites for fathers.   7 So also Plato, *Gorgias*, 80 (524).
8 Hesiod, *Works and Days*, 110.   9 Marillier, *La survivance de l'âme*.
10 W. Ellis, *Polynesian Researches*, chap. ix.   11 Marillier, op. cit.

in savage Virginia only nobles and priests were supposed to survive after death.[1] The North American Mandans (of Dakota), according to one view, assign to the brave in the hereafter the delightful villages of the gods.[2] When souls are supposed to enter into animals different animals are assigned to nobles and common men.[3] Kings and nobles retain their superiority of position and are sometimes attended by their slaves and officers.[4]

75. The manner of death is sometimes significant. The Karens hold that persons killed by elephants, famine, or sword, do not enter the abode of the dead, but wander on the earth and take possession of the souls of men.[5] In Borneo it is supposed that those who are killed in war become specters.[6] The belief in the Marquesas Islands is that warriors dying in battle, women dying in childbirth, and suicides go up to the sky.[7] In regard to certain modes of death opposite opinions are held in the Ladrone (Marianne) Islands and the Hervey group: in the former those who die by violence are supposed to be tortured by demons, those who die a natural death are believed to be happy; according to the view in the latter group these last are devoured by the goddess of death, and the others are happy. In the one case violent death, it would seem, is supposed to be due to the anger of the gods, and to be a sign of something bad in the man; in the other case happiness is compensation for the misfortune of a violent death, and natural death, being the fate of ordinary people, leaves one at the mercy of the mistress of the other world.

76. The advance to the conception of moral retribution hereafter could take place only in communities in which earthly life was organized on a moral basis. The beginning of the movement is seen in certain savage tribes. Savages have their codes, which generally recognize some ethical virtues among the tribal obligations.

1 Smith, *Virginia*, p. 36.
2 Will and Spinden, *The Mandans* (*Papers of the Peabody Museum of American Archæology and Ethnology*, Harvard University), p. 133.
3 So among the Betsileos and the Zulus (Marillier, op. cit.)
4 So in Madagascar. Cf. Ezek. xxxii, 18 ff.; Isa. xiv, 4 ff.
5 *Journal of the American Oriental Society*, iv, 312 f.
6 S. St. John, *The Far East*, 2d ed., i, 182 f.; cf. i, 184.
7 Marillier, op. cit. Here suicide appears to be regarded as a heroic act, and the women in question perish in doing a service to the tribe.

Stealing, lying, failure in hospitality, cowardice, violation of marital rights — in general, all the acts that affect injuriously the communal life — are, as a rule, condemned by the common sense of the lowest peoples, and the moral character of the gods reflects that of their worshipers. By reason of the sense of solidarity the faults of individuals affect not only themselves but also their communities, and the gods care for communities as well as for individuals. Whenever, then, there is an inquest in the other world, these faults, it is likely, will be punished. On account of the paucity of our information, it is not possible to make a general statement on this point, but examples of future moral control occur in many savage creeds.[1] In such systems the nature of the life beyond the grave is variously conceived: sometimes as cheerless and gloomy (as in Finland), sometimes as pleasant (as in Samoa, New Guinea, New Caledonia, Bowditch Islands, some North American tribes, Brazil).[2]

77. In tracing the growth of the conception of distinctions in the other world,[3] we find first a vague opinion that those who do badly in this life are left to shift for themselves hereafter;[4] that is, there is no authority controlling the lives of men below. In the majority of cases, however, distinctions are made, but these, as is remarked above, are based on various nonmoral considerations, and have small cultural value.[5]

78. In the published reports of savage beliefs there is not always mention of a formal examination of the character of the dead, and probably nothing of the sort was imagined by the lowest tribes. It appears, however, in such relatively advanced peoples as the Fijians[6] and the Khonds.[7]

---

[1] Dixon, The *Northern Maidu*, p. 261 ; Westermarck, *Moral Ideas*, Index, s. v. *Future Life*; Hobhouse, *Morals in Evolution*, ii, 271 ff. ; Tylor, *Primitive Culture*, ii, 83 ff.

[2] Castrén, *Finnische Mythologie*, p. 126; Turner, *Samoa*, p. 259; Lawes, " New Guinea," in *Journal of the Anthropological Institute*, viii, 370 ; Rochas, *Nouvelle Calédonie* (*Bulletin de la Société d'anthropologie*, 1860), p. 280 ; Lister, *Journal of the Anthropological Institute*, xxi, 51 ; Dixon, op. cit., p. 262 ; Müller, *Amerikanische Urreligionen*, p. 289 (Brazil).

[3] See Westermarck, loc. cit.   [4] Hawkins, *Creek Country*, p. 80.

[5] For details on this point see L. Marillier, *La survivance de l'âme*.

[6] Williams and Calvert, *Fiji*, p. 193 f.

[7] *Journal of the Royal Asiatic Society*, 1842, p. 172, and 1852, p. 211 ; Hopkins, *Religions of India*, p. 530 f.

79. Moral retribution proper is found only in great civilized nations and not in all of them; the early Semites appear to have retained the old conception of punishment for ritual faults or failures, and for offenses against the national welfare. For the Hebrews the proof is found in the Old Testament passim; in the Babylonian and Assyrian literature, as far as published, there is one sign of departure from the scheme sketched in the *Descent of Ishtar*: Hammurabi (ca. 2000 B.C.) invokes the curses of the gods on any one who shall destroy the tablet of his penal code, and wishes that such a one may be deprived of pure water after death. In regard to the South Arabians, the pre-Mohammedan North Arabians, and the Aramæans, we have no information; and for the Phœnicians there is only the suggestion involved in the curse invoked on those who violate a tomb, and in the funeral ceremonies.[1] But the same general religious ideas prevailed throughout the ancient Semitic area, and we may probably assume that the Hebrew conception was the universal one.

80. In Egypt, India, China, Persia, Greece, Rome, however, and among the Jews in the Greek period,[2] higher ethical conceptions were carried over to the Underworld; judgment, it was held, was pronounced on the dead, and rewards and punishments dealt out to them according to their moral character. The Jews and the Persians went a step further, and conceived of a final general judgment, a final winding-up of human history, and a permanent reconstruction of the world on a basis largely moral, though tinged with local religious elements — a grandiose idea that has maintained itself up to the present time, embodying the conviction that the outcome of life depends on character, and that ethical retribution is the essence of the world.

[1] Sepulchral inscriptions of Tabnit and Eshmunazar, and the inscriptions of Antipatros (*Corpus Inscriptionum Semiticarum*, vol. i, part i, p. 9 ff.; Lidzbarski, *Handbuch der nordsemitischen Epigraphik*, part ii, pl. iv, 1, 2; part i, p. 117; Rawlinson, *Phœnicia*, p. 394 f.).

[2] Breasted, *Egypt*, p. 173 ff.; Bloomfield, *Religion of the Veda*, p. 252; Hopkins, *Religions of India*, pp. 336, 380, 443; *Texts of Taoism*, ed. J. Legge, ii, 6 f. (in *Sacred Books of the East*, vol. 40); Legge, *Religions of China*, p. 82; De Groot, *Religion of the Chinese*, pp. 6, 25, 54, 70 ff., 117; Spiegel, *Eranische Alterthumskunde*, ii, 158 ff.; Plato, *Republic*, 614 (story of Er); Book of Enoch passim.

81. This ethical constitution of the life hereafter led to the local separation of the good from the bad. Such a separation was imagined by comparatively undeveloped peoples whose ethical principle was chiefly ritualistic, as, for example, the Fijians, the American Indians, and by civilized peoples in their early stages, the Vedic Hindus [1] (Yama's abode in the sky, and a pit) and the Greeks (the Homeric Elysian Fields, and Tartarus).[2]

82. In fact, a recognition of a place of happiness and a place of punishment in the other life accompanies sooner or later a certain stage of ethical culture in all communities. In India it appears in the late Vedic and post-Vedic periods, together with the ethical doctrine of metempsychosis, and though, as is natural in such a stage of development, various ideas are held respecting the destinies of the good and the bad, the ethical distinction between these classes of persons, with a systematic awarding of rewards and punishments, becomes firmly established : Yama becomes an ethical judge. In the Brahmanas, Manu, and the Mahabharata, we find a sort of heaven for the virtuous and a hell for the vicious. While the academic thought of Brahmanism and the altruistic systems of Jainism and Buddhism looked to the absorption of the departed into the All, the popular Hindu faith held fast to the scheme of happiness and wretchedness in the future.[3] As in Dante's *Divina Commedia*, the heaven was somewhat colorless, the hell more distinct and picturesque ; pain is acute and varied, happiness is calm and uniform.

83. The later Egyptian eschatological development was not unlike the later Hindu. The good were rewarded with delightful habitations in the West or with the Sun ; the bad were tortured in a gloomy place.[4]

---

1 W. Ellis, *Polynesian Researches*, chap. xv ; Will and Spinden, *The Mandans*, p. 133 ; Dixon, *The Northern Maidu*, p. 261 ; *Rig-Veda*, i, 356 ; vii, 104. Cf. article " Blest, abode of the " in Hastings, *Encyclopædia of Religion and Ethics*.

2 Tartarus is as far below Hades as the earth is below the sky (*Iliad*, viii, 16).

3 Hopkins, *Religions of India*, p. 379 ff.

4 Wiedemann, *Egyptian Doctrine of Immortality*, p. 50 f.; Maspero, *Dawn of Civilization*, p. 183 ff. ; Breasted, *History of Egypt*, pp. 64, 173 ff. Different conceptions, however, appear in different stages of eschatological thought. Probably the older view was that all the dead descended to the Underworld. According to another view, the good ascended to heaven and accompanied the sun on his daily voyage over the heavenly ocean.

84. As regards the early Greek eschatological scheme, it is suggested by S. Reinach[1] that the descriptions of punishments in Tartarus (as in the cases of Tantalus and others) arose from misunderstood representations of the condition of the dead in the other world, they being represented either as engaged in the occupations of this life, or as they were at the moment of death. The great punishments, in fact, are assigned only to heroic mythical offenders, but there seems to be no reason why the idea of retribution should not be supposed to enter into such descriptions. Separation of the good from the bad on ethical grounds appears in Greece in the time of Plato. In various passages he describes the savage places (Tartarus and others) to which criminals go after death, and the happy abodes of the virtuous.[2] These abodes were not with the gods; the occasional translations to heaven (Heracles, Ganymede) are exceptional honors paid to heroes and favorites.

85. The Jewish conception of a punitive future belongs to the Greek period of Jewish history, and was probably developed on Hebrew lines under Greek and Egyptian influence. A combination of the Old Testament view of future retribution on earth with the conception of torture in the other world is given in Enoch.[3] In some circles Sheol was placed in the West and divided into two regions, one of happiness, the other of punishment,[4] or the good dwell with the angels in heaven,·the bad in hell.[5] By others the abodes of the dead were placed ·in the heavenly regions: of the seven heavens, the second was assigned to the bad and the third to the good.[6] With all the variation of locality, the separation of the bad from the good is made permanent, and this distinction is maintained in the New Testament, which throughout assigns the wicked to hell (Gehenna or Tartarus), while the righteous dwell some-·times on the renovated earth, sometimes in the heavenly regions.[7]

[1] *Revue archéologique*, 1903, and Reinach, *Orpheus* (Eng. tr.), p. 88 f.
[2] *Gorgias*, 523-526; *Republic*, x, 614; *Laws*, x, 904 f; *Phædo*, 113 f.
[3] Isa. lxv, 17-21; lxvi, 24; Enoch, x, 12-22.   [4] Enoch, xxii.
[5] Enoch, civ, 6; xcix, 11.
[6] *Secrets of Enoch*, chaps. vii-x. For the third heaven cf. 2 Cor. xii, 2-4. Varro also (quoted in Augustine, *De Civ. Dei*, vii, 6) assigned the souls of the dead to a celestial space beneath the abode of the gods.
[7] Matt. xxv, 46; 1 Thess. iv, 17; 2 Pet. ii, 4; iii, 13; Rev. xx, 15; xxi, 1; 2 Cor. xii, 2-4.

86. The Jewish and Christian books mentioned above content themselves with the general statement that the punishment of the wicked will be torture by fire and cold. Succeeding Christian books elaborated the picture of torture with great ingenuity; the *Apocalypse of Peter*, following and expanding the description .of Plato and Enoch, has an elaborate barbarous apparatus of punishment, and this scheme, continued through a series of works,[1] has its culmination in Dante's Inferno, where, however, the ethical element is pronounced, though colored by the poet's likes and dislikes.

87. *Purgatory.* The wicked dead were not always left hopeless in their place of punishment. Kindly human feeling (shown in early stages by pious care for the well-being of the dead) and the analogy of earthly procedures, civil and religious, led to the view that, after the expiation of faults by suffering, the evildoer might be freed from his prison and gain a place of happiness. Pardon and purification were effected on earth by punishments (scourging, imprisonment, etc.) or by ritual processes (ablution, fastings, etc.) — why not in the other life? In some systems of transmigration the man, forced after death to assume a lower form, may rise by good conduct to a higher form. In Plato's imaginative construction of the Underworld[2] those who have lived neither well nor ill are purified in the Acherusian lake and then receive rewards according to their deserts; and those who have committed great but not unpardonable crimes may come to the lake (after having suffered the pains of Tartarus) and be freed from trouble if they obtain pardon from those they have wronged. But as here, so hereafter, certain offenses were regarded as unpardonable. The purgatorial conception passed into patristic and Roman and Eastern Christianity and Talmudic and Medieval Judaism.[3]

88. *Resurrection.* The doctrine of the resurrection of the dead, which has been fully developed only by the Persians and the Jews (and from them taken by Christianity and Islam), appears to have

---

[1] See, for example, the *Revelation of the Monk of Evesham*, Eng. tr. by V. Paget (New York, 1909).   [2] *Republic*, x, 614.

[3] Herzog-Hauck, *Real-Encyklopädie*, Index, s.v. *Fegfeuer*; *Jewish Encyclopedia*, article " Purgatory."

grown from simple beginnings. It is the expression of the conviction that the perfect man is made up of soul and body, and its full form is found only in periods of high ethical culture.

But in very early times the belief in the intimate connection between body and soul appears in the care taken among certain peoples to preserve the bones or the whole body of the deceased as a possible future abode for the soul; [1] and, on the other hand, as the soul, it was held, might return to the body and be dangerous to the living, means were sometimes employed to frighten it off. It seems to have been believed in some cases that the destruction of the body involved the destruction of the soul (New Zealand). An actual entrance of a departed soul into a human body is involved in some early forms of the doctrine of reincarnation, [2] but this is not the restoration of the dead man's own body. It was held in Egypt (and not improbably elsewhere) that the soul after death might desire to take possession of its own body, and provision was made for such an emergency; but this belief seems not to have had serious results for religious life. A temporary reunion of soul and body appears in the figure of the vampire, which, however, is a part of a popular belief and religiously not important. But these passing beliefs indicate a general tendency, and may have paved the way for the more definite conception of bodily restoration.

89. The more developed Hindu doctrine (Brahmanic, Jainistic, Buddhistic) recognized a great variety of possible forms of reincarnation (human and nonhuman), and made a step forward by including the continuity or reëstablishment of moral life and responsibility (the doctrine of karma). [8] It, however, never reached the form of a universal or partial resurrection.

[1] American Indians (H. C. Yarrow, *Introduction to the Study of Mortuary Customs among the North American Indians*, p. 5 ff.); Egypt (Wilkinson, *The Ancient Egyptians*, chap. x); see article " Funérailles " in *La Grande Encyclopédie*. Grant Allen, in *The Evolution of the Idea of God*, chap. iii, connects the idea of bodily resurrection with the custom of inhumation and the idea of immortality with cremation, but this view is not borne out by known facts.

[2] Frazer, *Golden Bough*, 2d ed., i, 262, 278.

[8] The doctrine of reincarnation in India followed on that of Hades, and stood in a certain opposition to it. Cf. Hopkins, *Religions of India*, pp. 204 ff., 530 n. 3; Bloomfield, *Religion of the Veda*, pp. 211, 252 ff.

90. The birthplace of this latter doctrine appears to have been the region in which Mazdaism arose, the country south of the Caspian Sea. Windischmann infers from Herodotus, iii, 62, that it appears as a Mazdean belief as early as the sixth century B.C.[1] This is doubtful, but it is reported as a current belief by Theopompus.[2] Its starting-point was doubtless the theory of reincarnation, which, we may suppose, the Iranian Aryans shared with their Indian brethren. Precisely what determined the Iranian movement toward this specific form of reincarnation we have no means of knowing. It may be due to the same genius for simple organization that led the Zoroastrians to discard the mass of the old gods and elevate Ahura Mazda to the chief place in the pantheon; their genius for practical social religious organization may have induced them to select human reincarnation as the most natural and the most effective morally, and to discard other forms as unworthy.[3] The dead man's own body would then be the natural dwelling place of his soul; but a refined body (as in 1 Cor. xv) might be regarded as better suited to the finer life of the future. Whatever the cause, they adopted this conception, and probably through their influence it passed to, or was formulated by, the Jews, among whom it appears in the second century B.C. (in the Book of Daniel).[4] In Daniel and 2 Maccabees resurrection is confined to the Jews; in Enoch it is sometimes similarly confined, sometimes apparently universal.[5] In the New Testament also the same diversity of statement appears; resurrection seems to be confined to believers in some

---

[1] *Zoroastrian Studies*, p. 236. Prexaspes says that " if the dead rise again " Smerdis may be the son of Cyrus. He may mean that this is not probable. Smerdis, he would in that case say, is certainly dead, and this pretender can be the son of Cyrus only in case the dead come to life.

[2] Diogenes Laertius in Müller, *Fragmenta Historicorum Græcorum*, i, 289; cf. Plutarch, *Isis and Osiris*, 47, and Herodotus, i, 131-140. See Spiegel, *Eranische Alterthumskunde*, ii, 158 ff.

[3] Occasional reincarnation in human form is found elsewhere. The Mazdeans made it universal.

[4] There is no certain or probable reference to it in the Old Testament before this. Ezek. xxxvii, 1-14, is obviously a figurative prediction of national (not individual) resuscitation, and the obscure passage Isa. xxvi, 19 seems to refer to the reëstablishment of the nation, and in any case is not earlier than the fourth century B.C. and may be later.   [5] Dan. xii; 2 Macc. vii, 14; Enoch, xci, 10; xxii.

passages[1] and to be universal in others.[2] In the former case it is regarded as a reward of piety and as a consequence of the intimate relation between the man and God or Christ; unbelievers then remain in hades, where they are punished. But universal resurrection was probably thought of as involved in the grandiose conceptions of a final judgment and a final moral restoration.[3]

5. POWERS OF THE SOUL

91. Savage lore takes account of the powers of the separated soul only; the qualities and functions of the earthly incorporate soul are accepted as a part of the existing familiar order, and are not analyzed or discussed. It was different with the departed soul, which, because of its strangeness and mystery, was credited with extraordinary powers, and this part of savage science was gradually developed, through observation and inference, into an important system. In the search for causes, the Shade, its independent existence once established, came to be regarded as the agent in many procedures of which no probable account could otherwise be given.

92. The greatest activity of the departed soul is found in the earliest known period of culture, when it was not yet relegated to hades or to the sky, but dwelt on earth, either near its former habitation or in a distant region from which it might return. Its powers of movement and action are then held to be all that imagination can suggest. Such souls move through the air or under the ground, enter houses through obstacles impenetrable to the earthly man, pass into the human body, assume such shapes as pleases them. Divested of gross earthly bodies, they are regarded as raised above all ordinary limitations of humanity. Of these conceptions, that of the ghost's superhuman power of movement remains in the popular faith to the present day.

93. The practical question for the early man is the determination of the relation of departed souls to earthly life. Among savage tribes their attitude is sometimes friendly, sometimes unfriendly,

---

[1] 1 Cor. xv, 23; Rom. vi, 4; viii, 11; John vi, 54.
[2] Acts xxiv, 15; John v, 28 f. [3] Apokatastasis (Col. i, 20; cf. Rom. xi, 32).

more often the latter.[1] To fear the unknown is a human instinct. Shades are looked on as aliens, and aliens are generally enemies. In particular, ghosts are conceived of as sometimes wandering about in search of food or warmth, or as cherishing enmity toward persons who had wronged them in their earthly life. They are supposed to be capable of inflicting disease or pain, and precautions are taken against them. Cases are reported of persons who killed themselves in order that, as ghosts, they might wreak vengeance on enemies.[2] On the other hand, to the members of its own family the departed soul is sometimes held to be friendly, or not unfriendly, but among savages it is not thought of as a potent and valuable friend.

94. In the more advanced cults the functions of the departed souls become larger and more important. They are regarded as having the power of foretelling the future, and are consulted.[8] They become guardian spirits, and a cult of souls arises.[4] In some higher forms of religion (Judaism, Christianity, Islam) they are regarded as mediators between man and the deity, or as advocates for man in the heavenly court.

95. *Prayer for the dead.* Before the ethical stage of religion the moral condition and needs of the dead did not come into consideration; their physical wants were met by performance of funeral rites and by supplying them with food and other necessities of life,[5] and they later came to be looked on as helpers rather than as needing help; but when this old view passed away, and the conceptions of judgment and ethical retribution after death were reached, the moral status of the dead became a source of anxiety to the living. It was held that the divine judge might be reached — by intercession or by petitions, or by the performance of certain ceremonies — and his attitude toward the dead modified.

---

[1] Cf. Steinmetz, *Ethnologische Studien zur ersten Entwicklung der Strafe*.
[2] Westermarck, *Moral Ideas*, ii, 234, 245 f.   [8] See below, on necromancy, § 927.
[4] See § 360 ff. (ancestor-worship) and § 350 ff. (divinization of deceased persons).
[5] In Egypt there grew up also an elaborate system of charms for the protection of the dead against hostile animals, especially serpents, — a body of magical texts that finally took the form of the " Book of the Dead " (Breasted, *History of Egypt*, pp. 69, 175 ; Steindorff, *Religion of the Ancient Egyptians*, p. 153 ff.).

96. A trace of such care for the deceased may be found in the Brahmanic ceremonies intended to secure complete immortality to fathers.[1] In Egypt, in the later times, there was an arrangement for securing for the deceased immunity from punishment for moral offenses : a sacred beetle of stone, inscribed with a charm beginning :" O my heart, rise not up against me as a witness," laid on the breast of the mummy, silences the heart in the presence of Osiris, and the man, even though guilty, goes free. Forms of charms were prepared by the priests, and the name of any one who could pay was inserted in blanks left for this purpose.[2] This sort of corrupting procedure was reproduced in some periods of Christianity. In the early Church a custom existed of receiving baptism on behalf of such as died unbaptized ;[3] here, apparently, a magical efficacy was ascribed to the act. The first mention of prayer for the dead occurs in a history of the Maccabean wars, where a sin-offering, accompanied by prayer, effects reconciliation for certain soldiers who died in a state of sin (idol symbols were found on their persons).[4] Prayer for the dead has been largely developed in Christianity and Islam.[5]

6. Genesis of Spirits

97. As early science identified life with the soul, it logically attributed a soul to everything that was regarded as living. This category seems to have embraced all the objects of the world — human beings, beasts, plants, weapons, rocks, waters, heavenly bodies. Savages rarely formulate their ideas on such a subject, but the belief in the future existence of nonhuman as well as human things is fairly established by the widespread practice of slaying animals at the tomb and burying with the dead the objects they are supposed to need in the other world. This custom exists among many tribes at

---

[1] *Çatapatha Brahmana*, xii, 9, 3, 12. Cf. W. Ellis, *Polynesian Researches*, i, 193 f.
[2] Breasted, op. cit., p. 249.   [3] 1 Cor. xv, 29.
[4] 2 Macc. xii, 40 ff. Possibly the custom came to the Jews from Egypt. For later Jewish ideas on this point see *Jewish Encyclopedia*, article " Kaddish."
[5] Smith and Cheetham, *Dictionary of Christian Antiquities*, article " Canon of the Liturgy " ; Hughes, *Dictionary of Islam*, article " Prayers for the Dead."

the present day, and the contents of ancient tombs prove its existence in former times. The dead are provided with clothing, implements of labor, weapons, ornaments, food, and as these objects remain in their mundane form by or in the grave, it is held that their souls pass with the souls of their possessors into the world beyond. Further, the belief in transformation from human to nonhuman forms and vice versa involves the supposition of life in all such things. That the heavenly bodies, similarly, are supposed to be animated by souls appears from the fact that they are regarded as manlike in form, thought, and manner of life: the sun is frequently represented as a venerable man who traverses the sky — the moon being his wife, and the stars their children; and sun and moon sometimes figure as totems. This general conception has been expanded and modified in a great variety of ways among different peoples, but the belief in the anthropomorphic nature of the astral bodies has been an element of all religions except the highest.

98. The apparent incongruities in the savage theory — that all things are endowed with life — need occasion us no difficulty. Complete consistency and tenability in such theories is not to be expected. Early men, like the lower animals, were doubtless capable of distinguishing between things living and things dead: a dog quickly discovers whether a moving object is alive. Man and beasts have in such questions canons of criticism derived from long experience.[1]

99. But man differs from the beast in that he feels the necessity of accounting for life by the hypothesis of a soul, and as he seems to himself to find evidence of life in plants and minerals (movement, growth, decay), he is justified in attributing souls to all things. He is interested, however, only in movements that affect his welfare. Whatever his general theory about rocks, a particular rock, as long as it does not affect his life, is for him an inert and worthless mass, practically dead; but if he discovers that it has power to harm him, it becomes instinct with life, and is treated as a rational being. Man has shown himself practical in all stages of religion; he is always the center of his world, and treats objects and theories with sole regard to his own well-being.

[1] On savage logic cf. Jevons, *Introduction to the History of Religion*, chap. iv.

100. The world of the savage was thus peopled with souls, and these came to have an independent existence. That this was the case with human souls is pointed out above,[1] and by analogy the separateness was extended to all souls. Thus there arose tree-spirits, river-spirits, and other similar extrahuman beings. It is convenient to employ the term 'spirit' as the designation of the soul in a nonhuman object, isolated and independent, and regarded as a Power to be treated with respect. The term is sometimes used of a disembodied human soul, and sometimes of a deity resident in an object of nature. It is better to distinguish, as far as possible, between these different senses of the word. The functions of a spirit are sometimes practically identical with those of a god. The difference between these two classes of extrahuman agents is one of general culture ; it is especially determined in any community by the extent of the organization of such agents that has been effected by the community. The cult of spirits is considered below in connection with the description of divine beings.[2]

<hr>

[1] See § 18 ff.   [2] See § 635 ff.

CHAPTER III

EARLY RELIGIOUS CEREMONIES

101. The earliest known forms of social life are characterized by the performance of public ceremonies, which are almost always religious. Religion in some form enters into all the details of early life — there is no event that is not supposed to be caused or affected by a supernatural Power or influence. A vaguely conceived force (*mana*), an attribute of life, is believed to reside in all things, and under certain circumstances has to be reckoned with. Mysterious potencies in the shape of souls, spirits, gods, or mana are held to preside over and control all affairs — birth, sickness, death, hate and love, hunting and war, sowing and reaping. There is no dogma except belief in this extrahuman influence — no conception of moral effort as based on and sanctioned by a definite moral ideal, no struggle of the sort that we call spiritual. Religion consists of a body of practices whose authority rests on precedent; as it is supposed they have existed from time immemorial, they are held to be necessary to secure the well-being of the tribe (a sufficient supply of food, or victory over enemies); to the question why such and such things are done, the common reply of the savage is that without them the thing desired could not be got.

102. In the earliest stages known to us these procedures are already elaborate and distinct; they are generally conducted by the tribal leaders (old men, chiefs, magicians), by whom they are handed down from generation to generation.[1] Their precise origin is lost in the depths of antiquity. Doubtless they arose from social needs, and their precise forms were suggested by crude observation and

---

[1] As to the efficiency of such tradition, compare the way in which mechanical processes are transmitted by older workmen to younger, always with the possibility of gradual improvement. In literary activity, also, tradition plays a great part; a young people must serve an apprenticeship before it can produce works of merit.

reasoning. Reflection on processes of nature, guided sometimes by fortunate or unfortunate accidents, may have led to the establishment of methods of procedure for gaining social and individual ends; and, as at this formative period the whole life of the community was permeated by religious conceptions, the procedures either were originally religious or speedily took on a religious coloring.

103. Two characteristics belong to early ceremonies: they are communal, and they are generally sacred mysteries. Whatever be the origin of the tribal and clan institutions of society, these are practically universal in the world as it is now known. Even in the few cases where men live in the comparative isolation of individual family groups (as the Eskimo, Fuegians, and others are said to do [1]), there is a communal feeling that is shown in the identity of customs and ideas among the isolated groups. In early man there is little individuality of thought or of religious experience,[2] and there is no observable difference between public and private religious worship. Ceremonies, like language, are the product of social thought, and are themselves essentially social. When a man performs an individual religious act (as when he recognizes an omen in an animal or bird, or chooses a guardian animal or spirit, or wards off a sickness or a noxious influence), he is aware that his act is in accordance with general usage, that it has the approval of the community, and that its potency rests on the authority of the community. It is true that such communal character belongs, in some degree, to all religious life — no person's religion is wholly independent of the thought of his community; but in the lower strata the acceptance of the common customs is unreflective and complete. When definite individualism sets in, ceremonies begin to lose their old significance, though they may be retained as mere forms or with a new interpretation.

---

[1] Spencer, *Principles of Sociology*, i, sec. 35; Westermarck, *Human Marriage*, p. 43 ff.; Pridham, *Ceylon*, i, 454 (Veddas); *United States Exploring Expedition*, i, 124 (Fuegians); Fison and Howitt, *Kamilaroi and Kurnai*, p. 278 (Australian Groundditch); Fritsch, *Die Eingeborenen Süd-Afrikas*, p. 328 (Bushmen); Schoolcraft, *Indian Tribes of the United States*, i, 207 (North American Snake tribes); Rivet, in *The American Anthropologist*, 1909 (" The Jivaros of Ecuador ").

[2] Cf. I. King, *The Development of Religion*, p. 66 ff.

104. That the ceremonial observances are usually sacred is obvious from all the descriptions we have of them. Their power is not always attributed to the action of external personal, supernatural agencies (though such agencies may have been assumed originally); in many cases, it is held to reside in themselves.[1] They are sacred in the sense that they are mysterious, acting in a way that is beyond human comprehension and with a power that is beyond human control.[2] They are efficacious only when performed by persons designated or recognized by the community. Here there is undoubtedly a dim sense of law and unity in the world, based on an interpretation of experiences. This is a mode of thought that runs through the whole history of religion — only, in the earliest stages of human life, it is superficial and narrow. The earlier ceremonial customs contain the germs and the essential features of the later more refined procedures.

105. Without attempting to give an exhaustive list, the principal early ceremonies may be divided into classes as follows:

EMOTIONAL AND DRAMATIC CEREMONIES

106. The dances that are so common among savage tribes are in many instances now (and doubtless this has always been the case) simply the expression of animal joyousness.[3] They are like the caperings of young animals — only, the human feeling of rhythm asserts itself, the movements are often measured and graceful. There is naturally an accompaniment of noise — shouting and beating on pieces of wood, bone, or metal, with songs or chants, the beginnings of vocal and instrumental music.

Words and melodies are simple and rude; they are the productions of individual singers, often, of course, made from a stock

---

[1] Even in higher forms of religion, as the Vedic, sacrifice and other ceremonies are supposed to have a magical power over the gods.

[2] This is a part of the belief in the mysterious energy (*mana*) potentially resident in all things.

[3] See, for example, the bird dances described by Haddon (*Head-hunters*, p. 358); compare W. Matthews, *Navaho Legends*, p. 83 al. Dances are now often given for the amusement of the public. Clowns often form a feature of such ceremonies; see Matthews, *Navaho Legends*, p. 230; R. B. Dixon, *The Northern Maidu* (*Bulletin of American Museum of Natural History*, xvii, part iii, p. 315 ff.).

of material common to all members of the clan or the tribe. In Australia songs are thought to be obtained by bards during sleep from the souls of the dead (sometimes from Bunjil), or the bard is possessed by the soul of a beast; chants are employed in magical ceremonies, and there are lullabies and other children's songs.[1] The Muscogee "Song of the Sabbea" is very sacred.[2] In West Africa minstrels recite song-stories, every story being attached to an object (bone, feather, etc.).[3] Songs are chanted at festivals in Guiana (and at night men tell endless stories).[4]

107. The movements of the dance are sometimes in imitation of those of animals,[5] sometimes spontaneous, and sometimes from our point of view indecent. The indecency and obscenity originated and has continued in a period when no moral element entered into such performances — they simply follow animal instincts and impulses, are controlled by them, and appear usually not to affect the customs relating to marriage and chastity (so in the Areoi festivities of Tahiti, and among the Central Australians[6]).

108. In accordance with the law by which religion appropriates social customs, the dance is devoted to religious purposes and acquires a sacred character.[7] It is a common ceremony as a preparation for war: the warriors of the tribe jump about with violent gesticulations and shouts, brandishing weapons and mimicking the acts of attacking and slaying enemies.[8] Here, doubtless, the object is partly to excite the men to fury and thus prepare them for combat, but there is also the conviction that the ceremony itself has a sacred potency.[9] A similar occult power is attached to dancing

---

[1] Howitt, in *Journal of the Anthropological Institute*, xvi, 327 ff.

[2] Miss Fletcher, *Indian Ceremonies*, p. 263 n.   [3] Miss Kingsley, *Studies*, p. 126.

[4] E. F. im Thurn, *Indians of Guiana*, vii, iv, 5.   [5] E. F. im Thurn, op. cit., vi.

[6] Of the same simple festive nature as dances are the plays or sports that are not infrequent among savages and half-civilized tribes. In the Areoi dramatic performances priests are ridiculed (W. Ellis, *Polynesian Researches*, p. 187).

[7] Miss Fletcher, "Emblematic Use of the Tree in the Dakotan Group" (in *Proceedings of the American Association for the Advancement of Science*, 1896).

[8] So among the hill tribes of North Arracan (*Journal of the Anthropological Institute*, ii, 239) and the North American Indians (Featherman, *Races of Mankind*, division iii, part i, p. 37 etc.). Such dances are performed by the Tshi women in the absence of the men (A. B. Ellis, *The Tshi*, p. 226).

[9] See below, § 905, on imitative magic.

in Timorlaut, where, when a ship is at sea, the girls sing and dance on the beach daily to bring the men back.[1] There are dances in commemoration of the dead[2] — apparently a combination of affection and homage, with the general purpose of conciliating the departed and procuring their aid; the belief being, apparently, that the dead see these demonstrations and are pleased with them. A Ghost Dance formerly performed in California had for its object bringing back the dead.[3]

109. At a later time such ceremonies were connected with the worship of gods : sometimes they were of the nature of offerings of homage to the supernatural Powers, as in the Young Dog Dance ;[4] sometimes they took on a symbolic and representative or dramatic character. Among the Redmen the dramatic dances are elaborate, often representing the histories of divine persons, these latter frequently appearing in the form of animals.[5] The accompanying songs or chants relate stories that are intended to explain, wholly or in part, the details of the rite.[6]

110. Thus combined with other ceremonies, dances become important means of religious culture. In Greece dances were connected with many cults, among others with the Dionysiac ceremonies, out of which grew the Greek drama. Among the Hebrews the ancient ceremonial dance appears as late as the time of David,[7] though it was then, perhaps, falling into desuetude, since his wife, Michal, is disgusted at his procedures. The violent movement of the dance excites not only warlike rage but also religious ecstasy, and has been used abundantly for this purpose by magicians, prophets, and

---

1 Riedel, in *Zeitschrift für Ethnologie*, xvii.   2 Haddon, *Head-hunters*, p. 139.
3 *Journal of American Folklore*, xvii, 32. Cf. the dance for the benefit of a sick man (R. B. Dixon, " Some Shamans of Northern California," op. cit., xvii, 23 ff.).
4 *Journal of American Folklore*, iv, 307. Cf. Will and Spinden, *The Mandans*, pp. 129 ff., 143 ff. The gods themselves, also, have their festive dances (W. Matthews, *Navaho Legends*, p. 83), and are sometimes represented as the authors of the sacred chants (ibid. p. 225).   5 See W. Matthews, loc. cit.
6 See, further, *Journal of American Folklore*, iii, 257 ; iv, 129 ; xii, 81 (basket dances) : R. B. Dixon, *The Northern Maidu*, p. 183 ff. (numerous and elaborate, and sometimes economic); Robertson, *Kafirs of the Hindu-Kush*, chap. 33 ; N. W. Thomas, *Australia*, chap. 7. Thomas describes many Australian games, and Dixon (*The Shasta*, p. 441 ff.) Californian games. For stories told by the natives of Guiana see above, § 106.
7 2 Sam. vi, 5.

mystics; the performer is regarded as a vehicle of divine revelation, all abnormal excitement being ascribed to possession by a spirit.[1]

111. With dances may be classed processions, in which usually a god is invoked or praised. In Ashanti-land, in time of war, when the men are with the army, processions of women, wives of the warriors, march through the streets, invoking the gods on behalf of the absent men.[2] Often the performers bear a sacred object, as a stone (sometimes inclosed in a box [3]), a boat, or an image; in early times such objects not only represent the gods but actually embody them, or are themselves superhuman Powers.

112. A peculiar form of procession is that in which the worshipers move round a sacred object, perhaps the adoption of a natural form of play. The original design in such movements may have been simply to show respect to the object in question and secure its favor, the circular movement being a natural way of keeping in touch with it. In certain cases the circumambulation is connected with the movement of the sun in the sky — probably a later interpretation of the ceremony. Examples are found in Hindu, Greek, and Roman practices, and in some modern Christian usages (in the Greek and Roman churches). As a magical efficiency was held to attach to the ceremony, its effect was sometimes held to depend on the direction of the movement: if it was to the right — passing from east through south to west (the worshiper facing the east) — it was good, but bad if in the opposite direction. Though traces of solemn circumambulation are found in some lower tribes, it has been, and is, practiced chiefly in the higher cults.[4]

113. Sacred dances and processions are natural human expressions of emotions that have been adopted by religious sentiment, and are often supposed to have potency in themselves. They tend to disappear with the progress of general refinement and of ethical conceptions of life and of deity. They continue, however, far into the civilized period, in which we find dramatic representations (as

---

[1] Tylor, *Primitive Culture*, ii, 133 f., 409 f.   [2] A. B. Ellis, *The Tshi*, p. 226.
[3] So, probably, the Old-Hebrew ark.
[4] See the references in article " Circumambulation " in Hastings, *Encyclopædia of Religion and Ethics*.

the Eleusinian rites and the medieval Mystery Plays), processions
of priests bearing or conducting sacred objects, processions of
devotees with music, and pilgrimages to shrines. Such ceremonies,
while they are regarded by educated persons simply as expressions
of reverence and accompaniments of prayer, are still believed by
many to have an innate or magic potency, insuring prosperity
to the participants.

DECORATIVE AND CURATIVE CEREMONIES

114. Love of ornament is found among all savage peoples; the
value they attach to beads and all colored things is well known to
travelers and traders. It has been plausibly argued that the origin
of clothing is to be found in the desire of each sex to make itself
beautiful in the eyes of the other.[1] However that may be, the
employment of leaves for headdresses and waistbands is general
among lower tribes.[2]

115. Equally popular is the adornment of the body by colored
marks made with red ocher, pipe-clay, turmeric, charcoal, and such
like things as are furnished by nature. Elaborate designs, of straight
and curved lines, are traced on the skin, and these are gradually
differentiated and become marks of rank and function. The war
paint of the American Indians is governed by fixed rules, the object
being to make the warrior terrible to enemies.[3] Rings, quills, sticks,
and stones, worn in holes made in ears, nose, lips, and cheeks,
are all originally decorative; and so also prickings and gashes in
the body, often in regular outlines.[4]

116. These latter, made according to tribal custom and law, become tribal marks (tattoo), and are then essential to one's standing
in the community. This custom is general in Polynesia and in

[1] Westermarck, *Human Marriage*, 3d ed., p. 541. This sexual instinct is carried
back by Darwin (*Descent of Man*, chap. xii) to the lower animals.

[2] Cf. Gen. iii, 7. There is no conclusive evidence that the concealment of parts
of the body by savages is prompted by modesty (cf. Ratzel, *History of Mankind*, i,
93 ff.), but it may have contributed to the development of this feeling.

[3] Cf. Y. Hirn, *Origins of Art*, chap. xvi. For the Maori usage see R. Taylor, *New
Zealand and its Inhabitants*, chap. xviii.

[4] Cf. Lucien Carr, " Dress and Ornaments of Certain American Indians " (in *Proceedings of the American Antiquarian Society*, 1897).

parts of North America.[1] The use of oil and other unguents early established itself as a custom of savage society. They were probably useful in a variety of ways. For the hair they made up for the absence of comb and brush; in combat they enabled the warrior to slip from the grasp of his enemy; they defended the naked body from rain, and from soiling and injury produced by contact with the earth and hard bodies; and in sickness they were regarded as curative.[2] Oil was abundantly used as an article of food.

117. All these materials of decoration are transferred to the service of religion. The headdress becomes a mask to represent an animal in a sacred ceremony,[3] or a priestly tiara. In such ceremonies (especially in those of initiation) the painting of the body plays an important part, the traceries varying according to the thing represented and the symbolism of the action.[4] It is often difficult to see the precise significance of the paintings, but in certain cases they are totemic marks, and represent whatever is sacred in totemic belief.[5]

118. It is possible to construe the development in two ways: the paintings may be regarded as originally totemic or other clan marks, and as afterwards employed as ornaments, or the order of movement may be taken to be in the reverse direction; but when we consider the primitive character of decoration, the second suggestion seems the more probable. The same remark applies to the practice of pricking, scarring, and tattooing.[6] For the body-markings blood is sometimes employed, perhaps in part on account of its decorative color, but also probably with a religious significance.[7]

---

1 Ratzel, op. cit., Index, s.v. *Tattooing*; Boas, *The Central Eskimo*, p. 561; Frobenius, *Childhood of Man,* chap. ii. Among some tribes (as the Fijians) untattooed persons are denied entrance into the other world. Naturally the origin of tattoo is by some tribes referred to deities: see Turner, *Samoa*, p. 55 f.; *Journal of the Anthropological Institute*, xix, 100 (New Zealand); xvii, 318 ff. (Queen Charlotte Islands and Alaska). The Ainu hold that it drives away demons (Batchelor, *The Ainu*, p. 22).   2 Turner, op. cit., p. 141.

8 Spencer and Gillen, *Native Tribes of Central Australia*, chap. vi.

4 Frobenius, *Childhood of Man*, p. 31 ff.; cf. chap. i.

5 Spencer and Gillen, op. cit., chap. vii.

6 On a possible connection between tattoo marks and stigmata cf. W. R. Smith, *Religion of the Semites*, 2d ed., p. 334.

7 See § 23. Blood of men is sometimes drunk, simply to assuage thirst, or as a curative (Spencer and Gillen, *Native Tribes of Central Australia*, pp. 462, 464).

119. Decoration has been and is largely employed in structures and dress connected with religious life. Posts and beams of houses, totem posts and masts of vessels are covered with figures in which artistic feeling is discernible ;[1] and in late periods all the resources of art are devoted to the form and adornments of temples, altars, and images. The designs are taken from familiar objects, mostly from plants and animals. The ultimate motive is love of ornament, which, while it finds abundant expression in ordinary social life, has its greatest development in religion — a natural result of the fact that in a large part of human history religion has been the chief organizing factor of society.

120. The tendency has been to make the dress of ministers of religion ornate.[2] This tendency has arisen partly from love of ornament, and partly, doubtless, it is the transference of court customs to religious ceremonial.[3]

121. Symbolism has entered largely into religious decoration. In very early times figures of animals, plants, and human beings were used as records of current events, and were sometimes supposed to have magical power, the picture being identified with the thing represented. In a more advanced stage of culture the transition was easy to the conception of the figures as representing ideas, but the older conception is often found alongside of the later — a symbolical signification is attached to pictures of historical things. These then have a spiritual meaning for higher minds, while for the masses they may be of the nature of fetishes.[4] In both cases they may serve a good purpose in worship by fixing the mind on sacred things.

---

[1] Seligmann, *The Melanesians of British New Guinea*, Index, s.v. *Art, decorative* ; *Journal of American Folklore*, vol. xviii, no. 69 (April, 1905).

[2] So the dress of the Jewish high priest (Ex. xxviii), that of the Lamas of Tibet (Abbé Huc, *Travels in Tartary, Tibet, and China*, ii, chap. ii ; Rhys Davids, *Buddhism*, p. 250), and costumes in some Christian bodies.

[3] Of the same nature is Jeremy Taylor's view (*An Apology for authorized and set forms of Liturgy*, Question I, § 7 ff.) that, as earthly monarchs are not addressed in the language of everyday familiar intercourse, so it is not proper that the deity should be approached with other than choice and dignified words— public prayers should be carefully worded.

[4] Cf. A. C. Haddon, article "Art" in Hastings, *Encyclopædia of Religion and Ethics*.

Economic Ceremonies

122. The first necessity of savages is a sufficient supply of food, and this, they hold, is to be procured either by the application of what they conceive to be natural laws, or by appeal to superhuman Powers. Among economic ceremonies, therefore, we may distinguish those which may be loosely described as natural, those in which a supernatural element enters, and those in which the two orders of procedure appear to be combined.

123. Savages are generally skillful hunters. They know how to track game, to prepare nets and pits, and to make destructive weapons. The African pygmies have poisoned arrows, with which they are able to kill the largest animals.[1] The people of British New Guinea organize hunts on a large scale.[2] In Australia, Polynesia, and America there is no tribe that is not able to secure food by the use of natural means.

124. But such means are often supplemented by ceremonies that involve some sort of supernatural influence. These ceremonies appear to assume a social relation between man and beasts and plants; in some cases there is assumed a recognition by animals of the necessities of the case and a spirit of friendly coöperation; in other cases a magical power is called into play.

125. Desire to propitiate the hunted animal, in order not only to avert the anger of its kin but also to obtain its aid, appears in the numerous cases in which excuses are made for the killing, and the animal is implored to make a friendly report of the man to its friends and to return in order that it may be killed.[3] Formal prayer is sometimes made to the animal in important tribal ceremonies, as in British Columbia a boy is ordered by the chief to pray to the first salmon sighted for a good catch;[4] here the good will of the salmon tribe and the quasi-human intelligence of the fish are assumed.

---

[1] A. de Quatrefages, *The Pygmies*, p. 157.
[2] Seligmann, *The Melanesians of British New Guinea*, Index, s.v. *Hunting*.
[3] Batchelor, *The Ainu* (the hunting of the bear) ; and so many American tribes, and, in part, some half-civilized peoples, as the Arabs of North Africa.
[4] Teit, in *Jesup North Pacific Expedition*, ii, 280.

126. Precautions are taken to guard against antagonistic extra-human influences; there are taboos and rules of purification in preparation for hunting. In New Guinea hunters are required to abstain from certain sorts of food and to perform purificatory ceremonies.[1] Among the Nandi some men are forbidden to hunt, make traps, or dig pits for game;[2] these men, it would seem, are supposed to be, for ceremonial reasons, antipathetic to the animals to be hunted, as, on the other hand, there are men who attract game.[3] The taboos of food and other things imposed are doubtless intended to guard against malefic spirits or mana. The particular rules are determined by local conditions.

127. Certain rules about eating the food secured by hunting appear to have come from the desire to act in an orderly manner and with due respect to the animal. When it is prescribed that a bone shall not be broken this may be for fear of giving offense to the animal kin and thus insuring failure in further hunting.[4] The provision that each man shall gather of a fruit or vegetable only so much as will suffice for a single day may have had an economic ground, the desire to avoid waste; or it may have been made also partly in the interest of orderliness, and so have had originally no reference to any superhuman being.[5] Naturally it was taken up into religion and given a religious sanction.

128. In Central Australia, where every clan is charged with the duty of procuring a particular food (its totem) for the tribe, the custom is that when the product of hunting or gathering is brought in to be thrown into the tribal store, the principal men of the hunting group begin by eating a little of the food, after which the food is

---

[1] Seligmann, *The Melanesians of British New Guinea*, p. 291 ff.

[2] Hollis, *The Nandi*, p. 8 (cf. p. 24).

[3] Hollis (op. cit., p. 6 f.) relates that on a certain occasion when his party was driven from its wagons by a swarm of bees, a Nandi man appeared, announced that he was of the bee totem, and volunteered to restore quiet, which he did, going stark naked into the swarm. His success was doubtless due to his knowledge of the habits of bees.

[4] So in the Tsimshian ceremony in eating the first fish caught (Boas, in *Fifth Report of the British Association for the Advancement of Science*, vol. lix, p. 51). Cf. the Jewish rule (Ex. xii, 46), which may have had a similar origin.

[5] Teit, in *Jesup North Pacific Expedition*, ii, 282. A similar provision is mentioned in Ex. xvi, 16–20.

licit for the rest of the tribe but illicit for the hunters.[1] This custom has been held to have a sacramental significance; it has been suggested that the food is sanctified by the touch of the elders and thus made lawful for the tribe, or that, as naturally sacred, it secures, when eaten, union between the eater and a superhuman Power. But there is no hint of such a conception in the Australian ceremony or elsewhere. The procedure is obligatory and solemn — to omit it would be, in the feeling of the people, to imperil the life of the tribe; but all such usages are sanctified by time. We should rather seek for the origin of the custom in some simple early idea. It is not unusual, in parts of Australia and in other lands, that a man, though he may not eat his totem, may kill it for others; the eating in this case is the important thing — there is magical power in it — and the economic obligation to provide food overbears the sense of reverence for the totem. The only obscure point in the ceremony under consideration is the obligation on the killer or gatherer to taste the food before he gives it to his fellows. This may be a survival of the rule, known to exist among some tribes, that in a hunting party he who kills an animal has the first right to it. The Australian hunter cannot eat his totem, but he may hold to his traditional right; the result will be the custom as it now exists. With our present knowledge no quite satisfactory explanation of the origin of this particular rule can be given.

129. The employment of magical means for procuring food appears in the performance of ceremonial dances, in the use of charms, the imitation of animals, and other procedures. In California the supply of acorns and animals is supposed to be increased by dances.[2] The New Guinea Koita give their hunting dogs decoctions of sago and other food into which are put pieces of odoriferous bark;[3] these charms are said to have been got from the Papuans, the lowest race of the region. A Pawnee folk-story (which doubtless reflects a current idea) tells how a boy by his songs (that is, magic

---

[1] Spencer and Gillen, *Native Tribes of Central Australia*, p. 167 f., and *Native Tribes of Northern Australia*, p. 308 etc.; Strehlow, *Die Aranda- und Loritjastämme in Zentralaustralien*, part ii, p. 59 etc.   [2] Dixon, *The Northern Maidu*, p. 285 f.
[3] Seligmann, *The Melanesians of British New Guinea*, p. 177 f.

songs or charms) brought the buffalo within reach of his people.[1] Among the Melanesians of New Guinea the hunting expert plays a great rôle — his presence is necessary for the success of an expedition.[2] He fixes the date of the hunt, prepares himself by a series of abstinences,[3] and at the appointed time assembles the men, recites spells addressed to ancestors, and passing along the lines of the hunters imitates the movements of the animal sought.[4]

130. Very elaborate ceremonies including imitations of animals (imitative or sympathetic magic) are found in Central Australia.[5] When any animal is to be hunted the old men of the appropriate totemic group, dressed to imitate the totem and accompanied by some of the young men, repair to a spot regarded as sacred, and, along with other ceremonies, trace on the sacred rock, with blood drawn from the young men, a picture of the animal, or figures representing its growth — in general, something that sets forth its personality. These ceremonies, very numerous and extending over a long space of time, constitute the main business of the elders, as, in fact, the procuring of food is the chief concern of the people.

131. There is no perceptible religious element in these Australian ceremonies — no utterance of charms or prayers, no mention of any supernatural being. The acts appear to be simply procedures of imitative magic, customs sanctified by long usage. They relate to the life of the tribe ; this life, like all life, is mysterious and therefore sacred.[6] The belief in the potency of the ceremonies appears to come from belief in the vital identity of the two groups, human and nonhuman — the latter is supposed to respond, in some occult way, to the expression of kinship involved in the official proceedings.

132. The employment of blood (considered as the locus of life) may indicate more definitely a sense of the unity of life-force ; the human blood is, perhaps, supposed to stimulate life in the kindred animal group, and so to produce a large supply of individuals. In

---

1 Dorsey, *The Skidi Pawnee*, p. 149.   2 Seligmann, op. cit., p. 291 ff.
8 Here again the taboos are precautions against injurious supernatural influences.
4 He is said also to imitate the cries of animals — that is, he combines natural means with supernatural.   5 Spencer and Gillen, and Strehlow, loc. cit.
6 This feeling for the tribal life may be called germinal public spirit. Cf. above, § 103.

the published accounts there is no hint that the blood is supposed to have atoning power. There is no sense of wrongdoing or unworthiness on the part of the performers, or of any relation to a deity. The theology of Central Australia is still obscure — the general religious situation in that region has much that is enigmatical.

133. A more advanced ritual occurs among certain agricultural tribes, among whom is found a more elaborate use of blood and a definite recognition of superhuman beings. In these communities it is regarded as necessary to profitable tilling to fertilize the soil with the blood of a slain victim, sometimes human (as among the Khonds of Orissa, the Pawnees, and others[1]), sometimes bestial (as in Southern India[2]); parts of the victim's flesh are buried, or blood is sprinkled on the seed, and homage is paid to a sacred stone or some similar object.

134. In more civilized agricultural communities these ceremonies persist in attenuated form. There is a sacrifice of first-born animals to a deity and an offering of the first fruits of the field ; and as children, no less than crops, are the gift of the gods, whose bounty must be recognized, it is not surprising to find that, along with the first fruits of the field, first-born children are sometimes sacrificed to the deity. Such a custom is reported as existing or having existed in New South Wales, Florida, East Africa, heathen Russia, the Fiji Islands, and Northern India.[3] A trace of the custom among the early Hebrews is, probably, to be recognized in the provision of the Old Testament code that the first-born children are to be redeemed by an animal sacrifice.[4]

135. In the course of time many ceremonies grew up in connection with the procuring and housing of crops and other supplies. In Australia the men of the clan charged with assuring any sort of food were unarmed and fasted during their ceremony.[5] Among the Kondyan plowing and sowing are solemn seasons, an auspicious

---

[1] Frazer, *Golden Bough*, 2d ed., ii, 238 ff.   [2] Hopkins, *Religions of India*, p. 526.
[3] Frazer (*Golden Bough*, 2d ed., ii, 43 ff.) refers to B. Smyth, *Aborigines of Victoria*, ii, 311 ; Strachey, *Historie*, p. 84 ; Krapf, *Travels*, p. 69 f.; Mone, *Geschichte des Heidenthums im nördlichen Europa*, i, 119. See, further, T. Williams and Calvert, *Fiji*, p. 181 f.; W. Crooke, *Popular Religion and Folklore of Northern India*, ii, 169.
[4] Ex. xxii, 29 [28] ; xiii, 12, 13.   [5] Spencer and Gillen, op. cit., chap. vi.

day is chosen, and there are religious songs and choruses.[1] For the Hos of Northeastern India the harvest home is a great festival, held with sacrifice and prayer (though also with great license of manners).[2] A dim conception of law underlies all these procedures. The law is sometimes natural, as in imitative processes, sometimes religious, as when blood is employed or the agency of religious official persons is called in.

136. The economical importance of rain has led to various quasi-scientific and magical devices for securing it, and to the rise of professional rain makers. The methods commonly employed are mimic representations of rainfall or of a storm.[3] The Australian Arunta have a rain clan whose function is to bring the desired supply by nonsacred dancing festivals and sacred ceremonies. A more advanced method is to dip a stone, as rain-god, into a stream.[4] Certain American tribes assign the duty of rain making to secret societies or to priests.

137. All such economical ceremonies disappear with the progress of knowledge, though traces of them linger long in civilized communities. Messrs. Spencer and Gillen note the gradual disappearance of the economical and magical aspect of ceremonies in parts of Australia, and a similar process is to be observed elsewhere.[5]

APOTROPAIC CEREMONIES

138. The savage and half-civilized belief (a belief that has survived to some extent in civilized communities) is that the ills that afflict or threaten a community (such as epidemics and shortage of crops) are due not to natural causes but to supernatural agencies.

---

[1] *Journal of the Anthropological Institute*, xxv, 104 ff.

[2] Frazer, *Golden Bough*, 2d ed., iii, 78.

[3] *Journal of the Anthropological Institute*, xxiii, 18 ; xxvi, 30. Other examples are given by Frazer in his *Golden Bough*, 2d ed., i, 81 ff., 163 ; he cites cases of persons (priests and kings) held responsible for rain, and put to death if they failed to supply it.

[4] Turner, *Samoa*, p. 145. On certain Roman ceremonies (that of the lapis manalis and others) that have been supposed to be connected with rain making see Wissowa, *Religion und Kultus der Römer*, p. 106 ; W. W. Fowler, *Roman Festivals of the Period of the Republic*, iii.

[5] Spencer and Gillen, *Northern Tribes of Central Australia*, p. 23.

But man, it is held, may control the hostile supernatural agents —
they are subject to fear and other emotions, and though powerful are
not omnipotent; they may be expelled or otherwise got rid of —
violence may be used against them, or the aid of stronger supernatural Powers may be called in. In pursuance of these ends
ceremonies have been devised in many parts of the world; though
differing in details they are alike in principle; the question is how
man may become the master of the demons. The ceremonies are
sometimes performed on the occasion of particular afflictions, sometimes are massed at stated seasons, as at the beginning of the year
or in connection with some agricultural festival.

139. Man's defensive attitude toward the supernatural world
appears in many usages connected with ordinary life. Fear of the
hostility of ghosts has led surviving friends to take precautions
against their return — their own houses are closed to them and
they are driven away with blows.[1] They are too near akin to be
trusted, and they are believed to be able and willing to do harm.[2]
At the other extreme of life, when the child comes into the world,
mother and child must be guarded against hostile demonic influences.[3] When a demon is known to have entered into a human
being, producing sickness or madness, exorcism must be resorted
to; magicians, prophets, and saints are able by ceremonies or by
prayer to expel the intruder and restore the afflicted to health.
Ritual taint (which is supernatural), incurred, for example, by touching a dead body, is removed by sprinkling with sacred water.[4]

140. But the term "apotropaic" is generally used of expulsive
ceremonies in which a whole community takes part. In the simplest forms of procedure the hostile spirits are driven out of the
village by shouts and blows; crowds of men rush through the
streets, searching houses, expelling spirits at every possible point
of ingress, and finally forcing them outside the limits of the community. Examples of such a custom are found in the Pacific

---

[1] Tylor, *Primitive Culture*, i, 454; Westermarck, *Origin and Development of the Moral Ideas*, i, 52 ff.; ii, 532 ff.
[2] There is, of course, another side to the character of ghosts — sometimes they are friendly. [3] Ploss, *Das Kind*, 2d ed., i, chap. iv. [4] Numb. xix.

Islands, Australia, Japan, Indonesia, West Africa, Cambodia, India, North America (Eskimo), South America (Peru),[1] and there are survivals in modern Europe. In China this wholesale expulsion is still practiced in a very elaborate form.[2] Among the Ainu, it is said, on the occasion of any accident the " spirit of accidents " (a useful generalization) is driven away by the community.[3] In these cases the spirits are thought of as being in a sort corporeal, sensitive to blows, and also as afraid of noise. There is sometimes a combination of natural and supernatural conceptions : while the violent expulsive process is going on the household utensils are vigorously washed by the women ; washing, known to cleanse from mere physical dirt, here also takes on, from its association with the men's ceremony of expulsion, a supernatural potency — it removes the injurious mana of the hostile spirits.

141. Less violent methods of riddance may be employed. Evil, being a physical thing, may be embodied in some object, nonhuman or human, which is then carried forth or sent away to some distant point, or destroyed. With this principle of transference may be compared the conception of solidarity of persons and things in a tribe or other community :. what one unit does or suffers affects all — the presence of an accursed thing with one person brings a curse on his nation,[4] and conversely, the removal of the evil thing or person removes the curse, which may, under certain circumstances, be shifted to some other place or person.

142. The particular method of expulsion or transference is immaterial.[5] The troublesome evil may be carted or boated away according to local convenience, or it may depart in the person of an animal. Leprous taint is transferred to a bird, which, having been dipped in the blood of a sacred animal, is allowed to fly away carrying the taint off from the community.[6] Even moral evils (sin) may thus be got rid of. In the great Hebrew annual ceremony of atonement not only the ritual impurity of the sanctuary and

---

[1] Frazer, *Golden Bough*, 2d ed., iii, 39 ff.

[2] J. J. M. de Groot, *Religion of the Chinese*, chap. ii.

[3] Batchelor, *The Ainu*, new ed., p. 321 f.   [4] Josh. vii (story of Achan).

[5] Examples are given in Frazer's *Golden Bough*, loc. cit.   [6] Lev. xiv, 1–9.

the altar, but also the sin of the nation, is laid on a goat and sent away to the wilderness demon, Azazel.[1]

143. Examples of human apotropaic vehicles occur in the ancient civilized world. In the Athenian Thargelia the Pharmakos was supposed to bear in his person crimes and evils, and was driven forth from the city.[2] The same conception is found, perhaps, in the Roman Mamuralia and Lupercalia. In the first of these Mamertius is driven forth from the city and consigned to the keeping of hostile persons;[3] in the second, young men ran about the streets beating the women with strips of goatskin, the skin being that of a sacred animal — a proceeding that was regarded as purificatory, and seems to be naturally explicable as an expulsion of evil spirits or injurious mana.[4]

144. In another direction expulsion of evil, or protection against it, is effected by the blood of a sacrificed (and therefore sacred) animal. A well-known example of this sort of ceremony is the Hebrew *pesah* (the old lamb ceremony, later combined with the agricultural festival of unleavened bread, at the time of the first harvest, the two together then constituting the passover); here the doorposts and lintel of every house were sprinkled with the blood of a slain lamb by the master of the house,[5] and the hostile spirits hovering in the air were thus prevented from entering. The sacred blood seems to have been conceived of as carrying with it the power of the family god (who was also the clan god), which overbore that of the demons (in the earliest period, however, the efficacy was doubtless held to reside simply in the blood itself). The ceremony belonged to each family, but it belonged also to the clan since it was performed by every family, and ultimately it became a national usage.

---

[1] Lev. xvi. Cf. the vision (Zech. v, 5 ff.) in which wickedness (or guilt), in the shape of a woman, is represented (in no brotherly spirit) as being transferred from Jewish soil to Shinar (Chaldea).

[2] Miss J. E. Harrison, *Prolegomena to the Study of Greek Religion*, p. 95 ff.

[3] Later the festival was certainly connected with the driving forth of winter, but its earlier form was, probably, as given above.

[4] W. W. Fowler, *Roman Festivals*, Index, s.v. *Mamurius, Lupercalia*. The beating was supposed also to have fertilizing power; cf. S. Hartland, *Primitive Paternity*, i, 100 ff.   [5] Deut. xvi; Ex. xii.

145. Apotropaic ceremonies appear to have been performed originally at various times during the year as occasions arose; the increasing pressure of occupations,[1] the necessity of consulting people's convenience, and the demand for order and precision led here (as in other cases) to the massing of the observances. When so massed they begin to lose their original significance, to yield to the knowledge of natural law, to be reinterpreted from time to time, and finally to become mere social events or to be dropped altogether. Apotropaism has hardly survived at all in the higher religions.[2] In popular customs it appears in the reliance placed on horseshoes and other objects as means of keeping witches and similar demonic things out of houses.[3]

Ceremonies of Puberty and Initiation

146. Ceremonies in connection with the arrival of young persons, male and female, at the age of maturity appear to be universal, and they yield in importance to no other class of social procedures. The basis of most of these is civil; their object is to prepare young persons for entering on the active duties of what may be called citizenship. They involve a distinct idea of the importance of the clan, the necessity of maintaining its life unimpaired, and, to that end, preparing with the utmost care the younger portion of the community to take up the duties of the older. The boys are to be trained to be the hunters and rulers of the clan, the girls are to be fitted to become the wives and mothers of the next generation. But while the ceremonies in question have their foundation in the needs of civil life, they inevitably receive a religious coloring, since religion is intimately connected with all the details of early life.

147. Among the details of the initiation of boys, tests of endurance occupy a prominent place. In various ways the capacity of the lad to endure physical pain or to face apparent dangers is

---

[1] In some savage tribes the older men seem to have nothing to do but arrange ceremonies.

[2] There is a faint survival, perhaps, in the use of incense in churches.

[3] A. Wuttke, *Der deutsche Volksaberglaube der Gegenwart*, ed. E. H. Meyer, Index: J. H. King, *The Supernatural*, i, 111 ff.

tested,[1] and in some cases one who fails to stand such tests is refused admission into the clan and forever after occupies an inferior and despised position. Such persons are sometimes treated as women; they are required to wear women's dress and to do menial work.[2]

148. The seclusion of girls on arriving at the age of puberty, with imposition of various taboos (of food, etc.), is a widespread custom. The mysterious change in the girl is supposed to be produced by some supernatural and dangerous Power, and she is therefore to be shielded from contact with all injurious things. The details of the procedure depend on local ideas, but the principle is the same everywhere. The object is the preparation of the girl for civic life, and the ceremony inevitably becomes connected with tribal cults of the supernatural Powers.[3]

149. A rearrangement of taboos is a frequent feature in ceremonies of puberty and initiation. Certain taboos, no longer needed, are removed and others are imposed; these latter refer, in the case of boys, to intercourse with the men and women of the clan or tribe — they are instructed not to speak to certain persons, and in general they are made acquainted with the somewhat elaborate social system that prevails in many early tribes. These taboos are intended to prepare the boys to understand their position as members of the tribe, responsible for the maintenance of its customs. The taboos relating to food have arisen from conditions whose origins belong to a remote and unrecorded past, and remain obscure.[4]

150. When the ceremony of initiation is elaborate and secret, it becomes mysterious to boys, is looked forward to by them with apprehension, and appeals to their imagination. Supernatural terrors are provided by the leaders — noises are heard (made by the bullroarer or some similar device), and the report is circulated that the

---

[1] *Journal of the Anthropological Institute*, xii, 129 ff. (Andaman Islands) ; ibid. xxv, 188 (East Africa) ; Frobenius, *Childhood of Man*, chap. iii; Frazer, *Golden Bough*, 2d ed., iii, 422 ff.

[2] A. L. Kroeber, in *University of California Publications in American Archæology and Ethnology*, ii, viii; Westermarck, *Origin and Development of the Moral Ideas*, chap. xliii (on homosexual relations).

[3] Frazer, *Golden Bough*, 2d ed., i, 326; iii, 204 ff. ; Hartland, *Primitive Paternity*, Index, s.v. *Puberty*; Crawley, *The Mystic Rose*, p. 55. [4] See below, under "Taboo."

initiate is in danger of death at the hands of a supernatural being. These methods testify to the importance attached by early societies to the introduction of the young into social and political life, and they furnish an early example of the employment of the supernatural for the government of the masses. The old men do not believe in their supernatural machinery, and the boys, after initiation, are let into the secret.

151. *Mutilation* of the body is a widespread custom in connection with initiation and arrival at the age of puberty.[1] In most cases the origin of mutilating customs is obscure. Imitation of the form or appearance of a sacred animal, embellishment of the initiate, or consecration of a part of the body to a deity have been suggested as motives; but there is no clear evidence of such designs. The knocking out of a tooth may be for convenience in taking food; it seems not to have religious significance except in so far as all tribal marks become religiously important.[2] Boring through the septum of the nose is perhaps for decorative purposes. The cutting of the hair is possibly for convenience, possibly for dedication to a deity.[3]

152. Among the most important of the customs of initiation are those connected with the organs of generation, excluding, as is remarked above, complete excision, which belongs to conceptions of religious asceticism (consecration to a deity, preservation against temptation) in the higher cults, and is not found among savages.[4] Partial excision occurs in circumcision, for males, and in similar operations for females.

153. *Circumcision of males.*[5] The most widely diffused of such customs of initiation is the gashing or the complete removal of the

---

1 Emasculation, of course, does not belong here; it is not a custom of initiation proper.   2 Cf. Crawley, *The Mystic Rose*, p. 135.

3 *Journal of the Anthropological Institute*, xxvii, 406 (Omahas). On mutilation as a general religious rite see H. Spencer, *Principles of Sociology*; i, 189, 290, and as punishment, Westermarck, *Origin and Development of the Moral Ideas*, Index, s.v. *Mutilation*.

4 Roscher, *Lexikon*, articles " Attis," " Kybele." Origen is a noteworthy example in Christian times ; cf. Matt. xix, 12.

5 For details of diffusion, methods, etc., see article " Circumcision " in Hastings, *Encyclopædia of Religion and Ethics*.

prepuce. It existed in ancient times among the Egyptians, the Canaanites, and the Hebrews (for the Arabs, the Syrians, and the Babylonians and Assyrians we have no information), not, so far as the records go, among the Greeks, Romans, and Hindus. At the present time it is found among all Moslems and most Jewish communities, throughout Africa, Australia, Polynesia and Melanesia, and, it is said, in Eastern Mexico. It is hardly possible to say what its original distribution was, and whether or not there was a single center of distribution. As to its origin many theories have been advanced. Its character as initiatory is not an explanation — all customs of initiation need to have their origins explained. It may be said at the outset that a usage prevalent in low tribes and clearly beginning under savage conditions of life must, probably, have sprung from some simple physical need, not from advanced scientific or religious conceptions. We may briefly examine the principal explanations of its origin that have been offered.

154. It cannot be regarded as a test of endurance, for it involves no great suffering, and neither it nor the severer operation of subincision[1] (practiced in Australia) is ever spoken of as an official test.

155. A hygienic ground is out of the question for early society. The requisite medical observation is then lacking, and there is no hint of such a motive in the material bearing on the subject. Circumcision is employed in modern surgery for certain diseases and as a generally helpful operation, but such employment appears to be modern and of limited extent. The exact meaning of Herodotus's statement that the Egyptians were circumcised for the sake of cleanliness, preferring it to beauty,[2] is not clear; but in any case so late an idea throws no light on the beginnings.

156. Somewhat more to the point is Crawley's view that the object of the removal of the prepuce is to get rid of the dangerous emanation from the physical secretion therewith connected.[3] Such an object would issue from savage ideas of magic, the secretions of the human body (as urine and dung) being often supposed to contain the power resident in all life. But this view, though

---

[1] This is an incision of the penis from the meatus down to the scrotal pouch.
[2] Herodotus, ii, 37.   [3] Crawley, *The Mystic Rose*, p. 137 f.

conceivably correct, is without support from known facts. There is no trace of fear of the secretion in question, and the belief in power, when such a belief appears, attaches rather to the oblated prepuce (which is sometimes preserved as a sort of charm, or hidden, or swallowed by the boy or by some other person) than to the secretion. Nor does this theory account for the custom of subincision.

157. As circumcision is often performed shortly before marriage it has been suggested that its object is to increase procreative power by preventing phimosis.[1] The opinion that such is its effect, though it has no scientific support, has been and is held by not a few persons. Such an object, however, is improbable for low stages of society — it implies an extent of observation that is not to be assumed for savages; and there is, besides, the fact that certain tribes (in Australia and elsewhere) that practice circumcision do not connect the birth of children with sexual intercourse. In general it is not to be supposed that savages make well-considered physical preparation for marriage in the interests of procreation. The choice of mates is determined by tribal law, but in other respects the individual is generally left free before marriage to satisfy his appetite — it is instinct that controls the relations between the sexes.

158. There is no clear evidence that the origin of circumcision is to be traced to religious conceptions. It has been held that it is connected with the cult of the generative organs (phallic worship).[2] It is true that a certain sacredness often attached to these organs; this appears, for example, in the oath taken by laying the hands upon or under the thigh, as in the story of Abraham.[3] In some parts of Africa circumcision is directly connected or combined with the worship of the phallus.[4] But, on the other hand, each of these customs is found frequently without the other: in India we have phallic worship without circumcision, in Australia circumcision without phallic worship; and this separateness of the two may be said to be the rule. The cult of the phallus seems not to exist among the lowest peoples.

159. The view that circumcision is of the nature of a sacrifice or dedication to a deity, particularly to a deity of fertility, appears

---

1 Ploss, *Das Kind*, 2d ed., i, 368 f.   3 Gen. xxiv, 2 f.
2 On phallic cults see below, § 388 ff.   4 A. B. Ellis, *The Yoruba*, p. 66.

to be derived from late usages in times when more refined ideas have been attached to early customs. The Phrygian practice of excision was regarded, probably, as a sacrifice. But elsewhere, in Egypt, Babylonia, Syria, and Canaan, where the worship of gods and goddesses of fertility was prominent, we do not find circumcision connected therewith. In the writings of the Old Testament prophets it is treated as a symbol of moral purification. Among the lower peoples there is no trace of the conception of it as a sacrifice. It is not circumcision that makes the phallus sacred — it is sacred in itself, and all procedures of savage veneration for the prepuce assume its inherent potency.

160. Nor can circumcision be explained as an attenuated survival of human sacrifice. The practice (in Peru and elsewhere) of drawing blood from the heads or hands of children on solemn occasions may be a softening of an old savage custom, and the blood of circumcision is sacred. But this quality attaches to all blood, and the essential thing in circumcision is not the blood but the removal of the prepuce.

161. The suggestion that the object of detaching and preserving the foreskin (a vital part of one's self) is to lay up a stock of vital energy, and thus secure reincarnation for the disembodied spirit,[1] is putting an afterthought for origin. The existence of the practice in question is doubtful, and it must have arisen, if it existed, after circumcision had become an established custom. Savages and other peoples, when they feel the need of providing for reincarnation, commonly preserve the bones or the whole body of the deceased.

162. *Circumcision and other operations performed on females.* Circumcision of girls is practiced by many African savage tribes (Nandi, Masai, Mandingos, and others), by Malays and Arabs, Gallas and Abessinians and others. Introcision appears to be confined to Australia. Infibulation is practiced in Northeastern Africa and by the Mohammedan Malays.[2] The effect, and doubtless the

---

[1] J. G. Frazer, in the *Independent Review*, iv, 204 ff.

[2] Circumcision of females is the removal of the clitoris and the labia minora; introcision is the enlargement of the vaginal orifice by tearing it downwards; infibulation is the closing of the labia just after circumcision. Cf. Ploss, *Das Weib*, 2d ed., i, chap. v.

purpose, of the first and second of these operations is to facilitate coition ; the object of the third is to prevent coition until the proper time for it arrives. They are all connected more or less with initiation or with arrival at the age of puberty, and they are, naturally, sometimes associated with other ceremonies.

163. *Origin of circumcision.* The preceding review may be taken to make it probable that the origin of circumcision is not to be referred to reflection or to religious ideas. We must look for a cruder motive, and several considerations point to the desire to facilitate coition as the starting-point of the custom (so also R. F. Burton). Reports from all over the savage world testify to the prominence of sexual intercourse in the lower forms of human life. Folk-stories are full of coarse details of the practice. Popular festivals are often characterized by gross license. To lend a wife to a guest is in many places a recognized rule of hospitality.¹ In all this there is nothing immoral — it is permitted by the existing law and is in accord with the current ideas of propriety. Early man seems in this regard to have obeyed his animal appetite without reflection. This form of pleasure occupied (and occupies) a great part of his life, and it was not unnatural that he should seek to remove all hindrances from it. It is quite conceivable that early observation led him to regard the prepuce as a hindrance.

164. About the motives of early man in the adoption of these customs of excision we have, of course, no direct information ; but some later usages favor the explanation suggested above. The operations performed on females are obviously dictated by considerations of convenience or propriety in coition. Various means are adopted of increasing the pleasure of sexual intercourse (in Indonesia and elsewhere).² These procedures are purely animal, nonmoral, and without ulterior design ; there is no thought of progeny or, in general, of preparation for marriage — the frame of mind is appropriate to the lowest grade of life.

¹ Cf. also the great extent to which masturbation prevails among savages. Cf. Westermarck, *Origin and Development of the Moral Ideas*, chap. xliii.

² A rod is thrust through the glans of the penis ; see Roth, in *Journal of the Anthropological Institute*, xxii, 45 (the palang) ; cf. Ploss, *Das Weib*, 2d ed., i, chap. xi ; J. Macdonald, *Journal of the Anthropological Institute*, xx, 116.

165. In the course of time, however, all such customs tend to become sanctified and to take on new meanings. When the importance of circumcision was generally felt, it was natural that it should be performed at puberty and at initiation.[1] It would thus come to be regarded as an introduction to the tribal life — not as preparation, but as a custom established by unwritten law. Its origination would be put far back in the past and sometimes ascribed to supernatural personages — the Central Australians refer it to the mythical ancestors, the later Jews to the command of the national deity issued to the legendary or mythical ancestor Abram.[2] Under certain circumstances it might become a tribal mark; the Hebrews thus distinguished themselves from their neighbors the Philistines, and "uncircumcised" was a term of reproach.[3]

166. Apart from its use in initiation the cultic rôle of circumcision has been small. It does not appear as an element in the worship of any deity, neither in that of such gods as Osiris, Tammuz, Adonis, Attis, nor in that of any other. It is not represented in ancient records as a devotion of one's self or an assimilation of one's self or of a child to the tribal or national god. Its performance is generally a religious duty, as is true of every established custom, but this fact throws no light on its origin. The prepuce is sometimes treated as an amulet or in general as a magically powerful or sacred thing; but many other parts of the body (hair, finger nails, etc.) are so treated.

167. In the higher religions circumcision is generally viewed as an act of physical purification or as a symbol of moral purification. The former view, perhaps, prevailed in Egypt, though on this point the records appear to be silent.[4] The latter view is that of the Old Testament prophets and the New Testament.[5] It has

---

[1] Cf. the defloration of young women (by certain officially appointed men) on the occasion of their arriving at the age of puberty; Rivers, *The Todas*, p. 503; Spencer and Gillen, *Native Tribes of Central Australia*, p. 93; Crawley, *The Mystic Rose*, p. 347.

[2] Gen. xvii. Islam has no divine sanction for circumcision; it is not mentioned in the Koran, doubtless because Mohammed took it for granted as a current usage.

[3] 1 Sam. xvii, 26.

[4] Article "Circumcision (Egyptian)" in Hastings, *Encyclopædia of Religion and Ethics*, and the literature there cited.   [5] Deut. x, 16; Jer. ix, 25 f.; Rom. ii, 28 f.

now ceased to have any effective religious significance, and is retained in some communities merely as a national social tradition or as an ancient divine ordinance.

168. The origin of circumcision suggested above seems to account sufficiently for all usages and ideas connected with it ; the possibility of several different origins need not be denied, but the practical identity of the customs in all parts of the world in which the institution exists, makes the simpler hypothesis the more probable.

169. Certain features of ceremonies of initiation appear to be designed to secure *union* between the initiate and the clan. Such, for example, is the custom found in New South Wales of the initiate's drinking the blood of his companions. In other cases there is a union with other parts of the body. Such usages arise from the idea that physical union is essential to social union — a conception which elsewhere takes the form of blood-brotherhood.[1] This is a scientific rather than a religious idea, depending on the belief that the body is an essential part of the personality.[2]

170. Another noteworthy custom is the feigned *resurrection* of the initiate. In Australia the women are informed that the youth during the process of initiation is slain by a supernatural being and brought to life again. Elsewhere the initiate is supposed to forget his former life completely and to be obliged, on emerging from the ceremony, to recover slowly his knowledge of things.[8] The origin of this custom is obscure, but it appears to express the idea that the youth now enters on an entirely new life, and having come into new relations and responsibilities, is to forget what he was and what he did before — a profound conception which has been taken up into some of the most advanced religions (as, for example, in baptism and confirmation).

171. In certain half-civilized tribes a higher type of initiatory ceremonies is found. The youth must perform a lonely vigil, going

---

1 Article " Brotherhood (artificial) " in Hastings, *Encyclopædia of Religion and Ethics*.

2 Cf. H. C. Trumbull, *The Blood-Covenant*, passim ; W. R. Smith, *Religion of the Semites*, new ed., Index, s.v. *Blood Covenant*.

8 Frazer, *Golden Bough*, 2d ed., iii, 422 ff. ; cf. Gatschet, *Migration Legend of the Creeks*, p. 185 f.

into the forest or some other solitary place, and there wait for the vision or revelation of a supernatural protector.[1] This procedure is connected with the advance of individualism, the old totemic or other relation being superseded by an individual relation to a guardian spirit. The development of this higher religious conception will be discussed below.[2]

172. Finally, instruction forms a part of most initiation ceremonies. The youth is told the secrets of the tribe, and is thus inducted into its higher and more intimate life.[3] This confiding of tribal secrets (the tradition and the knowledge of sacred things) to the young man about to enter on public life is a political necessity, but in the nature of the case connects itself with religious conceptions. Generally, also, moral instruction is given.[4] The ethical code is usually good so far as intratribal relations are concerned (foreigners are not considered): the youth is told that he must obey his elders, respect the rights of his fellow clansmen, and especially be careful in his attitude toward women. In some cases a supernatural sanction for such instructions is added; it is impressed on the youth that some supernatural being will punish him if he disobeys these instructions. The moral code in question is one which springs naturally and necessarily from the relations of men in society, and the supernatural sanction affixed to it is a consequence of the belief that the tribal deity is the lord of the tribe and the natural and most effective guardian of its rights.

173. From this brief statement of initiation ceremonies it appears that they rest substantially on social ideas and necessities. Religion enters into them, as is pointed out above, when a superhuman being is represented as the patron of the clan and the protector of its ceremonies, or when the moral teaching is referred to such a being, or when the initiate seeks a supernatural patron with whom to enter into relations, or when, as in some North Australian tribes, the

---

[1] Alice Fletcher, *Indian Ceremonies*, p. 278.   [2] §§ 533, 1095 ff., 1161 ff.
[3] *Journal of the Anthropological Institute*, xxv, 295 (South Australia); Howitt, *Native Tribes of South-East Australia*, p. 531 f.
[4] *Journal of the Anthropological Institute*, xiii, 296 (Queensland); Howitt, loc. cit.; Spencer and Gillen, *Native Tribes of Central Australia*, pp. 221, 223, and *Native Tribes of Northern Australia*, p. 361.

supernatural being is believed to be angry at the omission of the ceremonies. This last case might recall the displeasure of the Greek gods when sacrifices to them were withheld or diminished ; but more probably it involves simply the belief that all important ceremonies and affairs are under the control of the being in question, who demands obedience to him as lord.

174. In later stages of savage or semicivilized life the clan constitution as a rule has been succeeded by the formation of secret societies, and then initiation into a society takes the place of the old initiation into the clan.[1] Initiation into such a society is often elaborate and solemn — it is carried out in great detail in many Polynesian, African, and North American tribes — but its general features are the same as those of the earlier procedure. Savage societies and civilized mysteries all have their secrets and their moral instruction, and they all represent an advance in individualism. Still later the church takes the place of the mysteries, and here the process of initiation, though more refined, is still in essence identical with the earlier forms.[2] Naturally in the increasing refinement of the ceremonies there is an increasing prominence of the supernatural element, for the reason that the special care of religion recedes more and more from general society (which tends to occupy itself with civil and political questions solely), and is intrusted to special voluntary organizations.

Marriage Ceremonies

175. Marriage is so important a fact for the communal life that it has always been regulated to a greater or less extent by the community, which defines its methods, rights, and obligations.[3]

---

[1] H. Webster, *Primitive Secret Societies,* chap. ii ff.

[2] The office of sponsor exists in embryonic form in many savage communities ; for boys the sponsor is the father or other near relation, for girls an old woman. The duties of savage sponsors usually continue only during the period of initiation.

[3] Westermarck, *Human Marriage* ; H. N. Hutchinson, *Marriage Customs in Many Lands* ; Ch. Letourneau, *The Evolution of Marriage and of the Family* ; Crawley, *The Mystic Rose* ; and the references in G. E. Howard's *History of Matrimonial Institutions,* i, chaps. i–iv ; cf. Hartland, *Primitive Paternity.*

176. In the lowest known tribes the ceremony of marriage is simple: the woman is given to the man by the constituted author- ities — that is, the relatives of the parties and the elders of the clan or tribe — and by that act the two become husband and wife. At this stage of social growth the stress is laid on preparation for marriage in the ceremonies of puberty and initiation. The members of the tribe being thus prepared for union, marriage is merely the assignment of a given woman to a given man. The wife is selected according to established custom; that is, in accordance with custom- ary law, which in most cases defines precisely from what group of the tribe the woman proper to a given man shall be taken.

177. Though the origin of this law goes back to a remote an- tiquity and is involved in obscurity, it seems to have been origi- nally simply a matter of social agreement. It came to be, however, connected with systems of totemism and taboo, and thus to have acquired a certain religious character; and, as being important for the tribal life, it would come under the control of the tribal god when there is such a god. A similar remark may be made in regard to exogamy. Why marriage between members of the same tribe, clan, or phratry should be prohibited is not clear.[1] The rule arose, doubtless, from some social feature of ancient society, and only later was involved in the general religious atmosphere.[2]

178. Gradually greater freedom of choice was allowed men and women, and the ceremonies of marriage became more elaborate. Certain of these seem intended to secure the complete union of husband and wife; such, for example, are the customs of eating together, of the inoculation of each party with the blood of the other or with some bodily part of the other, and the giving of

[1] See below, § 429 ff.

[2] Similar restrictions existed in Greece and Rome. An Athenian citizen was not allowed to marry a foreign woman. In Rome connubium held in the first instance between men and women who were citizens, though it might be extended to include Latins and foreigners. In India marriage came to be controlled by caste. These local and national rules gradually yielded to rules based on degrees of consanguinity. Marriage between near relations was looked on with disfavor in Greece and Rome and by the Hebrews, and the Old Testament law on this point has been adopted (with some variations) by Christian nations. For the Arab customs see W. R. Smith, *Kinship and Marriage in Early Arabia*, chap. iii.

presents by each to the other. All these rest on the conception that union between two persons is effected by each taking something that belongs to the other; each thus acquires something of the other's personality. This is a scientific biological idea; and though it had its origin doubtless in some very crude notion of life, it has maintained itself in one form or another up to the present time.

179. Among many communities the custom is for the bride to hide herself and to be pursued and taken by the bridegroom. This custom, again, is in its origin obscure. Almost certainly it does not point to original marriage by capture, for of such a customary method of acquiring wives there is no trace in savage communities (though in particular cases women may have been captured and married). Possibly it reflects merely the coyness of the woman; or it may be simply a festive procedure, an occasion of fun for the young people, as indeed a wedding now commonly is. In many cases, however, it appears to represent the transference of the woman from her own tribe to that of her husband. Though she was thus transferred bodily and brought into civic relations with the latter, certain taboos, arising from her original tribal position, often clung to her. The right to dwell in her own house in her own tribe, and to receive there her foreign husband, belongs to a relatively late social stage.[1]

180. The defloration of the woman before marriage is rather a preparation for marriage than a marriage ceremony; or it may represent the social right of the elders of the tribe and the relatives of the bride to the possession of her, perhaps symbolizing her entrance into a family.[2] The hypothesis that such a custom points to primitive promiscuity is ably combated by Westermarck, and is involved in great difficulties; it is, however, maintained by Messrs. Spencer and Gillen in their two works on Australian tribes, whose customs seem to them to be inexplicable except on the supposition

---

[1] Cf. Crawley, *The Mystic Rose*, p. 462 ff.; W. R. Smith, *Kinship and Marriage in Early Arabia*, 1st ed., p. 62 ff.; Hartland, *Primitive Paternity*, chaps. v, vi.

[2] In some cases, among the Todas of South India for example, the defloration takes place shortly before the girl reaches the age of puberty (Rivers, *The Todas*, p. 703); more generally it is performed when she reaches this age. This difference of time is not essential as regards the significance of the ceremony.

of primitive promiscuity, in spite of Westermarck's arguments; and in support of this view the sexual license granted in many tribes to unmarried girls may be adduced. However this may be, the custom in question appears to be civil and not religious. The same thing is true of the ceremonies in which bridegroom and bride are hailed as king and queen — a very natural form of merrymaking.[1] The purchase of wives is probably a simple commercial act.

181. The marriage ceremonies mentioned above appear to be all social in their nature. Into them the supernatural is introduced in proportion as the conception of a divine control of society obtains.[2] On the other hand, those customs which are intended to ward off evil spirits or general evil influences from the married pair are religious or magical.

182. Mr. Crawley[8] holds that all marriage ceremonies are essentially religious, as involving the conception of something strange and dangerous in the contact of men and women; they are intended, he thinks, to neutralize dangers by reversing taboos and by assimilating the two persons each to the other, the dangers in question being not merely distinctly sexual but those of contact in general. Though he carries his application of the principle of taboo too far, he has collected a large number of examples which illustrate the separation between the sexes in early society, and the taboos which hold in their social intercourse. The separation of the sexes in early times seems to have resulted largely from the difference in their occupations and the consequent isolation of each from the other. Possibly one result of this isolation was that each saw something strange and wonderful in the other; but it must be remembered that the taboo laws were made by men and are therefore directed particularly against women. The belief in the sacredness of life would act more particularly on the ideas concerning birth.

---

[1] Cf. Frazer, *Golden Bough*, 2d ed., i, 224. For the Old Testament Song of Songs see Budde's commentary on that book.

[2] Sacrifices to local or other deities formed a part of marriage ceremonies in Greece and Rome; Hera and Juno were guardians of the sanctity of marriage. No religious ceremony in connection with marriage is mentioned in the Old Testament; a trace of such a ceremony occurs in the book of Tobit (vii, 13).

[8] *The Mystic Rose*, p. 322, etc.

183. Among many half-civilized peoples and generally in Christian communities marriage is regarded both as a religious ceremony and as a civil contract, and is controlled in the one case by the religious authorities, in the other case by the civil authorities. In Mohammedan communities marriage is simply a civil contract, but religious ceremonies are often connected with it.[1]

Ceremonies at Birth

184. It is possible that early man was so impressed by the fact of life and the wonderfulness of the birth of a human being that he included this latter fact in the sphere of the supernatural, and that the taboos connected with it arose from his dread of supernatural, dangerous influence.[2] Many of the ceremonies connected with the birth of a child may be explained easily as resulting from the natural care for mother and child. Both of these are, in the modern sense of the term, sacred; and even in very early times ordinary humane feeling would seek to protect them from injury.[3]

185. Thus the curious custom of the couvade,[4] in which the husband, and not the wife, goes to bed on the birth of the child, may be an effort on the man's part to share in the labor of the occasion, since he has to take care of the child; or it may be primarily an economical procedure — the woman must go out to work and the man must therefore stay at home to take care of the house and the child. But probably something more than this is involved — there seems to be fear of supernatural danger. It is not necessary to suppose that the man takes the woman's place in order to attract to himself the malevolent spirits that figure on such occasions; but the belief in the intimate vital connection between father and child may induce the desire to guard the former against injury. Similar precautions are taken in regard to the mother;[5] some of these have

---

[1] Hughes, *Dictionary of Islam*, article "Marriage."

[2] The danger might continue into early childhood and have to be guarded against; for a Greek instance see Gardner and Jevons, *Greek Antiquities*, p. 299.

[3] For details see Ploss, *Das Kind*, and works on antiquities, Hebrew, Greek, and Roman.   [4] Cf. Frazer, *Totemism and Exogamy*, i, 72 ff.; iv, 244 ff.

[5] Dixon, *The Northern Maidu*, p. 228 ff., and *The Shasta*, p. 453 ff.; Rivers, *The Todas*, p. 313 ff.; Hollis, *The Nandi*, p. 64 f.; D. Kidd, *Savage Childhood*, p. 7; Lev. xii; article "Birth" in Hastings, *Encyclopædia of Religion and Ethics*.

a natural basis in her physical condition which necessitates a certain carefulness. Where such customs connected with birth prevail, departure from them is thought to be dangerous or fatal; but such a feeling exists in regard to all social customs.

186. The belief that the newborn child is the reincarnation of an ancestor is scientific rather than religious. In Central Australia every child is held to be the reincarnation of a spirit ancestor; a similar idea is found in North America, in Western Africa, and in Orissa.[1] In searching for the cause of birth it is not unnatural that it should be ascribed to a preëxistent being who desires to enter again into human life.[2]

187. The ablutions or sprinklings of water practiced in some places appear to be merely the expression of welcome into the community.[3] The choice of a name for the child is frequently connected with religious ideas. Among many tribes the custom is to seek for some hint from the child itself, as by repeating a number of names and observing which of them the child seems to recognize or accept. The help of a deity is sometimes invoked, as in Borneo, where a pig is killed and its spirit thus sent as messenger to a particular god, who is asked to approve.[4] In Samoa a tutelary spirit is sometimes chosen for the infant;[5] during childhood the child bears the name of a god, who seems to be regarded as its protector. The identification of person and name, common among savages, is also scientific rather than religious. At the entrance into a secret society the novitiate may receive a new name.[6] The adoption of a child's name by the father (teknonymy) may be simply the expression of paternal pride, or possibly it is

1 See above, § 55 f.

2 Tylor (*Primitive Culture*, ii, 3 ff.) suggests that such an idea may have been supposed to account for the general resemblance between parents and children.

3 R. H. Nassau, *Fetichism in West Africa*, p. 212.

4 Haddon, *Head-hunters*, p. 353 ff.

5 Turner, *Samoa*, chap. iii. In some Christian communities the saint on whose festival day a child is born is adopted as the child's patron saint. In the higher ancient religions there were religious observances in connection with the birth and rearing of children, special divine care being sought; see, for example, the elaborate Roman apparatus of divine guardians.

6 Dixon, *The Northern Maidu*, p. 231; H. Webster, *Primitive Secret Societies*, p. 40 f.

the expression of the father's protection or of his identification with the child. The adoption of a secret name that involves the man's personality and is therefore to be withheld from enemies belongs to adult life.

188. The taboos imposed on the mother during pregnancy and after the birth of the child, often numerous and oppressive, are derived from local conditions, and are generally regulated by religion. With the growth of refinement they tend to disappear, while the attendant ceremonies take on a moral and spiritual character, culminating, in the great religions, in the conception that the babe, as a child of God, is to be taken into the religious fellowship of the community and trained for a good life.

Burial Ceremonies [1]

189. Among savage peoples grief for the dead expresses itself in a variety of violent ceremonies of mourning, such as wailing, and cutting and gashing the body. These are partly expressions of natural sorrow,[2] but may be intended in part to propitiate the dead, who thus sees that honor is paid him.

190. The belief that the dead person is powerful expresses itself in the care with which the grave is guarded, it being held that injury to the grave is an injury to the dead, and likely, therefore, to excite his anger. Further, savage science as a rule does not recognize natural causes of death. It regards death as murder, and there is accordingly search for the murderer, often by protracted ceremonies with the aid of a magician. The well-being of the dead man is provided for by placing food and drink, utensils and weapons in his grave, that he may have the means of enjoyment in the other world.[3] To assure him proper service his wives and slaves are sometimes slain, that their souls may accompany his;

---

[1] For methods of burial see article " Funérailles" in *La Grande Encyclopédie*.

[2] Robertson, *The Kafirs*, chap. xxxiii; Batchelor, *The Ainu*, chap. xlviii (the goddess of fire is asked to take charge of the spirit of the deceased).

[3] The food and drink (of which only the soul is supposed to be consumed by the deceased) are often utilized by the surviving friends; such funeral feasts have played a considerable part in religious history and survive in some quarters to the present day.

but this custom is not found among the lowest tribes — it belongs to a relatively advanced conception of the other life.[1] In many cases blood is sprinkled on the ground near the grave of the corpse, as in Borneo (the blood of a fowl);[2] the blood may be meant to be food for the dead, or its supernatural power may be supposed to guard against injury from him to the living.

191. A ban of silence is often imposed — the name of the dead person is not to be mentioned except by certain privileged men;[3] among certain North American tribes on the death of a child there is a ban of silence on the father.[4] The reason for this prohibition of the dead person's name is not certain. It may be respect for him, or it may be merely an expression of sorrow at his loss. More probably, however, it comes from the belief that the dead man is powerful and may be hurtful, and that therefore his name, which is identical with himself, is dangerous.[5]

192. In the cases mentioned above, the dead person is generally regarded as dangerous — to be feared and appeased. Among some tribes, indeed, precautions are taken to prevent his coming back to his house. Very generally the presence of the corpse is held to cause a certain pollution.[6] There is, however, another side to the attitude toward the dead. As he is regarded as powerful, parts of his body are preserved as amulets ; wives wear parts of the bones of the dead husband, and the skulls of the deceased are supposed to be especially powerful, in some cases to give oracular responses.[7]

193. In general, early burial ceremonies appear to be designed to assure the comfort of the deceased in the other world with a view to securing his friendship and aid for the members of his

[1] A. B. Ellis, *The Ewe* (Dahomi), chap. viii; A. G. Leonard, *The Lower Niger and its Tribes*, p. 160 f.; Herodotus, iv, 71 f. (Scythians) ; v, 5 (Thracians). Cf. the Greek Anthesteria and the Roman Parentalia.

[2] *Journal of the Anthropological Institute*, xxi, 121.

[3] Spencer and Gillen, *Native Tribes of Central Australia*, p. 498.

[4] For elaborate Sioux ceremonies on the death of a child see Miss Fletcher, *Indian Ceremonies* (the Shadow or Ghost Lodge).

[5] On the disposal of the corpse, by inhumation, cremation, exposure, etc., see article "Funérailles" cited above ; O. Schrader, in Hastings, *Encyclopædia of Religion and Ethics*, ii, 16 ff.   [6] This may be in part a hygienic precaution.

[7] Haddon, *Head-hunters*, p. 91. Cf. G. L. Kittredge, "Disenchantment by Decapitation," in *Journal of American Folklore*, vol. xviii, no. 68 (January, 1905).

family and clan in this life. As he is of the nature of a divine person, the ceremonies in question are naturally religious. Socially they are effective in binding the members of a community together — a large sense of solidarity is produced by the communal recognition of kinship with the dead. Special stress is laid on this conception in China.[1]

CEREMONIES OF PURIFICATION AND CONSECRATION [2]

194. The essence of religion is a helpful relation to the supernatural, but in early stages of culture man frequently finds himself exposed to conditions, either resident in himself or induced from without, that destroy this relation and disqualify him for the performance of sacred acts. The result is a state of ritual impurity or uncleanness, conceived of at first as purely physical, but tending to become gradually moralized. The removal of the disqualification constitutes purification ; the positive preparation for the performance of a sacred act constitutes consecration ; the two procedures represent two sides of the same idea, and they are related in a general way to ceremonies of initiation and atonement.

195. The occasions for purification are numerous, including all contacts or possibilities of contact with dangerous (sacred) things, and thus often coinciding with taboo conceptions.[3] All acts connected with procreation and birth ; contact with a corpse, or with a sacred person or thing, or with an object belonging to a sacred person ; return from a journey (in the course of which the traveler may have been exposed to some injurious supernatural influence) [4] — such things as these call for cleansing. Inanimate objects also, especially such as are connected with religious worship (altars, vessels, and instruments), require purification ; these are thought of originally as having souls, and as incurring defilement by the transmission of neighboring impurities. A moral conception may

---

[1] De Groot, *Religion of the Chinese*, chap. iii.
[2] Cf. Westermarck, *Origin and Development of the Moral Ideas*, chap. xxxvii ff. ; Saussaye, *Science of Religion* (Eng. tr.), chap. xviii ; and the references given in these works.   [3] See below, on removal of taboos.
[4] Frazer, *Golden Bough*, 2d ed., i, 306 f.

seem to be involved in the requirement of purification after the committal of a murder; certainly, in the more advanced stages of society, the feeling in this case is moral, but it is doubtful whether in earlier stages anything more is involved than the recognition of ritual defilement by contact with blood; homicide, as a social crime, is dealt with by the civil law, and is generally excluded from the benefits of acts of ritual atonement,[1] and so also all violations of tribal law.

196. The religious preparation for the performance of a sacred act usually concerns official persons (see below, under *consecration*, § 202), but sometimes involves the purification of others. The largest act of purification is that which includes a whole community or people;[2] the social mass is then regarded as a unit, and there is no reason, according to early thought, why such a mass should not, by a ceremony, be freed from all ritual disabilities, the idea of moral purification being, of course, absent or latent. Finally, ritual purification is sometimes a preliminary to pleasing and influencing the deity, who, as the most sacred and most dangerous object, must be approached with the greatest precautions.[8]

197. The various methods of purification may be included under a few heads, the principal of which are: the application of water (bathing, sprinkling); the application of sand, dung, bark, and similar things; exposure to fire; incantation and sacrifice; and fasting. In all these cases the virtue lies either in a sacred thing or act that has the quality of dissipating the mysterious defilement present, or in the removal or avoidance of the defiling thing; it is frequently required that the application of the cleansing substance be made by a sacred person, whose character adds potency to the act. The use of water for ceremonial purification has been, and is, practiced all over the world, alike by savages and by civilized peoples:[4] the newborn child, ritually impure by reason of the

---

[1] Cf. Westermarck, *Origin and Development of the Moral Ideas*, Index, s.v. *Homicide*. [2] See below, § 201; cf. the Athenian Anthesteria and Thargelia.

[8] In Ex. iv, 24 f., Yahweh is about to kill Moses, apparently for neglecting a ritual act.

[4] Examples in Tylor, *Primitive Culture*, ii, 429 ff.; cf. Knox, *Religion in Japan*, p. 39.

mystery of birth, is bathed or sprinkled; before the performance of a sacred act the officiator must bathe;[1] numerous ablutions are prescribed in the Old Testament; similar usages obtained among the Egyptians, the Hindus and the Persians, the Greeks and the Romans, the Chinese and the Japanese, the Mexicans and the Peruvians, and other peoples.

198. These usages have arisen doubtless from observation of the natural cleansing power of water and other things in conjunction with the belief in their sacred character. Adopted by the higher religions they have been more or less spiritualized by the infusion into them of ideas of penitence, forgiveness of sin, and regeneration — so in India, Persia, and Peru. Christian baptism seems to have come from Jewish proselyte baptism :[2] the proselyte was by immersion in water symbolically cleansed from sin and introduced into a new religious life, and such was the significance of the rite practiced by John, though his surname "the Baptizer" probably indicates that he gave it a broader and deeper meaning; he overstepped national bounds, receiving Jews as well as non-Jews.[3] Moslem ritual requires ablutions before the stated prayers and at certain other times; every mosque has its tank of water for the convenience of worshipers.

199. Where water cannot be had, usage in Islam and in some forms of Christianity permits the substitution of sand or dust — both thought to have cleansing power. Similar power is ascribed to urine and dung of domestic animals.[4] Such usages may originate in a belief in the physical cleansing efficacy of those substances (the Toda women employ dried buffalo's dung in household cleaning), or they may be supposed to derive their efficacy from the sacredness of the animals. The Todas also make much use of a

---

[1] See the practices described by Rivers, in *The Todas*, Index, s.vv. *Bathing*, *Purification*.

[2] Schneckenburger, *Proselytentaufe*; article " Proselyten " in Herzog, *Real-Encyklopädie*.

[3] In the New Testament baptism is said to be "for the remission of sins" (Acts ii, 38), and is called "bath of regeneration" (Tit. iii, 5); a quasi-magical power is attributed to it in 1 Cor. xv, 29.

[4] For the Mazdean use of urine see *Vendidad*, Fargard v, 160; xvi, 27, etc.; for use of buffalo's dung, Rivers, *The Todas*, pp. 32, 173 f., etc.

certain bark for purification.[1] The origin of these customs is obscure; they go back to times and conditions for a knowledge of which data are lacking — possibly to the early conception of the sacredness of all natural objects.[2] It is less difficult to explain the belief in the purifying power of fire. Its splendor and utility caused it to be regarded as a god in India and Persia, and if it was also destructive, it often consumed hurtful things. It was sacred, and might, therefore, be a remover of impurity. Its employment for this purpose is, however, not frequent; [3] it is oftener used to consume corpses and other unclean things.

200. In the more developed religious rituals, sacrifice is a common accompaniment of purifying ceremonies, the object being to procure the forgiveness of the deity for the offense held to be involved in the impurity; the conception of sin in such cases is sometimes physical, sometimes moral, and the ceremony is always nearly allied to one of atonement. In the Hebrew ritual a human bodily impurity and the apparatus of the temple alike require a sin-offering.[4] In India the bath of purification stood in close relation with a sacrifice.[5] In Greece the two were associated in the cults of Apollo and Dionysos and in ordinary worship in general.[6] Thus, men and gods take part in the process of freeing the worshiper from the impure elements of life: the man obeys the law of the ritual, and the god receives him into association with the divine.

201. Ancient examples of the purification of a whole community are the Hebrew ceremony on the annual day of atonement [7] (which is called in the text a purification), and the Roman Lupercalia.[8]

---

[1] Rivers, op. cit., p. 367.

[2] Compare, however, the use of natural pigments for decorative and religious purposes; see above, § 115 ff.

[3] The Toda ceremony of burning a woman's hand in the fifth month of pregnancy, and a child's hand on the occasion of a funeral (Rivers, *The Todas*, pp. 315, 374), may be purificatory, but this is not clear; cf. Frazer, in *Journal of the Anthropological Institute*, xi.   [4] Lev. xv, 30; xvi, 15 ff.

[5] Hopkins, *Religions of India*, p. 196.

[6] Gruppe, *Griechische Mythologie*, p. 888 ff.; Jevons, *Introduction to the History of Religion*, p. 375; Harrison, *Prolegomena to the Study of Greek Religion*, p. 150 ff.

[7] Lev. xvi.   [8] Fowler, *Roman Festivals*, Index, s.v.

An elaborate festival of this sort was observed every year by the Creeks;[1] it lasted eight days, included various cathartic observances, and ended in a physical and moral reconstruction of the nation. Among the Todas a similar ceremony for the purification of a village exists.[2]

202. Ceremonies of *consecration* are similar to those of purification, only usually more formal and solemn. Entrance on a sacred function, which involves special direct contact with a deity, requires special preparation. Even before a simple act of prayer it was felt to be proper to cleanse one's person;[3] how much more important was bodily cleansing and other preparation for one who was chosen by the community to represent it in its relations with the supernatural Powers! The preparation for such an office is in earlier times ritual and external, and becomes gradually moralized. Magicians must submit to purificatory restrictions, and prove their fitness by various deeds.[4] Initiation into secret societies (whose members had a certain official character) was, and is, often elaborate.[5] Priests in Egypt, Babylonia and Assyria, Canaan, India, Greece and Rome, were subject to conditions of purity, always physical and sometimes moral, that secured a daily consecration.

203. Methods of initial consecration were, probably, of the general character of those prescribed in the Hebrew ritual law.[6] Authority is often conferred by a high official, whose consecrating act is then generally regarded as essential.[7] The priest becomes invested with a quasi-divine authority. The consecration of kings follows the same general lines as that of priests. In both cases the desire is to have some visible form of the deity whose relations with men may be felt to be direct.

---

[1] The native name of the festival, *puskita* (busk), is said to mean 'a fast,' but the ceremonies are largely purificatory; Gatschet, *Migration Legend of the Creeks,* p. 177 ff.   [2] Rivers, *The Todas,* p. 300 ff.   [3] *Odyssey,* iv, 750.

[4] Westermarck, *Origin and Development of the Moral Ideas,* ii, 352; Dixon, *The Northern Maidu,* p. 269 f.

[5] H. Webster, *Primitive Secret Societies,* chap. ix; G. Brown, *Melanesians and Polynesians,* pp. 60-78.

[6] Lev. viii; cf. Copleston, *Buddhism,* chap. xviii; Lippert, *Priesterthum* (see references in the headings to the chapters).   [7] So in some Christian bodies.

204. No purificatory and consecrative usage has been more widespread than fasting.[1] It is found throughout religious history in the lowest tribes and in the most highly civilized peoples, has been practiced in a great variety of circumstances, and has been invested with a special sanctity and efficacy. It has been regarded as necessary before partaking of sacred food, before the performance of a sacred ceremony, after a death, in the presence of a great occurrence (as an eclipse or a thunderstorm, regarded as supernatural), as a part of the training of magicians, as a preparation for the search after a guardian spirit, as a part of ceremonies in honor of gods, as an act of abstinence in connection with a calamity (or in general as a self-denial proper to sinful man and pleasing to the deity as an act of humility), and, finally, as a retirement from fleshly conditions in preparation for spiritual exercises.

205. A great number of explanations of the origin of the custom have been proposed, and it is obvious that the particular usages come from somewhat different conceptions. Apparently, however, all these usages of purification by fasting go back to the idea that the body, which is identified with the human personality, is in its ordinary state nonsacred [2] and therefore unfit for the performance of a sacred act, and that it is rendered especially unfit by contact with a ritually unclean thing. Ordinary food, nourishing the body and becoming a part of it, thus maintains it in its nonsacred character. This point of view appears in the practice of administering a purge as a means of ceremonial purification; the Nandi, for example, give a purge to a girl before her circumcision, and in some cases to any one who has touched a taboo object.[3]

206. The essence of fasting is the avoiding of defiling food; this conception may be traced in all instances of the practice, though it may be in some cases reënforced by other considerations, and is sometimes spiritualized. The efficacy of sacred food would be

---

[1] The details are given at great length by Westermarck, op. cit., chap. xxxvii, with references to authorities.

[2] It is by nature nonsacred, and so remains so long as it has not been made sacred by the special ceremonies that abound in savage communities. We have here the germ of the dualistic conception of man's constitution — the antagonism between spirit and body.　　　　　[3] Hollis, *The Nandi*, pp. 58, 92.

destroyed if it came in contact with common food, or it might itself become destructive.[1] A sacred ceremony demands a sacred performer, one who has not taken a defiling substance into his being. Death diffuses defilement, and makes the food in the house of the deceased dangerous.

207. Other ideas may here come in : abstinence may be a sign or a result of grief, though this does not seem likely except in refined communities; or its ground may be fear of eating the ghost, which is believed to be hovering about the dead body;[2] it is hardly the result of "making excessive provision for the dead."[3] Special communion with supernatural Powers, by magicians and others (including conditions of ecstasy), requires ritual purity, and similar preparation of the body is proper when it is desired to avert the anger of a deity or to do him honor.

208. Once established, the custom has maintained itself in the higher religions[4] in connection with more or less definite spiritual aims and with other exercises, particularly prayer. The dominant feeling is then self-denial, at the bottom of which the conviction appears to be that the deity demands complete subordination in the worshiper and is displeased when he asserts himself. This conviction, which is a fundamental element in all religious thought, pertains properly only to inward experience, but naturally tends to annex nonspiritual acts of self-abnegation like fasting. As a moral discipline, a training in the government of self and a preparation for enduring times of real privation, fasting is regarded by many persons as valuable. Its power to isolate the man from the world and thus minister to religious communion differs in different persons. The Islamic fast of Ramadan is said to produce irritability and lead to quarrels. In general, fasting tends to induce a nonnatural condition of body and mind, favorable to ecstatic experiences, and favorable or not, as the case may be, to a genuine religious life.[5]

---

[1] Cf. the danger to a common man of eating a chief's food; see Frazer, *Golden Bough*, 2d ed., i, 321 f.

[2] Frazer, in *Journal of the Anthropological Institute*, xv, 94, quoted by Westermarck.

[3] H. Spencer, *Principles of Sociology*, i, § 140.

[4] In Christianity in connection with the eucharistic meal and other observances.

[5] The true principle is stated in Isa. lviii, 3 ff.

209. As with other religious observances, so with purificatory ceremonies the tendency is to mass and organize them — they are made to occur at regular times and under fixed conditions, as in the Christian Lent, the Moslem Ramadan, and the Creek Busk. Such arrangements give orderliness to outward religious life, but are likely to diminish or destroy spontaneity in observances. Ceremonies of this sort have great vitality — they are handed on from age to age, the later religion adopting and modifying and reinterpreting the forms of the earlier. In such cases the lower conceptions survive in the minds of the masses, and are moralized by the more spiritual natures, and their influence on society is therefore of a mixed character.

CEREMONIES CONNECTED WITH SEASONS AND PERIODS

210. Some of these have already been mentioned under "Economic Ceremonies." We may here take a general survey of festivals the times of whose celebration are determined by the divisions of the year, and thus constitute calendars.[1] The earliest calendars appear to have been fixed by observation of the times when it was proper to gather the various sorts of food — to hunt animals and gather grubs and plants (as in Central Australia), or this or that species of fish (as in Hawaii). The year was thus divided according to the necessities of life — seasons were fixed by experience.

211. At a comparatively early period, however, the phases of the moon attracted attention, and became the basis of calendars. Lunar calendars are found among savage and half-civilized tribes of various grades of culture in Polynesia, Africa, Asia, and the Americas, and were retained for a time by most ancient civilized peoples. Later observation included the movements of the sun; it is only among advanced peoples that festivals are connected with equinoxes and solstices. The more scientific calendars gradually absorbed the earlier, and it is probable that simple ceremonies that were originally neither agricultural nor astral were taken up into the later systems and reinterpreted.[2]

---

[1] Cf. article "Calendar" in Hastings, *Encyclopædia of Religion and Ethics.*

[2] For a series of dance seasons see Dixon, *The Northern Maidu*, p. 283 ff.; cf. Basset, in Hastings, *Encyclopædia of Religion and Ethics*, ii, 513.

212. When, from observation of climatic conditions and lunar changes, a general division of the year came to be made into spring, summer, autumn, and winter, or several similar seasons (sometimes with intermediate points), festivals gradually arranged themselves in the various periods. The terms designating the four seasons are, however, somewhat indefinite in regard to position in the year and duration, varying in these points in different places, and it is better, in considering agricultural ceremonies, to make a general division into times of planting and times of harvesting. It is not certain whether lunar or agricultural festivals came first in the development of public religious life, but as (omitting the lowest tribes) the former are found where there is no well-organized agricultural system, we may begin with them.

213. The new moon, as marking the beginning of the month, and other phases of the moon are frequently accompanied by observances of a more or less definitely religious character, with great variety of detail in different places. The Nandi[1] have two seasons (the wet and the dry) and twelve months named from meteorological phenomena, and each day in the month receives a name from the attendant phase of the moon. The great ceremonies are conducted in the period of the waxing of the moon, and its waning is an occasion of mourning. The new moon is greeted with a prayer that it may bring blessing. A similar custom exists among the Masai.[2] On the other hand the Todas, though the times of their festivals are all regulated by the moon, appear to have no lunar ceremony;[3] if there was ever any such ceremony, it has been absorbed by the buffalo cult. The South American Arawaks have six ceremonies in the year that seem to be fixed by the appearance of the new moon.[4] The Hebrew first day of the (lunar) month was observed with special religious ceremonies.[5] The full moon, the last phase of growth, is less prominent; where it marks a festival day it is generally in connection with an agricultural event, as among

1 Hollis, *The Nandi*, p. 94 ff.   2 Hollis, *The Masai*, Index, s.v. *Moon*.
3 Rivers, *The Todas*, Index, s.v. *Moon*.
4 Hastings, *Encyclopædia of Religion and Ethics*, ii, 835.
5 1 Sam. xx, 6 (clan festival); Isa. i, 13; Numb. xxviii, 11.

the non-Aryan Bhils of India[1] and in the later Hebrew calendar;[2] in both these cases the observance occurs only once in the year.

214. The new moon of the first month marks the beginning of the year, and new year's day is celebrated, particularly in the more advanced communities, with special observances. The Hindu *pongol* and similar festivals are seasons of merriment, with giving of presents, and religious exercises.[3] Though these occasions now include agricultural epochs, we may recognize in them an interest in the beginning of a new era in life. A like character attaches to the celebration of the Japanese new year's day.[4] Of Assyrian observances of the day little is known, but at Babylon it was celebrated with great pomp, and with it was connected the conception of the determination of human fortunes for the year by Marduk, the chief deity of the city.[5] The late Old Testament ritual makes it a taboo day (first day of the seventh month, September–October); no servile work is to be done, trumpets are to be blown (apparently to mark its solemnity), and a special sacrifice is to be offered;[6] in post-Biblical times the feature of the divine assignment of fates (probably adopted from the Babylonians) appears. The old Roman religious year began with the kalends of March, when the sacred fire of Vesta was renewed, a procedure obviously intended to introduce a new era; on the later civil new year's day (kalends of January) presents were exchanged,[7] a custom everywhere relatively late, a feature in the gradual secularization of ceremonies.

215. Solar festivals, as such, are less prominent than the lunar in religious ritual. Though the sun was a great god widely worshiped, it was little used in the construction of early calendars. Primitive astronomy knew hardly anything of solstices and equinoxes, and where these are noted in the more advanced rituals, they

---

[1] Hastings, op. cit., ii, 555.

[2] Lev. xxiii, 33; Ps. lxxxi, 4 [3]. On the Sabbath as perhaps full-moon day, see below, § 608.   [3] Hopkins, *Religions of India*, p. 449 ff.

[4] Buckley, in Saussaye's *Lehrbuch der Religionsgeschichte*, 2d ed., p. 83.

[5] Jastrow, *Religion of Babylonia and Assyria*, p. 677 ff.

[6] Lev. xxiii, 23 f.; Numb. xxix, 1 ff. The Hebrew text of Ezek. xl, 1, makes the year begin on the tenth day of some month unnamed; but the Hebrew is probably to be corrected after the Greek. Cf. Nowack, *Hebräische Archäologie*, ii, 158 f.

[7] Fowler, *Roman Festivals*, p. 278.

appear to be attachments to observances founded on other considerations — so the Roman Saturnalia, celebrated near the winter
solstice, and apparently the plebeian festival of the summer solstice
attached to the worship of Fortuna; and the same thing is probably true of the Semitic and Greek festivals that occurred near the
equinoxes and solstices.[1]

216. Elaborate solstitial ceremonies are practiced by the North
American Pueblos.[2] A well-developed solar system of festivals
existed in Peru, where the sun was the central object of worship;
equinoxes and solstices were observed with great ceremonies, and
especially at the summer solstice the rising of the sun was hailed
with popular rejoicing as a sign that the favor of the deity would
be extended to the nation.[3] Similar ceremonies may have existed
in Mexico and elsewhere, but in general, as is remarked above, the
astronomical feature at solar epochs yielded to other associations.
Occasional festivals occur in connection with the worship of stars
(especially the morning star);[4] the Pleiades are objects of observation among some low tribes, and in some cases (Society Islands,
Tahiti, Hawaii, New Zealand) the year began with the rising of these
stars, but apparently no festivals are dedicated to them.[5] In the later
theistic development various deities are brought into connection
with heavenly bodies, and their cults absorb earlier observances.[6]

217. Socially the agricultural festivals are the most important
of the early festival ceremonies;[7] they unite the people in public
observances, thus furthering the communal life, and they satisfy
the popular demand for amusement. Doubtless under any social
conditions gatherings for merrymaking would have arisen, but, by
reason of the constitution of early society, they necessarily assume
a religious character. Whether for planting or for reaping, the local
god must be considered; it is he whose aid must be invoked for

---

[1] Cf. A. Mommsen, *Feste der Stadt Athen* (1898), p. 55.

[2] J. W. Fewkes, "The Winter Solstice Ceremony at Walpi" (in *The American Anthropologist*, xi).   [3] Prescott, *Peru*, i, 104, 127.

[4] A Saracen cult is described in *Nili opera quædam* (Paris, 1639), pp. 28, 117.

[5] Hollis, *The Nandi*, p. 100; Rivers, *The Todas*, p. 593 ff.; cf. Dorsey, *The Skidi Pawnee*, p. xviii f.; Hastings, *Encyclopædia of Religion and Ethics*, iii, 132 f.

[6] For some fasting observances in astral cults see Westermarck, *Origin and Development of the Moral Ideas*, ii, 312 f.   [7] As food is the most pressing need.

coming crops, and he must be thanked for successful seasons. The festivals occur at various times in the year among various peoples, but the tone of merriment is the predominant one — it is only in a few cases that a touch of seriousness or sadness is found. Early festal calendars are largely agricultural. In Greece, Rome, and Peru there was a succession of festivals, connected with planting and reaping, running substantially through the year; other ceremonies, of course, stood side by side with them, but these were relatively few.

218. Joyous festivals occur especially at the time of the ripening of crops and harvest. The old Canaanite autumn feasts, adopted by the Hebrews, were seasons of good cheer.[1] In Greece the Panathenæa fell in July–August, the Thesmophoria in October, and the Anthesteria in February,— all agricultural, with joyous features;[2] of the similar Roman festivals the Feriæ Latinæ fell in April, the Feriæ Jovi in August, the Saturnalia in December, and with these should perhaps be included the Ambarvalia (in May) and the festival of the horse sacrifice (in October).[3] Other ceremonies of this nature occur in India, New Zealand, Torres Straits islands, and in the old Peruvian cult.

219. Popular festivities easily pass into license; examples are the Roman Saturnalia and the Hindu Holi[4]; the harvest festival of the Hos of Northeastern India is a debauch,[5] and with it is connected the expulsion of evil spirits — an example of the coalescence of festivals. A peculiar feature in certain of these ceremonies is the exchange of places between masters and servants; this abandonment of ordinary social distinctions is an expression of the desire for freedom from all restraints, and is found in carnivals generally (in the Saturnalia and elsewhere).[6]

---

1 Judg. ix, 27; Neh. viii, 10.

2 A. Mommsen, *Feste der Stadt Athen* (1898), Index, s.vv.; Gardner and Jevons, *Greek Antiquities*, pp. 287 f., 290, 292.

3 Fowler, *Roman Festivals*, pp. 95 ff., 157 ff., 268 ff., 114, 124 ff., 241 ff.; cf. article " Mars " in Roscher, *Lexikon*, col. 2416 f.

4 Hopkins, *Religions of India*, p. 453 ff.   5 Frazer, *Golden Bough*, 2d ed., iii, 78 f.

6 A Babylonian festival of this sort (Sakea) is mentioned by Athenæus (in *Deipnosophistæ*, xiv, 639) on the authority of Berosus, and " Sakea " has been identified with "zakmuk," the Babylonian New Year's Day (cf. the story in Esth. vi); but the details of the festival and of the Persian Sakæa (Strabo, xi, 8) are obscure.

220. Ceremonies of a serious character occur in connection with the eating of the first fruits of the year. In developed cults (as in the Hebrew) the deity is recognized as the giver by the presentation of a portion of the new crop.[1] In very early cults there are other procedures, the origin and significance of which are not always clear. So far as the ceremonial eating, a preliminary to general use, is concerned, this may be understood as a recognition, more or less distinct, of some supernatural Power to whom (or to which) the supply of food is due. The obscurest form of such recognition is found among the Australian Arunta.[2] The Nandi practice is clearer — the god is invoked to bless the grain.[3] In the Creek Puskita (Busk) there is perhaps a worship of the sun as the source of fertility.[4] Probably the element of recognition of extrahuman power (the object being to secure its favor) is to be found in all first-fruits ceremonies. A natural result of this recognition is that it is unlawful (that is, dangerous) to partake of the new food till it has been properly offered to the deity. The ceremonial features (such as the choice of the persons to make the offering) are simply the carrying over of general social arrangements into religious observances — the ministrant is the father of the family, or the chief of the tribe, or the priest or other elected person, according to the particular local customs.

221. The sadness or gloom that sometimes attaches to these ceremonies has been variously explained, and is due doubtless to various orders of ideas; it comes probably from the coalescence of other cults with the agricultural cults proper. The remembrance of ancestors is not unnatural at such a time, and sorrow may be expressed for their death; such is perhaps the case in the Nandi usage mentioned above — the women sorrowfully take home baskets of elusine grain, and the bits that drop in the house are left to the souls of the deceased. Sorrow appears also in other agricultural seasons, as in the Roman Vestalia (in June) and the Greek Thesmophoria (in the autumn), in which cases more likely it is connected with the fear of evil influences.[5] So the great tribal

[1] Lev. xxiii.   [2] See above, § 128.   [3] Hollis, *The Nandi*, p. 46 f.
[4] Gatschet, *Migration Legend of the Creeks*, p. 177 ff.
[5] Cf. the ceremony of the pharmakos in the festival of the Thargelia (Miss Harrison, *Prolegomena to the Study of Greek Religion*, p. 95 ff.).

purification of the Creeks, at the beginning of a new year, naturally coincides with the gathering of the new crop.

222. A further extension of the conception of the sacredness of food (whether or not of the first eating) appears in the Mexican custom (in May and December) of making dough images of gods, the eating of which sanctifies the worshiper;[1] here the god dwells in the bread of which he is the giver.

223. In addition to the astral and agricultural festivals above described there has been the observance of long periods to which a religious significance was sometimes attached. The Egyptian Sothis period[2] (of 1461 years), the Greek period of eight years (oktaeteris), and the Mexican period of fifty-two years were calendary — attempts to harmonize the lunar and solar years ; in Mexico the new cycle introduced a new religious era — a great ceremony was held in which domestic fires were rekindled from the sacred fires. The Hebrew jubilee period (of fifty years), apparently a late development from the sabbatical year, was intended, among other things, to maintain the division of landed property among the people — all alienated land was to return finally to its original owner — participation in the blessings bestowed by the national deity being conditioned on having a share in the land, of which he was held to be the proprietor ; the proposed arrangement turned out, however, owing to changed social conditions, to be impracticable.

224. It thus appears that ceremonies of various sorts have played a very important part in religious life. They have been the most popularly effective presentation of religious ideas, and they have preserved for us religious conceptions that without them would have remained unknown. Their social character has insured their persistence[3] — ceremonies of to-day contain features that go back to the earliest known stratum of organized religious life. While the

---

[1] Frazer, *Golden Bough*, 2d ed., ii, 337 ff.

[2] This period has been generally held to be calendary. Its calendary reality is denied by Legge (in *Recueil des travaux*, xxxi) and Foucart (in Hastings, *Encyclopædia of Religion and Ethics*, article " Calendar [Egyptian] ").

[3] A noteworthy instance of this persistence appears in the history of the Bene-Israel, a body of Jews living in the Bombay Presidency (article " Bene-Israel " in Hastings, *Encyclopædia of Religion and Ethics*) ; they preserve the Jewish religious festivals, but under Indian names.

motives that underlie them (desire to propitiate supernatural Powers, demand for an objective presentation of ideas, and love of amusement) are the same throughout the world, their forms reflect the various climatic, economic, and general cultural conditions of clans, tribes, and nations. They acquire consistency with the organization of society; they tend to become more and more elaborate, just as in other points social intercourse tends to produce formal definiteness; they grow decrepit and have to be artificially strengthened and revived; they lose their original meanings and must be constantly reinterpreted to bring them into accord with new ideas, social, moral, and religious. Their history, in a word, is the history of the development of human ideas, and it sets forth the religious unity of the race. The selections given above are only a small part of the known material, a full treatment of which would require a separate volume.

CHAPTER IV

EARLY CULTS

225. The lowest tribes known to us regard the whole world of nature and the human dead as things to be feared and usually as things to be propitiated. In most cases they conceive of some anthropomorphic being as the creator or arranger of the world. But in all cases they regard animals, plants, and inanimate objects as capable of doing extraordinary things. All these beings they think of as akin to men; transformations from human to nonhuman and from nonhuman to human are believed to be possible and frequent.

226. From the point of view of the savage mind this theory of the world is inevitable. Ignorant of what we call natural law, they can see no reason why the phenomena of life should not be under the control of any of the powers known to them; and for sources of power they look to the things around them. All objects of nature are mysterious to the savage — stones, hills, waters, the sky, the heavenly bodies, trees, plants, fishes, birds, beasts, are full of movement, and seemingly display capacities that induce the savage to see in them the causes of things. Since their procedures seem to him to be in general similar to his own, he credits them with a nature like his own. As they are mysterious and powerful, he fears them and tries to make allies of them or to ward off their injurious influences.

227. But while he excludes nothing from his list of possible powers, he is vitally interested only in those objects with which he comes into contact, and he learns their powers by his own experience or through the wisdom inherited from his forefathers. His procedure is strictly scientific; he adopts only what observation has shown him and others to be true. Different tribes are interested in different things — some are indifferent to one thing, others to another, according to the topographical and economic milieu. The savage is not without discrimination. He is quite capable of distinguishing between the living and the dead. Not all stones are held by him to be alive in any important sense, and not all beasts to be powerful. He is a practical thinker and deals with each phenomenon as it presents itself, and particularly as it shows itself to be connected with his interests. He is constantly on the alert to distinguish between the profitable and the unprofitable, the helpful and the injurious. He himself is the center of his whole scientific and religious system, and the categories into which he divides all things are determined by his own sense of self-interest.[1]

228. It is often by accident that one object or another displays itself as helpful or harmful, just as, in a later and higher form of religious belief, a theophany is often, as to time and place, a matter of accident. Indeed, most manifestations of extrahuman power in the earliest times may be said to come to man incidentally, since he does not generally demand them from the gods or make experiments in order to discover them. But in the nature of the case many things meet him as to which he is obliged to use judgment, and of these a certain number appear to him to be powerful.

229. These objects are held by him to be in some sort akin to man. This seems to be his view of certain dead things in which a mysterious power is held to reside. When such objects are parts of animals (bones, feathers, claws, tails, feet, fat, etc.), or of vegetables that are used as charms, it may be supposed that they simply retain the power resident in the objects of which they are parts — objects originally living and sacred. In other cases an indwelling supernatural being is assumed, as, for example, in minerals whose shape and color are remarkable.

230. Fetish objects in West Africa are believed to be inhabited by spirits.[2] The Australian sacred object called *churinga* — a thing

---

[1] See above, §§ 4, 7.

[2] The word "fetish" (from Portuguese *feitiço*, 'artificial,' then 'idol, charm,'), devised originally as a name of charms used by the natives of the West African coast, is often employed as a general name for early religious practices. Its proper use is in the sense of a dead object, as a piece of clay or a twig, in which, it is held, a spirit dwells. The fetish is often practically a god, often a household god; the interesting thing about it is that the spirit, generally a tutelary spirit, can enter the object or depart at will, may be brought in by appropriate ceremonies, and may be dismissed when it is no longer considered useful.

of mysterious potency — is believed to be the abode of the soul of an ancestor endowed with extraordinary power. Many such fetish objects are found all over the world.

231. Further, the conception of a life-force, existing in many things (perhaps in all things), appears to have been prominent in savage religious systems. Life implies power; but while it is held to reside in all things, its manifestations vary according to the relations between things and human needs. The life-force in its higher manifestations has been isolated in thought by some more advanced savages, especially in North America and Polynesia, and has been given a definite name; in Polynesia and Melanesia it is called *mana*, and other names for it occur elsewhere.[1]

232. It shows itself in any object, nonhuman or human, that produces extraordinary effects. In the Pacific islands all great achievements of men are attributed to it — all great chiefs possess it in an eminent degree;[2] it is then nearly equivalent to what we call capacity or genius. When it resides in an inanimate thing it may produce a physical effect: it comes up in the steam of the American sacred sweat lodge, and gives health to the body (and thus buoyancy to the mind);[3] here it is identical with the soothing and stimulating power of the steam. It is, in a word, a term for the force residing in any object.[4] Like sickness and other evils, blessings, and curses, it is conceived of as having physical form and may be transmitted from its possessor to another person or object. In some cases its name is given to the thing to which it is attached.[5]

233. How widely the conception exists is uncertain; further research may discover it in regions where up to now it has not

---

[1] Algonkin *manito* or *manitu* (W. Jones, in *Journal of American Folklore*, xviii, 190); Iroquois *orenda*; Siouan *wakonda*; Chickasa *hullo* (*Journal of American Folklore*, xx, 57); cf. the Masai *n'gai*, 'the unknown, incomprehensible' (Hinde, *The Last of the Masai*, p. 99), connected with storms and the telegraph. Other names perhaps exist.

[2] Codrington, *The Melanesians*, Index, s.v. *Mana*.   [3] W. Jones, op. cit.

[4] It has therefore been compared to the modern idea of force as inherent in matter.

[5] The American *manitu* is an appellation of a personal supernatural being. The Siouan *wakonda* is invoked in prayer (Miss Fletcher, *The Tree in the Dakotan Group*).

been recognized. Scarcely a trace of it exists in the higher ancient religions. The Latin *genius*, the indwelling power of the man, bears a resemblance to it. The Old Testament " spirit of God " is said to "come on" a man or to be "poured out on" him, as if it were a physical thing — it gives courage and strength to the warrior and knowledge to the worshiper;[1] the power or energy is here (in the earlier Hebrew writings) identified with the spirit or animus of the deity, which appears to be thought of as physical.

234. Mana is conceived of by the peoples mentioned above not as a vague influence diffused through the world, but as a power resident in certain definite persons or things. It is impersonal in the sense in which any quality, as courage, is impersonal, but it is not itself an object of worship; worship is directed toward the thing that possesses or imparts mana. It may reside in a natural object or in a supernatural being — the object will be used to secure it, the supernatural being will be asked to bestow it. In both cases the act will be religious.

235. Mana is itself, strictly speaking, a scientific biological conception, but it necessarily enters into alliance with religion. Belief in it exists along with belief in ghosts, spirits, and gods — it is not a rival of these, but an attachment to them. As a thing desirable, it is one of the good gifts that the great Powers can bestow, and it thus leads to worship. It is found in distinct form, as is pointed out above, only in superior tribes — it has not been discovered in very low communities, and appears not to belong to the earliest stratum of religious beliefs. But it rests on the view that all things are endowed with life, and this view may be taken to be universal. The doctrine of mana gradually vanishes before a better knowledge of the human constitution,[2] a larger conception of the gods, and a greater trust in them.[3]

236. Things and persons endowed with peculiar power, whether as seats of mana or as abodes of spirits, are set apart by themselves,

---

[1] Judg. xiv, 19; 1 Sam. xix, 23; Ezek. xxxix, 29. Fury also is said to be poured out. Cf. Mark v, 30, where power (δύναμις) is said to go out of Jesus.

[2] Cf. the Greek *energeia* and *entelecheia*.

[3] Cf. I. King, *The Development of Religion*, chap. vi.

are regarded with feelings of awe, and thus become "sacred."
In process of time the accumulated experience of generations builds
up a mass of sacred objects which become a part of the religious
possessions of the community. The quality of sacredness is sometimes attached to objects and customs when these are regarded
as necessary to the well-being of the community, or highly convenient. A house, for example, represents the life of the family,
and is therefore a thing to be revered; and in many tribes the
walls, which guard the house against intrusion, and the door and
the threshold, which offer entrance into it, are considered sacred;
the hearth especially, the social center of the dwelling, becomes a
sacred place.

237. The savage communities with which we are acquainted all
possess their stock of such things — the beliefs concerning sacred
objects are held by all the members of the tribe. The development
of the idea of 'sacred' is a social communal one, but it is impossible for us to say precisely how all the individual sacred objects
were selected, or what was the exact attitude of primeval man
toward all the things that are now regarded as sacred.

238. The conception of power resident in certain things to control human life is represented by our term "luck." The formulation
of " luck " systems goes on in savage and half-civilized communities
up to a certain point, and is then checked by the rise of higher
religious ideas and by the growth of the conception of natural
law. But long after the grounds of belief in luck have ceased to
be accepted by the advanced part of the community, many individual forms of good luck and bad luck maintain themselves in
popular belief.[1] Some of these beliefs may be traced back to their
savage sources, especially those that are connected with animals;
the origin of most of them is obscure. They coalesce to some
extent with conceptions derived from magic, divination, and taboo.
The persistence of such savage dogma into civilized times enables us to understand how natural this dogma was for early
forms of society.

[1] Examples in J. H. King, *The Supernatural.* Cf. T. S. Knowlson, *Origins of
Popular Superstitions*, etc.; T. Keightley, *Fairy Mythology.*

239. In the practices mentioned above there is no worship proper. Mana is not thought of as being in itself a personal power, and worship is paid only to objects regarded as having personality. The fetish derives its value from the spirit supposed to be resident in the fetish objects; these are commonly worn as charms, and the attitude of the man to such a charm, though he regards it as powerful, seems to be not exactly that of worship — he keeps it as a protection so long as it appears to be useful, but, as is remarked above, he acts as if he were its master. He believes that the efficient factor is the indwelling spirit, but he commonly distinguishes between this spirit and a god proper. When, however, the fetish is regarded as a tutelary divinity, it loses its lower character and takes its place among the gods.

240. We turn now to man's attitude toward other objects, similarly regarded as sacred, but invested with distinct personality, and supposed to act consciously on human life. These are all such things as men's experiences bring them into intimate relations with, this relationship forming the basis of the high regard in which they are held. They are animals, plants, mountains, rivers, heavenly bodies, living men, and ghosts. These are objects of cults, many of them in some cases being worshiped at the same time in a single community. A chronological order in the adoption of such cults it is not possible to determine. All objects stand together in man's consciousness in early cultural strata, and the data now at command do not enable us to say which of them first assumed for him a religious character; the chronological order of cults may have differed in different communities when the general social conditions were different. We may begin with the cult of animals without thereby assuming that it came first in order of time.

ANIMALS

241. Of all nonhuman natural objects it would seem to have been the animal that most deeply impressed early man.[1] All objects were potentially divine for him, and all received worship, but none

---

[1] Cf. Tylor, *Primitive Culture*, 3d ed., ii, 229 ff.; article "Animals" in Hastings, *Encyclopædia of Religion and Ethics*.

entered so intimately into his life as animals. He was doubtless struck, perhaps awed, by the brightness of the heavenly bodies, but they were far off, intangible; mountains were grand and mighty, but motionless; stones lay in his path, but did not approach him; rivers ran, but in an unchanging way, rarely displaying emotion; plants grew, and furnished food, but showed little sign of intelligence. Animals, on the other hand, dwelt with him in his home, met him at every turn, and did things that seemed to him to exhibit qualities identical with his own, not only physical but also mental — they showed swiftness, courage, ferocity, and also skill and cunning. In certain regards they appeared to be his superiors, and thus became standards of power and objects of reverence.

242. At a very early period the belief in social relations between men and animals appears. The latter were supposed to have souls, to continue their existence after death, sometimes to come to life on earth after death. Their social life was supposed to be similar to that of men;[1] in Samoa the various species form social units,[2] the Ainu see tattoo marks on frogs and sparrows,[3] the Arabs recognize a clan organization in beasts.[4]

243. From identity of nature comes the possibility of transformation and transmigration.[5] An Australian of the Kangaroo clan explained that he might be called either kangaroo or man — it was all the same, man-kangaroo or kangaroo-man, and the Australian legends constantly assume change from human to animal and from animal to human.[6] The same belief appears in Africa and North America, and may be assumed to be universal among savages. It survives in the Greek transformation stories and in the werwolf and swan maiden of the European popular creed. It is the basis of a part of the theory of the transmigration of souls.[7]

---

[1] This may have been simply the transference to them of human custom, or it may also have been suggested by the obvious social organization of such animals as bees, ants, goats, deer, monkeys.   [2] Turner, *Samoa*, pp. 21, 26.

[3] Batchelor, *The Ainu*, p. 27.

[4] W. R. Smith, *Religion of the Semites*, (new ed., see p. 106) p. 128 f.

[5] A. Lang, *Myth, Ritual, and Religion*, i, 117 ff.

[6] Spencer and Gillen, *Native Tribes of Central Australia*, pp. 389, 401. Some Australians believed in an original gradual transformation of animals and plants into human beings.   [7] On the conception of animals as ancestors see below, § 449 f.

244. The relations of early man with animals are partly friendly, partly hostile. A friendly attitude is induced by admiration of their powers and desire for their aid. Such an attitude is presupposed in the myths of intermarriage between beasts and men. It is perhaps visible also in the custom of giving or assuming names of animals as personal names of men, though this custom may arise from the opinion that animals are the best expressions of certain qualities, or from some conception underlying totemistic organization; the general history of savage proper names has not yet been written. Beast tales, likewise, bear witness to man's opinion of the cleverness or folly of his nonhuman brethren, and perhaps originally to nothing more. The distinctest expression of friendliness is seen in certain religious customs spoken of below.

245. On the other hand, early man necessarily comes into conflict with animals. Against some of them he is obliged to protect himself by force or by skillful contrivance; others must be slain for food. With all of them he deals in such a way as to secure his own well-being, and thus comes to regard them as things subservient to him, to be used in such way as he may find profitable. Those that he cannot use he gradually exterminates, or, at a later stage, these, banished to thickets, mountains, deserts, caves, and other inhospitable places, are excluded from human society and identified with demons.[1]

246. The two attitudes, of friendliness and of hostility, coexist throughout the savage period, and, in softened form, even in half-civilized life. They represent two points of view, both of which issue from man's social needs. Early man is logical, but he comprehends the necessity of not pushing logic too far — he is capable of holding at the same time two mutually contradictory views, and of acting on each as may suit his convenience; he makes his dogma yield to the facts of life (a saving principle not confined to savages,

---

[1] A demon may be defined as a supernatural being with whom, for various reasons, men have not formed friendly relations. Cf. W. R. Smith, *Religion of the Semites*, new ed., p. 119 ff., on the Arabian jinn; De Groot, *Religion of the Chinese*, p. 13 ff., for the Chinese belief in demonic animals. On the origin, names, and functions of demons and on exorcismal ceremonies connected with them see below, § 690 ff., and above, §138 ff.

but acted on to a greater or less extent by all societies). He slays sacred animals for divinatory and other religious purposes, for food, or in self-defense; he fears their anger, but his fear is overcome by hunger; he offers profuse apologies, explains that he acts without ill will and that the bones of the animal will be preserved and honored, or he declares that it is not he but some one else that is the slayer — but he does not hesitate to kill.[1]

247. This fact — the existence of different points of view — enables us to understand in part the disrespectful treatment of sacred animals in folk-tales. Such tales are the product of popular fancy, standing apart from the serious and solemn conceptions of the tribal religion. The reciter, who will not fail at the proper time to pay homage to his tribal patron, does not hesitate at other times to put him into ridiculous and disgraceful situations.[2]

248. Man's social contact with the lower animals is doubtless as old as man himself, but there are no records of his earliest life, and it is not possible to say exactly when and how his religious relations with them began. His attitude toward them, as is remarked above, was a mixed one; in general, however, it may be assumed that constant intercourse with them revealed their great qualities and impressed on him the necessity of securing their good will. This was especially true of those of them that stood nearest to him and were of greatest importance for his safety and convenience. These, invested with mystery by reason of their power and their strangeness, were held in great respect as quasi-gods, were approached with caution, and thus acquired the character of sacredness. Gradually, as human society was better and better organized, as conceptions of government became clearer, and as the natures of the various animals were more closely studied, means were devised of guarding against their anger and securing their friendship and aid. Our earliest information of savage life reveals in every tribe an inchoate pantheon of beasts. All the essential apparatus of public religion is present in these communities in embryonic form — later

---

[1] So the Eskimo, the Ainu, the Redmen, and modern Arabs in Africa; many other instances are cited by Frazer in his *Golden Bough*, 2d ed., ii, 386 ff.

[2] Examples are found in many folk-stories of savages everywhere.

movements have had for their object merely to clarify ideas and refine procedures.

249. The animals revered by a tribe are those of its vicinage, the inhabitants of its hunting grounds. Some of these man uses as food, some he fears. His relation to plains, mountains, forests, lakes, rivers, and seas, influences his choice of sacred beasts. Usually there are many of them, and the natural inference is that originally all animals are sacred, and that gradually those most important for man are singled out as objects of special regard.

250. Thus, to mention the principal of them : in Africa we find lion, leopard, hyena, hippopotamus, crocodile, bull, ram, dog, cat, ape, grasshopper ; in Oceania, kangaroo, emu, pig, heron, owl, rail, eel, cuttlefish ; in Asia, lion, elephant, bear, horse, bull, dog, pig, eagle, tiger, water wagtail, whale ; in Europe, bear, wolf, horse, bull, goat, swan ; in America, whale, bear, wolf, fox, coyote, hare, opossum, deer, monkey, tiger, beaver, turtle, eagle, raven, various fishes. The snake seems to have been generally revered, though it was sometimes regarded as hostile.[1] Since animals are largely valued as food, changes in the animals specially honored follow on changes in economic organization (hunting, pastoral, and agricultural stages).

251. Often animals are looked on as the abodes or incarnations of gods or spirits : so various birds, fishes, and beasts in Polynesia (in Samoa every man has a tutelary deity, which appears in the form of an animal[2]), Siberia, Mexico, and elsewhere. In other cases they are revered as incarnations of deceased men.[3] Where a species of animal is supposed to represent a god, this view is probably to be regarded not as a generalization from an individualistic to a specific conception (a process too refined for savages), but as an attempt to carry over to the animal world the idea of descent

---

[1] For other sacred animals see N. W. Thomas, article "Animals" in Hastings, *Encyclopædia of Religion and Ethics.*   [2] Turner, *Samoa*, p. 238.

[3] Frazer, *Golden Bough*, 2d ed., ii, 430 ff. ; Thomas, article "Animals" cited above ; Shortland, *Traditions of New Zealand*, iv ; Marsden, *Sumatra*, p. 292 ; Schoolcraft, *Indian Tribes*, i, 34 ; v, 652 ; Waitz, *Anthropologie*, iii, 190 ; Callaway, *Amazulus*, p. 196 ; A. B. Ellis, *The Tshi*, p. 150 ; Mouhot, *Indo-China*, i, 252 ; J. Wasiljev, *Heidnische Gebräuche der Wotyaks*, pp. 26, 78, etc. ; G. de la Vega, *Comentarios Reales*, bk. i, chap. ix, etc. (Peru) ; Miss Kingsley, *Travels*, p. 492.

from a common ancestor combined with the idea of a special creator for every family of animals.[1]

252. In the course of religious growth the beast-god may be replaced or succeeded by an anthropomorphic god, and then the former is regarded as sacred to the latter — the recollection of the béast form still remains after the more refined conception has been reached, and the two, closely connected in popular feeling, can be brought into harmony only by making one subordinate to the other.[2] A certain element or flavor of divinity clings to the beast a long time, but finally vanishes under the light of better knowledge.

253. While the cases, very numerous, in which animals are associated in worship with gods — in composite forms (as in Egypt, Babylonia, and Assyria) or as symbols of deities or sacred to them — point probably to early beast-cults, Egypt alone of the ancient civilized nations maintained the worship of the living animal.[3] For the better thinkers of Egypt beasts doubtless were incarnations or symbols of deities; but the mass of the people appear to have regarded them as gods in their own persons.

254. Reverence for animals persists in attenuated form in civilized nations in various superstitions connected with them. Their appearances and their cries are believed to portend success or disaster. The great number of "signs" recognized and relied on by uneducated and educated persons at the present day bear witness to the strong hold that the cult of animals had on early man.[4]

255. It is in keeping with early ideas that savages often, perhaps generally, ascribe the creation or construction of the world (so far as they know it) to animals. The creation (whether by beasts or

---

[1] Turner, op. cit., p. 242; Castrén, *Finnische Mythologie*, pp. 106, 160, 189, etc.; Parkman, *Jesuits in North America* (1906), pp. 61 f., 66; Brinton, *Myths of the New World*, pp. 3, 105, 127, 161, 175, 272; cf. Acosta, *Historia de las Indias*, bk. v, chap. iv.

[2] So Zeus and bull, Artemis and bear, Aphrodite and dove, and many other examples. In such cases it is generally useless to try to discover a resemblance between the character of the god and that of the associated animal. There is simply, as a rule, a coalescence of cults, or an absorption of the earlier cult in the later.

[3] The particular conditions that induced this cult in Egypt escape us. See the works on Egyptian religion by Maspero, Wiedemann, Erman, Steindorff, and others.

[4] On the curious attitude of medieval Europe toward animals as legally responsible beings see E. P. Evans, *The Criminal Prosecution and Capital Punishment of Animals*.

by other beings) is not conceived of as produced out of nothing; there is always preëxisting material, the origin of which is not explained; primitive thought seems not to have considered the possibility of a situation in which nothing existed. The " creation " conceived of is the arrangement of existing material into the forms familiar to man — every tribe accounting thus for its own environment. The origin of the land, of mountains, defiles, lakes, rivers, trees, rocks, sun, moon, and stars, wind and rain, human beings and lower animals, and sometimes of social organizations and ceremonies, is explained in some way natural to the thought of the time and place. Not all these details occur in the cosmogony of every tribe or clan, but the purpose of every cosmogony is to account for everything in the origin of which the people are interested.

256. The creator in the cosmogonies known to us is not always an animal — he is sometimes a man, sometimes a god; it is possible, however, that human and divine creators are the successors of original animal creators. In Central Australia the production of certain natural features of the country and the establishment of certain customs are ascribed to ancestors, mythical beings of the remote past, creatures both animal and human, or rather, either animal or human — possibly animals moving toward the anthropomorphic stage.[1] However this may be, there are instances in which the creator is an animal pure and simple, though, of course, endowed with extraordinary powers. The beast to which the demiurgic function is assigned is selected, it would seem, on the ground of some peculiar skill or other power it is supposed to possess; naturally the reason for the choice is not always apparent. For the Ainu the demiurge is the water wagtail;[2] for the Navahos and in California,[3] the coyote or prairie wolf; among the Lenni-Lenâpé, the wolf.[4] Various animals — as elephants, boars, turtles,

---

[1] Spencer and Gillen, *Native Tribes of Central Australia*, chap. x. Two superhuman creators are said to have transformed themselves into lizards (ibid. p. 389 ff.).

[2] Batchelor, *The Ainu*, p. 35 ff.

[3] Matthews, *Navaho Legends*, pp. 80, 223; Dixon, *The Northern Maidu*, p. 263.

[4] Brinton, *Myths of the New World*, p. 269; cf. article " Animals " in Hastings, *Encyclopædia of Religion and Ethics*.

snakes — are supposed to bear the world on their backs. The grounds of such opinions, resting on remote social conditions, are obscure.

257. Though, in early stadia of culture, animals are universally revered as in a sort divine, there are few recorded instances of actual worship offered them.[1] Whether the Bushmen and the Hottentots worship the mantis (the Bushman god Cagn) as animal is not quite clear.[2] The bear, when it is ceremonially slain, is treated by the Ainu as divine — it is approached with food and prayer, but only for the specific purpose of asking that it will speak well of them to its divine kin and will return to earth to be slain. The Zuñi cult of the turtle and the Californian worship of the bird called *panes* [3] present similar features. The non-Aryan Santhals of Bengal are said to offer divine worship to the tiger.[4] Such worship appears to be paid to the snake by the Naga tribes and the Gonds of India, and by the Hopi of North America.[5]

258. In these and similar cases it is sometimes difficult to say whether the animal is worshiped in its own person merely, or as the embodiment or representative of a god or of ancestors. The usages in question are almost entirely confined to low tribes, and disappear with the advance of civilization; wild animals are banished from society and cease to be sacred, and the recollection of their early character survives only in their mythological attachment to deities proper. For a different reason domesticated animals lose their sacredness — they become merely servants of men. The Egyptian cult of the bull is the best-attested instance of actual worship of a domestic animal, and parallels to this it is hard to find; the Todas, for example, for whom the buffalo is the central sacred object, do not now pay worship to the animal — they may have done so in former times.

---

[1] See above, § 253, for the Egyptian cult.

[2] References to Stow's *Native Races of South Africa* and Merensky's *Beiträge* are given in Hastings, *Encyclopædia of Religion and Ethics*, i, 522.

[3] Cushing, in *The Century Magazine*, 1883; Tylor, *Primitive Culture*, ii, 243 f.

[4] Crooke, *Popular Religion and Folklore of Northern India*, ii, 213.

[5] Hopkins, *Religions of India*, pp. 539, 527; Crooke, op. cit.; Fewkes, "The Winter Solstice Ceremony at Walpi," p. 17 ff.

259. The sacredness of animals, and the fact that they are regarded as embodying the souls of things and human beings, have led to a coalescence of their cults with other religious observances. They are abundantly employed in magical procedures and in sacrifices ; they are often identified with spirits of vegetation, any locally revered animal being chosen for this purpose ; they are brought into connection with astral objects and their forms are fancifully seen in sun, moon, and constellations ; they play a great rôle in apotropaic and purificatory ceremonies ; and they appear in myths of all sorts,[1] especially in the histories of gods.

260. But, though they are in many cases regarded as tutelary beings, it is doubtful whether they ever develop into anthropomorphic deities.[2] The creation of such deities followed a different line [3] and dispensed with the lower quasi-divine forms. Such manlike attributes as beasts were supposed to have were taken up into the distincter and nobler conceptions of tribal gods to whom beasts were more and more subordinated. The latter were allegorized and spiritualized, and came to serve merely as material for poetry.

261. Yet beast worship, such as it was and is, has played an important part in religious development. It has furnished a point of crystallization for early ideas, and has supplied interesting objects in which man's demand for superhuman companionship could find satisfaction.[4] It has disappeared when it has been no longer needed.

PLANTS

262. The cult of plants has been as widespread as that of animals, and, if its rôle in the history of religion has been less important than that of the latter, this is because plants show less definite signs of life than animals and enter less intimately than they into the social

---

[1] For a fanciful connection between the sun-myth and the spider see Frobenius, *Childhood of Man*, chap. xxiii.

[2] A somewhat vague Naga (snake) being of this sort is noted (Hopkins, *Religions of India*, p. 539). The relation between the Australian supernatural being Bunjil (or Punjil) and the eagle-hawk is not clear. Cf. Howitt, *Native Tribes of South-East Australia*, Index ; Spencer and Gillen, *Native Tribes of Central Australia*, Index.

[3] See below, § 635 f.

[4] A special form of man's relations with animals is considered below under " Totemism."

interests of man. But, like all other things, they are regarded by early man as living, as possessing a nature similar to that of man, and as having power to work good or ill. Trees are represented as thinking, speaking, entering into marriage relations, and in general doing whatever intelligent beings can do. Through thousands of years in the period before the dawn of written history man was brought into constant contact with the vegetable world, and learned by experience to distinguish between plants that were beneficial and those that were harmful. His observation created an embryonic science of medicine, and his imagination an embryonic religious cult.

263. The value of certain vegetable products (fruits, nuts, wild plants) as food must have become known at a very early time, and these would naturally be offered to the extrahuman Powers. At a later time, when cereals were cultivated, they formed an important part of sacrificial offerings, and were held — as, for example, among the Greeks and the Hebrews — to have piacular efficacy.

264. Among the discoveries of the early period was that of the intoxicating quality of certain plants — a quality that came to play a prominent rôle in religious life. Valued at first, probably, for the agreeable sensations they produced, such plants were later supposed to possess magical power, to exert a mysterious influence on the mind, and to be the source or medium of superhuman communications. Thus employed by magicians they were connected with the beginnings of religious ecstasy and prophecy. Their magical power belongs to them primarily as living things, but came to be attributed to extrahuman beings.

265. Plants as living things were supposed to possess souls.[1] Probably the soul was conceived of at first as simply the vital principle, and the power of the plant was thought of as similar

---

[1] For example, in Sumatra, offerings are made to the "soul of the rice"; there is fear of frightening the rice-spirit, and ceremonies are performed in its honor; see Wilken, *Het Animisme bij de Volken van den Indischen Archipel*; Kruyt, *De Rijstmoeder van den Indischen Archipel*, 389. It has been suggested that the prohibition of yeast in the Hebrew mazzot (unleavened bread) festival may have come originally from fear of frightening the spirit of the grain. It may have been, however, merely the retention of an old custom (if the grain was eaten originally without yeast), which later (as sometimes happened in the case of old customs) was made sacred by its age, was adopted into the religious code, and so became obligatory.

to the power of an animal or any other living thing. In the course of time this soul, the active principle, was distinguished from the vital principle, was isolated and regarded as an independent being dwelling in the plant. To it all the powers of the latter were ascribed, and it became a friend or an enemy, an object of worship or of dread.[1]

266. This difference of attitude on man's part toward different plants probably showed itself at an early period. Those that were found to be noxious he would avoid; the useful he would enter into relations with, though on this point for very early times there is in the nature of the case little information.[2] Unfriendly or demonic spirits of plants are recognized by savage man in certain forests whose awe-inspiring gloom, disease-breeding vapors, and wild beasts repel and frighten him. Demons identified with plants or dwelling in them are of the same nature as animal demons, and have been dealt with in the same way as these.[3]

267. The progress of society brought men into association with useful plants, such as medicinal and edible herbs, and fruit-bearing and shade-giving trees; these, conceived of as inhabited by anthropomorphic spirits, fulfilled all the functions that attach to friendly animals. They became guardians and allies, totems and ancestors.[4] Several of the Central Australian totems are plants, and form part of the mythical ancestral population constructed by the imagination or ethnographic science of the people.[5] In Samoa a plant is often the incarnation of a spirit friendly to a particular family[6] — a conception that is not improbably a development from an earlier view that a certain plant had a special relation to a certain clan.[7]

---

1 This conception survives in the expressions " spirit of wine," etc., and Cassio's " invisible spirit of wine " easily passes into a " devil."

2 This distinction is made in a somewhat formal way by the Ainu, a very rude people (Batchelor, *The Ainu*, chap. xxxiii).

3 W. R. Smith, *Religion of the Semites*, 2d ed., p. 132 f.

4 Frazer, *Totemism and Exogamy*, Index, s.vv. *totems, ancestors.*

5 Spencer and Gillen, *Native Tribes of Central Australia*, pp. 112, 116. Many other plant totems are mentioned by Frazer in his *Totemism and Exogamy.*

6 Turner, *Samoa*, pp. 32, 39, 43, 72.

7 This relation was not necessarily totemic — it may have been of a general character, of which totemism is a special form.

In general, a plant important in a given region (as, for example, the tobacco plant in North America) is likely to be invested with a sacred character.

268. Trees, by reason of their greater dignity (size, beauty, protective character), have generally been singled out as special cultic ·centers.[1] A great tree sometimes served as a boundary mark or signpost; under trees chiefs of clans sat to decide disputes. Thus invested with importance as a sort of political center as well as the abode of a spirit, a tree naturally became a shrine and an asylum.[2] In India and Greece, and among the ancient Celts and Germans, the gods were worshiped in groves, by the Canaanites and Hebrews "under every green tree." To cut down a sacred tree was a sacrilege, and the spirit of the tree was believed to avenge the crime.[3]

269. As might be expected, there is hardly a species of tree that has not been held sacred by some group of men. The Nagas and other tribes of Northeast India regard all plants as sacred,[4] and every village has its sacred tree. In Babylonia and Assyria, it is said, there were hundreds of trees looked on as invested with more or less sanctity. The oak was revered in some parts of Greece, and among the Romans and the Celts. The cult of particular species, as the pipal (*Ficus religiosa*), the vata or banyan (*Ficus Indica*), the karam and others, has been greatly systematized in India.[5]

270. Vegetable spirits in some cases have developed into real gods. A notable example of such growth is furnished by the history of the intoxicating soma plant, which in the Rig-Veda is represented not only as the inspiring drink of the gods but as itself a deity, doing things that are elsewhere ascribed to Indra, Pushan, and other

[1] Frazer, *Golden Bough*, 2d ed., i, 179 ff.

[2] Cf. articles "Asylum" in Hastings, *Encyclopædia of Religion and Ethics*, and *Jewish Encyclopedia*.

[3] W. R. Smith, *Religion of the Semites*, 2d ed., pp. 133, 195; Hopkins, in *Journal of the American Oriental Society*, xxx (1910), 4, p. 352.

[4] Miss Godden, in *Journal of the Anthropological Institute*, xxvi, 186 ff.

[5] W. Crooke, *Popular Religion and Folklore of Northern India*, new ed., ii, 85 ff.; cf. Hopkins, "Mythological Aspects of Trees, etc.," in *Journal of the American Oriental Society*, September, 1910.

well-established deities.[1] The spirit, coming to be regarded as an anthropomorphic person, under peculiar circumstances assumes the character of a god. A similar development appears in the Iranian haoma, and the cultic identity of soma and haoma shows that the deification of the plant took place in the early Aryan period.[2]

271. Another example has been supposed to be furnished by corn-spirits. The importance of cereal crops for human life gave them a prominent position in the cult of agricultural communities. The decay and revival of the corn was an event of prime significance, and appears to have been interpreted as the death and resurrection of the spirit that was the life of the crop. Such is the idea in the modern popular customs collected by Mannhardt and Frazer.[3] The similarity between these ceremonies and those connected with the Phœnician Tammuz (Adonis) and the Phrygian Attis makes it probable that the two are based on the same ideas; that is, that Adonis and Attis (and so also Osiris and Ishtar) were deities of vegetation. This, however, does not prove that they were developed out of spirits of vegetation; they may have been deities charged with the care of crops.[4] The Phœnician name Adon is merely a title ('lord') that might be given to any god; he whom the Greeks called Adonis was a Syrian local deity, identical in origin with the Babylonian Tammuz, and associated in worship with Astarte, whom the Greeks identified with their Aphrodite.

272. A sacred tree often stood by a shrine; that is, probably, the shrine was put in the spot made sacred by a tree, and a ritual connection between the two was thus established. Later, when a shrine for any reason (in consequence of a theophany, for example) was built where there was no tree, its place was supplied by a wooden post, which inherited the cultic value of a sacred tree. In the Canaanite cult, which was adopted by the Hebrews, the sacred post (called "ashera") stood by the side of every shrine, and was

---

[1] *Rig-Veda*, ix al.; Muir, *Original Sanskrit Texts*, v; Hillebrandt, *Vedische Mythologie*, i, 450; Hopkins, *Religions of India*, p. 112 ff.

[2] Spiegel, *Eranische Alterthumskunde*, ii, 114 ff.; Tiele-Gehrich, *Geschichte der Religion im Altertum*, ii, ii, p. 234 ff.

[3] Mannhardt, *Baumkultus* and *Antike Wald- und Feldkulte*; Frazer, *Golden Bough*, Index, s.v. *Corn-spirit*.   [4] Cf. below, § 751 ff.

denounced by the prophets as an accompaniment of foreign (that is, non-Yahwistic) worship.[1] The transition from tree to post is illustrated, perhaps, by the conventionalized form of trees frequent on Babylonian seal cylinders.[2] How far the sacred post was an object of worship by the people we have no means of knowing; but by the more intelligent, doubtless, it came to be regarded simply as a symbol, a sign of the presence of a deity, and was, in so far, in the same category with images.[3]

273. It is not impossible that totem posts may be connected with original totem trees or other sacred trees. A tree as totem would naturally be the object of some sort of cult, and when it took the form of a post or pole, would have totemic symbols carved on it. Oftener, probably, it was the sacred pole of a village (itself descended from a sacred tree) that would be adorned with totemic figures, as among the Indians of Northwestern America.[4] In all such cases there is a coalescence of totemism and tree worship.

274. It was natural in early times, when most men lived in forests, which supplied all their needs, that trees should be looked on as intimately connected with human life. A tree might be regarded as in itself an independent personality, having, of course, a body and a soul, but not as dependent on an isolated spirit. A group of men might think itself descended from a tree — a conception that may have been widespread, though there is little direct evidence of its existence.[5] Indirect evidence of such a view is found in the custom of marrying girls to trees,[6] and in the belief in "trees of life," which are sometimes connected with individual men in such a way that when the tree or a part of it is destroyed the man dies, as in the case of Meleager whose life depended on the preservation of a piece of wood,[7] the representative, probably, of a tree, and the priest

---

[1] The connection between such posts and the North-Semitic goddess Ashera is uncertain.　　　　[2] Ward, *Seal-cylinders of Western Asia.*

[3] Cf. the suggestion of A. Réville (in his *Prolégomènes de l'histoire des religions*) that images arose in part from natural woods bearing a fancied resemblance to the human form.

[4] Boas, *The Kwakiutl*; Swanton, "Seattle Totem Pole," in *Journal of American Folklore*, vol. xviii, no. 69 (April, 1905).　　　[5] See below, "Totemism," § 449 f.

[6] Crooke, *Popular Religion and Folklore of Northern India*, ii, 115 ff.

[7] Pausanias, x, 31, 4; Roscher, *Lexikon*, article "Meleagros."

of Nemi whose life was bound up in the "golden bough"[1]; sometimes the tree has a magical power of conferring life on whoever eats of its fruit, as in the case of the tree of Eden.[2]

275. These stories involve the conception of blood-kinship between man and tree. Closely related to the " tree of life " is the "tree of knowledge" — life is knowledge and knowledge is life. In the original form of the story in Genesis there was only one tree — the tree of the knowledge of good and evil [3] — whose fruit, if eaten, made one the equal of the gods;[4] that is, the tree (in the original form of the conception, in remote times) was allied in nature (that is, in blood) to gods and to men, so that whoever partook of its substance shared its attribute of knowledge in sharing its life, and the command not to eat of it was due apparently to Yahweh's unwillingness that man should equal the gods in knowledge. The serpent-god, who belongs to the inner divine circle, but for some unexplained reason is hostile to the god of the garden,[5] reveals the secret.

276. Probably, also, it is from this general order of ideas that the conception of the cosmic tree has sprung. The Scandinavian Yggdrasil is the source of life to all things and represents also wisdom; though the details may contain Christian elements, the general conception of the world as a tree or as nourished by a tree is probably old.[6] The same conception appears in the cosmic tree of India.[7] Such quasi-philosophical ideas of the unity of the life of the world suppose, doubtless, a relatively advanced stage of culture, but they go back to the simple belief that the tree is endowed with life and is a source of life for men. The transition to the cosmic conception may be found in those quasi-divine trees that grant wishes and endow their friends with wisdom and life.

---

[1] Frazer, *Golden Bough*, 2d ed., iii, 391 ff.

[2] Gen. iii; cf. Hopkins, in *Journal of the American Oriental Society*, September, 1910. Whether the golden apples of the Hesperides had the life-giving quality is doubtful.

[3] This appears from a comparison of Gen. iii, 3 with ii, 17.   [4] Gen. iii, 5, 22.

[5] He is, perhaps, a diminished and conventionalized form of the old chaos dragon.

[6] On the various names and characters of this cosmic tree see Saussaye, *Religion of the Teutons*, p. 347 ff.   [7] *Rig-Veda*, x, 81, 4.

277. The divinatory function of trees follows as a matter of course from their divine nature (whether this was regarded as innate or as due to an indwelling spirit). Their counsel was supposed to be expressed by the rustling of their leaves,[1] or in some way that was interpreted by priests or priestesses (as at Dodona and elsewhere) or by diviners (so, perhaps, the Canaanite " terebinth of the diviners ").[2] The predictions of the Cumæan sibyl were said to be written on leaves that were whirled away by the wind and had to be gathered and interpreted. To what method of divination this points is not clear — possibly to supposed indications in the markings of the leaves; it may, however, be merely an imaginative statement of the difficulty of discovering the sibyl's meaning.[3]

278. The passage from the conception of the tree as a divine thing or person (necessarily anthropomorphic) to the view that it was the abode of a spirit was gradual, and it is not always easy to distinguish the two stages one from the other. The tree-spirits, in the nature of the case very numerous, were not distinguished by individual names, as the trees were not so distinguished.[4] The spirits resident in the divine trees invoked in the Vedas are powerful, but have not definite personality, and it is hard to say whether it is the tree or the spirit that is worshiped. The Indian tree-spirits called Nagas appear to be always nameless, and are not mentioned in the list of deities that pay reverence to the Buddha (in the Maha Samaya).[5] The large number of trees accounted sacred in Babylonia were doubtless believed to be inhabited by spirits, but to no one of these is a name given.

279. Thus the divine tree with its nameless spirit stands in a class apart from that of the gods proper. A particular tree, it is true, may be connected with a particular god, but such a connection is generally, if not always, to be traced (as in the parallel case of animals [6]) to an accidental collocation of cults. When a deity has become the numen of a tribe, his worship will naturally coalesce

---

[1] 2 Sam. v, 24. [2] Judg. ix, 37. [3] See below, § 935 ff.
[4] This is the case with all spirits that social needs do not force man to give names to. [5] Rhys Davids, *Buddhist India*, p. 232. [6] See above, § 252 f.

with the veneration felt by the tribe for some tree, which will then be conceived of as sacred to the god. Such, doubtless, was the history of the oak of Dodona, sacred to Zeus; when Zeus was established as deity of the place, the revered tree had to be brought into relation with him, and this relation could only be one of subordination — the tree became the medium by which the god communicated his will. There was then no need of the spirit of the tree, which accordingly soon passed away; the tree had lost its spiritual divine independence. The god who is said to have appeared to Moses in a burning bush, and is described as dwelling in the bush, is a local deity, the *numen loci*, later identified with Yahweh, or called an angel.[1] That a tree is sacred to a god means only that it has a claim to respect based on its being the property or instrument of a god.

280. While the tree-spirit has undoubtedly played a great rôle in early religious history, there is not decisive evidence of its ever having developed into a true god, with name, distinct personality, and distinct functions.[2] There are many Greek and Roman titles that connect gods with trees,[3] but these may be explained in the way suggested above: Zeus Endendros is a god dwelling in a tree, but the tree is only an abode, not a god, and the god Zeus does not come from the tree — rather two distinct sacred things have been brought together and fused into a unity, or the tree is a rude, incipient image. The Dionysos hermes-figures may be explained in the same way.[4]

281. It appears to be the aloofness of trees that prevents their becoming gods; they are revered and worshiped, but without becoming personalities. Babylonian seal engravings and wall pictures often represent a tree before which men or higher beings stand in adoration; according to Maspero[5] there was actual worship of trees in Egypt, and similar cults are found among the wild tribes of India.[6] Adoration, however, does not necessarily imply a god;

---

[1] Ex. iii, 2 ff.; Deut. xxxiii, 16; Acts vii, 30, 35.
[2] See *Journal of the American Oriental Society*, xxx, 353 f., for possible examples.
[3] A list of such titles is given by C. Boetticher in his *Baumkultus der Hellenen und Römer*, chap. iv.   [4] Dionysos is a bull-god as well as a tree-god.
[5] *Dawn of Civilization*, p. 12.   [6] Hopkins, *Religions of India*, p. 533.

the Buddhist's worship under the bo-tree is not directed to any being; it is only the recognition of something that he thinks worthy of reverence.[1]

282. The cult of the corn-spirit is referred to above,[2] and doubt is there expressed as to whether such a spirit has grown into a true god. The question is confessedly a difficult one on account of the absence of full data for the period involved. The chief ground for the doubt as to the development in question lies in what we know of early gods. The term ' Adon,' as is remarked above, is the Phœnician title of the local deity. The origin of such deities is involved in the obscurity of the remote past, but they are, each in his community, universal powers; their functions embrace all that their communities desire, and they represent each the total life of a people. It is the general rule that any popular custom may be introduced into the cult of the local god; of such sort of procedure there are many examples. In the case under consideration the god may have become the hero of a ceremony with which he had originally nothing to do, as the Hebrews when they entered Canaan connected Canaanite festivals with their national god, Yahweh, and later a cult of the wilderness deity Azazel[3] was adopted and modified by the Yahwist leaders. Various cults attached themselves to the worship of Zeus, Apollo, Dionysos, and other Greek deities.[4]

283. A similar explanation may be given of the ceremonies of death and resurrection connected with Attis and Osiris. Of Attis we have only late accounts, and do not know his early history. Osiris is an old underground deity (later the judge of the Underworld), with functions that included more than the vivification of vegetation, and the absorption of the corn-spirit into his cult would be natural. The collocation of a male with a female deity, common to the three cults, may be merely the elaboration of the myth in accordance with human social usage (the dead deity is mourned by his consort).[5] The descent of Ishtar has been

---

[1] On the Soma cult see above, § 270.   [2] § 271.   [3] Lev. xvi.

[4] Gruppe, *Culte und Mythen*; Roscher, *Lexikon*. Cf. the developed cults of Vishnu and Çiva.   [5] On Osiris and Isis see below, § 728 f.

interpreted of the weakening of the sun's heat in winter; but as she is obviously a deity of fertility and, in her descent, disappears entirely from among men, while the sun does not disappear entirely, she rather, in this story, represents or is connected with the decay and rebirth of vegetation.

284. It is thus possible that, though many ancient ceremonies stand in relation to the corn-spirit and also to a god, the explanation of this fact is not that the spirit has grown into a god, but that it has coalesced with a god. In all such explanations, however, our ignorance of the exact processes of ancient thought must be borne in mind.

285. Trees have been widely credited with the power of bestowing blessings of all sorts. But, like animals, they rarely receive formal worship;[1] the reason for this is similar to that suggested above[2] in the case of animals. The coalescence, spoken of above, of tree ceremonies with cults of fully developed gods is not uncommon, and trees figure largely in mythical divine histories.

STONES AND MOUNTAINS

286. Like all other objects stones have been regarded, in all parts of the world, as living, as psychologically anthropomorphic (that is, as having soul, emotion, will), and, in some cases, as possessing superhuman powers.[3] The term 'sacred,' as applied to them, may mean either that they are in themselves endowed with peculiar powers, or that they have special relations with divine beings; the first meaning is the earlier, the second belongs to a period when the lesser revered objects have been subordinated to the greater.

287. The basis of the special belief in their sacredness was, probably, the mystery of their forms and qualities, their hardness, brilliancy, solidity. They seem to have been accepted, in the earliest known stages of human life, as ultimate facts. When

---

[1] Some instances of worship are given in Frazer's *Golden Bough*, 2d ed., i, 181, 189, 191. Frazer sometimes uses the term 'tree worship' where all that is meant is respect for trees as powerful things.   [2] See § 253 ff.

[3] See *Revue de l'histoire des religions*, 1881.

explanations of their presence were sought, they were supposed to have been deposited by ancestors or other beings, sometimes as depositories of their souls.[1] Meteorites, having fallen from the sky, needed no other explanation. Popular science (that is, popular imagination), perhaps from fancied resemblances to the human 'form, assumed of some stones that they were human beings turned to stone, and stories grew up to account for the metamorphoses. In many different ways, according to differences of physical surroundings and of social conceptions, men accounted for such of these objects as interested them particularly.

288. That stones were believed to be alive and akin to men is shown by the stories of the birth of men and gods from stones,[2] the turning of human beings to stone (Niobe, Lot's wife), the accounts of their movements (rocks in Brittany).[3]

289. Small stones, especially such as are of peculiar shape, are in many parts of the world regarded as having magic power; the peculiarity of shape seems mysterious and therefore connected with power. Doubtless accidental circumstances, such as the occurrence of a piece of good fortune, have often endowed a particular stone with a reputation for power. Certain forms, especially flat disks with a hole in the center, have preserved this reputation down to the present day. The Roman lapis manalis is said by Festus to have been employed to get rain.[4]

290. Magical stones were, doubtless, believed to possess souls. In accordance with the general law such stones and others were regarded later as the abodes of independent movable spirits.[5]

---

[1] So in Central Australia (Spencer and Gillen, *Native Tribes of Central Australia*, pp. 123 f., 137).

[2] The rock whence came the stones thrown by Deucalion and Pyrrha (the origin of the human race) also gave birth to Agdistis *mugitibus editis multis*,, according to Arnobius, *Adversus Nationes*, v, 5. Mithra's birth from a rock (Roscher, *Lexikon*) is perhaps a bit of late poetical or philosophical imagery.

[3] For various powers of stones, involving many human interests, see indexes in Tylor's *Primitive Culture*, Frazer's *Golden Bough*, and Hartland's *Primitive Paternity*, s.v. *Stone* or *Stones*.

[4] Festus, p. 2 ; see the remarks of Marquardt, *Römische Staatsverwaltung*; Aust, *Religion der Römer*, p. 121; and Fowler, *Roman Festivals*, p. 232 f. On the relation between the lapis and Juppiter Elicius, see Wissowa, *Religion und Kultus der Römer*, p. 106; cf. Roscher, *Lexikon*, article "Iuppiter," col. 606 ff.   [5] See above, § 97 ff.

When the power of a fetish seems to be exhausted, and a new object is chosen and by appropriate ceremonies a spirit is induced to take up its abode in it, there seems to be no theory as to whether the incoming spirit is the old one or a new one, or, if it be a new one, what becomes of the old one, about which little or no interest is felt.[1] The pneumatology is vague; the general view is that the air is full of spirits, whose movements may be controlled by magical means: spirits, that is, are subject to laws, and these laws are known to properly trained men.

291. Reverence for divine stones continues into the period of the rise of the true gods. When god and stone stand together in a community, both revered, they may be and generally are combined into a cultic unity: the stone becomes the symbol or the abode or the person of the god.[2] It was, doubtless, in some such way as this that a stone came to be identified with the Magna Mater of Pessinus. When this stone was brought to Rome toward the end of the Second Punic War, the Roman leaders may have regarded it simply as a symbol of the goddess, but the people probably looked on it as itself a divine defense against Hannibal.[8] The Israelite ark, carried out to the battle against the Philistines,[4] appears to have contained a stone, possibly a meteorite, possibly a piece taken from the sacred mountain Sinai, itself divine, but in the Old Testament narrative regarded as the abode of Yahweh (a Sinaitic god), though it was probably of independent origin and only gradually brought into association with the local god of the mountain.

292. Similar interpretations may be given of other stones identified or connected with deities, as that of Zeus at Seleucia,[5] that of Aphrodite at Paphos,[6] that of Jupiter Lapis,[7] and the black

---

[1] On processes of capturing a god in order to inclose him in an object, or of transferring a god from one object to another, see W. Crooke, "The Binding of a God," in *Folklore*, viii.

[2] In pre-Islamic Arabia many gods were represented by stones, the stone being generally identified with the deity; so Al-Lât, Dhu ash-Shara (Dusares), and the deities represented by the stones in the Meccan Kaaba.   [8] Livy, xxix, 10 f.

[4] 1 Sam. iv.   [5] Head, *Historia Numorum*, p. 661.

[6] Tacitus, *Hist*. ii, 3 ; it was conical in shape.

[7] Fowler, *Roman Festivals*, p. 230 ff.; cf. above, the "lapis manalis," § 289.

stone that represented the Syrian Elagabalos at Emesa.[1] The remark of Pausanias, after he has described the thirty sacred stones of Pheræ, that the early Greeks paid divine honors to un-hewn stones, doubtless expresses the traditions and beliefs of his time;[2] and it is probable that in antiquity there were many divine stones, and that these were frequently in later times identified with local gods. In many cases, however, there was no identification, only a collocation and subordination : the stone became the symbol of the deity, or a sacred object associated with the deity.[8]

293. This seems to be the later conception of the character of the sacred stones mentioned in the Old Testament, as the one that Jacob is said to have set up as a masseba and anointed.[4] The Canaanite massebas, adopted as cultic objects by the Israelites,[5] were stone pillars standing by shrines and regarded as a normal if not a necessary element of worship ; originally divine in themselves (as may be inferred from the general history of such objects), they came to be regarded as mere accessories ; there is no indication in the Old Testament that they were looked on as gods, though they may have been so regarded by the people[6] — their presence at the Canaanite shrines, as a part of foreign, non-Yahwistic worship, sufficiently explains the denunciation of them by the prophets.[7]

294. In the story of Jacob he is said to have given the name Bethel to the place where he anointed the stone. It does not appear that he so called the stone itself ; Bethel (in Hebrew, " house of God "[8]) seems to have been an old sacred place, and terms compounded with ' beth ' in Hebrew are names of shrines. The relation between this name and the Semitic word whence,

---

1 Herodian, v, 3, 10.

2 Pausanias, vii, 22. Cf. Tylor, *Primitive Culture*, ii, 160 ff.

3 H. Spencer, *Principles of Sociology*, i, 335 ; Saussaye, *Manual of the Science of Religion* (Eng. tr.), p. 85 ff.

4 Gen. xxviii, 18 ; cf. Smith, *Religion of the Semites*, 2d ed., p. 203 f.

5 Hos. iii, 4.

6 The reference in Jer. ii, 27, Hab. ii, 19 (stones as parents and teachers), seems to be to the cult of foreign deities, represented by images.

7 On the interpretation of the masseba as a phallus or a kteis see below, §§ 400, 406.

8 And so in Assyrian and Arabic.

probably, comes Greek *baitulos*[1] (Latin *baetulus*) is not clear; this last is the designation of a sacred stone held to have fallen from heaven (meteoric). Such an one is called by Philo of Byblos "empsuchos," 'endowed with life or with soul.'[2] Pliny describes the baetulus as a species of ceraunia (thunderstone).[3] The Greek word is now commonly derived from *betel* ('bethel') — a derivation possible so far as the form of the word is concerned.[4] According to this view the stone is the abode of a deity — a conception common in early religion. Such an object would be revered, and would ultimately be brought into connection with a local god.[5] If Hebrew bethel was originally a stone considered as the abode of a deity, then in the Old Testament the earlier form of the conception has been effaced by the later thought — the word 'bethel' has become the name of a place, a shrine, the dwelling place of God.[6]

295. The origin of the black stone of the Kaaba at Mecca is unknown — it was doubtless either a meteorite or in some way connected with a sacred place; it was, and is, regarded as in itself sacred, but whether it represented originally a deity, and if so what deity, is not known.[7]

296. The belief in the sacred character of stones may account, at least in part, for the custom of casting stones on the grave of a chieftain (as in Northern Arabia), though this may be merely intended to preserve the grave. So also the stones thrown at the foot of a Hermes pillar may have been meant as a waymark, yet with the feeling that the stone heap had a sacred character of its

---

[1] There is no Greek etymology for *baitulos*, and if it came from without, a Semitic origin is the most probable.

[2] Eusebius, *Praeparatio Evangelica*, i, 10, 18.

[3] *Hist. Nat.*, bk. xxxvii, chap. 51.

[4] Cf. F. Lenormant, in *Revue de l'histoire des religions*, iii, 31 ff.; Gruppe, *Griechische Mythologie*, p. 775 f.

[5] For Phœnician customs see Pietschmann, *Phönizier*, p. 204 ff.

[6] Cf. Deut. x, 2; Ex. xxv, 16; 2 Chr. v, 10, where the stone in the ark seems to have become two stone tables on which the decalogue was written by the finger of Yahweh — an example, if the view mentioned above be correct, of the transformation of a thing originally divine in itself into an accessory of a god.

[7] Cf. Hughes, *Dictionary of Islam*, s.v. *Kaaba*; Wellhausen, *Reste arabischen Heidentumes*, pp. 99, 171.

own.[1] The stone circles at Stonehenge and Avebury may have had a religious significance, but their function is not clear. Boundary stones seem to have had at first simply a political function, but were naturally dedicated to the deities who were guardians of tribal boundaries (Roman Terminus, various Babylonian gods, etc.).

297. It is by virtue of their divine character that stones came to be used as altars.[2] As things divine in themselves or as representing a deity they receive the blood of the sacred (that is, divine) sacrificial animal, which is the food of the god. Originally a part of the blood is applied to the stone, and the rest poured out or eaten (as sacred food) by the worshiper. In process of time, when the god has been divorced from the stone, the latter becomes a table on which the victim is offered;[3] the old conception survives in the custom of slaying the victim by the side of the altar, and applying the blood to the horns of the altar as a representative part of the sacred structure. In the late Jewish ritual this application of blood is interpreted as a purification of the altar from ceremonial defilements.[4]

298. Originally, it seems, it was only natural stones that were sacred or divine and were employed as representatives of deities; but by a natural process of thought the custom arose of using artificial stones in the same way. By means of certain ceremonies, it was held, the deity could be induced to accept an altar or a house, or to take up his abode in an image, as a spirit is introduced by the savage into a fetish object.[5] The basis of this sort of procedure is first the belief in the amenableness of the deity to magical laws, and, later, the belief in his friendly disposition, his willingness to accede to the wishes of his worshipers provided they offer the proper tribute; but even in very late ceremonies a trace of the magical element remains.

---

[1] On the relation between the stone heaps and the Hermes pillars cf. Welcker, *Griechische Götterlehre*, ii, 455, and Roscher, *Lexikon*, i, 2, col. 2382. With Hermes as guide of travelers cf. the Egyptian Khem (Min), of Coptos, as protector of wanderers in the desert, and perhaps Eshmun in the Sardinian trilingual inscription (see Roscher, *Lexikon*, article " Esmun "; *Orientalische Studien Nöldeke gewidmet*).

[2] See below, § 1080.

[3] W. R. Smith, *Religion of the Semites*, 2d ed., pp. 202, 341; cf. Jevons, *Introduction to the History of Religion*, chap. xi; article " Altar " in Hastings, *Encyclopædia of Religion and Ethics*. [4] Lev. xvi, 19.

[5] For some methods of such introduction see W. Crooke, in *Folklore*, viii.

299. The significance of the high pillars, of stone or of metal, that stood at the entrance of certain Semitic temples, is not clear. Examples are: in Tyre, the temple of the local Baal (Melkart);[1] Solomon's temple of Yahweh in Jerusalem, and the temple planned by Ezekiel in imitation of that of Solomon;[2] compare the temple of the Carthaginian Tanit-Artemis, a form of Ashtart, the votive stela from the temple of Aphrodite in Idalium (in Cyprus), and similar figures on Cyprian coins.[8] Of the various explanations offered of these pillars that which regards them as phallic symbols may be set aside as lacking proof.[4] It is not probable that they were merely decorative; the details of ancient temples, as a rule, were connected with worship. It has been suggested that they were fire altars,[5] in support of which view may be cited the figures on Cyprian coins (mentioned above), and the fact that sailors sacrificed at Gades at a place where there were two high pillars;[6] but such a custom does not prove that the sacrifices were offered on the pillars, and these latter are generally too high to serve such a purpose; they are too high also to be convenient candelabra.[7] It seems more probable that they were developments from sacred stones (such as the Canaanite massebas), which originally represented the deity, came to be conventional attachments to temples, and then were treated in accordance with architectural principles. They would be placed in pairs, one pillar on each side of the temple door, for the sake of symmetry, and dignity would be sought by giving them a considerable height.[8] They might also be utilized, when they were not too high, as stands for lamps or cressets, but this would be a secondary use. The obelisks that stood in front of Egyptian temples, likewise, were probably sacred monuments reared in honor of deities.[9]

---

[1] Herodotus, ii, 44; he identifies Melkart with Herakles.

[2] 1 Kings, vii, 15–22; Ezek. xl, 49.

[8] Perrot and Chipiez, *Histoire de l'art*, vol. iii; cf. Pietschmann, *Phönizier*, p. 203 ff.; Rawlinson, *Phœnicia*, p. 338.   [4] Cf. below, § 399 ff.

[5] W. R. Smith, *Religion of the Semites*, 2d ed., p. 487 ff.   [6] Strabo, iii, 5, 5.

[7] Those of Solomon's temple are described as being 27 feet in height, and without stairways. Cf. the structures connected with the Hierapolis temple (Lucian, *De Syria Dea*, 28).

[8] Desire for height appears also in the Egyptian pyramid and the Babylonian ziggurat, but both these had means of ascent to the higher levels. Cf. below, § 1085.

[9] Maspero, *Egyptian Archæology*, p. 100 ff.

300. Images of gods and other extrahuman beings arise through the natural human impulse to represent familiar objects of thought. Very rude tribes have stone or wood carvings of spirits and gods, good and bad. These images are generally in human shape, because all Powers are thought of as anthropomorphic. Sometimes, as Réville suggests, a root, or branch of a tree, bearing some resemblance to the human face or figure, may have led to the making of an image; but the general natural artistic tendency is sufficient to account for the fact.[1]

301. The character assigned to images varies with stages of culture. In low communities they are themselves divine — the gods have entered into them and they are not thought of as different from their divine indwellers. In such cases they are sometimes chained to prevent their getting away; if they are obstinate, not listening to prayers, they are cuffed, scourged, or reviled.[2] This conception lingers still among the peasants of Southern Europe, who treat a saint (a rechristened old god) as if he were a man to be won by threats or cajolements. In a more refined age the image becomes simply a symbol, a visible representation serving to fix the attention and recall divine things. Different races also differ in the extent of their demand for such representations of deity.

302. Stones and rocks, like other natural objects, are startingpoints for folk-stories and myths. All over the world they lie on the ground or rise in the shape of hills, and, being mysterious, require explanation. The explanations given, and handed down from generation to generation, are always connected with superhuman or with extraordinary persons, ancestors, heroes, spirits. To each stone or rock a story is attached, a creation of the fancy suggested by the surroundings and by the popular traditions; and each story forms an episode in the history of the hero or spirit. The stones and rocks thus come to constitute a book chronicling the history of the tribe and the deeds of its great men — a book quite

---

[1] The movement from aniconic to anthropomorphic forms is seen in the image of the Ephesian Artemis, the upper half human, the lower half a pillar (Roscher, *Lexikon*, i, 1, cols. 588, 595).

[2] Examples in Tylor's *Primitive Culture*, 2d ed., ii, 170 f.; cf. his *Early History of Mankind*, chap. vi.

legible to the man who has been taught the stories. These grow with every generation, receiving such additions as fancy and reflection dictate, and gradually taking on literary form. In the territory of the Australian Arunta every stone is connected with some incident in the careers of the mythical ancestors, and the stories taken together form the legendary history of the origin of customs.[1] In Samoa and New Guinea many stones are pointed out as having been set in place by local heroes. In North America innumerable rocks and stones are connected with the mythical ancestors and creators of the tribes.

303. Mountains have everywhere been regarded as abodes of spirits or deities, and therefore sacred. Their height and massiveness invested them with dignity (even as now they appeal mightily to the imagination), and their lofty summits and rugged sides were full of danger and mystery. Sacred mountains are found in North America, Bengal, Africa, and elsewhere. Naturally they are often abodes of gods of rain; they are feared on account of the spirits inhabiting them, but they are also resorted to as places where divine revelations may be obtained.[2] The Semitic, Hindu, and Greek examples are familiar: the Hebrew and Canaanite Sinai (or Horeb), Nebo, Carmel, Hermon; the Arabian Arafat, near Mecca; the Babylonian Ekur; in India, Meru, Mandara, Himavat, and other mountains; in Greece, Olympus and Parnassus.

304. Mountains are also worshiped as being themselves divine.[8] The cult, however, has not been important; the physical mass is too solid, lacking in movement, and human interest naturally centered in the spirit or deity who dwelt therein.[4]

305. Mythological fancy has made them the abodes and places of assembly of gods and glorified saints, usually in the north. The

---

[1] Spencer and Gillen, *Native Tribes of Central Australia*, p. 188, etc.

[2] Matthews, *Navaho Legends*, Index, s.v. *Mountains*; article " Bengal " in Hastings, *Encyclopædia of Religion and Ethics*; Tylor, *Primitive Culture*, ii, 260; Hollis, *The Nandi*, p. 48.

[3] Hopkins, *Religions of India*, pp. 358 ff., 537, and *Journal of the American Oriental Society*, September, 1910.

[4] On a general relation between gods and local hills see Rivers, *The Todas*, p. 444.

mythical Ekur was the dwelling place of Babylonian deities.[1] In India various peaks in the Himalayas, inaccessible to men, were assigned to groups of deities, and the mythical world-mountain Meru was the special abode of great gods, who there lived lives of delight.[2] On the highest peak of the Thessalian Olympus Zeus sat, surrounded by the inferior gods; here he held councils and announced his decrees.[3] The two conceptions of the home of the gods — on mountains and in the sky — existed for a time side by side, having in common the feature of remoteness and secrecy; gradually the earthly abode was ignored, and the gods were assigned to the more dignified heavenly home.

WATERS

306. To early man waters, fire, winds, are interesting because of their relation to his life, and sacred because of their power and mysteriousness.[4] They are regarded by him not as " elements " of the world, but as individual phenomena that affect well-being. His conception of them is not cosmogonic or analytic, but personal; they are entities with which he has to deal.

307. The mobility of masses of water, seeming to be a sign of life, naturally procured them a definite place among sacred things. Any spring, pond, lake, or river with which a tribe was brought into intimate relations was regarded as a source of life or of healing, and of divination. Dwellers by the sea regarded it with awe; its depths were mysterious and its storms terrible.

308. As in the case of animals, plants, and stones, so here: the earliest conception of water masses is that they are divine in themselves (every one, of course, having its own soul), and are potent for bodily help or harm, and for divination. The waters of the

---

[1] Jastrow, *Religion of Babylonia and Assyria*, pp. 541, 638; cf. Isa. xiv, 13. Many Babylonian temples, considered as abodes of gods, were called " mountains."

[2] Hopkins, in *Journal of the American Oriental Society*, loc. cit., where the mythical mountains of the Mahabharata are described.　　　[3] *Iliad* viii, 2 al.

[4] Bastian, " Vorstellungen von Wasser und Feuer," in *Zeitschrift für Ethnologie*, i; Tylor, *Primitive Culture*, 2d ed., ii, 209 ff., 274 ff.; W. R. Smith, *Religion of the Semites*, lecture v.

Nile, the Ganges, the Jordan, were held to heal the diseased and purify the unclean; and a similar power is now ascribed to the water of the well Zamzam in the Kaaba at Mecca. Hannibal swore, among other things, by the waters,[1] and the oath by the river Styx was the most binding of oaths, having power to control even the gods; the thing by which an oath is taken is always originally divine. In the Hebrew ordeal of jealousy the sacred water decides whether the accused woman is guilty or not.[2] The sea is treated as a living thing, whose anger may be appeased by gifts; it is a monster, a dragon.[3] The Spartan Cleomenes, about to start on a voyage, sacrifices a bull to the sea.[4] Offerings to the sea are made in the Maldive Islands.[5]

309. Water is abundantly employed in religious ritual as a means of purification from ceremonial defilement, and in services of initiation. A bathing-place often stood by a shrine (as in pre-Islamic Arabia and in Islam now), and immersions came to play a prominent part in highly developed systems (Jewish, Christian, Mithraic). The purification was generally symbolic, but in some forms of Christian belief the water of baptism is held to have regenerating power[6] — a survival of the ancient conception of the divinity of water.

310. It is often hard to say whether a body of water is regarded simply as itself a living thing, or is conceived of as the dwelling place of an isolated or independent spirit. In savage systems the details on this point are hardly ever recorded or obtainable; but the beliefs involved in later folk-lore make it probable that this latter stage of the construction of creeds is passed through in savage life. The water maidens of Greek mythology and the Germanic nixies and water kelpies are developed forms of spirits. Sacred springs and wells are still believed to be inhabited by beings that are not gods, but possess superhuman power.

311. While wells and streams of a domestic character (such as are freely used by human beings) are generally friendly, they have their unfriendly side. The spirits that dwell in them are sometimes

---

[1] Polybius, vii, 9. [2] Num. v. [3] Job vii, 12. [4] Herodotus, vi, 76.
[5] *Journal of the Royal Asiatic Society*, x, 179; Bell, *Maldive Islands*, p. 73.
[6] In Titus iii, 5, the reference seems to be to baptism.

regarded as being hostile to man. They drag the incautious wanderer into their depths, and then nothing can save him from drowning. Fear of these malignant beings sometimes prevents attempts to rescue a drowning person ; such attempts are held to bring down the vengeance of the water-demon on the would-be rescuer.[1]

312. In the course of time true water-gods appear. In Greece every river had its deity, and in India such deities are found in the Mahabharata.[2] When in the Iliad the river Xanthos rises to seize and drown Achilles, it may be a question whether the stream or the god of the stream is the actor. Nor is it always possible to say whether the extrahuman Power inhabiting a water mass is a true god or a spirit ; the latter form may pass by invisible gradations into the former.

313. Waters originally divine tend to become the abodes of the deity of the place, or sacred to him, and healing or other power is ascribed to his presence or agency.[3] Sacred water, being unwilling to retain anything impure, thus becomes a means of detecting witches and other criminals, who, when thrown in, cannot sink, but are rejected by the divine Power.

314. Deities of streams and springs do not play an important part in worship or in mythology ; their physical functions are not definite enough, and their activities are naturally merged in or subsumed under those of the greater or more definite local gods. If, for example, the Canaanite Baals are gods or lords of underground irrigation,[4] this is because they, as divine lords of the particular regions, control all phenomena ; they are, in fact, also gods of rain and thunderstorms, harvests and war. So rain-gods in general are to be regarded as local deities, among whose functions that of bestowing rain was regarded as specially important. In the lowest systems the rain-giver may be a sacred stone, dipped in a stream,[5] or a royal or priestly magician who is held responsible and is punished

---

[1] De Groot, *Religion of the Chinese*, p. 10 f.; cf. the German Lorelei.

[2] Frazer (in *Anthropological Essays presented to E. B. Tylor*) sees a river-god in the figure mentioned in Gen. xxxii, 24. [3] Cf. John v, 4 (in some MSS.).

[4] This is W. R. Smith's contention in *Religion of the Semites*, lecture v. See his account of Semitic water-gods in general.

[5] Turner, *Samoa*, p. 345 f. Cf. the Roman lapis manalis ; see above, § 136.

if the expected result is not attained.[1] In such cases the procedure is often one of imitative magic.[2]

315. If there be, in the next higher stratum of belief, a local or tribal god, it is he who is looked to for the rain supply; so the early Hebrews looked to Yahweh,[3] and the Canaanites, doubtless, to the Baals. The economic importance of rain led, even in low tribes, to the conception of a special deity charged with its bestowal.[4] In more elaborate mythologies various deities are credited with rain-making power. In India, for example, Dyaus, the Maruts, Parjanya, Brihaspati, Indra, Agni,[5] all concerned with rain, have, all except Agni, evidently grown from local figures with general functions; this appears from the great variety of parts they play. The same thing is true, perhaps, of Zeus and Jupiter in their character of rain-gods — as all-sufficient divine patrons they would be dispensers of all blessings, including rain; they seem, however, to have been originally gods of the sky, and thus naturally the special guardians of rain.[6]

316. Great masses of water have given rise to myths, mostly cosmogonic. The conception of a watery mass as the primeval material of the world (in Egypt, Babylonia, India, Greece, Rome) belongs not to religion but to science; in a relatively advanced period, however, this mass was represented as a monster, the antagonist of the gods of light and order, and from this representation has come a whole literature of myths. In Babylonia a great cosmogonic poem grew up in which the dragon figures of the water chaos (Tiamat, Mummu, Kingu) play a great part,[7] and echoes of this myth appear in the later Old Testament books.

---

[1] A large number of examples are given by Frazer in his *Golden Bough*, 2d ed., i, 81 f., al.

[2] Brinton, *Myths of the New World*, p. 17; Spencer and Gillen, *Native Tribes of Central Australia*, p. 189 f.

[3] One signification (not a probable one) proposed for the name Yahweh is, 'he who causes (rain) to fall.'

[4] Examples of such gods, in Africa, America, and Asia, are given in Tylor's *Primitive Culture*, ii, 259 ff.　　　[5] Hopkins, *Religions of India*, p. 99 ff.

[6] So in the *Secrets of Enoch* (ed. R. H. Charles), chaps. iv–vi, the treasuries of rain and dew in the lowest heaven are guarded by angels.

[7] Jastrow, *Religion of Babylonia and Assyria*, Index, s.vv.

317. In the more elaborate pantheons the local deities of streams and springs tend to disappear, and gods of ocean appear : in Babylonia, Ea ; in Greece, Okeanos and Poseidon ; in Rome, Neptune; and along with these are numerous subordinate figures—attendants on the great gods, and intrusted with various particular duties.

FIRE

318. There was, doubtless, a time when man had not learned to produce fire, and there may now be tribes unacquainted with its domestic uses. But such ignorance, if it exists, is rare ; savages generally know how to make fire, and to use it for warmth and for the preparation of food. When men began to reflect on the origin of things, fire seemed to them so wonderful that they supposed it must have been discovered or invented, and the knowledge of it bestowed on men by higher beings, gods or demigods ; such benefactors are Hastsezini (of the Navahos), Lightning (of the Pawnees), the Beaver and the Eagle (of the Thompson River Indians of British Columbia), Maui (of the Maoris), Agni, Prometheus.[1]

319. Though, like other mysterious things, it has been regarded generally (perhaps universally) as sacred, there is no clear proof that it has been worshiped as divine. What may have been the case in remote ages we cannot tell, but, according to the information we possess, it has been, and is, merely revered as in itself mysterious or sacred,[2] or as the abode or production of a spirit or a deity. Possibly in the early stages of culture known to us there is a fusion of the element with the indwelling or controlling god or spirit.[3] The divine patrons of fire are found in all parts of the world, varying

---

[1] Matthews, *Navaho Legends*, p. 37 ; Dorsey, *The Skidi Pawnee*, p. 8 ; Teit, *Thompson River Indians*, p. 56 f ; R. Taylor, *New Zealand and its Inhabitants*, p. 130 ; Hopkins, *Religions of India*, p. 168, n. 1 ; Roscher, *Lexikon*, article "Prometheus." Accounts of the original production or the theft of fire are found in savage mythology the world over ; see Frobenius, *Childhood of Man*, chaps. xxv–xxvii ; Seligmann, *The Melanesians of British New Guinea*, p. 379 ; Tylor, *Primitive Culture*, ii, 277 ff. ; O. T. Mason, *Origins of Invention*, chap iii.

[2] So among the Todas (Rivers, *The Todas*, p. 437) and the Nandi (Hollis, *The Nandi*, p. 85).

[3] On an identification of Agni with fire see Bloomfield, *Religion of the Veda*, p. 158 ff.

in form and function according to the degrees of advancement of the various communities, from the beast-gods of the Redmen to the departmental deities of the Maoris, Babylonians, Mexicans, and others, and to the more complicated gods of Hindus, Greeks, and Romans.[1]

320. The most elaborate and most interesting of all fire-cults is the Persian. The ritual of the Avesta appears at times to describe a worship of the element itself: in Fargard xviii the fire implores the householder to rise, wash his hands, and put pure wood on the flame; Yaçna lxi is a hymn of homage and petition addressed to the fire, which is called the son of Ahura Mazda — the householder asks that all the blessings of life may be his as a reward for his sacrifice. The numerous temples devoted to the fire-cult, mentioned by later writers,[2] might seem to look in the same direction. But a comparison of other parts of the Avesta makes it doubtful whether in the passages just cited anything more is meant than that the fire, as a creation of Ahura Mazda and sacred to him, is for his sake worthy of reverence and through him a source of blessing. Thus Yaçna xvii is a hymn in honor of Ahura Mazda and all his creatures, among which are mentioned the law of Zarathustra, the fire (and five different fires are named), the soul of the ox, and pure deeds, along with the Amesha-Spentas, the heavenly bodies, and good men. This collection shows vagueness in the conception of the divine and the sacred, and, to say the least, leaves it uncertain whether the singer does not think of the fire simply as a symbol of the Supreme God.

321. The relation of fire to the gods, and especially its use in sacrifice, have led to a number of religious ceremonies in which it plays a principal part.[3] Certain fires must be kindled by specially appointed sacred persons: among the Todas of Southern India, when a new dairy is visited or an old dairy is reconsecrated;[4] among

---

[1] See Chap. VI.

[2] Shahrastani (12th century), *Kitab al-Milal wa'l-Nihal*, a sketch of religions and philosophical sects, Moslem and other (Germ. tr. by Haarbrücker, p. 298 f.).

[3] Hopkins observes (*Religions of India*, p. 105) that originally fire (Agni), in distinction from sun and lightning, is the fire of sacrifice. Cf. Bloomfield, *Religion of the Veda*, p. 157.

[4] Rivers, *The Todas*, p. 437 ; cf. the ceremony described on page 290 f.

the Lacandones of Central America, on the occasion of the renewal
of the incense-bowls;[1] in the Peruvian temple at the feast of
Raymi, when the flame was intrusted to the care of the Virgins
of the Sun, and was to be kept up during the year;[2] in the temples
of Hestia and Vesta; throughout Greece, when the fires had been
polluted by the presence of the Persians, it was ordered that they
should be put out and rekindled from the sacred fire at Delphi.[3]

322. The purificatory power of fire was, doubtless, a fact of early
observation.

323. As the physical means of sacrifice, fire acquired a certain
symbolic significance; in the Hebrew ritual "fire-offerings" are regarded as specially important. By Carthaginians, Moabites, and
Hebrews children were devoted to the deity by fire.[4]

324. By reason of its brightness fire connects itself in religious
imagery with the sun, with lightning, and with light in general, and
so appears frequently as a representation of the glory of the deity.[5]

325. Light is sometimes regarded as an independent thing, and
as sacred.[6]

WINDS

326. Traces of an early cult of the physical wind may be found,
perhaps, in certain customs that survive in modern communities;
as, for example, in the offering of food to the wind that it may be
placated and do no harm.[7] The belief of sailors that wind may be
called up by whistling rests on a process of imitative magic that
may be connected with an early cult. Wind is said to be regarded
as a divine being in some American tribes.[8] But generally it is the
spirit or god of a wind (and usually of a definite wind) that is

---

[1] A. M. Tozzer, *Comparative Study of the Mayas and the Lacandones*, p. 133.

[2] Prescott, *Peru*, i, 106 f.   [3] Plutarch, *Aristides*, 20.

[4] The Hebrew expression, rendered in the English version " cause to pass through
fire," means simply 'devote by fire.'

[5] Ex. xix, 18; Ezek. i, 4; Ps. xviii, 9 [8]; *Rig-Veda*, iii, 26, 7 (Indra).

[6] Rivers, *The Todas*, p. 437. In Gen. i, 3, light appears before the creation of the
heavenly bodies.

[7] So in Carinthia, the Tyrol, and neighboring districts (Wuttke, *Der deutsche
Volksaberglaube der Gegenwart*, p. 86).

[8] Dorsey, *The Skidi Pawnee*, p. xix.

invoked. Examples of wind-gods are found in all parts of the world.[1] A wind may be the vehicle or the messenger of a deity.[2]

327. As in the cases of other elements, referred to above, it is often hard to say whether it is the thing or the deity that is invoked: Achilles's appeal, for instance, seems to be to the physical winds, but Iris, who goes to summon them, finds them carousing like men, and they act like gods.[3] It must be borne in mind, however, that in early thought all active things are conceived of as being anthropomorphic, and there is the difficulty, just mentioned, of determining where the anthropomorphic object stops and the spirit or god begins.

HEAVENLY BODIES

328. The heavenly bodies seem to have been regarded at first merely as objects somehow thrown up into the sky or in some other way fixed there by gods or men.[4] Later, under the general anthropomorphizing tendency, they are conceived of as manlike beings, and their characters and histories are worked out in accordance with local ideas. Their origin is ascribed at first to such creative beings as appear in the various early communities; for example, among the Navahos to the First Man, the First Woman, and the coyote.[5]

329. In half-civilized peoples elaborate cosmogonies arise, in which the sky is introduced along with sun, moon, and stars. The most noteworthy of these representations of the origin of the sky is one that occurs in almost identical forms in Egypt and New Zealand, among the Masai of Central East Africa, and elsewhere: two beings lie in marriage embrace — one is lifted up and stretches from horizon to horizon as the sky, the other remains as the earth.[6] The sun is commonly male but sometimes female,[7] and

---

[1] See below, § 662, etc.   [2] Ps. xviii, 11 [10]; civ, 3 f.   [3] *Iliad*, xxiii, 194 ff.

[4] Spencer and Gillen, *Native Tribes of Central Australia*, chap. xviii; Rivers, *The Todas*, p. 595.   [5] W. Matthews, *Navaho Legends*, pp. 80, 223.

[6] Breasted, *History of Egypt*, p. 55; Taylor, *New Zealand*, p. 119; Hollis, *The Masai*, p. 279; cf. Turner, *Samoa*, p. 283.

[7] Teit, *Thompson River Indians*, p. 55 (the present sun is the daughter of a man sun).

there is also diversity of views as to the sex of the moon. The stars are often called the children of the sun and moon.

330. Savage fancy sees in the groups of stars resemblances to human persons and objects.[1] Such resemblances are worked out by civilized peoples, a descriptive science of constellations arises, and stories are invented to explain the origin of their names. These stellar myths, brought into connection with others, play a great part in developed mythologies.

331. Among higher communities there are diverse conceptions of the sex of the great luminaries. The word for 'sun' is feminine in Sanskrit, Anglo-Saxon, German, and often in Hebrew; masculine in Babylonian, Assyrian, Greek, and Latin. 'Moon' is masculine in Anglo-Saxon and German, and generally in Sanskrit and the Semitic languages; feminine in Greek and Latin. The reasons for these differences are to be sought in the economic relations of the communities to sun and moon, and in the play of imagination, but the history of the variations is not clear. One proposed explanation is that to those who traveled by night on land or on sea the moon was the strong guide and patron, and by day the sun appeared as a splendidly beautiful woman. Other explanations have been offered, but no general determining principle can be stated.[2]

332. The early anthropomorphic figures of sun and moon appear to be on the verge of becoming true gods. It is, however, often difficult to decide whether in the widespread veneration of the sun it is to be regarded as a living thing (it is frequently represented as a man, a great chief,[3] dwelling in the sky), or a physical object inhabited by a spirit, or a fully developed god.[4] The transition to the higher conception is gradual, and will be discussed below,[5] along with the representations of the moon and the stars.

333. The view that the sky and the earth are the original progenitors of things appears among many peoples, low and high (notably among the Chinese); the two are sometimes taken for

[1] See examples in Tylor's *Primitive Culture*, i, 290 ff.
[2] On the position of the sun and moon in the later cults see below, Chap. VI.
[3] Teit, op. cit., p. 54.
[4] See the elaborate Pawnee history of gods (Dorsey, *The Skidi Pawnee*).
[5] See Chap. VI f.

granted, but it is probable that there were always stories accounting for their origin. The sky is sometimes female, usually in the older myths (Maori, Egyptian), sometimes male (Greek, Roman).[1]

334. Thunder and lightning are regarded in early systems of thought as independent things, only locally or accidentally combined. They are awful and terrible to savage feeling,[2] but they have never received religious worship. A quasi-scientific explanation of thunder found among certain peoples (North American, Brazilian, Bakuana, Karen, and others) is that it is produced by the flapping of the wings of a mighty bird.[3] More commonly thunder is the voice of a deity, and lightning is his arrow,[4] or these are said simply to be sent by a god.[5]

WORSHIP OF HUMAN BEINGS [6]

335. We might naturally suppose that human beings, as well as animals, plants, and inanimate things, would be objects of religious reverence to undeveloped communities; men, it might seem, would be thought worthier objects of worship than beasts, plants, and stones. In fact, the cult of human beings has been and is widespread, but in this cult the savage mind makes a sharp distinction between the living and the dead. Living men are tangible and intelligible, affected with human frailties, and therefore offer less food for the imagination than beasts; the souls of dead men are remote, intangible, mysterious, and it is they that have most inspired religious emotion. The history of these cults is in some

---

[1] On the genesial (urano-chthonic) conception of the world in Polynesia see Tautain, in *Anthropologie*, vii (1896). [2] Hollis, *The Nandi*, p. 113.

[3] Tylor, *Primitive Culture*, i, 363; ii, 262. [4] Ps. xxix, 3; xviii, 14, 15 [13, 14].

[5] *Iliad*, viii, 76 f.; xxi, 198, etc. The thunderbolt of Zeus is said in Hesiod, *Theogonia*, 140 f., to be forged by the Cyclops.

[6] Bastian, *Beiträge*; H. Spencer, *Principles of Sociology* and *Principles of Ethics*; Grant Allen, *Evolution of the Idea of God*; Waitz-Gerland, *Anthropologie der Naturvölker*; Lippert, *Allgemeine Geschichte des Priesterthums*; Tylor, *Primitive Culture*; Codrington, *The Melanesians*; Frazer, *Golden Bough*; Wilken, *Handleiding voor de Vergelykende Volkenkunde van Nederlandsch-Indië*; Steinmetz, *Ethnologische Studien zur ersten Entwicklung der Strafe*; Westermarck, *Origin and Development of the Moral Ideas*, Index, s.vv. *Kings, Man-gods*; Religions of Egypt (Maspero, Meyer, Wiedemann, Breasted, Steindorff), Babylonia (Jastrow), India (Barth, Hopkins), China (De Groot), Greece (Gruppe), Rome (Auer), etc.

points obscure; though many facts have been collected, the data are not full and exact enough to furnish a complete explanation of the details of usage, diffusion, origin, and development.

THE CULT OF THE LIVING

336. Savages appear to put no limit to the possible powers of men. In the absence of any exact knowledge of natural law there is no reason why a man should not be thought capable of inflicting sickness and death, bringing rain, securing food, and doing all that relates to human life. Magicians, prophets, ascetics, and saints are credited with such powers in early and later times. Polynesian chiefs are supposed to be imbued with a sacredness that makes contact with them dangerous, and everything that they touch becomes thereby taboo to the ordinary man; the same sort of sacredness clung to the Roman flamen dialis, to the emperor of Japan, and to many other high officials. This reverence, however, is simply fear of the mysterious, and does not, in itself, reach the height of worship, though it prepares the way for it and may sometimes be scarcely distinguishable from worship proper. The magician is the mouthpiece of a god, and in popular belief is often invested with power that is practically divine.

337. Many cases, in fact, are reported in which living men are worshiped as gods; but such reports are often open to doubt and need confirmation. Travelers and other observers are not always in position to state the facts precisely; particularly they do not always distinguish between awe and religious worship, and the statements of savages on this point are often vague. Frazer has collected a considerable number of examples of alleged worship of living men.[1] One of these, that of the dairyman (*palol*) of the Todas of Southern India, is not supported by the latest observer, who says that the palol is highly respected but not worshiped.[2] An apparently clear case of worship is the Panjab god Nikkal Sen, said to be General Nicholson;[3] and it is not improbable that

---

[1] *Golden Bough*, 2d ed., i, 139 ff.   [2] Rivers, *The Todas*, p. 448.
[3] Monier-Williams, *Religious Life and Thought in India*, p. 259. See the cases mentioned by Hopkins, *Religions of India*, p. 522 n.

in other cases mentioned by Frazer (Marquesas Islands, Raiatea, Samoa, Fiji) actual deification takes place.

338. Among many more-advanced communities divinity has been ascribed to living monarchs: to the kings of ancient Egypt; to many early Babylonian kings; to the emperor of China; to some of the Ptolemies and Seleucids; to certain Roman emperors; to the kings of Mexico and Peru; and in more modern times to the emperor of Japan. Whether such titles involve a real ascription of divinity, or are only an assertion of kinship with the gods, or express nothing more than the adulation of courtiers, it may not be easy always to determine; probably all these conceptions have existed at various times. The conception that men are akin to gods, that there is no difference of nature between the two classes, is an old one, and the ascription of divinity to a king might involve, in earlier stages of civilization or even in relatively advanced stages, no break in the order of things. The custom once established, it might continue to be observed, long accepted seriously by the mass of the people, but coming gradually to be regarded by the educated classes as a mere form.

339. The development of the custom appears most plainly in *Egypt*.[1] The identification of the king with Horus (apparently the ancient patron deity of Egypt) runs through the history down to the Persian conquest: he is called " Horus " or " Golden Horus," and sometimes (as, for example, Mentuhotep IV) " heir of Horus," or is said to sit on the throne of Horus, and has a " Horus name," the affirmation of his divine character; even the monotheistic reformer Amenhotep IV is called " Golden Horus." At the same time he is styled the " son " of this or that deity — Re, Min, Amon, Amon-Re, Osiris — according to the particular patron adopted by him; the liberal interpretation of such filial relation is illustrated by the title " son of the gods of the Northland " given to one monarch. The king is " the good god "; at death he flies to heaven (so, for instance, Totmose III, of the eighteenth dynasty).

340. The official honorific character of divine titles appears as early as the fifteenth century, when Queen Hatshepsut is officially

[1] For the documents see Breasted, *Ancient Records of Egypt.*

declared to be the daughter of Amon. By such an official procedure Alexander, though not akin to any Egyptian royal house, was declared to be the son of Amon; Ptolemy Philadelphus became the son of the sun-god, and his wife Arsinoë was made a goddess by a solemn ceremony. Possibly the recognition of the divine title, in educated Egyptian circles, as a conventional form began at a relatively early time — the easy way in which a man was made a god may have been felt in such circles to be incompatible with real divinity. Nevertheless the cult of the divinized king was practiced seriously. In some cases the living monarch had his temple and retinue of priests, and divine honors were paid him.[1]

341. The case was different in the *Semitic treatment of kings* styled divine. The custom of so regarding them is found only in early Babylonia. The evidence that they were held to be divine consists in the fact that the determinative for divinity (Sumerian *dingir*, Semitic *an*) is prefixed to their names in the inscriptions.[2] It appears that the determinative occurs at times during a period of about a thousand years (ca. 3000–2000 B.C. — the chronology is uncertain), and is then dropped. The data do not explain the reasons for this change of custom; a natural suggestion is that there came a time when the conception of the deity forbade an ascription of divinity to human beings. However this may be, the nominal divinization of kings seems not to have had any effect on the cultus. As far as the known evidence goes, the king seems never to have been approached with divine worship.[3]

342. It may be doubted whether the Babylonian usage can properly be called Semitic. As such a custom is found nowhere

<hr>

[1] Rawlinson, *Egypt*, ii, 40 f., 84; Ed. Meyer, *Geschichte des Alten Aegyptens*, p. 252.

[2] When in a compound name the name of a god stands first, the determinative may refer simply to the god; it is evidence for the man only when it stands immediately before the nondivine element of the royal name. The inscriptions are given in Schrader, *Keilinschriftliche Bibliothek*, III, i; Thureau-Dangin, *Sumerisch-Akkadische Königsinschriften*. In the Code of Hammurabi (ca. 2000 B.C.) the king in one place (col. 5, ll. 4, 5) calls himself "the Shamash of Babylon," but this is of course a figure of speech; the code is given him by Shamash, the god of justice, and he assumes to be no less just than the god whom he here represents.

[3] For a different view see S. H. Langdon, article "Babylonian Eschatology" in *Essays in Modern Theology and Related Subjects* (the C. A. Briggs memorial volume).

else in the Semitic area, and as the early Babylonian Semites borrowed much from the non-Semitic Sumerians (they borrowed their system of writing and some literary material), it is conceivable that they adopted this practice from them. There is, to be sure, no proof, except from the inscriptions, that the practice was Sumerian; but, as it is found in some Asiatic non-Semitic lands,[1] there is the possibility that it existed among the Sumerians, of whose history, however, we unfortunately know little. It is to be noted that the cessation of the practice appears to be synchronous with the establishment of the first great Semitic dynasty at Babylon.

343. No ascription of divinity to men is found among the *Hebrews*. The Elohim-beings (called " sons of God " in the English translation of the Bible) are gods. The code forbids men to curse God (not " judges ")[2] — judges are not called " gods." There is nothing going to show that the old Hebrew kings were looked on as divine. Frazer's hypothesis that the king was identified with the God Adonis[3] is not supported by the statements of the Old Testament; the title ' my lord ' (*adoni*) given him is simply the ordinary expression of respect and courtesy. He is " the anointed of Yahweh," as many ancient official persons (kings and priests) were inducted into office by the pouring of oil on their heads, but, as a mouthpiece and representative of the deity, he is inferior to the prophet; at best, flattery, such as that of the woman of Tekoa, might liken him to an angel.[4] The epithet *el gibbor* (English Bible, " mighty God "), applied to a Jewish prince, must probably be rendered ' mighty hero.'[5] The title ' gods ' has been supposed to be given to men (judges) a couple of times in the Psalter,[6] but the reference there seems to be to Greek deities regarded as acting as judges.

---

1 Cf. the Chinese and Japanese views mentioned above. Among the Mongols there seems to be no trace of such a cult (Buckley, in Saussaye, *Lehrbuch der Religionsgeschichte*, 2d ed.), but a similar one is found in Tibet in Lamaism.

2 Ex. xxii, 28 [27]. Cursing the deity (that is, the national or the local god) is mentioned several times in the Old Testament. Eli's sons committed this offense (1 Sam. iii, 13, corrected text), and Job feared that his sons might have been guilty of it (Job i, 5, where the old Jewish scribes, *causa reverentiae*, have changed " curse " into " bless,"— so also in i, 11 ; ii, 5, 9).   3 *Adonis Attis Osiris*, p. 15 ff.

4 2 Sam. xiv, 17.   5 Isa. ix, 6 [5].

6 Ps. lviii, 1 [2] ; lxxxii, 1, 6. This last passage, however, is understood in John x, 34 f., to refer to Jewish men. The Hebrew text of Ps. xlv, 7 [6], is corrupt.

344. The ascription of divinity to human beings is lacking in *Arabia* also and among Semitic Moslems generally. The Ismailic and Babist dogmas of the incarnation of God in certain men are of Aryan (Indian) origin.

345. The *Chinese* conception of the all-pervading and absolute power of the Universe naturally invests the emperor with divinity.[1] All human beings are supposed to possess some portion of the divine essence, but he alone, as head and representative of the nation, possesses it in full measure. He is theoretically perfect in thought, word, and deed, and is entitled not only to the reverence and obedience of his subjects, but also to their religious homage. Larger acquaintance with other peoples has doubtless led educated Chinese to regard him as only one among several great kings in the world, but for the people at large he is still practically a god. Other living men also are worshiped as divine.

346. The *Japanese* formal divinization of the emperor appears to have begun with the establishment of the monarchy (in the sixth or seventh century of our era), but, like the Chinese, goes back to the crude conception of early times. It has been generally accepted seriously by the people, but has not received philosophical formulation. It is now practically given up by the educated classes, and will probably soon vanish completely.[2]

347. Among the *Greeks* and the *Romans* the belief in the divinity of living men and women was of a vague character. In Homer the epithet *dios* when applied to human beings (individuals or peoples) means little more, if any more, than ' of exalted character' (except in the case of mythical heroes, like Achilles, who were of actual divine parentage). At a later time such divinization was sometimes treated jestingly. If Plutarch may be accepted as authority,[3] Alexander did not take his own godhead seriously, did not believe in it, but allowed it merely for its effect on others.

---

[1] De Groot, *Religion of the Chinese*. This is the philosophical form of the dogma. The root of the conception is to be found, doubtless, in the old (savage) view that the chief of the tribe has quasi-divine attributes.   [2] Knox, *Religion in Japan*, p. 64.

[3] In *Alexander*, 28. In the case of Alexander the influence of Egypt is apparent, and it may be suspected that this influence affected the later Greek and Roman custom.

It was little more than a farce when the Syrian-Greek Antiochus II, for services rendered to a city, was called " Theos " by the grateful citizens;[1] it was the baldest flattery when Herod's oration[2] was greeted by a tumultuous assembly as the " voice of a god." Augustus, though he allowed temples and altars to be consecrated to him in the provinces, did not permit it in Rome, being, apparently, ashamed of such procedures.[3] The most infamous of the early emperors, Caligula, received divine honors in his lifetime by his own decree.[4] Apart from these particular cases, however, the general conception of the possibility of a man's being divine had a notable effect on the religious development in the Roman Empire.[5] The custom, for example, of burning incense before the Emperor's statue (which faithful Christians refused to do), while it strengthened the idea of the presence of the divine in human life, doubtless debased it.

348. Deification of living men is not found in the great national religions of *India* and *Persia*. Mazdaism, like Hebraism, kept the human distinctly apart from the divine : Ahura Mazda is virtually absolute, and Zoroaster and the succeeding prophets, including the savior Çaoshyanç-, are men chosen and appointed by him.[6] Vedism developed the nature-gods, and in Brahmanism the goal of the worshiper was union with the divine, but not independent divinity ; the muni by ascetic observances might attain a power equal or superior to that of the gods and feared by them,[7] but he remained (like the old magician) a powerful man and did not receive divine worship.[8] In recent times the followers of the Brahma-Samaj leader Sen are said to have worshiped him as a god[9] — apparently an isolated phenomenon, the origin of which is not clear. Buddha was

---

[1] Appian, *De Rebus Syriacis*, lxv.   [2] Acts xii, 22.

[3] Boissier, *La religion romaine* (1878), i, 131 ff.   [4] Suetonius, *Caligula*, xxii.

[5] On the demand for a universal religion in the Roman Empire, and the preparation in the earlier cults for the worship of the emperors, see J. Iverach's article "Cæsarism" in Hastings, *Encyclopædia of Religion and Ethics*; Boissier, op. cit., bk. i, chap. ii.   [6] Spiegel, *Eranische Alterthumskunde*, bk. iv, chap. iii.

[7] See the story of the power and fall of a great muni in Lassen's *Anthologia Sanscritica*.

[8] So, many Christian and Moslem saints have been wonder-workers without being divinized.   [9] Monier-Williams, *Brahmanism and Hinduism*, p. 510 f.

purely human to himself and his contemporaries. The ascription of divinity to the Tibetan Grand Lamas is a product of the transformation of Buddhism under the influence of a crude non-Aryan population that retained the old conception of the essential identity of nature of men and gods.

349. When chiefs and kings are divinized, offerings are usually made to them as to other gods; their cult becomes a part of the polytheistic system. But it is rare that they displace the old local deities or equal them in influence. Their worship passes with the passing of polytheism.

The Cult of the Dead

350. In the history of religion the veneration of the dead, as is remarked above, is more widely diffused and more effective than that of the living. We may distinguish between the cult of known historical persons after death (which is closely related to that of living men), the deification of mythical ancestors, and the worship of ghosts.

351. *Historical persons.* In simple communities commanding personalities that have impressed the imagination of the people by proofs of power and by conferring benefits on communities may not unnaturally receive divine honors after death. Lyall reports a case of this sort in recent times: the French officer Raymond in Hyderabad is said to have been worshiped as a god.[1] Other cases are reported as occuring in Samoa and in India.[2] Rivers mentions traditions among the Todas of Southern India which, he thinks, may vouch for the worship of gods who were originally men, but implicit reliance cannot be placed on such traditions.[3] Two apparently definite instances of deification are given by Ellis,[4] both of cruel kings (one dethroned in 1818), to whom temples with complete rituals are dedicated; but the deification in one of these cases (and probably in the other) was a deliberate act of political leaders,

---

[1] *Fortnightly Review*, 1872.

[2] Stair, *Samoa*, p. 221; article " Bengal " in Hastings, *Encyclopædia of Religion and Ethics* (Brahmans often become evil spirits).

[3] *The Todas*, pp. 193, 203, 446.   [4] *The Ewe-speaking Peoples*, p. 88 ff.

and not a product of spontaneous popular feeling. Two other local gods mentioned by Ellis were, according to the tradition, two men who began the trade that made Whydah the chief port of the west coast of Africa; but here also the tradition is not perfectly trustworthy.

352. Egyptian kings were regularly deified after death, being identified with Osiris; their cult, though not equal in sanctity to that of the gods proper, was still prominent and important.[1] It is probably to be regarded as a revision and magnification of the cult of the dead kin, combined with the desire to honor great representative men. No such custom is known to have existed among Semitic peoples, by whom a sharp distinction was made between the divine and the human. In India it was chiefly the ascetic sages that were religiously eminent, and in the prevailing pantheistic system these (as is remarked above), absorbing the divine essence, sometimes became as powerful as gods, but passed after death into the cosmic All, and remained human. The Mazdean faith, like the Israelite, made it impossible to accept a deceased man as a god.

353. Examples of the occasional divinization of deceased men in the Hellenic world are given below.[2] In Rome the custom arose at a comparatively late period, and it was the work not of spontaneous Roman thought but of political philosophy.[3] The deification of the Roman emperors after death had its ground in the reconstruction of Roman life undertaken by Augustus. He recognized a principle of unification in the resuscitation of the old national religion, in which the people believed, whether he himself did or not. Religion in Rome was largely an affair of the state; the leaders of the public religion were great state officials. Augustus was made pontifex maximus, and it was only one step farther to elevate the chief magistrate to the rank of a god. The good sense of the time generally forbade the bestowment of this honor during the imperator's lifetime, but an apotheosis was in accord with the veneration paid to the manes and with the exalted position of the

---

[1] Breasted, *Records of Ancient Egypt.*   [2] § 357.
[3] Here, as in the case of the divinization of living men (§ 347 n., above), outside suggestion is probable.

Emperor as absolute lord of the Western world.[1] Popular feeling appears to have accepted this divinization without question and in sincerity; educated circles accepted it as an act of political policy. The elevation of Julius Cæsar and Augustus to the rank of gods established the rule, and deceased emperors received divine honors up to the triumph of Christianity.[2]

354. In China, Confucius was deified as the special exponent of the state religion and the authoritative teacher of the principles of social and political life. His religious cult is practiced by the government (officially) and by the masses of the people; how far it is sincerely accepted by the educated classes is uncertain. In China and in Japan the gods of war are said to be historical persons deified.

355. The divinization of the Calif Ali by some Shiah sects was the product of religious fanaticism under the guidance of Aryan conceptions of the incarnation of the divine.[8]

356. *Mythical ancestors.* Mythical ancestors are usually eponymous; the tendency in all ancient peoples was to refer their names and origins to single persons. Such an eponym was the product of imagination, a genealogical myth (Hellen, Ion, Dorus, Jacob, Israel), and was revered, but was not always the object of a religious cult; such cults do not appear among the Semites[4] or in the native Roman rites. Nor does the custom seem to have originated in the earliest periods; it was rather a creation of quasi-scientific reflection, the demand for definite historical organization, and it appears first in relatively late literary monuments.[5]

357. Still later arose the worship of these ancestral founders. In Greece shrines were erected by various cities to their supposed founders, and where, as in Athens, the tribes had their eponyms, these received divine worship, though they never attained equal

---

[1] Cf. article "Cæsarism" in Hastings, *Encyclopædia of Religion and Ethics.*

[2] Boissier, *La religion romaine*, i, 182. An illustration of religious ideas in the third century is afforded by the enrollment of Caracalla among the heroes, a divinizing decree of the Senate having been extorted by the turbulent and mercenary soldiery (Dio Cassius, ed. Boissevain [Eng. tr. by H. B. Foster], lxxix, 9).

[8] A. Müller, *Islam*, i, 494; W. Muir, *The Caliphate*, p. 553 ff.

[4] In Isa. lxiii, 16, 'Abraham' appears to be a synonym of 'Israel,' and the reference then is to the nonrecognition of certain Jews by the national leaders.

[5] The narratives of the Pentateuch; Herodotus, v, 66; Pausanias, i, 5, 1.

rank with the gods proper. From Greece this cult was brought into Italy. It was probably under Greek influence, and at a relatively late time, that Romulus was created, made the immediate founder of Rome, and took his place among the objects of worship;[1] on the other hand, Æneas (a Greek importation), though he was accepted as original founder, never received divine worship, doubtless because Romulus (nearer in name to the city Roma) already held the position of divine patron. The cult of eponyms tended naturally to coalesce with that of divine 'heroes'[2] — the two figures were alike in character, differing mainly in function, and eponyms were styled 'heroes.'[3]

358. The inverse process, the reduction of divine beings to simple human proportions, has gone on in early cults and in early attempts at historical construction to a not inconsiderable degree. Thus, to take a relatively late example, by Saxo Grammaticus and in the Heimskringla (both of the thirteenth century) the god Odin is made into a human king and the history of his exploits is given in detail.[4] It is, however, especially in the treatment of the old divine heroes, originally true gods, that the process of dedivinization appears. These figures, because of their local character and for other reasons, entered into peculiarly close relations with human societies, of which they thus tended to become constituent parts, and the same feeling that gave the gods human shapes converted the heroes into mere men, who are generally reconstructers of society. Examples of this sort of anthropomorphizing are found in myths all over the world: the Babylonian Gilgamesh; the "mighty men" of Genesis vi, 4, originally demigods, the progeny of human mothers and of the Elohim-beings (the Benē Elohim, 'sons of the gods,' members, that is, of the divine circle); Heracles and Hercules; the Scandinavian (apparently general Teutonic) Valkyrs, Nornas, and Swan-maidens.[5]

---

[1] Article "Romulus" in Roscher's *Lexikon*.   [2] See below, § 652.
[3] Herodotus, v, 66 al.   [4] Saussaye, *Religion of the Teutons*, pp. 163, 170, 206.
[5] The Ojibwa god Manabozho (described in Schoolcraft's *Algic Researches*) by some inadvertence got the name 'Hiawatha,' and so appears in Longfellow's poem. The real Hiawatha was a distinguished Iroquois statesman (supposed to be of the fifteenth century), the founder of the Iroquois League, honored as a patriot, but never worshiped as a god. See H. Hale, *Iroquois Book of Rites*, Index, s.v. *Hiawatha*; Beauchamp, in *Journal of American Folklore*, October, 1891.

359. The Sicilian Euhemeros (of the latter part of the fourth century B.C.), after extensive travels to great places of worship, formulated the theory that all the gods were deified men. Some grounds for his theory he doubtless had, for, according to ancient opinion, gods might and did die, and their places of burial were sometimes pointed out (the grave of Zeus, for instance, in Crete). How far this view had been held before the time of Euhemeros is uncertain, but he gave it vogue, and it is called, after him, Euhemerism.[1] In recent times it has been revived in part by Herbert Spencer and Allen, who derive all gods from ghosts.[2] Similar to it is the rationalizing of myths, which has met with favor at various times.

360. *The dead kin.* Apart from the special cases mentioned above, the dead have been the objects of particular care in all parts of the world. Some of the observances connected with them might perhaps, in themselves considered, be ascribed to natural affection. It cannot be denied that savages have some love of kindred, and this feeling, in conjunction with the ideas concerning the future state, might lead the survivors to do such things as it was believed would secure the comfort of the deceased — decent burial in accordance with tribal customs, and provision of food and attendants and other necessaries. But, while the existence and influence of natural human kindliness need not be denied, observation of savage life favors the conclusion that the greater part of the early usages connected with the dead have their origin in the desire to conciliate them, to avert their displeasure and gain their aid, and thus come to constitute a cult of the dead that runs through all phases of civilization.[3]

361. Such usages must be very ancient, for they are found in the lowest tribes, and appear to be based on the earliest known conceptions of the nature of departed souls.[4] These latter are held

---

[1] F. Pfister, *Der Reliquienkult im Altertum.*

[2] Spencer, *Principles of Sociology*, i; Grant Allen, *Evolution of the Idea of God.* See below, § 631 ff.

[3] Westermarck, *Origin and Development of the Moral Ideas*, Index, s.v. *Dead*: Grant Allen, op. cit.; article "Ancestor-worship" in Hastings, *Encyclopædia of Religion and Ethics.*   [4] Cf. above, Chap. II.

to have all the ordinary affections of the living, but to be endowed with extraordinary powers : they have their likes and dislikes, their kindliness, jealousy, anger, revengefulness, all on the lower moral grade of undeveloped life ; they are, in many regards, not subject to the ordinary limitations of the living — they are invisible, move swiftly from place to place through obstacles impervious to the living, enter their bodies, produce sickness and death, aid or destroy crops. On the other hand, they need food and other necessities of ordinary life, and for these things are dependent on the living. Hence the desirableness of securing their good will by showing them respect and supplying their needs, or else of somehow getting rid of them.

362. There are, then, two sorts of ghosts, or, more precisely, two sorts of ghostly activity — the friendly and the unfriendly — and corresponding to these are the emotions of love and fear which they call forth. On account of paucity of data it is difficult to say which of these emotions is the commoner among savages ; probably the feeling is a mixed one, compounded of fear and friendliness.[1] In general it is evident that with the better organization of family life a gentler feeling for the dead was called forth ; but it is probable that in the least-developed communities fear of the mysterious departed was the prevailing emotion.

363. Though the accessible evidence does not enable us to determine with certainty the motives of all savage customs connected with the dead, there are some distinctions that may be made with fair probability. To supply the dead with food and cooking-utensils may very well be, as is remarked above, the impulse of affection, and even where slaves and wives are slain that their ghosts may minister to the ghost of the master and husband, this may not go beyond pious solicitude for the comfort of the deceased. But the mourning-usages common with savages are too violent to be merely the expression of love ; the loud cries and the wounding of

---

[1] Steinmetz (*Ethnologische Studien zur ersten Entwicklung der Strafe*, p. 280 ff.) has attempted a collection and interpretation of the usages of nearly two hundred tribes, but his reckoning is not satisfactory — his enumeration is not complete, and the facts are not sufficiently well certified. He concludes that cases of fear are twice as numerous as those of love.

the person are meant more probably to assure the deceased of the high regard in which he is held;[1] in some cases, as among the Central Australians, men gash themselves so severely as to come near producing death.[2] These excessive demonstrations are softened as general culture increases, and finally dwindle to an apparatus of hired mourners. A similar explanation holds of the restriction of food, the seclusion of the widow or the widower, and the rule against mentioning the name of the deceased: abstinence and silence are marks of respect.

364. Funeral feasts also testify respect:[3] they appear to be extensions of the practice of providing food for the dead, feasts in which the mourners, from motives of thriftiness, take part; the ghost consumes only the invisible soul of the food, and it is proper that what is left should furnish refreshment for the living.[4] The funeral festivities are sometimes protracted, and become occasions of enjoyment to the circle of kinsfolk, in some cases at a ruinous expense to the family of the deceased, as is true now sometimes of Irish and other wakes. The honor of the family is involved, and this fact, together with the natural desire for pleasure, has contributed to the development of the custom in savage as well as in civilized life. In general the solemnity of the various ceremonies and other usages testifies to a profound conviction of the necessity of keeping on good terms with the dead.[5]

365. The reports of savage customs show a certain number of cases in which the benevolent and the malevolent activities of the dead are equally prominent: so, for example, among the Australian Kurnai,[6] the New Zealanders,[7] the Melanesian peoples,[8] the

---

[1] Westermarck, *Origin and Development of the Moral Ideas*, chap. xlv.

[2] Spencer and Gillen, *Northern Tribes of Central Australia*, pp. 516 f., 520 f.

[3] Cf. Codrington, *The Melanesians*, p. 271 f.

[4] The conception of such meals as physical and spiritual communion with the dead was a later development.

[5] The buffoonery that was sometimes practiced at Roman funerals seems to have come from the natural love of fun, here particularly, also, through the reaction from the oppressive solemnity of the occasion.

[6] Howitt and Fison, *Kamilaroi and Kurnai*, p. 246 ff.

[7] Taylor, *New Zealand*, pp. 104, 108.

[8] Codrington, *The Melanesians*, pp. 194, 253 f.; Powell, *Wanderings*, p. 170.

Vezimbas of Madagascar,[1] the Zulus,[2] the Ewe-speaking tribes on the west coast of Africa.[3] It is probable that the list might be greatly extended by exact observation. When we find two peoples, dwelling near together and of the same grade of general culture, credited the one with fear, the other with friendly feeling toward the dead, it seems likely that different sets of usages have met the eyes of the observers; a certain amount of accident must color such reports.

366. It is natural to suppose that fear of ghosts is commoner among less-developed peoples, kindly feeling more usual in higher communities; and when civilized peoples are taken into account this sort of progression is obvious. But the reports of savages show such a mixture of customs that it is difficult to see any line of progress. Dread of ghosts is certified in Central Australia and North Queensland, in Tonga (Polynesia), Central Africa, Central Asia, among the North American Chippewas, Navahos, and Southwest Oregon Indians, and the South American Araucanians; friendly feeling is found in Tasmania, Western Africa, South Africa, California, and among the Iroquois and the Zuñi Indians.[4] In such lists there is no clear sign of a division according to general culture.

367. Friendly relations with the dead do not in themselves necessarily involve worship, but a more or less definite *cult of ghosts* is found in various parts of the world. They are, or were, regarded as tutelary spirits in Tasmania, Ashanti, and Dahomi (where shrines are dedicated to them), and by the Zuñi Indians; prayers are addressed to them in Samoa and the Hawaiian Islands (where there is a definite family worship), in Yoruba, by the Banyas and the Zulus, by the Ossetes, the Veddahs of Ceylon, and the North American Dakotas; offerings are made to them — sometimes to influential persons, chiefs, and others, as in the Gilbert Islands, in parts of Melanesia, in Borneo, and by the Cakchiquels of Central America — sometimes to all the dead, as in the Solomon Islands,

---

[1] Ellis, *Madagascar*, i, 23, 423.   [2] Callaway, *The Amazulu*, pp. 145, 151.

[3] A. B. Ellis, *The Ewe*, p. 102 f.

[4] Steinmetz, *Ethnologische Studien zur ersten Entwicklung der Strafe*. A. L. Kroeber (in *Journal of American Folklore*, 1904) gives an account of a 'ghost-dance' in Northwest California, the object of which was said to be that the dead might return, though the details are obscure.

the New Hebrides, Fiji, Torres Straits, and by the Zulus, the Veddahs of Ceylon, the Kolarians of Bengal, and the Ossetes.[1]

368. These lists include peoples of very different grades of culture; the inference suggested is that the cult of the dead is of very early origin — its basis is the same among all communities that practice it, though the particular ceremonies of worship vary.

369. Besides forms of actual worship there are several usages that involve religious veneration of the dead. Graves are regarded as asylums by the Kafirs (graves of chiefs)[2] and in Tonga.[3] The Bedawin of Arabia held (in pre-Islamic times), and still hold, graves sacred;[4] they sometimes become shrines, and oaths are sworn by them. The custom of swearing by the dead is widespread. In their character of powerful spirits they are agents in processes of magic and divination. Parts of dead bodies are used as charms. The skull especially is revered as an oracle.[5]

370. Among the lower tribes, savage and half-civilized, it is chiefly those who have died recently that are worshiped. A Zulu explained to Callaway that his people forgot those who died long ago — they were supposed to be not helpful — and hope of gain has always been the basis of worship. Among the Kafirs of the Hindu Kush it is the custom to erect an effigy to the memory of every adult one year after his decease. Women, as well as men, are thus honored, and may be put on an equality with men by being given a throne to sit on. No worship is offered to these images, but it is believed that their presence brings prosperity; bad weather is ascribed to their removal. There are solemn dances in honor of the illustrious dead and sacrifices are offered to them.[6]

371. The worship of the dead in the great civilized communities, though more elaborate and refined than the savage cult, is in

---

[1] Some such custom seems to be referred to in Deut. xxvi, 14.

[2] Fritsch, *Die Eingeborenen Süd-Afrikas.* [3] Mariner, *Tonga*, p. 149.

[4] Wellhausen, *Reste arabischen Heidentumes*, p. 162 f.; Goldziher, in *Revue de l'histoire des religions*, x. So the Egyptian fellahin to-day.

[5] Codrington, *The Melanesians*, p. 219 f.; Bonney, in *Journal of the Anthropological Institute*, xiii, 122 ff.; Haddon, *Head-hunters*, pp. 91 f., 183; G. Allen, *Evolution of the Idea of God*, chap. iii.

[6] Sir G. S. Robertson, *The Kafirs of the Hindu-Kush*, pp. 645 ff., 615 ff., 414 f.

substance identical with it. The Egyptians provided the departed soul with food and honored the dead man with laudatory notices of his earthly life ; the royal ancestor of a king, it was believed, might act as mediator between him and the gods.[1] The Babylonians, while they lamented the departure of men to the gloomy existence in the Underworld, recognized the quasi-divine power of the dead and addressed prayer to them.[2] The Hebrews offered food to the dead, had funeral feasts, and consulted ghosts who were regarded as divine.[3] The Hindu "fathers," though kept distinct from the gods, were yet conceived of as possessing godlike powers and were worshiped as gods.[4] The Persian "forefathers" (*fravashis*), particularly the manes of eminent pious men, were held to be bestowers of all the blessings of life ; offerings were made and prayers addressed to them.[5]

372. Early notices of a cult of the dead among the Greeks are scanty. There was the usual kindly provision of food, arms, and other necessaries for them.[6] Odysseus in Hades pours out a libation (honey, wine, water, to which meal is added) to all the dead, addresses vows and prayers to them, and promises to offer to them a barren heifer on his return to Ithaca, and a black sheep separately to Teiresias.[7] From the sixth century onward the references in the literature show that the worship of the dead (including children) was then general (and of course it must have begun much earlier). The offerings made to them were both vegetable and animal ; the sacrificed animal was slaughtered in the same way as in the sacrifices to chthonic deities — the dead were, in fact, regarded as underground deities.[8] The flesh of the animals offered was not eaten by the worshipers.

373. Among the dead thus honored is to be included one class of heroes. A Greek "hero" was sometimes an eminent man,

---

[1] Breasted, *Egypt*, p. 421, etc.

[2] Jastrow, *Religion of Babylonia and Assyria*, p. 604 f.

[3] Deut. xxvi, 14 ; Hos. ix, 4 ; Ezek. xxiv, 17 (revised text) ; Isa. viii, 19 ; 1 Sam. xxviii, 13.   [4] *Rig-Veda*, x, 15 ; Hopkins, *Religions of India*, p. 143 f.

[5] Spiegel, *Eranische Alterthumskunde*, ii, 91 ff.

[6] *Odyssey*, xi, 74 ff. ; cf. xxiv, 63 ff.   [7] *Odyssey*, x, 519 ff. ; xi, 25 ff.

[8] Stengel and Oehmichen, *Die griechischen Sakralaltertümer*, p. 99 f.

sometimes such a man divinized, sometimes an old god reduced to human dimensions, reckoned in some cases to belong to the circle of the gods proper.[1] Such personages might be worshiped as gods, with the sacrifices appropriate to the gods, or as departed men, with the sacrifices that custom fixed for the dead. The hero-cult included many men of note recently deceased, like Brasidas and those that fell at Marathon.[2]

374. The cults just mentioned dealt with the departed as friendly souls, the protectors of the family, the clan, or the state. The state cult of the dead was elaborate and solemn. The Greek citizen was surrounded by a host of the eminent dead who kept him in touch with the past and offered him ideals of life.[3] Another attitude toward the dead is indicated by the great apotropaic spring festival, the Anthesteria of Athens, the object of which was to rid the city of the ghosts that then wandered about.[4] This double attitude is precisely that of the savage tribes referred to above. The same difference of feeling appears in the Roman cults: the *manes* are the friendly or doubtful souls of dead ancestors; the Parentalia is a festival in honor of the dead kin; in the Lemuria, on the other hand, the father of the family performs a ceremony at midnight intended to rid the house of ghosts.[5]

375. Among modern peoples it is the Chinese that have organized the worship of the dead in the completest way; it is for them the most important part of the popular religion.[6] Similar veneration of ancestors exists in Japan.[7]

---

[1] Gardner and Jevons, *Greek Antiquities*, p. 158 ff.; Gruppe, *Griechische Mythologie*, Index, s.v. *Heros*; Deneken, article " Heros " in Roscher, *Lexikon*. Lists of heroes are given by F. Pfister, in *Der Reliquienkult im Altertum*.

[2] Thucydides, v, 11; Pausanias, i, 32. For other examples, and for the details of the cult, see Stengel and Oehmichen, *Die griechischen Sakralaltertümer*, p. 96 ff.

[3] Similar functions are performed by saints in some Buddhist, Christian, and Moslem communities.

[4] Pauly-Wissowa, *Real-Encyclopädie der classischen Altertumswissenschaft*; Miss J. E. Harrison, *Prolegomena to the Study of Greek Religion*, chap. ii, and the references in these works. On the *Keres* as ghosts see Crusius, in Roscher's *Lexikon*, s.v. *Keren*, and Harrison, op. cit., chap. v.

[5] Ovid, *Fasti*, v, 429 ff., *manes exite paterni*; cf. the Greek proverbial expression θύραζε κᾶρες (Suidas, s.v. θύραζε).   [6] De Groot, *Religion of the Chinese*, chap. iii.

[7] Aston, *Shinto*; Knox, *Religion in Japan*, p. 66 f.

376. The venerated dead stood apart, as a rule, from the nature-spirits and the gods, but these different classes sometimes coalesced, as has been remarked above, in popular usage. The powers and functions of the dead were not essentially different from those of the divinities proper, particularly in the simpler stages of society. They were able to bestow all the blessings and to inflict all the misfortunes of life. In process of time the advance of knowledge relegated them to a subordinate place, but they long retained a considerable importance as friends of families and states, as disseminators of disease, and as predictors of human fortunes.

377. In the exercise of these functions they were often not to be distinguished from the higher and lower deities. King Saul, on the eve of a great battle, having failed to get an answer from the national deity by the ordinary legitimate methods, had recourse to necromancy and obtained from the ghost of Samuel the information that Yahweh had refused to give.[1] The Greek *kēres* and the wandering ghosts of West Africa do exactly what is ascribed to the malefic spirits of Babylonia.[2] Examples of such identity of function between the various superhuman Powers are found all over the world.

378. This fact does not show that these Powers have the same origin. The savage accepts agents in human life wherever he can find them — in beings inhabiting mountains, rocks, trees, caves, springs, and in the souls of departed men. Doubtless he thinks of the forms of these various actors as being all of the same sort, a sublimated manlike body ; but he keeps them in different categories, and in the course of time the tendency is for ghosts and spirits to sink out of sight and for the gods to absorb all extrahuman activities.

379. The ethical power of the cults so far discussed resides in the human association to which they give rise and the sanctions they supply to conduct. Of these two effects the former is the more important. The moral character of a ghost or spirit or deity never rises above that of its circle of worshipers : its approval or disapproval is the echo of current usage, and has special efficiency only in the accompanying power of reward or punishment ; it appeals

[1] 1 Sam. xxviii.   [2] Cf. also the Teutonic valkyrs and nornas.

to the hopes and fears of men. This police function is doubtless valuable in restraining from crime and inciting to good conduct, but it has no regenerative power. The enlargement of human association, on the other hand, increases sympathy and coöperation among men, and paves the way to the cultivation of the mutual respect and regard which is the basis of social virtue.

380. Among the lower cults ancestor-worship may be expected to take the highest place, for the reason that it tends to strengthen family unity and the solidarity of the clan, tribe, or nation ; all such knitting together of men makes for the increase of honesty and kindliness. The data are lacking, however, for the determination of this point. It may be said in general that the attitude toward the dead becomes finer with advance in civilization ; but before a specific moral power in ancestor-worship can be proved, it will be necessary to have exact details of moral ideas and conduct in all the lower tribes, together with some information regarding the attitude of individuals toward questions of conduct, and the motives that impel toward this or that action. The question of ethical growth in society is a complicated one, and the most that can be said for any element of social constitution is that it tends to strengthen or weaken the individual's confidence in and regard for his fellows.

381. The part played in religious history by the worship of the dead is so important that some writers have derived all religion from it.[1] This view is now generally rejected for the reason that it does not accord with known facts ; it is only by forced (though often ingenious) interpretations that a plausible case is made out for it. To reply in detail to the arguments advanced in its favor would be to go over the whole ground of the origin of religious observances; the answer is furnished by setting forth the nature of the various cults, as is attempted in this and following chapters. If, for example, there is reason to believe that savages have always regarded the lower animals as powerful beings, there is no need, in accounting

---

[1] See above, § 359. The wide prevalence of the theory in ancient times is indicated by its adoption in the Græco-Jewish *Wisdom of Solomon* (of the first century B. C.), chap. xiv, and by some Roman writers.

for the veneration given them, to resort to the roundabout way of assuming a misinterpretation of names of men derived from beasts.

382. Between Euhemerism and the theory that explains myths as a " disease of language " there is little or no essential difference of principle. Both theories assume that man, having devised certain epithets, later came to misunderstand them and to build up histories on the misunderstanding. Both thus rest the immense mass of human religious customs and beliefs, which form so large a part of human history, on the precarious foundation of passing fancy and inadvertence, and they must be put into the same category with the naïve theory, once popular, that religion is the invention of priests who sought to control men through their fears.

383. Ancestor-worship is the feeling of kinship with the dead, invested by religion with peculiar intensity and solemnity. It has been one of the great constructive forces of society.

Cults of Generative Powers

384. The origin of religion is not to be referred exclusively to any one order of ideas; it springs out of man's total life. All objects and processes have been included in men's construction of nature, and the processes, when they have been held to bear on human well-being, have been ascribed to a force inherent in things or to the activity of supernatural beings.

385. The study of processes has gone hand in hand with the creation of divine beings who are supposed to manifest themselves in the processes. The great spectacle of nature's productivity has been especially recognizable in the vegetable world and in the world of man ; in both of these life has been perpetually unfolding itself under men's eyes as a mysterious process, which, by virtue of its mysteriousness, has become religious material and has entered into systems of religious worship.

386. The relation of vegetable life to religious cults is referred to elsewhere,[1] and a brief survey may now be given of usages and ideas that have been connected with the production of human life.

---

[1] § 262 ff.

387. It is obvious that not all customs that include the function of generation are of the nature of religious observances. The promiscuity that obtains in many savage communities before marriage is a naïve unreflective animal procedure. Exchange of wives (as in Central Australia) and the offering of a wife to a guest are matters of social etiquette. Festivals in which sexual license is the rule are generally merely the expression of natural impulses. Holidays, being times of amusement, are occasions used by the people for the satisfaction of all appetites : there is eating and drinking, buffoonery, disregard of current conventions, unbounded liberty to do whatever exuberant animalism prompts. Such festivities abound among existing savages,[1] were not uncommon in ancient civilized times,[2] and have survived in diminished form to the present day.[3] In the course of time they often become attached to the worship of gods, are organized, explained by myths, and sanctified. In such cases of coalescence we must distinguish between the true worship offered to a divine being, and the observances, generally originating in desire for animal amusement and enjoyment, that have been attached to them.

388. *Cult of generative organs.* Men's attention must have been directed very early to those organs that were believed to be connected with the genesis of human life. At what stage this belief arose it is hardly possible to say; there are peoples among whom it seems r.ot to exist ;[4] but it is found over a great part of the world, and was doubtless an outcome of popular observation.[5] As it was intimately connected with life it passed naturally into the domain of religion, and in process of time became a more or less prominent part of religious observances ; the organs in question, both male and female, became objects of religious devotion.

389. Here again it must be noted that not all usages connected with the organs of generation were religious of origin. It

---

1 For example, in Australia, Fiji, New Guinea, and India.

2 Greece, Rome (Lupercalia), Egypt, and apparently in Israel (Ex. xxxii, 6 ; Numb. xxv). 8 In carnivals and many less elaborate customs. 4 See above, § 34.

5 It was observable in the lower animals, but in their case was not regarded as religiously important. See below, § 419, for the connection of animals with phallic cults.

is pointed out above[1] that the origin of circumcision and excision is to be sought in another direction. Ithyphallic images are sometimes merely attempts at realism in art; a nude figure (as in modern art) must be represented in its full proportions. Such seems to be the nature of certain images among the Western Bantu,[2] and this may have been the case with the images of the Egyptian Khem and Osiris and similar deities. In general this sort of representation in savage and ancient civilized communities is often either simple realism or indecency. Folk-stories abound in details that sound indecent to modern ears, but were for the authors often merely copies of current usages.

390. All important members of the human body have been regarded as to a greater or less extent sacred, their importance depending on their subservience to man's needs. The head of an enemy gives the slayer wisdom and strength; an oath sworn by the head or beard of one's father is peculiarly binding; the heart, when eaten, imparts power; a solemn oath may be sworn by the sexual organs. In no case does the sacredness of an object necessarily involve its worship; whether or not it shall receive a true cult depends on general social considerations.

391. Though phallic cults proper cannot be shown to be universal among men, they have played a not inconsiderable part in religious history. They appear to have passed through the usual grades of development — simple at first, later more complicated. The attitude of savages and low communities generally, non-Christian and Christian, toward the phallus, suggests that in the earliest stage of the cult some sort of worship was paid the physical object itself considered as a creator of life; satisfactory data on this point, however, are lacking. It was at so early a period that it was brought into cultic connection with supernatural beings that its initial forms escape us.

392. It seems not to exist now among the lowest peoples. There are no definite traces of it in the tribes of Oceania, Central Africa, Central Asia, and America. The silence of explorers on this point cannot indeed be taken as proof positive of its

---

[1] § 158 ff. [2] Hastings, *Encyclopædia of Religion and Ethics*, ii, 361.

nonexistence; yet the absence of distinct mention of it in a great number of carefully prepared works leads us to infer that it does not play an important part in the religious systems therein described.[1] It seems to require, for its establishment, a fairly well-developed social and political organization. Some of the tribes named above have departmental deities, mostly of a simple sort, but apparently it has not occurred to them to isolate this particular function, which they probably regarded as a familiar part of the order of things and not needing special mention. The gift of children was in the hands of the local god, a generally recognized part of his duty as patron of the tribe, and all sexual matters naturally might be referred to him. Also, as is remarked above, in certain tribes there was no knowledge of the connection between the birth of children and the union of the sexes,[2] and such tribes would of course ascribe no creative power to the phallus.

393. The best example of a half-civilized phallic cult is that which is now practiced in Yoruba and Dahomi, countries with definite government and institutions. The cult is attached to the worship of a deity (Elegba or Legba), who appears to be a patron of fertility; the phallus occupies a prominent place on his temples, and its worship is accompanied by the usual licentious rites.[3] These are expressions of popular appetite, and it does not appear that the cult itself is otherwise religiously significant.

394. In modern India the Çivaite phallicism is pronounced and important. The linga is treated as a divine power, and, as producer of fertility, is especially the object of devotion of women;[4] though Çivaism has its rites of unbridled bestialism, the worship of

---

[1] See Ratzel, *History of Mankind*; Waitz, *Anthropologie der Naturvölker*; Müller, *Amerikanische Urreligionen*; Spencer and Gillen, *Native Tribes of Central Australia*; Codrington, *The Melanesians*; W. Ellis, *Polynesian Researches*; Hartland, article "Bantu" in Hastings, *Encyclopædia of Religion and Ethics*; Callaway, *Amazulus*; Featherman, *Races of Mankind*; Grünwedel, "Lamaismus" in *Die orientalischen Religionen* (I, iii, 1, of *Die Kultur der Gegenwart*) ; Brinton, *Myths of the New World*, p. 149 ; Matthews, Dorsey, Teit, Boas, Hill-Tout, opp. cit. (on American Indians).

[2] § 34.

[3] A. B. Ellis, *Yoruba* and *Ewe*. Ellis does not say that the cult exists in Ashanti, where we should expect it to be found; its absence there is not accounted for. On phallic worship in Congo see H. H. Johnston, in *Journal of the Anthropological Institute*, xiii.   [4] Hopkins, *Religions of India*, pp. 453, 470.

the linga by women is often free from impurity; it is practically worship of a deity of fertility. The origin of the Indian cult is not clear. As it does not appear in the earliest literature, it has been supposed to have come into Aryan worship from non-Aryan tribes. Whatever its origin, it is now widely observed in Aryan India, and has been adopted by various outlying tribes.[1]

395. While it is, or was, well established in Japan, it apparently has had no marked influence on the religious thought of the people. Phallic forms abound[2] in the land, in spite of repressive measures on the part of the government, but the cult partakes of the general looseness of the Shinto organization of supernatural Powers. It is said to have been adopted in some cases by Buddhists. It appears to have been combined with Shinto at a very early (half-civilized) time, for which, however, no records exist.

396. It is among the great ancient civilized peoples that the most definite organization of phallic cults is found.

397. For Egypt there is the testimony of Herodotus,[3] who describes a procession of women bearing small phallic images and singing hymns in honor of a deity whom he calls Dionysos — probably Khem or Osiris or Bes; such images are mentioned by Plutarch,[4] supposed by him to represent Osiris. Both Khem and Osiris were great gods, credited with general creative power, and popular ceremonies of a phallicistic nature might easily be attached to their cults. Bes, a less important deity, seems to have been fashioned largely by popular fancy. These ceremonies were doubtless attended with license,[5] but they probably formed no part of Egyptian serious worship. The phallus was essential in a realistic image, but it appears to have been regarded simply as a physical part of the god or as an emblem of him; there is no evidence that worship was addressed to it in itself.

398. The evidence that has been adduced for a cult of the phallus among Semitic peoples is of a doubtful nature. No ithyphallic

---

[1] Cf. Crooke, article " Bengal " in Hastings, *Encyclopædia of Religion and Ethics.*
[2] Griffis, *Religions of Japan*; Aston, *Shinto*; Buckley, in Saussaye, *Lehrbuch der Religionsgeschichte*, 2d ed.; Florenz, in *Die Kultur der Gegenwart.*
[3] Herodotus, ii, 48 f.   [4] *Isis and Osiris*, 51.
[5] An example of naïve popular festivities is given in Herodotus, ii, 60.

images or figures of gods have been found. Religious prostitution there was in all North Semitic lands,[1] but this is a wholly different thing from a phallicistic cult. It is supposed, however, by not a few scholars that descriptions and representations of the phallus occur in so many places as to make some sort of cult of the object probable. In a passage of the Book of Isaiah, descriptive of a foreign cult practiced, probably, by some Jews, the phallus, it is held, is named.[2] The passage is obscure. The nature and origin of the cult referred to are not clear; it is not elsewhere mentioned. The word (*yad*, usually 'hand') supposed to mean 'phallus' is not found in this sense elsewhere in the Old Testament or in later Hebrew literature. But, if the proposed rendering be adopted, the reference will be not to a cult of the phallus but to sexual intercourse, a figurative description of idolatry.

399. A distinct mention of phalli as connected with religious worship occurs in Pseudo-Lucian's description of the temple of a certain goddess at Hierapolis.[3] He gives the name to enormously high structures standing in the propylæa of the temple, but mentions no details suggesting a phallic cult. Twice a year, he says, a man ascends one of them, on the top of which he stays seven days, praying, as some think, for a blessing on all Syria — a procedure suggesting that the pillar was simply a structure consecrated to the deity of the place (probably Atargatis, who is often called " the Syrian goddess ")[4]. However, if there was a phallic cult there (the phallus being regarded as a symbol of the productive function of the deity), it is not certain that it was Semitic. Hierapolis had long been an important religious center in a region in which Asiatic and Greek worships were influential, and foreign elements might easily have become attached to the worship of a Semitic deity. The cult

---

[1] The Gilgamesh epic (Jastrow, *Religion of Babylonia and Assyria*, p. 477); Amos ii, 7; Deut. xxiii, 17 f.; Herodotus, i, 199; Strabo, xvi, 1, 20; Epistle of Jeremy, 42 f.; Lucian, *De Syria Dea*, 6 ff. But Hos. ii, Ezek. xvi, xxiii, Isa. lvii, 8, are descriptions of Hebrew addiction to foreign idolatrous cults.

[2] Isa. lvii, 8: " Thou didst love their bed, the yad thou sawest." The renderings in the English Revised Version are not possible.   [3] Lucian, op. cit., 28, cf. 16.

[4] The Aramean Atargatis, properly Attar-Ate, is substantially identical with Ashtart and Ishtar.

of the Asian Great Mother (whom the Greeks identified with their Leto) had orgiastic elements. Lucian's reference to a custom of emasculation suggests Asian features at Hierapolis.[1]

400. In Babylonia and Palestine stones, held by some to be phalli, have been found.[2] While the shape of some of these objects and their occurrence at shrines may be supposed to lend support to this view, its correctness is open to doubt. There is no documentary evidence as to the character of the objects in question, and they may be explained otherwise than as phalli. But, if they are phalli, their presence does not prove a phallic cult — they may be votive objects, indicating that the phallus was regarded as in some sort sacred, not that it was worshiped. Decision of the question may be reserved till more material has been collected. There is no sufficient ground for regarding the stone posts that stood by Hebrew shrines as phallic symbols; they are naturally explained as sacred stones, originally embodying a deity, later attached to his shrines as traditional objects entitled to veneration.[3]

401. In Asia Minor and the Hellenic communities (both in Ionia and in Greece proper) the phallicistic material is extensive and complicated. A symbolic signification appears to have been superimposed on early realistic anthropomorphic figures that were simply images of supernatural Powers. In various regions such figures came to be associated with the generative force of nature in human birth, and the tendency to specialization assigned these divine beings special functions; of this nature, probably, were the local Athenian deities Orthanes, Konisalos, and others.[4] At a later period such functions were attributed to the well-developed gods of fertility; rituals sprang·up and were explained by myths, and various combinations and identifications were made between the prominent gods.

---

[1] Lucian, *De Syria Dea*, 15.

[2] J. P. Peters, *Nippur*, Index, s.v. *Phallic symbols*; Bliss and Macalister, *Excavations in Palestine*, p. 136; Macalister, *Bible Side-lights*, p. 72 f.

[3] These objects (Hebrew *masseba*) are denounced by the prophets because they were connected with the Canaanite non-Yahwistic worship. The same thing is true of the sacred wooden post (the *ashera*) that stood by shrines ; Deut. xvi, 21 f., etc.

[4] Roscher, *Lexikon*, s.v. *Priapos*. Diodorus Siculus, iv, 6, mentions also Ithyphallos and Tychon.

402. The most interesting figure of this character is Priapos, an ithyphallic deity of uncertain origin; his special connection was with Lampsakos, and he may have been an Asian creation. From the variety of his functions (he was patron of gardens and viticulture, of sailors and fishermen, and in some places a god of war)[1] it may be surmised that he was originally a local deity, charged with the care of all human interests, in an agricultural community the patron of fertility, and at some time, and under circumstances unknown to us, especially connected with sexual life. Whatever his origin, his cult spread over Greece, he was identified with certain Greek deities, licentious popular festivals naturally attached themselves to his worship, and his name became a synonym of sexual passion. In the later time the pictorial representations of him became grossly indecent; his cult was an outlet for popular and artistic license.[2] On the other hand, in the higher thought he was made the representative of the production of universal animal life, and rose to the rank of a great god.[3]

403. The Greek deities with whom Priapos was oftenest identified were Dionysos and Hermes — both gods of fertility. They, as great gods of such a nature, would naturally absorb lesser phallicistic figures; but they were specialized in other directions, and Priapos remained as the distinctest embodiment of phallicistic conceptions. Other such figures, as Pan, Titans, Sileni, and Satyrs, were beings connected with fields, woods, and mountains, products of a low form of civilization, to whom realistic forms and licentious festivals naturally attached themselves.

404. Rome had its native ithyphallic deity, Mutunus Tutunus (or Mutinus), a naïve symbol of generative power.[4] Little is known of his cult beyond the fact that he figured in marriage ceremonies in a peculiarly indecent way; by later writers he is sometimes identified with Priapos.[5] The Romans adopted the cult of Priapos as well as other phallicistic forms of worship; his original character appears in his rôle of patron of gardens.

1 Roscher, *Lexikon*. 2 S. Seligmann, *Der böse Blick und Verwandtes*, ii, 191 ff.
3 Diodorus Siculus, i, 88.
4 Roscher, *Lexikon*, s.v. *Indigitamenta. Muto* is 'phallos.'
5 So Augustine, *De Civitate Dei*, iv, 11, 34 al.

405. Phalli as amulets occur in all parts of the world ; as symbols and perhaps as abodes of deities, they have been held potent to ward off all evils.[1]

406. The female organ (*yoni, kteis*) appears frequently in figures of female deities, ordinarily without special significance, religious or other, except as a sign of sex. In the rare cases in which it is the object of religious veneration (as in India) it is subordinated to the phallos [2] — there is little or no evidence for the existence of a yonistic cult proper.[3] Female deities act as fully formed anthropomorphic Powers, embodiments of the productive energies of nature ; they are generally treated as persons, without special reference to bodily parts. The most definite formulation of this conception appears in Çaktism, the worship of the female principle in nature as represented by various goddesses, often accompanied, naturally, by licentious rites.[4]

407. *Androgynous deities* represent attempts to combine in a single person the two sides of the productive power of nature. Such attempts are relatively late, implying a considerable degree of reflection and organization ; how early they began we have not the data to determine. They are not found among savage or half-civilized peoples.

408. In Semitic lands no artistic representations of a bisexual deity are now known, but evidence is adduced to show that this conception existed in early times. It has been sought in two old Babylonian inscriptions published by the British Museum.[5] The first of these (written in Sumerian) reads : " For [or, in honor of] the (divine) king of countries, the (divine) Nana [Ishtar], the lady Nana, Lugaltarsi, king of Kish, has constructed," etc. Barton takes

---

[1] S. Seligmann, *Der böse Blick und Verwandtes*, ii, 196 ff.

[2] Cf. Hopkins, *Religions of India*, p. 490, n. 4.

[3] On the yoni as amulet see Seligmann, *Der böse Blick und Verwandtes*, ii, 203.

[4] Hastings, *Encyclopædia of Religion and Ethics*, ii, 491 f., and the references there to Gait's *Assam* and other works.

[5] III Rawlinson, pl. i, no. 12155, and IV Rawlinson, col. 2, ll. 25–28. The androgynous sense is maintained by G. A. Barton, in *Journal of the American Oriental Society*, xxi, second half, p. 185 ff. Other renderings of the first inscription are given by Thureau-Dangin in *Revue d'Assyriologie*, iv, and Radau, *Early Babylonian History*, p. 125.

the two titles "the divine Ishtar" (= 'king of countries,' masculine) and "the lady Ishtar" to refer to the same deity, in whose person would thus be united male and female beings. If, however, the king of countries and Ishtar be taken to be two different deities (as is possible), there is no bisexuality. The second inscription, which is bilingual, has the expressions "the mother-father Enlil," "the mother-father Ninlil" (Sumerian), rendered in Semitic "the father-mother Enlil," "the father-mother Ninlil." These expressions probably signify not that the two deities are bisexual, but that each of them fulfills the guarding and nourishing functions of a father and a mother.

The expression in a hymn to Ishtar that "she has a beard like the god Ashur" may be satisfactorily explained as an astrological statement, the meaning of which is that the planet Dilbat (Ishtar, Venus) at certain times equals the sun (represented by Ashur) in brilliancy, her rays being likened to a beard.[1] A similar astrological interpretation is offered by Jastrow of a passage (to which attention was called by François Lenormant) in which a female Dilbat and a male Dilbat are spoken of. Other astrological texts indicate that the terms 'male' and 'female' are employed as expressions of greater or less brilliancy.[2] Lajard's view, that all Babylonian and Assyrian deities were androgynous, hardly needs discussion now.[3]

409. Of a more definite character are expressions in two Phoenician inscriptions. In an inscription of Eshmunazzar II (probably early in the fourth century B.C.) the great goddess of Sidon is called "Ashtart *Shem* Baal."[4] The word *shem* means 'name,' and, if it be so interpreted as to give the goddess the name of a male divinity, she may be understood to have partly male form. But such change

[1] Text in Craig, *Assyrian and Babylonian Religious Texts*, i, pl. vii, obv. 6, and by Meek, in *American Journal of Semitic Languages*, xxvi; translation in Jastrow's *Religion Babyloniens und Assyriens*, i, 544 f., and discussion by him in article "The 'Bearded' Venus" in *Revue archéologique*, 1911, i.

[2] See for Lenormant's view *Gazette archéologique*, 1876 and 1879, and Jastrow's criticism in the article cited in the preceding note.

[3] Lajard, *Recherches sur le culte de Vénus*. He is followed by A. Jeremias, *The Old Testament in the Light of the Ancient East* (Eng. tr.), i, 123.

[4] *Corpus Inscriptionum Semiticarum*, i, i, p. 13.

of name is hardly probable, and this is not necessarily the natural force of the phrase. In Hebrew to " call one's name on a person or thing " is to assert ownership in it or close connection with it.[1] In the West Semitic area some personal names signify simply ' name of such and such a deity,' as, for example, Shemuel (Samuel), ' name of El,' Shemzebul, ' name of (the god) Zebul,' denoting devotion or subordination to the deity in question. " Shem Baal " as a title of Ashtart may then indicate her close relation with the god, or, perhaps, if the expression be understood more broadly, her equality with him in power (the name of a deity involves his attributes) — he was the great god, but she, the expression would say, is not less mighty than he ; or, less probably, *baal* may be taken not as proper name but as title, the sense then being that the goddess is the lord of the city.[2] Another proposal is to read " Ashtart shamē Baal," ' Ashtart of the heaven [sky] of Baal.'[3] There is a Phœnician Baal-shamem, ' lord of the sky,' but nowhere else is the sky described as the abode of a baal, and the transference of the local city-goddess to that region would be strange ; nor in the expression ' Baal-shamem ' is Baal a proper name — it is merely a title.

410. Another phrase, occurring in many Carthaginian inscriptions, makes mention of " Tanit face of Baal,"[4] an expression that may point to a female body with male face. Its indefiniteness — it does not state the nature of the face (it may point to a beard) — makes it difficult to draw from it any conclusions as to the character of the deity named.[5] But the probability is that it is identical

---

[1] 1 Sam. xii, 28; Deut. xxviii, 10. The angel in whom is Yahweh's name (Ex. xxiii, 21) has the authority of the deity.

[2] Cf. Dillmann, in *Monatsbericht der Akademie der Wissenschaften* (Berlin, 1881). The feminine form given to Baal in Rom. xi, 3 f., may refer to the disparaging term ' shame ' (Heb. *boshet*, for which the Greek would be *aischunē*) often substituted by the late editors of the Old Testament for Baal. Saul's son Ishbaal (' man of Baal ') is called Ishbosheth, Jonathan's son Meribbaal is called Mephibosheth, etc.

[3] Dillmann (loc. cit.) combines *shamē* with Ashtart, as if the sense were ' the heavenly Ashtart of Baal ' — an impossible rendering ; but he also interprets the phrase to mean ' Ashtart the consort of the heavenly Baal.' Halévy, *Mélanges*, p. 33 ; Ed. Meyer, in Roscher's *Lexikon*, article " Astarte."

[4] *Corpus Inscriptionum Semiticarum*, i, i, no. 195 ; i, ii, no. 1, al. Tanit appears to be identical in character and cult with Ashtart.

[5] See below, § 411 f. ; cf. W. R. Smith, *Religion of the Semites*, 2d ed., p. 478.

in sense with the one mentioned above. Tanit was the great goddess of Carthage; she is called "Adon," 'lord,' and her equality with Baal is indicated by the statement that she had his face, the word 'face' being here equivalent to 'personality' and ' power.'[1]

411. At a later period (early in the fifth century of our era) two authors, Servius and Macrobius, make definite statements concerning a bisexual cult, apparently Semitic.[2] Both statements occur in connection with Vergil's use of the masculine *deus* (*ducente deo*) as a title of Venus, in explanation of which the cases of supposed bisexualism are cited.[3] What is said is that there was in Cyprus a deity whose image was bearded — a god of virile nature, but dressed as a woman, and regarded as being both male and female. Further, Philochorus is quoted to the effect that men sacrificed to her in women's dress and women in men's dress. This last remark does not necessarily point to an androgynous deity, for exchange of dress between men and women sometimes occurs where there is no question of the cult of such a deity.[4] But the Cyprian deity is said also to have been called Ἀφρόδιτον (Aphroditos? or Aphroditon?)[5] — apparently a male Aphrodite.

412. Leaving aside a few other notices that add nothing to our knowledge of the point under consideration, we should naturally conclude, if we give any credit to the statements of Servius and Macrobius, that there was a report in their time of a bisexual deity in Cyprus. As regards Vergil's " deus," that may be merely a poetical expression of the eminence and potency of the goddess. But the assertions of her bisexual character are distinct, even if the " beard " be discarded. This latter may have come from a misunderstanding of some appearance on the face of the statue; or,

---

[1] A similar interpretation is given by Bæthgen in his *Semitische Religionsgeschichte*, p. 267 f. His "monistic" view, however, that various deities were regarded as manifestations of the supreme deity is not tenable.

[2] Servius, Commentary on Vergil, *Æn.* ii, 632 ; Macrobius, *Saturnalia*, iii, 8, on the same passage.

[3] There are manuscript variations in the text of Servius, but these do not affect the sense derived from the two authors, and need not be considered here.

[4] Cf. Frazer, *Adonis Attis Osiris*, p. 428 ff.

[5] Servius, " they call her " ; Macrobius, "Aristophanes calls her." But who this Aristophanes is, or where he so calls her, we are not informed.

as has been suggested, there may have been a false beard attached to it permanently or occasionally,[1] and from this may have sprung the belief in the twofold nature of the deity. We are not told, however, that such a nature was ascribed to Aphrodite, or that a beard was attached to her statue; and, if this was done, it is difficult to suppose that a popular belief in the bisexuality of a deity could have arisen from such a procedure. Some better ground for the statements of Servius and Macrobius there seems to have been, though we do not know their authorities. In any case it may be concluded that the cult in question, if it existed, was late, popular, and without marked influence on the Semitic religious development. No figures or other traces of a bisexual deity have been discovered in Cyprus or elsewhere (unless the Carthaginian Tanit be an exception), and all that is otherwise known of the character and cult of the Babylonian Ishtar, the Phœnician Ashtart, and the Carthaginian Tanit (= Ashtart) is against the supposition of bisexuality. Ishtar, originally a deity of fertility, became, through social growth, a patron of war and statecraft; but there is no indication that an attempt was ever made to combine these two characters in one figure.

413. The Phrygian figure Agdistis, represented in the myths as androgynous [2] (the myths being based on cults), is connected with the worship of the Great Mother, Kybele (the embodiment of the female productive power of nature), with whom is associated Attis (the embodiment of the male power).[3] The myths identify Agdistis on the one hand with Kybele, on the other hand with Attis — he represents in his own person the combination of the two generative powers. But it is doubtful whether this was his significance in the actual worship, in which he hardly appears; he was

---

[1] So Jastrow, in the article cited above. Remarking on the statement of Lydus (in *De Mensibus*, ii, 10) that the Pamphylians formerly worshiped a bearded Venus, he calls attention to the Carian priestess of Athene (Herodotus, i, 175; viii, 104), who, when misfortune was impending, had (or grew) a great beard — a mark of power, but presumably not a genuine growth. Exactly what this story means it is hard to say.

[2] Pausanias, vii, 17; Arnobius, v, 5.

[3] Roscher, *Lexikon*, articles " Agdistis," " Attis"; Frazer, *Adonis Attis Osiris*, p. 219 f.; H. Hepding, *Attis*; cf. Pseudo-Lucian, *De Syria Dea*, 15 (Attis assumes female form and dress).

probably a divine figure of the same character as Kybele and Attis, worked up by myth-makers and woven into the larger myth. His self-castration reflects the practice of the priests and other worshipers of Kybele.[1] Thus cultually he is of little or no importance.

414. There is no evidence that this Phrygian figure was derived from Semitic sources. A certain similarity between Phrygian and Syrian cults of gods and goddesses of fertility is obvious, and the social relations between Asia Minor, Syria, and Cyprus make borrowing in either direction conceivable. But cults of such deities might grow up independently in different regions,[2] and the supposition that the Phrygian worship was native to Asia Minor is favored by the great elaboration of its ceremonies and by their barbarous character. This character suggests that the worship may have originated with savage peoples who preceded the Aryans in the country.[8]

415. The most definite androgynous figure is the Greek Hermaphroditos. It was only in Greece that such a compound name arose, and that the composite form became established in art. It is not certain when the Greek form was fixed. If the statement that Aristophanes used the term "Aphroditos"[4] (or "Aphroditon") is to be relied on, it must be concluded that the conception existed in Greece prior to the fifth century, probably in that case as a popular usage that was unorganized and unimportant, since it is not referred to in the existing literature. But of this Aristophanes we know nothing, and the vague statements of Servius and Macrobius may be neglected as being without significance for the figure in question.

416. The name Hermaphroditos is said to occur for the first time in the fourth or third century B.C.[5] This would indicate a gradual formulation of the idea, the result being the combination of two divine forms into a single form. Aphrodite would naturally be chosen for the female side, and the ithyphallic Hermes is

---

1 This practice seems to be an exaggerated form of the savage custom of self-wounding in honor of the dead (to obtain their favor), interpreted in developed cults as a sacrifice to the deity or as a means of union with him.

2 On the wide diffusion of cults of mother-goddesses see below, §§ 729, 734, 762, etc.

8 Cf. Pseudo-Lucian, *De Syria Dea*, 15; Ed. Meyer, *Geschichte des Altertums*, 2d ed., i, 649, 651; Lagrange, *Études sur les religions sémitiques*, 2d ed., p. 241; Hepding, *Attis*, p. 162.   4 See above, § 411.

5 In Theophrastus, *Characters*, article 16 (Roscher, *Lexikon*, s.v. *Hermaphroditos*).

appropriate for the male side — possibly the Hermes pillar with Aphrodite bust was the earliest form.[1] The representations of Hermaphroditos show a male body with female bust; the name Aphroditos would rather suggest a female body with male additions. Other Greek bisexual figures are forms of Priapos and Eros.

An historical connection between the Greek and the Phrygian forms is possible, but is not proved. In India the bisexual form of Çiva, which seems to be late,[2] connects itself with the licentious character of his rites. Its historical origin is uncertain.

417. It does not appear that the cult of the Greek androgynous deities entered seriously into the religious life of the people. In late philosophic circles they were treated merely as symbols of the creative power of nature, and thus lost their character as persons.

418. The starting-point for the development of the hermaphrodite figure may perhaps be found in two facts, the interchange or change of sexual characters [3] and the combination of two deities to express a broader idea than either of them represents. The assumption of female dress and sexual habits by males, and of male dress and habits by females, has prevailed over a great part of the world.[4] The embodiment of this fact in a composite divine form would be not unnatural at a time when there was a disposition to give expression, in the person of gods, to all human experiences. Such definite embodiment is, however, rare in religious history, probably, as is suggested above, because it involves a large generalization and a more or less distinct symbolism. The first movement in this direction may have been naïvely sensuous; later, as is remarked above, the symbolic conception became predominant.

419. The association of certain *animals* with certain phallic deities (as the bull with Dionysos, the goat with Pan, the ass with Priapos) is a part of the general connection between gods and animals, the grounds of which are in many cases obscure.[5] Pan's rural character may explain his relation to the goat; the bull, the ass, and

---

[1] Roscher, article cited.   [2] Hopkins, *Religions of India*, pp. 447, 492.
[3] H. Ellis, *Psychology of Sex*, i, passim.
[4] Westermarck, *Origin and Development of the Moral Ideas*, chap. xliii.
[5] Cf. § 251 ff.

many other animals regarded as sacred, may have been brought into ritual connection with gods by processes of subordination of divine beasts and through collocation of cults. There is no evidence to show that the animals connected with phallic gods were selected on account of their salacious dispositions or their sexual power.

420. Phallicistic cults, attenuated by advance of refinement, survived long, even into Christian times, under modified forms.[1] In such cases they become merely devices of ignorant piety. When the aid of a Christian saint is sought in order to secure fertility, the trust in the phallus-symbol involves no unworthy desire; and what is true of medieval European peoples may have been true of ancient peoples. In the ancient world these cults took many forms, ranging from naïve faith to frank obscenity on the one hand and philosophic breadth on the other hand. They take their place as part of the general worship of the forces of nature, and follow all the variations of human culture.

[1] Dulaure, *Des divinités génératrices.* Cf. Hartland, *Primitive Paternity*, chap. ii.

CHAPTER V

TOTEMISM AND TABOO

421. Totemism and taboo are both of them intimately connected with the history of early religion, but in different ways. Totemism is not essentially religious if religion be held to involve worship of superhuman or extrahuman beings; it has, however, in many cases coalesced with religious practices and ideas, and it is sometimes difficult to draw the line distinctly between it and religion proper. Taboo, on the other hand, is founded on magical conceptions, and these are nearly allied to the basis of early religion; it is more or less prominent in all early cults, and has survived in the higher religious systems, though in these it is generally spiritualized. The two lines of development, totemism and taboo, appear side by side in early cults, and influence each the other; but their functions in the social organization of religion have been different, and they are best treated separately. As the collections of material for their history are still incomplete, accounts of them must be regarded as, to a greater or less extent, provisional.

TOTEMISM

422. The natural attraction of human beings for one another and the necessity of providing effective means of defense against enemies have led men to associate themselves together in clans and tribes. In such associations some form of organization arose as a matter of course; experience early showed that men could not live together except under the guidance and control of authoritative regulations. Such regulations dealt with fundamental facts of life, which in the beginnings of society are mostly physical. The points requiring regulation are: the relation of man to nonhuman things

(animals, plants, and inanimate objects); the maintenance of rights
of life and property; and the sexual relations between human beings, especially marriage as the basis of the family. The determination of what things may be eaten belongs more particularly under
" taboo," and is considered below. Customs and rules designed
to protect life and property have always coalesced with religious
systems; they are mentioned in connection with the ethical element
in religion.[1] The other points — relations to nonhuman things and
sexual relations — may be conveniently considered together here;
but, as the second point belongs rather to sociology than to the
history of religion, it will be sufficient, with an introductory word
on marriage restrictions (under *Exogamy*), to give the facts in
connection with the various totemic organizations.

423. *Exogamy*.[2] All over the savage world the general rule
prevails (though not without exceptions) that a man must not
marry a woman of his own clan; though the family proper (husband, wife, and children) exists, the clan is the fundamental social
unit. When a tribe contains several clans it is commonly divided
into groups (phratries), each phratry including certain clans, and
the rule then is that a man shall not marry a woman of his phratry.
Usually the number of phratries is two, but in some cases (as among
the Australian Arunta and adjoining tribes) these are divided so that
there are four or eight exogamous groups (subphratries). When
the totem is hereditary the totemic clans are exogamous; otherwise
(as among the Arunta) marriage between persons of the same clan
is permitted.

424. Whether the clan or the phratry preceded in time it is hardly
possible to determine — clans may have united to form a larger
group, or an original group may have been divided into clans. But
in the latter case this original group was practically a clan, so
that the question of precedence in time is not important. Where
clan exogamy exists without phratries it is possible that these also

---

1 See below, Chap. XI.
2 J. F. McLennan, *Studies in Ancient History*; Frazer, *Totemism and Exogamy*;
A. Lang, *Social Origins*; A. E. Crawley, in *Anthropological Essays presented to E. B.
Tylor*; N. W. Thomas, ibid.

formerly existed and have been dropped in the interests of freedom — that is, they limited the choice of a wife to an extent that
proved inconvenient.[1]

425. An almost universal feature of the marriage rules of low
tribes is the classificatory system of relationship. According to this
system, the community being divided into groups, terms of relationship indicate not kinship in blood but tribal status in respect
of marriageability; thus, the same term is used for a child's real
father and for every man who might legally have become the
husband of his mother, and the same term for the real mother
and for every woman whom the father might have married;
the children of such possible fathers and mothers are the child's
brothers and sisters; all possible spouses are called a man's
"wives" or a woman's "husbands"; and similarly with all relationships.[2]

426. The system has many varieties of form, and gives way in
time to the formal recognition of blood kinship. It has been held
to point to an earlier system of "group marriage," in which all
the men of one group had marital relations with all the women of
another group, and further to a primitive custom of sexual promiscuity.[3] In the nature of the case these hypotheses do not admit of
proof or disproof. All that is certain is that the classificatory system
has been and is an accompaniment of one stage of social and religious
development.

427. The effect of exogamous arrangements has been to prevent marriage between persons related in blood.[4] In totemic
organizations, when the totem is inherited, a division into two
exogamous groups makes marriage of brother to sister impossible,
since all the children of one mother are in the same group; and

---

[1] Frazer (*Totemism and Exogamy*, iv, 135), thinks it possible that exogamy of
totemic clans is always exogamy in decay.

[2] L. H. Morgan (the discoverer of the system), *Ancient Society*; W. H. R. Rivers
in *Anthropological Essays presented to E. B. Tylor*.

[3] For the supposition of promiscuity are Morgan (op. cit., p. 54), Spencer and
Gillen (*Native Tribes of Central Australia*, p. 100 ff.), and others; against are
Westermarck (*Human Marriage*, chap. iv), Crawley (*The Mystic Rose*, p. 479 ff.),
and others.   [4] Cf. Morgan, op. cit., p. 27, and part ii, chap. i.

if there are four such groups and children are assigned to a group different from that of the father and that of the mother, marriage between parent and child is impossible. When the totem is not inherited (as is the case among the Australian Arunta) similar results are secured by a further subdivision.

428. The particular exogamic customs vary considerably among early tribes, the differences following, in general, differences of social organization. In some more settled savage communities (as, for example, the Kurnai of Southeast Australia), in which there are neither classes nor totemic clans, marriage is permitted only between members of certain districts.[1] Well-organized social life tends to promote individual freedom in marriage as in other things. Marriage with a half-sister was allowed by the old Hebrew law,[2] and Egyptian kings often married their sisters.

429. *Theories of the origin of exogamy.* Exogamy has been referred to a supposed scarcity of women, which forced the young men to seek wives abroad.[3] On the assumption of early sexual promiscuity it has been regarded as a deliberate attempt to prevent the marriage of blood relations.[4] It has been supposed to result from the absence of sexual attraction between persons who have been brought up together.[5] An original human horde being assumed, it has been suggested that the patriarch, who had possession of all the women of the horde, would, from jealousy, drive the young men off to seek wives elsewhere.[6] From the point of view of the totem as divine ancestor, exogamy has been supposed to arise from religious respect for the clan blood, which is held to share the divinity of the totem, and would be polluted (with danger to the clan) by outside marriages.[7]

---

[1] Howitt, *Native Tribes of South-East Australia*, p. 269 ff.

[2] Gen. xx, 12; the rule was later abrogated (Ezek. xxii, 11; Lev. xviii, 9).

[3] J. F. McLennan, *Studies in Ancient History*, first series, p. 90 ff.; second series, chap. vii.

[4] L. H. Morgan, *Ancient Society*, p. 424 ff.; Frazer, *Totemism and Exogamy*, i, 164 ff.

[5] Westermarck, *Human Marriage*, chaps. xiv–xvi; Crawley, *The Mystic Rose*, p. 222. Cf. Darwin, *Variation of Animals and Plants under Domestication*, ii, 103 f.

[6] J. J. Atkinson, *Primal Law* (in volume with Lang's *Social Origins*, p. 210 ff.).

[7] E. Durkheim, in *Année sociologique*, i, 1–70.

430. Objections may be raised to all these theories. It is doubtful whether a scarcity of women existed in early times; and supposing that there were not women enough in a clan for the men of the clan, this would not stand in the way of men's taking as wives their clan women.[1] The assumption of primitive sexual promiscuity, likewise, cannot be said to be distinctly borne out by known facts.[2] Morgan's theory, however, is not dependent on this assumption — it need only suppose repugnance to the marriage of blood relations. Such repugnance granted, the main objection to the theory rests on the difficulty of supposing savages capable of originating so thoughtful and elastic a scheme as the exogamous system. This is a point on which it is not possible to speak positively. The lowest tribes have produced languages of wonderfully intricate and delicate construction, and, supposing the process of constructing marriage regulations to have gone on during a very long period, modifications introduced from time to time, to meet conditions felt to be important, might conceivably result in such exogamous systems as are now found.

431. As to absence of sexual attraction between persons brought up together,[3] this seems to be a result rather than a cause of the prohibition of sexual relations between certain classes of persons. The argument from habits of the lower animals is indefinite — no general habit has been proven. In orgies in India and elsewhere no repulsion appears between persons of the same family. In the ancient world marriage between such persons was legal and not uncommon.

432. The human horde, with its jealous patriarch, appears to be a creation of the scientific imagination. It, again, was derived by its author from the procedure of certain beast-herds in which the strongest male drives away his rivals. It is supposed, however, that in the human horde the young men, having found wives, are allowed to come back bringing their wives with them, and these last the patriarch is supposed not to appropriate. The theory is supported by no facts of actual usage.

---

1 Frazer, *Totemism and Exogamy*, iv, 75 ff.   2 See references in § 426.
3 H. Ellis, *Psychology of Sex*, i, 36 f.; Crawley, in *Anthropological Essays presented to E. B. Tylor.*

433. The supposition that the young men of a clan or tribe go off to seek food, and thus found a new clan, has more in its favor. Being compelled to seek wives in their new surroundings, they might thus initiate a habit of outside marriage that would in time become general usage and therefore sacred. Secession from tribes does occur, and may have been frequent in prehistoric times, but concerning these times we have little or no information. It may be said that movements of this sort would furnish a more probable starting-point for savage customs than the ideas and schemes mentioned above.

434. Proof is lacking also for Durkheim's theory. It is not probable that the totem was regarded as divine in the period in which exogamy arose — by the tribes whose ideas on this point are known the totem is looked on as a friend and an equal but not as a god. And, as is pointed out above, there is no such general religious respect for the clan blood as would forbid sexual intercourse between persons of the same clan. The demand for revenge for the murder of a clansman arises from the sense of clan solidarity and the necessity of self-defense — it is only in this regard that the blood of the clan is regarded as sacred.

435. Horror of marriage or of sexual intercourse in general, within the prohibited degrees or areas, is universal in low communities; violation of the tribal law on this point is severely punished, sometimes with death. Whence this feeling sprang is not clear.[1] It cannot have arisen from respect for the purity of women or from a belief in the sanctity of the family — intercourse with girls before their marriage is freely allowed, and lending or exchange of wives is common. Magical dangers are supposed to follow on infringement of marriage rules, but, as such results come from violation of any tribal custom, this throws no light on the origin of the feeling of horror in question. Absence of sexual attraction between persons brought up together,[2] though the absence of such feeling is said to have been observed in some of the lower animals, is not assured for savages; its existence in civilized communities

[1] See above, § 431.
[2] See above, § 429, and compare Howard, *History of Matrimonial Institutions*, i, 121 ff.

is due to the acceptance of the established usage, which makes certain unions impossible, so that they are not considered, and the germ of such a public opinion may perhaps be assumed for early tribes. Probably the horror of incest is a derivation from economic and other situations and laws that arose naturally in early society — it is a habit hardened into an instinct.

436. Though exogamy differs from totemism in origin and function, the two are often found associated — their conjunction may be said to be the general rule. There are, however, exceptions.[1] Totemic clans are not exogamous in Central Australia, the Melanesian Banks Islands, among the Nandi of East Africa, and the Bakuana of South Africa. On the other hand, exogamy is found without totemism in the tribes just mentioned, among the Todas of Southern India, in Sumatra, among the African Masai and Ashanti, and in Southern Nigeria, and local exogamy among tribes (for example, the Kurnai of Southeast Australia, and the Californian Maidu and Shasta) in which totemic divisions are not perceptible.

437. In all such cases, however, the absence of records makes the history of the organizations uncertain — we do not know whether or not one of the elements, totemism or exogamy, formerly existed and has yielded to disintegrating influences. Thus local exogamy may have superseded clan exogamy in many places, the former representing the more settled habit of life, and the absence of the totemic constitution may indicate a process of decay of totemism. No general rule for the decision of the question can be laid down — every case must be judged for itself.[2]

438. Since a custom of exogamy presupposes at least two social groups (clans), and totemism appears to be connected originally with single clans, the natural inference is that the latter has everywhere preceded the former in time. Both have undergone great changes produced by similar sets of circumstances, and in both cases the simplest form is probably the oldest, though here again definite data are lacking. However, comparison of the known exogamous systems points to a two-group arrangement as that from which the existing forms have come.

---

[1] Details are given in Frazer's *Totemism and Exogamy*.   [2] Cf. below, § 442.

439. Exogamy served a good purpose in early stages of society, both by preventing marriages between blood relations and by inducing a sense of the sacredness of the marriage bond. Its long persistence shows that it was regarded by most tribes as necessary for the maintenance of the tribal life. Its restriction of individual freedom in the choice of wives was an evil, and was in time modified and finally thrown off; but it seems to have been the only means, discoverable by early society, by which clans and tribes could live peaceably side by side, and it paved the way for the establishment of the family proper.

440. This brief account of the most important adjunct of totemism may serve to clear the way for the consideration of the totemic system.

441. Among the various relations that undeveloped communities sustain to nonhuman things totemism has the peculiarity that it is an alliance between a human group (clan or tribe) and a species of animals or plants, or an inanimate natural object (as sun or moon), or, rarely, an artificial object (usually an implement of labor).[1] The nonhuman thing is regarded as a friend, and is respected and cared for accordingly. When it is a species (animal or plant) every individual of the species is held to bear this friendly relation to every individual of the allied human group. Generally there is believed to be not only similarity or identity of nature between the two (such identity of nature between man and nonhuman things is everywhere an article of the creed of savages) but a special intimacy, commonly a kinship of blood. While the men of a group respect their ally, it, on its part, is supposed to refrain from injuring them, and even in some cases to aid them. It is credited with great power, such as in savage life all nonhuman things are supposed to possess. The members of the human group regard one another as brothers; this feeling, however, can hardly be said to be peculiar to totemic organizations — it exists, more or less, in all early associations, particularly in any one association as against others.

---

[1] On two supposed human totems, Laughing Boys and Nursing Mothers, see Frazer, *Totemism and Exogamy*, i, 160, 253; ii, 520 f.

442. While, therefore, we may take a certain clan alliance as a fundamental fact of totemism, we find in various communities other features of organization more or less closely combined with this into a social unity. In every such case it is necessary to inquire whether the feature in question is a universal or general accompaniment of clan alliance, and whether it is peculiar to the latter or is found in other systems also.

443. (a) *Exogamy.* It is pointed out above [1] that totemism and exogamy are mutually independent arrangements, differing in function and origin, each being found without the other. Yet in many cases, perhaps in the majority of cases, the two are found combined. Exogamy supposes a body of clans, and, given a group of totemic clans, it would naturally be attached to these, and so become an organic part of their social constitution. Where there is no totemism the question of union, of course, does not come up. Where totemism is not accompanied by exogamy it is sometimes probable that the union of the two once existed,[2] or that exogamy is excluded by the peculiar form of the totemism.[3] Exogamy may thus be regarded as a natural and frequent accompaniment of totemism, but it is not a universal and necessary element of the totemic constitution.

444. (b) *Names.* As a general rule the totemic clan bears the name of its totem. The exceptions appear to be found in somewhat advanced communities, as the Fijians and the Kwakiutl (but not the northern branch of this tribe).[4] There are also many larger exogamous groups (as, for example, in Australia) the meaning of whose names is obscure — they may or may not contain the name of the totem; but such groups may have a different origin from that of the totemic clans.

445. In some cases clans and tribes have distinctive *crests* or *badges*, generally totemic figures or parts of such figures. These are carved on beams of houses and on house poles, or cut or drawn on men's persons, and are used as signs manual, serving thus to indicate to strangers a man's clan connections. Such emblems are

---

[1] § 436.　　[2] So, apparently, among the Nandi (Hollis, *The Nandi*, pp. 6, 61).

[3] As among the Australian Arunta (Spencer and Gillen, *Native Tribes of Central Australia*, pp. 116, 125 ff.).

[4] Frazer, *Totemism and Exogamy*, ii, 136; iii, 321; Boas, *The Kwakiutl*, p. 328 ff.

employed in the Torres Straits islands and British New Guinea,[1] in the Aru Islands (southwest of New Guinea), and in North America among the Lenâpé (Delawares), the Pueblo tribes, the Tlingit, the Haidas, and the Kwakiutl.[2]

446. In America the crest is not always identical in name with the totem, and sometimes coalesces with the guardian animal-spirit. The myths that give the origin of the crest usually describe some adventure (marriage or other) of a man with the crest animal, involving sometimes, but not always, the origin of the clan.[3] The relation between totem and crest thus differs in different places, and its origin is not clear. The simplest form of this relation (that found in the New Guinea region) may indicate that the totem animal, being most intimately connected with the clan, is chosen on that account as its badge. Or possibly totem and crest have arisen, independently of each other, from some early affiliation with animals, and therefore do not always coincide. Such a mode of origination would help to explain the fact that in Northwestern America a clan may have several crests, and a man also may acquire more than one. The relation of crest to clan is looser than that of totem to clan — the same crest or crests are found in different clans. When the totemic constitution of the tribe or clan is weakened, the crest may become more important than the totem, as is the case among the Haidas. But the adoption of the crest name does not invalidate the general rule that the clan bears the name of its totem.

447. Names of families and of persons do not come into consideration here. They arise from various local and personal peculiarities that, as a rule, have nothing to do with totemism, and they become more prominent and important as the latter declines.

448. The origin of clan totemic names is closely connected with the origin of the totemic organization, and will be more conveniently considered in connection with this point.[4]

---

[1] Haddon and Rivers, *Expedition to Torres Straits*, v, 158 ff.; Seligmann, *The Melanesians of British New Guinea*, pp. 51, 320.

[2] Frazer, *Totemism and Exogamy*, ii, 200; iii, 40, 227, 267, 281, 322.

[3] Swanton, *Tlingit Myths* (*Bulletin 39*, Bureau of American Ethnology).

[4] See below, § 544 ff.

449. (c) *Descent from the totem.* Details so far reported as to this belief are regrettably few and often indefinite, and it is not possible to give more than a provisional sketch of it.[1] In Central Australia it is held that all the members of a clan come into being as spirit children, who are the creation of mythical half-human, half-animal beings of the olden time; the clan bears the name of the mythical ancestor (its totem), and its members regard themselves as identical in blood and nature with the totem.[2] Similar beliefs are reported as existing in New South Wales and West Australia, and a definite conception of descent from the totem has been found in the Santa Cruz group in Southern Melanesia, in Fiji in Eastern Melanesia, and apparently in Tonga and Tikopia.[3] In North America the belief is reported as existing among the Lenâpé (Delawares) and other Eastern tribes.[4] In South America it appears among the Arawaks of Guiana,[5] and perhaps elsewhere. For Africa there is little information on this point, and what we have is not always definite;[6] one of the clearest expressions of descent is found in the title "grandfather" given to the chameleon by the Chameleon clan of the Herrero of German Southwest Africa, but a comparison with the similar title given by the Zulus to a sort of divine ancestor, and with the Herrero mythical stories of the origins of certain clans, suggests that the conception is vague.

450. In addition to the more direct statements there are traditions or myths that connect the origin of clans with animals or plants through the intermediation of gods or human beings, by marriage, or some other relation. The Bushbuck clan of the East African Baganda worship a lion-god, who is called an ancestor and is said to have turned into a lion at his death. Fluctuating opinions (some persons holding to direct descent from a nonhuman object, others to friendly relations between it and the ancestor) are

---

[1] For the details of totemic customs reference may be made, once for all, to Frazer's encyclopedic *Totemism and Exogamy.*

[2] Spencer and Gillen, *Native Tribes of Central Australia*, pp. 415, 423, etc.

[3] Rivers, *Journal of the Royal Anthropological Institute*, xxxix; *Man*, viii.

[4] Brinton, *The Lenâpé*, p. 39.   [5] E. F. im Thurn, *Indians of Guiana*, p. 184.

[6] For the Mandingos of Senegambia see *Revue d'ethnographie*, v, 81, cited in Frazer's *Totemism and Exogamy*, ii, 544.

reported in Sumatra, Borneo, and the Moluccas. The Hurons regarded the rattlesnake as a kinsman of their ancestor. The origin of the clan or family is referred to marriage with an animal by the Borneo Dyaks and various tribes on the African Gold Coast, and to marriage with a plant by some of the Upper Liluet;[1] and the origin of the crests in Northwestern America is ascribed to adventures with crest animals.[2] In the Trobriand group of islands (lying to the northeast of British New Guinea) the totems are said to have been brought by the first men; naturally it is not explained whence and how the men got them.[3]

451. These instances of indirect origination (to which others of the sort might be added) show a variety of points of view, and may be variously interpreted. They may be regarded as declensions from an earlier belief in the direct descent of the clan from the totem, or as independent conceptions that never grew into this belief. Both these ideas of the form of descent are found in widely separated regions and in communities differing one from another in general culture and in the degree of importance they attach to the totemic constitution. The possibility of general agreement in myths, with difference in details, between tribes remote from one another is illustrated by the creation myths of the Australian Arunta (who have an elaborate totemism) and the Thompson River Indians of Northwestern America (who have no clan totems, secret societies, or dramatic ceremonies); both relate transformations of primitive unformed persons, but in the former the creators are half-human, half-animal, in the latter they are men who transform half-human, half-animal beings. Such widespread variations point to early differences in social conditions and in intellectual endowments with the nature of which we are not acquainted.[4]

452. (d) *Refusal to kill or eat the totem.* The usages in regard to killing or eating the totem are so diverse, and often so uncertain,

---

[1] Teit, *Thompson River Indians,* p. 95.

[2] Swanton, *Tlingit Myths,* and *Jesup North Pacific Expedition,* v, 231; Boas, *The Kwakiutl,* pp. 323, 336 f.

[3] Seligmann, *The Melanesians of British New Guinea,* p. 679; in the Louisiade group belief in direct descent is said to exist (p. 743).

[4] Cf. the remarks of Boas in the Introduction to Teit's *Thompson River Indians.*

that it is not possible to lay down a general rule of prohibition. An edible totem is only a peculiar sort of sacred animal or plant, and respect for such objects often leads to refusal to kill or eat them — an interdiction of this sort does not in itself show whether or not the object in question is a totem. But within totemic areas the usage varies in a remarkable manner, as, for example, in Australia. In the north there is complete prohibition, sometimes including the totems of a man's father, mother, and father's father. Among the central tribes a man kills his clan totem only for the benefit of other clans, and eats a little of it ceremonially. In the southeast the Dieri, it is said, kill and eat their totems freely, while other tribes, the Wotjoballuk and others, eat them only at a pinch.[1] The northeastern tribes have many food taboos, which, however, relate not to the totemic clans but to the exogamous subclasses. A modified regard for the totem or crest (kobong) appears in West Australia, according to Sir George Grey's report[2]; it is not allowable to kill a family kobong while it is asleep, and it is always with reluctance that it is killed.

453. Abstention from killing and eating the totem holds, as a rule, in the Torres Straits islands, while in New Guinea the custom varies — the totem is eaten by some tribes, not eaten by others.

454. In Melanesia the food restrictions connected with animal patrons or friends of clans are less definite than in Australia. Here, also, there are local differences of usage. Prohibition of eating or using the totem (fish, grass, fowl, and so forth) was found by Rivers in the Santa Cruz group (in Southern Melanesia) but not in the northern New Hebrides.[3] In the central islands the prohibition refers to the exogamous classes, and a similar usage is reported as existing in the Duke of York group (in the north). The Fijians refrain from eating their tribal sacred animals.

---

[1] On the other hand, the Kurnai, who are not totemic, refrain, apparently, from eating their sex-patrons.

[2] This report was made in 1841, before the natives had come in contact with the whites.

[3] In the Banks Islands the restrictions of eating relate to the patrons of individual persons; see *Journal of the Royal Anthropological Institute*, xxxix, 165 f.

455. In Polynesia family gods appear instead of totems, and the incarnations of gods (in animals and plants) are not eaten; such is the rule in Samoa and Tonga, and this was formerly the practice in Hawaii. The food restrictions in Borneo and Sumatra are not definitely totemic.

456. The non-Aryan tribes of India generally refrain from eating their totems, or, in some cases, from injuring or using them; and this is true even of those tribes (for example, the Khonds and Oraons of Bengal) that have somewhat developed theistic systems. Occasionally exemptions from the rule of abstention are procured, perhaps under Aryan influence; such influence has affected many of the tribes, but has not usually destroyed the old totemic customs. Among the Todas (in the south), however, Rivers found only feeble suggestions of totemic objects and food restrictions; the buffalo-cult seems to have ousted all others.[1]

457. Among the native tribes of Africa there is special respect for the object with which the clan or tribe has particularly definite relations. The Bakuana do not eat the animal whose name is borne by the clan; if an animal (the lion, for example) is dangerous, it is killed with an apology. The Herrero (of German Southeast Africa) abstain from the flesh of the chameleon, and will not eat gray sheep or oxen. Among the half-civilized Baganda, of the east, certain of the clans refrain from eating the object from which a clan takes its name; the noteworthy political organization of these people seems to have obliterated old clan functions in part. In the west (Senegambia, Ashanti, Dahomi, Nigeria, Congo) there are food restrictions, but these are not generally connected with totemic social organizations.

458. There is little evidence for totemic food restrictions in North America. The custom of apologizing to an animal on killing it, frequent elsewhere, is reported as existing among the Algonkin Ottawas and Menomini; but this is not necessarily totemic. The more advanced tribes of the East and South (Algonkin, Iroquois, Creeks, Choctaws, Chickasas, Cherokees, Natchez), the peoples of the Pacific Coast, and the agricultural tribes of the middle of the

---

[1] Rivers, *The Todas*, Index, s.v. *Food, restriction on.*

continent (Pueblos, Mandans, and others) appear to be free from restrictions as to eating. The Navahos are said to refrain from the flesh of fish, turkeys, swine, and bears, but the grounds of the interdiction are not clear.[1] The distinctest evidence of totemistic clan food-taboos are found among the Siouan Caddos (of the southern Mississippi Valley) and the Omahas (of the Middle West). Both these groups are in part agricultural, and it does not appear how they have come to differ from their neighbors in this regard. Food restrictions are reported for the Northwest region.[2]

459. There is no clear report of totemic food restrictions in Central America or in South America;[3] but these regions have as yet not been thoroughly examined for clan usages.

460. (e) *Magical ceremonies for increasing the supply of food.* Such ceremonies exist, or have existed, in many regions and among peoples of various grades of culture, civilized as well as savage, but the cases in which they are, or were, conducted by totemistic clans are comparatively few. This sort of economic function of the totem clan is most definite and important in Central and parts of Southeast Australia, where every clan is charged with the duty of increasing the supply of its totem for the benefit of its connected clans; and magical rites are performed in the fertile coast region no less than in the arid region about Lake Eyre — that is, in these cases the employment of magic seems not to be conditioned on the natural resources of the land. Similar totemic clan functions appear in the islands of Torres Straits, the Turtle and Dugong clans performing ceremonies to increase the supply of turtles and to attract dugongs. Magical control of totems for the benefit of the whole community is reported to be found in the Siouan Omaha clans (in the center of the North American continent). The tribes just mentioned are those in which the social organization is definitely totemistic.

---

[1] Cf. Matthews, *Navaho Legends*, p. 239, note 169; Franciscan Fathers, *Ethnologic Dictionary*, p. 507.   [2] Teit, *Thompson River Indians*, p. 77.

[3] Cf. A. M. Tozzer, *Comparative Study of the Mayas and the Lacandones* (of Yucatan), and the literature given in articles " America, South " and " Brazil " in Hastings, *Encyclopædia of Religion and Ethics*.

461. Elsewhere the economic function attaches to other bodies than totemic clans, as in parts of Southeast Australia, and in West Australia (where the ceremonies are conducted by the exogamous classes). In New Guinea the totemic character of the performances appears to be doubtful. A single instance of clan action has been found among the East African Baganda — the women of the Grasshopper clan undertake to increase the supply of their totem; why this duty is assigned to the women is not clear — the custom appears to involve a relaxation of totemistic rules. The economic festivals and "dances" of the Siouan Mandans and Hidatsa are general tribal ceremonies. Among the Pueblo Indians such rites are the care of religious fraternities;[1] the Zuñi Frog clan performs a ceremony to procure rain, but this duty is mainly committed to rain-priests. In Northwestern America the magical performances are not connected with totemic clans.

462. *Definition of totemism.* It appears, then, that not one of the points just mentioned is found invariably in the systems of organization commonly called totemic. Exogamy is an independent phenomenon; the clan does not always bear the name of the totem, and is not always held to have descended from it; usages in regard to eating it vary greatly; magical economic ceremonies are performed by other than totemic bodies. There is no known clan that includes all these elements in its organization, though in Central Australia there is an approach to complete inclusion; the features lacking are clan exogamy and absolute prohibition of eating the totem, but practically a clan does not eat its totem, and exogamy, for reasons given above, may be left out of consideration. The Central Australian system may be said to be substantially complete; with it the North American systems stand in sharp contrast, and from it many others diverge.

463. But, with all these differences, the fact remains that in totemism the human group stands in a peculiar relation to some

---

[1] J. W. Fewkes is of opinion that the great Snake dance (an economic function) was formerly conducted by the Snake clan (*Sixteenth Annual Report of the Bureau of American Ethnology*, p. 304).

nonhuman object.[1] This general statement must, however, be defined in two particulars: the relation is an alliance for the benefit of both parties; and the nonhuman object is not regarded as a god and is not worshiped. The first of these particulars marks totemism off from that general regard that is paid by savages to animals, plants, certain heavenly bodies, and other physical things;[2] the second particular distinguishes it from the cult of ghosts and gods proper. We may therefore define it as an alliance, offensive and defensive, between a human group and a nonhuman group or object that is not worshiped, the friendly relation existing between every member of the one group and every member of the other group.[3]

464. This relation having been formed, the various features mentioned above will naturally become attached to it in various ways and to different extents. The clan will somehow get a name, when and how we need not now ask; usually its name is that of the totem — this is in keeping with the intimate connection between the two. To trace the origin of the clan to the totem is only to do what is done abundantly among uncivilized and civilized peoples (Hebrews, Greeks, and others); the eponymous ancestor is constructed out of the current name of the clan. To refrain from killing or eating a friendly animal or plant is a simple mark of respect. The conception of special ability in a clan to insure a supply of its totem for food is in accord with savage ideas of magical endowment. When the custom of exogamy arose it would naturally attach to the clan as the social unit.

465. In view of the diverse physical surroundings of the tribes of the earth and their intellectual differences, it cannot be surprising

---

[1] The choice of the object is determined by local conditions that are not known to us. Sometimes, probably, the object is the one most important for the welfare of the community; sometimes it may have come from accident. See below, § 554 ff.

[2] The artificial objects that are regarded, in a few cases, as totems are probably of late origin, the product of reflection, and thus differing from the old totems, which arise in an unreflective time. However, the artificial totems are doubtless sometimes looked on as powerful; in some cases they may be little more than badges.

[3] This is Frazer's definition (in his *Totemism*, p. 1), supplemented by the words "not worshiped." Cf., on the whole subject, Tylor, in *Journal of the Anthropological Institute*, xxviii, 144; F. Boas, in *American Journal of Psychology*, xxi; A. A. Goldenweiser, "Totemism," in *Journal of American Folklore*, xxiii (1910).

that they have combined these elements of organization in various ways. In their efforts to secure food, good marriage relations, protection of property, and defense against enemies, they have from time to time adopted such measures as the circumstances made desirable and possible. There is evidence that in some instances clans have changed their social regulations, sometimes by a process of internal growth, sometimes by borrowing from without. It is not always possible to trace such movements, and it is impossible now to say what the earliest social constitution of men was. The probability is that the earliest state was an unformed one, without governmental or other institutions, and that totemism was one of the first attempts to introduce order into society. In accordance with what is said above, the term ' totemism ' may be used to mean particularly a simple alliance between men and nonhuman things, and then more generally to mean such an alliance combined, in whatever way, with one or more of the particular customs described in preceding paragraphs.[1]

466. *Geographical survey of totemistic usages.* If totemism be taken in the simpler sense, as a certain sort of intimate relation between men and nonhuman things, it will be found to be widely distributed in the noncivilized world. Its occurrence becomes rarer in proportion as adjuncts are attached to it; as is remarked above, it is hardly possible to find a clan whose constitution embraces all adjuncts. Where usages like exogamy occur, or where there is reverence for an object, without belief in a definite, nontheistic relation between a human clan and a nonhuman object, we cannot recognize totemism proper; such usages must be treated as belonging to man's general attitude toward his nonhuman associates. The question whether they represent germinal or decadent totemism, or neither, must be considered separately in every case.

467. The two great totemistic regions of the world are Australia and North America, and in each of these the variations of custom run through the gamut of possible differences. In each of them also the native population may include different stocks, though on

---

1 For a preciser definition of totemism see below, § 520.

this point there is uncertainty. Differences of climate and topographical situations there are, but these do not always account for the diversities of culture and custom.[1]

468. *Australia.* In the heart of Central Australia (the home of the Arunta and other tribes) there are clans that bear the names of their totems, and trace their descent from half-human totem ancestors, with whom they consider themselves to be identical; totems, however, are not hereditary, but are determined by the ancestor connected with the place where the mother first becomes aware of the child within her; each clan performs magical ceremonies to secure a supply of its totem for the associated clans, and, when the totem is an animal or a plant, hunts or gathers it and brings it to be distributed; at the distribution the headman of the providing clan must eat a little of the food ceremonially, and at other times clansmen eat of it sparingly;[2] the rule of exogamy relates not to the totemic clans, but to the phratries or subphratries.

469. In the South Central region these features are found, with an exception in the rule concerning eating one's totem. Sometimes, as in the Urabanna tribe, such eating is forbidden. But among the Warramunga there is a relaxation of the rule in the case of old people — for them the food restriction is removed (apparently a humanitarian provision); on the other hand, for other clansfolk there is an extension of the rule — the prohibition includes two subclasses of the moiety to which the clan belongs, and conditionally includes the whole moiety (this is perhaps a cautionary measure, to guard against the possibility of unlawful eating on the part of clansmen).

470. The special feature in North Australia (on the shores of the Gulf of Carpentaria) is the absolute prohibition of eating the totem. In regard to the performance of magical ceremonies for increase of the totem also there is the peculiarity that a clan is not bound to conduct such performances — it is optional with it to do

---

[1] The details are given in Frazer's *Totemism and Exogamy.*

[2] Certain Arunta traditions appear to point to a time when the totem was freely eaten. The bird-mates of the clans may be regarded as secondary totems — perhaps a survival from a time when a clan might have more than one totem.

so or not; it has magical power, but is not required by custom to exercise it. It is suggested by Spencer and Gillen that this variation from the usage of the Central region is to be attributed to the more regular rainfall on the coast, which insures a more regular supply of food and thus does away with the necessity for magic.[1] Possibly, also, this climatic feature may account for the stricter rule of prohibition mentioned above; as the rule is sometimes relaxed when it is hard to get food, so, on the other hand, it may be strictly enforced when food is plentiful.

471. Still a different situation appears in the southeastern part of the continent (New South Wales and Victoria) — several prominent features of the Central system are absent. The Dieri clans bear the names of their totems, from which also they think themselves descended, but they eat them freely. Some adjacent tribes eat them only at a pinch, others refrain from them. The clans of the Narrinyeri are mostly localized, and the clan-names are not now those of the totems;[2] the totems are eaten. The Kurnai show the greatest divergence from the ordinary type — they have neither totemic clans nor exogamous classes; their rule of exogamy relates to districts. Throughout the southeast the conduct of magical economic ceremonies by clans, every clan being responsible for its own totem, seems not to exist.

472. In certain tribes (the Wotjoballuk, the Yuin, the Kurnai, and others) there are sex-patrons, animals intimately related to all the males or all the females of the tribe; the belief is said to be that the life of any individual of the animal group is the life of a man or a woman, and neither sex group will kill its patron animal. So far as regards the conception of identity with the animal and reverence for it, the institution agrees with the usual totemic type; but since it is not connected with clans, some such designation for the animal as " patron " or " guardian " is to be preferred to " totem." [3] Such animals, protectors of sexes, are of rare occurrence, having been certainly found so far only in

---

[1] Spencer and Gillen, *Northern Tribes of Central Australia*, pp. 173, 318.

[2] The clan-names may formerly have been totemic, but data for the decision of this point are lacking.   [3] So Frazer, *Totemism and Exogamy*, iv, 173.

Southeast Australia, and they occur in a body of tribes that show a disposition to discard the clan constitution. In this region individual men also sometimes have animal guardians, so that a general tendency toward individualism may be recognized. It is not unnatural to connect this tendency with the fertility of the south coast, which may weaken the clan organization. The organization by sex is a singular phenomenon, of the history of which there are no records. It is doubtless a special development of the widespread separation of the sexes, combined with an increasing recognition of the property rights and the social equality of women. At an early age boys were often kept apart from girls. Special taboos, of food and other things, were imposed on women. On the other hand, they were in some cases the owners of the tribal property, and were sometimes admitted to membership in secret societies. The organization of the sex would follow under peculiarly favorable conditions.[1]

473. The remaining districts of Australia have been less carefully investigated than the central and southern parts, and information about their totemistic customs is not always satisfactory. So far as the accounts go there is a widespread divergence from simple clan organization in these districts. In Northeast Australia (Queensland) there are exogamous subclasses, and no clan taboos. In the southwest not clans but families are the social units; these trace their descent from animals, and there are individual animal patrons. In the northwest no clan organization is reported; there is class exogamy, and in the magical ceremonies the performers are taken from the exogamous classes.

474. *Torres Straits Islands.* These noteworthy variations in the totemism of the Australian continent appear to be connected in a general way with differences of climate and the degree of isolation of the clans and tribes. Similar variations appear in the Torres Straits islands and in British New Guinea. In the western islands of the Straits (the only part in which distinct totemism has been

---

[1] Cf. H. Webster, *Primitive Secret Societies*, pp. 1, 121 ff.; Crawley, *The Mystic Rose*, pp. 41 f., 45, 350, 454 ff.; Westermarck, *Origin and Development of the Moral Ideas*, ii, 28 ff.; Hobhouse, *Morals in Evolution*, i, 183 ff., 188 ff.

found) the social organization is to a certain extent independent of totemic relations: the clans are locally segregated, and marriage is mainly regulated by blood-kinship. On the other hand, an intimate relation between a man and his totem is recognized — the latter, as a rule, is not eaten by the related clansmen (there are exceptions), magical economic ceremonies are performed by certain clans, and there is clan exogamy. A possible survival of an early social arrangement is the existence of subsidiary totems.

475. There is also a rudimentary cult of heroes: two of these (animal in form) have shrines and effigies, annual dances are performed in their honor, and stones are shown in which their souls are supposed to dwell. The resemblance of this cult to certain forms of worship in Polynesia (in Samoa, for example) is apparent; the stones may be compared with similar abodes of superhuman animals or spirits in Central Australia and elsewhere; the myths connect the two animal heroes with the origin of totems — a common procedure. One hero, Kwoiam of Mabuiag, is said to have been a real man, and to have been almost deified; divinization of dead men is not unusual in Polynesia.

476. *New Guinea.* In the eastern portion of British New Guinea the peculiarities of organization are [1] that the people live in hamlets; that there is generally a combination of totems in a clan; and that special regard is paid to the father's totem. There is no report of belief in descent from the totem.[2] The hamlets tend to become family groups, but clan exogamy is observed. The system of "linked totems" seems to be designed to secure superhuman aid from all departments of the nonhuman world: ordinarily there will be a bird, a fish, a snake, and a plant — the bird has come to be the most important of these. A man may kill his own totem but not his father's — a rule that has arisen perhaps from a displacement of matrilineal descent (according to which a man's totem is that of his mother) by descent through the father. So far as appears, there

---

[1] C. G. Seligmann, *The Melanesians of British New Guinea*, chaps. xxxv, l.

[2] Such a belief is said to exist in the Aru archipelago (Papuan) west of New Guinea. There the family, and not the clan, is the social unit; every family has its badge or crest.

are no magical ceremonies for increase of the supply of food. In both New Guinea and the Straits the fact that old customs are disappearing under foreign influence increases the difficulty of determining whether certain usages are primitive or decadent.

477. *Melanesia.* The social organization in the vast mass of islands called Melanesia[1] has not been fully investigated, but the existence of some general features has been established. Society is divided not into clans or tribes, but into exogamous classes, and the classificatory system of relationships is general. The rules governing marriage are less elaborate than in Australia, the method of initiation is simpler, and the political organization is more definite. In regard to other usages commonly associated with totemism the reported details are not numerous. There appears to be a movement away from Australian totemism, growing more pronounced as we go eastward, and culminating in Fiji, in which totemic features are very rare.

478. In the Bismarck Archipelago every class has connected with it certain animals regarded as relatives, but in New Britain, apparently, not as ancestors.[2] In New Ireland dances imitating the movements of the sacred animals are performed. Such animals are treated with great respect, and the relation to them constitutes a bond of union between members of a class.

479. Some peculiarities appear in the Solomon Islands. While there is the usual regard for the sacred objects (called *buto*), so that these are not to be eaten (in some cases not to be touched or seen), the names of the classes are not always those of the sacred things, and there is difference of opinion among the natives as to whether the latter are ancestors or merely associated with an ancestor: a man (particularly a chief) may announce that after death he will be incarnate in a given thing, as, for example, a banana — this then becomes sacred. But in some cases[3] the god of the class is regarded as the ancestor; instead of a number of sacred animals

---

[1] Melanesia is here taken to include the Bismarck Archipelago (New Britain, New Ireland, and adjacent islands) and the islands lying to the eastward as far as the 180th meridian of longitude, though in this area there is in some places Polynesian influence.   [2] So Reverend George Brown, *Melanesians and Polynesians*, p. 28.

[3] This usage is reported for Florida Island.

there is a theistic system with regular worship — a state of things quite distinct from totemism.[1]

480. In the New Hebrides group there is mention of a slight magical ceremony performed by a member of a class to attract a class animal, but there is no rule against eating the object whose name the class bears. The usage in the Santa Cruz group in regard to eating, and the belief as to descent from the sacred object, differ in different islands; they are sometimes lax and vague, sometimes strict and definite.

481. Belief in a vital connection between a man and some object chosen by himself is found in the Banks Islands; there is an obvious similarity between such an object and the North American manitu. Further, the belief is reported by Rivers that in these islands the character of a child is determined by an edible object from which the mother, before the birth of the child, received some sort of influence; the child will resemble the object or be identified with it, and will not, throughout life, eat of it.[2]

482. In the easternmost group, the Fijian, the relation between the tribes and their associated sacred animals and plants was, and is, various. The rule was that these should not be injured, and, if edible, should not be eaten. But alongside of such sacred objects real gods are found; these dwell or are incarnate in certain birds, fish, and plants, and sometimes in men. In one district, in the interior of the large island Viti Levu, Rivers learned that every village had its deity, which in many cases might turn into an animal, and the animal would then become taboo;[3] the familiar custom of not eating a sacred thing was thus extended to any new object of this sort. The functions of the tribal sacred animals approached in some points those of gods: they were consulted by magicians on important occasions (war, sickness, marriage). It was supposed (somewhat as in the Banks Islands) that the tribal sacred animal appeared to a mother just before the birth of her child.

---

[1] On the question whether these gods are a development out of totem animals see below, § 577.

[2] On the relation of this idea to Frazer's theory of " conceptional totemism " see below, § 548.

[3] It might then seem that the deity was originally the animal; see below, § 577.

483. Thus in Melanesia, along with a large mass of sacred objects connected more or less intimately with social units (but not with clans proper), there are usages and ideas that are commonly found associated with clan totemism (belief in descent from a sacred thing and refusal to eat it when it is edible), but also other ideas and usages (omens from animals; superhuman determination, before a child's birth, of its character; creation of a new sacred thing by an individual man) that look away from clan organization to an individualistic form of society.[1]

484. *Micronesia and Polynesia.* The character of the social organization in Micronesia (the Caroline and Pelew groups, with which may be included the little island of Tikopia, southeast of the Santa Cruz group) is not very well known, but the published reports indicate a considerable divergence from clan totemism. The westernmost island of the Carolines, Uap (or Yap), according to a recent observer,[2] retains many old beliefs, is without an exogamous system, and has a large apparatus of spirits and gods. Elsewhere in the Carolines and in Tikopia there are nonexogamous social groups, sacred animals greatly revered, and in some places belief in descent from an animal-god. Sacred animals and village gods (with exogamous families) are found in the Pelew group.[3] The diversity in Micronesian customs may be due in part to mixture of tribes resulting from migrations.

485. In Polynesia the family is generally the social unit, and there is a fairly good political organization, with more or less developed pantheons. Gods are held to be incarnate in animals and trees, but there are also great gods divorced to some extent from phenomena. The theistic development is noteworthy in Hawaii, New Zealand, Samoa, Tahiti, and Tonga, and there are elaborate forms of worship with priests and temples. The existing organization is not totemic, but here, as elsewhere in similar cases, the question has been raised whether or not the gods have arisen from sacred

---

[1] As to the significance of this fact cf. below, § 529 ff.

[2] W. H. Furness, 3d, *The Island of Stone-Money.*

[3] On the large theistic material of the Pelews see Frazer, *Adonis Attis Osiris,* pp. 386, 428 ff., with references to J. Kubary, " Die Religion der Pelauer " (in A. Bastian's *Allerlei aus Volks- und Menschenkunde*).

(or, more definitely, totemic) animals and plants,[1] and whether, in general, the existing organization was preceded by one approaching totemism.[2]

486. *Indonesia.* The Battas of the interior of Sumatra have clan exogamy (but the clans live mixed together), and every clan has sacred animals which it is unlawful to eat. One clan on the west coast asserts its descent from a tiger. In the Moluccas villages claim descent from animals or plants, and these are taboo. The indications of totemic organization in Borneo are slight: there are sacred animals that are not eaten, and there is a vague feeling of kinship with animals — phenomena that are not necessarily totemic. The belief of the Sea Dyaks in individual guardians is to be distinguished from general respect for sacred animals.

487. *India.* The non-Aryan peoples of India are divided into a large number of exogamous clans, each with its sacred object, which it is unlawful to injure or use.[8] A departure from ordinary totemic usage appears in the fact that in many cases the sacred objects receive worship. The social constitution of these peoples seems to have undergone modifications, partly through adoption of agriculture (which has occurred generally), partly by direct Hindu religious influence; the history of the non-Aryans, however, is obscure in many points. The Aryans of India have exogamy but not totemism, and this is true in part of the Assamese. Totemism has not been observed in Burma[4] and China, or in the Malay Peninsula.

488. *North America.* The North American native tribes, scattered over a large territory, with widely different climatic and topographical features, and themselves divided into half a dozen linguistic stocks, show great diversities of social organization. While exogamous groups (clans, phratries, and local groups) are found

---

[1] Cf. below, § 577.

[2] Exogamy is said to exist in the atoll Lua Niua, in the Lord Howe group; the population is described as Polynesian (Brown, *Melanesians and Polynesians*, p. 414 ff.) ; Dr. Brown thinks it probable that exogamous classes formerly existed in Samoa, to which place the Lua Niua people, he holds, are ultimately to be traced.

[8] Certain septs (among the Telugus and others) are named from inanimate (some times artificial) objects.

[4] The usages mentioned in article " Burma " in Hastings, *Encyclopædia of Religion and Ethics*, iii, 24, do not necessarily show totemism.

almost everywhere, there is little precise information about certain fundamental points of totemic systems, particularly customs of killing and eating the totem and belief in descent from it. With a general apparatus that often suggests an original totemism, the American·social type differs considerably from the Australian, resembling in some respects the Melanesian and the Polynesian, but with peculiarities that difference it from these. Among the Eskimo and the Californians no definite signs of totemism have been discovered. Among the other peoples the Rocky Mountain range makes a line of demarcation — the tribes of the Pacific Coast differ in organization decidedly not only from their eastern neighbors but also from all other known savage and half-civilized peoples. There are points of similarity to these, but the general Pacific Coast type is unique.

489. Beginning with the *Eastern* tribes, we find that the Iroquois and their allies (Mohawks, Senecas, and others),[1] mainly agricultural, had the tribe or the phratry rather than the clan as their political and religious unit. The Iroquois League, organized by the great statesman Hiawatha in the fifteenth century, was a federal union of five (later of six) tribes that showed remarkable political wisdom and skill. The great festivals were tribal. The clan is recognized in a myth that describes the metamorphosis of a turtle into a man who became the progenitor of the clan of that name, and it was socially influential by reason of the brotherhood that existed among members of clans having the same name in different tribes, and through the fact that a man's personal name was the property of the clan. The totem figure was used as a badge. Whether or not the totem was killed and eaten is not known. In the form, then, in which it is known, the Iroquois organization cannot be called totemic — whether it was originally such must be left undetermined.

490. The Cherokees, belonging to the southern division of the Iroquois stock (living formerly in Tennessee and North Carolina), killed the animals they respected, but with ceremonies. Their Green

[1] The Iroquois stock occupied an immense territory, partly in Canada, partly in the region now including the states of New York, Pennsylvania, Kentucky, Tennessee, Georgia, Alabama, and the Carolinas.

Corn dance, the object of which was to insure a good crop, was expiatory, and was accompanied by a general amnesty.[1]

491. Wyandot (Huron) myths[2] account for their Snake and Hawk clans by stories of marriages between women and a snake or a hawk; here human beings are assumed to have existed before the genesis of the clan (a difference from the Australian scheme), but it is true that the clan is held to have descended in part from an animal.

492. In the great Algonkin stock[3] the evidence for a distinct totemic organization is similarly indefinite. The Lenâpé (Delawares), who were agricultural and well advanced in manufacture, gave prominence to families rather than to clans, and the totem was a badge. The Ojibwas, hunters (dwelling by the Great Lakes and in the valley of the St. Lawrence),[4] also used their sacred animal forms as badges; whether they ate such animals or claimed descent from them we are not informed. The friendly relation existing between the Otter and Beaver clans is explained by a story of a marriage between an Otter clansman and a Beaver woman. · For the Potawatamies it was lawful to kill and eat the totem. The Ottawas (of Canada) and the combined Sauks and Foxes (of the Mississippi Valley) had traditions of descent from the totem. The Menomini (of the same region) would kill the totem, but always with an apology to it; their myths embody varying conceptions of the relation of eponymous animals to clans: sometimes the origin of a clan is referred to the action of a supernatural being who changed a bear, for example, into a man, or to adventures of animals; sometimes eponymous birds (eagle and hawk) are described as being spirits or deities. Such introduction of supernatural beings involves a deviation from the conception of the eponymous animal as independent creator of a clan.[5]

---

1 Cf. Gatschet, *Migration Legend of the Creeks*, p. 24 ff.

2 The Wyandots, who were allied to the Iroquois, dwelt in the district north of Lake Ontario.

8 The Algonkins formerly ranged over a large territory extending along the Atlantic coast as far south as North Carolina and reaching westward to the Mississippi.

4 It was from the Ojibwas that our word 'totem' was taken.

5 A similar rôle, somewhat vague, is assigned to two supernatural beings in Australia (Spencer and Gillen, *Native Tribes of Central Australia*, p. 388; cf. p. 246).

493. For the tribes bordering on the Gulf of Mexico no signs have been preserved of an organization based on the relation between clans and eponymous animals, plants, and other objects. The great Maskoki stock (including Creeks, Seminoles, Choctaws, Chickasas, and some other less important tribes) had a well-formed political system, and their religion was represented by the Chief Magician or Priest (Medicine Man). They performed magical ceremonies for increase of food, but these were tribal, and the Creek annual fast (*puskita*, busk) had high religious and ethical significance.[1]

494. The Caddoan group, dwelling formerly west of the Mississippi, in Texas, Louisiana, and Arkansas, had an approach to specific totemism. In the Caddo tribe clansmen refrained from killing the eponymous animal; but all members of the tribe refrained from killing eagles and panthers. Whether this custom represents former clan restrictions is uncertain. For the related Skidi Pawnee (who formerly dwelt in the Nebraska region) there is evidence, from folk-tales, of a belief in the origin of clans from marriages between human beings and animals, and of belief that through such marriages benefits accrued to the people. But such beliefs appear not to have affected the Pawnee social organization.[2]

495. The Nakchi (Natchez) people (of the lower Mississippi Valley) dwelt in villages that had such names as "pond-lily people," "hickory people," "swan people," "forest people." These are possibly survivals of totemic names, but there is no account of the existence of totemic groups among them. On the other hand, they had a highly developed sun-worship, with human sacrifices.

496. Customs in the Siouan stock vary. In the Dakota tribe there is no known evidence of totemism. The Omahas (of the

---

[1] Gatschet, *Migration Legend of the Creeks*, p. 177 ff. It was expiatory, and was accompanied by a moral reconstruction of society, a new beginning, with old scores wiped out. Cf. the Cherokee Green Corn dance (see article "Cherokees" in Hastings, *Encyclopædia of Religion and Ethics*).

[2] Dorsey, *The Skidi Pawnee*, p. xviii. The Pawnee had a fairly well-developed pantheon, and a civil government based on rank (chiefs, warriors, priests, magicians). They lived in endogamous villages; in every village there was a sacred bundle, and all the people of the village were considered to be descendants of the original owner of the bundle.

Missouri Valley), who are partly agriculturalists, partly hunters, refrain from eating or using eponymous objects, certain clans are credited with magical power over such objects, and there are traces, in ceremonies and myths, of the descent of clans, each from its eponym. This combination of more definite totemistic conceptions is not found in any other member of the Siouan stock. The Osages had a tradition or myth of their descent from animals, but their civil organization was nontotemic — they were divided into two groups, termed respectively the Peace Side and the War Side, and the members of the former group took no animal life, though they ate flesh that they obtained from the War Side. The origin of this custom is uncertain — the two divisions of the tribe, the hunters and the tillers of the soil, exchanged products, but how this division of labor arose (whether from a union of two tribes or otherwise) is not clear. Among the Hidatsa, it is reported, there was a belief that spirit children might enter into a woman and be born into the world. The resemblance to the Central Australian belief is striking, but it does not appear that such entrance of spirit children was supposed to be the only mode of human birth. The Mandans (living on the Missouri River, in North Dakota) now have no totemic system; but little or nothing is known of their early history.[1] In the Siouan tribes the figure of the individual animal guardian (the manitu or " medicine ") plays a prominent rôle.

497. There are indications that the institutions of the Pueblo tribes (who are now wholly agricultural) have undergone modifications, perhaps under foreign (Spanish) influence. Hopi myths represent clans as descended from ancestors originally animal, and transformed into human shape by deities. But the elaborate sun-worship and the complicated solstice ceremonies are tribal.[2] The Zuñi economic ceremonies appear to have passed from under clan control. Thus, the magical ceremony for procuring rain, properly the function of the Frog clan, is now in the hands of rain-priests;

---

1 Will and Spinden, *The Mandans* (*Papers of the Peabody Museum of American Archæology and Ethnology*, Harvard University, vol. iii, 1906), p. 129 ff.

2 J. W. Fewkes, *The Winter Solstice Ceremony at Walpi* (reprint from *The American Anthropologist*, vol. xi, 1898), with bibliography.

and the magical, dramatic performances for insuring a supply of food are conducted by nontotemic religious fraternities. The great Snake " dance" may have been originally a totemic ceremony intended to secure rain and corn.[1]

498. For a former totemic organization among the Navahos, Apaches, and Mohaves (these last live on the Colorado River) there are only vague traditions and other faint traces; the taboos on foods now touch not a particular clan but a whole tribe.

499. The coast tribes of Northwest America (in British Columbia and the United States)[2] differ in social organization from the other Indians in several respects, and particularly in the importance they attach to rank, in their employment of the crest or badge, and in the prominence they give to the individual guardian animal or spirit.

500. In the civil organization of the Carrier division of the Déné, the Salish, the Kwakiutl, and other tribes, three or four castes or groups are recognized : hereditary nobles ; the middle class, whose position is based on property ; and the common folk ; and to these is to be added among some tribes the class of slaves. In the summer ceremonies the men are seated according to class and rank. The family pride of the nobles is great — every family has its traditions and pedigrees. In such a scheme the zoönymous clan plays an insignificant part. Classes and clans are mixed in the villages in which, for the most part, these people live, and trade is prominent in their life. The curious custom of the " potlatch " — a man invites his friends and neighbors to a gathering and makes them magnificent presents, his reputation being great in proportion to the extent of his gifts — appears to be a device for

---

[1] Fewkes, *Journal of American Ethnology and Archæology*, iv, and *Journal of American Folklore*, iv.

[2] The stocks or groups are, going from north to south : the Déné or Athabascans (middle of Alaska and running east and west) ; the Tlingit (Southern Alaska) ; the Haidas (Queen Charlotte Islands and adjacent islands) ; the Tsimshians (valleys of the Nass and Skeena rivers and adjacent islands) ; the Kwakiutl (coast of British Columbia, from Gardiner Channel to Cape Mudge, but not the west coast of Vancouver Island) ; the Nootkas (west coast of Vancouver Island) ; the Salish (eastern part of Vancouver Island, and parts of British Columbia, Washington, Idaho, and Montana) ; the Kootenay (near Kootenay Lake and adjoining parts of the United States). See the authorities cited by Frazer in *Totemism and Exogamy*.

laying up property; the host in his turn receives presents from friends and neighbors.

501. The employment of a sacred object as a badge or crest, a sign of tribal or clan position, is found, as is noted above,[1] in various parts of the world: in the Torres Straits islands, in the Aru archipelago (west of New Guinea), and in North America among the Iroquois, the Lenâpé (Delawares), the Pueblos, and perhaps among the Potawatamies. In these tribes, however, the rôle of the badge is relatively unimportant — it is employed for decorative purposes, but does not enter fundamentally into the organization of the clan or the tribe. In Northwest America, on the other hand, it is of prime significance both in decoration and in organization — it, to a great extent, takes the place occupied elsewhere by the totem, and it is not always identical with the eponymous object of the clan, though this may be an accidental result of shifting social relations (new combinations of clans, or a borrowing of a device from a neighbor).

502. *The crest.* The origin of this function of the crest and its relation to the function of the totem is not clear; it may have arisen in different ways in different places, or different conceptions may have been combined in the same place. The decorative use is an independent fact, having no necessary connection with clan organization; the demand for decoration is universal among savages, and the employment of sacred objects for this purpose is natural. Figures of such objects are used, however, in magical procedures — abundantly, for example, in Central Australia — and it is conceivable that such use by a clan may have converted the totemic object into a symbol or device. The artistic employment of figures of sacred objects has been developed on the American Pacific Coast to a remarkable extent; the great poles standing in front of houses or erected in memory of the dead have carved on them histories of the relation of the family or of the deceased person to certain animals and events. These so-called totem poles presuppose, it is true, reverence for the sacred symbol, but the custom may possibly have grown simply out of artistic and historical (or biographical) motives.

1 § 445 f.

503. Perhaps, however, we must assume or include another line of development. The crest may be regarded either as the non-artistic modification or degradation of an original true totem (due to diminished reverence for animals and other causes), or as an employment of sacred objects (for purposes of organization) that has not reached the proportions of totemism proper. Which of these views will seem the more probable will depend partly on the degree of importance assigned to certain traditions and folk-stories of the Northwestern tribes, partly on one's construction of the general history of totemistic observances. In so obscure a subject a definite theory can hardly be maintained. The large number of stories in which the beginnings of clan life are attributed to marriages between clansmen and eponymous animals, or to beneficent or other adventures with such animals, may appear to indicate that there was an underlying belief in the descent of clans from animals. On the other hand, in certain low tribes (in New Britain and the Solomon Islands and elsewhere) the feeling of kinship with animals is said to exist without the belief that they are ancestors, or the animal is regarded as the representative of a human ancestor rather than as itself the ancestor. This latter view may be a bit of euhemeristic rationalism.[1]

504. While *guardian spirits* (generally in animal form) are found abundantly in America and elsewhere,[2] their rôle in the tribes of the Pacific Coast appears to be specially important, for there they largely take the place occupied in Central Australia by the clan totems. They are not wholly lacking, however, in Australia. Among the nontotemic Kurnai of Southeast Australia there are animal patrons of the sexes and of shamans and other individuals. In like manner the shamans of the Pacific Coast Haidas and Tlingit have their guardians, and sometimes secret societies are similarly provided; in the winter ceremonies of the Kwakiutl the youth is supposed to be possessed by the patron of the society to which he

---

[1] Cf. the divergent native accounts of the Melanesian *buto* (Codrington, *The Melanesians*, p. 31 ff.).

[2] In North America, in the Iroquois, Algonkin, Maskoki (Creek), and Siouan stocks; in Central America and South America; in Borneo and East Africa; and elsewhere.

belongs. We thus have, apparently, similar and mutually independent developments in Australia and America out of the early relations of men with animals.

505. The Eskimo live in small groups, and marriage is locally unrestricted. There is the usual reverence for animals, with folk-stories of animal creators and of transformations, but no well-defined marks of totemism, and no recognition of individual protecting animal-spirits.

506. In the Californian tribes, which are among the least developed in America, no traces of totemistic organization have been found.[1] The people live, or lived, in villages. The shamans, who are important members of the communities, have their familiar spirits, acquired through dreams and by ascetic observances; but these belong to the widespread apparatus of magic, and differ in their social function from guardian spirits proper.

507. There are no definite marks of totemism in Central and Northeastern Asia, and few such marks in Africa. The Siberian Koryaks believe in a reincarnation of deceased human beings in animals, but their social organization is not determined by this belief. Certain clans of the Ainu (inhabiting the northernmost islands of the Japan archipelago) are said to regard as ancestors the animals whose names they bear, but this belief appears to be socially unimportant. Marriage is not controlled by clan relations.

508. Throughout savage Africa sacred animals, plants, and other objects play a great part in life, but generally without assuming a specifically totemistic rôle.

509. In the great Bantu family the usages vary greatly.[2] One of the most interesting systems is that of the Bakuana (in the south). Here the eponymous animal approaches divinity — not only is it killed with regret, it is a thing to swear by, and has magical power; but independence of the totem appears in the fact that it may be changed; that is, it is a friend adopted by men at their

[1] R. B. Dixon, *The Northern Maidu* (Central California), p. 223; id., *The Shasta* (Northern California and Oregon), p. 451; id., *The Chimariko Indians* (west of the Shasta, on Trinity River), p. 301; A. L. Kroeber, article "California" in Hastings, *Encyclopædia of Religion and Ethics.*

[2] Article "Bantu" in Hastings, *Encyclopædia of Religion and Ethics.*

convenience. It is in accord with this conception that the Bakuana (who are pastoral and agricultural) have clan gods. Beyond taboos on sacred objects there is nothing in the Bantu territory that clearly indicates a totemistic organization of society.

510. In the half-civilized and higher savage communities of the eastern and western parts of the continent totemism proper, if it has ever been predominant, has been expelled or depressed by higher forms of organization. It seems not to exist among the Masai, a vigorous people with an interesting theistic system. The neighboring Nandi, who have clan totems, lay stress rather on the family than on the clan in their marriage laws, and their taboos include more than their totems; their excessive regard for the hyena may be due simply to their fear of the animal.[1]

511. The half-civilized Baganda (of the British Uganda Protectorate) refrain from injuring clan totems, but the functions of the clans are now political and religious (relating, for example, to the building of temples) under the control of a quasi-royal government; there is almost complete absence of magical ceremonies for the multiplication or control of sacred objects.[2] Old marriage laws are relaxed — a king may marry his sister (as in ancient Egypt). Free dealing with totems is illustrated by the adoption of a new cooking-pot as totem by one clan. The cult of the python obtains here, as in West Africa. Among the neighboring Banyoro, and among the Bahima (west of Victoria Nyanza), who are herdsmen with a kingly government, there is the usual reverence for animals, but eponymous animals are not important for the social organization.

512. In West Africa also definite totemistic organization has not been found. Everywhere there is reverence for the eponymous sacred thing, and, when it is edible, refusal to eat it; but the taboos are sometimes, as in Siena (which is agricultural), more extensive than the list of sacred things. In Southern Nigeria at

---

[1] Hollis, *The Masai*, Index, and *The Nandi*, p. 5 f.

[2] A hint of an earlier usage is given in a legend which relates that totemic clans were ordained by a king to the end that certain sorts of food might be taboo to certain families, and thus animals might have a better chance to multiply.

funerals (and sometimes on other occasions) the totem animal or plant is offered, in the form of soup, to the dead; the animal or plant in such cases is regarded, apparently, simply or mainly as acceptable food for ghosts — the offering is a part of ancestor-worship. In Congo families have sacred animals (as in Samoa) which they abstain from eating. Here and there occurs belief in the reincarnation of deceased human beings in animals. A negro fetish, becoming intimately associated with a clan, sometimes resembles a totem. The half-civilized Ashanti, Dahomi, and Yoruba have elaborate theistic systems, with monarchical governments that leave no place for a totemistic organization.[1]

513. Madagascar, before it came under European control, had a well-defined religious and political hierarchy.[2] Along with its very elaborate tabooism the island has beliefs concerning animals that are found in totemic systems but do not take the form of totemism proper. The animal is regarded as an ancestor or a patron, but clans do not take their names from animals, there is no general rule of exogamy, and there is no word corresponding exactly to the word 'totem.' The question arises whether the Malagasy system is a stage antecedent to totemism proper or an attenuated survival of it.[3]

514. *Alleged survivals of totemism among civilized peoples.* Though totemism, as a system of social organization, is not recognizable in any civilized community, ancient or modern, it is held by some scholars that the fragments or hints of such a system that are certified bear witness to its former existence in these communities.[4]

[1] See the volumes of A. B. Ellis on these countries (chapters on "Gods" and on "Government"). [2] A. van Gennep, *Tabou et totémisme à Madagascar*, p. 314.
[3] On this point see below, § 522 ff.
[4] For the details see W. R. Smith, *Kinship and Marriage in Early Arabia* (includes the Hebrews) ; Joseph Jacobs, "Are there Totem-clans in the Old Testament?" (in *Archæological Review*, vol. iii) ; A. Lang, *Custom and Myth* (on the Greek *genos*), and *Myth, Ritual, and Religion*, i, 266 ff. ; ii, 226 ; S. Reinach, *Cultes, mythes et religions* (Greek and Celtic) ; Gardner and Jevons, *Greek Antiquities*, p. 68 ff., etc.; Fowler, *Roman Festivals*, p. 84 f.; G. L. Gomme, "Totemism in Britain" (in *Archæological Review*, vol. iii) ; N. W. Thomas, "La survivance du culte totémique des animaux et les rites agraires dans le pays de Galles" (in *Revue de l'histoire des religions*, vol. xxxviii).

515. In fact certain ideas and customs that occur in connection with savage totemism are found abundantly among ancient Semites, Greeks and Romans, and in Celtic and Teutonic lands. They are such as the following: a tribe or clan bears an animal name, and regards itself as akin to the animal in question and as descended from it; this animal is sacred, not to be killed or eaten (except ceremonially), and, when it dies, is to be buried solemnly; sacred animals aid men by furnishing omens, or even by protecting from harm; they are sacrificed on critical occasions (sometimes once every year), and in some cases the killing of the sacrificial animal is treated as a crime; animal-gods are worshiped, and gods are thought to be incarnate in animals; men change into animals and animals into men; certain animals are sacred to certain deities; human worshipers dress in imitation of animal forms (by wearing skins of beasts and by other devices); a man's tribal mark is derived from the form of an animal; the death of the sacrificial animal comes to be regarded as the death of a god; the form of social organization in certain ancient communities is similar to that with which totemism is usually found associated.

516. Not all of these points are found in any one case, but their occurrence over so wide an area, it is argued, is most naturally explicable by the assumption of an original totemism of which these are the survivals. It is suggested also that they may be an inheritance from savage predecessors of the civilized peoples.

517. It will be sufficient to mention a few examples of the beliefs and usages that appear to point to an original totemism.[1] Names of clans and tribes derived from animals or plants are not uncommon: Hebrew Raḥel (Rachel, ewe), perhaps Kaleb (dog) and Yael (Jael, mountain goat);[2] Greek Kunnadai (dog), and perhaps Myrmidon (ant); Roman Porcius (hog), Fabius (bean); Irish Coneely (seal); Teutonic clan-names like Wolfing and the like. Belief in a general kinship of men and animals existed among Semites, Greeks, and Romans. On the other hand, belief in the descent of a clan from an animal rarely appears: it is apparently

---

[1] Names are omitted that appear to belong only to individuals or to places.
[2] G. B. Gray, *Hebrew Proper Names*, p. 86 ff.

not found in the Semitic area; the Ophiogeneis of Parium (in Asia
Minor) are said to have regarded themselves as akin to snakes and to
have traced their genos (family or clan) to a hero who was at first
a snake;[1] the Myrmidons, according to one tradition, were transformed ants, and some of the Irish Coneely clan are said to have
been changed into seals. Transformations of men into animals are
common in Greek mythology. Taboos of certain foods were observed abundantly in the ancient world: by Egyptians,[2] Hebrews,[8]
Greeks,[4] and Romans,[5] and by Celts.[6] Among the various omen-
giving animals some may have been totems. Solemn annual sacrifices, followed by mourning for the victims, were performed in
Egypt,[7] and the slaying of the sacrificial animal was treated as
murder in various Greek cities.[8] Living animals were worshiped in
Egypt, and everywhere in antiquity gods assumed animal forms, and
certain animals were sacred to certain gods. Worshipers clothed
themselves in the skins of sacrificed animals in Egypt, Cyprus, and
Rome.[9] Tribal marks and ensigns were sometimes derived from
figures of animals.[10] Finally, there are traces, in the early history
of the ancient civilized peoples, of the form of social organization
with which savage totemism is found associated.[11]

519. It is possible that such facts as these may point to a
primitive totemistic stage of ancient civilized society. But it is to
be noted that the usages in question almost all relate to the general
sacredness of animals (or of plants), not to their specific character
as totems. They occur in lower tribes in cases where totemism does
not exist.[12] Animal clan-names and tribe-names, belief in kinship

---

1 Strabo, *Geographica*, xiii, 588.
2 Herodotus, ii, 37, 42; Diodorus Siculus, *Bibliotheke Historike*, i, 70.
8 Lev. xi; Deut. xiv.
4 Stengel and Oehmichen, *Die griechischen Sakralaltertümer*, p. 27.
5 Frazer, *Golden Bough*, 2d ed., i, 241 f.   6 Cæsar, *De Bello Gallico*, v, 12.
7 Herodotus, ii, 42.
8 Pausanias, i, 24, 4. On the death of the god cf. Frazer, *The Dying God*.
9 Herodotus, ii, 39 ff.; W. R. Smith, *Religion of the Semites*, 2d ed., additional
note G; the Roman Lupercalia.
10 Diodorus Siculus, i, 86 (Egypt); cf. Pliny, *Historia Naturalis*, x, 4 f.
11 W. R. Smith, *Kinship and Marriage in Early Arabia*, chap. viii (Semites).
12 See above, §§ 441 ff., 466, and below, § 526; Frazer, *Totemism and Exogamy*,
Index, s.vv. *Animals* and *Totems*.

with animals and plants and in descent from them, exogamy, transformations, refusal to eat certain animals except ceremonially, apologies for killing them, omens derived from them, worship of animal-gods, incarnations of gods in animals, animals sacred to gods, tribal marks derived from animals — all these are found in such diverse social combinations that it is impossible to infer merely from the occurrence of this or that custom the existence of the peculiar form of social organization to which the name 'totemism' proper is given above. The same remark holds of inferences from the general constitution of early society; a custom of matrilineal descent, for example, by no means carries totemism with it.

519. The evidence for the existence of totemism among the ancient civilized peoples, consisting, as it does, of detached statements of customs that are found elsewhere without totemism, is not decisive. Animal-worship has played a great rôle in religious history, but the special part assigned to totemism has often been exaggerated. It has been held that the latter is at the base of all beliefs in the sacredness of animals and plants, or that certain usages (such as those mentioned above) are inexplicable except on the supposition of an original totemism. These positions are not justified by known facts, and it will conduce to clearness to give totemism its distinct place in that general regard for animals and plants of which it is a peculiar part.

520. Totemistic forms of society, as far as our present knowledge goes, are found only among the lower peoples, and among these a perplexing variety of conditions exists. As our review of what may be called totemistic features shows,[1] the one permanent element in the relation between men and nonhuman, nondivine objects is reverence for these last on men's part; and the conception of an alliance, defensive and offensive, between the two groups has been proposed above as an additional differentia of totemism, a sense of kinship being involved. If we further add the condition that the social organization (not necessarily exogamous) must be determined by this alliance, we have all that can safely be demanded in a definition of totemism; but as much as this seems necessary if totemism is to be marked off as a definite institution.

[1] See above, § 443 ff.

521. From the point of view of religious history the important thing in any social organization is its character as framework for religious ideas and customs. If the central social fact is an intimate relation between a human group and a nonhuman class of natural objects, then conceptions regarding this relation may gather about it, and these will be as various as the tribes of men. The elements of social and religious institutions spring from the universal human nature and attach themselves to any form of life that may have been suggested by circumstances. Thus the term 'totemism' may be used loosely to denote any combination of customs connected with the idea of an alliance between man and other things, and the alliance itself may exist in various degrees of intimacy. The restricted definition suggested above is in part arbitrary, but it may serve as a working hypothesis and as a norm by which to estimate and define the various systems or cults involving a relation between human groups and individuals on the one side and nonhuman things on the other side.

522. *Conditions favorable and unfavorable to totemistic organization.* The questions whether totemism was the earliest form of human social life and whether existing freer forms are developments out of definite totemism may be left undetermined. Data for the construction of primitive life are not accessible, and how far decay or decadence of institutions is to be recognized must be determined in every case from such considerations as are offered by the circumstances. We may, however, distinguish between social conditions in connection with which some sort of totemism flourishes and those under which it is nonexistent or feeble; we may thus note unfavorable and, by contrast, favorable general accompaniments. These may be roughly described as economic, individualistic, political, and religious.

523. *Economic conditions.* Of savage and slightly civilized tribes some live by hunting or fishing, some are pastoral (nomadic or settled), some practice agriculture. Without undertaking to trace minutely the history of these economic practices it may be assumed that they are fixed in general by climatic and topographical conditions. Where food is plentiful, thought and life are likely to be freer. In general, savage peoples are constantly on the alert to discover supplies of food, and they show ingenuity in devising economic methods — when one resource fails they look for another. Hunters and fishers are dependent on wild animals for food, and stand in awe of them. The domestication of animals leads men to regard them simply as material for the maintenance of life — the mystery that once attached to them vanishes; they are considered not as man's equals or superiors but as his servants. The same result follows when they are used as aids in tilling the soil or in transportation. Agricultural peoples also have generally some knowledge of the arts of life and a somewhat settled civil and political organization, and these tend to separate them from the lower animals and to diminish or destroy their sense of kinship with them.

524. We find, in fact, that in many cases totemic regulations are less strict where the food supply is plentiful and where agriculture is practiced. The correspondence is not exact — other considerations come in, such as isolation and the unknown quantity of natural tribal endowments; but the relation between the economic and totemic conditions is so widespread that it cannot be considered as accidental.

525. Thus, for example, the contrast between the social system of sterile Central Australia and that of certain tribes on the comparatively fertile southeast coast is marked; the Kurnai have practically no clan totemism. In the islands of Torres Straits and in New Guinea agriculture marks a dividing line between stricter and looser organizations based on regard for the totem. The agricultural Melanesian and Polynesian tribes, with great regard for animal patrons, lay stress on the family or on voluntary associations rather than on the clan. In Africa the partially civilized peoples, such as the Baganda and adjacent tribes in the east, and Yoruba, Dahomi, and Ashanti in the west, have fairly well-developed religious organizations, in which totems play a subordinate part. The customs of certain tribes in the south are especially worthy of note: the pastoral Herrero have a double system of clans, maternal and paternal, and their food restrictions are curiously minute, relating to parts of animals or to their color; the Bakuana, who are pastoral and agricultural, kill the clan eponymous animals, though unwillingly, and appear not to regard them as ancestors. The non-Aryan tribes of India have been so long in contact with Aryan civilization that in many cases, as it seems, their original customs have been obscured, but at present among such agricultural tribes as the Hos, the Santhals, and the Khonds of Bengal, and some others, totemic organizations are not prominent, and the Todas, with their buffalo-cult, show no signs of totemism.

526. In North America the variety of climatic and other economic conditions might lead us to expect clear testimony as to the relation between these conditions and totemic development; but the value of such testimony is impaired by the absence of information concerning early forms of organization. In the period for which there are details it appears that in the Eastern groups (Iroquois, Algonkin, Creek, Natchez, Siouan, Pueblo) the effective rôle of totemism is in inverse proportion to the development of agriculture and to stable civil organization: there are clans bearing the names of animals and other objects, with mythical stories of descent from such objects, and rules of exogamy, but the civil, political, and religious life is largely independent of these conditions; there are great confederations of tribes with well-devised systems of government that look to the well-being of the whole community, the clan-division being of small importance. The mode of life appears to be determined or greatly influenced by climate, though different climatic situations sometimes lead to similar results: agriculture naturally arises from fertility of soil, but the Pueblo tribes have been driven (perhaps under civilized influences), by the aridness of their land, to till the soil. Throughout the East the known facts suggest that a nontotemic organization has followed an earlier form in which quasi-totemic elements are recognizable.

527. The interesting social organization of the Northern Pacific Coast, on the other hand, appears to be independent of agriculture. The people live by hunting and fishing; families and villages are the important social units; instead of totems there are crests or badges; society in some tribes is marked by a division into classes differing in social rank. The history of all these tribes, however, is obscure: there have been modifications of organization through the influence of some tribes on others; the details of the various social schemes are not all accurately known. The settled village life and the half-commercial, half-aristocratic constitution of society must be referred to racial characteristics and other conditions with which we are not acquainted. As in the East, so here there is the suggestion of a movement away from a form of organization that resembles true totemism. The Northwest has a remarkable system of ceremonies, but in definiteness and elevation of religious conceptions it is greatly inferior to the East.

528. The fact that some of the least-advanced American tribes, particularly the Eskimo and the California tribes, show no signs of totemistic organization [1] makes against the view that totemism was the initial form of human society, but its historical background is not known. In any case it does not invalidate what is said above of the rôle of agriculture in the modification of savage institutions. The lines of savage growth have been various — a general law of development cannot be laid down; the history of every community must be studied for itself, and its testimony must be given its appropriate value. In this way it will be possible to give a sketch of totemistic forms and suggestions, if not a history of totemism.

529. *Individualistic institutions.* The development of individualism, a universal accompaniment of general social progress, is unfavorable to totemism, since in this latter the individual is subordinated to the clan. To assert one's self as an individual is practically to ignore the totem, whose function pertains to the clan as a whole, without separate recognition of its members. Revolt against the supremacy of the clan (if that expression is allowable) has shown itself from an early social stage and in all parts of the world. The principal forms in which it appears are the institution of voluntary societies, and the adoption of personal guardians by individuals.

530. *Secret societies.* It is a common custom in the lower tribes to keep the sexes separate and to distinguish between the initiated

[1] So, also, in Northeastern Asia, in the Japan archipelago (the Ainu), and in low African tribes.

and the uninitiated. There are often men's houses in which the young unmarried males are required to live.[1] Women and boys are forbidden to be present at ceremonies of initiation when, as in some instances, the secrets of the tribe are involved. Thus there arise frequently secret associations of males, who conduct tribal affairs. But these associations are not voluntary — all initiated men belong to them perforce — and they are not divorced from totemic relations. The real voluntary society is of a quite different character. In general, in its most developed form, it ignores differences of age, sex, and clan. There are, however, diversities in the constitution of the various organizations that may be called voluntary;[2] conditions of membership and functions vary.

531. Such organizations are of two sorts, one mainly political or governmental, the other mainly religious. The best examples of the first sort are found in Melanesia, Polynesia, and West Africa. The clan government by the old men, of which a simple form exists in Central Australia, has passed into, or is represented by, a society of men that undertakes to maintain order, exact contributions, and provide amusements for the people. The Dukduk of the Bismarck Archipelago,[3] the Egbo of Old Calabar, and the Ogboni of Yoruba,[4] to take prominent examples, are police associations that have managed to get complete control of their respective communities and have naturally become instruments of oppression and fraud. They have elaborate ceremonies of initiation, are terrible to women and uninitiated males, and religion usually enters only casually and subordinately into their activities, chiefly in the form of magical ceremonies. A partial exception, in regard to this last point, occurs in the case of the Areoi society of Tahiti, which, as it is the best-organized society in Polynesia, is also the most tyrannical, and the broadest in its scope; its members enjoy not only a large share of the good things of this life, but also the most desirable positions in the future life.[5]

---

[1] Where sexual license before marriage prevails, young girls are allowed to go to these houses.   [2] H. Webster, *Primitive Secret Societies.*

[3] G. Brown, *Melanesians and Polynesians*, p. 60 ff.

[4] Mary Kingsley, *West African Studies*, p. 384, and *Travels in West Africa*, p. 532 ff.; Ellis, *Yoruba*, p. 110.

[5] H. Webster, *Primitive Secret Societies*, p. 164 ff.

532. On the other hand, the North American voluntary societies are mainly concerned with the presentation of religious ideas by the dramatization of myths, and by demanding for membership some sort of religious experience. How far such societies existed in the Eastern tribes it is not possible to say. Among these tribes, as among the Skidi Pawnee, the Navahos, and other groups of the Middle West, the control of religion has largely passed into the hands of priests—an advance in religious organization. Where ceremonies are conducted by societies, membership in these is often conditioned on the adoption of a personal divine patron by every member.

533. This adoption of a *guardian spirit* by the individual is the most definite early divergence from the totemistic clan organization. An intermediate stage is represented by the sex-patrons of Southeast Australia,[1] who embody a declaration of independence by the women. In this region, moreover, among the Kurnai, not only shamans but all other men have each his special "brother" and protector.[2] Naturally, where the family, in distinction from the clan, is the social unit, family protectors arise. The Koryaks of Northeastern Asia have a guardian spirit for every family and also for every person.[3] A curious feature of Dahomi religion is the importance that is attached to the family ghost as protector, the ghost, that is, of a former member of the family, ordinarily its head; he has a shrine, and becomes practically an inferior deity. Still more remarkable is the worship that the West African native, both on the Gold Coast and on the Slave Coast (communities with well-developed systems of royal government), offers to his own indwelling spirit;[4] the man's birthday is sacred to the spirit and is commenced with a sacrifice.[5] In Samoa a guardian spirit (conceived of as incarnate in some animal) is selected for a child at its birth.[6] Some such custom is said to exist among the Eskimo of the Yukon district

---

1 Frazer, *Totemism and Exogamy*, i, 495 ff.

2 Frazer, loc. cit. Cf. A. Lang, *Secret of the Totem*, p. 138.

3 *Jesup North Pacific Expedition*, vi, 1, 32 ff., 43 ff.

4 So worship was offered to the Roman *genius* (Horace, *Carm.* iii, 17; *Epist.* i, 7, 94).   5 A. B. Ellis, *Ewe*, p. 105; *Tshi*, p. 156; *Yoruba*, chap. vii.

6 Turner, *Samoa*, p. 78 f. So the κουροτρόφος (Farnell, in *Anthropological Essays presented to E. B. Tylor*).

in Alaska; a guardian animal is selected by a boy when he arrives at the age of puberty, or it is selected for him in his early childhood by his parents.[1]

534. While these examples indicate a tendency toward the adoption of individual patrons, and may suggest that the custom is, or was, more widespread than now appears, it is among the North American Redmen that this sort of individualism is best developed and most effective socially and religiously.[2] There are traces of it in the Eastern tribes; but it is in its Western form that it is best known — it is explicit among the Western Algonkins and the Siouan tribes, and on the Northwest Pacific Coast. Most men, though not all, seek and obtain a guardian spirit (usually represented by an animal) which shall protect from injury and bestow prowess in war, success in love, and all other goods of life. The spirit is, as a rule, independent of the clan totem — is found, indeed, in nontotemic tribes; it is often identical with the eponymous animal of some religious society. It is sometimes inherited, but rarely — the essence of the institution is that the guardian shall be sought and found. The preparation for the quest is by fasting; the revelation of the guardian comes in a dream or a vision, or by some strong impression made otherwise on the mind.

535. Among the Siouan Indians there are religious societies, each of which bears the name of some animal and has a ritual composed of chants and songs which, it is often claimed, have been received in a supernatural manner.[3] The youth who aspires to become a member of one of these societies goes off alone to the forest, and there, fasting and meditating, waits for the vision of the sign. This comes usually in the form of an animal, and the youth enters the society whose distinguishing mark this animal is. First, however, he must travel until he meets the animal he saw, when he must slay it and preserve the whole or a part of it. This

---

[1] W. H. Dall, *Alaska and its Resources*, p. 145, cited by Frazer, *Totemism and Exogamy*, iii, 442 f.

[2] The acquisition of a supernatural inspirer by a shaman is analogous to this custom, but belongs in a somewhat different category: see below, § 540.

[3] Miss Alice Fletcher, "Indian Ceremonies" (in *Report of the Peabody Museum of American Archæology and Ethnology*, Harvard University, 1883).

trophy is the sign of his vision and is the most sacred thing he can possess, marking as it does his personal relation to the supernatural being who has appeared to him.

536. A similar ceremony is found among the Kwakiutl in North-western America.[1] The novice is supposed to stay some time with the supernatural being who is the protector of his society. From this interview he returns in a state of ecstasy, and is brought to a normal state by the songs and dances and magical performances of the shaman; but before he is permitted to take part in the ordinary pursuits of life he must undergo a ceremonial purification. In these tribes, as is remarked above, the totemic groups have been replaced by clans, and in the winter ceremonial these clans (according to one report) are again replaced by the secret societies, whose function is political only in the sense that its members form a part of the aristocracy. Recently societies of women have been established — a fact that illustrates the divergence of the new system from the old.

537. The details of initiation or of acquisition of the guardian spirit vary (for example, it is not always required that the youth kill his patron animal), but in all cases there is recognition of the emotional independence of the individual, and there is involved a certain largeness of religious experience in the modern sense of the term. The demand for the supernatural friend represents a germinal desire for intimate personal relations with the divine world; and, though the particular form that embodied the conception has given way before more refined ideas, the conception itself has survived in higher religions in the choice of patron saints.[2]

538. *Political conditions.* Political organization, in unifying a community under the control of a central authority, tends to efface local self-governing groups. This process is visible in the increased power of Melanesian chiefs, in the royal governments of Polynesia and Western and Eastern Africa, and in the inchoate constitutional federations of Eastern North America. In all these cases the simple clan system is reduced to small proportions, and totemism loses its social significance. The way in which the functions of totemic

---

[1] F. Boas, *The Kwakiutl*, p. 393 f.
[2] Cf. Frazer, *Totemism and Exogamy*, iii, 450 ff.

groups are thus modified appears plainly in such governmental systems as that of the East African Baganda (in which heads of clans have become officers of the king's household)[1] and the Iroquois Confederation (in which the tribes act through their representatives in a national Council or Parliament).

539. *Religious conditions.* The personal guardian spirit and the totem, when it assumes this character, sometimes receive worship — they are treated as gods. But their rôle as divinities is of an inferior nature, and it does not last long. Deities proper came into existence as embodiments of the sense of an extrahuman government of the world by anthropomorphic beings; they are direct products of the constructive imagination.[2] When the true gods appear the totemic and individual half-gods disappear. We find that totemism is feeble in proportion as theistic systems have taken shape, and that where personal guardians are prominent there are no well-defined gods. In Central Australia there is only a vague, inactive form that may be called divine; a more definite conception is found in Southeastern Australia, where the strictness of totemism is relaxed. Melanesia and Polynesia show an increased definiteness of theistic figures. Northwestern North America is, in comparison with the East, undeveloped in this regard. Similar relations between totemism and theism appear in India and South America. In a certain number of cases the facts suggest that the former system has been superseded by the latter.

540. Cults of the totem and of individual guardian spirits are to be distinguished from certain other forms of worship with which they have points of connection. The West African fetish is the abode of a tutelary spirit, and finally is absorbed by local gods; it arises, however, from belief in the sacredness and power of inanimate things, and is without the sense of identity with the spirit that characterizes the North American relation. The family sacred symbols that are worshiped in some places[3] are really family gods

---

[1] This process is similar to the gradual reduction of the European independent barons to the position of royal officers.   [2] See below, § 633 f.

[3] As, for example, by the Marathas of the Bombay Presidency (Frazer, *Totemism and Exogamy*, ii, 276 ff.).

(whether or not they were originally totems), developed, probably, under Brahmanic influence. The worship of a tutelary spirit has sometimes coalesced with that of an ancestor, but this is doubtless due to the collocation of two distinct cults; at a certain stage an ancestor is naturally regarded as friend and protector. The general potency termed " mana " is not to be connected particularly with any one cult; it represents a conception that probably underlies all ancient forms of worship.

541. It thus appears that several lines of social progress have proved unfavorable to totemism, and to these movements it has generally succumbed. Its home has been, and is, in isolated hunting communities; agriculture and social intercourse have been fatal to it as to all early forms of society based on a belief in kinship with nonhuman natural objects.

542. It remains to mention the principal theories of the origin of totemism that are or have been held, and to ask what part it has played in the history of religion.

543. *Theories of the origin of totemism.* These may conveniently be divided into such as refer the origin to individual action, and such as refer it to the action of clans.

544. *Individualistic theories.* Among the earliest of theories were those that explained the totemic constitution as due to a confusion in the minds of savages between names and things. Individuals or families might be named after animals, plants, and other objects, and these, it was supposed, might come to be regarded as intimately associated with human persons, and might be looked on with affection or reverence and even worshiped.[1] Or, more definitely, it was held that, the origin of such names being forgotten, reverence for the ancestors led to reverence for the things after which they were named and identification with them — a man whose ancestor was called " the Tiger " would think of himself as descended from a tiger and as being of the tiger stock.[2] It is now

---

[1] Lord Avebury (Sir John Lubbock), *Prehistoric Times*, 2d ed., p. 598, and 6th ed., p. 610; id., *Origin of Civilisation* (1902), p. 275 ff.; and his *Marriage, Totemism, and Religion*.

[2] Herbert Spencer, *Fortnightly Review*, 1870, and *Principles of Sociology*, i, § 171.

generally recognized, however, that the origin of so widespread and influential a system of organization as totemism cannot be referred to a mere misunderstanding of nicknames; and whether such misunderstanding was general or natural in early times is open to doubt.

545. It sometimes happens that a man (generally a chief) announces that after death he will take the form of this or that animal or plant, and this procedure, it has been supposed, would found a totemic family — his descendants would revere the object in question as the embodiment of the spirit of the ancestor, would take its name, and, when it was edible, would refrain from eating it.[1] It is true that the belief was, and is, not uncommon among savages that a deceased person might take the form of some natural object; but the reported cases are rare in which a man deliberately enjoins on his descendants reverence for such an object with the result that a quasi-totemic group arises.[2] This custom is not frequent enough to account for totemism.

546. A theory suggested by the fact that many clans perform magical ceremonies (for the purpose of increasing the supply of food) is that, when the magical apparatus of some body of persons consisted of parts of an animal, the animal would become sacred, a magical society might be formed by an individual magician, and thus a totemic magic-working clan might be created. For this hypothesis there is no support except in the fact that changes in clan life are sometimes brought about by the old men; but such changes are modifications of existing usages, not new creations. The power of a savage man of genius may be admitted, but to account for the known totemic communities we should have to suppose a vast number of such men, in different parts of the world, all working in the same direction and reaching substantially the same results.

547. The belief that a man might deposit his soul in an animal or a plant or some other object is found in West Africa, North America, and probably elsewhere. As such objects would, as a

---

[1] This view is provisionally indorsed by E. B. Tylor, in *Journal of the Anthropological Institute*, xxviii.

[2] One such case is mentioned in Codrington's *Melanesians*, p. 33.

rule, not be killed (and every individual of a group would be thus respected), it has been supposed that, when various persons deposited their souls in the same object, a totemic body would come into existence.[1] This view would account for totemic reverence and for the sense of kinship, but the objection to it is that in most totemic organizations the belief in question has not been certified.

548. The "conceptional" theory refers the origin of totemism to the belief, found among certain peoples, that conception is produced by the entrance into the mother's womb of some object (animal, plant, or other) with which the child is identified.[2] In Central Australia it is held that what passes into the woman is a spirit child which has a certain object for its totem; but in this case the previous existence of the totem is assumed. In certain islands (Mota and Motlav) of the Banks group, however, there exists, it is said, the belief that a child is the object from which the mother received some influence at conception or at some other period of pregnancy — the child resembles the object, and may not eat it if it is edible.[3] The persons thus identified with a given object would, if united, constitute a group totemic in the respects that they believe themselves to be one with the object in question and refrain from eating it.[4] The totemic object is selected, in the case of every child, by the fancy of the mother, and is, therefore, not inherited; totemic groups, thus, would be found distributed through the larger groups (phratries or tribes), and might also gradually coalesce and form local groups. If the belief in this origin of birth (identity of the child with some object) were found to be widespread, and generally effective as the ground of early social organization, it would furnish a satisfactory explanation of totemistic beginnings. But in point of fact it has so far been found, in full form, only in a small region in Melanesia, and its history in this

---

[1] Frazer, *Golden Bough* (1890), ii, 332 ff. This theory has since been abandoned by Frazer (*Totemism and Exogamy*, iv, 54 f.).

[2] Frazer, *Fortnightly Review*, July and September, 1905, pp. 154–172 (reprinted in *Totemism and Exogamy*, i); *Totemism and Exogamy*, ii, 89 ff.; iv, 57 ff.

[3] Rivers, "Totemism in Polynesia and Melanesia" (in *Journal of the Royal Anthropological Institute*, xxxix [1909], 172); Frazer, *Totemism and Exogamy*, iv, 59 ff.

[4] This is the theory adopted by Frazer in his latest work on the subject.

region is not known; back of it may lie some other system of organization. And in this region clan totemism is lacking or faint. Further testimony is needed before it can be accepted as the solution of the problem of totemic origins.[1]

549. A similar remark must be made in reference to theories based on the belief that the souls of the dead are incarnate in animals and plants. Such a belief is a natural outgrowth from the conception of the identity of nature of human beings and animals, and it occurs in so many parts of the world (Oceania, Africa, America) that it might naturally be regarded as having been at one time universal, though it is not now found everywhere. Reverence for an ancestor might be, and sometimes is, transferred to the object in which he is supposed to be incarnate; from this object a man holds himself to be descended, and he refrains from eating or injuring it.[2] This view, a combination of reverence for ancestors and reverence for animals and plants, thus supplies two features of totemistic organization, but proof is lacking that it is the basis of this organization. If it be the determining consideration in some cases, there are many cases in which its influence is not apparent. There are myths tracing the totemism of clans to ancestors having animal forms, but these myths are relatively late savage philosophical explanations of existing institutions.

550. The relation of the individual patron and guardian to the clan totem has been variously defined. Such a patron, it is sometimes held (obtained by a dream or a vision), descends from the original possessor to his children (or, in a matrilineal system, to his sister's children), and thus becomes the patron (the totem) of a family or kin; and a larger group, formed by the union of several kins, may similarly have its protecting spirit. Cases in which descent is through the mother here make a difficulty — a

---

[1] The widespread belief that birth may be independent of the union of the sexes does not, of course, carry with it an explanation of totemism.

[2] Lippert, *Die Religionen der europäischen Culturvölker*, p. 12; G. A. Wilken, " Het Animisme bij de Volken van den Indischen Archipel," in *De Indische Gids*, 1884 (cf. Tylor, in *Journal of the Anthropological Institute*, xxviii, 1899); G. M. Theal, *Records of South-eastern Africa*, vii, and *History and Ethnography of South Africa*, i, 90.

man's guardian spirit would not then be inherited. Granting that the personal patron of a shaman or of an ordinary man may be inherited, such inheritance appears to be of rare occurrence, and there is no trustworthy evidence that it ever leads to the formation of a totemic clan.

551. It is true there is a resemblance between a man's relation to his clan totem and his relation to his personal guardian — in both cases the sacred object is revered and spared. It is sometimes the case also (as, for example, among the Australian Arunta) that the totem comes through an individual (the mother) and is not transmissible, and yet endogamous clans arise by the union of persons having the same totem. But here the resemblance ceases — the Arunta child's totem is determined for him before his birth, but a man chooses his personal guardian for himself, and joins others having the same guardian, not in a clan but in a secret society. Furthermore, the institution of the personal guardian is very rare except in North America, and there flourishes in inverse proportion to the strength of clan life proper.

552. On the supposition of the primitive predominance of the rule of descent through the mother individualistic theories of the origin of totemism, with one exception, are out of the question — the totem is first chosen by a man, but children would have the totem not of the father but of the mother. The exception is the conceptional theory, in which the totem is determined by the mother — especially the Mota (Banks Islands) form, in which the choice of a sacred object by the woman is unlimited. In a small community a certain number of women would, however, choose the same object, and thus totemic groups would arise. This scheme of organization, though not open to the objection mentioned above, is geographically limited.

553. *Theories based on clan action.* Here the starting-point is the clan, which is supposed to have come into existence somehow ; it is not essential to determine precisely the method of its origination, though the question of method is sometimes included in the discussion of a theory. The clan finds itself confronted by various natural objects with which, it believes, it must form helpful relations; or some sort of relation is forced on it by the conditions of life. The question is how a human group came to enter into the totemic relation.

554. The simplest answer is that the primitive clan deliberately chose among all associated objects some one to be its particular friend or its special associate,[1] naturally valued and respected this object, refrained from eating it when it was edible, took its name, came to regard it as ancestor, and created myths explanatory of these conceptions. This general theory has assumed various forms, but the objection usually made to its central supposition is that such deliberate choice is out of keeping with the known methods of early societies. Though a certain amount of reflection must be assumed for primitive men (the lower animals, indeed, show reflection), it is held that so elaborate a system as totemism, like other institutions, must have been the product of accidental experiences, developed through a long period of time. Something more definite, it is said, is required in order to account for the details of the system — all that can be safely assumed is that early man, constantly on the alert to better his condition, took advantage of every situation to strengthen himself by taking precautions against enemies or by securing the aid of surrounding objects, human and nonhuman.

555. The totem is supposed by some to have been originally merely the mark or badge by which a human group distinguished itself from neighboring groups. In hunting expeditions and migrations such a mark would be necessary or, at any rate, useful.[2] More generally, it was natural for a clan to have a name for itself, as it had names for its individual members and for other objects. It might take its name from an associated animal or plant or heavenly body or from a place. The badge and the name once adopted, other totemic features would follow. Such badges are common in Northwestern America, and are found elsewhere, and the term ' totem ' has been explained by natives as meaning ' badge.'

---

1 F. B. Jevons, *Introduction to the History of Religion*, 1st ed., p. 101.

2 F. M. Müller, *Anthropological Religion*, p. 121 ff.; Pikler and Somló, *Ursprung des Totemismus*, p. 7 ff.; A. K. Keane, *Ethnology*, p. 10; cf. G. M. Theal, *History and Ethnography of South Africa*, i, 17.

But this explanation is late, and the employment of the sacred object as badge is not widely diffused. When it gives a clan its name it is, of course, a distinguishing mark, but this does not show that such distinction was in all cases its original function. Nor would the badge come into use till the name had been fixed.

556. The view just mentioned does not attempt to explain how a particular name came to be attached to a clan. This lack is supplied by the theory that a clan was named by its neighbors after the kind of food on which it chiefly subsisted.[1] The objection to this theory is that no group of men is known to confine itself to one article of food — savages eat whatever they can find — and moreover contiguous groups would feed on the same kinds of food. A view not open to this objection is that names of clans, also given from without, expressed fancied resemblances of the persons named to animals and other objects, or peculiarities of person or speech, or were derived from the place of abode.[2]

557. It is obviously true that human groups have names derived from objects with which they are somehow specially connected; in the lists of clan-names in Oceania, Africa, India, America, animal names predominate, but many are taken from plants, and some from inanimate objects;[3] when groups become settled they are sometimes called after their places of abode. The other supposition in these "name theories" — that the names are given from without — is less certain. There are examples of such naming by outsiders — nicknames, sometimes respectful, sometimes derisive.[4] But the known cases are not numerous enough to establish a general rule — the origin of names of clans and tribes is largely involved in obscurity.[5] There is no improbability in either theory of the method of naming, native or foreign — both modes may have existed, one in one region, one in another, and one group may at different times have been called by different names.

---

[1] A. C. Haddon, in *Report of the British Association for the Advancement of Science*, 1902.   [2] A. Lang, *The Secret of the Totem*, chap. vi.

[3] Lists are given in Frazer's *Totemism and Exogamy*.

[4] Lang, *The Secret of the Totem*, loc. cit.; Theal, *History and Ethnography of South Africa*, i, 92.

[5] Cf. A. W. Howitt, *Native Tribes of South-East Australia*, p. 154.

558. " Coöperative " theories suppose that a number of groups united for economic purposes, to each being assigned the duty of increasing by magical means the supply of a particular sort of food or other necessity, and procuring a portion for the general store.[1] Such coöperation, however, assumes too great a capacity of organization to be primitive. It is hardly found outside of Central Australia, in which region there are indications of a long period of social development.[2]

559. The theory that the totem is a god, immanent in the clan, incarnate in every member of the clan, a divine ancestor, the center of the clan's religion,[3] is contradicted by the actual relation between a clan and its totem : the latter is cherished as a kinsman and friend, but not worshiped as a god.[4]

560. *Summing-up on the origin of totemism.* This brief survey of proposed theories of the origin of totemism is sufficient to show the complexity of the problem. Not one of the hypotheses just mentioned is universally accepted, and no one of them appears to account satisfactorily for all the known facts. Some of them are based obviously on data derived from limited areas. Australian usage suggested the coöperative theory, and Australia and Melanesia the conceptional theory. The identification of totemism with ancestor-worship comes from South Africa ; its connection with the belief in transmigration is due to Indonesia ; its derivation from the individual guardian is based on a North American institution ; and North America probably suggested the badge theory also. It may be frankly confessed that in the present state of knowledge all theories are guesses.

561. As there are communities in which it is probable or possible that totemism has never existed, so it is conceivable that it has been developed in different ways in different places. Considering the variety of circumstances in primitive life, it would not be strange if human groups found themselves impelled to take various

---

[1] Frazer, in *Fortnightly Review*, 1899 (this theory was afterwards abandoned by him) ; B. Spencer, in *Journal of the Anthropological Institute*, xxviii (1899).

[2] Cf. Durkheim, in *Année sociologique*, v.

[3] Durkheim, in *Année sociologique*, v.   [4] See below, § 577.

paths in their attempts at effective organization. The starting-point being reverence for animals and other objects of nature, and belief in their kinship with men, one human group may have been led by some accidental experience to regard some nonhuman group or object as its ally. In another case a name, adopted by a group of its own accord or given it from without, may have induced such an alliance. Individuals may have imposed their guardian animals or plants on communities. A badge, chosen for convenience, may have been the beginning of a totemic organization. In these and other ways a group of men may have come to form intimate relations with a nonhuman group or other object.

562. This fundamental relation having been established (with aversion to eating or injuring the sacred object), various usages would attach themselves to it in accordance with general laws of social development. In many cases a rule of exogamy, for the better regulation of marriage, would be adopted. When tribes, consisting each of several clans, came into existence, a coöperative economic system would sometimes arise : magical methods of producing results, common in early stages of life, would be so organized that to every clan would be assigned the duty of producing a supply of some sort of food. Following the general tendency to genealogical construction, the belief in kinship with the sacred object would lead a clan to imagine an ancestor of the same kind, animal or animal-human or plant or rock, and myths explaining the origin would be devised. Various other usages and ideas would coalesce with those belonging to totemism proper : belief in the superhuman power of nonhuman things, including the conception of mana; the belief that every newborn child is the reincarnation of an ancestor; recognition of omens from the movements of such things; belief in the magical power of names; reverence for ancestors — a natural feeling, in itself independent of the totemic conception ; totems regarded as creators ; the employment of totemic animals as emissaries to the supernatural Powers. Thus the resultant social system would be a congeries of beliefs and usages, and in such a system, when it appears, the totemic element must be distinguished from its attachments, which must be referred each to its appropriate source.

563. *Function of totemism in the development of society.* The service of totemism to society lies in the aid it has given to the friendly association of men in groups. Common social feeling, the perception of the advantage to be gained by combination in the quest for food and for defense against human enemies, originated the formation of groups. Totemism strengthened union by increasing the sense of brotherhood in the clan and facilitating the cooperation that is a condition of social progress. This sort of service was rendered in early times by all systems in which social relations were connected with relations to animals and other natural objects; but totemism made a special appeal to the emotions and gave all the members of a human group one and the same object of devotion about which sentiments of loyalty and brotherhood could crystallize. It is a crude, initial political form that has given way to more definite forms.

564. It cannot be said that totemism has contributed to *economic* progress except in so far as every stable organization may be favorable to general progress. It has been claimed that it effected the domestication of animals and plants.[1] In support of this claim it is urged that, apart from reverence for these objects, there is nothing in savage ideas and customs that could lead to domestication. Early man, seeking food, would try all accessible animals and plants — but why, it is asked, should he desire to keep them as attachments to his home and cultivate them for his own use? Would his purpose be amusement? But, though savages sometimes have animals as pets, the custom is not general, and such pets are freely killed. Could the motive be utility? The answer is that savages have neither the ability to perceive the advantage, for food and labor, that would accrue from domestication, nor knowledge of the fact that seeds must be kept, in order to secure a crop, from one year to another, nor the self-restraint to practice present abstinence for the sake of future good.

---

[1] Frazer, in his *Totemism* (this view is now given up by him); F. B. Jevons, *Introduction to the History of Religion*, Index; S. Reinach, *Cultes, mythes et religions*, i, 86 ff.; Hahn, *Die Haustiere*, pp. 28 ff., 42, and his *Demeter und Baubo*, p. 19 ff. (domestication of cattle and use of milk as food connected with moon-cult). Cf. H. Ling Roth, in *Journal of the Anthropological Institute*, xvi, 102 ff.

565. On the other hand, it is said, semireligious reverence for animals preserves them from injury, they lose their fear of man, and those that are domesticable become tame and are appropriated and used by men ; and sacred plants are retained from one year to another for ritual purposes, and their seeds produce a succession of crops. Totem animals are not eaten — a pastoral people does not eat its cattle, it keeps them for their milk. In a word, animals, it is held, are not tamed by man of set purpose, but grow tame when not molested, and those that are edible or capable of rendering service are gradually domesticated ; and similarly, through religious use of plants, the possibility of cultivating certain plants becomes known.

566. This argument rests on the assumption of the universal mental incapacity of early men — a subject admittedly obscure. Certainly they appear to be quite lacking in knowledge and reflection in some regards ; yet they sometimes show remarkable skill in hunting (so, for example, the African Pygmies), and they have created remarkable languages. But, if we leave the question of intellectual capacity aside, there are facts that seem to throw doubt on the totemic origin of domestication. In the first place, the conditions under which reverence for a totemic animal may make it tame do not appear to have existed in totemic society. For such taming it is necessary that the animal be perfectly safe within a considerable area. But this is not possible where a group of men is composed of various clans, a given animal being spared by one clan but freely hunted and killed by all the other clans [1] — a state of things that was presumably universal.

567. Further, it is difficult to discover any historical connection between the actual cases of domestication of animals and reverence for these as totems. It is unfortunate for the decision of this question that in the two principal totemic centers, Australia and North America, there are very few native domesticable animals — only one (a species of dog) in Australia, and two (dog and bison) in North America. The history of the dog in North America, however,

---

[1] The totem belongs not to a tribe (Jevons, *Introduction to the History of Religion*, p. 114 f.) but to a clan.

is suggestive: it has been domesticated by totemic Redmen for hunting purposes and by nontotemic Eskimo for drawing sledges — that is, its economic use seems to be independent of totemic considerations. Other cases of divergence between employment of animals and their position as totems have been cited in Uganda, for example ;[1] but civilization is relatively far advanced in Uganda, and in such cases we cannot infer original conditions from existing customs.

568. It may fairly be surmised that observation in some cases led to the domestic use of animals. The value of the milk of cattle, goats, and mares as food may have been suggested to men who were acquainted with the life of these animals; and valuing them for their milk, their owners would abstain from eating them except under pressure of hunger or for ceremonial purposes. Such a procedure does not seem to be beyond the capacities of very simple communities. Chance may have suggested the function of seeds in the growth of plants, and, agriculture once entered on, the labor of animals would gradually be utilized. So far as regards artistic representations, these are found everywhere, and their occurrence on totemic poles (as, for example, among the Haidas of Queen Charlotte Islands) cannot be regarded as a special product of totemism.

569. Considering the obscurity of the subject, it is doubtless wise to refrain from offering a universal theory of the origin of domestication of animals and plants. All that is here contended for is that the large rôle sometimes assigned to totemism in this regard is not supported by the facts now known to us. Future investigations may bring with them new constructions of early history.

570. *Relation of totemism to religion.* As the beginnings of totemism are obscure it is not possible to say exactly what a man's attitude toward his totem was in the earliest period. But, when the totemic relation became a definite feature of social organization, the feeling was that the totem was in the nature of a clansman, of the same blood as the human group, and entitled to all the respect and affection with which men regarded their clan-brethren. The sentiment, in this point of view, was sacred in the sense in which this term may be used of the feeling existing between persons of

---

[1] Frazer, *Totemism and Exogamy*, iv, 19.

the same human group; it involved a certain sense of obligation toward fellow members — to respect their rights and to defend them against enemies was an imperative duty.

571. Totemic clanship, however, differed from ordinary human clanship in that the nonhuman clan-brother was regarded as a specially powerful being, endowed with the superhuman qualities with which all animals and plants and certain other objects were credited. Regard for the totem was, thus, part of the regard paid to nonhuman objects in general, only emotionalized and intensified by the belief that the nonhuman group was in a peculiar way allied to the human group. There was not only unwillingness to injure the totem— there was fear that one would suffer by such an act. The totem, it was believed, was able in its turn to inflict injury; and this belief added an element of awe to the feeling with which it was regarded.

572. In another respect, also, the totem shared the powers of other nonhuman objects — it could aid its friends. The expectation of totemic aid is, however, vague in the earlier stages of organization, that is, in communities in which totemism proper is well-defined — it appears to amount to little more than a feeling that things will go well if respect is paid to the totem. In cases where there is more definite aid there is always the question whether the aid is afforded by the totem in its specific character of clan-brother or merely in its character of nonhuman powerful thing. Omens, for example, are given by all natural objects; when an object of this sort happens to be a totem, it is not clear that its capacity of omen-giving belongs to it simply as totem.

573. There is similar uncertainty in the case of the Queensland practice, when a man, on lying down at any time or rising in the morning, whispers the name of the animal after which he is called or the name of the animal belonging to his group-division, in the belief that it will give him success in his affairs;[1] here the animal is not a clan totem, and the evidence does not show that it has come from such a totem — it may be a sacred animal that has somehow been brought into special connection with the man or

1 W. E. Roth, quoted in Frazer's *Totemism and Exogamy*, i, 532.

with his group. Personal guardians that confer magical powers
on a man do not here come into consideration.

574. The relation between totemism and the practice of magic
appears to be essentially one of coexistence in a community. The
two belong to the same stage of culture and the same order of
ideas; but the fact that each is found without the other shows that
neither is dependent on the other. Naturally they are sometimes
combined, as sometimes happens in North America and particularly
in Central Australia (where every totemic clan is charged with certain magical ceremonies); yet this close alliance is rare. Magical
practice rests on a conception of man's relation to nature that is
distinct from the conception of kinship between a human clan and
a nonhuman species or individual object.

575. Secret societies sometimes perform magical ceremonies;
but such societies are not totemic — either they have risen above
the totemic point of view, or they have sprung from ideas and
usages that are independent of totemism proper.[1]

576. It is difficult to find a clear case of the offering of religious
worship to a totem as totem. There are the ceremonies performed
by the Australian Warramunga for the purpose of propitiating or
coercing the terrible water snake Wollunqua.[2] This creature is a
totem, but a totem of unique character — a fabulous animal, never
visible, a creation of the imagination; the totem proper is a visible
object whose relations with human beings are friendly, the Wollunqua is savage in nature and often hostile to men. He appears
to be of the nature of a god, but an undomesticated one — a demon,
adopted by a tribe as totem, or identified with a previously existing
totem. The situation is an exceptional one and cannot be regarded
as evidence of general totemic worship.

577. The question whether a totem ever develops into a god is
a part of the general question whether a sacred animal ever becomes a god.[3] The complications of early ideas and customs and

---

[1] See above, § 529 ff.

[2] W. E. Roth, *North Queensland Ethnography*; Spencer and Gillen, *Northern
Tribes of Central Australia*, p. 226 ff.

[3] See below, § 635 ff.; cf. A. Lang, *Myth, Ritual, and Religion*, ii, 197, etc.; S. Reinach, *Orpheus* (Eng. tr.), p. 81 ff.; Frazer, *Totemism and Exogamy*, iv, 30 ff.

the paucity of data for the formative period of early religion make an answer to these questions difficult. As far as regards the evolution of the totem into a true divine figure the evidence is not decisive. The identification of heroes or gods with animals, their transformations into animals, and their incarnations in animal forms may, indeed, suggest such an evolution. Thus, in the island of Yam (between Australia and New Guinea) two brothers, Sigai and Maiau, have their shrines, in which they are represented by a shark figure and a crocodile figure respectively, and to them food is presented, songs are sung, dances are danced and prayers are offered. Other heroes, Kwoiam (a totem-bringer), Sida (an introducer of the arts of life), Yadzebub (a warrior), and some unnamed are revered in islands of Torres Straits.[1] In the Rewa district in Fiji every village, it is said, has a deity, and these deities have the power of turning into animals, which are then not eaten — that is, it may be supposed, the god is a developed totem.[2] In the Wakelbura tribe of Southeast Australia the totem animal is spoken of as " father," a title frequently given to clan gods. Household gods are considered to be incarnate in animals and other objects in some of the Caroline Islands, in Tonga and Tikopia, and in Samoa, and in these islands, except Samoa, the people are supposed to have descended from the animals in question. Similar ideas seem not to exist in the Americas or in Africa; in India the influence of Hindu cults has largely effaced or greatly modified non-Aryan usages so that their original form cannot generally be determined.[3]

578. The cases just mentioned are susceptible of other explanations than that of an evolution from totem to god. The history of the cult of heroes in Yam and other Torres Straits islands is obscure, but from known facts the indications are that the hero figures have arisen independently of the totem figures and have been, by a natural process, identified with these.[4] The peculiarity

---

[1] Haddon, in *Anthropological Essays presented to E. B. Tylor*, 183 ff.

[2] Rivers, in *Man*, viii (1908).

[3] Cf. Frazer, *Totemism and Exogamy*, iv, 31 ff. The Bushman god Cagn, who has the form of a mantis, and the Hindu monkey-god Hanuman seem to have no connection with totemism.

[4] Cf. the remarks of Haddon, op. cit.

of the Rewa deities is that they assume animal forms at will, and
such animals, not being eaten, are held to be totems. Whether totems
or not they are sacred and might easily be identified with gods who
stood alongside of them ; an obvious explanation of this identity
would be that the god assumed the form of the animal.[1] A similar
explanation may be given of incarnations of gods in animals — a
metamorphosis is a temporary incarnation. The Samoan Moso is
incarnate in half a dozen different objects, and some deities are
incarnate in men. As for the title " father," it belongs of course
to the object from which a clan is supposed to be descended.

579. The sacramental eating of the totem, where such a custom
exists, involves a certain identity of nature of totem and clan god,
but the two are regarded as distinct — their distinctness is, indeed,
a necessary condition of the sacrificial efficacy of the totem as a
means of placating the deity.[2]

580. Our review seems, thus, to lead to the conclusion that there
is no good ground for the opinion that a totem has ever grown
into a god. The question, belonging, as it does, to a period for
which we have no contemporary records, must be admitted to be
difficult, and answers to it must be of the nature of hypotheses ;
but gods and spirits appear to have taken shape through processes
of thought different from those that lie at the basis of totemism.[3]

TABOO

581. So far we have been considering the growth of the simpler
religious ideas and the parallel development of a quasi-religious
social organization. The ethical development is no less important
than the religious and the political, with which it has always been
closely connected. Ethical ideas and customs are in their origin
independent of religion. Religion deals with the relation between
human beings and supernatural Powers ; ethics has to do with the
relation between man and man.[4]

---

[1] So Zeus and other Greek gods.   [2] See below, § 1041 ff.   [3] See below, § 635.

[4] The moral perfection of the individual is an ideal that has arisen out of social
relations ; it is demanded by the deity because the moral standard of a deity is that
of his human society.

582. Thus, the necessity for the protection of life and property (including wives and children) has produced certain rules of conduct, which are at first handed on orally and maintained by custom, and gradually are formulated in written codes. The protection of the tribal life is secured by the tribal leaders as representatives of society. The protection of individual interests is at first in the hands of the individuals concerned, but always under the sanction of society. The murderer, the thief, and the adulterer are dealt with by the person injured or by his clan or family, in accordance with generally recognized regulations. As social life becomes more elaborate, such regulations become more numerous and more discriminating; every new ethical rule springs from the necessity of providing for some new social situation. In all communities the tendency is toward taking the protection of interests out of the hands of the individual and committing it to the community; this course is held to be for the advantage of society.[1]

583. As men are constituted, to account for the growth of moral customs we need to assume only social life; practically all our requirements that refer to the relations between men are found among early tribes, and it may be taken for granted that any body of human beings, living together and having some form of activity, would work out some such system of rules, mostly negative or prohibitive but also to some extent positive. Even the law of kindness, a product of natural human sympathy, exists among the lowest known peoples. The reference of moral growth to social necessities does not involve the denial of a germinal sense of right and wrong or of germinal moral ideals, but this sense and these ideals arise, through reflection, from experience. We are here concerned only with the actual conduct of men traceable in the early forms of society.

584. But while social life is the basis of ethical construction, the actual ethical constitution of men has been influenced by religion, in later times by the supplying of lofty ideals and sanctions, in early times by a magical determination of things injurious. It is this second category that is covered by the term 'taboo,' a

---

1 In international relations this tendency appears in the demand for arbitration.

Polynesian word said to mean ' what is prohibited.' Prohibitions arising from natural human relations constitute civil law; those arising from extrahuman or other magical influences constitute taboo.[1]

585. Early man, regarding all objects as possibly endowed with power, selects out of the whole mass by observation and experience certain objects which affect his life, his relations with which he finds it desirable to define. These are all mysterious;[2] some are helpful, some harmful. The helpful objects become lucky stones, amulets. The injurious or dangerous objects are the more numerous; in an atmosphere of uncertainty the mysterious is dreaded, avoided, and guarded against by rules.[3]

586. The objects affected by the conception of taboo are as various as the conditions of human life — they include things inanimate and animate, and events and experiences of all sorts. Sometimes the danger is supposed to be inherent in the object, sometimes the quality of dangerousness is imposed on it or infused into it by some authority; but in all cases there is present the force (mana) that, in savage theory, makes the external world a factor in human destinies.[4] This force may be transmitted from one object to another (usually by contact[5]), and thus the taboo infection may spread indefinitely, a silent and terrible source of misfortune, sometimes to a single person, sometimes to a whole community. Ceremonies connected with taboo are designed to protect against this destructive influence.

1 N. W. Thomas, article " Taboo " in *Encyclopædia Britannica*, 11th ed.; Codrington, *The Melanesians*; Thomson, *Story of New Zealand*; A. van Gennep, *Tabou et totémisme à Madagascar*; Wallace, *Malay Archipelago*, p. 149 f.; J. G. Frazer, *Early History of the Kingship*; Marett, " Is Taboo a Negative Magic? " (in *Anthropological Essays presented to E. B. Tylor*).

2 Cf. the Chickasa *hullo*, said to mean ' mysterious' (Speck, in *Journal of American Folklore*, xx, 57).

3 The danger from such objects is referred to a supernatural presence, whose attitude toward human beings may be doubtful; only, when the phenomenon observed is thought to be nonnatural and is afflictive (as in the case of death, for example), this attitude is judged to be hostile.

4 Purely economic and other social considerations are sometimes combined with the mana conception.

5 The physical unity produced by contact may be brought about, according to savage philosophy, in other ways.

587. The principal taboo usages may be classed roughly under certain heads, which, however, will sometimes overlap one another.

588. *Taboos connected with the conception of life.* For early man the central mystery of the world was life, and mystery and danger attached to all things connected with its genesis, maintenance, and cessation — to pregnancy, birth, death, corpses, funerals, blood. Against these things precautions, in the form of various restrictions, had to be taken. Pregnancy was sometimes regarded as due to supernatural agency, and in all cases was noted as a mysterious condition in which the woman was peculiarly exposed to evil influences; she was sometimes required to keep her head covered or to avoid moonshine, or to live separated from her husband.[1]

589. Care for women during pregnancy and after the birth of a child might be induced by natural human kindliness. But certain usages in connection with birth indicate fear of superhuman dangers. In many regions (Central Asia, Africa, Oceania, China) the mother is taboo for a certain time, being regarded apparently as a source of danger to others, as well as being herself exposed to danger. The child also is surrounded by perils. Mother and child are protected by isolation, ablutions (baptism), amulets, conjurations, and by consecration to a deity.[2] The intimate relation between father and child may make it necessary to impose taboos on the former — he is sometimes required to go to bed (the *couvade*, or man-childbed), to abstain from work and from certain foods held to be injurious, and to avoid touching weapons and other dangerous things; thus, through the identity of father and child, the latter is guarded against the hostile mana that may be lurking near. The seclusion of the mother sometimes varies in duration according to the sex of the child; in most cases, apparently, the period is longer for a male child;[3] in the Jewish ritual the period for the maid-child is twice as great (eighty days) as that for the male;[4] the difference

---

[1] Ploss-Bartels, *Das Weib*, i, 591; cf. E. S. Hartland, *Primitive Paternity*; **Avesta**, *Vendidad*, xv, 8.

[2] Article " Birth " in Hastings, *Encyclopædia of Religion and Ethics.*

[3] Ploss-Bartels, *Das Weib*, ii, 345 ff.

[4] Lev. xii. In the modern Parsi usage a woman after giving birth is secluded forty days.

in the points of view, perhaps, is that the evil influence may direct itself particularly against, or be more serious for, the male as socially the more important, or it may be more dangerous for the female as the weaker.[1]

590. *Taboos connected with death.* The danger to the living arising from a death is of a twofold nature: the corpse, as a strange, uncanny thing, is a source of peril; and there are possible external enemies — the spirit that produced the death, and the ghost of the departed. Against these dangerous things avoidance of the corpse is the common precaution — a dead body must not be touched, or, if it is touched, he who touches must undergo purification.[2] Perhaps the various modes of disposing of corpses (exposure, inhumation, cremation) were originally attempts to get rid of their dangerous qualities; later other motives came in. The body of a suicide was especially feared, and was staked down on a public way to prevent its reappearance; it was perhaps the abnormal and desperate character of the death that produced this special fear. The dread of a corpse is, however, not universal among savages — in many cases it is eaten, simply as food or to acquire the qualities of the deceased, or for other reasons. It is feared as having hurtful power, it is eaten as being sacred or helpful.

591. The house in which a death occurs shares the evil power of the dead body, and sometimes must be destroyed, together with all its furniture, or abandoned or purified.[3] Death diffuses its baleful influence through the atmosphere, making it unfavorable for ordinary work, which, accordingly, is often then suspended for a time.[4] Seclusion is sometimes enjoined on widower or widow,[5] and mention of the name of the deceased is forbidden — the identity of spouse or name with the dead effects the transmission of what is

---

[1] On the relation between birth customs and systems of relationship (patrilineal and matrilineal) see the references in Hastings, *Encyclopædia of Religion and Ethics*, ii, 636.

[2] Numb. xix, 11 ff. For the Mazdean rules see Tiele-Gehrich, *Geschichte der Religion im Altertum*, ii, 340 ff.

[3] Sanitary purposes may have entered into such customs.

[4] Seligmann, *The Melanesians of British New Guinea*, chap. xxiii, p. 138, etc.; Turner, *Samoa*, p. 145 f.; Kidd, *The Essential Kafir*, p. 253.

[5] Ellis, *The Ewe-speaking Peoples*, p. 160.

dangerous in him. In another direction the earthly dwelling of a dead person is protected—a curse is pronounced on one who violates it.[1]

592. *Taboos connected with woman and the relations between the sexes.* Among many peoples there is dread of the presence of women and of their belongings under certain circumstances.[2] The ground of this fear may lie in those physiological peculiarities of woman which are regarded as mysterious and dangerous, and the antagonism of feeling may have been increased by the separation between the sexes consequent on the differences in their social functions and their daily pursuits. Woman seems to move in a sphere different from that of man; she acts in ways that are strange to him. Whatever its ground, the feeling of dread is a real one: a case is reported of a man who, on learning that he had lain down on his wife's blanket, became violently ill.

593. Various restrictions are imposed on women at periods of sexual crisis. The girl on reaching the age of puberty is generally (though not always[3]) immured, sometimes for weeks or months, to shield her from noxious influences, human and nonhuman. During menstruation a woman is isolated, may not be looked on by the sun, must remain apart from her husband, and her food is strictly regulated.[4] It is not infrequently the case that certain foods are permanently forbidden women, for what special reasons is not clear.[5] The rule forbidding a wife to eat with her husband may have come originally from nonreligious social considerations (her subordination to the man, or the fact that she belonged to a social group different from his), but in that case it later acquired a religious character. Women have commonly been excluded in savage communities from solemn ceremonies (as those of the initiation of males) and from tribal councils;[6] such rules may have originated in the natural differentiation of social functions of the sexes or in the

---

[1] Cicero, *De Legibus*, ii, 26 (Athens); Roman *Digests*, xlvii, 12; *Corpus Inscriptionum Semiticarum*, i, 13 (Phœnician); and so among many savage and half-civilized peoples.   [2] Crawley, *The Mystic Rose*, chap. iii.

[3] Seligmann, *The Melanesians of British New Guinea*, p. 140.

[4] Ploss-Bartels, *Das Weib*, i, 296, 302, 374, 618.

[5] Frazer, article "Taboo" in *Encyclopædia Britannica*, 9th ed.

[6] Seligmann, *The Melanesians of British New Guinea*, p. 466; Crawley, *The Mystic Rose*, p. 52 ff.

desire of men to keep the control of tribal life in their own hands, but in many cases the presence of women was supposed to vitiate the proceedings supernaturally. In industrial enterprises, such as hunting and fishing, they are sometimes held to be a fatal influence.[1] In family life a wife's mother was debarred from all social intercourse with her son-in-law.[2]

594. Where procreation was ascribed to the union of the sexes, sexual intercourse, as being intimately connected with life, was credited with supernatural potency, generally unfavorable to vigor.[3] It has been largely prohibited on all important public occasions, such as hunting and war, and particularly in connection with religious ceremonies.[4] Various considerations may have contributed to the establishment of such customs, but in their earliest form we have, probably, to recognize not any moral effort to secure chastity, but a dread of injurious mana resident in women.[5] We may compare the fact that women have often been regarded as specially gifted in witchcraft.[6]

595. *Taboos connected with great personages.* The theory of mana includes the belief that special supernatural power resides in the persons of tribal leaders, such as magicians, chiefs, priests. It follows that danger attaches to their bodies (particularly to head, hair, and nails), to their names, and to their food and other belongings. These things must be avoided : their food must not be eaten by common folk ; their houses and other property must not be used ; their nail-cuttings must be buried so that danger may be averted from the community ; their names must not be mentioned. They themselves, being peculiarly sensitive to malign influences, must be protected in the house and when they walk out ; and it is

---

[1] G. Brown, *Melanesians and Polynesians*, p. 241 ; W. H. Furness, 3d, *The Island of Stone-Money*, p. 38 f.   [2] Crawley, *The Mystic Rose*, p. 399 ff.

[3] A physiological basis for this view seems to lie outside the resources of savage observation, but prohibition of intercourse just after childbirth may have a humanitarian basis.

[4] G. Brown, *Melanesians and Polynesians*, pp. 68, 80, 200 ; Seligmann, *The Melanesians of British New Guinea*, p. 292 ; W. R. Smith, *Religion of the Semites*, additional note C.

[5] Cf. Westermarck, *Origin and Development of the Moral Ideas*, ii, 406 ff. ; Hobhouse, *Morals in Evolution*, Index, s.v. *Chastity*.

[6] See below, § 895 ff. ; Westermarck, op. cit., i, 620 ff.

in some cases not safe for the common man to look on the chief as he passes through the village.

596. Not all these regulations are found in any one community, but the principle is the same everywhere. The greatest development of taboo power in chiefs occurs in Polynesia, the home of taboo. There they are all-powerful. Whatever a chief touches becomes his property. If he enters a house, steps into a canoe, affixes his name to a field, it is his. His control appears to be limited only by the accident of his momentary desire. No one thinks of opposing his decisions — that would be fatal to the opposer. This social situation passes when a better form of civil government is established, but some features of the old conception cling to later dignitaries: till recently the nail-parings of the emperor of Japan were carefully disposed of lest, being inadvertently touched, they should bring misfortune.

597. A priest also may carry taboo infection on his person. In Ezekiel's scheme of ritual organization it is ordered that when the priest, having offered sacrifice, goes forth into the outer court where the people are, he shall put off the garments in which he ministered and lay them in a sacred place, and put on other garments, lest some one touching him should be made ritually unclean, that is taboo, forbidden to mingle with his fellows or to do his ordinary work for a certain time (generally till the evening).[1] In many regions there have been and are numerous restrictions on priests, some of which are in their own interests (to preserve their ritual purity), some in the interests of others (to guard them against the infection of taboo).[2] Other quasi-official or devoted persons (as, for example, the Hebrew Nazirite[3]) were subject to restrictions of

[1] Ezek. xliv, 19. The term "sanctify" of the English Version means 'make ritually sacred,' not to be touched. Cf. Shortland, *Southern Districts of New Zealand*, p. 293 f.; Wellhausen, *Reste arabischen Heidentumes*, p. 106 f.

[2] For Jewish rules see Lev. xxi. The onerous restrictions on the Roman flamen dialis and his wife are given in Frazer's *Golden Bough* (see Index, s.v. *Flamen dialis*) and the authorities cited by him.

[3] The prohibition of the products of the grapevine to the Nazirite (Numb. vi, 3 f.) seems to have been originally part of the attempt to follow the old pastoral life, in contrast with the Canaanite agricultural life; later it received a religious coloring. The prohibition might begin at the moment of the child's conception (Judg. xiii, 4, 14).

food. Strangers, who in a primitive period were frequently put
to death, in a more humane period were subjected to purifying
processes in order to remove the taboo infection that might cling
to them.[1]

598. *Industrial taboos.* The customs of certain Polynesian
chiefs, described above, cannot be said to aid industry, but there
are taboo usages designed to protect and further popular occupations. These doubtless have a natural nonmagical basis — the
necessity of making good crops and protecting private property
would be recognized everywhere, and would call forth legal enactments; but it was inevitable, in certain communities, that such
enactments should be strengthened by supernatural sanctions such
as those offered by the conception of taboo.

599. Protective arrangements of this sort abound in Oceania
and Indonesia. In Samoa the sweet-potato fields are taboo till
the crop is gathered.[2] Hawaiian fisheries are protected by the simple device of forbidding the taking of certain fish at certain seasons;
here the economic motive is obvious, but taboo penalties are an-
nexed.[3] During planting time in New Zealand all persons employed
in the work were taboo for other occupations and obliged to give
all their time to the planting; and the same rule held for hunting
and fishing.[4] The Borneo Kayans refrain from their usual occupations during planting, harvesting, and the search for camphor.[5]
Similar restrictions, of an elaborate kind, are in force in Sumatra,[6]
and in Assam.[7]

600. The property of private persons was protected: the common man might impose a taboo on his land, crops, house, and garments, and these were then safe from depredation. It was true,
however, in New Zealand as elsewhere, that the potency of the imposed taboo depended on the influence of him who imposed it;
chiefs, as uniting in their persons civil and religious authority, were

---

[1] Frazer, *Golden Bough*, 2d ed., i, 299 ff.   [2] Turner, *Samoa.*
[3] Alexander, *Short History of the Hawaiian People.*
[4] R. Taylor, *New Zealand*, chap. viii.
[5] Furness, *Home Life of the Borneo Head-hunters*, p. 160 ff.
[6] C. S. Hurgronje, *The Achehnese*, p. 262 ff.
[7] T. C. Hodson, in *Journal of the Anthropological Institute*, xxxvi.

the most powerful persons in the community, and taboos ordered by them were the most effective. In Melanesia taboo is largely employed for the protection of private property — curses are pronounced against trespassers, and the authority of the tabooer is reënforced by that of the local spirit or ghost (*tindalo*);[1] here taboo has become definitely an element of civil law, in which it tends to be absorbed.

601. *Taboos connected with other important social events.* It appears that all occurrences supposed to affect the life of the community have been, and often still are, regarded as bringing with them, or as attended by, supernatural influences (resident in mana or in spirits) that may be dangerous. Against these perils the usual precautions are taken, one of the commonest (as in cases mentioned in the preceding paragraphs) being abstinence from ordinary work; the belief, apparently, is that such work is tainted with the injurious influence with which the atmosphere is charged.

602. Among religious ceremonies the expulsion of evil spirits was naturally attended with danger, and work was prohibited. Such was the custom in Athens at the Anthesteria and on the sixth day of the Thargelia, and in Rome at the Lemuria.[2] Among existing tribes there are numerous examples of this sort of restriction: it is found in West Africa[3] and in Indonesia (Kar Nicobar, Bali[4]); in Assam it takes the form of a taboo (*genna*) for laying to rest the ghosts of all who have died within the year[5] (an All Souls ceremony).

603. In general, sacred seasons, times of great communal ceremonies, demand the avoidance of ordinary pursuits, which, it is feared, may imperil the success of the ceremonies by necessitating contact with things infected or nonsacred. The earlier Hebrew usage recognized such seasons (new moon, sabbath, and perhaps others); the later usage increased the number of tabooed

---

[1] Codrington, *The Melanesians*, p. 215 ff.

[2] Harrison, *Prolegomena to the Study of Greek Religion*, pp. 50, 96 ff.; Fowler, *Roman Festivals*, p. 106 ff.   [3] Frazer, *Golden Bough*, 2d ed., iii, 76 f.

[4] *Journal of the Anthropological Institute*, xxxii; Frazer, op. cit., iii, 80.

[5] T. C. Hodson, "The Genna amongst the Tribes of Assam" (in *Journal of the Anthropological Institute*, xxxvi).

days as the ritual was expanded and organized.[1] For Greece we have. the Plynteria, on the principal day of which work was suspended;[2] in Rome the feriae were such days, regular or occasional.[3] The inbringing of first fruits was a peculiarly solemn occasion, when gratitude to the deity mingled with fear of hostile influences; so among the Hebrews[4] and at Athens[5] and in Tonga.[6] Polynesian restrictions on the occasion of ceremonies are given by Ellis.[7] All such days of abstinence from ordinary work tend to become holidays, times of popular amusement, and a taboo element may be suspected in such festivals as those of the later Hindu period.[8] Naturally, also, days of restriction become sacred to deities.

604. Great nonreligious tribal events and peculiar situations demand restrictive precautions. Warriors prepare for an expedition by remaining apart from their wives.[9] Women whose husbands are absent are sometimes immured or forbidden all intercourse with human beings; by reason of the identity of husband and wife supernatural harm to the latter will affect the former. Afflictive occurrences, such as famines, pestilences, earthquakes, are signs of some hostile supernatural power, defense against which requires the avoidance of ordinary pursuits. Arbitrary enactments by chiefs may attach restrictions to a particular day. Sometimes restrictive usages, of obscure origin, become communal law. Thus, every Toda clan has certain days of the week (not the occasion of special ceremonies) in which it is forbidden to follow ordinary occupations; among the things forbidden are the giving of feasts, the performance of funeral ceremonies, the cutting of nails, and shaving; women and dairymen may not leave the village, and the people and buffaloes may not move from one place to another.[10] Doubtless this system of prohibitions is the outcome of many generations of experience — the organization of various local usages.

[1] Lev. xxiii; Numb. xxviii f.
[2] Stengel and Oehmichen, *Griechische Sakralaltertümer*, p. 170.
[3] Wissowa, *Religion der Römer*, p. 365 ff.   [4] Numb. xxviii, 26.
[5] The Thargelia; Harrison, op. cit., chap. iii.   [6] Mariner, *Tonga*, p. 483.
[7] W. Ellis, *Polynesian Researches*, iv, 388, etc.
[8] Cf. Hopkins, *Religions of India*, p. 448 ff.
[9] Cf. W. R. Smith, *Religion of the Semites*, additional note C.
[10] Rivers, *The Todas*, p. 405 ff.

605. *Taboos connected with the moon.* Unusual celestial phenomena, such as eclipses, meteors, and comets, have always excited terror, being referred to some hostile supernatural agency, and have called forth special placative and restrictive ceremonies. They are accounted for in savage lore by various myths.[1] But the permanently important taboos have been those that are associated with the phases of the moon. These periodical transformations, unexplained and mysterious, seemed to early man to have vital relation with all earthly life — the waxing and waning of the moon was held to determine, through the sympathy existing between all things, the growth and decay of plants, animals, and men.[2] Hence arose the widely diffused belief that all important undertakings should be begun while the moon was increasing, and innumerable regulations for the conduct of affairs were established, not a few of them surviving in civilized popular belief and practice to the present day.

606. Sometimes the changes in the moon are minutely observed. The Nandi describe every day of the month by the appearance of the moon or by its relation to occupations.[3] Natural observation in some cases divided the lunar month into four parts: the Buddhist uposatha days are the four days in the lunar month when the moon is full or new or halfway between the two;[4] in Hawaii the 3d–6th, 14th–15th, 24th–25th, 27th–28th days of every month were taboo periods;[5] the Babylonians had five such periods in certain months (four periods with one period intercalated). But, though the quartering of the lunation may seem to us the most natural division of the month, in actual practice it is rather the exception.[6] The simplest division, indeed, is that into two parts, determined by new moon and full moon (Cambodia, Siam; cf. the Mexican period of thirteen days). The division into three periods

---

[1] Tylor, *Primitive Culture*, i, 288, 354.

[2] For details see Frazer, *Adonis Attis Osiris*, bk. iii, chap. viii f.

[3] Hollis, *The Nandi*, p. 95 f.

[4] Rhys Davids, *Buddhism* (in *Non-Christian Religious Systems*), p. 140 f. Thus, as the author remarks, uposatha is a weekly festival; and there is an approach to a true seven-day week.   [5] Alexander, *Short History of the Hawaiian People*.

[6] Details of the week are given in the article " Calendar " in Hastings, *Encyclopædia of Religion and Ethics*, with references to authorities.

of ten days each (Egypt, Greece, Annam, Japan) ignores lunar phases and seeks a convenient and symmetrical arrangement. With this decimal system is perhaps connected the division of the month into six periods of five days each (Yoruba, Java, Sumatra, and perhaps Babylonia). The Romans had a somewhat irregular official division of the first half of the month into three parts (Kalends, Nones, Ides) corresponding in a general way to lunar phases, and also commercial periods of eight days (*nundinae*), perhaps of similar origin. A seven-day division is found in Ashantiland (and perhaps in Peru), and in Java there is reported a division of a year into thirty periods of seven days each.

607. It appears, then, that in several communities there has been a division of the month in the interests of convenience, without regard to lunar phases; that in several cases a seven-day week has been fallen upon; and that of the phases of the moon new moon and full moon have been most frequently looked to as chronological marks. The new moon, apart from its function of indicating the beginning of the lunar month, has also by many tribes been hailed with joy as a friend restored to life after seeming extinction.[1] The full moon, while it has not entered so intimately into the emotional life of man, has played an important part by marking the division of the month into two equal parts.

608. *The Hebrew sabbath.* Taboo days are days of abstinence from work, set apart as seasons of rest.[2] Such was the original form of the Hebrew sabbath — it is described in the earlier Old Testament notices simply as a day on which ordinary work was unlawful.[8] The history of its precise origin and development is, however, by no means clear. Theories that derive it from the cult

---

[1] Hollis, *The Nandi*, p. 79; Frazer, *Adonis Attis Osiris*, pp. 370 ff., 375.

[2] See the noteworthy Yoruban rest day, the first day of the five-day week (A. B. Ellis, *Yoruba*).

[8] For the literature on the sabbath see Herzog-Hauck, *Real-Encyklopädie*; Jastrow, in *American Journal of Theology* for 1898; Cheyne, *Encyclopædia Biblica*; Hastings, *Dictionary of the Bible*; *Jewish Encyclopedia*; F. Bohn, *Der Sabbat im Alten Testament*; Benzinger, *Hebräische Archäologie*; Nowack, *Hebräische Archäologie*; C. H. Toy, "The Earliest Form of the Sabbath," in *Journal of Biblical Literature* for 1899 (in which, so far as appears, the view that the Hebrew sabbath is a taboo day is stated for the first time).

of some particular deity or regard it as primarily a day for placating a supernatural Power[1] may be set aside. It may be assumed that it is an early institution somehow connected with the moon, and a definite indication of origin appears to be furnished by the fact that in a Babylonian inscription the term *shabattu*[2] is used for the full moon. The identification of Hebrew sabbath with full moon is favored by the collocation of new moon and sabbath in early Old Testament documents[3] as days on which trading was unlawful. These, obviously, were the two chief taboo days of the month; the fact that new moon stands first is doubtless due to its position in the month.

609. It is uncertain whether the Babylonian full-moon day was ritually particularly important, and it is not clear how the Hebrews came to invest this day, if it was their sabbath, with peculiar significance. In the earlier legal documents it is merely a restrictive period — man and beast are to rest from toil;[4] in later codes religious motives for the observance of the day are introduced — first, gratitude to Yahweh for the rescue of the nation from Egyptian bondage, and then respect for the fact that Yahweh worked in creating the world six days and stopped work on the seventh day.[5] In the sixth century we find the sabbath elevated to the position of specific sign of Yahweh's protective relation to the people, and still later it is regarded as a day of joyous obedience to divine law.[6] Thus, the process of moralization of the day was probably a long-continued one.[7]

---

[1] Any taboo day might be the occasion of placative ceremonies; but this is not a distinctive feature of the day.

[2] T. G. Pinches, in *Proceedings of the Society of Biblical Archæology*, xxvi, 51 ff.; Zimmern, in *Zeitschrift der deutschen morgenländischen Gesellschaft*, lviii, 199 ff., 458 ff.; J. Meinhold, *Sabbat und Woche im Alten Testament*. There is no good reason to doubt that this Babylonian term is formally identical with Hebrew *shabat*.

[3] 2 Kings iv, 23 ; Amos viii, 5 ; Isa. i, 13.   [4] Exod. xxiii, 6.

[5] Deut. v, 12 ff.; Exod. xx, 8 ff.; the term 'holy' here means set apart ritually, that is, taboo.

[6] Ezek. xx, 12 f., 16, 20 f., 24; Isa. lviii, 13 f.; cf. article "Sabbath" in *Jewish Encyclopedia*.

[7] The Hebrew stem *shabat* means 'to cease,' a signification that accords well with the character of a taboo day. But this sense has not been certainly found for the Babylonian stem, and the original force of the term *sabbath* may be left undecided.

610. In the various experimental divisions of the month, as we have seen, a week of seven days has been approached independently in several places (Babylonia, Hawaii, Java, Ashantiland). The basis of this division is doubtless the quartering of the lunation, and it has been reënforced, probably, by considerations of convenience — seven is an intermediate number, six days of work and one of abstinence and rest (holiday) commends itself as a practical arrangement. It appears among the Hebrews as early as the eighth century B.C.;[1] it may have been derived from or suggested by Babylonian usage, or it may have been an ancient Hebrew custom — data on this point are lacking. In any case the Jewish genius for religious organization seized on the seven-day scheme and wove it into the system of worship. A more important step taken by the Jews was the ignoring of lunar phases (except, of course, new moon as the beginning of the month) and reckoning the week and the seventh day (the sabbath) in a continuous line. We have noted cases in which lunar phases were ignored, but this Jewish arrangement appears to be unique, and its simplicity and convenience have commended it to the world.

611. *Lucky and unlucky days.* The malefic influences emanating from various objects and resident in the air attached themselves to certain days, and out of the vast mass of experiences in every community there grew up systems of days when things might or might not be done with safety and advantage. There were the great occasions, economic and astronomical, referred to above, and there were particular occurrences, such as a death or a defeat, that stamped a day as unlucky. There are many such beliefs, the origin of which is lost in a remote antiquity. The ancient civilized nations had their codes of luck. Egypt had a long list of unlucky days.[2] In Babylonia onerous restrictions were imposed on kings, seers, and physicians on certain days (the 7th, 14th, 19th, 21st, 28th) of the sixth and eighth months[3] (and perhaps of other months).

---

[1] Exod. xxiii, 12.

[2] Chabas, *Le calendrier des jours fastes et néfastes*; Maspero, *Études égyptiennes*, i, 28 ff.; Wiedemann, *Religion of the Ancient Egyptians*, chap. x.

[3] IV Rawlinson, plates, 32 f.; Jastrow, *Religion of Babylonia and Assyria*, p. 373 ff.

A brief list of days favorable and unfavorable to work is given by Hesiod.[1] The Roman *dies nefasti*, properly 'irreligious days,' were inauspicious, unlucky.[2] Similar lists of lucky and unlucky days are found among existing tribes,[3] and the popular luck codes in Christian communities are numerous and elaborate.[4] These have done, and still do, great harm by substituting irrational for rational rules of conduct.

612. In many of the cases cited above and in many totemistic regulations there are prohibitions of particular sorts of food. Such prohibitions, very numerous, are found in all grades of civilization.[5] They have arisen from various causes — climatic conditions, hygienic beliefs, religious conceptions (as, for example, the recognition of the sacred character of certain animals, and the connection of certain foods with supernatural beings and ceremonies [6]), sometimes, perhaps, from accidental experiences; the history of most of the particular usages escapes us. The fundamental principle involved is the identity of the food with him who eats it — when it is charged with supernatural power (by its own sacredness, or by its connection with a sacred person, or by ecclesiastical decree) it becomes malefic to an unauthorized person who partakes of it.

613. A peculiar form of prohibition of foods appears when a society is divided into groups that are kept apart from one another by social and religious traditions that have hardened into civic rules. In such cases the diet of every group may be regulated by law, and it may become dangerous and abhorrent for a superior to eat what has been touched by an inferior. The best example of this

---

[1] Hesiod, *Works and Days*, 763 ff.

[2] Wissowa, *Religion der Römer*, p. 365 ff.; Fowler, *Roman Festivals*, Index. The Romans, with their thoroughness where public religion was concerned, divided all the days of the year into the three classes, *dies festi* (festive, for worship), *dies profesti* (for ordinary business), and *dies intercisi* (mixed, partly for religion, partly for ordinary affairs).

[3] Hastings, *Encyclopædia of Religion and Ethics*, iii, 29 (Burma).

[4] J. H. King, *The Supernatural*, Index, s.v. *Luck*.

[5] Many examples are given in Westermarck's *Origin and Development of the Moral Ideas*, chap. xxxvii f.; cf. above, § 204 ff., on fasting.

[6] Howitt, *Native Tribes of South-East Australia*, p. 630 ff.

sort of organization is the Hindu system of castes, which has a marked and unhappy effect on the life of the people.[1] All such arbitrary social divisions yield gradually to the influence of education and civic freedom, and this appears to be the tendency in India at the present day.

614. *Punishment of violation of taboo.* Where the hostile power is inherent in an object, punishment is supposed to follow violation automatically — through contact the malefic influence passes into the man's body and works destruction. Many experiences seem to the savage to establish the certainty of such a result. Fervid belief, moreover, produced by long tradition, acts powerfully on the imagination, and in taboo-ridden communities thus often brings about the bodily ill called for by the theory: a man who ate of food that he found on the roadside, learning afterwards that it belonged to a chief, fell ill and died in a few hours.[2] When taboo regulations have been taken up into the civil law,[3] punishment for violations is inflicted by the civil authorities. The tendency to make taboo a part of the civil law, and to subordinate the former to the latter, increases with the advance of knowledge and political organization; and one result of this movement is that great personages are sometimes permitted to violate with impunity taboos imposed by inferiors. The native theory in such cases doubtless is that the great man's mana overcomes the taboo infection; but at bottom, we may surmise, lies the sense of the dominance of civil authority.

615. The chief's mana, however, sometimes comes into play as a means of relief. A man who has inadvertently (or perhaps, in some instances, purposely) violated a taboo may escape punishment by touching some part of a chief's body. Here the innate potency of the superior man expels or destroys the taboo force that has entered the inferior — another example of how the primitive theory of taboo is modified by conceptions of social rank and authority.

---

[1] E. A. Gait, article " Caste " in Hastings, *Encyclopædia of Religion and Ethics.*
[2] Frazer, *Golden Bough*, 2d ed., i, 321.
[3] Taboo thus helps the growth of civil law (especially of penal codes) by its collection of offenses, though only on condition of retiring from the field. Cf. Frazer, *Psyche's Task*, p. 17 ff.

616. *Removal of taboo.* In general, magical ceremonies may be employed to counteract the injurious influence resident in a thing or an act, or to destroy the evil consequences resulting from a violation of the taboo law. For this purpose sprinkling with water, bathing in water, and the employment of charms are held to be effective. Thus in the old Hebrew code the taboo resting on a house supposed to be infected with the plague is removed by sprinkling the house with water and the blood of a slain bird, and setting free a second bird alive, which is supposed to carry the plague-power off with it.[1] A woman is tabooed forty days at the birth of a male child, and eighty days at the birth of a female child; the taboo is removed by a holocaust and a sin-offering.[2]

617. A general taboo regulation may be set aside by tribal agreement in the interests of convenience or pleasure. On certain occasions the restrictions on the intercourse of the sexes are removed for a brief period, at the expiration of which the prohibitory law resumes its place.[8] Many special ceremonies in various parts of the world have to do with modifications of marriage laws.[4]

618. *Taboo and magic.* Reference is made above to magical procedures in connection with taboo customs. Taboo and magic have a common basis in the conception of an occult force (which may conveniently be called *mana*) resident in all things, but they contemplate different sides of this force, and their social developments are very different. Taboo recognizes the inherent malefic manifestations of the force (known by supposed experience), and avoids them; magic uses the mana energy to effect results impossible for unaided human power. In taboo man feels himself to be under the dominance of an occult law, and his virtue is blind obedience; in magic he feels himself to be the master of a great energy, and what he needs is knowledge. Taboo has originated a mass of irrational rules for the guidance of everyday life; magic

---

[1] Lev. xiv, 48–53. [2] Lev. xii.

[8] So in many popular festivals; see Spencer and Gillen, *Native Tribes of Central Australia*; Hopkins, *Religions of India*, p. 453 ff.; Westermarck, *Origin and Development of the Moral Ideas*, chap. xlii.

[4] Examples are given in Crawley's *Mystic Rose*, pp. 223, 480 ff., chap. x ff.

has grown into a quasi-science, with an organized body of adepts, touching religion on one side and real science on another side.

619. A closer relationship between magic and taboo has been assumed in view of the fact that both rest to some extent on the principle of the association of ideas, the principle that like procedures produce like results. It is true that some taboo rules depend on this conception: [1] the flesh of timid animals is avoided, that of courageous animals is eaten, under the belief that the man partakes of the character of the food he eats; association with women is sometimes supposed to make a man or a boy effeminate. It is to be expected that in the immense number of taboo prohibitions and precautions some should be found in which the association of ideas is the determining factor. But for the majority of taboo regulations this explanation does not hold. In the economic and sexual taboos mentioned above, in the dread of corpses, in the fear of touching things belonging to a chief, and in other cases there are customs that can only be referred to a belief in an injurious potency residing in certain objects. [2] Practically, savage tribes distinguish between taboo and magic.

620. Contamination of customs has always been the rule in human communities, early and late, savage and civilized. We have seen how there has often been a coalescence between taboo regulations proper and ordinary civil law. To state the case more fully, these have been fused into a unity of social life with individual initiative, magical notions, arbitrary enactments. The actual social constitution even of slightly developed tribes is composite, the outcome of long experience and experiment in which all the lines of social feeling and thought have gradually drawn together and been compacted into a more or less unitary mass. While these lines have influenced each the others, it is possible, to a considerable

---

[1] Tylor, *Early History of Mankind*, 3d ed., p. 129 ff.; Hubert and Mauss, in *Année sociologique*, vii; Frazer, *Early History of the Kingship*, lecture ii, especially p. 52 ff. (he defines taboo as "negative magic," magic, that is, employed to avoid malefic influences); cf. Crawley, *The Mystic Rose*, chap. ix, for the transmission of sex characteristics.

[2] Cf. R. R. Marett, " Is Taboo a Negative Magic?" (reply to Frazer), in *Anthropological Essays presented to E. B. Tylor*.

extent, to distinguish the sphere of each. Thus we can, in many cases, see where ordinary civil law comes in to adopt, modify, or set aside taboo rules, and so we can generally recognize the line of demarcation between definite taboo and the conception of association of ideas. In some cases the explanations offered of taboo customs are afterthoughts — imagined hypotheses to account for things already in existence.[1]

621. The despotism exercised by taboo systems over certain Polynesian communities is one of the extraordinary facts of human history. In New Zealand and Hawaii the restrictions on conduct were so numerous and were carried out so mercilessly that life under these conditions would seem to us intolerable.[2] In addition to a great number of particular prohibitions and to the constant fear of violating the sacredness of the persons of chiefs and trenching on their prerogatives, we find in New Zealand the amazing rule that on the occasion of a great misfortune (as a fire) the sufferer was to be deprived of his possessions — the blow that fell on him was held to affix a stigma to all that he owned. Besides the traditional taboos there were the arbitrary enactments of chiefs which might constantly introduce new possibilities of suffering. Yet with all this the people managed to live in some degree of comfort, somewhat as in civilized communities life goes on in spite of earthquakes, epidemics, bank failures, the injustices of law, and the tyranny of the powerful.

622. The duration of certain taboo periods among various peoples in various ages has varied greatly. Taboos relating to foods, chiefs, and the intercourse of the sexes are usually permanent everyday customs; those that relate to economic procedures are in force for the time demanded by each industry. In Hawaii the catching of certain species of fish was forbidden for half the year, and the Borneo harvest taboo (carrying prohibition of other work) lasts sometimes for weeks. There is mention in a Maori legend of a taboo of three years.[3] According to the later Hebrew law, in

---

[1] Cf. Marett, op. cit.

[2] R. Taylor, *New Zealand*, chap. viii; Alexander, *Short History of the Hawaiian People*.   [3] Shortland, *Maori Religion*.

every seventh year all agricultural operations ceased.[1] A portent
may demand a long period of restriction, as in the case of the
Roman nine-day ceremony (*novendiales feriae*).[2] As has been remarked above, economic taboos are often dictated by convenience
— they are prudential rules to which a supernatural sanction has
been attached.

623. *Diffusion of taboo.* Polynesia, particularly New Zealand
and Hawaii, is the special home of taboo — the only region in
which it is known to have taken the form of a well-compacted,
all-embracing system. It exists in Melanesia, but it is there less
complicated and general,[3] and the same thing is true of British
New Guinea.[4] In parts of Borneo it is found in modified form:
there are two sorts of taboo, one, called *mali*, absolutely forbidding
work on certain occasions, the other, called *penti*, allowing work if
it is begun by a person not *penti*; before the birth of a child the
latter form of taboo rests on both parents.[5] The Land Dyaks
have their *lali* days and the Sea Dyaks their *pemate*,[6] these terms
being the equivalents of *taboo*.

624. Though there is no proof of the existence of all-pervading
taboo systems among the peoples of Asia and America, there are
notices of taboo regulations in particular cases in these regions. At
the birth of a child the Hindu father was subject to certain restrictions along with the mother, and his taboo was removed by bathing.[7] Among the Sioux Indians on the death of a child the father
is taboo for a period of six months or a year.[8] In West African
Calabar there are taboos (called *ibet*) on individuals, connected
with spirits, the guardians of children.[9] In Assam economic and
other taboos are elaborate and well organized.[10] Such observances,

---

[1] Exod. xxiii, 10 f.   [2] Livy, i, 31.

[3] Codrington, *The Melanesians*, p. 215 ff.; George Brown, *Melanesians and Polynesians*, p. 273 ff.

[4] Seligmann, *The Melanesians of British New Guinea*, Index, s.v. *Taboo*.

[5] H. Ling Roth, *The Natives of Sarawak and British North Borneo*, i, 98.

[6] On *permontong* see W. H. Furness, 3d, *Home Life of the Borneo Head-hunters*,
p. 160 ff.   [7] Manu, v, 62.   [8] Miss Alice Fletcher, *Indian Ceremonies*, p. 297 f.

[9] Miss Mary Kingsley, *Travels*, Index.

[10] T. C. Hodson, "Genna amongst the Tribes of Assam," in *Journal of the Anthropological Institute*, xxxvi (1906).

in connection with death, are found among the Kafirs[1] and the Eskimo.[2]

625. For the ancient civilized peoples there is no proof of the existence of general taboo systems. Various particular prohibitions, involving a sense of danger in certain things, are mentioned above ; they relate chiefly to corpses, to infected houses, to women in connection with menstruation and childbirth,[3] to certain official persons (as the Roman flamen dialis). There are also the lists of unlucky days (Egyptian, Babylonian, Greek, Roman). The origin of food prohibitions (Hebrew, Pythagorean) is uncertain ;[4] they may have arisen, as is suggested above, from general regard for sacred animals and plants, or from totemistic relations, or from other conditions unknown to us ; the Hebrew lists of forbidden animals may have been gradually expanded under the guidance of antagonism to surrounding non-Yahwistic cults. Whether the ancient taboo usages are the remains of older more extensive systems or represent the extreme point to which tabooism was carried by the communities in question the data do not enable us to decide.

626. In various places, outside of the Polynesian area, we find terms that bear a more or less close resemblance in signification to taboo.[5] Melanesian *tambu* is that which has a sacred character.[6] The Borneo terms (*lali, pemate, mali, penti*) are mentioned just above, and there is the *pomali* of Timor (in the Malayan Archipelago). The Malagasy *fady* is defined as 'dangerous, prohibited.'[7] In Gabun (West Africa) *orunda* is said to mean 'prohibited to human beings.'[8] The Hebrew *tamē* is used of things dangerous, not to be touched, ritually defiling,[9] and this sense sometimes

---

[1] Kidd, *The Essential Kafir*, Index.

[2] Boas, in *Sixth Annual Report of the Bureau of American Ethnology*, and *Bulletin XV*, American Museum of Natural History.   [3] Lev. xii–xv.

[4] Deut. xiv ; Lev. xi ; Diogenes Laertius, *Pythagoras*, xvii.

[5] On *tabu* (or *tapu*) see E. Tregear, *Maori-Polynesian Comparative Dictionary* ; W. Ellis, *Polynesian Researches*, iv, 385.   [6] Codrington, *The Melanesians*, p. 215.

[7] A. van Gennep, *Tabou et totémisme à Madagascar*.

[8] R. H. Nassau, *Fetichism in West Africa*, p. 211.

[9] The taboo sense proper is not found in Greek ἅγιος (ἅγος), ἐναγής, and Latin *sacer*, which rather mean what is accursed, detestable on account of wrong committed.

attaches to the term *qadosh* (rendered in the English version by
' holy '), which involves the presence of a supernatural (and therefore dangerous) quality.[1]

627. From all the facts known it may be concluded that the
conception of taboo exists or has existed in some form in a great
'part of the world,[2] though its development has differed greatly in
different regions. In general its prevalence appears to have been
in inverse proportion to that of totemism — it is lacking or feeble
in the chief totemic centers, Australia and North America, and
strongest in Polynesia, where totemism is hardly recognizable. It
may be said that, while totemism appears in those forms of social
life that have been created by hunting communities,[3] taboo is the
product of more settled societies, in which agriculture plays an
important part. But while this is true, at least in a general way,
we are not able to trace all the influences that have determined
the development of totemism and taboo ; some of these are lost
in the obscurity of the remote past, and, unfortunately for purposes of investigation, both taboo and totemism, as we now meet
them in actual operation, are in process of decay. Why, for instance,
taboo has flourished in Hawaii with its fishing industries and has
not flourished in certain half-civilized, partly agricultural North
American tribes we are unable to explain precisely. We may fall
back on the vague statement that every community has accomplished that for which its genius fitted it, but how the genius of
any one people has fitted it for this or that particular task it is
not always possible to say.

628. *The disappearance of the taboo system* in civilized nations is
to be referred to the general advance in intelligence and morality.
Usually this movement is a gradual and silent one, marked by
a quiet dropping of usages as they come to be held unnecessary
or oppressive. Sometimes a bold individual rebels against the
established custom and successfully introduces a new era : thus

---

[1] Sacred books " defile the hands."

[2] Cf. articles " Taboo " in *Encyclopædia Britannica*, 9th ed. (by Frazer) and 11th
ed. (by Thomas).

[3] The relation between totemism and man's attitude toward beasts and plants is
discussed above, §§ 524 ff., 564 ff.

in Yoruba, under an old custom, when a king died his eldest son was obliged to commit suicide ; this custom was set at defiance by a certain Adelu in 1860, and has not since been observed.[1] All the influences that tend to broaden thought go to displace taboo. The growth of clans into tribes, the promotion of voluntary organizations, secret societies, which displace the old totemistic groups, the growth of agriculture and of commercial relations—all things, in a word, that tend to make the individual prominent and to further family life lead naturally to the abrogation of oppressive taboos.

629. Doubtless also among lower tribes intercourse with higher communities has had the same result. One of the most remarkable episodes in the history of taboo is its complete overthrow in the Hawaiian Islands in the year 1819 by a popular movement.[2] The movement was begun by members of the royal family, particularly by one of the queens, and was eagerly followed by almost the whole population — the result was the final overthrow of the system. This was before the arrival of Christian missionaries ; but as foreigners had visited the islands many years before (Captain Cook first came in 1778), it is possible that the suggestion of the reform came from observation of the fact that the taboos were disregarded by those men without evil effects. In any case it was the acceptance of better ideas by the people that led to the revolutionary movement.

630. *Rôle of taboo in the history of religion.* The relation of taboo to morality and religion and to the general organization of society appears from the facts stated above. It has created neither the sense of obligation nor the determination of what is right or wrong in conduct. The sense of obligation is coeval with human society — man, at the moment when he became man, was already potentially a moral being (and a religious being as well).[3] His experience of life induced rules of conduct, and these, with the concurrence of some hardly definable instincts, became imperative for

---

[1] A. B. Ellis, *Yoruba*, p. 167.

[2] Alexander, *Short History of the Hawaiian People*, chap. xxii.

[3] On the question whether a germinal sense of moral obligation is found in the lower animals see above, § 12.

him — the conception involved in the word 'ought' gradually took shape. The practical content of the conception was determined by all sorts of experience; the decisive consideration was whether or not a given thing was advantageous. The belief arose that certain disadvantageous things were to be referred to extrahuman influences, and such things were of course to be avoided — this ·belief produced the taboo system.

631. The prohibitions of morality sprang from social relations with human beings, the prohibitions of taboo from social relations with superhuman beings — duties to both classes of beings were defined by experience. The rule " thou shalt not kill thy clansman" was a necessity of human society; the rule " thou shalt not touch a corpse " sprang from the fear of a superhuman, malign, death-dealing Power. Avoidance of poisonous herbs was an obligation founded on common experience; avoidance of a chief's food and certain other foods arose from dread of offending a spirit or some occult Power. And so with all taboo prescriptions as contrasted with others relating to conduct.[1]

632. Taboo is in essence religious, not moral. In so far as it supplies a supernatural sanction for moral conduct proper and maintains rational social relations (as when a man's wife and other property are made taboo to all but himself), it is often beneficent. On the other hand, it is antimoral when it elevates to the rank of duties actions that have no basis in human relations or are in any way antagonistic to a healthy human instinct of right. This it has often done, and there has accordingly resulted a conflict between it and morality — a conflict that has formed no small part of the ethical history of the race, its echoes remaining to the present day. In all religions it has been hard to bring about an intelligent harmony between the moral and the ritual. Taboo was not originally irrational — it sprang from the belief (rational for the early time) in the presence of the supernatural in certain objects, and this belief was held to be supported by early experience, according to which it seemed that violations of taboo were followed by sickness

---

[1] Naturally, the origin of all the particular taboos escapes us; it depends in most cases on unknown conditions.

or death or other misfortunes. It came to be thought irrational with the progress of knowledge and reflection.

633. Taboo, being a religious conception, has been adopted and fostered by all popular systems of religion. It has been set aside not by religion as such but by all the influences that have tended to rationalize religion. Religious leaders have modified it so far as modification has been demanded by public opinion. So enlightened and spiritualminded a man as the apostle Paul declared that an unworthy participation in the eucharistic celebration produced sickness and death.[1] Innumerable are the taboos that have passed silently into oblivion.

634. Taboo, then, is a concomitant of man's moral life that has sometimes opposed, sometimes coalesced with natural morality. Like all widely extending institutions it has tended in part to weld men together; like all irrational restrictions it has tended also to hold men apart. Like all positive law it has fostered the sense of moral obligation, but like all arbitrary law it has weakened the power of intelligent and moral obedience. It has been not the guardian of morality, but a temporary form (useful in a primitive stage of society) in which a part of the moral law expressed itself. The real moral force of society has been sympathetic social intercourse, which, under the guidance of an implicit moral ideal, has been constantly employed in trying to spiritualize or to reject those enactments of taboo that have been proved by experience, observation, and reflection to be injurious.[2]

[1] 1 Cor. xi, 27–30.
[2] On the social organization of law cf. Darwin, *Descent of Man*, p. 108; article "Aryan Religion" in Hastings, *Encyclopædia of Religion and Ethics*.

CHAPTER VI

GODS

635. The climax of the organization of external religion appears in the conception of gods proper; this conception is always associated with more or less well-developed institutions. Early religious life expresses itself in ceremonies; the god is the embodiment of man's ideal of the extrahuman power that rules the world. It is not always easy to distinguish the true gods from the other supernatural beings with which early man's world is peopled.[1] As far as concerns power, the ghosts and the spirits appear to do all that the gods are credited with doing; the sphere of ghostly action is practically unlimited, and the spirit that dwells in a spring, in a river, or in a mountain, is as mighty in his sphere as Indra or Apollo in his sphere; the difference between them and gods is a difference of intellectual and moral culture and of the degree of naturalization in a human society — a god might be defined as a superhuman Being fashioned by the thought of a civilized people (the term 'civilized' admitting, however, of many gradations). Still, gods proper may be distinguished from other Powers by certain characteristics of person and function. Ghosts are shadowy doubles of human beings, sometimes nameless, wandering about without definite purpose except to procure food for themselves, uncertain of temper, friendly or unfriendly according to caprice or other circumstances, able to help or to harm, and requiring men to be constantly on the alert so as not in an unguarded moment to offend them. Souls of recently deceased ancestors, more highly organized ghosts, conceived of also as attenuated bodies, have powers not essentially different from those of the simpler ghosts, but are differentiated from these in function by their intimate relations with

---

[1] See above, § 240 ff.

the family or clan to which they belong, and by their more definite human nature; they are as a rule permanently friendly, are capable of definite sympathetic social intercourse with living men, and are sometimes controllers and patrons, hardly to be distinguished from local or departmental gods. Spirits are ethereal beings residing in, or closely connected with, certain objects (trees, rivers, springs, stones, mountains, etc.), sometimes permanently attached to these objects, sometimes detached; roaming about, sometimes kindly, more generally inimical, authors of disease and death, to be feared and to be guarded against, but sometimes in function (though not in origin) identical with ancestral ghosts. Totems, in their developed form, are revered, but rarely if ever worshiped. The term ' animal-gods ' may mean either living animals regarded as divine, or animals believed to be the forms assumed by gods; in the latter case they may be taken to be real gods of an inferior type.

In distinction from the four classes of Powers just mentioned, a true god is a supernatural being with distinct anthropomorphic personality, with a proper name or a distinctive title, exercising authority over a certain land or people or over a department of nature or a class of phenomena, dwelling generally in a sanctuary on the earth, or in the sky, or in the other world, and in general sympathetic with men. Gods have rational human qualities, human modes of procedure, and are human beings in all things except power.[1]

636. The god appears to have been at the outset a well-formed anthropomorphic being. His genesis is different from that of the ghost, spirit, ancestor, or totem. These, except the spirit, are all given by experience: totems are familiar objects plainly visible to the eye; ghosts and ancestors are known through dreams and appearances by day, and by tradition; and the conception of the spirit is closely allied to that of the ghost, though it is in part a scientific inference rather than a fact of experience. In distinction from these a god is a larger product of imagination, springing from the necessity of accounting for the existence of things in a relatively refined

---

[1] In a cannibal community, for example, the gods will be cannibal; see A. Lang, *Myth, Ritual, and Religion*, new ed., i, 6, 263 f.

way. The creator is a beast only in low tribes, and in process of
time, if the tribe continues to grow in culture, is absorbed in the
cult of a true god. It is rarely, if ever, that a beast, whether a
totem or only a sacred thing, becomes a god proper.

The best apparent examples of such a growth are the Egyptian
bull Apis, who had his temple and ministers, the Hindu monkey-
god Hanuman, and the divine snake of the Nagas of India.[1] But,
though in these cases the beast forms receive divine worship, it is
not clear whether it is the beast that is worshiped or a god incarnate in the beast; the question is difficult, the data being meager.
The myths in which gods appear in beast forms do not prove a
development of the former out of the latter. It is not necessary to
suppose that Zeus was once a bull, Artemis a bear or a sow, Adonis
a boar, and Aphrodite a sow or a dove. The myths may be naturally
explained as arising from the coalescence of cults, the local sacred
beast becoming attached to a local deity who had a different birth.

The god is a figure of slow growth. Beginning as a sort of headman, identified sometimes with an ancestor, sometimes with a beast,
his character is shaped by all the influences that go to form the
tribal life, and he thus embodies from generation to generation the
tribe's ideals of virtue.

637. The list of classes of supernatural Powers given above
must be regarded, as is there intimated, as a general one. One
class appears sometimes to shade into another; in the theistic
schemes of low tribes it is often difficult to define the conceptions
of supernatural beings with precision.

Early mythical founders of culture. Before proceeding to a consideration of true gods, a class of beings must be mentioned that
appears to stand on the borderland between divine animals, spirits,
and gods. There are various sorts of beings that appear sometimes
in animal form, sometimes in human form, their function being the
arranging of the affairs of the world, the origination of institutions,
and sometimes a definite creation of various things. The title
" founders" or " transformers " or " culture-heroes " has been given

---

[1] Rawlinson, *History of Ancient Egypt*, i, 414 f.; ii, 85, 506; Breasted, *History of
Egypt*, pp. 46, 575; Hopkins, *Religions of India*, pp. 368, 502; ibid., p. 538 f.

them. They arise, just as the true gods do, from the necessity of accounting for the beginnings of things,[1] and, from a comparison of the ideas of various tribes, a certain growth in the conception may be recognized.

638. In some cases the figure is that of a mere trickster, a mischievous being, the hero of countless stories, who acts from caprice or malice, though his actions may result in advantage to men. Such are many of the animal forms of the North American Indians : the coyote of the Thompson River Indians,[2] the raven of North British Columbia,[3] the mink and the blue jay of the North Pacific Coast.[4] In other cases, as also to some extent in the Thompson River region, he appears in a more dignified form as a benevolent organizer.

This growth of the trickster into the real culture-hero may be referred to a progress in thought and refinement.[5] Among the Northern Maidu of California there is a sharp distinction between the two characters : the coyote is tricky and mischievous in the bad sense, with no desire to do anything profitable to men ; the benevolent and useful work of the world is ascribed to a personage called " the creator," who is always dignified and regardful of the interests of man.[6] This sort of distinction, intended to account for the presence of both good and evil elements of life, is found in inchoate form among other low peoples (as, for example, the Masai and the Australians[7]), but reaches its full proportions only in the great civilized religions.

---

[1] They sometimes coalesce in functions with ghosts and spirits.

[2] Teit, *Thompson River Indians*, p. 19 ff.

[3] L. Farrand, " Traditions of the Chilcotin Indians " in *Jesup North Pacific Expedition* (vol. ii of *Memoirs of the American Museum of Natural History*), i, 14 ff.; Farrand and Kahnweiler, " Traditions of the Quinault Indians," ibid., iii, 111 ; Boas, *Indianische Sagen*, p. 194 ff.; C. Hill-Tout, articles in *Journal of the Anthropological Institute*, vols. xxxiv, xxxv, xxxvii.

[4] Boas, Introduction to Teit's *Thompson River Indians*, p. 16, and " Reports on the Indians of British Columbia " in *Reports of the British Association for the Advancement of Science*, vols. lix, lx, lxi, lxiv, lxv. A tricksy character is ascribed to Loki in some of the Norse stories (Saussaye, *Religion of the Teutons*, p. 263). Loki, however, as he appears in the literature, is a highly complex figure.

[5] See Boas's Introduction in Teit's *Thompson River Indians*.

[6] R. B. Dixon, *The Northern Maidu*, p. 263.

[7] A. C. Hollis, *The Masai*, p. 264 f.; Lang, *Myth, Ritual, and Religion*, 1st ed., ii, 4 f.

639. In this class of vaguely conceived creators or transformers we may place the Central Australian Arunta ancestors, who embodied the idea of the identity of beasts and human beings, and are the originators of all the arts and institutions of the tribes; they established the totemic groups and the ceremonies, and, in the developed myth, perpetuate their existence by entering the bodies of women and being born as human beings.[1] The relative antiquity of this conception of the origin of things is uncertain; in one point of view it is crude, but in another it is an elaborate and well-considered attempt to explain the world. These Arunta ancestors, notwithstanding their half-bestial forms, are represented as acting in all regards like human beings, and as having planned a complete system of tribal organization, but no religious worship is offered them — they figure only in sociogonic myths and in the determination of the totemic status of newborn children. Among the Navahos we find a combination of beast and man in the work of creation.[2] In their elaborate cosmogonic myth the first actors are Coyote, First Man, and First Woman, and there is discord between Coyote and his human coworkers. Here again the object seems to be to account for the diverse elements of the tribal life.

640. Many such personages, originators or introducers of the arts of life and the distribution of territory, are described in the folk-tales and myths of the North American tribes. The conception, it may be concluded, existed all over the world, though for many communities the details have not yet been brought to light.[3] A noteworthy personage of this class is the Melanesian Qat (especially prominent in the Banks Islands), a being credited with almost plenary power, the creator or arranger of seasons, the introducer of night, therefore an important cultural power, yet mischievous, the hero of numerous folk-stories; he does not appear in animal form but lives an ordinary family life. He is not worshiped — he is regarded rather as the explanation of phenomena, a genuine

---

1 Spencer and Gillen, *Native Tribes of Central Australia*, p. 123 ff.
2 W. Matthews, *Navaho Legends*, pp. 69 ff., 73 ff.
8 See Brinton, *Myths of the New World* and *American Hero-Myths*; *Journal of American Folklore*, passim. On the ' Hiawatha' myth see Hale, *Iroquois Book of Rites*, p. 180 ff., and Beauchamp, in *Journal of American Folklore*, October, 1891.

product of early cosmogonic science. He appears to be the nearest approach in Melanesia to a real creator (with the exception perhaps of a somewhat uncertain female being called Koevasi); but alongside of him stand a number of spirits and ancestral ghosts who play an important part in the organization of society.[1] For the Koryaks of Northeastern Siberia the " Big Grandfather " is an arranger of all things out of preëxisting material;[2] the Chukchee, on the other hand, regard as creator a benevolent being residing in the zenith. Vague stories of similar arrangers are found among the East African Nandi, and the South African Zulus.[3]

641. Traces of this function of organizing society appear in the mythical figures of some higher religions. Among such figures may be reckoned the Babylonian Gilgamesh, the Old Testament Cainides, the Greek Heracles, Theseus, Orpheus, and others.[4] But these personages generally take on human form and are treated as factors in the regular social development.

642. The " culture-hero " thus seems to be a natural product of incipient civilization. He represents the vague feeling that the institutions of society arose out of human needs and that the origination of these institutions demanded more than human wisdom and power.[5] He partakes of the nature of both men and gods — he is all-powerful, yet a creature of caprice and a slave of accident. To him society is supposed to owe an incalculable debt; but his mixed nature affords a wide field for bizarre myths and folk-stories, and he of necessity gives way to more symmetrical divine figures.

[1] Codrington, *The Melanesians*, pp. 28, 167, and Index, s.v. *Qat*.

[2] He is called also the " Big Raven," belonging under this title in the cycle of raven myths of the North Pacific Ocean (both in Asia and in America); see Jochelson, in *Jesup North Pacific Expedition*, vi, i, 17 f.

[3] Hollis, *The Nandi*, p. 98 f.; Callaway, *The Amazulu*, p. 1 ff.; cf. the Japanese mythical emperor Jimmu (Knox, *Development of Religion in Japan*, pp. 46, 63).

[4] Jastrow, *Religion of Babylonia and Assyria*, Index, s.v.; Gen. iv; articles in Roscher's *Lexikon*, s.vv.; Gruppe, *Griechische Mythologie*, Index, s.vv.

[5] It is noteworthy that among the numerous ætiological myths there seems to be no attempt to account for the origin of language. Language was thought of as so simple and natural a thing that no explanation of its beginnings was necessary. Adam, in Gen. ii, is able, as a matter of course, to give names to the animals. In early myths beasts have the power of speech. In a Nandi folk-story (Hollis, *The Nandi*, p. 113) what excites the wonder of the thunder and the elephant is not man's capacity of speech, but the fact that he can turn over when asleep without first getting up.

643. The god, in the true sense of the word, is the highest generalization of the constructive religious imagination. In his simplest and earliest form he appears as a venerable supernatural man, wise according to the wisdom of his place and time — such is the natural conception of the lower tribes. His position is described by the titles " the old one," " the father," " the grandfather " ;[1] he is a superhuman headman or chief, caring for his people, giving them what they need, sharing their ethical ideas and enforcing their ethical rules. He is an all-sufficient local ruler or overseer, his functions touching the whole life of his people and of no other people. In the progress of myth-making (that is, in the construction of early scientific theology) such gods are not infrequently represented as men who have gone up to the sky ; this is a natural way of accounting for their superterrestrial abode. Savage conceptions of the origin and history of such figures are usually vague, and their theologies fluctuating and self-contradictory ; but there are two points as to which opinion is firm : the god is like men in everything except power, and his functions are universal. He represents not a monotheistic creed (which takes the whole world as the domain of God), but a narrow tribal acceptance of the sufficiency of the local divine patron.[2]

Clan Gods

644. The character just described is that of the earliest known gods ; it is embodied in certain figures found in various parts of the world. Such divine figures belong to the simplest form of social organization, the clan ; it is in the clan that they are shaped, and they reflect the conceptions, political and ethical, of the clan. In Southeast Australia the personages called Daramulun, Baiame, Bunjil, correspond to this description : they are supernatural old men who have always existed ; they are taken for granted without inquiry into their origin ; they direct the affairs of the tribe in a

---

[1] For female deities the title " grandmother " occurs (Batchelor, *The Ainu* [1901], p. 578). The devil's grandmother figures in Teutonic folk-stories ; see *Journal of American Folklore*, xiii, 278 ff. ; Frazer, *Golden Bough*, 1st ed., i, 336.

[2] Attempts to prove a primitive monotheism usually fail to take this distinction into account.

general way in accordance with the moral ideas of the place and time.[1] The Australians have other beings with vaguely expressed characters and functions, but our information regarding these is so meager that it is not possible to form a distinct judgment of their character. Similar figures are the Klamath Indian "Old Man"[2] and the Zulu Unkulunkulu, an old man, the father of the people, only dimly understood by the natives who have been questioned on this point; they are uncertain whether he is dead or alive, but in any case he is revered as a great personage.[3]

645. Other such deities are reported in South Africa, as the Qamata of the Xosa, Morimo of the Bakuana, and farther north Molungu.[4] On the West Coast also, in Ashanti, Dahomi, and Yoruba, a number of deities exist which were in all probability originally local.[5] Such appears to be the character of certain gods of the non-Aryan tribes of India, as the Kolarian Sunthals and Koles.[6] Perhaps also the god Vetala was originally such a local deity with the savage characteristics proper to the time and place, though later he was half Brahmanized and became a fiend.[7] Among the Todas every clan has its god, who was the creator and instructor of the people. The large number of gods now recognized by the various Toda communities are essentially the same in character and function, and the existing system has doubtless been formed by the coalition of the clans.[8] In North America the Navahos have a number of local deities, the *yei* (Zuñi, *yeyi*), some of which are called by terms that mean ' venerable.'[9] The Koryak guardians of occupations and houses may be of the nature of such objects of worship in the clans,[10] and so also the Patagonian family-gods. Cf. the Greek κουροτρόφος. In Japan the early system of supernatural beings has been obscured by the great religions of

---

1 Howitt, *Native Tribes of South-East Australia*, p. 488 ff.
2 Boas, Introduction to Teit's *Thompson River Indians*, p. 7.
3 Callaway, *The Amazulu*, p. 1 ff.   4 Kidd, *The Essential Kafir*, p. 101 ff.
5 A. B. Ellis, *Tshi*, chaps. v–vii; *Ewe*, chap. v; *Yoruba*, chap. iii. Cf. C. Partridge, *Cross River Natives* (South Nigeria), p. 282 ff.
6 W. Crooke, *The Popular Religion and Folklore of Northern India* (1907) chap. ii.   7 Hopkins, *Religions of India*, p. 537 f.
8 Rivers, *The Todas*, chap. xix.   9 Matthews, *Navaho Legends*, p. 35 ff.
10 Jochelson, in *Jesup North Pacific Expedition*, vi, i, 36–43.

the later time — Shinto in its developed form, and Buddhism — but the indications are that the general term *kami*, a designation of all supernatural things, included local deities.[1]

646. It is not clear how early the practice began of giving these beings proper names. In the lowest known tribes we meet descriptive titles such as "old one," "grandfather," "grandmother"; and so among some civilized peoples, as the Semites, whose local deities are often known simply as *baals* ('possessors,' 'lords'), sometimes as lords of particular places, as, for example, the Arabic Dhu ash-Shara (Dusares), 'lord of the Shara.' A god identified with a particular object may be called by its name; so 'Heaven' is said to have become the proper name of a Huron deity (cf. Zeus, Tien, Shangti).[2] Names of Pawnee gods are Bright Star (Evening Star), Great Star (Morning Star), Motionless One (North Star), and many other such; the Navahos have The Woman Who Changes (apparently the changing year), White Shell Woman, Child of Water;[3] the Kolarian Sunthals, Great Mountain;[4] the Brazilian Arawaks, River-born.[5] A proper name becomes necessary as soon as definite social relations with a god are established. Divine names in civilized religions, of remote origin, are often inexplicable.

647. Among the simple clan gods divinized men should be included. In many parts of the world, as is remarked above, chiefs and other great personages are regarded as divine; this attribution of divinity is a part of that general early conception according to which there was an element of power in all things, naturally embodied in a special way in important men. This sort of divinization is particularly prominent in Melanesia and parts of Polynesia; it exists also in Japan and in West Africa. As a rule it is only the recently dead that are thus regarded as divine objects of worship, and the cult would thus be substantially a part of the worship of ancestors; but such divinized men frequently

1 Aston, *Shinto*, Index, s.v. *Kami*; Knox, *Religion in Japan*, p. 27 ff.
2 Tylor, *Primitive Culture*, ii, 255; cf. ii, 337.
3 Dorsey, *The Skidi Pawnee*, p. xix; Matthews, *Navaho Legends*, p. 34 f.
4 Hopkins, *Religions of India*, p. 532.
5 Spence, in Hastings, *Encyclopædia of Religion and Ethics*, ii, 835.

bore a peculiarly intimate relation to the clan or community and became specific protectors.[1] So far as their origin is concerned, this class of divine patrons differs essentially from the old clan god, whose genesis probably belongs to a remote antiquity and is based on the general consciousness of some powerful influence in nature.[2]

648. Clan gods are found abundantly among the ancient civilized peoples, Egyptian, Babylonian, Canaanite, Arabian, Greek, Roman, and probably existed among other peoples as to whom we have no exact information. In Old Egypt every hamlet had its protecting deity; these continued to be the objects of popular worship down to a very late time, the form of the deity being usually that of a living animal.[3]

649. A similar religious constitution obtained among the old Semitic peoples. This is obvious in the case of the Canaanites (including the Phœnicians), where every clan or community had its divine lord (the Baal), who was a universal deity sufficient for all the needs of the living, though particularly connected with the dominant interests of his people.[4] Such, probably, was the original form of the Hebrew Yahweh (Jehovah); in his Sinaitic home he was naturally connected with the phenomena of desert and mountain, and in Canaan, whither the Israelites brought his cult, he was after a while recognized as the giver of crops also, and gradually became a universal god in the larger sense of the term.[5] The Phœnician Baals — such as the Tyrian Melkart, ' the king of the city ' — are obviously local deities.[6] The same thing is true of the various gods that appear in pre-Mohammedan Arabia; the

---

[1] A. B. Ellis, *Ewe* (Dahomi), p. 104.

[2] On the ascription of divinity to men in great civilized religious systems see above, § 351 ff.

[3] Maspero, *Dawn of Civilization*, p. 120 ff. ; Ed. Meyer, *Geschichte des Alten Aegyptens*, p. 31 ff.; Wiedemann, *Religion of the Ancient Egyptians*, p. 109; Erman, *Handbook of Egyptian Religion*, pp. 21 f., 39.

[4] Cf. W. von Baudissin, *Studien zur semitischen Religionsgeschichte*, i, 28 f.

[5] R. Smend, *Alttestamentliche Religionsgeschichte*, p. 33 f. In regard to the original home of Yahweh and the diffusion of his cult among other peoples than the Hebrews exact information is lacking.

[6] Pietschmann, *Phönizier*, pp. 170 f., 182 ff.

deity of any particular clan or tribe was known to the people as
"the god" (Arabic *Allah*, that is, *al-Ilahu*), and the title "Allah,"
adopted by Mohammed as the name of the supreme and only god,
thus in so far fitted in with the usage of the people.[1]

650. In Babylonia also a very large part of the divine names
found in the inscriptions must be understood to refer ultimately
to local deities, each supreme in his own territory; the later theologians (probably priests) endeavored to organize these into a sort
of pantheon, but never succeeded in differentiating the various
deities distinctly. In general it may be said that all these old
Semitic gods had one and the same character; each in his place
was supreme, and it is difficult to find any difference in real character and function among the great gods, as Ea, Bel, Marduk,
Sin, Shamash, Ishtar, Nabu, Ashur, Eshmun, and others.[2]

651. The same remark will probably hold good of the popular
worship of the old Greeks. When Pausanias traveled through
Greece he found everywhere local cults which bore evidence of
primitiveness, and obviously pertained to the clan gods of the
various regions. In many cases these had been identified with
old animal-gods or had been interwoven into the general later
scheme and had been merged with the great gods of the developed
pantheon.[3] The functions ascribed to various deities in the Veda
suggest a similar origin for them. When we find that many of
them are credited with the same larger or smaller acts of creation,
protection, or blessing, we may suspect that they were originally
clan gods that have been incorporated in the great theologic system, and that "henotheism" is mainly a survival from this earlier
scheme or an extension of it.[4] Similar local gods appear in Peru[5]
and Mexico.[6]

[1] Hastings, *Encyclopædia of Religion and Ethics*, i, 664.

[2] Jastrow, *Religion of Babylonia and Assyria*, Index, s.vv.; articles in Roscher's
Lexikon; "Eshmun" in *Orientalische Studien Nöldeke gewidmet*.

[3] See, for example, Pausanias, i, 37, 3 (Zeus Meilichios); ii, 19, 3 (Apollo Lykios);
iii, 13, 2 (Kore Soteira — Persephone, the protectress); v, 25, 6 f. (Heracles);
viii, 12, 1 (Zeus Charmon).

[4] Macdonell, *Vedic Mythology*, p. 15 ff.; Bloomfield, *Religion of the Veda*, p. 90.

[5] Sir C. R. Markham, *The Incas of Peru*, p. 104.

[6] L. Spence, *The Mythologies of Ancient Mexico and Peru*, p. 24 f.

652. One class of *Greek "heroes"* may be considered as belonging in the category of clan gods.[1] When the hero appears to be originally a god his worship is identical in character with that offered to local deities; so in the case of Achilles and many others.[2] Such an one is often a divine patron of a definite (usually small) territory, has his sacred shrine with its ministers, and his specific sacrificial cult. A trace of this type may perhaps be recognized in Hesiod's " halfgods," [3] the heroes of the Trojan war and others, whom he places just after the age of bronze and just before his modern age of iron; their origin is thus made relatively late, as was natural if they descended cultually from old gods.

653. A similar view appears in the fact that a hero is sometimes of mixed parentage — his father or his mother is divine: a local god, standing in close cultic connection with a greater deity, is easily made into a son of the latter. In general, in the popular worship there seems to be no distinction between old heroes and gods. Where such a hero stood in close relations with a community — if, for example, as was sometimes the case, he was the patron or tutelary divinity of a family, or a mythical ancestor — there was doubtless a peculiar tenderness in the feeling for him. But his general function probably was simply that of local patron.[4]

654. Clan gods are specially important in the history of worship — they form the real basis of the great theistic development. Ghosts and spirits continue to be recognized and revered or dreaded, but they are not powerful social bonds — it is the local deity about whose person organized public worship grows up, and it is he whose functions are gradually enlarged till he becomes a universal god. The initial forms of religion are everywhere limited locally and intellectually; it is only by loyalty to the home as a center and standing-place that man's religious affections and ideals have expanded so as to embrace the world, and reach a high standard of ethical purity and logical consistency.

---

1 See above, § 647.   2 Roscher, *Lexikon*, article " Heros," col. 2473 ff.
3 *Works and Days*, 155 ff.
4 He appears to be usually beneficent; but, like all the dead, he might sometimes be maleficent.

DEPARTMENTAL GODS

655. It must be regarded as an advance in religious conceptions and religious life when natural phenomena are divided into classes and assigned each to its special deity; such a scheme brings men into more intimate and sympathetic relations with the gods. It presupposes a relatively advanced observation of nature and some power of coördination and generalization, and seems to be found only in communities that have some well-organized communal life. In general it belongs to the agricultural stage and to the higher civilizations that have grown out of this stage. Care for food appears to be the starting-point; later, all sorts of social interests demand consideration.

656. This specialization of functions is possibly in part an elevation of the old scheme of spirits according to which every object in the world was conceived of as inhabited or controlled by some spiritlike being. It is not probable that the departmental gods are always developed directly out of spirits — they appear sometimes to belong rather in the clan system, are anthropomorphic, human, lending themselves more readily than spirits do to human intercourse.[1] It is true that the lower cults of animals and spirits persist alongside of the higher religious forms, and the various groups often appear to blend with one another, as is generally the case in transitions from one system of thought to another.

657. Deities with this sort of specialized functions appear in all parts of the world and at various periods of culture. The particular sort of specialization differs according to climatic conditions and social organization — that is, it depends in any community on the nature of the phenomena that touch the life of the community closely. But the general principle remains the same — it is the effort to penetrate more deeply into the nature of the supernatural Powers, and to enter into more intimate and helpful relations with them; it is the beginning of a more practical study of theology proper.

658. A somewhat low and vague form of specialization of function is found in Melanesia, where certain beings appear as patrons

---

[1] But these origins, going far back into prehistoric times, are obscure.

of work.[1] These are said by Codrington to be ghosts, yet to be prayed to just as if they were gods; and in fact, being men with indefinitely great powers, they can hardly be distinguished from such deities as Daramulun and Unkulunkulu, except in the fact that their function is specific. In Australia the published reports do not describe departmental gods proper, with the possible exception of an undefined being in the North. A more developed scheme exists in Polynesia. In New Zealand there were deities of food-planting and of forests.[2] The highest point of Polynesian civilization seems to have been reached in the Hawaiian Islands, where, besides several great gods, there were deities of the sky, the sea, winds, and lightning, of agriculture, and of various occupations and professions, such as fishing, and even robbing.[3]

659. The Sea Dyaks have a god of rice-farming and one of war.[4] In the Malay Peninsula there is a confused mingling of supernatural beings of various sorts, with a great development of magic; the determination of the functions of the better-developed gods is rendered difficult by the fact that the Malays have been much affected by Hindu influence.[5] Such influence is possibly to be recognized also in the systems of the Dravidian and Kolarian tribes, though in them there seems to be a native non-Aryan element. The Khonds have gods of rain, fruit, hunting, and boundaries. Among all these tribes the chief deity is the sun-god, by whose side stands the earth-god; these may well be primitive, though their present form may be due to Hindu influence.[6]

660. The Masai of Eastern Africa have two chief gods — one black, said to be good; the other red, said to be bad.[7] The only trace of a recognition of cosmic powers appears in their myth that

---

[1] Codrington, *The Melanesians*, p. 132.

[2] Tregear, in *Journal of the Anthropological Institute*, xix, 97 ff.; Grey, *Polynesian Mythology*, p. 164.   [3] Alexander, *Short History of the Hawaiian People*.

[4] E. H. Gomes, *Southern Departments of Borneo*.

[5] Skeat, *Malay Magic*, chap. iv; Skeat and Blagden, *Pagan Races of the Malay Peninsula*, ii, 245 ff.

[6] Hopkins, *Religions of India*, p. 529 f.; Crooke, *Popular Religion and Folklore of Northern India*, i, chap. ii.

[7] Hollis, *The Masai*, p. 264. The related Nandi worship the sun (Asista) mainly, but have also a thunder-god (Hollis, *The Nandi*, p. 40 f.).

the sky and the earth were once united in one embrace; [1] but it is not clear that they recognize a god of the sky and one of the earth. Among the Bantu, who are largely, though not wholly, pastoral, there appears to be no trace of an apportionment of natural phenomena among supernatural beings.[2] On the West Coast of Africa there is a somewhat elaborate scheme of departmental deities. The sky is the chief god, but in Dahomi and Ashanti there are gods of lightning, fire, the ocean, the rainbow, war, markets, silk, cotton, and poison trees, smallpox, sensual desire, discord, and wisdom; in Dahomi there is a tutelary god of the royal family. The Yorubans have a similar system, embracing gods of the Niger, nightmare, wealth, gardens, and divination.[3] This more elaborate system corresponds to their more highly developed scheme of social organization.

661. The tribes of Northeastern Asia are less developed religiously. The Koryaks are said to have benevolent and malevolent deities, but appear not to have made much progress in the recognition of the distinct departments of nature.[4] The Ainu have a large number of specific deities: the goddess of fire, whose title is " Grandmother "; gods of the kitchen, of doors, of springs, and of gardens.[5] As the Ainu culture resembles that of Northeastern Asia in several respects, it is possible that in the latter region there exists a more highly specialized scheme than has yet been reported. In Central Asia also it seems that no great progress has been made in this direction by native thought. The statement of Herodotus [6] that the Thracians in time of thunderstorms used to shoot arrows at the sky and threaten the god, may point to a recognition of a god of the sky or of storm. In the greater part of Central Asia the conception of local spirits has prevailed and still prevails (Shamanism), a phase of religion that stands below that of the division of nature into departments. In certain districts of Mongolia, in which

---

1 Hollis, op. cit., p. 279.

2 With them, as everywhere else, there is occasional discrimination in the functions of magicians, different men healing or inflicting different sicknesses; cf. article " Bantu " in Hastings, *Encyclopædia of Religion and Ethics*.

3 A. B. Ellis, *Ewe*, chap. v; *Tshi*, chap. v; *Yoruba*, p. 45.

4 Jochelson, in *Jesup North Pacific Expedition*, vi, i, 33 ff., 27 ff.

5 Batchelor, *The Ainu*, chap. li.   6 Herodotus, iv, 94.

the theistic system is complicated, departmental deities are now found, but the obvious dependence of this region on Buddhism (Lamaism) and other outside cults makes it doubtful whether or how far this scheme of gods is of native origin.[1]

662. In North America the Algonkin and Maskoki nations and the Skidi Pawnee have deities of the sky, the heavenly bodies, the winds, and fire.[2] In the western part of the continent the theistic systems are less developed, but the details of the cults have not yet been fully collected ; so far as appears, a departmental organization has not been made. In Brazil there is a trace of such a conception among the Tupis ; but the South American tribes remain at a low level of theistic development.[3]

663. The three greater religions of America, the Maya, the Mexican, and the Peruvian, offer much more interesting material, in regard to which the information which has been handed down to us is often unfortunately meager. Particularly, little definite is known of the Maya system ; the indications are that the Mayas were superior in civilization to the Aztecs, and their religious customs and conceptions correspondingly higher than those of the latter.[4]

664. The Aztec religion is that which the Spaniards on their arrival found to be the dominant one in Mexico. It was the religion of a conquering race, formed in part by a coalition of tribes and a combination of cults. From the records (none of which are contemporaneous) it appears that there was a very considerable specialization of function in the Aztec deities. These were probably local gods with universal functions gradually differentiated. Huitzilopochtli, apparently a patron of vegetation (with three annual festivals corresponding to agricultural seasons), became especially the god of war, in accordance with the character of the Aztecs. Another side of social life was embodied in the conception of

---

[1] Demetrius Klementz, article " Buriats " in Hastings, *Encyclopædia of Religion and Ethics.*

[2] Brinton, *The Lenâpé*, p. 65 ff.; Dorsey, *The Skidi Pawnee*, p. xviii ff. On gods of air and winds see J. H. Keane, in article " Air and Gods of the Air " in Hastings, *Encyclopædia of Religion and Ethics.*   [3] Hastings, op. cit., i, 382 ff., and ii, 837.

[4] Brinton, *American Hero-Myths*, chap. iv ; A. M. Tozzer, *Comparative Study of the Mayas and the Lacandones* (of Yucatan), pp. 80, 93 ff. ; H. H. Bancroft, *Native Races of the Pacific States of North America*, ii, chap. xx ff.

Tezcatlipoca, who represented law and justice, but naturally became also a god of war. In sharp contrast with these stands Quetzalcoatl, a milder god, apparently a representative of general culture and good life. But he is commonly held to be of foreign origin. If a foreigner, he was nevertheless adopted by the Aztecs and embodied one side of their life, particularly, perhaps, the protests against the human sacrifices, which were so prominent a feature in the cults of the other two deities. There were further a god of rain, a goddess of harvest, and a goddess of sensual pleasure, besides a great number of minor specialized deities. With this specialization of function, however, there was no corresponding development of character in the gods, no pantheon proper. The myths which have been preserved relate to the origin of social customs and to the birth of gods. They appear to have been developed only a step beyond the myths of the Redmen.[1]

665. The Peruvian cult differs from the Mexican in that it recognizes, in its developed form, one preëminent deity, the sun-god, from whom issues all authority. Along with him stand two prominent figures, Viracocha and Pachacamac, who also are credited with great powers. Apparently they were local universal deities who were incorporated into the Peruvian system and subordinated to the sun-god. All three are only vague, general figures, having no histories except a few stories of origins, and the Peruvian myths do not differ in essential character from those of the Aztecs.[2]

666. In this category we may include a large number of minutely specialized deities of the Egyptians, the Greeks, and the Romans. As among some lower tribes already referred to, so here many common objects and pursuits are regarded as being under the fostering care of specific deities. In Egypt the ripe ear of the grain, the birth of a child and its naming, and other things had their special divinities.[3]

---

[1] J. G. Müller, *Geschichte der amerikanischen Urreligionen*, p. 577 ff.; Lang, *Myth, Ritual, and Religion*, chap. xiv; L. Spence, *Mythologies of Ancient Mexico and Peru*; E. Seler, *Gesammelte Abhandlungen*. For earlier authorities see Winsor, *Narrative and Critical History of America*, vol. i, chaps. iii, iv.

[2] J. G. Müller, *Geschichte der amerikanischen Urreligionen*, p. 313 ff.; Prescott, *Peru*, i, 91 ff.; C. R. Markham, *The Incas of Peru*, chap. viii; and see preceding note.

[3] Maspero, *Dawn of Civilization*, ii, 81, note 2; p. 82, notes 1 and 2.

667. The Greeks had such divine patrons of the corncrib, beans, plowshare, cattle, city walls, banquets, potters, physicians, athletic contests, and even one hero known as the " frightener of horses " and a deity called the " flycatcher." [1]

668. The Romans carried out this specialization in even greater detail. Almost every object and every event of the communal life had its patron deity : the house, the hearth, the field, the boundary stone, sowing and reaping, the wall, breath, marriage, education, death ; the Lares were the special protectors of the house or of the field, and all patrons of the home were summed up under the general designations *dii penates* and *dii familiares.* Most of these beings have proper names, but even where there are no such names, as in the case of the *dii penates*, there can be little doubt that they were looked on as personal individualized beings.[2] The tendency was, as time went on, to add to the number of these specialized patrons, as appears from the Roman *indigitamenta*,[3] lists of such divine beings redacted by the priests, who were disposed, naturally, to make the objects of worship as numerous as possible ; but herein they doubtless responded to a popular impulse.

669. This disposition to define practical functions minutely appears also in the cultic history of the greater gods of the old Roman religion : the rôle of Jupiter as god of sky and rain was definitely fixed, and Tellus was not the divine mother of the human race but the beneficent bestower of crops. As the functions of such greater gods became more numerous and more definitely fixed, epithets were employed ; Jupiter had a dozen or more of such adjectival additions, and it appears that at a later time such epithets were personalized into deities ; but this academic or priestly procedure does not set aside the fact that the early Roman religion recognized a vast number of divine beings as the specific patrons of certain things and acts.

670. It was quite natural for the practical Roman mind to place everything of importance under the care of a divine being — a

---

[1] Usener, *Götternamen*, p. 122 ff. ; L. R. Farnell, " The Place of the ' Sonder-Götter ' in Greek Polytheism " (in *Anthropological Essays presented to E. B. Tylor*).
[2] Farnell, op. cit. ; cf. T. R. Glover, *Conflict of Religions in the Early Roman Empire*, p. 12.   [3] Roscher, *Lexikon*, s.v.

procedure which is simply carrying out in greater detail modes of
thought which we have seen to be common in many of the lower
tribes. Augustine thinks this specialization amusing, ridiculous, and
difficult to understand. He brings up the whole question of origin
when he asks why it was necessary to have two goddesses for the
waves of the sea — one, Venilia, representing the wave as advancing
to the shore; the other, Salacia, representing the wave as receding.[1]
This seems, to be sure, an unnecessary specialization; but, considered in connection with the whole Roman system, it is not less
intelligible than the multiplication of deities attending upon the
birth and education of a child, on the processes of farming, and on
the fortunes of war. Since human life is guided by the gods,
thought the Romans, there is no act that may not have its god;
this system is the objectivation of the conception of divine special
providence.[2]

671. To certain Semitic deities highly specialized functions have
been supposed to belong; but the known facts hardly warrant this
supposition. In the names Baal-Marqod, Baal-Marpe, Baal-Gad,
the second element may be the name of a place; that is, the Baal
may be a local deity (as the Baals elsewhere are). The title Baal-
berit [3] has been interpreted as meaning " lord of a covenant " — that
is, a deity presiding over treaties; but the expression is not clear.
Baal-zebub is in the Old Testament the god of the Philistine city
Ekron, where he had a famous oracle; [4] it is highly improbable that
the name means " lord of flies " (which would rather be Baal-zebu-
bim), but the sense is obscure. The New Testament Baal [Beel]-
zebul [5] (the only correct form) has been variously explained.
The second element, *zebul*, occurs in the Old Testament as a name
of the heavenly abode of the deity,[6] and the title has been regarded
as the Semitic rendering of a Greek or Roman title of a god of
heaven (Zeus Ouranios; cf. Caelestis, epithet of Jupiter); as foreign

---

[1] Augustine, *De Civitate Dei*, vii, 22; cf. bks. vi, vii, passim.
[2] Cf. Wissowa, *Religion der Römer*, pp. 15, 145 ff.   [3] Judg. viii, 33.
[4] The name occurs only once, in 2 Kings, i, 2. It is incorrectly adopted in the
English Version of the New Testament.
[5] Found only in the Synoptic Gospels, Mk. iii, 22; Matt. x, 25; xii, 24, 27; Luke
xi, 15, 18, 19.   [6] Isa. lxiii, 15.

deities wcrc called "demons" by the later Jews, the chief of these deities, it is held, might well be taken to be the "prince of demons." However this may be, Beelzebul cannot be ranked among the deities with highly specialized functions.[1]

672. The scheme of gods just described is closely allied to that of tutelary deities for individual human beings. A transitional step may be recognized in the assignment of special divine protectors to every house or village or grove, as among the Ainu (with whom the tutelary power is the head of a bear), in Borneo (where every house has a human skull as protector), among the Khonds, in the Vedic Vastoshpati, the "lord of the house," in the Hindu "house goddess," and in the Chinese tutelary god for every year.[2] From such a scheme to the assignment of a protecting spirit to every human being there is but a step, and this is made natural or necessary by the increasing sense of the value of the individual. Such tutelary spirits or deities are found in Polynesia and Africa.[3] The North American manitu and the Central American nagual,[4] referred to above, are not only special objects of worship but also constantly present guardians of individual men. The Iroquois have special tutelary spirits.[5] In Ashanti such a function is performed by the indwelling spirit, which is scarcely distinguishable from the man himself.[6] The Roman genius represents the man's individual life, but becomes also his guardian;[7] and the daimon of Socrates was possibly originally a being of the same sort,[8] though he may have identified it with conscience.

---

[1] On these Semitic titles see articles "Baal" and "Baalzebub" in Hastings, Encyclopædia of Religion and Ethics; article "Beelzebul" in Cheyne, Encyclopædia Biblica; various articles in Brown, Driver, Briggs, Hebrew and English Lexicon.

[2] Batchelor, The Ainu, chap. x; Furness, Home Life of the Borneo Head-hunters, p. 64 f.; Hopkins, Religions of India, p. 530, note 2; De Groot, Religion of the Chinese, p. 129 f.

[3] Turner, Samoa, p. 18 f.; Nassau, Fetichism in West Africa, pp. 67, 163 ff.

[4] On "manitu" see Handbook of American Indians, s.v. (and cf. article "Wakonda"); W. Jones, in Journal of American Folklore, xviii, 183 ff. On "nagual" see Bancroft, Native Races of the Pacific States of North America, iii, 458; Brinton, in Journal of American Folklore, viii, 249.   [5] Journal of American Folklore, viii, 115.

[6] Cf. M. H. Kingsley, West African Studies, p. 132 f.

[7] Roscher, Lexikon, i, 2, col. 1616.

[8] Cf. article "Daimon" in Roscher, op. cit.

673. In the great religions of antiquity every city and every state had its special divine protector. The Persian fravashis are the guardians of individual human beings. The later Jews held that there was a guardian angel for every nation and for every person.[1] All such conceptions embody the human sense of dependence on divine aid and the demand for specific divine protectors standing near to man and sustaining special relations with individuals. In some forms of Christianity the function of protection is assigned to patron saints.

674. Certain classes of departmental or specific gods may be mentioned here for the purpose of indicating their development.

675. *Creators.* The work of the creation of the world is assigned among various peoples to a great variety of beings. In the earliest strata of religious belief animals play a great rôle as creators. The known examples of their creative function are so numerous that we may well be disposed to regard it as universal. In general it is the best-known animal, or the one credited with the greatest sagacity, that is regarded as creator.[2]

676. But the natural progress of thought involved the advance to the conception of anthropomorphic creators. A transitional stage is presented by the Australian Arunta, in whose mythical system the authors of tribal institutions and the makers of heavenly bodies are the half-animal, half-human ancestors; this seems to be an attempt at a transformation of the old scheme of creation by animals — unwilling to abandon the earlier conception, these tribes have satisfied themselves by the theory that the ancestors and creators, though animals in nature, must at the same time have been human.[8] We may compare with these the Melanesian and Samoan supernatural beings who are incarnate in animal forms and are at the same time originators of civilization.[4] These zoömorphic beings are not necessarily totems, as in Australia; outside of the Arunta it does not appear that totems as such are ever regarded

---

[1] Spiegel, *Eranische Alterthumskunde*, ii, 91 ff.; Dan. x, 20; xi, 1; xii, 1; Matt. xviii, 10.   [2] Examples are given above, § 255 f.

[8] Spencer and Gillen, *Native Tribes of Central Australia*, chap. x.

[4] Codrington, *The Melanesians*, pp. 150 f., 158 f., 168 f.; Turner, *Samoa*, pp. 7, 52.

as creators [1] — they are ancestors, but at that point their function appears to cease.

677. There are however ghosts, which, while of course representing ancestors, are regarded not specially in their ancestorial capacity, but rather as powerful beings who have been more or less active in framing the constitution of society. This form of ghost occurs in Melanesia, where also spirits, vague beings who never were human, play a great rôle. The best authorities find it somewhat difficult to distinguish between such ghosts and spirits on the one hand, and gods on the other hand.[2] The Qat of the Banks Islands is in one sense a creator, since he determines the regular courses of the seasons and is the introducer of night; yet, since he does not actually create the world, but only rearranges the existing material, he belongs rather in the category of transformers or initiators. Real anthropomorphic gods appear as creators in very early tribes. Such, for example, are Baiame, Daramulun, Bunjil of Australia,[3] perhaps Supu of the Melanesian island of Vate.

678. In Polynesia there is a better-defined cosmogonic anthropomorphism. The Hawaiian creators Kane and Tangaloa appear to be fully formed deities.[4] The Maoris have the divine figures Heaven and Earth, whose children are the producers of all things in the world. But Maui, who seems to be a general Polynesian figure, is rather a culture-hero than a god, though his achievements were of a very serious sort. The Tapa of the Borneo Land Dyaks,[5] and the Boora Pennu of the Khonds [6] may be regarded as real gods. On the West Coast of Africa the Yorubans, the most advanced of the coast tribes, with a well-developed pantheon, have deities who may be called creators; such are Obatala, who, according to one account, made the first human pair out of clay, and Ifa, the restorer of the world after the flood.[7] In North America the

---

[1] Here again a distinction must be made between animals simply sacred and those that are specifically totemic.   [2] Codrington, *The Melanesians*, pp. 248 f., 253 ff.

[3] Lang, *Myth, Ritual, and Religion*, chaps. xii f.

[4] So the Samoan Tangaloa (Tylor, *Primitive Culture*, 3d ed., ii, 344 f.).

[5] St. John, *The Far East*, i, 180.   [6] Hopkins, *Religions of India*, p. 528 ff.

[7] A. B. Ellis, *Yoruba*, pp. 38 ff., 56 ff.; cf. M. H. Kingsley, *West African Studies*, p. 117 ff.

New England Kiehtan and the Virginian Oki have creative functions.[1] The Navahos ascribe the creation of certain animals to a
god Bekotsidi, whose character and rôle, however, are vague.[2] The
Brazilian Tupan and Jurupari appear to be divine creators.[8] For a
good many tribes in all parts of the world the published reports
give no precise information regarding the beginning of things, but
it seems probable that fuller acquaintance with them would reveal
conceptions similar to those described above.

679. The great civilized nations, with their well-formed anthropomorphic deities, have constructed elaborate cosmogonies, which
commonly begin with the conception of an unshaped mass of
material out of which the gods arise and create the world. There
is no great difference in these various schemes : Babylonians and
Greeks have fallen upon substantially the same general view of
creation ; the variations among the various peoples are due to circumstances of place and culture. It is noteworthy that the Maoris
have a cosmogony which is not unlike that of the great civilized
nations of antiquity, but the origin of their scheme of the world is
not clear.[4]

680. *Gods of the other world.* The class of departmental
gods includes those who have charge of the other world. As soon
as the abode of men after death is definitely fixed, it is natural
that a deity presiding over this other world should arise. Among
the lower tribes this sort of god is not frequent.[5] One of the
clearest cases of such organization occurs in Fiji.[6] Here, in addition to other deities who deal with the dead on their entrance into

1 Lang, *Myth, Ritual, and Religion*, preface to new edition.
2 Matthews, *Navaho Legends*, p. 34.
8 Article " Brazil " in Hastings, *Encyclopædia of Religion and Ethics*.
4 G. Grey, *Polynesian Mythology*, p. 1 ff.; Taylor, *New Zealand*, chap. vi; cf.,
for Polynesia, W. Ellis, *Polynesian Researches*, chap. xiii. The abstract ideas reported
by Taylor are remarkable : from conception came increase, from this came swelling,
then, in order, thought, remembrance, desire ; or, from nothing came increase and so
forth ; or, the word brought forth night, the night ending in death. The significance
of this scheme (supposing it to be correctly stated) has not been explained. The
rôle assigned to " desire " in the Rig-Veda creation-hymn (x, 129) is the product of
learned reflection (cf. Schopenhauer's "blind will"), and sounds strange in the
mouth of New Zealand savages.   5 Cf. Tylor, *Primitive Culture*, ii, 308 ff.
6 Williams and Calvert, *Fiji*, p. 193 f.

this farther world, the great deity Ndengei has his abode, and one of his functions is to pass on the merits of those who present themselves from the world of living men. He is, however, in part an otiose deity and can hardly be said to rule over this other-worldly realm. Similar undeveloped deities are found among the Maoris and the Finns.[1]

681. But fully formed and effective divine rulers of the other world occur only in the more advanced religions, such as the Babylonian, the Egyptian, the Hindu, the Persian, the Greek, the Roman.[2] From the nature of their abode such deities have very little to do with the life on earth except when, as in the Egyptian system and to some extent in the Fijian, there is a judge of conduct, with authority to assign the dead their places, good or bad. In such cases they become important moral factors in life.

682. An ethical god of the other world appears not to have been created by the Semites. The Babylonian Underworld goddess or god has nothing to do with moral character, and among the Hebrews, so far as the statements in the Old Testament go, no special deity was assigned to the other world; whether such an Underworld deity once existed and was lost by the Hebrews, or has been expunged by the later editors of the Old Testament books, must remain uncertain;[3] in the late pre-Christian period the

---

[1] Grey, *Polynesian Mythology*, p. 15; Castrén, *Finnische Mythologie*, p. 1.

[2] Jastrow, *Religion of Babylonia and Assyria* (English and German editions), Index, s.vv. *Allatu, Nergal*; id., *Aspects of Religious Belief and Practice in Babylonia and Assyria*, p. 368 ff.; Wiedemann, *Religion of the Ancient Egyptians*, p. 217; Erman, *Handbook of Egyptian Religion*, p. 94 ff.; Macdonell, *Vedic Mythology*, pp. 171 ff., 169 ff.; Bloomfield, *Religion of the Veda*, p. 144 f.; Hopkins, *Religions of India*, p. 128 ff.; Spiegel, *Eranische Alterthumskunde*, ii, 163 (but the old Persian god of the Underworld, if there was one, was absorbed, in Zoroastrianism, by Ahura Mazda); Jackson, in Geiger and Kuhn's *Grundriss der iranischen Philologie*, ii, 652, § 52; Farnell, *Cults of the Greek States*, ii, 513 ff.; iii, chap. v; Wissowa, *Religion der Römer*, p. 187 ff.; Aust, *Religion der Römer*, p. 52; Rohde, *Psyche*, 3d ed. i, 205, ff.; articles on Hades, Plutos, Hermes, Dionysos, Nergal, and related deities, in Roscher's *Lexikon*.

[3] Cf. Jastrow, *Aspects of Religious Belief and Practice in Babylonia and Assyria*, pp. 356 f., 372 f.; F. Schwally, *Das Leben nach dem Tode*, p. 65 ff.; R. H. Charles, *Eschatology*, p. 18 f. For the Arabs see Wellhausen, *Reste arabischen Heidentumes*, iii, 22 ff., 42 ff.; Nöldeke, article " Arabs (Ancient) " in Hastings, *Encyclopædia of Religion and Ethics*; for the Phœnicians, Pietschmann, *Phönizier*, p. 191 f.

national god, Yahweh, was regarded as controlling the Underworld as well as Heaven and Earth.[1] The Greek Aïdes or Ploutōn
and the Roman Pluto also are not ethical gods in the higher sense,
as indeed no early deity of any people has such a moral character.
At a later period ethical distinctions were introduced into the administration of the other world.

By reason of paucity of data it is difficult to determine the precise characters of various Celtic, Slavic, and Germanic deities
whose names appear in the records. They are gods of clans and
of departments of nature; none of them can properly be reckoned among the great gods.[2]

683. *Division into good and bad Powers.* Among many savage
and half-civilized peoples we find that a distinction is recognized
between good and bad ghosts and spirits — a distinction at first
vague, based on passing experiences in which all the fortunes of
men, favorable and unfavorable, are referred to these beings.
Their morals are those of the human communities with which
they are connected: they may be amiable or malignant, beneficent
or revengeful, but the ethical element in their characters and deeds
is not distinctly recognized and is not made the basis of the distinction between the two classes. The world is seen to be full of
Powers that make for weal or for woe — a conception that contains the germ of all the later development but is at first nebulous.

684. In a somewhat higher form of culture these two classes
of Powers may be unified respectively into, or replaced by, two
gods, one helpful, the other harmful. Such appears to be the
scheme of the Masai, who have their black god and red god.[8] A
Californian cosmogonic myth describes a nonmoral conflict of
work between the good " Creator " and the malicious Coyote.[4]

---

[1] Ps. cxxxix.

[2] See article " Celts " in Hastings, op. cit.; Saussaye, *Lehrbuch der Religionsgeschichte*, 2d ed.; Usener, *Götternamen*; article "Aryan Religion" in Hastings,
op. cit., p. 38 f. and passim.

[8] Hollis, *The Masai*, p. 264. The neighboring Nandi, according to Hollis (*The
Nandi*, p. 41), have a similar pair.

[4] A. C. Dixon, *The Northern Maidu* (*Bulletin of the American Museum of Natural
History*, xviii, iii), p. 263. For other such conceptions see Tylor's discussion in
Primitive Culture, ii, 320 ff.

A real unification appears, however, to be rare; it supposes in fact a degree of reflection and organization that we should not expect to find among lower peoples. The story, for example, that has been told of a well-developed dualistic system of the Iroquois is based on a misconception.[1] Dualism proper is not recognizable among the savages of America, Polynesia, Asia, or Africa.[2] In the Old Testament prior to the sixth century B.C. the spirits, good and bad, which are not essentially different from those we find among the lower tribes, are massed under the control of Yahweh, and do his bidding without moral reflection; when he sends a lying spirit into the mouth of Ahab's prophets[3] this spirit goes without malice merely to perform the will of the supreme god. This massing of all spirit Powers under the control of one god is a step toward unity and clearness in the conception of the government of the world.

685. At a later stage of social growth there appears the conception of a cosmic struggle, the conflict between the natural forces that tend to disorder and those that tend to order. Philosophical reflection led to the supposition of an original chaos, a medley of natural forces not combined or organized in such a way as to minister to the needs of human life; and a similar conception of conflict may have arisen from observation of the warring elements at certain seasons of the year.

686. The adjustment of the rival forces and the establishment of a system of physical order is referred to the great gods. Such a picture of the original state of things is contained in the elaborate Babylonian cosmologies that have come down to us; in these the dragon of disorder (Tiamat) is completely conquered by the god Bel-Marduk, who represents the Babylonian civilization of the time in which the cosmology arose. Of the same nature is the Egyptian myth of the contest between Horus (the light) and Set (the dark), in which, however, the victory of Horus is not described

---

[1] Brinton, *Myths of the New World*, p. 63; H. Hale, *Iroquois Book of Rites*, p. 74.

[2] A possible exception is the Khond myth of the struggle between the sun-god (Boora Pennu), the giver of all good things, and the earth-goddess (Tari), the author of evil things (Hopkins, *Religions of India*, p. 529 f.; Macpherson, *India*, p. 84); but the origin of this myth is uncertain.   [3] 1 Kings xxii, 19–23.

as being absolute [1] — a representation suggested, possibly, by the
recognition of the persistence of the good and bad elements of the
world ; compare the cosmologies of the Maidu and the Khonds
mentioned above (§684). In the Greek and Teutonic myths in
which the Giants are the enemies of the great gods a more humane
and settled government of the world is introduced by Zeus and
Wodan. Traces of this construction of the universe are to be
found also among the Maoris, the Hawaiians, and other peoples
of a like grade.[2]

687. In the original form of these myths there is no moral element beyond the fact that the settlement of the cosmic powers was
necessary in order to the establishment of good social life. Individual wicked deities do not appear at this stage, but the way is prepared for them by the picture of cosmic struggle in which powers
friendly and unfriendly to men are opposed to one another. A
similar conception is found in the figures of the Fates, who are the
embodiment of the course of events in the world — the immovable,
remorseless, absolute fortune of men, good and bad — a picture
of life as it has presented itself, doubtless, to men in all periods of
history. Out of this came the abstract conception of Fate, the
impersonal power that controls all things.

688. The deeper conception of a conflict between the moral good
and the moral evil in life belongs to the latest period in religious
history. Here the determining fact is the control of the world by
the high gods, who have their adversaries, but in general prove
victors. At the foundation of this scheme of the world lies the conception of order, which is particularly defined in the Vedic *arta* and
the Avestan *asha* [3] — the regulation of the world in accordance
with human interests, in which the ethical element becomes more
and more prominent as human society is more and more formed
on an ethical basis.

[1] Ed. Meyer, *Geschichte des Alten Aegyptens*, p. 71 f.; Maspero, *Dawn of Civilization*, pp. 172, 177.

[2] R. Taylor, *New Zealand*, pp. 114 ff., 132; Jean A. Owen, *The Story of Hawaii*,
p. 70 f.

[3] Mills, in *Journal of the American Oriental Society*, xx, 31 ff.; Bloomfield,
Religion of the Veda, p. 125 ff.

689. Ethical dualism is most fully embodied in the Persian conception of two gods, good and bad, with the understanding that the good god, Ahura Mazda, exercises a certain restraint on the bad god, Angro Mainyu, who is finally to be crushed.[1] This optimistic point of view, which has no doubt existed in germinal shape among all peoples, appears also in the modified dualism of the Old Testament and the late Jewish and Christian schemes. The Old Testament Satan is originally a divine being, one of the " sons of the Elohim" (that is, he belongs to the Elohim, or divine, class); his function is that of inspector of human conduct, prosecutor-general, with a natural tendency to disparage men and demand their punishment. As a member of Yahweh's court and council he makes regular reports to his divine lord and pleads cases before the divine court.[2] In this character he is suspicious and mischievous but not immoral; but a little later a trace of malice appears in him,[3] and in the uncanonical Jewish book of the Wisdom of Solomon and in the New Testament he advances to the position of the head of the kingdom of moral evil, so that he is called also " the god of the present age "[4] — that is, he is the controller of the existing unregenerate element in human society, and is to be displaced when the ideal age shall be established.

690. *Man's attitude toward demons.* Demons[5] (the term being taken to include all early malefic superhuman beings, whether ghosts or spirits) are feared and guarded against, but rarely receive worship. As they are the authors of all physical ills that cannot be explained on natural grounds, measures, usually magical, are taken to thwart their purposes — to prevent their intervention or to overcome and banish the evil begun by them. As they are not credited with moral principle, hostility to them rests not on ethical feeling but merely on fear of suffering.[6] If they are placated, it is in cases in which they approach the character of gods and in so far cease to be demons in our sense of the word. They serve a useful purpose

---

[1] Spiegel, *Eranische Alterthumskunde*, ii, 21 ff., 121 ff.

[2] Zech. iii, 1–5; Job i, ii.   [3] 1 Chr. xxi, 1.   [4] 2 Cor. iv, 4.

[5] The Greek *daimon*, properly simply a deity, received its opprobrious sense when Jews and Christians identified foreign deities with the enemies of the supreme God.

[6] Tylor, *Primitive Culture*, ii, 318 ff.

in that, taking on their shoulders all the ills of life, they leave the clan gods free from the suspicion of unfriendliness to men.[1] On the other hand, the belief in them has created a pseudo-science of relief from suffering and a great host of pseudo-doctors who for a long time exercised a large control over society and bound men in fetters of ignorance.

691. In early societies demons have not individual names. In savage societies there are malefic deities, with individual names, connected with sicknesses and other ills; but such deities are not demons. Demons do not enter into friendly social relations with men,[2] and observation of experiences is not carried so far as to assign every ill to a separate author. In more advanced societies, as, for instance, the Babylonian,[3] demons are divided into classes according to their various lines of activity, and to these classes names are given. If some individual demon, representing a particular ill, becomes specially important, it may receive an individual name. In general, the demonic name-giving follows the theistic, but lags behind it. Clan gods have at first some such appellation as Old One, Grandfather, or a descriptive epithet (as among some American Indian tribes), and later, Lord, Lady, Mighty One, Exalted One; in process of time they receive proper names, which must have arisen at a relatively early period, since the meaning of the names of most of the old deities was to the ancients, as it is to us, unknown. In the case of the demonic world this development has not been carried so far, for the reason stated above, namely, that these beings, unlike gods, have not become real citizens of the communities with which they are connected.

692. In like manner the organization of demons has not kept pace with that of gods. In most regions they have remained a mob, every individual pursuing his way independently. It is only in

---

[1] Great gods also send suffering, but only when they are angered by men's acts, as by disrespect to a priest (Apollo, in *Iliad*, i) or to a sacred thing (Yahweh, 1 Sam. vi, 19; 2 Sam. vi, 7). In the high spiritual religions suffering is treated as educative, or is accepted as involving some good purpose unknown to men.

[2] W. R. Smith, *Religion of the Semites*, 2d ed., p. 126 f.

[3] Jastrow, *Religion of Babylonia and Assyria*, p. 260 ff.; O. Weber, *Dämonenbeschwörung bei den Babyloniern und Assyriern* (in *Der Alte Orient*, 1906).

advanced cults that they form a community with a head. In China and Persia the sharp division of supernatural forces into two classes was the outcome of great religious reformations that followed the usual savage chaos of the hordes of demons. The Jewish demonology (probably influenced by the Persian) chose for the head of its kingdom of evil an old god (the Satan) or the similar figure Azazel.[1]

693. It does not appear that religious worship has ever been offered to a being regarded as morally bad and in honor of moral badness. The "devils" reported by early (and some recent) travelers as the recipients of religious homage turn out on inquiry to be clan gods whose anger is feared.[2] The cult of many savage and many civilized deities has been, and is, characterized by gross cruelty and licentiousness; but it is certain that human sacrifice and sexual indulgence were, and are, in these cases not regarded as morally wrong. Durga (Kali), wife of Çiva, most terrible and repulsive of female deities, while she is feared, is also revered as the giver of all good gifts; and the Thugs, when they offered her their strangled victims, ascribed no more moral blame to her than to themselves — their work they regarded not as murder but as pious sacrifice.[3] The Gnostic sects, Ophites and Cainites, looked on the serpent and Cain as friends of the supreme Deity and of man; they were enemies only of the Demiourgos, the Jewish god Yahweh, who, they held, wished to keep man in ignorance.[4] The Mesopotamian Yezidis also (the so-called devil-worshipers) revere only beings that they regard as morally good or as destined to become good. Their peculiar attitude toward Satan (a mingling of fear and respect) is based not on his connection with evil but on their expectation that, though he is now fallen from his high angelic estate, he is ultimately to be restored to his original dignity.[5]

---

[1] The Ethiopic Book of Enoch (ed. R. H. Charles), chaps. liii, vi–x; the Slavonic Enoch, or Secrets of Enoch (ed. R. H. Charles), chap. xxxi. For the later Jewish view (in Talmud and Midrash) see *Jewish Encyclopedia*, article "Satan."

[2] The "demons" of 1 Cor. x, 20 (King James version, "devils") are foreign deities.

[3] Hopkins, *Religions of India*, pp. 416, 492 ff.

[4] Herzog-Hauck, *Real-Encyklopädie*, articles "Ophiten," "Kainiten."

[5] J. Menant, *Les Yézidiz* (in *Annales du Musée Guimet*); Isya Joseph, *Yezidi Texts* (reprinted from *American Journal of Semitic Languages and Literatures*, xxv (1909), no. 2 f.). Cf. the idea of restoration in Col. i, 20.

694. Thus, it cannot be said that a demon has ever developed into a god. The malefic Powers of savages have generally been absorbed by higher beings or have otherwise disappeared. Some gods, such as the Hebrew Satan and certain Greek deities, have been degraded to the demonic class. In some cases, particularly in the Zoroastrian system, a being who is the consolidation of all malign supernatural activities has been credited with all-but divine power and authority.[1] But the two classes remain distinct — the true " god " is a friendly member of a human society, and when he is angry may be placated; the true " demon " is essentially hostile to men and must be thwarted and expelled.[2]

695. *Gods of abstractions.* Gods of abstractions, found in certain theistic systems, are to be distinguished on the one hand from deities that are simply personalizations of physical objects (such as Vesta and Agni) and on the other hand from poetical personifications, such as that of Wisdom in the Jewish books of Proverbs, Ecclesiasticus, and the Wisdom of Solomon, and from concrete figures like the Logos of Philo and the Fourth Gospel. Though these abstract forms appear to be relatively late (posterior to the formation of the greater gods), the meagerness of our data makes it difficult to describe their genesis and the conceptions of their character by the peoples among whom they arise. Some facts known to us, however, may help us to understand in part the process by which they came into existence.

696. We have already considered the tendency in human communities to particularize the divine objects of worship and to personalize external objects; everywhere, it would appear, there is a disposition to assign a particular divine control to every fact that is specially connected with human interests. We have to note, further, the tendency to concretize, as, for example, in many cases in which evil, physical or moral, is regarded as a concrete thing that may be removed bodily from the community.[3] This sort of

---

[1] So the Christian Satan.

[2] When, in the reports of travelers and other observers, demons are said to be placated, examination shows that these beings are gods who happen to be mischievous. Of this character, for example, appear to be the " demons " mentioned in Hastings, *Encyclopædia of Religion and Ethics*, ii, 122. [3] Frazer, *Golden Bough*, 2d ed., iii, 39 ff.

conception we may suppose to be connected with early psychological theory, according to which anything that affects man is credited with manlike form and power. The facility with which the abstract and the concrete may be identified is illustrated by such modern terms as deity, majesty, highness, state, government, direction, counsel; in these expressions the abstract quality or act is incarnated in certain persons, and so we may imagine that at a certain stage of society any quality or act might be isolated and regarded as a personal thing. A series of victories, for example, might suggest the conception of 'victory' as a thing present in these events, and the tendency to personalize would then create the divine figure Victory. Historically a personalization may have arisen, in some cases, through the isolation of an epithet of a deity (so, for example, Fides may have come from Dius Fidius),[1] but in such cases the psychological basis of the personalization is the same as that just stated. From these, as is remarked above, must be distinguished poetical and philosophical abstractions.

697. Whatever be the explanation of the process, we find in fact a large number of cases in which such abstractions appear as deities and receive worship.

698. *Semitic.* The material for the Semitic religions on this point is scanty.[2] The Arabic divine names supposed by Nöldeke to represent abstractions are Manāt (fate), Sa'd (fortune), Ruḍā (favor), Wadd (love), Manāf (height), 'Aud (time). Whether these are all abstract terms is doubtful. *Wadd* means also ' lover,' divine friend or patron. *Sa'd* occurs as adjective ' fortunate,' is the appellation of certain stars, and the god Sa'd is identified by an Arab poet with a certain rock[3] — the rock is doubtless an old local divinity.

---

1 But see below, § 704.

2 Baethgen, *Beiträge zur semitischen Religionsgeschichte*; Wellhausen, *Skizzen*, iii, 25 ; Nöldeke, in *Zeitschrift der deutschen morgenländischen Gesellschaft*, 1886, 1888, and article "Arabs (Ancient) " in Hastings, *Encyclopædia of Religion and Ethics*; Pinches, article "Gad," and Driver, article "Meni," in Hastings, *Dictionary of the Bible*; Cheyne, article " Fortune " in *Encyclopædia Biblica*; Commentaries of Delitzsch, Duhm, Marti, Skinner, and Box on Isa. lxv, 11.

3 Lane, *Arabic-English Lexicon*, s.v. The Old Testament title " Rock " given to Yahweh (Deut. xxxii, 18, "the Rock that begat thee ") is figurative, but may go back to a divine rock.

Ruḍā is found apparently only as a divine name (in Palmyrene and Safa inscriptions and as a god of an Arabian tribe) — the form may be concrete, in the sense of 'favoring,' divine patron. As " time " (*dahr, zaman*) often occurs in Arabic poetry in the sense of ' fate,' the god 'Auḍ may be an embodiment of this conception.[1] *Manāf*, if understood, as is possible, in the sense ' high place,' is not abstract but concrete, though in that case the original reference of the term is not clear.

699. Manāt is one of the three great goddesses of Mecca, the others being Al-Lât ('the goddess') and Al-Uzza ('the mighty one'); as these two names are concrete, there is a certain presumption that *Manāt* likewise is concrete. The original meaning of the word is obscure. It does not occur as a common noun, but from the same stem come terms meaning ' doom, death,'[2] and, if it be allied to these, it would be an expression for ' fate ' (like *'Auḍ*). However, the stem is used in the sense ' number, determine, assign,' and Manāt may be the divine determiner of human destinies. From this same stem comes the Biblical *Meni*, and apparently the Assyrian *Manu*.[8] The ordinary North Semitic conception of the source of human destinies is that they are determined by the gods and written on tablets or in a book,[4] and the same conception may have existed in the South Semitic area.[5] The other deity mentioned in Isaiah lxv, 11, is Gad; the word means in Arabic and Hebrew ' fortune, good fortune,' and occurs as the name of a deity in Phœnician and Aramaic inscriptions, but the data are not sufficient to fix its original sense. It is the name of a Hebrew tribe, which

---

[1] On the Hebrew place-name (Job i, 1) and perhaps personal name (Gen. xxxvi, 28) Uṣ (Uz), which seems to be formally identical with 'Auḍ, see W. R. Smith, *Kinship and Marriage in Early Arabia*, 1st ed., p. 260 f., and his *Religion of the Semites*, p. 43 ; Wellhausen, *Skizzen*, iii ; Nöldeke, in *Zeitschrift der deutschen morgenländischen Gesellschaft*, xl, 183 f.   [2] *Maniya*, plural *manāyā*.

[8] Isa. lxv, 11 ; III Rawlinson, 66.

[4] Jastrow, *Religion of Babylonia and Assyria*, pp. 420, 428 (the tablets of fate given to Kingu and snatched from him by Marduk) ; R. F. Harper, *Assyrian and Babylonian Literature*, p. 304 f. (Marduk seizes the tablets of fate from Zu) ; Ps. cxxxix, 16 ; Dan. vii, 10 ; Rev. v, 1, and other passages.

[5] As far as the forms are concerned, a concrete sense for *manāt, manu, meni*, seems possible; cf. Wright, *Arabic Grammar*, 2d ed., i, § 231; Barth, *Semitische Nominalbildungen*, p. 163 ff.; Delitzsch, *Assyrian Grammar*, p. 158 ff.

is perhaps so called from the tribal god, and the name of a tribal god is probably concrete.[1]

700. It seems, then, that for most if not all of the names of the Semitic deities just mentioned abstract senses, though possible, are not certain. Nöldeke remarks that most of these terms are poetical — they may be ornate epithets given to old concrete divine figures, in which case the real cults were attached to these latter and not to abstractions. It must be regarded as doubtful whether Semitic religion created any abstract deity.

701. *Egyptian.* The most prominent Egyptian abstract deity is Maat, ' truth.' She fulfilled an important function in the judgment-hall of Osiris in the Underworld, and was widely revered, but had no mythical history, and seems to have been rather a quasi-philosophical creation than a vital element of the Egyptian religious life. A god Destiny is mentioned, who generally bestowed a happy fate.[2]

702. *Roman and Greek.* The most fully developed form of this conception is found in the Roman cult.[8] The civic genius of the Romans led them to give prominence to the maintenance of public and private rights ; thus among their deities appear public safety or salvation (Salus Publica), public faith or fidelity to engagements (Fides), civic harmony (Concordia), connubial purity (Pudicitia), filial devotion (Pietas), the boundary of property (Terminus), victory (Victoria), liberty (Libertas). There are further the gods Youth (Juventus and Juventas) and Desire [4] (Cupido), perhaps as things fundamental in human life.[5] Fortune (Fortuna) is the mass of evidence determining life by the will of the gods, with which the utterances of the gods (Fata) are identical, and the embodiment of the determining agencies is the Parcæ. Several of these deities

---

[1] The etymologies in Gen. xxx, 11 ff. are popular. In " Baal-Gad " (Josh. xi, 17) *Gad* may be the name of a place ; cf. Stade, *Geschichte des Volkes Israel,* i, 271, note.

[2] Erman, *Handbook of Egyptian Religion,* chap. iii. For a list of other Egyptian gods of abstractions, such as eternity, life, joy, see Wiedemann, " Religion of Egypt," in Hastings, *Dictionary of the Bible,* v, 191.

[8] Boissier, *La religion romaine,* i, 4 ff. ; Wissowa, *Religion der Römer,* p. 46 ff. ; Usener, *Götternamen,* p. 364 ff. (cf. Farnell, in *Anthropological Essays presented to E. B. Tylor*) ; Fowler, *Roman Festivals,* pp. 190 f., 341 ; Frazer, *Adonis Attis Osiris,* p. 169 ff.   [4] Cf. above, § 679, note.   [5] Not all of these had public cults.

have their correspondents in the Greek theistic system:[1] Eros (desire); Tuche (that which is allotted one by the gods or by the course of events); Moira (Aisa), the unification of all the powers that determine man's destiny. The god Kronos was by some improperly identified with "time" (χρόνος).[2]

703. Aryan. Among the Aryans of India the god Kama (desire) appears to be identical with Cupido. Some other abstractions, such as Piety and Infinity, are akin to Mazdean conceptions.[3] Brahma, originally 'magical formula,' then 'prayer,' and later 'pious thought,' becomes finally Brahma, the all-embracing god. Rta (arta), ' order,' at first, perhaps, the proper order of the sacrificial ritual, becomes finally 'moral order or righteousness' and 'cosmic order.' This conception is still more prominent in the Avesta,[4] in which Asha (Order) is one of the Amesha-spentas, only inferior to the supreme god; the other companions of Ahura Mazda have similar titles and may equally be regarded as the personalization of abstract ideas.[5] In the same category may be included the Mazdean conceptions Endless Time (Zrvan Akarana) and Endless Space (Thwasha), which appear to be treated in the Avesta as personal deities.[6] The organizers of the Mazdean faith,

[1] See articles in Roscher's *Lexikon* ("Eros," "Moira," and similar terms); on Phoibos, cf. L. Deubner, in *Athenische Mittheilungen*, 1903.

[2] Cicero, *De Natura Deorum*, ii, 25.

[3] Hopkins, *Religions of India*, p. 135 f.; Bloomfield, *Religion of the Veda*, pp. 191, 243 ff.; Macdonell, *Vedic Mythology*, p. 115 ff.

[4] Spiegel, *Eranische Alterthumskunde*, ii, 34 ff.; A. V. Williams Jackson, *Iranische Religion* (in Geiger and Kuhn's *Grundriss der iranischen Philologie*, ii, 637).

[5] The six are: Vohumanah (Good Thought or Good Mind), Khshathra Vairya (Best or Wished-for Righteous Realm or Law), Spenta Armaiti (Holy Harmony), Asha Vahista (Perfect Righteousness or Piety), Haurvatat (Well-being), Ameretat (Immortality).

[6] On these and certain minor divinized conceptions of time see Spiegel, op. cit., ii, 4-17. On the Hindu personification of time see Bloomfield, *Religion of the Veda*, p. 244 ff. In these and similar cases time, containing all things, is conceived of as the producer of all things, and the line between personification and hypostatization is not always clearly defined. For the influence of astrology on the deification of time, see Cumont, *Les religions orientales parmi les peuples romains*, chap. vii (on astrology and magic), p. 212 f., paragraph on new deities, and notes thereto. Hubert, "La représentation du temps dans la religion et la magie" (in *Mélanges de l'histoire des religions*), p. 190, distinguishes between the notation of favorable and unfavorable times (and the nonchronological character of mythical histories) and the calendar, which counts moments continuously.

having discarded almost all the old gods, invested the supreme
god with certain moral qualities, and these, by a natural process
of thought, were concretized (Ahura Mazda is sometimes included
in the list of Amesha-spentas). Thus arose a sort of pantheon,
an echo of the old polytheism; but the history of the process of
formulation is obscure.[1]

704. Most, if not all, of the abstract conceptions mentioned
above are also placed, in the various theistic systems, under the
control of great gods. Thus, for example, Jupiter is the guardian
of boundaries and has the epithet " Terminus," and Zeus is the
patron of freedom (Eleutherios).[2] It is, however, not necessary to
suppose that the abstractions in question are taken from the functions of the great gods. Rather these epithets of the gods are to
be explained from the same tendency that produced gods of abstractions. It was the sense of the importance of the boundary
in early life that led both to the creation of the god Terminus and
to the assignment of the epithet "Terminus" to Jupiter. The desire
or love that was so important an element in human life both
fashioned itself into a personality and was put under the guardianship of a special deity. Public safety was a cherished idea of the
Romans and was doubtless held to be maintained by every local
or national god, yet could none the less become an independent
deity. The data are not sufficient to enable us to determine in all
cases the question of chronological precedence between the deification of the abstraction and the assignment of the epithet to a
god. We know that in the later Roman period abstractions were
personalized, but this procedure was often poetical or rhetorical.[3]

705. A general relation may be recognized between the intellectual character of a people and the extent to which it creates abstract gods. The Semitic peoples, among whom the development

---

[1] On a supposed relation between the Amesha-spentas and the Vedic Adityas see
Roth, in *Zeitschrift der deutschen morgenländischen Gesellschaft*, vi, 69 f.; Macdonell,
Vedic Mythology, p. 44; Bloomfield, *Religion of the Veda*, p. 134 f. Cf. also L. H.
Gray (on the derivation of the Amshaspands from material gods), in *Archiv für
Religionswissenschaft*, vii (1904), 345.

[2] Cf. J. B. Carter, *De Deorum Romanorum Cognominibus*.

[3] Cf. Boissier, *La religion romaine*, i, 9.

of such gods is the feeblest, are characterized by objectiveness
of thought, indisposition to philosophical or psychological analysis, and a maintenance of local political and religious organization ; it is natural that they should construct concrete deities
exclusively or almost exclusively. Egypt also was objective, and
carried its demand for visible objects of worship to the point of
incarnating its gods in living animals ; such living gods tend to
banish pale abstractions, and such conceptions played an insignificant part in Egyptian religion. In India, with its genius for philosophical refinement, we might expect to find this latter class of
gods ; but Indian thought speedily passed into the large pantheistic and other generalizations that absorbed the lesser abstractions.
Greece appears to have had the combination of philosophy and
practicalness that favors the production of a certain sort of abstract gods, and a considerable number of these it did produce ;[1]
but here also philosophy, in the form of large theories of the constitution and life of man, got the upper hand and repressed the
other development. The Romans had no pretensions to philosophic or æsthetic thought, but they had a keen sense of the value
of family and civic life, and great skill in using religion for social
purposes. It is they among whom specialized deities, including
abstractions, had the greatest significance for the life of the people
— family and State.

706. With the growth of general culture all specialized divinities tend to disappear, absorbed by the great gods and displaced
by better knowledge of the laws governing the bodily and mental growth of men.[2] The divinities of abstractions, so far as they
were really alive, had the effect of making great civic and religious
ideas familiar to the people. Later (as in modern life) such ideas
were cherished as the outcome of reflection on domestic and
national relations — in the earlier period they were invested with
sacredness and with personal power to inspire and guide. Exactly
what their ethical influence on the masses was it is hardly possible

[1] Cf. Farnell, *Cults of the Greek States*, v, 442 ff.

[2] They survive in later times to some extent in the form of patron and other local
saints, Christian and Moslem.

to determine; but it may be regarded as probable that they helped to keep alive certain fundamental conceptions at a time when reflection on life was still immature.

NATURE GODS

707. The term "nature gods" may be taken as designating those deities that are distinguished on the one hand from natural objects regarded as divine and worshiped, and on the other hand from the great gods, who, whatever their origin, have been quite dissociated from natural objects; in distinction from these classes nature gods are independent deities who yet show traces of their origin in the cult of natural objects.[1]

708. These three classes often shade into one another, and it is not always easy to draw the lines between them. It is worth while, however, to keep them separate, because they represent different stadia of religious and general culture; the nature gods are found in societies which have risen above the old crude naturalism, but have not yet reached the higher grade of intellectual and ethical distinctness. But as they are in a real sense dissociated from natural objects, they tend to expand as society grows, and it is unnecessary to attempt to deduce all their functions from the characteristics of the objects with which they were originally connected. In some cases, doubtless, they coalesce with the local clan gods whose functions are universal; and in general, when a god becomes the recognized deity of his community, the tendency is to ascribe to him a great number of functions suggested by the existing social conditions. In some cases the particular function of the god may be derived from the function of the natural object whence he is supposed to spring; but the number and variety of functions that we often find assigned to one deity, and the number of deities that are connected with a single function, indicate the complexity of the processes of early religious thought and make it difficult to trace its history in detail.

[1] Cf. Bloomfield's classification of deities (*Religion of the Veda*, p. 96) partly according to the degree of clearness with which characters belonging to physical nature appear: "translucent" gods are those whose origin in nature is obvious; "transparent" gods are half-personified nature objects.

709. Among natural objects the heavenly bodies, sun, moon, and stars, and particularly the suń and moon, have very generally attracted men's attention and become objects of worship. The deification of the sun may be traced through all stadia of development, from the crudest objectivism to a highly developed monolatry or a virtual monotheism.[1] Veneration of the physical sun, or a conception of it as a supernatural man, is found in many parts of the world.[2] It has not been observed, apparently, in Australia, Melanesia, Indonesia, and on the North American Pacific Coast;[3] these regions are all backward in the creation of gods — devoting themselves to the elaboration of social organization they have contented themselves largely with an apparatus of spirits and divine animals. In Central and Northern Asia and among the Ainu of Jesso, while there appears to be a recognition of the sun as divine, it is difficult to distinguish real solar divinities.[4] In Japan mention is made of a sungoddess but she plays an insignificant part in the religious system.[5]

710. The cult is more developed in Eastern and Central North America, particularly in the former region. The Navahos (in the center of the continent) have a vague deity of the sun, but the cult is most prominent among the Algonkin (Lenâpé) and Natchez tribes; the last-named especially have an elaborate cult in which the sun as deity seems to be distinct from the physical form.[6]

711. The highest development of this cult in America was reached in Mexico and Peru. In both these countries, which had worked out a noteworthy civilization, the solar cult became supreme, and in Peru it attained an ethical and universalistic form which entitles it to rank among the best religious systems of the lower civilized nations.[7]

---

[1] Cf. Tylor, *Primitive Culture*, ii, 285 ff.   [2] See above, § 328 ff.

[3] Spencer and Gillen, *Native Tribes of Central Australia*, p. 561 ff., and *Northern Tribes of Central Australia*, p. 182 ; Codrington, *The Melanesians*, p. 348 ; Roth, in *Journal of the Anthropological Institute*, xxi, 125 ; Boas, *The Kwakiutl*, p. 410 f.

[4] Cf. Batchelor, *The Ainu* (1901), p. 63 f.   [5] Cf. Aston, *Shinto*, p. 35.

[6] J. G. Müller, *Amerikanische Urreligionen*, p. 58, and Index, s.v. *Sonnendienst*; Matthews, *Navaho Legends*, p. 33; Brinton, *The Lenâpé*, p. 65 (cf. his *American Hero-Myths*, p. 230) ; Gatschet, *Migration Legend of the Creeks*, p. 216 f.

[7] Prescott, *Mexico*, i, 57 ff.; id., *Peru*, i, 92 ff.; E. J. Payne, *History of the New World called America*, i, 463, 550 ff.; C. R. Markham, *The Incas of Peru*, pp. 63, 67, 104 ff.

712. The Egyptians, with their more advanced civilization, finally carried sun-worship to a very high point of perfection. The hymns to Ra, the sun-god, reached the verge of monotheism and are ethically high, yet traces of the physical side of the sun appear throughout.[1] The same thing is true of the old Semitic sun-cult. The Babylonian and Assyrian Shamash is in certain respects an independent deity with universal attributes, but retains also some of the physical characteristics of the sun.[2] In Africa, outside of Egypt, the only trace of an independent sun-god appears to be in Dahomi, where, however, he is not prominent; why such a god should not be found in the neighboring countries of Ashanti and Yoruba is not clear; climatic conditions would affect all these countries alike.[3]

713. In the Veda the sun-god Savitar has a very distinguished position as ethical deity, but earlier than he the similar figure Surya represents more nearly the physical sun, and this is true perhaps also of Mitra.[4] With the latter it is natural to compare the Avestan Mithra; he is held by some to have been originally a god of light, but he seems also to have characteristics of the sun in the Avesta,[5] and in late Persian the word *mihr* (' sun ') indicates that he was at any rate finally identified with the sun. It is noteworthy that a distinct sun-worship is reported among certain non-Aryan tribes of India, particularly the Khonds;[6] this cult may be compared with that of the Natchez mentioned above,[7] though the Khonds are less socially advanced than these American tribes.

714. The cultic history of the moon is similar to that of the sun, but in general far less important. In addition to its charm as illuminer of the night, it has been prominent as a measurer of time — lunar calendars appear among many tribes and nations, uncivilized (Maoris, Hawaiians, Dahomi, Ashanti and Yorubans, Nandi, Congo tribes, Bantu, Todas, and others) and civilized (the early Babylonians, Assyrians, Hebrews, Greeks, Romans,

---

1 *Records of the Past*, first series, ii, 129 ff.; viii, 105 ff.

2 Jastrow, *Religion of Babylonia and Assyria*, p. 71.   8 A. B. Ellis, *Ewe*, p. 65.

4 Macdonell, *Vedic Mythology*, pp. 30, 32, 29, cf. p. 23; Bloomfield, *Religion of the Veda*, p. 86; Hopkins, *Religions of India*, p. 40 ff.   5 *Yasht* x, 67.

6 Hopkins, *Religions of India*, p. 529 f.   7 § 710.

perhaps the early Egyptians, and now all Mohammedan peoples). Naturally it has been associated with the sun in myths, standing to it in the relation of brother or sister, husband or wife. Among existing noncivilized peoples it sometimes receives worship as a god [1] or as connected with a god. [2] In these cases it retains to a great extent its character as an object of nature. So the Greek Selenē and the Roman Luna, standing alongside of the lunar gods proper, probably indicate an early imperfect deification of the moon.

715. Though the stars were generally regarded, both among savages and in ancient civilized communities, as animated (possessed of souls), and in a sort divine, [3] instances of the deification proper of particular stellar bodies are rare. In Egypt they were reverenced, but apparently not worshiped. [4] The Babylonian astronomers and astrologers began early to connect the planets with the great gods (Jupiter with Marduk, Venus with Ishtar, etc.), and stars, like other heavenly bodies, were held by them to be divine, but a specific divinization of a star or planet does not appear in the known literature. [5] The same thing is true of China, where, it may be supposed, reverence for the stars was included in the general high position assigned to Heaven. [6] In the Aryan Hindu cults stars were revered, and by the non-Aryan Gonds were worshiped, but there is no star-god proper. [7]

716. In the Old Testament and the Apocrypha there are passages in which stars and planets are referred to in a way that indicates some sort of a conception of them as divine: they are said to have fought against Israel's enemies, and in the later literature they are (perhaps by a poetical figure of speech) identified

---

[1] W. Crooke, *Popular Religion and Folklore of Northern India*, i, 12 ff.; *Journal of the Royal Asiatic Society*, xviii, 373 ff. (the Lurka Coles) ; Hopkins, *Religions of India* (Dravidians, Kolarians) ; and for a modern, more civilized cult see Hopkins, op. cit., p. 480, note 3 ; Payne, *History of the New World called America*, i, 546 ff.

[2] Turner, *Samoa*, Index, s.v. *Moon*; Matthews, *Navaho Legends*, pp. 86, 226.

[3] See above, § 328 ff.; cf. Tylor, *Primitive Culture*, i, 290 f.

[4] Erman, *Handbook of Egyptian Religion*, pp. 88, 91.

[5] Jastrow, *Religion of Babylonia and Assyria*, pp. 356 ff., 457.

[6] De Groot, *Religion of the Chinese*, p. 5 (cf. J. Edkins, *Religion in China*, p. 105 ff.).

[7] Hopkins, *Religions of India*, pp. 204, 266, 526.

with foreign deities or with angels.[1] But there is no sign of Israelite worship offered them till the seventh century B.C., when, on the irruption of Assyrian cults, incense is said to have been burned in the Jerusalem temple to the mazzalot (probably the signs of the zodiac) and to all the host of heaven (the stars);[2] and there is still no creation of a star-god.[3] The early Hebrews may have practiced some sort of star-worship; there are traces of such a cult among their neighbors the Arabs.

717. The Arab personal name Abd ath-thuraiya, ' servant (worshiper) of the Pleiades,' testifies to a real cult,[4] though how far it involves a conception of the constellation as a true individual deity it may be difficult to say. It has been supposed that the pre-Islamic Arabs worshiped the planet Venus under the name Al-Uzza,[5] but this is not certain. It is true that they worshiped the morning star, and that ancient non-Arab writers identified the planet with Al-Uzza because it was with this goddess that the Roman goddess Venus was generally identified by foreigners. But Al-Uzza was an old Arabian local deity who gradually assumed great power and influence, and it is certain that she could not have been originally a star. It must, therefore, be considered doubtful whether the Arabs had a true star-god.

718. A well-defined instance of such a god is the Avestan Tistrya.[6] His origin as an object of nature appears plainly in his functions — he is especially a rain-god, and, as such, a source of all blessings. Alongside of him stand three less well defined stellar Powers. The Greeks and Romans adopted from Chaldean astronomy the nominal identification of the planets with certain gods (their own divine names being substituted for the Babylonian);

---

[1] Judg. v, 20; Isa. xxiv, 21 ff.; Job xxxviii, 7; Enoch xviii, 12; xxi, 1 (cf. Rev. ix, 1); cf. Neh. ix, 6. See Baudissin, *Semitische Religionsgeschichte*, i, 118 ff.; article " Astronomy and Astrology " in Hastings, *Dictionary of the Bible*.   [2] 2 Kings xxiii, 5.

[3] The corrupt and obscure passage Amos v, 26, cannot be cited as proving a cult of a deity Kaiwan (Masoretic text Kiyyun, Eng. R.V. " shrine ") identical with Assyrian kaiwan or kaiman, the planet Saturn; there is no evidence that this planet was worshiped in Assyria.   [4] Hastings, *Encyclopædia of Religion and Ethics*, i, 660.

[5] Cf. W. R. Smith, *Kinship and Marriage in Early Arabia*, chap. vi, note 8; Hastings, *Encyclopædia of Religion and Ethics*, loc. cit.

[6] Spiegel, *Eranische Alterthumskunde*, ii, 70 ff.

this did not necessarily carry with it stellar worship,[1] but at a late period there was a cult of the constellations.[2]

To some savage and half-civilized peoples the rainbow has appeared to be a living thing, capable of acting on man's life, sometimes friendly, sometimes unfriendly.[3] It figures largely in myths, but is not treated as a god.

THE GREAT GODS

719. Along with the deities described above there is a class of higher gods with well-defined personalities, standing quite outside physical nature and man, with definite characters, and humanized in the higher sense. In contrast with the bizarre or barbarous anthropomorphic forms of the earlier deities these have the shape of refined humanity, capable of taking part in the life of the best men; they are the embodiment of a reflective conception of the relations between men and the great world. Inchoate divine forms of this sort may be recognized among certain half-civilized communities, but in their full form they are found only among civilized peoples, being indeed the product of civilization; and among such peoples they exist in varying degrees of approach to completeness.

720. The process of growth from the clan deities and the nature gods up to these higher forms may be traced with some definiteness in the great civilized nations of antiquity. We can see that there has been a scientific movement of separation of gods from phenomena. There is the distinct recognition not only of the difference between man and physical nature, but also of the difference between phenomena and the powers that control them.[4] At the same time there is an increasing belief in the predominance of reason in the government of the world, and along with this a larger conception of the greatness of the world and finally of its unity. Artistic feeling coöperates in the change of the character of divine

---

[1] Cf. Gruppe, *Griechische Mythologie*, Index, s.vv. *Stern* and *Sternbilder*.

[2] Cumont, *Les religions orientales parmi les peuples romains*, chap vii.

[3] The Franciscan Fathers, *Ethnologic Dictionary of the Navaho Language*, Index, s.v.; Tylor, *Primitive Culture*, i, 293 f.

[4] This is the full development of what had doubtless been felt vaguely from the beginning of religious history.

beings — the necessity of giving symmetry and clearness to their persons, whereby they more and more assume the form of the highest human ideals. Necessarily the ethical element advances hand in hand with the intellectual and artistic; it becomes more and more difficult to conceive of gods as controlled by motives lower than those recognized by the best men.

721. This general progress of thought is in some cases embodied in the conception of a succession of dynasties — one set of gods is overthrown or succeeded by another set; the most extreme form of the overthrow appears in the conception of the death of a whole community of gods, but this occurs not in the form of natural development, but only when one stadium or phase of religion is overmastered and expelled by another.

722. In Babylonia the earliest pair of deities, Lakhmu and Lakhamu, vague forms, were succeeded by a second pair, Anshar and Kishar, somewhat less vague, and these in their turn yielded to the more definite group represented by Ea, Bel, and Marduk — deities who became the embodiments of the highest Babylonian culture; in Assyria Ashur and Ishtar occupied a similar position. In the long religious history of the Hindus many of the gods prominent in the Veda disappear or sink into subordinate positions, and deities at first unimportant become supreme. The Greek succession of dynasties resembles the Babylonian. The ancient Heaven and Earth are followed by Kronos,[1] and he is dethroned by Zeus, who represents governmental order and a higher ethical scheme of society. The Romans appear to have borrowed their chronology of the gods from the Greeks: the combination of Saturnus with Ops (who belongs rather with Consus), the identification of these two respectively with Kronos and Rhea, and the dynastic succession Cælus,[2] Saturnus, Jupiter, seem not to be earlier than the Hellenizing period in Rome.

723. These changes, when original, may have been due partly to the shifting of political power — the gods of a particular dominant

---

[1] On Kronos and the Titans cf. article " Kronos " in Roscher's *Lexikon*.

[2] Cælus (or Cælum) was sometimes called the son of Æther and Dies (Cicero, *De Natura Deorum*, iii, 17, 24).

region may have come into prominence and reigned for a time, giving place then to deities of some other region which had secured the hegemony; the history of the earliest gods lies far back in a dim region without historical records and therefore is not to be reconstructed definitely now. But such light as we get from literary records of later times rather suggests that the dynastic changes are the product of changes in the conception of the world, and these are as a rule in the direction of sounder and more humane thought.

724. There is a general similarity between the great deities that have been created by the various civilized peoples, since civilization has been practically the same everywhere. But the gods differ among themselves according to the special characters, needs, and endowments of the various peoples, so that no deity can be profitably studied without a knowledge of the physical and mental conditions of the community in which he arose. But everywhere we find that any one god may become practically supreme. Here again the political element sometimes comes in — a dominant city or state will impose its special god on a large district. There is also the natural tendency among men to concentrate on an individual figure. As legendary material has always gathered around particular men, so the great attributes of divinity gather about the person of a particular god who, for whatever reason, is the most prominent divine figure in a given community. Such a god becomes for the moment supreme, to the exclusion of other deities who under different circumstances might have had similar claims to precedence; and under favorable conditions a deity thus raised to the highest position may maintain himself and end by becoming the sole deity of his people and of the world. In any case such a divine figure becomes an ideal, and thus influences more or less the life of his worshipers.

725. In Oriental polytheistic systems the desire to secure completeness in the representation of divine activity shows itself in the combination of two or more forms into a unity of action. On the lower level we have the composite figures of Egypt and Babylonia, congeries of bodies, heads, and limbs, human and nonhuman — the result partly of the survival of ancient (sometimes outgrown) forms or the fusion of local deities, partly of the imaginative collocation of attributes. Many compound names may be explained in this way; in some cases they seem to arise from accidental local relations of cults.

As illustrations of lines of growth in divine figures we may take brief biographies of some of the greater gods. It is in comparatively few cases that the development of a god's character can be satisfactorily traced. There are no records of beginnings — we can only make what may be judged to be probable inferences from names, cults, and functions. The difficulty of the subject is increased by the fact that mythologians and theologians have obscured early conceptions by new combinations and interpretations, often employing familiar divine figures simply as vehicles of late philosophical ideas or some other sort of local dogmas.

726. *Egypt.*[1] The cult of the sun in Egypt issued in the creation of a group of solar divinities, the most important of whom are Horus (Har or Hor) and Ra (or Rê).

Horus appears to have been the great god of united Egypt in the earliest times about which we have information. The kings of the predynastic and early dynastic periods are called " worshipers of Horus," a title that was adopted by succeeding monarchs, who had each his " Horus name." [2] He was also the special patron of some small communities — a fact that has been variously interpreted as indicating that the god's movement was from local to general patron,[3] or that it was in the opposite direction[4]; the former of these hypotheses is favored by what appears elsewhere in such changes in the positions of deities. As Horus is always connected with light he may have been originally a local sun-god; it is possible, however, that he was a clan god with general functions, who was brought into association with the sun by the natural progress of thought. In any case he became a great sun-god, but yielded

---

[1] Ed. Meyer, *Geschichte des Alten Aegyptens* (and cf. his *Geschichte des Altertums,* 2d ed.); Maspero, *Dawn of Civilization*; Wiedemann, *Religion of the Ancient Egyptians,* and article " Religion of Egypt " in Hastings, *Dictionary of the Bible,* vol. v; Erman, *Handbook of Egyptian Religion*; Breasted, *History of Egypt.*

[2] Breasted, op cit., pp. 36, 46; id., *Ancient Records of Egypt,* under the various kings.   [3] So Ed. Meyer, in article " Horos " in Roscher's *Lexikon.*

[4] So Steindorff, *Religion of the Ancient Egyptians,* p. 26 f.

his position of eminence to Ra. The myth of his conflict with Set, the representative of darkness, is probably a priestly dualistic construction, resting, perhaps, on a political situation (the struggle between the North and the South of the Egyptian territory).[1]

727. The general development of Ra is plain, though details are lacking. It may be inferred from his name (which means ' sun ') that he was originally the physical sun. Traces of his early crudeness appear in the stories of his destruction of mankind, and of the way in which Isis, by a trick, got from him his true name and, with it, his power.[2] With the growth of his native land (Lower Egypt) he became the great lord of the sun, and finally universal lord ;[3] his supremacy was doubtless due in part to the political importance of On (Heliopolis), the seat of his chief shrine. What other circumstances contributed to his victory over Horus are not recorded ; in general it may be supposed that political changes occasioned the recedence of the latter.

The primacy of Ra is illustrated by the fact that Amon was identified with him. Amon, originally the local god of Thebes,[4] became great in the South as Ra became great in the North, rising with the growth of the Theban kingdom. His hold on the people, and particularly (as was natural) on the priests, is shown in a noteworthy way by the episode of Amenhotep IV's attempt to supplant him by establishing a substantially monotheistic cult of the sun-god Aton; the attempt was successful only during the king's life — after his death Amon, under the vigorous leadership of the Theban priests, resumed his old position and maintained it until the first break-up of the national Egyptian government. But it was Amon-Ra that became supreme from the fourteenth century onward. The combination of the names was made possible by the social and political union of the two divisions of the land, and it was Ra who gave special glory to Amon.[5]

---

1 Cf. Steindorff, op. cit., p. 30 f.

2 *Records of the Past*, vi, 105 ff. ; Steindorff, op. cit., p. 107 ff.

8 See, for example, the hymn in *Records of the Past*, viii, 105 ff.

4 He was, therefore, doubtless a god of fertility.

5 *Records of the Past*, ii, 129 ff. The names of other deities also were combined with that of Ra.

728. A different line of growth appears in the history of Osiris — he owed his eminence mainly to his connection with the dead. Where his cult arose is not known; he was a very old god, possibly prominent in the predynastic period;[1] at a later time the importance of Abydos, the chief seat of his worship, may have added to his reputation. But the ceremonies of his cult and the myths that grew up about his name indicate that he was originally a deity of vegetation, the patron of the underground productive forces of the earth, and so, naturally, he became the lord of the Underworld,[2] and eventually (as ethical conceptions of life became more definite in Egypt) the embodiment of future justice, the determiner of the moral character and the everlasting fate of men. Why he and not some other underground god became Underworld judge the data do not make clear. His association with the death and revivification of plants gave a peculiarly human character to his mythical biography and a dramatic and picturesque tone to his cult.[3] Of all ancient lords of the Otherworld it is Osiris that shows the most continuous progress and reaches the highest ethical plane — a fact that must be referred to the intense interest of the Egyptians in the future.[4]

729. The three most prominent female deities of the Egyptian pantheon, Hathor of Dendera, Neith (Nit, Neit) of Sais, and Isis of Buto, exhibit one and the same type of character, and each is occasionally identified with one of the others. Hathor was widely worshiped, but was not otherwise especially noteworthy. The famous inscription said to have stood in the temple of Neith at Sais ("What is and what shall be and what has been am I — my veil no one has lifted"[5]) seems not to be immediately connected with

[1] Egyptian civilization, as appears from recent explorations, began far back of Menes; cf. Ed. Meyer, *Geschichte des Altertums*, 2d ed., vol. i, part ii, § 169.

[2] Cf. Breasted, *History of Egypt*, p. 58; Frazer, *Adonis Attis Osiris*, bk. iii, chap. v.

[3] Plutarch, *Isis and Osiris*, 18; Frazer, loc. cit.; Breasted, op. cit., p. 171 f.

[4] His identification by some ancient theologians with the sun (Frazer, op. cit., p. 351 f.) or with the moon (Plutarch, op. cit., 41) is an illustration of the late tendency to identify any great god with a heavenly body.

[5] Such is the wording given by Proclus. The form in Plutarch (*Isis and Osiris*, 9) is substantially the same: "I am all that has been and that is and that shall be, and my veil no mortal has lifted." See Roscher, *Lexikon*, article "Nit," col. 436. Doubts have been cast on the reality of the alleged inscription.

any important religious movement, though it is in keeping with the
liberal and mystical tendency of the later time. The third goddess,
Isis, had a more remarkable history. Her beginnings are obscure,
and she appears in the inscriptions later than the other two. She
may have been a local deity,[1] brought into association with Osiris
(as his sister or his wife) through the collocation of their cults, and
thus sharing his popularity ; or she may have been a late theological
creation.[2] Whatever her origin, as early as the sixteenth century B.C.
she appears as a great magician (poisoning and healing Ra by magic
arts),[3] then (along with Osiris) as civilizer, and finally as model wife
and mother, and as serene and beneficent mistress of the land. It
was, apparently, in this last character that she became the gathering-
point for the higher religious and ethical ideas of the time, and the
central figure in a religious scheme that was widely adopted in and
out of Egypt and seemed to be a formidable rival of Christianity.[4]

730. India. It is in India that we find the most varied and most
sweeping development in the functions and positions of deities —
a result due in part to the long-continued movement of philosophic
thought, partly to changes in the popular religious point of view
occasioned by modifications of the social life.[5]

The etymology of the name Varuna is doubtful, but the representation of him in the Rig-Veda points to the sky as his original
form — he is a clear example of a sky-god who becomes universal.
Of his earliest history we have no information — in the most ancient
records he is already fully formed. In the Rig-Veda he embraces
the whole of life — he is absolute ruler and moral governor, he
punishes sin and forgives the penitent. In conjunction with Mitra
he is the lord of order.[6] Mitra, originally the physical sun, is naturally associated with Varuna, but in the Rig-Veda occupies a generally subordinate position, though he appears sometimes to have the

---

1 Maspero, *Dawn of Civilization*, p. 131.
2 So Ed. Meyer, in Roscher, *Lexikon*, article " Isis," col. 360.
3 Steindorff, *Religion of the Ancient Egyptians*, p. 107 ff.
4 See Drexler, in Roscher, *Lexikon*, article " Isis," col. 424 ff.
5 Barth, *The Religions of India* (Eng. tr.) ; Hopkins, *Religions of India* ; Hillebrandt, *Vedische Mythologie* ; Macdonell, *Vedic Mythology* ; Bloomfield, *Religion of
the Veda*. See the bibliography in Hopkins, op. cit., p. 573 ff.
6 *Rig-Veda*, viii, 41, 1. 7 ; i, 23, 5 (*ṛta*, ' order ').

attributes of his associate; the two together embody a lofty ethical conception. In accordance with the Hindu fondness for metaphysical abstractions and generalizations the nature god Varuna in the course of time yielded the primacy to Prajapati, ' lord of beings,' [1] who in his turn gave way to the impersonal Brahma. In the popular cults as well as in philosophical systems Varuna sank (or perhaps returned) to the position of patron of phenomena of nature — there was no longer need of him.

731. A god of somewhat uncertain moral character is Indra, who as a nature god is closely connected with the violent phenomena of the air (rain, thunder, and lightning). In this relation he is often terrible, often beneficent, but with low tastes that it is difficult to explain. His fondness for soma, without which he attempts nothing, is perhaps a priestly touch, a glorification of the drink that played so important a part in the ritual; or he may herein be an expression of popular tastes. The sensuous character of the heaven of which he (as air-god) is lord arose doubtless in response to early conceptions of happiness; [2] it is not unlike the paradise of Mohammed, which is to be regarded not as immoral, but only as the embodiment of the existing conception of happy family life. Yet Indra also became a universal god, the controller of all things, and it was perhaps due to his multiform human character as warrior and rain-giver [3] (in his victorious conflict with the cloud-dragon), and as representative of bodily enjoyment, that he became the favorite god of the people. It is not hard to understand why Agni, fire, should be associated with him and share his popularity to some extent; but the importance of fire in the sacrifice gave Agni a peculiar prominence in the ritual.

732. The most curious case of transformation and exaltation is found in the history of Soma, at first a plant whose juice was intoxicating, then a means of ecstatic excitement, a gift to the gods,

---

[1] *Rig-Veda*, x, 121.

[2] Early imagination apparently connected the future social life of gods and men not with the calm sky, but with the upper region that was the scene of constant and awful movements. But the ground of the choice of Indra as lord of heaven rests in the obscurity of primeval times.

[3] For economic reasons a rain-god must generally be prominent and popular.

the drink of the gods, and finally itself a god invested with the greatest attributes. This divinization of a drink was no doubt mainly priestly — it is a striking illustration of the power of the association of ideas, and belongs in the same general category with the deification of abstractions spoken of above.[1]

733. An example of a god leaping from an inferior position to the highest place in the pantheon is afforded by Vishnu, a nature god of some sort, described in the early documents as traversing the universe in three strides. Relatively insignificant in the earlier period and in the Upanishads, he appears in the epic, and afterwards, as the greatest of the gods, and, in the form of his avatar Krishna, becomes the head of a religion which has often been compared with Christianity in the purity of its moral conceptions. By his side in this later time stands his rival Çiva, the chief figure in a sect or system which shared with Vishnuism the devotion of the later Hindus. The rise of these two gods is to be referred probably to the dissatisfaction in the later times with the phenomenal character which still clung, in popular feeling, to the older deities. Varuna, once supreme, sank after a while to the position of a god of rain, and Indra, Agni, and Soma were frankly naturalistic, while the impersonal Brahma was too vague to meet popular demands. What the later generation wanted was a god personal and divorced from physical phenomena, supreme, ethically high, but invested with warm humanity. These conditions were fulfilled by Vishnu and Çiva, and particularly by Krishna; that is, the later thought constructed these new deities in accordance with the demand of the higher and the lower religious feeling of the time: the two sides of the human demand, the genial and the terrible, are embodied, the first in Vishnu, the second in Çiva.

734. The primeval pair, Heaven and Earth, though represented as the parents of many gods and worshiped with sacrifices, play no great part in the Hindu religious system. Dyaus, the Sky, never attained the proportions of the formally identical Zeus and Jupiter. His attributes are distinctly those of the physical sky. The higher rôle is assigned to Varuna, who is the sky conceived

[1] § 703.

of as a divíne Power divorced from merely physical characteristics;[1] the mass of phenomena connected with the sky (thunder,
lightning, and such like) are isolated and referred to various
deities. Prithivi, the Earth, in like manner, retains her physical attributes, and does not become the nourishing mother of all things.[2]

With a partial exception in the case of Ushas[3] (Dawn) the
early Hindu pantheon contains no great female figure; there are
female counterparts of male deities, but no such transcendent
personages as Isis, Athene, and Demeter. Whether this fact is to
be explained from early Hindu views of the social position of
women, or from some other idea, is uncertain. In certain modern religious cults, however, the worship of the female principle
(Çakti) is popular and influential. It is probable that in early
times every tribe or district had its female divine representative
of fertility, an embryonic mother-goddess. If the Aryan Hindus
had such a figure, she failed to grow into a great divinity. But
the worship of such deities came into Aryan India at a relatively
recent date, apparently from non-Aryan sources, and has been
incorporated in Hindu systems. Various forms of Çakti have
been brought into relation with various gods, the most important
being those that have become attached to the worship of Çiva.[4]
To him is assigned as wife the frightful figure called Durga or
Kali (and known by other names), a blood-loving monster with
an unspeakably licentious cult. Other Çakti deities are more
humane, and there is reason to suppose that the ground of the
devotion shown to Kali, especially by women, is in many cases
simply reverence for the female principle in life, or more particularly for motherhood.[5]

735. The original character of the Hindu lord of the Otherworld, Yama, is obscured by the variety of the descriptions of

---

[1] The history of this distinction between Dyaus and Varuna is lost in the obscurity of the beginnings.

[2] This conception appears in germinal form in *Rig-Veda*, v, 84, vi, 515, but is not
there or elsewhere developed.   [3] Macdonell, *Vedic Mythology*, § 20.

[4] Cf. Hastings, *Encyclopædia of Religion and Ethics*, article " Bengal," p. 491 ff.,
and the references there given to authorities.

[5] One form of Çaktism is described (in Hastings, loc. cit.) as being the general
worship of the Mothers of the universe represented as the wives of the gods.

him in the documents. In the Rig-Veda he appears both as god and (as it seems) as man. He is the son of the solar deity Vivashant (Vivashat); he is named in enumerations of gods, and Agni is his friend and his priest; he receives worship, and is besought to come to the sacrifice.[1] On the other hand, he is never called "god," but only "king";[2] he is spoken of as the "only mortal," and is said to have chosen death; he is associated in heaven with the "fathers."[3] The modern interpretations of his origin have followed these two sets of data. By some writers he has been identified with the sun (particularly the setting sun), and with the moon.[4] But these identifications are set aside for the Veda by the fact that in lists of gods he is distinguished from sun and moon.[5] By others he is regarded as the mythical first man, the first ancestor, with residence in the sky, deified as original ancestors sometimes were, and, as the first to die and enter the world beyond, made the king of that world.

Though Yama is not the sun in the Veda, it is possible that he was so regarded in the period preceding the Vedic theological construction, and in support of this view it may be said that the sun setting, descending into the depths, is a natural symbol of the close of man's life,[6] and rising, represents the man's life in the beyond — thus the sun would be identified with man, and not unnaturally with the first man, the first to die. In support of the other view may be cited the great rôle ascribed by many peoples to the first man: in savage lore he is often the creator or arranger of the world,[7] and he is sometimes, like Yama, the son of the sun.[8]

[1] Rig-Veda, x, 64, 92, 135, 21, 52, 14.

[2] Ibid., x, 14; ix, 113. However, this title is given to Varuna also (x, 14): Yama and Varuna are the two kings whom the dead man sees when he reaches heaven.

[3] Ibid., x, 10, 13, 14 (cf. Atharva-Veda, xviii, 13).

[4] Hillebrandt, Vedische Mythologie, i, 394 ff., but only for the Indo-Iranian period.

[5] Rig-Veda, x, 64.

[6] Cf. Müller, Lectures on the Science of Language, second series, p. 534 f.; Tylor, Primitive Culture, ii, 314; Bergaigne, La religion védique, ii, 94, note 3; Frobenius, Childhood of Man, chap. xxii. Cf. the Egyptian conception of Osiris (Maspero, Dawn of Civilization, p. 195).

[7] Matthews, Navaho Legends, p. 80; other examples are given in W. Ellis's Polynesian Researches, i, chap. v, and Tylor, op. cit., ii, 312 ff.

[8] Ellis, loc. cit.; Dorsey, The Skidi Pawnee, p. 6.

Such an one, entering the other world, might become its lord, and in process of time be divinized and made the son of the creator sun.[1] The Hindu figure is often compared to the Avestan first man, Yima; but Yima, so far as appears, was never divinized, and is not religiously of great importance. Nor do the late Jewish legends and theosophical speculations bear on the point under consideration : in Paradise, it is said, Adam was waited on by angels, the angels were commanded by God to pay him homage (so also in the Koran), and he is described as being the light of the world; and Philo and others conceived of a first or heavenly man (Adam Kadmon), free from ordinary human weakness, and identical with the Logos or the Messiah — therefore a judge in the largest sense of the word.[2] But, while these conceptions testify to the strong appeal made to the imagination by the figure of the mythical first man, they throw little light on the original form of Yama — the early constructions do not include the judge of the other world, and the later ones are too late to explain so early a figure as the Vedic king of that world.

736. In the Rig-Veda Yama is specifically the overlord of the blessed dead — the pious who were thought worthy to dwell in heaven with the gods and to share to some extent their divinity; with the wicked he seems to have nothing to do. The general history of the conception of the future life suggests that in the earliest Indo-Iranian period there was a hades to which all the dead went.[3] If there was a divine head of this hades (originally an underground deity, like Osiris, Allatu, and Ploutos) he would accompany the pious fathers when, in the later Hindu theologic construction, they were transported to heaven; and if the first ancestor occupied a distinguished place among the dead,[4] he might be fused with the divine head into a sort of unity, and the

---

[1] Hopkins, *Religions of India*, p. 128 ff.; Macdonell, *Vedic Mythology*, § 77; Bloomfield, *Religion of the Veda*, Index, s.v .*Yama*; and see the references in these works to other authors.

[2] *Jewish Encyclopedia*, articles "Adam" and "Adam Kadmon"; *Koran*, ii, 29 ff.; cf. 1 Cor. xv, 45 ff.   [3] See above, §§ 67 ff., 82.

[4] On the relation between the two "first ancestors," Yama and Manu, cf. Bloomfield, op. cit., p. 140 f.

result might be such a complex figure as Yama appears to be. However this may be, the Vedic Yama underwent a development in accordance with the changes in the religious ideas of the people, becoming at last an ethical judge of the dead.[1]

737. *Persia.* The Mazdean theistic system presents special difficulties.[2] The nature of its divine world is remarkable, almost unique, and the literature that has come down to us was edited at a comparatively late period, probably not before the middle of the third century of our era, so that it is not always easy to distinguish the earlier and the later elements of thought. It is generally regarded as certain that the two branches of the Aryan race, the Indian and the Persian, once dwelt together and formed one community, having the same general religious system : the material of spirits is substantially the same in the two and they have certain important names in common — to the Indian Asura, Soma, Mitra, the Persian Ahura, Haoma, Mithra correspond in form exactly. But in the way in which this material was modified and organized the two communities differ widely.

738. The peculiarity of the Persian system is that it practically disregards all the old gods except Mithra and Anahita, substituting for them beings designated by names of qualities, and organizes all extrahuman Powers in two classes — one under the Good Spirit (Spenta Mainyu), the other under the Bad Spirit (Angro Mainyu). The former is attended by six great beings, Immortal Spirits (Amesha-spentas) : Good Mind, Best Order or Law, Holy Harmony or Wisdom, Piety, Well-being, Immortality.[3] In the Gathas, which are commonly held to be the most ancient Zoroastrian documents, these attendants of the supreme god are often nothing but qualities, but on the other hand are often personified and worshiped. The rival of the Good Spirit is surrounded similarly by lying spirits (*drujas*), among whom one, Aeshma, holds a prominent place. The two divine chiefs stand side by side in the earliest

[1] Hopkins, *Religions of India*, p. 379 ff.
[2] Tiele-Gehrich, *Geschichte der Religion im Altertum*, vol. ii, part i.
[3] See above, § 703. Cf. articles by L. H. Mills in *Journal of the American Oriental Society*, vols. xx and xxi; L. H. Gray, in *Archiv für Religionswissenschaft*, vii (1904), p. 345.

literature almost as coequal powers; but it is explained that the wicked one is to be destroyed with all his followers.

739. In some of the early hymns (Yaçnas) Mithra is closely attached to Ahura Mazda — the two are called " the lofty and imperishable ones." The goddess Anahita, first mentioned in an inscription of Artaxerxes II, and described only in the late Fifth Yasht, appears to have been originally a deity of water. It was, doubtless, her popularity that led to her official recognition by Artaxerxes; possibly her formal recognition by the Mazdean leaders was a slow process, since she does not appear in the older Avesta. In the Yasht she receives worship (being in the form of a beautiful young woman) as the dispenser of all blessings that come from pure water; she is said to have been created by Ahura Mazda, and is wholly subordinated to him. Besides these two a great number of lesser gods are mentioned; the latter, apparently the old local gods and spirits here subordinated to the supreme god, are unimportant in the official cult. The souls of the departed also become objects of worship.

740. It thus appears that Zoroastrianism was a reform of the old polytheism. The movement closely resembles the struggle of the Hebrew prophets against the worship of the Canaanite Baals and other foreign gods. In both cases there is evidence going to show that popular cults continued after the leaders of the reform had thrown off the offensive elements of the old system: the Hebrew people continued to worship foreign gods long after the great prophets had pronounced against them; and the official recognition of Ahura Mazda in the Achæmenian inscriptions[1] by no means proves that lower forms of worship were not practiced in Persia by the people.[2]

741. If we ask for the grounds of this recoil from the old gods, we must doubtless hold that ethical feeling was a powerful motive in the reform, though economic and other considerations were, doubtless, not without influence.

[1] *Records of the Past*, vols. v, ix.
[2] Many lesser divine beings are mentioned by Spiegel (in *Eranische Alterthumskunde*, ii, 66 ff.) ; the advance to a real monotheistic cult was not achieved in Persia without many generations of struggle.

Since Ahura Mazda is ethically good and his worship ethically pure, there is clearly in its origin hostility to low modes of worship and to materialistic ideas. Possibly also we have here a struggle of a clan for the recognition of its own god, as among the Israelites the Yahweh party represented exclusive devotion to the old national god. If there was such a clan or party in Persia, it is obvious that it produced men of high intelligence and great moral and organizing power, and all that we know of the religious history leads us to suppose that the establishment of the supremacy of Ahura Mazda was the result of a long development.

742. As to the provenance of the Mazdean supreme lord, not a few scholars of the present day hold that he was identical with the Indian Varuna. It is in favor of this identification that the qualities of the two deities are the same, and there is also the noteworthy fact that Ahura Mazda is coupled with Mithra as Varuna is coupled with Mitra; according to this view the Mazdean deity was originally the god of the sky, by whose side naturally stands the sun. In a case like this, involving a general agreement between two systems of thought, there are two possible explanations of the relation between them · it may be supposed that one borrowed from the other (in the present case the borrowing would be on the part of the Persians); or the explanation may be that the two communities developed original material along the same general lines, though with local differences. In the absence of historical data it is perhaps impossible to say which of these explanations is to be preferred. There is, however, no little difficulty in the supposition that one community has actually borrowed its religious system from a neighbor; the general probability is that each followed its own line.

743. Nor is it probable that the rejection of the old divine names by the Persians was the result of hostility toward their Indian neighbors. It is doubtless a curious fact that the Indian name for 'evil spirit,' *asura*, is in Persian the name of a good spirit, Ahura, while the Indian *diva*, the general term for a god, is in Persian the designation of a wicked spirit, *daeva*. The Persian employment of *daeva* for 'evil spirit' may be explained as a protest not against

Indian gods, but against the deities of their own land; so the Hebrew prophets or their editors apply opprobrious names, " no-god " and other terms, to deities regarded by them as inadequate. The abstractions of the Mazdean system have been referred to above. They seem to have been resorted to from a feeling of pro-found disgust at the worship of some class of people. Unfortunately we have not the historical data that might make the situation clear. In the Gathas the people of Ahura Mazda are suffering from the incursions of predatory tribes, and the greater part of the appeals to the deity are for protection for the herds against their enemies. We thus have a suggestion of a struggle, political and religious, between the more civilized Aryans and the savage Tataric tribes around them.

744. In the later period of Mazdeanism the old titles of supreme deity were succeeded (though not displaced) by the terms " Bound-less Time" and " Boundless Space," the latter doubtless suggested by the vault of heaven. These generalizations, however, had little influence on the development of the theological side of the religion, which has continued to regard Ahura Mazda and Angro Mainyu as the two heads of the world and the determiners of human life. The rituals of the Mazdean and Hindu faiths were influenced by the ethical developments of the two, becoming simpler and more humane with the advance toward elevated conceptions of God and man.

745. In view of such facts as are known it may be surmised that the Mazdean system originated with an Aryan agricultural tribe or body of tribes dwelling near the Caspian Sea, in contact with hostile nomads. These Aryans, we may assume, had the ordinary early apparatus of spirits and nature deities (gods of the sun, water, etc.), but, at the same time, a disposition to concentrate worship on a single god (probably a sky-god), who became the chief tribal deity and was naturally regarded as the source of all things good, the Good Spirit; the phenomena of life led them (as it led some other early peoples) to conceive of a rival spirit, the author of things hostile to life. With economic conditions and intellectual character-istics very different from those of their Hindu brethren, they de-veloped no capacity for organizing an elaborate pantheon — they

were practically monolatrous, were content with an all-sufficient
Good Spirit (the Bad Spirit being tolerated as an intellectual necessity), gradually subordinatèd to him such gods as the popular feeling retained, and relegated to the sphere of evil the host of inferior
hurtful spirits or gods (*daevas*) whose existence they could not
deny.[1] The religious leaders, representing and enforcing the tribal
tendency of thought, in the course of time gave more and more
definite shape to the cult; perhaps Zoroaster was a preëminent
agent in this movement. Ethical purification, as a matter of course,
went hand in hand with cultic organization. The old gods or spirits,
associates of the supreme god, became embodiments of moral conceptions, and a ritual of physical and moral purity was worked out.
Such may have been the general history of the official system; data
for a detailed chronological history are lacking.[2]

746. China. Chinese religion is characterized by a remarkable
restraint in ecclesiastical development : simple religious customs, no
native priestly order, few gods, almost no myths. The basis of the
popular religion is the usual material, comprising ancestors, spirits
(including tutelary spirits), a few departmental gods (of war, of the
kitchen, etc.), some of which are said to be deified men. The
system is thus nearly the same as that of the central Asiatic
Mongolians.[3]

747. The reflective movement (which must have begun long
before the sixth century B.C., the period of Confucius and Lao-tsze)
is marked by the attempt to perfect the social organization, regard
being paid mainly to visible, practical relations. Stress is laid on the
principle of order in family and state, which is held to reflect the
order of the universe;[4] speculation is avoided, there is a minimum
of religion. In the more developed religious system the two prominent features are, first, the dominant conception of the unity of

---

[1] Cf. the similar process in the Arabian treatment of the jinn (W. R. Smith,
Religion of the Semites, new ed., p. 122 f.).

[2] Cf. A. V. Williams Jackson, *Zoroaster*, and his sketch in Geiger and Kuhn's
Grundriss der iranischen Philologie; D. Menant, *Zoroaster d'après la tradition parsie*, in *Annales du Musée Guimet*, vol xxx.

[3] De Groot, *Religion of the Chinese*, chaps. i and iii; pp. 62 ff., 112 f., 129 f.

[4] With this conception we may compare the similar principles in the Vedic and
Mazdean systems.

the family and of the state led to the emphasizing of the worship of ancestors — a cult which, going back to a very early time, has been interwoven in China with the individual and communal life in a thoroughgoing way, with a constant infusion of moral ideas; and in the next place, the order of society and of the external world is represented by Heaven.[1]

748. Originally, doubtless, Heaven was the physical sky (as among the Hindus and Persians and many other peoples), but at an early period came to be practically the supreme god. A sort of monotheistic cult has thus been established as the official religion. The emperor is the Son of Heaven and the High Priest of the nation, and in the great annual sacrifices performed by him the host of minor powers is practically ignored and worship is addressed to the controlling powers of the world. This official worship does not set aside the cult of the various spirits, whose existence is recognized by the minor officials as well as by the people. The cult of local spirits has grown to extraordinary dimensions. They fill the land, controlling the conditions of life and demanding constant regard; and the experts, who are supposed to know the laws governing the action of the spirits (for example, as to proper burial-places), wield enormous power, and make enormous charges of money. These spirits are treated as of subordinate importance in the official religion. The process by which China has reached this religious attitude must have extended over millenniums, and, as is stated above, the intellectual movement in the direction of simplicity and clearness has been attended by an advance in ethical purity.

749. The tendency of Chinese thought is illustrated by the two systems of philosophy which in the sixth century B.C. formulated the conception of a universal dominant order:[2] Confucius represents the extreme logical development of natural order in human life as a product of cosmic order — he is content absolutely to deal with

---

[1] The all-controlling order, as is remarked above, is that of the universe, which furnishes the norm for human life; but in the universe the grandest object is heaven.

[2] Legge, in *Sacred Books of the East*, xxxix, xl; De Groot, *Religious System of China*, and his smaller works, *Religion of the Chinese* and *Development of Religion in China*.

the practical affairs of life and discourages attempts to inquire into
the nature of gods or into the condition of men after death. Lao-
tsze, on the other hand, similarly taking the Way (*tao*), or Universal
Order, as the informing and controlling power of the world, appears
to have laid the stress on the relation between it and the human
soul — a conception that has affinities with the Stoic Logos. But
it is Confucianism that has remained the creed of educated China.
Taoism, beginning, apparently, as a spiritual system, did not appeal to the Chinese feeling, and speedily degenerated into a system
of magical jugglery. Thus the Chinese, with the feeblest religious
sense to be found in any great nation, have nevertheless reached
the grandiose conception of the all-embracing and all-controlling
supreme Heaven. In their case the governing consideration has
been the moral organization of social life, and Nature has swallowed up all great partial deities.

750. *Japan.* Japan has produced no great god ;[1] out of the mass
of nature gods reported in the Kojiki not one becomes preëminent.
There is recognition of Heaven and Earth as the beginning of
things, and of the sun as a deity, but neither the sky-god nor the
sun-goddess becomes a truly high god. Japanese theistic development appears to have been crippled at an early period by the
intrusion of Chinese influences; the very name of the national
religion, Shinto, ' the Way of the Gods,' is Chinese. The emperor
was deified, and ancestor-worship became the principal popular
cult ;[2] but Confucianism and Buddhism overlaid the native worship
at an early period. The later forms of Shinto have moved rather
toward the rejection of the old deities than toward the creation of
a great national god.

751. *Semitic peoples.* Among the various Semitic peoples there
is so marked a unity of thought that, as Robertson Smith has
pointed out,[3] we may speak of the Semitic religion, though there are

[1] W. E. Griffis, *Religions of Japan*; E. Buckley, in Saussaye, *Lehrbuch der Religionsgeschichte*, 2d ed.; Aston, *Shinto*; Knox, *Development of Religion in Japan*;
Longford, *The Story of Old Japan*, chap. ii.

[2] Whether the worship of ancestors, now so important an element of the national
life, is native or borrowed is uncertain.

[3] W. R. Smith, *Religion of the Semites*, new ed., p. 13 ff.

noteworthy local differences. Generally we find among these communities, as elsewhere, a large number of local deities, scarcely
distinguishable in their functions one from another.[1] A noteworthy
illustration of the long continuance of these local cults is given in
the attempt of the last king of Babylon, Nabonidus, to centralize
the worship by bringing the statues of the local deities to Babylon; the result was a general popular protest. Similarly an attempt
was made by King Josiah in the seventh century B.C. to centralize
all Israelite worship in Jerusalem, but the history of the succeeding
generations shows that the attempt was not successful. The local
gods represent the clannic and tribal organization, to which the
Semites appear to have clung with peculiar fondness.

752. Semitic religion shows an orderly advance through the
medium of tribal and national feeling in conjunction with the
regular moral and intellectual growth of the community. First one
god and then another comes to the front as this or that city attains
leadership, but these chief gods are substantially identical with one
another in functions. The genealogical relations introduced by the
priestly theologians throw no light on the original characters of the
deities and are often ignored in the inscriptions. A natural division
into gods of the sky and gods of the earth may be recognized, but
in the high gods this distinction practically disappears.

753. Turning first to the Tigris-Euphrates region, we find certain
nature gods that attained more or less definite universal character.[2]
The physical sky becomes the god Anu, who, though certainly
a great god, was never so prominent as certain other deities, and
in Assyria yielded gradually to Ashur. Why the Semites, in marked
contrast with the Indo-Europeans and the Chinese, have shown a
relatively feeble recognition of the physical heaven we are not able
to say; possibly the tribal feeling referred to above may have led

---

[1] Compare Baethgen, *Beiträge zur semitischen Religionsgeschichte*, p. 262 f.

[2] Jastrow, *Religion of Babylonia and Assyria*; id., *Aspects of Religious Belief and
Practice in Babylonia and Assyria*; Jeremias, in Saussaye, *Lehrbuch der Religionsgeschichte*; Zimmern, article "Babylonians and Assyrians" in Hastings, *Encyclopædia
of Religion and Ethics*; Ed. Meyer, *Geschichte des Altertums*, i, part ii, 2d book. In
our survey of Babylonian deities the question of Sumerian influence may be left
out of the account.

to a centering of devotion on those deities that lay nearer to everyday life, or in the case of Babylonia it may be that the city with
which Anu was particularly connected lost its early importance, and
its deity in consequence yielded to others.[1] The sun is a more definite and more practically important object than the expanse of the
sky, and the Semitic sun-god, Shamash, plays a great rôle from the
earliest to the latest times. The great king Hammurabi (commonly
placed near the year 2000 B.C.), in his noteworthy civil code, takes
Shamash as his patron, as the inspirer of wisdom and the controller of human right; and from this time onward this deity is
invoked by the kings in their inscriptions. The worship of the
sun was established in Canaan at an early time (as the name of
the town Bethshemesh, 'house of Shemesh,' shows), and under
Assyrian influence was adopted by a large number of Israelites in
the seventh century B.C.; the prophet Ezekiel represents prominent
Israelites as standing in the court of the temple, turning their backs
on the sacred house and worshiping the sun;[2] but as to the nature
of the sun-god and his worship in these cases we have no information. Other nature deities that rose to eminence are the moon-god,
Sin, and the storm-god, Ramman.

754. The other deities of the Babylonian and Assyrian pantheons seem not to be connected by their names with natural
phenomena. They are attached to particular cities or districts,
and each district or city, as it becomes a great religious center,
raises its favorite god to a position of preëminence. Generally
the choice of a special deity by a particular city lies back of historical documents, and the reason for such choice therefore cannot be
definitely fixed. The attributes and functions of the resulting great
gods, as has already been remarked, are substantially everywhere
the same, and where one function becomes prominent, it is often possible to explain its prominence from the political or other conditions.

755. Moreover, as in all theological constructions that follow
great political unifications, it was natural to extend the domain

---

[1] Compare Jastrow, *Religion of Babylonia and Assyria*, p. 481; id., *Aspects of
Religious Belief and Practice in Babylonia and Assyria*, pp. 23, 45, 121.
[2] Ezek. viii, 16.

of a principal god to whatever department of life or of nature appealed especially to the theologian. When we find certain gods invested with solar functions it does not follow that they were originally sun-gods — such functions may be a necessary result of their preëminence. Out of the great mass of Babylonian and Assyrian deities we may select a few whose cults illustrate the method of development of the religious conceptions. As non-Semitic (Sumerian) religious and other ideas and words appear to have been adopted by the Semitic Babylonians, it is not always easy to distinguish between Semitic and non-Semitic conceptions in the cults as known to us.

756. *Babylonia.* The god Ea appears to have been originally the local deity of Eridu, a city which in early times stood on the Persian Gulf. This proximity to the sea may account for the fact that Ea was generally associated with water (in Babylonia, as elsewhere, there were many deities of waters). It is not certain that this was his original rôle, but it was, in any case, assigned him in the course of the theistic construction. It is not improbable that in the original form of the Babylonian epic it was Ea who sent the flood and saved one man — a natural representation for the god of Eridu; in later recensions of the poem it is first Bel and then Marduk who assumes the principal rôle. As Eridu was probably a prominent political center, Ea, as its chief god, naturally became the creator, the bestower of wisdom, the author of the arts of life, in general a universal god. As the political center shifted, the popular interest changed and Ea yielded more or less to other gods, continuing, however, throughout the whole Babylonian and Assyrian period to receive high consideration.

757. Enlil, the god of Nippur, had a similar career; originally local, he became supreme. A peculiar feature of his history is the fact that the title Bel, 'lord' (which is the Semitic equivalent of the non-Semitic Enlil), clung to him in a peculiar way and practically ousted the original name. This title was assigned to various gods (so in Canaan the title Baal), and its special appropriation by the god of Nippur must be referred to the preponderant importance of that city in the period before the rise of Babylon. In the

Babylonian system he is lord of the lower world, that is, apparently, the divine king of the earth; his original domain, the district of Nippur, was extended to embrace the whole world — a sort of extension that was common in all ancient religions. His importance is evident from the fact that he was a member of the early triad, Anu, Bel, Ea, names that have been supposed to represent three divisions of the world into heaven, earth, and ocean. It seems probable, however, that this triadic grouping was the work of relatively late constructionists; it is more likely that the original prominence of these three deities was due to the fact that they represented the more important political communities.[1]

758. A particularly good illustration of the dependence of a god's position on the political position of his region is furnished by the god Marduk, a name the meaning of which is uncertain. He is first clearly mentioned in the inscriptions of Hammurabi (ca. 2000 B.C.), but mentioned in such a way that his cult must go back to a much earlier time. From the devotion paid him by Hammurabi, and much later by Nebuchadrezzar II (sixth century B.C.), it is generally assumed that he was the local god of Babylon. He rose with the fortunes of this city, finally becoming supreme: he was regarded as creator, and invested with all the highest functions; in the later astronomical constructions he is represented as the arranger of the zodiacal system and all that was connected with it, but, as is pointed out above, this is no ground for regarding him as having been originally a sun-god. A glimpse into the method of theological reconstruction is afforded by the representation in the cosmogonic epic where he is invested with supreme power by the older gods — this investiture is with probability regarded by Assyriologists as representing the leadership attained by the city of Babylon (ca. 2000 B.C.), whose religious hegemony lasted throughout the existence of the Babylonian state.

---

[1] Jastrow, *Aspects of Religious Belief and Practice in Babylonia and Assyria*, p. 82. The Babylonian and Assyrian triads were loosely constructed, and had, apparently, no significance for the local and royal cults. In this regard they differed from the Egyptian triads and enneads, which were highly elaborated and organized (Maspero, *Dawn of Civilization*, p. 104 ff.; Breasted, *History of Egypt*, p. 56.; Steindorff, *Religion of the Ancient Egyptians*, p. 29).

759. *Assyria.* The Assyrian pantheon is in general identical with that of Babylon, but has certain features which are due to the peculiar character of the Assyrian civilization. The god Ashur, originally the local god of the city or district of Ashur, and then the chief god of Assyria, was naturally a war-god — Assyria was essentially a military nation, differing in this regard from Babylonia. He is, however, more than a mere god of war — he has all high attributes, and came to represent in Assyria that approach to monotheism which in Babylon was embodied in the later cult of Marduk.

760. Babylonian and Assyrian *female deities* are of two classes: those who are merely consorts of the male deities, and those who represent fertility. The first class we may pass over — the goddesses of this class are vague in character and functions and play no important part in the religious system; they appear to be artificial creations of the systematizers. The deities of the second class, however, are important. From a very early time the fertility of nature has been referred appropriately to female Powers, and in the Semitic pantheon a large number of such divinities occur. A deity of this sort naturally becomes a mother-goddess, with all the attributes that pertain to this character; in some cases a mother-goddess becomes supreme.

761. A very early female divinity is Bau, worshiped particularly at the city Lagash and by King Gudea. Her function as patron of productiveness is probably indicated in the spring festival held in her honor on New Year's Day, in which she is worshiped as the giver of the fruits of the earth. There are several local female deities that seem to be substantially identical in character with Bau. Innanna (or Ninni) in Uruk (Erech) was the mistress of the world and of war, and Nana is hardly to be distinguished from her.[1] In Agade Anunit has a similar rôle; in Lagash Nina was the determiner of fate, and the mother of the goddesses.

762. These names appear to be titles signifying 'mistress,' 'lady,' and this is probably the meaning of the name of the great

[1] Cf. article "Astarte" (by Ed. Meyer) in Roscher, *Lexikon.*

goddess who finally ousted or absorbed her sisters, Ishtar.[1] In the earliest form in which Ishtar appears, in the old poetry, she is the deity of fertility; when she goes down to the Underworld all productiveness of plants and men ceases; and her primitive character at this time appears in the account of her marriages with animals, in which there is to be recognized the trace of the old zoölatrous period; but as patron of fertility she becomes in time a great goddess and takes on universal attributes — she is the mother of gods and men, universal protector and guide. Where war was the chief pursuit she became a goddess of war; in this character she appears in Babylonia as early as the time of Hammurabi, and later in Assyria. In the genealogical constructions she was brought into connection, as daughter, wife, or other relation, with any god that the particular conditions suggested. As the Assyrians grew morally she was endowed with all the highest virtues (so in the Penitential Psalms), and occupied so preëminent a position that under favorable circumstances she might perhaps have become the only god of the land.

763. If her name signified originally 'lord' or 'lady,' the occurrence of several Ishtars in Assyria (particularly Ishtar of Nineveh and Ishtar of Arbela) is easily understood; so in Canaan, as we learn from the Old Testament, there was a great number of local Ashtarts.[2] We can thus also explain the male deities Ashtar in Moab and Athtar in South Arabia.[3] None of these, however, attained the eminence of the Babylonian and Assyrian Ishtar; her

---

[1] For the cuneiform material see Delitzsch, *Assyrisches Handwörterbuch*, and, for various etymologies proposed for the name, Barton, *Semitic Origins*, p. 102 ff.; Haupt, in *Journal of the American Oriental Society*, xxviii, 112 ff.; Barton, ibid., xxxi, 355 ff. The frequent expression *ilani u ishtarâti*, 'gods and goddesses,' suggests that the original sense of *ishtar* is simply 'a deity'; it is not probable that a proper name would become a common noun and have a plural; cf. the treatment of the title *ilu*, 'a god.'

[2] As the title *bel*, 'lord,' became the proper name of a particular god, so the title *ishtar*, 'mistress,' 'lady,' might become the proper name of a particular goddess; in neither case is the detailed history of the process known to us.

[3] They were probably local "lords"; in Moab Ashtar was combined with a deity called Kemosh, of whom nothing is known except that he was a Moabite national god (cf. G. F. Moore, article "Chemosh" in *Encyclopædia Biblica*). For a different view of Ashtar and Athtar see Barton, *Semitic Origins*, Index, s.vv. *Chemosh, Athtar*; he regards these deities as transformations of the mother-goddess Ashtart.

supremacy in Mesopotamia was due doubtless in part to the political importance of the cities that adopted her. She had her rivals, as we have seen, in Marduk and Ashur and others; and that she was able to maintain herself is to be ascribed in some measure to the importance attached by her worshipers to the fertilizing power of nature.

764. The other Semitic peoples, with the exception of the Hebrews, offer little material for tracing the development of the great gods. For the Aramean region the records are sparse; Aramean deities appear to be of the same character as the Canaanite.[1] In Canaan (including Phœnicia) out of the vast number of local divinities, the Baals and Ashtarts, few attained to eminence, and it is doubtful whether any one of them deserves the title " great." [2] The divine patrons of cities were locally powerful; such were the Baal of Tyre, called Melkart ('the king of the city'), the Ashtart of Sidon, and Tanit of Carthage; [2] these owed their reputation to their official positions, and there is no other record of their development. The same thing is true of the Moabite Kemosh, the Ammonite Malkom (Milkom), and the Philistine Dagan (Dagon) and Baalzebub. None of these became ethically great or approached universality. The Phœnician Eshmun was known to the Greeks, and was identified by them with their Asklepios (Æsculapius), probably because among the various functions attaching to him as local deity healing was prominent; but of his theologic history little is known.[3] Several North Arabian deities, especially Dusares (Dhu ash-Shara) and the goddesses Al-Lât and Al-Uzza, were widely worshiped, their cults extending over the whole Nabatean region; but the communities to which they belonged never produced a great civilization or attained great political significance, and these deities always retained traces of their local

[1] Baethgen, *Beiträge zur semitischen Religionsgeschichte*, p. 66 ff.; Jeremias, " Syrien und Phönizien " (in Saussaye's *Lehrbuch der Religionsgeschichte*).

[2] Rawlinson, *History of Phœnicia*; Pietschmann, *Geschichte der Phönizier*; Jeremias, op. cit.

[3] Article " Esmun " in Roscher's *Lexikon*; article in *Orientalische Studien Nöldeke gewidmet*. Of the vague group known as the Kabiri (the 'great ones,' seven in number, with Eshmun as eighth) we have little information; on the diffusion of their cult in Grecian lands see Roscher, op. cit., article " Megaloi Theoi."

nature.[1] The same remark is to be made of the South Arabian gods known to us; they were locally important, but we have little information concerning their characters.[2]

765. The clearest example of the orderly advance of a deity to preëminence is afforded by the Hebrew Yahweh (Jehovah). Originally, it would seem, a local deity, the god of certain tribes on the northern boundary of Arabia,[3] he was adopted by the Hebrews under conditions which are not quite clear, and was developed by them in accordance with their peculiar genius. At first morally and intellectually crude, he became as early as the eighth century B.C. ethically high and practically omnipotent.[4] For many centuries he was regarded merely as the most powerful of the gods, superior to the deities of other nations, and it was only after the beginning of our era that the Hebrew thought discarded all other gods and made " Yahweh " synonymous with " God." In each period of their history the conception that the Hebrews had of him was in accord with the economic and intellectual features of the time.[5]

766. A word may be added respecting the Semitic titles Ilu, or El, and Elohim, which have been supposed by some recent writers to prove the existence of an early monotheism, particularly in Southern Arabia. The terms mean simply ' god,' and were applied by early Semitic communities to any deity, particularly to the local god. In the Arabia of Mohammed's time a tribe would call its deity simply " the god," a sufficient designation of him for the

1 Wellhausen, *Reste arabischen Heidentumes*, pp. 21 ff., 45 ff.; W. R. Smith, *Kinship and Marriage in Early Arabia*, chap. vi, note 8; chap. viii, note 2; article " Dusares " in the *Anthropological Essays presented to F. W. Putnam*.

2 Mordmann, *Himyarische Inschriften*; Mordmann and Müller, *Sabäische Denkmäler*; Barton, *Semitic Origins*, p. 127 ff.

8 His original seat is uncertain; by some scholars he is regarded as an old North Semitic deity, but the grounds for this view are not convincing. The occurrences of the name outside of the Hebrew region throw little or no light on his origin. Cf. Delitzsch, *Paradies*; Baudissin, *Studien zur semitischen Religionsgeschichte*; Barton, *Semitic Origins*, chap. vii.

4 On his position in the seventh century cf. W. F. Bade, in *Transactions of the American Philological Association*, 1908.

5 For the Old Testament statements see C. G. Montefiore, *Origin and Growth of Religion as illustrated by the Religion of the Ancient Hebrews* (Hibbert Lectures, 1892), Index, s.v. *Yahweh*.

place ;[1] this designation, in Arabic *al-ilahu*, came to be pronounced
" Allah," and this familar term, as is remarked above, was adopted
by Mohammed and expanded (probably under the influence of
some advanced Arabian circle of thinkers of his time) into the con-
ception of the one only god, which he and others had derived from
Christians and Jews. In certain parts of the Old Testament also
" Elohim " stands for the national god, conceived of as all-sufficient.
But these are late conceptions. There is no proof that in South
Arabia or in Babylonia the term Ilu meant anything else than the
local deity, though such a deity would naturally receive all the attributes that his worshipers demanded in their religious constructions.
Most of the appellations of Semitic deities are epithets, and while
this mode of conceiving of the gods militated against the development of them into distinct personalities and the construction of a
pantheon, it was favorable, on the other hand, to isolation and to the
tendency to elevate any favorite deity to a position of preëminence.

767. *Greece.* The Greeks, with their rich imagination and artistic feeling, filled the world with divine figures, well-defined types of
Greek character, ideals of Greek thought. Greece alone has constructed a true pantheon, a community of gods all individualized,
but all compacted into a family or a body of government. The
question of their historical development involves great difficulties,
partly because the wide diffusion of their cults in Hellas occasioned
many local expansions of the original conceptions in the various
regions, partly because most of the deities appear fully or almost
fully formed in the earliest literary monuments, so that we are
dependent on cultic procedures and passing allusions for a knowledge of their preliterary character. Without, then, attempting an
investigation of the obscure prehistoric theogonic period, the general lines of growth of some of the principal divine personages
may be followed (as far as the data permit) as examples of the way
in which the great gods were gradually created.[2]

---

[1] He was thus supreme for the particular tribe, though not universal; cf. article
"Arabs (Ancient) " in Hastings, *Encyclopædia of Religion and Ethics.*

[2] Farnell, *Cults of the Greek States*; Gruppe, *Griechische Mythologie*; articles on
the various deities in Roscher's *Lexikon.*

768. Zeus, originally doubtless a sky-god (not the sun), represents an old Indo-European divine conception, found substantially also among all the great peoples of antiquity, as well as in many half-civilized tribes. But nowhere has he attained so eminent a position as in Greece. The Hindu Dyaus (the ' shining one ') [1] is not prominent in the Vedic mythology or in later times, and the Mazdean Ahura Mazda, if he was originally the sky, had dropped his physical characteristics and become only a spirit; the Latin Jupiter approaches Zeus most nearly in name and character. A sky-god is naturally conceived of as universal ruler,[2] but in any particular region he assumes the characteristics of the ruling human personages of the place and time. Zeus appears first as a barbarian chieftain with the ordinary qualities of such persons. Stories that have come down about him reflect a period of what now seems immorality, though it was the recognized morality of the time; he is deceitful and changeable and completely unregardful of any definite marriage laws. His cult in some places (for example, in Arcadia) had savage features. Whether he had originally in the Hellenic world a special home, and if so what it was, cannot now be determined.[3]

769. In the historical period he appears as a chief god in many places in Greece, gradually absorbs the functions of other gods, and receives numerous titles derived from places and functions. He is the father of gods and men, but not the sole creator of the world. His gradual rise in moral character may be traced in the literature. In Homer he is a universalized Agamemnon, with very much the intellectual and moral qualities of Agamemnon; a process of growth

[1] Formally the names Dyaus, Zeus, and Ju (in Jupiter) are identical; and to these may probably be added the Teutonic Tiu (Tyr).

[2] In early thought the sky (like the earth) is in itself a powerful thing, a personality, and the god who is later supposed to inhabit and control it is a definite figure, like, for example, a tree-god.

[3] From the ancient notices of Kronos it is hardly possible to fix definitely the relation between him and Zeus. It is probable that he represents an older cult that was largely displaced by that of Zeus. The custom of human sacrifice in his cult led to the identification of him with the Phœnician (Carthaginian) Melek (Moloch), and his name has been interpreted (from κραίνω) as meaning ' king' (= melek); but this resemblance does not prove a Semitic origin for him. Whether his rôle as king of the Age of Gold was anything more than a late construction is not clear.

in the conception of him in the Homeric poems is indicated by the incongruities in his portraiture — at one time he is a creature of impulse and passion, at another time a dignified and thoughtful ruler. In Pindar and the tragedians of the fifth century he has become the representative of justice and order in the world, and in later writers he comes to be more specifically the embodiment of everything that is good in the universe. He represents the Greek conception of civic authority, and thus the nearest approach to monotheism discoverable in the Greek mythological system; and as embodying the finer side of religious feeling he both punishes and forgives sin.

770. Next in importance to Zeus as representative of Greek religious thought stands Apollo. The meaning of the name and the original seat of the god are obscure; he appears to have been a Pan-Hellenic deity; he was definitely shaped by the whole mass of Hellenic thought. Originally, perhaps, the local deity of some hunting and pastoral region, and possessing the quasi-universal attributes of such deities, the wide diffusion of his cult (through conditions not known to us) brought him into relation with many sides of life. While he shares this many-sidedness with several other gods, the Greek genius of theographic organization assigned him special headship in certain distinctively Hellenic conceptions. Zeus embodied the theocratic idea, and Apollo the ideas of Pan-Hellenic civic unity, artistic feeling, and the more intimate ethical and religious experience. He became the patron of the Amphictyonic assembly and of literature and art, and, especially in connection with the Delphic oracle, the fosterer of ethical conceptions of ritual and of sin. How it came to pass that these particular departments were assigned him it is not possible to say. Such specialization was natural to the Greeks, but the determining conditions in particular cases have not been recorded, and can only be surmised. His growth kept pace with that of the Hellenic people — in the Iliad he is a partisan, and his words and deeds do not always command our respect, but in the later theological constructions he throws off his crudeness. His connection with the sun was a natural consequence of his rise to eminence; he is not a sun-god in the earliest literary remains.

771. Poseidon, second only to Zeus in power, is also of obscure origin.[1] His specific marine character is certain, though as a great god he had many relations and functions.[2] Possibly he was originally the local deity of some marine region, and by reason of the importance of his native place, or simply through the intimate relationship between the Greek communities, and in accordance with the Greek spirit of organization, came to be generally recognized as the god of the ocean.[3] Though he was widely revered he remained largely a nature god — he never attained the majesty and moral supremacy of Zeus, never, indeed, represented specifically any refined moral or religious conception. Whether this ethical and religious meagerness was a consequence of the vagueness of the relation between the sea and human life, or of some other fact, is a point that can hardly be determined.

772. Hermes, to judge from his history, was the creation of some pastoral community, an ideal of rustic excellence: fleet of foot, a leader in popular amusements, skilled in simple music, eminent in an art much valued in early times — the art of stealing cattle. When he was taken into the circle of Greek theological thought his swiftness recommended him to the position of messenger of the gods,[4] and his function as psychopompos, the guide of souls to the other world, would then follow naturally; from this function it cannot, however, be inferred that he was originally a chthonic deity — a character that does not accord with the early portraitures of him. Like other gods he grew morally, but he never reached ethical distinction. Skill in theft was in early times often regarded as a virtue,[5] and in general he who got the better of his

[1] The etymology of his name is doubtful.

[2] On his titles "earth-shaker" and "earth-upholder" cf. Gruppe, *Griechische Mythologie*, p. 1139, note 2.

[3] Possibly he was originally the ocean itself conceived of as a living and powerful thing, as Zeus (and so Varuna and Ahura Mazda) was originally the physical sky; Okeanos is a great god (*Iliad*, xiv, 201; Hesiod, *Theogony*, 133).

[4] By many writers he is considered to have been originally a wind-god; but wind, though it might suggest swiftness (and, with some forcing, thievishness), cannot account for his other endowments.

[5] Gen. xxx, 37 ff.; xxxi, 9; Wellhausen, *Reste arabischen Heidentumes*, p. 196; Westermarck, *Origin and Development of the Moral Ideas*, ii, 17–19.

fellows was esteemed a master of good luck and prosperity; and a bestower of outward prosperity Hermes came to be.[1] His main quality was cleverness, in contrast with the intellectual power of Apollo.

773. On the other hand, another rustic figure, the Arcadian herd-god Pan,[2] never developed into a great Hellenic god. His worship was widely diffused; he appears often in artistic representations, and Pindar thought him worthy of a hymn (of which, unfortunately, only fragments survive), but in general he remained uncouth and half savage, a goatlike figure, the companion of satyrs, or (as the Homeric hymn depicts him) a merrymaker. He seems to have been an embodiment of the lower rustic pleasures, a local god, probably not a divinized goat.[3]

774. His name, however, taken to mean 'all,' gave occasion to fanciful interpretations. He was so called, it was said, because he gave delight to all the Immortals;[4] or his person and his musical and other instruments were supposed to represent universal nature — his horns the rays of the sun and the horns of the moon, his spotted fawnskin the stars, his pipe of seven reeds the harmony of the heavens, his crook the year, which returns on itself, and so on.[5] The Stoics and the Orphic writers made him Universal God, the creator of the world.[6] In the popular cult, however, he remained the merry patron of herds. The most satisfactory explanation of his name is that which derives it from the stem *pa*, 'feed' — he is then "the goatherd."[7] The story told by Plutarch, of a voice heard crying on the coast of Epirus, "Great Pan is dead," arose from some misapprehension, but no

---

[1] *Odyssey*, xv, 319 f. Lang lays too much stress on this fact (*Myth, Ritual, and Religion*, 1st ed., ii, 257).

[2] Gruppe (*Griechische Mythologie*, p. 1384) thinks (on grounds not clear) that he was originally of Crete.   [3] So Gruppe, op. cit.   [4] *Homeric Hymn to Pan*.

[5] Servius on Vergil, *Eclogue* ii, 31.

[6] Roscher, in *Lexikon*, article "Pan," col. 1405, and in *Festschrift für Joh. Overbeck*, p. 56 ff. On the influence of the Egyptian cult of the goat-god of Mendes on the conception of Pan see Roscher, *Lexikon*, article "Pan," cols. 1373, 1382.

[7] Mannhardt, *Antike Wald- und Feldkulte*, p. 135 f.; Roscher, op. cit., col. 1406; Farnell, *Cults of the Greek States*, v, 431, and many others. To this etymology Gruppe (op. cit., p. 1385) objects that such a name for a deity is not probable for primitive savage times; he offers nothing in its place.

precise explanation of its origin has been given.[1] Poets like Pindar
and Vergil, disposed to preserve and dignify the old traditions,
treat Pan respectfully and sympathetically, but such constructions
are nonpopular.[2]

775. Ares seems to be the creation of a war-loving tribe; in
the Iliad he is a fierce warrior, armed cap-a-pie, delighting in
battle and slaughter. Through the machinations of Hera and
Athene he is overcome by human heroes, the poet's feeling being,
possibly, contempt for the mere savage fighter; in fact, Ares in
the Iliad is, from our point of view, hardly a respectable character — he violates his promise, and when wounded cries out like
a hurt child. But as war-god he was widely revered in Greece;
in Thebes especially he was honored as one of the great gods.
Hesiod makes him the son of Zeus and Hera,[3] but he never
attains moral or other dignity; in the popular cult he remained,
probably, merely the patron of war. In the later artistic representations he is the ideal of warlike vigor and grace. In the
Homeric hymn (which may be of Orphic origin) he is transformed into a lover of peace and a source of all pure and lofty
aspirations — a violent procedure, induced by the poet's unwill
ingness that an Olympian should represent anything but what
was morally good.

776. The process of development of a god's character is illustrated with special clearness by the history of Dionysus. It is
generally agreed that he was of foreign origin, an importation
from Thrace. The features of his earliest cult known to us are
marked by bald savagery. His worshipers indulged in wild
orgies, probably excited by intoxicating drinks, tore to pieces a
goat (as in Thrace) or a bull (as in Crete) and ate the flesh raw;[4]
and the evidence goes to show that they practiced human sacrifice. All these procedures have parallels in known savage cults.
Omophagic orgies are described by Nilus (among the Saracens),

---

[1] Plutarch, *De Defectu Oraculorum*, 17; Reinach, *Orpheus* (Eng. tr.), p. 41.
[2] Pindar, ed. W. Christ, *Fragments*, 95 ff.   [3] *Theogony*, 922 f.
[4] Euripides, *Bacchæ*, 131 f. (cf. Æschylus, *The Seven against Thebes*, 541; Porphyry, *De Abstinentia*, § 13).

and such customs are reported as existing or having existed in the Fiji Islands and elsewhere.[1] Among many tribes intoxication is a common preparation for the work of the shaman; and human sacrifice has been practiced in all parts of the world. There is nothing peculiar in the office of soothsayer that accompanied the Dionysiac cult; mantic persons and procedures have formed a prominent part of the constitution of the lower peoples everywhere.

777. Dionysus, in a word, was originally the local god of a savage community; the data are not sufficient to fix precisely his original place and the original conception of him. His mantic function does not necessarily show that he was a ghost. It is true that the dead were often consulted (and necromancy long survived among civilized peoples), but any spirit or god might take possession of a worshiper and make him the vehicle of revelation. Nor is the phallus-cult peculiar to Dionysus; this cult is widely diffused, and its origin is to be referred not specifically to the recognition of the general generative power of nature, but to the mystery of human life.[2] In his original home Dionysus seems to have represented everything that touched the life of his people. When, at a certain time, he passed into Hellas (carried, doubtless, by immigrants), he took on the character necessitated by his new surroundings — a process of transformation began. Exact chronological data are lacking, but as in the Iliad[3] he is the son of Zeus, he must have been adopted by the Greeks very early. In his new home he became the patron of the vine.[4] In a vine-growing region any prominent deity may become a wine-god;[5] but the special connection of Dionysus with wine in Greece suggests that in his earlier home he was somehow identified with intoxicating drinks. With vegetation in general also he may have been connected in Thrace — such a relation would be natural for

---

[1] *Nili Opera*, p. 27; Smith, *Religion of the Semites*, 2d ed., p. 338 f.; Spencer, *Principles of Sociology*, i, 288.   [2] See above, § 384 ff.   [3] *Iliad*, xiv, 325.

[4] Perhaps the description of him in the *Iliad* (loc. cit.) as "a joy to mortals" refers to wine; cf. Hesiod, *Theogony*, 941, where he is called the "bright joyous one."

[5] As, for example, the Arabian clan god Dusares (Dhu ash-Shara), carried by the Nabateans northward, was brought into relation with the viticulture of that region. Cf. above, § 764.

a clan god — and in that case his Hellenic rôle as god of vegetation would follow as a matter of course; or, if he advanced from
the vine to the whole of vegetable nature, the development is
intelligible.

778. When and on what grounds he was accepted as one of
the Olympians is not clear; [1] perhaps it was on account of the
importance of vine culture, perhaps from the mysterious character of his cult, the enthusiasm of divine inspiration reflected in the
frenzy of the worshipers, or from these causes combined; his later
name, Bacchus, which seems to refer to cultic orgiastic shouting, would appear to indicate this element of the cult as a main
source of his popularity. Once established as a great god he
was credited with various functions. The Greek drama arose in
connection with his worship, and at Eleusis the old element of
seizure by the god was transformed by the higher thought of the
time into the conception of ethical union with the deity. Thus the
old savage god came to stand for man's highest aspirations.

779. As among other peoples, so among the Greeks the government of the Underworld was gradually organized, and a head
thereof appointed.[2] Already in the Iliad and in Hesiod [3] the universe is divided into three parts under the rule of the Kronids
Zeus, Poseidon, and Aïdes respectively; the earth, however, and
Olympos, says Poseidon, are the common property of them all —
there was no complete governmental separation between the
Underworld and the Upperworld. The Greeks, with their joy in
the present, gave comparatively little prominence to the future
(being herein sharply contrasted with the Egyptians).

780. The title generally given to the underground chief, Hades
(apparently ' the invisible one '), indicates the vagueness that attached to this deity.[4] In the Iliad he is a dark and dread divinity.
The precise significance of his title Plouton [5] is uncertain; but
under this name he is connected in the myths with processes of

---

[1] On this point cf. Miss J. Harrison, *Prolegomena to the Study of Greek Religion*,
p. 366.   [2] See above, § 680 f.   [3] *Iliad*, xv, 184 ff.; Hesiod, *Theogony*, 453 ff.
  [4] He is not always in mythological constructions distinct from Zeus — in *Iliad*,
ix, 457, it is Zeus Katachthonios who is lord below.
  [5] Æschylus, *Prometheus Bound*, 806.

vegetation — it is Plouton who carries off Persephone, leaving the world in the deadness of winter. The figure of the underground deity appears to have taken shape from the combination of two mythological conceptions — the underground fructifying forces of nature, and the assemblage of the dead in a nether world or kingdom.[1] His only moral significance lay in his relation to oaths, wherein, perhaps, is an approach to the idea of a divine judge below the earth.[2]

781. The *female deities* of the Greeks are no less elaborately worked out than the male gods, and, like these, are types of human character and representatives of human pursuits.[3]

782. The great goddess Hera is in Homer attached especially to Argos, Sparta, and Mycenæ, but at a very early time was Pan-Hellenic. The meaning of her name and her origin are uncertain. There is no good ground for regarding her as having been originally a moon-goddess (Selene was the real moon-goddess). What is certain is that she had a special relation to women and particularly to childbirth; but such a function is so generally attributed to some goddess that we can only suppose that she rose to eminence through local conditions unknown to us. The most interesting point about her is that she came to be the representative of the respectable Greek matron, jealous of her wifely rights, holding herself aloof from love affairs, a home person, entitled to respect for the decency of her life, but without great womanly charm.

783. By a natural mythological law she was regarded as the consort of Zeus, and gradually acquired dignity without, however, ever coming to be a distinct embodiment of any form of intellectual or moral life. As Zeus embodied the conception of civil and political headship, so Hera appears to have embodied the idea of the wife as controller of the purely domestic affairs of the family, her business being the bringing up of children and the oversight of servants — duties that may have seemed at an early period not to require great moral and intellectual power.

---

[1] Cf. the development of Osiris (above, § 728).
[2] Cf. Greek Horkos, and the oath by the Styx.
[3] Cf. Miss Harrison, *Prolegomena to the Study of Greek Religion*, chap. vi.

784. A distincter form is that of Demeter, who, whatever the meaning of her name,[1] certainly represents the fertile earth — a figure similar to hundreds of others in the world, and doubtless existing at various points in Greece under local names; she probably represents a unification of the different conceptions of the fertile earth, a process that went on in the natural way in Greek thought, and was formulated by the poets. Her historical connection with the great Asian earth-goddess, the Mother-Goddess, is uncertain. Demeter, however, never became the great earth-mother; she remained attached to the soil, except that in the Eleusinian mysteries she (probably as patron of fertility) was allegorized into a representation of those moral conceptions of the future that gradually arose in Greece.

785. The group of deities that may be called maiden goddesses is of peculiar interest. A maiden goddess is originally an independent deity who, for whatever reason, has not been brought by the myth-makers into marriage relations with a male deity. Generally such independence is a result of the fact that the goddess is the representative of fertility. She may, in accordance with early customs of human society, choose temporary consorts at will (as is the case with Ishtar); she may be in her sole person (like the Dea Mater) the productive power of the world; or she may remain a virgin, occupied only with the care of some department of life (so Athene and Artemis). Which of these characters she takes depends on early social conditions and on the nature of the local theistic organization. In Greece these goddesses assume various shapes.

786. There is first the primitive divine Power of vegetation, called simply the Kore, the Maiden, a figure ultimately identical with Demeter and in the later constructions represented as her daughter. She is not necessarily to be regarded as a development out of an original corn-spirit. Her title "maiden" may be compared with the Semitic title "mistress," mentioned above, and with the names expressing family relations, " sister," "mother" — only this particular designation defines her simply as an unmarried

[1] Cf. Roscher, *Lexikon*, s.v.; Miss Harrison, *Prolegomena to the Study of Greek Religion*, p. 271 ff.

female divinity. The " corn-maiden " of modern European folk-lore may be the cultic degradation of an old deity.[1] The title Kore became almost a proper name, though the designation was not so definite as in the cases of Bel and Ishtar.[2]

787. As the Kore is the representative of vegetable life, so Hestia stands in general for the indoor life, the family. She long retained this local character, but gradually assumed the position of the great goddess of the home center, the hearth,[3] and was connected with the household fires and festivals. She represents the more intimate social life of the family in contrast with Hera, who stands for the government of the household.

788. The development of the functions of Artemis is comparatively clear. The origin of the name is doubtful, but in the earliest records she is connected with the fertile earth, with vegetable and also with animal life.[4] This character indicates that she was at one time a local, all-sufficient deity, though it is hardly possible to determine her original seat. As a local goddess in the hunting area she was naturally connected with the chase, and as a female divinity she was the patroness of marriage and the protector of human birth. Her original nature as the maiden appears in the representation of her as a virgin which occurs in Homer.[5] There is no contradiction between this character and her function of presiding over marriage and birth if we consider her as a local goddess who from one point of view was regarded as a simple maiden, from another point of view as the protector of women.[6] Thus invested with the control of these important features of life she naturally became a general patroness, a guardian. Later she was connected with Apollo as his sister, exactly by what steps we do not know;

---

[1] Compare Mannhardt, *Mythologische Forschungen*, p. 320 ff.; Frazer, *Golden Bough*, 2d ed., ii, 176 ff.   [2] Compare Miss Harrison, op. cit., p. 271 ff.

[3] By her name she is identified with the hearth, as similarly Zeus is identified with the sky. The hearth was the center of the home, and had wide cultic significance. The name Hestia embodies not the divinization of a concrete object, but the recognition of the divine person presiding over the object in question.

[4] Roscher, *Lexikon*; Farnell, *Cults of the Greek States.*   [5] *Odyssey*, xx, 71.

[6] The representation of her as the slayer of women with her " kindly arrows " (*Odyssey*, xx, 67), that is, by an easy death, is in keeping with the early idea that death was caused by some supernatural Power; so Apollo slays (*Iliad*, xxiv, 759).

and in the mythical constructions she was represented as the daughter of Zeus and Leto.[1]

789. The Hellenic goddess Artemis is to be distinguished from the Ephesian deity to whom the Greeks gave the same name, though when the Greeks came into close contact with Asia Minor the two were identified. And in fact, though in historical origin the two deities are to be kept apart, they doubtless go back to the same conception. The Ephesian goddess was the Great Mother — she stood specifically for the idea of maternity which lies at the basis of the world; the Greek divinity, beginning as a local protectress, took on larger functions which gave her general resemblance to the universal mother.

790. The relation between Artemis and Hekate is an illustration of the process of coördination and harmonization that went on continually among the Greeks. Hekate does not appear in Homer, but in Hesiod she has the full form of a great deity — she exercises control over heaven, earth, and sea;[2] and at a later period she becomes similarly connected with the Underworld. This variety of functions can be explained only by the supposition that she also was a local deity, who, like all local deities, was regarded as universal.[3] As the meaning of her name is uncertain and her original region unknown, it can be only surmised that her cult spread gradually in Greece through the growing unification of the Hellenic states. Like Artemis she presided over human birth. The functions of the two goddesses being so nearly the same (they appear to represent similar conceptions arising at different centers), it was natural that in the later times they should be identified or closely associated.

---

[1] Leto is a Titaness (Hesiod, *Theogony*, 404 ff.), an old local goddess, naturally a patron of children, and so of similar nature with Artemis, with whom she was often joined in worship. Her connection with Apollo arose possibly from a collocation of her cult with his in some place; in such collocations the goddess would become, in mythological constructions, the mother, sister, or wife of the god. This relation once established, stories explaining it would spring up as a matter of course. The fact that she was later identified with the Asian Great Mother indicates that she also had a universal character.   [2] Hesiod, *Theogony*, 411 ff.

[3] She was, perhaps, an underground deity, or the product of the fusion of two deities, one of whom was chthonic.

791. Athene is said in a late myth (not in the Iliad) to have been born from the head of Zeus, a representation that has led many recent scholars to regard her as the goddess of the thunderstorm, the lightning that cleaves the clouds, the divine warrior that slays the dragon. But ingenious and attractive as this interpretation is, to determine the origin of the goddess it is safer to go to the earlier forms of her cult. At a very early period she is connected with ordinary social occupations.[1] She is the patroness of the cultivation of the land ; in Athens, where the olive was important, it was she who bestowed this tree on the city ; here she is the maiden, the genius, the divine patron of vegetation. She presided over the domestic employments of women, spinning and weaving — that is, she is the goddess of household work.[2] As is the case with so many divine patrons of men's early simple employments, she grew with the community and became gradually a great goddess, and necessarily a patroness of cities. In her character of general patroness she became a goddess of war — a necessity for all ancient states. On the other hand, in a community (like Athens, for example) where intellectual insight was highly esteemed she would naturally become the representative of cleverness and wisdom.

792. The peculiar nature of the wisdom that is prized by men depends on time and place. In the earliest periods what Athene bestows is a high degree of common sense and skill in devising ways and means, such as Odysseus shows. In later times of larger cultivation she bestows wisdom in the higher sense, intellectual breadth. Exactly how it came to pass that the two figures Artemis and Athene developed on such different lines we are unable to say — the beginning of the divergence goes back to times of which we have no records ; but, as gods represent the elements of human life, it was natural that a gradual differentiation should take place ; the same general conception would be particularized in different ways in different places, just as divergent forms of the same original word

---

[1] Farnell, *Cults of the Greek States*; Roscher, *Lexikon*.
[2] Thus the Greeks endeavored to embody in divine figures all sides of family life. The division of functions between Hera, Hestia, and Athene is clear.

acquire different significations in speech.[1] As for the later combination of these deities with heavenly bodies and many other things, these are to be regarded as the product of later poetical imagination and the tendency to universalize all great deities.

793. Aphrodite exhibits more clearly than any other deity the process or the direction of the Hellenization of a foreign god. Her titles Cypris, Paphia, Cytherea, as well as her connection with Adonis, point, as is generally held, to a Semitic origin [2]; she seems to have been identical with the great Babylonian, Assyrian, and Syrian goddess Ishtar (Astarte).[8] Received into the Greek pantheon at a very early time (already in the Iliad she is one of the Olympians), she yet shows the main characteristics of the Semitic deity [4] — she is especially the representative of fertility and sexual passion, and also has relation to war. The lines of development, however, were different in different communities. In Babylonia and Assyria Ishtar became a great universal national deity, charged particularly with the care of all the interests of the state, while in Syria and Canaan the corresponding figures (Attar, Ashtart) remained to a great extent local, and were especially prominent in festivals.

794. In Greece the conception of Aphrodite was worked out in a non-Semitic way in two directions. By poets and philosophers she was made the beneficent producer of all things, shedding her charm over animate and inanimate nature ; [5] and the sentiment of love, for which she stood, was exalted into a pure affection, the basis of married life. The baser side of her cult, with its sexual license (Asiatic of origin), remained along with the higher conception of her,[6] but the latter was the special contribution that the Greeks made to her development.

---

[1] As, for example, ' fragile' and ' frail,' ' intension' and ' intention,' ' providential' and ' prudential,' and many other groups of this sort.

[2] For the view that she was a native Ægean deity see Farnell, *Greece and Babylon*, p. 97. Later Semitic influences, in any case, must be assumed.

[8] No satisfactory explanation of the name Aphrodite has as yet been offered.

[4] See above, § 762.

[5] *Homeric Hymn to Aphrodite* ; Euripides, *Medea*, 835 ff. ; Lucretius. Ishtar also is the mother of all things, but the idea is not developed by the Semites.

[6] Compare the details given in J. Rosenbaum's *Geschichte der Lustseuche im Altertume*.

795. The theistic scheme of the old Greek polytheistic period is the broadest and finest that the ancient polytheism produced. It recognized a divine element in all sides of human life, from the lowest to the highest; it marked out the various directions of human feeling and effort, and in its final outcome it reached the conception of a unity in the divine government of the world, and gave expression to man's best aspirations for the present and for the future. True, it gave way at last to philosophy; but it had recognized those elements of thought on which philosophy was based. The Persian and Hebrew systems expressed more definitely the idea of a divine monocracy, and lent themselves easily to the formation of a religious society, a church, but they did not escape the limitations of mere national feeling. The Greeks founded no church — they formulated universal ethical and religious conceptions, and left the development to the individual. All the great ancient religions reached a high ethical plane and a practical monotheism, but the Greek was the richest of all in the recognition of the needs of humanity.

796. *Rome.* The Roman pantheon (if the Italian divine community can properly be called a 'pantheon) had not the fullness and fineness of the Greek — in accordance with the Roman genius it included only deities having special relations with the family and its work and with the state.[1] The rich Roman development of specific gods of the home is referred to above.[2] The old nature gods long retained their place, doubtless, in popular worship, but were gradually subordinated to and absorbed in the larger divine figures. And the great gods themselves began at an early time to be assimilated to Greek deities and to assume their functions and even their names.[3]

797. The most important of the nature gods are Sol, Luna, and Tellus (primitive figures that soon gave way to deities divorced from

---

[1] Aust, *Religion der Römer*; Fowler, *Roman Festivals*; id. *The Religious Experience of the Roman People*; articles in Roscher's *Lexikon*; Mommsen, *History of Rome* (Eng. tr.), bk. i, chap. xii. [2] § 702 ff.

[3] Hence a confusion of names that appears even to-day, and in books otherwise careful, as, for example, in the Bohn translations of Greek works, in which the Greek deities are throughout called by Latin names.

the physical sun, moon, and earth), and the patrons of agricultural work, Consus and Ops, Liber and Libera, Silvanus and Faunus. The natural features represented by these deities did not disappear entirely from the greater deities, but were purified and elevated. Anna Perenna, for example, as representative of the round of years, remained by the side of Janus, but he embodied this conception in a larger civic way.

798. The greatest of the Roman gods, Juppiter[1] or Jupiter, is identical in name with Zeus, but differs from him in mythological development and in the final form of his character. As sky-god he was connected with atmospheric phenomena (rain and lightning) and so naturally with wine and other crops. But as chief god of the state he speedily rose above these connections, and as Optimus Maximus became the representative of all Roman virtues. Along with this native development he was in later times more or less identified with Zeus. By his side stood the national deity Quirinus, who remained a local patron and never rose to large proportions. Related to him are Sancus and Dius Fidius, who represented some primitive conceptions similar to those belonging to his early form, but they did not develop into great gods. These three were practically absorbed by him, but the history of this process is obscure.

799. Janus, the guardian of the entrance to the house (*janua*) — a function of prime importance in early times, had a prominent place in the cult. He was invoked at the beginning of the day, the month, and the year; in the Salian hymn he is called "god of gods" and "good creator"; he was served by the rex sacrorum, who was the first in priestly dignity. He may thus have been a chief god in the oldest Latin scheme.[2] Yet he seems never to have come to stand for anything intellectually or morally high except in late philosophical thought. Though the guardian of public as well

---

[1] So written in good manuscripts. The "piter" probably denotes fatherly protection, though it may have meant originally physical paternity. On this point cf. W. R. Smith, *Religion of the Semites*, lecture ii, and the various stories of the birth of Jupiter's children.

[2] On the significance of the doublefaced Janus (Janus Geminus) and of the ancient usage of opening the gates of his temple in time of war and closing them in time of peace, see article "Janus" in Roscher's *Lexikon*, col. 18 ff.

as private houses, he was not the patron of the city. He remained in the cult a sort of family and clan god, and represented only the ideas of a primitive mode of life, the great rôle being assigned to the sky-god.[1]

800. To judge from the old rituals Mars was in the earliest time of which there is any record a god of vegetation. The Arval Brothers, who were charged with the care of crops, addressed their petitions to him, and it was to him that the Roman husbandman prayed for a blessing on his labors.[2] What may have been his still earlier character we have no means of determining with certainty. The view that he was originally a god of the fructifying sunlight[3] seems to rest mainly on a precarious etymology, the derivation of his name from a stem *mar* meaning ' to shine '; but it does not appear that ancient peoples attributed the growth of crops to the sun.[4] Analogy would rather lead us to regard him as an old local deity, naturally connected with vegetation. However this may be, the importance of agriculture for the life of the community raised him to a position of eminence, his priestly college, the Salian (traditionally referred to Numa), was one of the greatest, he was connected with various departments of life, and for the warlike Romans he naturally became the patron of war. The cult of the old war-goddess Bellona maintained itself, but she never attained the highest rank; she is not the equal of Mars, with whom in the later constructions she was brought into connection. In the Hellenizing period he was identified with Ares.[5]

801. The name Saturn is generally connected with the stem *sa* (*sero*, *satum*, *sata*), to sow, and he is accordingly regarded as an agricultural deity, the special patron of agricultural work. Whether or how he differed originally from Mars is not clear — perhaps in original differentiation of functions, he being attached to the work of sowing, Mars to vegetation in general; or perhaps

[1] With his function as door-god compare the functions of other Roman door-gods, of Vesta, and of Hindu and other house-deities.

[2] Varro, *De Lingua Latina*, v, 85 ; Cato, *De Agri Cultura*, 141.

[3] So Roscher and others.   [4] Cf. Fowler, *Roman Festivals*, p. 35.

[5] The cult of Mars was widely diffused in Italy and, later, elsewhere. His original seat is uncertain. He was, perhaps, the tribal god of a conquering people.

they were two similar deities belonging originally to different regions, and differentiated when brought together in the same system. Information on this point is lacking. That Saturn was an ancient Latin god is probable from the fact that he was traditionally said to be an old king of Latium. Of his earliest cult in Rome little is known. The feast that bears his name, the Saturnalia (held on December 17 and some following days), was a time of popular festivity, when social distinctions were laid aside (slaves were on an equality with masters). Similar festivals are found elsewhere.[1] Midwinter, when the work of gathering in the harvest was over, was a natural time for festivities.[2] Saturn, or the figure from which he arose, may have presided over this season originally, or he may have been gradually connected with an old ceremony. The process of Hellenizing him began early. He was identified with Kronos, made the father of Jupiter and the head of a pre-Jovian divine dynasty, and, in accordance with the tendency to regard the former days as better than the present, the *Saturnia regna* became the golden age of the past.[3] Apart from this he seems to have had no ethical significance.

802. In the case of certain deities, as Volcanus, Neptunus, Mercurius, Sancus, a pronounced Roman development cannot be traced, partly because of the lack of full data, partly, in the case of Volcan, Neptune, and Mercury, because of an early and complete identification with the Greek gods Hephaistos, Poseidon, and Hermes.

803. The Roman *female deities* [4] are far less developed than the Greek — their functions are simple, their mythological interest small. The members of the group representing the productive power of the earth — Bona Dea, Dea Dia, Libera, Fauna, Ceres, Proserpina,[5] and others — were not worked up by the Romans into great personalities.

804. Juno, an independent deity, originally not the wife of Jupiter, is, in the developed cult, the special patron of the maternal

---

1 Cf. also the Ancillarum Feriæ (July 7).   2 See above, § 217 ff.

3 Vergil, *Eclogues*, iv, 6. Cf. above, § 768, note (Kronos).

4 Aust, *Religion der Römer* ; Farnell, *Cults of the Greek States* ; Fowler, *Roman Festivals* ; articles in Roscher's *Lexikon*.

5 She appears to have been a Greek deity adopted by the Romans.

side of the life of women, and, as such, is a great domestic power, the embodiment of a large part of family life. It was probably as great sky-goddess that she attained this position — the chief female deity is naturally the protector of women. The name came to designate the woman's personality as childbearer, and more generally her inner essence or self, as " genius " came to designate the male essence.[1] Whether this usage was simply an extension of the idea of ' protectress ' to that of ' self,' an identification of woman with her specific function in the family, or rested on some older conception, is not clear. However this may be, she became a great goddess, in the later construction the wife of Jupiter, and was identified with Hera, to whom in fact she is nearly related in function and character. Though her name appears to contain the same stem (*iu*) as ' Jupiter,' and her epithet ' Lucina ' the stem *luc*, ' to shine,' there is no proof that she was, in early times, regarded as a light-deity, or particularly as moon-goddess. She was sky-goddess, but not, for that reason, necessarily light-goddess.

805. The importance attached by the Romans to the family life is expressed in the cult of Vesta, the guardian of the hearth as the center of that life.[2] The Penates, however, the divine protectors of the household, were no less important in the family cult than she. The state also had its Vesta and its Penates. To this character of sacredness stamped on the life of the private family and the larger family, the state, ethical significance and influence must doubtless be ascribed.

806. Diana appears to have originated in the time when life was spent largely in forests, and trees were a special object of worship ; she was in historical times connected with groves.[3] Her cult was widely diffused in Italy, and she became (perhaps because she embodied the common feature of the old life) the representative of Italian unity. As great female deity she was the helper of women in childbirth. Her name is based on the stem *di*, ' to shine,' [4] which

---

[1] See above, § 43.

[2] Compare the Greek Hestia and the Hindu house-goddess (Hopkins, *Religions of India*, pp. 374, 530).

[3] On the Arician Diana see Frazer, *Golden Bough*, 2d ed., i, 230 f.

[4] Or, better, from *deiā*.

appears in ' Jupiter ' and ' Juno '; but she is not a sky-goddess —
the "shining" in her case is that of trees and plants, the green
color that gleams in the light, so that the grove is called *lucus*, the
'shining mass.'[1] Diana was soon identified with Artemis, and
was endowed with her attributes.

807. Another Italian goddess, Minerva, stood, probably, in the
earlier time for the simpler arts of a simple community — she was the
patroness of manual work and of the healing art. The expression
omnis Minervae homo, descriptive of a man capable in his line of
work, almost reduces her to an abstract idea. The name (as the
older form, Menerva, more clearly indicates) is based on the stem
man (found in Latin *mens*), and appears to mean ' endowed with
mind ' (or, ' spirit '), though exactly what was the range of this
conception in the earliest times is not clear.[2] Later her function was
extended to embrace intellectual capacity, but it was not until her
identification with Athene (not later than the third century B.C.)
that she attained her full cultic significance.[3]

808. Venus, though an old Italian deity (as her name and her
ancient temples show), was so early Hellenized that her proper
native development was cut short. The fact that she was in early
times the patroness of gardens [4] suggests that she was originally a
deity of the productive field; probably she belonged in the group
of goddesses (Libera, Bona Dea, and others) [5] who presided over fertility. It would seem that every region in Italy had such a *numen
loci* (naturally mainly agricultural). It is not clear to what particular
spot Venus was originally attached,[6] or how she came to be revered
over a wide region. Under ordinary Italian conditions she might
have become a deity like Ceres. But in Sicily, at Mount Eryx,

---

[1] The prevailing view is that the grove is an opened place into which light enters,
and it is thus distinguished from the dark and gloomy forest. The verbs *nitere*,
nitescere, *virere*, are used by Ovid and other writers to describe this gleaming of
leaves, plants, trees, groves, and of the earth.

[2] An early divine name expressive of intellectual power is not probable.

[3] On her origin cf. Wissowa, *Religion der Römer*, p. 203 ff.

[4] Varro, *De Re Rustica*, i, 1.   [5] See above, § 803.

[6] In favor of Ardea, twenty miles south of Rome, as her original seat, cf. Wissowa, *Religion der Römer*, p. 235.

according to tradition, her cult came into contact with that of Aphrodite, whose qualities she soon assumed.[1]

809. In the third century B.C. the cult of the Sicilian Venus (Venus Erycina) was brought to Rome by direction of the Sibylline Books, and from this time onward her advance to prominence was continuous. As a great goddess she became (like Ishtar and Aphrodite) in a warlike community the patron of war (Venus Victrix). When the Æneas myth was adopted in Rome she took the place of Aphrodite as mother of that hero (who became the founder of the Roman state), and was honored by Julius Cæsar and others as Venus Genetrix. The old Roman moral feeling appears in the dedication of a temple (114 B.C.) to Venus Verticordia as atonement for the unchastity of three Vestals.[2] In general the later functions and cult of Venus were reproductions or imitations of those of Aphrodite. Such a divine figure, it seems, the Romans would never have developed out of their own resources.

810. The general characteristics of the great ancient national religions are indicated in the preceding descriptions. In the sacrificial cult and the general apparatus of worship there is no important difference between them, but they differ notably among themselves in the construction of the divine world. The simplest theistic system is the Chinese, which regards the world as order controlled by Heaven. The western cults fall into two divisions, the Egypto-Semitic and the Indo-European. The Egyptian and the Semitic, though they differ in collateral points (divinization of kings, idea of the future life), agree in lacking a true pantheon. On the other hand, notwithstanding resemblances between the Hebrew and

---

[1] Her identification with the Greek goddess was perhaps furthered by a supposed relation between her name and the noun *venustas*, 'grace, beauty,' the special quality of Aphrodite. If that was the original sense of 'Venus,' it could hardly have indicated an æsthetic perception of nature (Wissowa, op. cit.) ; such a designation would be foreign to early ways of naming deities. Whether the stem *van* might mean 'general excellence' (here agricultural) is uncertain ; on the Greek epithets 'Kallisto,' 'Kalliste,' and so forth, cf. Gruppe, *Griechische Mythologie*, p. 1270 f. The name 'Venus,' if connected with the root of *venerari*, might mean simply 'a revered object,' a deity ; cf. Bona Dea and Ceres (creator).

[2] Roscher's *Lexikon*, s.v. " Fortuna," col. 1518 ; Fowler, *Roman Festivals*, p. 68. On licentious cults of Venus cf. J. Rosenbaum, *Geschichte der Lustseuche im Altertum*

the Persian, the difference between the Semitic group and the Indo-European is well-defined. This difference may be indicated by pointing out certain peculiarities of the Semitic theistic system.

811. *Features of Semitic theism.* 1. Paucity of departmental gods and absence of highly specialized gods. Of this latter class, so prominent in Greece and Rome, there is no clear trace in Semitic cults.[1] Departmental deities are not found in Arabia, Canaan (including Israel and Phœnicia), and Syria. The Hebrew Yahweh obviously controls all departments of nature and life. The Phœnician Eshmun (a name of uncertain meaning) was identified by the Greeks with their Asklepios as god of healing, but no special function of this sort is attributed to him in Semitic records. As he was somehow connected with the Kabiri, the "great gods," it is probable that he was a local divinity credited with general powers.[2] There is more ground for recognizing real departmental gods in Babylonia and Assyria, though even there the evidence is not quite satisfactory. The great gods, Ea, Bel, Sin, Shamash, Marduk, Ishtar, Ashur, preside over all human interests. Nabu stands for agriculture as well as for wisdom, and Ea for wisdom as well as for the great deep. Nergal is not the only god of war. Perhaps the distinctest case of specialization is Ramman (Ninib, Adad), the storm-god[3]: the "thunderbolts of Im [Ramman]" are mentioned in "The War of the Seven Evil Spirits"; yet Shamash stands with him against the storm-spirits. In general it appears that the recognition of special departments for gods is inchoate and feeble in Babylonia and Assyria. There is a separate deity for the Underworld, sometimes a goddess, sometimes a god, but they are vague figures.[4] The connection of certain gods with certain stars was a late construction, and seems to have had no significance for worship except a general deanthropomorphizing tendency.

---

[1] See above, § 671.

[2] Articles in Roscher, *Lexikon*, and in *Orientalische Studien Nöldeke gewidmet*.

[3] Inscriptions of Rammannirari and Nebuchadrezzar (Birs Nimrud); Jastrow, *Religion of Babylonia and Assyria*, Index, s.v.; id., *Aspects of Religious Belief and Practice in Babylonia and Assyria*, Index, s.v. *Adad*.

[4] There is no separate god of Sheol in the Old Testament. On Eve as such a deity see Lidzbarski, *Ephemeris*, i, 26; cf. Cook, *North Semitic Inscriptions*, 135.

812. 2. There is no trace of a cult of heroes in the Semitic area. The Babylonian Etana, Gilgamesh, and Nimrod (an enigmatical figure), and the Old Testament Nephilim do not receive worship.[1] The dead were consulted, but there was no cult of the great ancestors.[2] The divinization of Babylonian kings, referred to above,[3] seems not to have carried worship with it.

813. 3. The Semitic material of malefic spirits, while in general the same as that found elsewhere in the world, has a couple of special features. In Babylonia there was a sort of pandemonium, a certain organization of demons,[4] with proper names for some classes; demons usually have not proper names, but may receive such names when they come into specially definite relations with men. The demon Lilit mentioned in the Old Testament,[5] is probably Babylonian. The two great Hebrew hostile beings, Satan and Azazĕl, are rather gods than demons.[6] They were both most highly developed under Persian influence, and in the Book of Enoch take on the character and rôle of Angro Mainyu. Their history exhibits, however, the disposition of the later Jews to organize the realm of supernatural evil; about the first century B.C. the serpent-god of Genesis iii was identified with Satan.[7]

The Greek malefic beings, Ker, Harpy, Fury, Gorgon, Sphinx, and the like, appear to have been developed out of ghosts[8] — whether or not this is true of the Babylonian demons the known material does not enable us to say. Organization of such beings was carried out fully by the Persians, but not by any other Indo-European people and not by the Chinese.

---

[1] Gen. vi, 4, cf. Ezek. xxxii, 27; Philo of Byblos; Harper, *Assyrian and Babylonian Literature*.

[2] Isa. lxiii, 16 (" God is our father, though Abraham and Israel do not acknowledge us ") is regarded by some commentators as pointing to ancestor-worship. It seems, however, to be nothing more than the complaint of persons who were disowned by the community or by the leaders.   [3] § 341 ff.

[4] Jastrow, *Religion of Babylonia and Assyria*, p. 168 : " a pantheon of demons."

[5] Isa. xxxiv, 14.

[6] Satan is one of the Elohim-beings, old gods subordinated to Yahweh, and Azazel, if his name contains the divine title *el*, must be put into this class.

[7] Wisdom of Solomon, ii, 24.

[8] Harrison, *Prolegomena to the Study of Greek Religion*, chap. v. On Hindu demons see Hopkins, *Religions of India*, Index, s.v. *Devils*.

814. 4. On abstract gods and phallic cults see the discussions of these points above.[1]

815. 5. Semitic theistic myths differ from Indo-European in that they are almost wholly without the element of personal adventures of gods.[2] Since all known genuine Semitic myths seem to have their original home in Babylonia, and Babylonian mythical material bears marks of Sumerian influence, the question has been raised whether we have any genuinely Semitic mythical biographies of gods. However this question may be answered, it remains true that the Semites show little disposition to work out this line of thought.

816. Of the origin of these peculiarities of the Semitic theistic system, as of all such origins, it is impossible to give any satisfactory explanation. Geographical and climatic conditions have been appealed to : the Semitic area was small and isolated — the Semites were shut off by oceans, mountains, and rivers from the rest of the world, were disposed to migrate only within the limits of their area,[3] and long lived under the monotonous influence of the desert ; thus, it is said, their conception of the world became objective and limited — they were clannish, practical, unanalytic, and unimaginative. But the origin of races is obscure, and the genius of every ancient people was formed and developed in remote ages under conditions not known to us. We can do little more than note the characteristics visible in historical times.

817. Paucity of myths and the other features mentioned above accord with the later rôle of Semitic, especially Hebrew, theism — the tendency to conceive of the deity as on the one hand aloof and transcendent, and on the other hand standing in close social relations with man as his lord and protector. This proved to be socially the most effective idea of God, and has been adopted by all the great nations of the western world.

818. The contributions of the Indo-European religions to the religious thought of the world are indicated in the preceding

[1] §§ 698 ff., 398 ff.
[2] See below, Chapter vii. Here, again, Mazdaism forms an exception, resembling the Semitic scheme rather than the Hindu.
[3] A partial exception is found in the comparatively late movement from the south of Arabia over into Africa (Abessinia, Ethiopia).

sketches. What is to be learned from the Chinese the future must show. The general history of civilization leads us to expect a gradual combination and fusion of all lines of religious development, in which every system will contribute its best, and the lower elements will be discarded.[1]

---

[1] On the characteristics of the various great religions see Hegel, *Religionsphilosophie*; Santayana, *Reason in Religion* (vol. iii of *The Life of Reason*); E. Caird, *Evolution of Religion*; R. B. Perry, *Approach to Philosophy*; S. Johnson, *Oriental Religions*; J. F. Clarke, *Ten Great Religions*; S. Reinach, *Orpheus*. See below, Chapter ix.

CHAPTER VII

MYTHS

819. Myths represent the savage and half-civilized science of origins, the imaginary construction of the world. From the earliest times men have shown curiosity respecting the origin of the things that lie about them. In the presence of plains and mountains, trees and rivers, sun, moon, and stars, beasts and human beings, they have felt the necessity of accounting for the beginning of all these objects.[1] This attempt at giving a natural history of the world is in itself a scientific procedure, but in the earlier periods of humanity it naturally attached itself to the hypothesis of superhuman Powers — the production of this variety of mysterious things appeared to demand capacity above that of man. The science and the fancy of early man combined to produce a great mass of theories and stories which to their inventors seemed to be a satisfactory account of the origin of all things.

820. Myths thus furnish an important contribution to the history of early opinion, scientific and religious; in the absence of written records they often offer our only means of information concerning early thought. They describe the origin not only of the physical world but also of communities and social organizations and institutions. They have a noteworthy vitality, lasting from the beginning of human communal life into periods of advanced civilization; and, when adopted by great religious organizations and interwoven into their theories of salvation, they perpetuate to civilized times the

---

[1] But a certain substratum is usually assumed, no attempt being made to account for its existence.

[2] Cf. Tylor, *Primitive Culture*, chaps. viii–x; Jastrow, *Study of Religion*, Index, s.vv. *Myth, Mythology*; Lang, *Custom and Myth*, and *Myth, Ritual, and Religion*; articles "Mythologie" in *La Grande Encyclopédie*, and "Mythology" in *Encyclopædia Britannica*, 11th ed,

ideas of the crude period in which they originated. In many cases they stand side by side, and in sharp contrast, with elevated moral conceptions of the deity, and then have to be harmonized, usually with a great expenditure of exegetical ingenuity, with the higher ideas of society.

821. The mythopœic age, in the widest sense of the term, embraces the whole period in which appeal is made, for the explanation of phenomena, to other than natural agencies; but it is generally understood to extend only up to the time when, though a general divine Power is invoked for creation, this is regarded as working solely through the laws of nature.[1] And within this period the myth-making impulse lasted longer in some directions than in others. In general, the mythical theories concerning the larger processes, as, for example, the creation of the world, received no addition after the establishment of a settled civilization; but after this time even well-advanced communities continued to invent mythical accounts of the origin of customs, institutions, genealogies, and similar facts. Throughout the whole myth-making period a progression may be recognized in the character of the myths: from the earlier animal and human creators we pass to the higher anthropomorphic forms, the great gods; there is increased literary excellence, a molding and a remolding of the old crude stories, with a combination of them into well-ordered histories; they are constantly modified by the growing acquaintance with the laws of nature and by the higher intellectual conceptions of the deity; and they are more and more infused with ethical significance.

822. An examination of myths all over the world shows that the most of them, especially those relating to creation and to the histories of the gods, originated at a period when men stood intellectually and morally on a very low plane.[2] The first myth-makers were savages, with all the well-known characteristics of savage life. Having next to no knowledge of natural law, and holding to a practical identity of nature among men, beasts, and physical

---

[1] Belief in miracles, which is found in some higher religions, may here be left out of the account as belonging in a separate category.

[2] Lang, *Myth, Ritual, and Religion*, chaps. ii–iv.

things, they had no difficulty in imagining all sorts of transformations and creative procedures. No limit was conceived of for the power of beasts and men — there was no object in heaven or earth which, according to the current ideas, could not have been produced by some procedure which was similar to the procedures of ordinary life. The ethical character of the creators and of the introducers of general culture was that of the communities that imagined them ; naturally the stories were full of ethical barbarities and violations of all the moral rules recognized at a later period ; and, as is remarked above, these stories continued into civilized times, and had to be interpreted by various devices.

823. One of the most noteworthy facts in the history of mythology is the general similarity of the myths that are found all over the world. Allowing for continuous moral and intellectual progress and for local differences of surroundings, it may be said that the theories of the production of the earth and the heavenly bodies, of man and other objects, of customs and institutions, show substantially the same types everywhere. The question has been raised whether this virtual identity is to be explained by the supposition of independent origination at various points, or is to be attributed to a borrowing by one community from another. The question of the migration of myths is a part of the larger question of the migration of culture, and is attended with all the difficulties that attach to this latter. It is not possible at present to give an answer which shall embrace all the phenomena. Obviously any satisfactory solution of the problem must be preceded by a thorough examination of all particular myths, all social characteristics, and all geographical and migratory relations affecting the early communities ; and on these points there is yet much to learn.

824. It is well known that customs and beliefs have sometimes passed from one tribe or nation to another, when there has been close social intercourse between the two. It is known also that early men were capable of long journeys by land and by water : the migration legends of various peoples are full of the details of such movements ; in comparatively recent times there have been great migrations of large bodies of people, as, for example, from the Arabian desert to the north and northwest, and from the central Asiatic steppes westward and eastward; and the tribes of the Pacific Ocean appear to have traversed long distances in their canoes. And when we consider the great lapse of time, many thousands of years, that preceded the formation of the human society with which we are acquainted, it appears to be impossible to assign any limit to the possibility of tribal movements on the face of the earth. On the other hand, we do not know whether, or how far, such migrations issued in social fusion; and all the well-attested cases of borrowing of customs and ideas have sprung from long-continued social union.

825. Further, a distinction must be made between general resemblances and minute agreement or complete identity; there may be a similarity so great as to force on us the hypothesis of imitation, and there may be general similarities that may be ascribed to ordinary human thought working in different places under similar conditions. In fact, the conditions of existence have not varied very greatly over the globe. There are differences of climate and soil and surface-configuration, but everywhere there have been the sky with the heavenly bodies, the sequence of day and night, sunshine and rain, hunting and fishing, trees, rivers, beasts and birds, and the cultivable soil; and as man's problem was everywhere the same — namely, how to put himself into good relation with his surroundings — and as his intellectual equipment was everywhere substantially the same, it would not be surprising if he should fall on similar methods of thought and procedure independently in various parts of the world. It was natural to early man to think of the sun as a ball of fire which had somehow been thrown up into the sky, and of the moon as associated with the sun as sister or wife or husband, and of the stars as children of these two. For creative agents early man had to look to the beings about him, particularly to beasts, birds, and insects. The process of creation was simple — the story usually amounts merely to saying that such and such a beast or other being made this or that object; and there is very rarely, if ever, a conception of an absolute beginning; almost always a reconstruction of existing material is assumed.

826. Both explanations of the resemblances in myths, it thus appears, are reasonable in themselves, and every case must be considered separately. That a community has borrowed one story does not prove borrowing in the case of any other story ; and that a people has been a center of distribution of certain myths does not prove that it was the originator of all myths. These two propositions appear to be self-evident, but they have often been ignored in discussions of the provenance of mythical material.[1]

827. The similarities in myths all over the world extend over the whole domain of religion. Myths may be divided into those which deal with the creation of the world and of man (cosmogonic), those which deal with the origins of tribes and nations (ethnogonic), those which refer to the origin of customs and institutions (sociogonic), and those which are based on the forms and movements of the heavenly bodies, clouds, winds, and so forth (solar, lunar, procellar, and so forth).

828. *Cosmogonic myths.*[2] Among early tribes the creators are very often familiar animals, such as the coyote, the raven, the hare (North America), the wagtail (among the Ainu), the grasshopper (among the Bushmen) — in general, whatever animals appear to the men of a particular tribe to show skill and power. Reference is made above to the reasons which led early men to pay such high regard to the lower animals.[3] But in more advanced savage communities the creative function is ascribed to a man, as among the Thompson River Indians and in Southeast Australia ; in Central Australia the authors of creation or of the arrangement of things are beings who are indifferently men or animals, but are regarded as the ancestors of the tribes. In the higher religions the creators are nature gods and great gods, and finally the one God stands alone as creator.

829. The act of creation is commonly represented as a process. Mud is brought up from a pool, or an island is raised from the sea

[1] So with the theory of universal borrowing from one center advocated by Stucken (*Astralmythen*), Winckler (*Himmels- und Weltensbild der Babylonier als Grundlage der Weltanschauung und Mythologie aller Völker*), Jeremias (*Das Alte Testament im Lichte des Alten Orients*), Jensen (*Das Gilgamesch Epos*), and others.

[2] Cf. article "Cosmogony and Cosmology" in Hastings, *Encyclopædia of Religion and Ethics*. [3] § 225 ff.

(the Maoris, the Redmen), and these are stretched out so as to meet the needs of men; or a dragon or a giant is cut to pieces and the various parts of the universe are made from the pieces (Babylonia, India, Scandinavia); or, in still later times, an unformed mass of water is conceived of as the original state out of which all things are fashioned (Babylonians, Hebrews, Hindus, Greeks); or the universe issues from an egg (the origin of the egg being left unexplained),[1] or the earth is represented as the mother of all things (California). Elaborate cosmogonies are found in New Zealand (the Maoris), in North America (the Pawnees, the Lenâpé, and so forth), in Australia, and elsewhere. An interesting example is the Californian Achomāwi cosmogony. In the beginning, according to this scheme, were only the sea and the sky, and from the sky came down the Creator; or a cloud, at first tiny, grew large, condensed, and became the Silver-Gray Fox, the Creator, and out of a fog, which in like manner was condensed, came the Coyote, and these two made the earth and man.[2]

830. In all these cases the creation is out of already existing material[3] and the creator is really a culture-hero or transformer, a character that clings to deities in the most advanced religions, as the Egyptian, Babylonian, and Greek. The character of these early transformers and creators is that of the communities in which they originate. Morally they represent both the higher and the lower sides of life, and this is true in all periods — the Hindu Indra is as tricksy and unmoral as the North American Coyote, and the early form of Zeus resembles these and other savage figures.[4] The conceptions of the creator grew more and more ethically good, but the lower representations continued to exist side by side with the higher.[5]

---

[1] *Çatapatha Brahmana*, xi, 1, 6, 1.

[2] R. B. Dixon, *The Northern Maidu*, p. 335 f.

[3] Spiegel (*Eranische Alterthumskunde*, ii, 144) ascribes to the Eranians the conception of creation out of nothing. See also the Hawaiian representation of the origin of all things from the primeval void, and the orderly sequence of the various forms of life.   [4] A. Lang, *Myth, Ritual, and Religion*, chap. vi ff.

[5] See, for example, the two accounts of creation in the Book of Genesis. In the earlier account (chap. ii) the procedure of Yahweh is mechanical, and things do not turn out as he intended; in the later account (chap. i) there is no mention of a process — it is the divine word that calls the world into being.

831. It is not altogether strange that the two sorts of creative Powers should be early thought of as mutually antagonistic. The Maidu bad creator is constantly opposing and bringing to naught the work of his good rival, and their collision produces the actual state of things on the earth.[1] It is probably by way of explanation of the evil in the world that in this myth the bad Coyote finally overcomes his rival. The resemblance of this scheme to the Mazdean dualism, except in the outcome, is obvious. For a full account of these systems we must await further information; but at present there is no ground for holding that the similarity is due to borrowing.

832. In various early cosmogonies the representation is found of an earlier race or an early world that had been destroyed, sometimes by a flood (Babylonia, India, Greece, Polynesia, North America, South America), sometimes in other ways.[2] Flood stories probably arise from local inundations, and may therefore have been constructed independently in various regions. In some cases the general conditions favor the supposition of distribution from one point: it seems probable, for example, that the Babylonian flood story was adopted by the Canaanites and from them by the Hebrews (the supposition of common descent from an original Semitic myth is made improbable by the closeness of resemblance between the Babylonian and Hebrew forms); it may have passed to India, but the Hindu story may be accounted for from local conditions. But we know of no such intercourse between the Americas, Polynesia, and Western Asia, as would suggest a migration of the myth from the latter to the two former, though this is conceivable.

833. The origin of man is included in that of the world. He is made from clay or wooden figures or stones, or, as in Australia, out of a shapeless mass. The conception found in various parts of the world, that the present race of men was preceded by another, appears to be due sometimes to a real, though often confused, tradition of an earlier population, sometimes to a vague conception

[1] Dixon, *The Northern Maidu*, p. 263.
[2] See R. Andree, *Die Flutsagen*; article "Flood" in Hastings, *Dictionary of the Bible*.

of the conflict and incompleteness in the world. Traditions of predecessors are found in various parts of the world. In North America — as, for example, among the Navahos — a part of the early history is the conflict with certain mighty and evil beings who made good life impossible — a semidualistic scheme.[1] This view comes from the general disposition to conceive of the past as the time of mightier agencies, good and bad, than now exist.

834. A not uncommon representation is that man was originally not mortal, or that it was a question whether or not he should be mortal (death being generally regarded by early man as an abnormal event, produced by supernatural agency). In such cases mortality is brought about by an accident or an error: among the Maoris by a mistake of the hero Maui;[2] among the Hebrews by the disobedience of the first man, or by his failure to eat of the tree of life; in South Africa by the accident that the messenger who was to announce immortality was outrun by one who announced mortality.[3]

835. The belief that the earliest men were longer-lived and of larger stature than their successors is found among certain peoples.[4] Of the origin of this belief in ancient times we have no accounts. It may have been suggested by various objects supposed to be remains of men, or it may have been due simply to a tendency to conceive of the beginners of human society as superior beings (dedivinized gods). The Hebrew tradition ascribed great age to Abraham, Isaac, Jacob, Joseph, and Moses, on a generally descending scale; the longevity of the antediluvians is perhaps a speculative continuation of the series back of Abraham on an ascending scale, though special mythical traits here come in.

Connected with the general belief in the superiority of early conditions of life is the belief in a primitive earthly paradise; the history of this conception is not clear, but in some cases the paradise appears to have been the delightful abode of a deity, into

---

[1] Matthews, *Navaho Legends*, p. 37; cf. Dorsey, *The Skidi Pawnee*, p. 14 ff.
[2] Grey, *Polynesian Mythology*, p. 57 f.; cf. Tylor, *Primitive Culture*, i, 335.
[3] Callaway, *The Amazulu*, pp. 3, 4, 100, 138.
[4] Gen. v; vi, 4; Herodotus, iii, 23; Roscher, *Lexikon*, s.v. *Giganten*; cf. Tylor, op. cit., i, 385 ff.; Brinton, *American Hero-Myths*, p. 88.

which human beings were for various reasons admitted, or the primeval fair and happy earth.[1]

836. The belief that the world or the existing order is to be destroyed appears to be connected with the conception of history as involving a cycle of ages, and the theory of ages may have arisen from the tradition or the knowledge of social and political revolutions, the rise of each new phase of civilization involving the destruction of its predecessor. Traditions of past cataclysms may have helped toward the formulation of an expectation of coming destruction. This expectation, generalized under the influence of belief in a final judgment of men by God, would lead to the announcement of a final destruction of the present world. This destruction, which ushers in a new age, is accomplished in various ways, sometimes by water, wind, or fire,[2] sometimes by supernatural enemies.[3] The Hindu and the Persian schemes of successive ages are relatively late theological constructions, but they are based on the older idea that present things must have an end.[4] The Navaho series of five worlds represents, apparently, nothing but traditions of social changes, interspersed with minor ætiologic myths.[5]

837. Many other cosmogonic details, common to various peoples, might be added. Transformation from human to animal or mineral forms and the reverse are to be found, as we have seen, everywhere. The slaying of dragons by gods or heroes is often connected with creation, but belongs sometimes in the category of cultural or nature myths. Abnormal forms of birth and generation

---

[1] Brinton, *Religions of Primitive Peoples*, p. 126 f.; Maspero, *Dawn*, p. 158; Gen. ii, iii; *Avesta, Vendidad*, Fargard ii; Spiegel, *Eranische Alterthumskunde*, i, 463 ff.; Windischmann, *Zoroastrische Studien*, p. 19 ff.; Hopkins, in *Journal of the American Oriental Society* (September, 1910), pp. 362, 366; article "Hesperiden" in Roscher's *Lexikon*; commentaries of Kalisch, Dillmann, Driver, Skinner, and others on Gen. ii, iii; *Jewish Encyclopedia*, s.v. *Paradise*; Delitzsch, *Wo lag das Paradies?* On the character of the abode of the Babylonian Parnapishtim see Jastrow, *Religion of Babylonia and Assyria*, pp. 488, 496.

[2] 2 Pet. iii, 7, contrast with the old destruction by water; Hindu eschatology.

[3] The Norse myth of "the twilight of the gods" has perhaps been colored, in its latest form, by Christian eschatology.

[4] Hopkins, *Religions of India*, p. 421; Spiegel, *Eranische Alterthumskunde*, ii, 161; H. Warren, *Buddhism in Translations*, p. 315 ff.

[5] Matthews, *Navaho Legends*, p. 63 ff.

may be sometimes products of savage fancy, or they may be attempts to set forth the mysterious or the supernatural in certain beings, or they may be nature myths: in various mythologies a god or a hero is born from the side or the thigh or the head of the mother or the father; fecundation by other means than sexual union appears in North America, Egypt, Greece, and generally in savage tribes.[1] The representation of the primeval parents, Heaven and Earth, as having been originally united in a close embrace and then separated, Heaven being lifted up and Earth remaining below, is so remarkable that it might be doubted whether it arose independently in different places; yet, as it is found in New Zealand,[2] in Egypt,[3] in India,[4] among the Masai of Eastern Central Africa,[5] and as the supposition of borrowing for these widely separated communities would be difficult (except, perhaps, as between Egypt and the Masai land), it is simpler to regard the myth as a natural effort of early science.[6] It need hardly be added that with all the similarities in the various cosmogonic systems the diversities among different peoples are as numerous as the differences of surroundings and character.

838. Among most early communities the great figures of the past (creations of imagination) to whom are ascribed the introduction of the arts of life and the general betterment of society are regarded as demigods, descended from parents one of whom is divine and the other human; it is sometimes the father, sometimes the mother, that is divine.[7] This conception is a simple and natural explanation of the supposed extraordinary powers of the personages in question. A more refined conception represents man as receiving life from the breath of God,[8] whence easily comes the idea that man is the child of God and has in him a spark of divinity.

---

[1] Hartland, *Primitive Paternity*, chap. i.   [2] Grey, *Polynesian Mythology*, chap. i.
[3] Maspero, *Dawn*, p. 128 f.   [4] *Aitareya Brahmana*, iv, 27.
[5] Hollis, *The Masai*, p. 279; cf. Turner, *Samoa*, p. 198.
[6] Gruppe, *Griechische Culte und Mythen*. Cf. the birth-myth in Matthews, *Navaho Legends*, p. 71.
[7] So Heracles, Achilles, Æneas, and the heroes mentioned in Gen. vi, 4.
[8] Gen. ii, 7.

839. *Ethnogonic myths.* Early science has to account not only for the origin of the world and the human race, but also for the origin of particular tribes and their surroundings. The area involved is the known world, which among savage peoples is small in extent but increases with knowledge, the general method of accounting for social division remaining, however, the same. As a ·rule, the center of the distribution of mankind is the territory of the particular tribe in which the myth originates. There is always the conviction, expressed or implied, that the tribe in question is the čenter of the world and the favorite of the creative Power;[1] it being established in its place, the rest of the world is divided among other tribes — a conception that survives among civilized peoples of antiquity.[2]

840. The ethnogonic history generally takes the form of a genealogy — every tribe or other group is derived from a mythical ancestor, who among savages is frequently a beast, or half-beast half-human, or even in some cases a rock or a stone. Familiar examples are the genealogical systems of the Australians, the Maoris of New Zealand, the Samoans, the American Indians;[3] but the conception appears to be universal. There was indeed no other natural way of accounting for the origin of a tribe : as an existing family would reckon its beginning from the grandfather, so the tribe would come from some remote person, and so at a later time the nation, and then finally the human race. As there were no historical records of such beginning, the scientific imagination of early peoples constructed the first parents in various ways, often by personifying the tribe and transferring its name to the mythical ancestor. It is in this way that the genealogical lists of the post-Mohammedan Arabians arose; it is certain that they had no records of the past extending further than a few generations, and in some cases the origins of the names in genealogical

---

[1] So in Polynesia, North America, China, ancient Greece, and among the Hebrews.
[2] As, for example, the Hebrews (Deut. xxxii, 8 f.).
[3] Spencer and Gillen, *Native Tribes of Central Australia*, p. 119 ff.; Taylor, *New Zealand*, chap. xiv and p. 325 ; Turner, *Samoa*, p. 3 ff.; J. G. Müller, *Geschichte der amerikanischen Urreligionen*, pp. 33 ff., 179 ff., § 61.

lists may be fixed. The Greek method of naming ancestors is simple and obvious : the sons of Hellen are Dorus, Xuthus, Æolus ; the sons of Xuthus are Achæus and Ion ; and these are all descended from Deucalion. In like manner the Pelasgians are carried back to the ancestor Pelasgus, and the Peloponnesians to Pelops. The Roman Romulus, Remulus, Remus, are natural inventions based on the name of the city.

841. Genealogical elaboration was carried out more fully by the Hebrews than by any other ancient people. Not only were tribal names, Jacob, Israel, Judah, Joseph, Ephraim, and the rest, personified, but they were arranged in a well-shaped family system ; and, the same method being applied to all the nations known to them, these were carried up to the three sons of Noah, and finally through Noah up to the first man, whose Hebrew name, Adam, means simply man.[1] The table of nations in Genesis x is a remarkable example of ethnographic organization. As it is based on geographical relations, it does not in all particulars accord with modern ethnological schemes, but it is a noteworthy attempt to embrace the whole world in a family picture. The view that the division of the earth among the various peoples revolved around the Israelite territory is expressed in the poem cited above,[2] which is of the seventh century B.C., and it may be inferred that this large genealogical unification was completed among the Israelites at a time when they felt the influence of the great Assyrian civilization, with which they seem to have come into somewhat intimate contact. Later examples are found in Vergil's Æneid and Milton's " History of Britain " (in which he adopts early attempts at genealogical construction).

842. *Sociogonic myths.* Most of the customs and institutions of early peoples go back to a time when there were no records, and their introduction was naturally referred, so soon as reflection thereon began, to gods and heroes of primeval time.

---

[1] So the Hindu Manu (man), or Father Manu (*Rig-Veda*, ii, 33, 13), is the progenitor of the human race. Cf. the " first man," Yama. For the Old-Persian genealogical scheme see Spiegel, *Eranische Alterthumskunde*, i, 473, 500 ff.

[2] Deut. xxxii.

843. The arts of life are commonly explained in this mythical way. The beginnings of agriculture are referred in Melanesia to the Little One or to Qat, in Mexico to the god or culture-hero Quetzalcoatl, in Peru to Viracocha or Pachacamac, or to Manco Capac and his wife. For the Algonkins Michabo, the Great Hare, was the teacher of fishing and of other pursuits.[1] The Babylonian god Ea was the instructor of his people in all the arts of civilization.[2] In the Old Testament Cainite (Kenite) genealogy the originators of pastoral life, of metal-working, and of music, are the ancient ancestors.[3] In the Book of Enoch the employment of metals, the use of writing, and in general all the early arts of civilization are ascribed to the fallen angels, whose children are represented in the Book of Genesis [4] as the culture-heroes of the olden time. The introduction of writing into Greece is ascribed by the Greeks to the mythical hero or demigod Cadmus.[5] Fire is in India the production of the god Agni [6] (who is simply fire elevated to the rank of a personal divinity); in the Greek myth it is stolen and given to men by the demigod Prometheus [7] against the will of the gods, who are jealous of human progress.[8] Among various savage tribes there are similar histories of the derivation of the use of fire from superhuman beings.[9]

844. Early ceremonies, as we have seen,[10] are universally connected with religion, and their origin is ascribed to divine or semi-divine figures of the past. In Australia the initiation ceremonies, which take up a great part of the tribal life, are regarded as having been established by the mythical ancestors.[11] Among the

---

[1] Codrington, *The Melanesians*, p. 156 ff.; Réville, *Native Religions of Mexico and Peru*, p. 64; Brinton, *Myths of the New World*, p. 264, and *American Hero-Myths*, pp. 186 f., 195 ff.; cf. R. B. Brehm, *Das Inka-Reich*, p. 24 ff.

[2] Jastrow, *Aspects of Religious Belief and Practice in Babylonia and Assyria*, p. 89.

[3] Gen. iv, 16 ff.   [4] Gen. vi, 1, 2, 4 (verse 3 is an interpolation).

[5] Herodotus, v, 57 f.; Roscher, *Lexikon*, s.v. *Kadmos*.   [6] *Rig-Veda*, i, 93, 6.

[7] Hesiod, *Works and Days*, 49 ff.

[8] In the story in Genesis (ii, 17; iii, 5, 22–24) there is a trace of such jealousy; and it is by violation of the command of the deity that man attains the knowledge of good and evil.

[9] L. Frobenius, *Childhood of Man*, chap. xxv (and cf. chap. xxvi).

[10] Chapter iii.

[11] Spencer and Gillen, *Native Tribes of Central Australia*, p. 394 ff.

Hebrews when circumcision, an early initiation ceremony,[1] became religiously important, its establishment was referred to the ancestor Abraham, who is said to have acted by direct command of God,[2] but in earlier documents there are hints of other origins for the rite.[3] The ritual dances of the North American Indians, which are very elaborate, are accompanied by explanations in which the origin of every detail is referred to some event or person in the supernatural past ;[4] and similar explanations are given of the dances of Mexico.[5] In many cases the restrictions of food and other things are ascribed to the experiences of the ancestors or to the commands of deities : the Hebrew usage of not eating a certain sinew is connected with the story of the struggle between Jacob and a divine being.[6]

845. Festivals also were treated in this manner as soon as men began to reflect on the origin of society. As one feature in the festival sacred to Mars (March 1) was the dancing of the priests who carried curious shields, it was narrated, to account for this, that the shield of Mars fell down from heaven ;[7] and the goddess Maia, according to one conjecture, was invented to explain the name of the month of May.[8] A Greek explanation of the fact that children at a later period were not called by the mother's name was that in the contest between Poseidon and Athene for the control of the city of Athens the latter deity prevailed by the votes of the women, who were in the majority, and to appease the wrath of Poseidon this rule was then made by the men.[9] The Gileadite festival in which maidens lamented the death of the daughter of Jephthah [10] was doubtless an old rite in which the death of some divinity was bewailed. The Greek Boedromia was referred to the succor given by Theseus against the Amazons,[11] and in the

---

[1] See above, § 153 ff.   [2] Gen. xvii.   [3] Ex. iv, 24-26; Josh. v, 2 ff.

[4] W. Matthews, *Navaho Legends*, p. 40 ff.; J. W. Fewkes, *The Winter Solstice Ceremony at Walpi.*

[5] Réville, *Native Religions of Mexico and Peru* (Hibbert Lectures), pp. 94 f., 110 (cf. ib., p. 224 f., on Peruvian dances). See above, § 109, note 6.

[6] Gen. xxxii, 24 ff.   [7] Fowler, *Roman Festivals*, p. 38.

[8] Fowler, op. cit., p. 99 ff.; for another view see Roscher, *Lexikon*, article " Maia II " ; cf. Wissowa, *Religion der Römer*, p. 185.

[9] Augustine, *De Civitate Dei*, 18, 9.   [10] Judg. xi, 30 ff.

[11] Plutarch, *Theseus*, 27.

celebration of the Eleusinian mysteries ætiological myths connected with Demeter, Kore, and Dionysos formed the central part of the proceedings.[1] In the Old Testament the spring festival (Passover) is connected with the departure of the people from Egypt, and the autumn festival (Tabernacles) with the sojourn in the wilderness; and by the later Jews the midsummer festival (the Feast of Weeks, Pentecost) was similarly brought into connection with the giving of the law on Mount Sinai.

846. *Relation between myth and ritual.* The question whether myth comes from ritual or ritual from myth has been much discussed. Obviously universal precedence cannot be allowed to either of the two. There are cases in which primary mythical beliefs determine the form of religious procedure: the belief, for example, that a god, as anthropomorphic divine patron, must be placated and provided with all the accessories of a potentate, leads to the offering of food and other gifts and to the establishment of abodes and attendants; the sense of his aloofness and of his powerful and dangerous qualities induces cautionary rules for approach to his presence; because he has manlike intellectual and emotional limitations his favor must be secured by prayers and praises; if he has a son, this latter may act as mediator between his father and a suppliant, or one god may mediate with others in behalf of men.[2] On the other hand, there are many examples of myths that arise as explanation of ritualistic details.[3] It is sometimes hard to say on which side the precedence in time lies. In general, it seems, it is from broader and fundamental mythical conceptions that ritual arises, while mythical narratives spring from particular ritualistic observances.

847. Important religious changes which have come to pass through natural changes of thought, usually by the movement

---

[1] F. B. Jevons, *Introduction to the History of Religion*, chap. xxiii f.; Miss J. E. Harrison, *Prolegomena to the Study of Greek Religion*, chap. x; K. H. E. de Jong, *Das antike Mysterienwesen*, pp. 14, 16, 18; Preller, "Eleusinia" in Pauly's *Realencyclopädie*; Reitzenstein, *Hellenistische Mysterienreligion*.

[2] In Babylonia such rôles are ascribed to Ea and Marduk (Jastrow, *Religion of Babylonia and Assyria*, pp. 137, 139, 276).

[3] See above, § 844 f.; W. R. Smith, *Religion of the Semites*, 2d ed., pp. 18, 173 ff., *Records of the Past*, vi, 108.

toward greater refinement, are explained as having been introduced by some great reformer. The abrogation of human sacrifice
was a reform of great moment: in Mexico it is ascribed to the
god Quetzalcoatl,[1] and in the Old Testament to Abraham acting
by command of God.[2] One of the Incas of Peru is said to have
reached monotheistic views by a process of reasoning, and the post-
Biblical Jewish myths ascribed the same achievement to Abraham.[3]

848. As a rule sacred places were connected with stories of
the presence of divine personages or mythical ancestors. In Samoa,
the Hawaian group, and other Pacific islands many stones are
connected with stories of heroes, spirits, or gods.[4] In Central Australia every stone, rock, or tree has its myth of the half-bestial
ancestors.[5] In Greece, as Pausanias relates, there was hardly a
place that did not have its story of the origin of some sacred spot
or thing due to a god.[6] In the earlier books of the Old Testament
the sacred places, which were Arabian or Canaanite shrines adopted
by the Hebrews, are generally connected with the presence of
the patriarchs or other great men. The magical qualities of springs,
pools, and other bodies of water are explained by stories in which
a god or other divine person descends into them, or in some other
way communicates power.[7]

849. *Myths of heavenly bodies, winds, and vegetation.* As the
sun, the moon, and other objects of nature were regarded as anthropomorphic persons and naturally came into relation with men,

---

[1] The myths connected with Quetzalcoatl (see Brinton, *American Hero-Myths*,
and L. Spence, *Mythologies of Ancient Mexico and Peru*) do not relate mostly to the
movements and deeds of the sun or the winds, but arose from his character as local
deity with universal powers. Social and political events were woven into them. His
contest with Tezcatlipoca seems to reflect the struggle between two tribes; his defeat signifies the victory of the conquering tribe, and the expectation of his return
(by which the invading Spaniards, it is said, profited) was based on the political hope
of his people. Cf. similar expectations among other peoples.

[2] Gen. xxii.

[3] B. Beer, *Leben Abraham's nach Auffassung der jüdischen Sage*, p. 5 and note 34;
p. 102, note 30.   [4] Turner, *Samoa*, Index.

[5] Spencer and Gillen, *Native Tribes of Central Australia*, chap. xviii.

[6] Pausanias, *Description of Greece*, passim.

[7] Semitic and other examples are given in W. R. Smith's *Religion of the Semites*,
p. 173 ff.

their imagined adventures have produced a great mass of stories in all parts of the world. These stories are partly attempts to account for phenomena and partly are simply products of fancy; the myth-maker is very often a mere story-teller. The sun, conceived of usually as an old man, is supposed to live in a house up in the sky, to have his wife and children, to receive visitors, and to interfere to some extent in human affairs. An eclipse was obviously to be regarded as the work of an enemy of the sun, usually a dragon (so in many low tribes, and in India). A great excess of heat on the earth might be explained by the supposition that the chariot of the sun had been driven too near the surface.[1] The waning of the moon was supposed to be due to her sorrow at the loss of her children, the stars, which were devoured by the sun. The moon might be a fair woman who becomes enamored of a human being. At a later time in the progress of astronomical knowledge the planets and certain of the stars were individualized — they became actors in human history or, still later, the abode of supernatural beings.[2]

850. The beginnings of astrological theory are probably to be recognized at a very early period. The height of the sky above the earth, the persistence with which the stars seem to look down on men, the invariability of their courses, the mysteriousness of their origin would naturally lead to the belief that they had some control over human affairs. Meteors, regarded as falling stars, have always been objects of dread. The development of astrology has been due to the increase of astronomical knowledge and to the tendency to organize religion in its aspect of dependence on the supernatural Powers.[3]

851. Winds have played a less prominent part in theistic history than the heavenly bodies, but have given rise to not a few myths

---

[1] On the complicated myth of Phaëthon see the article in Roscher's *Lexikon.*

[2] Isa. xxiv, 21 ; Tylor, *Primitive Culture*, i, 356 ff.

[3] The Babylonians were the great astronomers and astrologers of antiquity, but their eminence in this regard belongs to their later period. After the fall of the later Babylonian empire (B.C. 539) the term 'Chaldean' became a synonym of 'astrologer' (so in the Book of Daniel, B.C. 165–164) ; cf. Jastrow, *Aspects of Religious Belief and Practice in Babylonia and Assyria*, p. 259 f.

in religions of different grades of culture and in different parts of the world.[1] In the Scandinavian myths the storm wind as a representative of the prevailing climatic condition has assumed special prominence. In the Iliad when a messenger is dispatched to the abode of the winds to secure their aid, these are found feasting like a human family.[2] Later, winds are, of course, subordinated to the great gods.

852. From time to time theories have arisen explaining many deities and heroes as representatives of the heavenly bodies, and many stories of gods and heroes as reflecting the phenomena of the sky or the air. Such theories have been carried so far sometimes as to explain everything in mythology as a solar or lunar or astral myth. These constructions leave much to the fancy, and it is not difficult to find in mythical narratives references to the movements of the sun or the moon or the stars or the winds. It is possible that such reference really exists in certain stories. It is probable also that simple myths representing such phenomena have been in later times elaborated and brought into connection with a more detailed astronomical knowledge. The same principles of interpretation should guide us here as are referred to above.

853. There are doubtless cases in which a hero or a god represents the sun or the moon, the correspondence between the adventures of the hero and the movements of the heavenly bodies being plain. The twelve labors of Heracles may represent the passage of the sun through the twelve signs of the zodiac; but if this be the case, it is certain that such construction was relatively late, and that the separate adventures must be referred to some more simple facts. If Heracles slays the Hydra, it is more natural to regard this as having represented originally some mundane phenomenon of nature or some simple conflict of the savage life.

---

[1] Brinton, *Myths of the New World*, passim; Hartland, *Primitive Paternity*, i, 149 f.; Grey, *Polynesian Mythology*, p. 1 ff.; Hickson, *Northern Celebes*; Lane, *Arabian Nights*, i, 30 ff.; Saussaye, *Religion of the Teutons*, p. 216 f.; *Iliad*, xxiii, 198 ff.; Tylor, *Primitive Culture*, i, 360 ff.; Ratzel, *History of Mankind* (Eng. tr.), passim.

[2] *Iliad*, xxiii, 200 f. For some wind-myths see Roscher, *Lexikon*, articles " Boreaden," " Boreas," " Harpyia." Cf. the Maori myths given in R. Taylor's *New Zealand*, chap. vi, and for Navaho winds see Matthews, *Navaho Legends*, p. 226, note 75.

The same thing is probably true of the adventures of the Babylonian hero Gilgamesh, who is sometimes considered to be the original of Heracles. Nothing is easier than to expound the story of Samson in the Old Testament as a series of solar and other phenomena,[1] but the probability is that he embodies the vague recollections of early tribal adventures, and, notwithstanding his name (which means ' solar,' that is, devoted to the sun), there is no good ground for supposing that his history has been astronomically worked over. A similar remark applies to many discussions respecting various deities, Hindu (as Indra), Egyptian (as Osiris), Semitic (as Nergal, Marduk, Nabu), and Greek (as Apollo). In all such cases it is necessary to inquire first whether the explanation of the myth may not be found naturally in some ordinary human experience or some very simple natural phenomenon, and a line of demarcation must be drawn between original forms of the myth and later learned constructions.

854. Another source of mythical narration is the history of vegetation, which at the present time has largely supplanted the solar theory. The amazing spectacle of the decay and revival of vegetation, naturally referred to superhuman power, and the importance of plants for human life, have led to the construction of stories (sometimes founded on ritual) in which the adventures of the spirit of vegetation are recounted. Obviously there is a sound basis for this view. The earth was necessarily regarded as the mother from whom came the corn and wine that supported human life. The study of the relatively modern European ceremonies[2] has brought out the persistence of such an idea, and the similarity between the new ceremonies and the old may be said to have demonstrated the existence of an early cult of the divine Power controlling vegetation.

855. The Asian Magna Mater and the Greek Mother (Demeter) or Maiden (Kore, Persephone) are identical in function with the

[1] As in Goldziher's *Hebrew Mythology* (Eng. tr.), a view later abandoned by the author.
[2] By Mannhardt, in *Mythologische Forschungen*, p. 224 ff.; Frazer, in *Golden Bough*, 2d ed. (see Index, s.v. *Corn*) ; and others.

corn maiden of modern times, and the latter figure may be a degraded or socialized descendant of an early deity. When we add
that ancient local deities all took account of the products of the
soil, it will not seem improbable that a great mass of stories should
have arisen describing the adventures of the Spirit of Vegetation.[1]
The descent of a hero or a god into Hades may be explained as
the passage of the sun from its summer warmth to its winter feebleness, or as the annual death and revival of vegetation. Which of these
views shall be adopted will depend in any case on the particular
coloring of the story, on the signification of the names involved, or
on the ceremonies accompanying the worship. It is not now possible to frame a theory that shall embrace all possible phenomena.

856. Certain great myths have in the course of time taken on
elaborate literary form, and in this form show traces of advanced
thought on some fundamental questions. Such myths occur among
half-civilized peoples. There is, for example, the great mythical
cosmogony of the Maoris of New Zealand — a scheme seemingly
so philosophic in form that it excites wonder as to how it could
have arisen in such a place.[2] The story of the adventures of Maui,
a general Polynesian figure, constitutes a Polynesian history of the
rise of civilization. Among the North American Indians the mythological systems of the Algonkins, the Pawnees, and other tribes,
include the origin of all forms of natural objects and all institutions
of society. The histories of the Great Hare of the Lenâpé, the
Thunder Bird of the West, and the various transformers or culture-
heroes, are scarcely less elaborate than the New Zealand stories.
The mythologies of the Finns also (given in the Kalevala) are
noteworthy. Passing to higher forms, it is sufficient to note the
suggestive story of Balder among the Scandinavians, and, in the
ancient world, the Egyptian Osiris myth, the Great Dragon myth of
the Babylonian cosmogony, the various forms of the story of a
primeval paradise, and the ceremonies and ideas that have arisen
in connection with the death of a god.

[1] Cf. Frazer, op. cit., chap. iii, § 16 f.; Roscher, *Lexikon*, articles " Kybele," " Attis," " Persephone," " Ceres "; and Farnell, *Cults of the Greek States.*
[2] See above, § 678.

857. The motif of the *antagonism between light and darkness* appears to be attached to or involved in certain myths, especially the great cosmogonies and stories in which solar deities figure prominently. The original unformed mass of matter is often, perhaps generally, conceived of as being in darkness, and its transformation is attended with the appearance of light[1] — light is an essential element in the conditions that make earthly human life possible; in contrast with the Upperworld the Underworld is dark. The diffusion of light is a main function of the sun, and the high gods dwell in continual brightness.[2] Light is the symbol of right, security, and happiness. But it is doubtful whether the expression of the antithesis and conflict of light and darkness is the immediate object of the early portraitures of deities and the mythical narratives of creation and the future of the world. The Egyptian Ra has no conflict with darkness, and the struggle between Osiris (and Horus) and Set, while it may be and often is interpreted in this sense, is susceptible of other interpretations. The motif in the Babylonian cosmogony is the bringing of order out of disorder, in which work the creation of light is an incident. In ethically advanced religious systems, such as the Hindu and the Persian, the good Powers are connected with light and the wicked Powers with darkness, but a conflict between these adjuncts is not brought out clearly. No such conflict appears in Greek mythology. Where a supernatural being intervenes in defense of light (as when a god destroys a dragon-creature who attempts to swallow the sun), this is simply an explanation of a physical phenomenon, and not a conflict between light and darkness.

858. The theory, widely held, that a great body of early myths, including the conception of the characters and functions of many deities, represent the struggle between light and darkness, is, therefore, not sustained by the facts. Such a generalization is found in late philosophic systems, but it does not belong to early religious thought, which deals with concrete personal agents.[3] A conflict between two gods is often to be explained as the rivalry of two

---

[1] Gen. i, 2 f.　　　　　　[2] Dan. ii, 22; Rev. xxi, 23.

[3] This is true even in the case of abstract deities; see above, §§ 696, 702 ff.

districts or of two forms of culture. Attacks on luminous bodies, or defenses of them, are common as ætiological myths, and an antagonism between light and darkness then naturally appears, as is observed above, as an accessory or incident, but not as an immediate object of mythical portraiture. The closeness of the relation between the light-and-darkness theory and the solar theory of myths is obvious.

859. *Myth and legend.* In the course of the formulation of myths they have naturally become mingled with legend. As they narrate the achievements of the great supernatural figures of the past, these achievements have often become blended in the twilight of tradition with actual (though embellished) experiences of the clan or tribe and of the great men therewith connected.[1] In such cases it is generally difficult to decide where legend ends and myth begins, and every story must be investigated separately, and its nature determined from what is known of the real history of the time and of the development of mythical ideas. Familiar examples of this combination of legend and myth appear in connection with the Homeric poems, certain Asian and Greek cults, and the early histories of Greece and Rome and Israel.[2] The elucidation of such narratives must be left to the technical investigator in the various historical periods. In general, it may be said, there is enough historical material to enable us to trace the development of tribes and nations with a fair degree of certainty; and the caution already expressed against excessive mythological interpretation is especially in place in such researches.[3]

The material published under the general title of "folk-lore" consists of various elements — purely religious usages and ideas, mythical and legendary narratives, and fanciful stories. As the term, defined precisely, refers only to popular survivals from

---

[1] A myth is a purely imaginative explanation of phenomena; a legend rests on facts, but the facts are distorted. The two terms are often confused the one with the other.

[2] Some peculiar combinations appear in the figures of Semiramis and the Kuretes and the Korybantes; see the articles in Roscher's *Lexikon* under these headings.

[3] Cf. Gomme, *Folklore as an Historical Science*; Van Gennep, *La formation des légendes.*

defunct religious systems, its material shows a constant process of
modification from generation to generation by newer ideas. The
mythical element, extricated from the general mass, must be treated
in accordance with the general principles of the criticism of myths.[1]

860. *Mythical biographies.* As gods and heroes are the actors
in mythical constructions of society, the stories in such constructions generally assume the form of anecdotal biographies of these
personages. Such sketches gather fresh material from generation
to generation, are gradually worked up into literary shape, and,
being brought into connection with historical traditions, assume
historical form, and are then sometimes accepted in their homes
and elsewhere as historical.[2] As they embody the ideas of the
times in which they originate, they have, in so far, historical and
psychological value. Charm of style has given some of these
stories literary value, and they have been accepted as part of the
literary treasure of the world. They are sometimes combinations
or fusions of myth and legend, and these two elements are not
always easily distinguishable the one from the other.[3]

861. In questions that touch the original nature of a god the
possible difference between earlier and later conceptions of him
must, of course, be borne in mind. When a deity has been definitely shaped and has become a patron of a community, he may
be identified by the people, or particularly by poets and priests,
with any object or idea that is of special interest to the community.
The baals of the agricultural Canaanites presided over irrigation,
but were not specifically underground gods;[4] they were rather
general divine patrons interested in all that interested the people.
A solar deity, becoming the favorite god of an agricultural community, may be regarded as connected with vegetation; or a god
of vegetation may be associated, in astronomical circles, with the
sun. A divine figure is often composite, the product of the coalescence of several orders of ideas. In general it may be said that

[1] See the various folk-lore journals; W. W. Newell, article " Folk-lore " in Johnson's *Universal Cyclopædia*; cf. Gomme, op. cit., and § 881 below.

[2] So in the cases of the Australian ancestors, the Polynesian, Teutonic, Finnic,
Slavic, Greek, Phrygian, and other heroes and gods, the Hebrew patriarchs, and many
other such figures.   [3] See above, § 859.   [4] See above, § 649.

the simplest and least socially refined function of a god is likely to indicate his original character. We must go behind the conceptions of cultivated times to the hints given in popular observances and poetry.

862. *Interpretation of myths.* For savage and half-civilized communities, and for the masses in civilized times, the stories of the achievements and adventures of gods, heroes, and ancestors, accepted as history, have been and are sources of enjoyment and of intellectual impulse. Narrated by fathers to their families, and recited or sung by professional orators and poets to groups and crowds throughout the land,[1] they have been expanded and handed down from generation to generation, receiving from every generation the coloring of its experiences and ideas, and in the course of time have taken literary shape under the hands of men of genius, and have been committed to writing. For the early times they not only formed a body of historical literature, but also, since they described relations between men and gods, came to be somewhat vague yet real sacred scriptures of the people.[2] As such, being regarded simply as statements of facts, they needed no outside interpretation; and being molded by human experience, they carried with them such moral and religious instruction as grew naturally out of the situations described. A more highly cultivated age, dissatisfied with bald facts, desired to find in the stories the wisdom of the fathers, and the imagination of poets and philosophers was long occupied with discovering and expounding their deeper meanings till further research set aside such attempts as useless. The treatment of mythical material thus shows three stadia: the acceptance of myths as genuine history; esoteric explanations of their assumed profound teachings; and finally, return to their original character as primitive science, having their origin in crude conceptions of life. A brief sketch may show how the

---

1 Such were the Greek rhapsodists (Müller and Donaldson, *History of the Literature of Ancient Greece*, i, 33 ff.), and probably the Hebrew mashalists (Numb. xxi, 27, Eng. tr., "they that speak in proverbs "). Such reciters are found in India at the present day.

2 On the value of myths for religious instruction cf. Schultz, *Old Testament Theology*, Eng. tr. (of 4th German ed.), i, chap ii.

interpretation of myths has come to be regarded as an historical and sociological science.

863. *Ancient interpretations of myths.* When the progress of thought, especially in Greece, made it impossible to accept the current beliefs concerning gods and their doings, it was felt necessary to put some higher meaning into them — they were rationalized and spiritualized by a process of allegorization. This process seems to have begun in Greece as early as the sixth century B.C.[1] It was the philosophers who undertook to reinterpret the Homeric mythical material, and the extent to which this procedure had been carried in the time of Plato is indicated by the fact that he ridicules these modes of dealing with the poet.[2] But Homer maintained his place in literature, and the demand for a spiritualizing of his works increased rather than diminished. A science of allegory was created, Pergamus became one of its chief centers,[3] and the Alexandrian Jew Philo applied the method to the interpretation of the Pentateuch. It was speedily adopted in the Christian world, and has there maintained itself, though in diminishing extent, up to the present day.[4] As a serious interpretation of ancient myths, outside of the Old Testament, it is no longer employed. Myths are, indeed, important as reflecting early opinions, religious and other — good doctrinal matter may be extracted from them, but this must not be ascribed to the intention of their authors and reporters. In the Old Testament itself the Jewish editors have socialized the mythical material (weaving it into the history, as in Genesis), or have brought it under the work of the national deity.

864. *Recent interpretations.* In recently proposed interpretations we may note first certain attempts at a *unification* of some body of myths or of all known mythical material. These attempts, almost without exception, take the sky and the heavenly bodies as their basis.

---

[1] Geffcken, article "Allegory" in Hastings, *Encyclopædia of Religion and Ethics.*
[2] *Phædrus*, 229; *Cratylus*, 406 f.; *Republic*, 378.
[3] Cf. Müller and Donaldson, *History of the Literature of Ancient Greece*, chap. xxvi.
[4] 1 Cor. ix, 9 f.; x, 1–4; Gal. iv, 24 ff.; Heb. vii, 2; Origen, Augustine, Thomas Aquinas, and commentators generally up to the sixteenth century and later.

At the end of the eighteenth century, when the theory of human unity had taken hold of the French revolutionists, C. F. Dupuis [1] undertook to explain all the cults of the world as having come from the worship of the universe — a conception broad enough to cover everything; but he practically reduces it to the worship of the heavenly bodies, particularly the sun, and derives all myths from stellar objects. His work is ingenious, learned, and suggestive, but in his day the facts of ancient mythology were insufficiently known.

865. In the next century the study of Sanskrit and Old Persian widened the field of knowledge, the science of Indo-European grammar was created, and on this followed attempts at the construction of an Indo-European mythology. The first definitely formulated unification was the theory of F. Max Müller,[2] which derived all Aryan (Indo-European) myths from phenomena of the sun and the dawn, largely, he held, through misunderstandings of the meaning of old descriptive terms (myths as a "disease of language"). It is conceivable that a word, originally used simply as descriptive of an actual fact, may have passed into a proper name and become personalized and the center of adventures; but the character of early man's thought, as we now know it, makes it impossible to regard such a view as a probable explanation of the mass of mythological material. Müller's services to the science of the history of religions were great, but his theory of the origin of myths has now been generally abandoned.[3]

866. The great discoveries of literary material made in Egypt and Babylonia since the middle of the nineteenth century have aroused special interest in the religions of these countries. Leadership in ancient civilization is claimed by Egyptologists and Assyriologists, each party for its own land. It is, however, Babylonia that has given rise to the largest theories of the unity of myths — a fact due in part to its development of astronomy, in part, perhaps, to the resemblance between the Babylonian mythical material and

---

[1] *Origine de tous les cultes ou religion universelle* (1794).
[2] *Science of Language*, 2d series; cf. his Hibbert and Gifford lectures.
[3] It is elaborated in G. W. Cox's *Mythology of the Aryan Nations.*

that of the Old Testament. Dupuis[1] had observed that the ancient Chaldeans taught that the heavenly bodies controlled mundane destinies, and, according to Diodorus, that the planets were the interpreters of the will of the gods. This is substantially the point of view of E. Stucken,[2] who, in common with Dupuis (though, apparently, independently), holds to the unity of ancient religions and the astral origin of all myths. From Babylonia, he thinks, myths passed to all parts of the world, Egypt, Asia, Europe, Polynesia, and America — in such migrations, however, it was the motif that passed; the personages might vary in different lands.[3] Finally he traces all sagas of all peoples to the creation myth.[4] This supreme unification is reached by arguments so far-fetched as to deprive them of force.

Stucken's position was adopted and elaborated by H. Winckler, who was followed by A. Jeremias and some others.[5] Winckler attempts to show that a single religion existed in the ancient Oriental world (with a single system of myths), and that this was dominated by the conception that there was a correspondence between the heavenly world and the lower world in such wise that all earthly affairs were indicated by the movements of the heavenly bodies, whence arose the whole religious system of Western Asia and Greece.

867. What is true in this theory (to which the name of " Panbabylonianism " has been given) is that Semitic mythology is a unit, with Babylonia as its birthplace, and that certain elements are common to the Egyptian, Semitic, Greek, and other mythological systems. The substantial identity of Babylonian, Aramean (Syrian), and Canaanite myths is generally acknowledged:[6] the Old Testament dragon-myth (which occurs also in the New Testament Apocalypse) is found in full shape only in Babylonian material;[7]

1 Op. cit., § 864. Cf. article " Panbabylonianism " in *Harvard Theological Review* for January, 1910.

2 *Astralmythen der Hebräer, Babylonier und Aegypter* (1896–1907).

3 So in folk-tales the same motif appears in a hundred different settings; but this is not necessarily a sign of borrowing.   4 Op. cit., p. 190.

5 See above, § 826, note.   6 No well-defined Arabian myths are known.

7 Most of the Old Testament mythical material has been worked over by Hebrew monotheistic editors.

the Syrian Adonis myth is at bottom the Babylonian story of Tammuz and Ishtar. The probability is that all early Semitic schemes of creation and prehistoric life are essentially one. Further, such conceptions as the origin of the world from an unshaped mass of matter and the origin of man from the earth are widely distributed over the earth.

868. Babylonia, then, is the chief mythopœic center for the Semitic region, but we are not warranted in extending its influence as myth-maker beyond this region. The myths of the Indo-European peoples have in general the stamp of independent creation. Loans there may be (as, for example, in the myths connected with Aphrodite and Heracles, and perhaps others), but these do not affect the character of the whole. The relation between the Semitic and the Egyptian mythologies is still under discussion.

869. The astral element of the theory, based on arbitrary parallelisms carried out without regard to historical conditions, is an unauthorized extension of the generally accepted fact that certain myths are astral. Winckler's assumption of an astral " system " that obtained throughout the Western world is supported only by unproved assertions of the sort just referred to.

870. Jensen's contention that all myths come from the Babylonian Gilgamesh story[1] exhibits the same general method as the theories of Stucken and Winckler (giving assertion in place of proof), differing from them only in the material of comparisons.

871. The fundamental vice of these theories (apart from the arbitrary character of the assertions made by their authors) is the failure to take into account the historical development of mythical conceptions, their beginnings in the rudest periods of human thought, and their gradual elaboration and distinct formulation in the great communities, in which process, along with the varieties of local conditions, certain fundamental resemblances remain throughout.[2]

872. Besides these more prominent or more definitely formulated theories there has been in some quarters a disposition to

---

[1] P. Jensen, *Das Gilgamesch Epos in der Weltliteratur.*
[2] Cf. article " Panbabylonianism " cited in § 866, note.

insist too strongly on lines of mythical development connected with the plant world, particularly with the death and revival of vegetation. All that we know of the history of mythical material among existing savages and in the earliest forms of belief of civilized nations forbids the limitation of the origin of myths to any one department of nature or to any one part of the world. Myths, like gods, may be composite: of this nature, probably, are some cosmogonic histories,[1] and the stories of Gilgamesh, Heracles, Perseus, and many others. The lines of origin mentioned above have, naturally, in some cases, coalesced, and their combination into single coherent narratives has been spread over long periods of time. For this reason there is always need of detailed investigations of particular myths as a preparation for a general history of mythology.[2]

873. *Modern critical methods in the interpretation of myths.* The treatment of myths has followed the general course of the development of thought in the world. In the old national religions they were incorporated in the substance of the religious beliefs. The reformers of thought either ignored them (so, for example, Confucius and Buddha), or denounced their absurdities (so Plato and others), or allegorized or rationalized them (so many Greek philosophers); the early Christian writers treated Old Testament myths as history, and ridiculed the myths of Greece and Rome. During the long period when the European peoples were assimilating the ideas of Christianity the study of myths remained in abeyance. After the classical revival there was a return to the allegorizing method, the fondness for which has not yet completely died out.[3]

874. The extension of knowledge in the eighteenth century gave an impetus to the study of religion, the results of which for mythological investigation appear in the works of Dupuis and others.[4] These authors were necessarily ignorant of many

---

[1] As, for example, those of New Zealand, Babylonia, and Greece.
[2] Cf. Keightley, *Fairy Mythology*, 2d ed., p. 14 f.
[3] Bacon, *Wisdom of the Ancients*; in Biblical exposition many recent writers.
[4] See above, § 864 ff.; cf. Jastrow, *Study of Religion*, p. 28 ff.

important facts, but they have the merit of having collected much material, which they treated as something that had to be explained in accordance with the laws of human thought.

875. The turning-point in the development of mythological science was the rise of the modern critical study of history, begun by Voltaire and Gibbon and carried on by Niebuhr and others. A vigorous group of writers arose in Germany. Creuzer,[1] indeed, holding that the myths of the ancients must embody their best thought, and falling back on symbolism, cannot be said to have advanced his subject except by his collection of materials; there is some basis for his position if the ancient myths are taken in the sense given them by the later poets and philosophers, but the supposition of a primary symbolism in myths is set aside by an examination of the ideas of undeveloped races. Creuzer's theory was effectively combated by Voss.[2] Other writers of the time adopted exacter methods of inquiry,[3] and K. O. Müller,[4] particularly, laid the foundation for a scientific treatment of myths by distinguishing between their real and their ideal elements, between the actual phenomenon and the imaginative (the true mythical) explanation of it.

876. The next generation witnessed two retrograde movements in the interpretation of myths. F. Max Müller, dazzled by the wealth of Sanskrit mythological material, revived the solar theory, with a peculiar appendage;[5] the defects of his theory must not blind us to the great service he performed in arousing interest in the comparative study of myths and leading the way to a formulation of the conception of the general history of religion. On another side the vast accumulation of the religious ideas and usages of lower tribes led Herbert Spencer to his euhemeristic view.[6] Neither of these theories has seriously affected the growth of the science of mythology.

---

[1] *Symbolik und Mythologie der alten Völker* (1810–1812).
[2] *Antisymbolik* (1824–1826).
[3] Buttmann, Welcker, Lobeck, and others.
[4] *Prolegomena zu einer wissenschaftlichen Mythologie* (1825).
[5] See above, § 865.
[6] See above, § 359. Cf. Grant Allen, *The Evolution of the Idea of God.*

877. A saner direction was given to investigation by the great biological and sociological studies made in the second half of the nineteenth century.[1] E. B. Tylor definitely stated the view that the origin of myths is to be found in all the ideas of early man. By a very large collection of facts [2] he showed that the same representations that are familiar in Egyptian, Semitic, Hindu, Greek, Roman, and other ancient myths occur also in the systems of half-civilized and savage communities; and he pointed out how such representations had their basis in the simple ideas of undeveloped men and how their survival is to be traced through all periods of history. This fruitful view has been illustrated and developed by later writers,[3] and much light has been thrown on the genesis and growth of myths by studies of existing popular customs in civilized communities.[4]

878. Interest in the subject has now become general, and collections of material are being made all over the world.[5] At the same time it is recognized that every local mass of myths must be studied first by itself and then in connection with all other known material, and that great caution must be exercised in dealing with questions of origin, transmission, and survival. Archæological and geographical discoveries have widened the known area of human life on earth; it is seen that the history of man's development is more complicated than was formerly supposed.

879. We are still without a general survey of myths arranged in some orderly fashion.[6] The material for such a collection is scattered through a great number of publications, in which the mythical stories are not always treated critically. The most useful principle of tabulation, perhaps, would be an arrangement according to motifs, under which geographical or ethnological and

---

1 Darwin and Spencer (evolution), Bastian (ethnology), and others.

2 In his *Early History of Mankind* and *Primitive Culture*. Cf. C. de Brosses (*Du culte des dieux fétiches*, 1760), who expressed a similar view.

3 A. Lang, *Custom and Myth* and *Myth, Ritual, and Religion*, and other works; Frazer, *Golden Bough*, 2d and 3d edd.; W. R. Smith, *Religion of the Semites*; and others.   4 Mannhardt, *Wald- und Feldkulte* and *Mythologische Forschungen*.

5 See the bibliography at the end of this book.

6 Beginnings for such a survey have been made in the Teutonic, American, and some other areas.

geographical relations might be noted. At the present time it would be possible only to make a beginning in such a work, since the obtainable material is not all recorded, and the complicated character of many myths makes an arrangement by place and motif difficult. Still, even an incomplete digest would be of service to students of mythology and would pave the way for a more comprehensive work. The importance of the study of mythology for the general history of religions is becoming more and more manifest. This study, in its full form, includes, of course, psychological investigation as well as collections of statistics; but the psychology finds its material in the facts — we must first know what men believe, and then explain why they believe.

880. It must, however, be added that myths have influenced mainly the dogmas and ceremonies of religion — their part in more intimate or spiritual worship, the converse of the worshiper with the deity, has been comparatively slight. Religious ceremonies are ordinary social customs and forms transferred to dealings with supernatural Powers. Dogmas are quasi-philosophical expressions of conceptions concerning the nature of these Powers and their relations with men, and sometimes contain mythical material which is then introduced into worship; if, for example, a man is divinized and worship is paid him, the tone of the worship is affected by the divine character thus ascribed to him. But in general, as men, in worship proper, approach a deity to get some advantage from him, the appeal is to him directly without regard to ceremonies or minute dogmas. Savages, though in theory they may make a god to be an animal or a plant, come to him devoutly as a superior being who can grant their requests. In higher religions the deity addressed is for the moment an omnipotent friend standing apart from the stories told of him. Rival sects lose sight of their differences in the presence of needs that drive them to God for help. Prayer is a religious unifier — communion with the Deity is an individual experience in which all men stand on common ground, where ritual and dogmatic accessories tend to fade or to disappear.

881. Long after myths in their original forms have ceased to be believed they persist in the form of "fairy tales," which retain something of the old supernatural framework, but sink into mere stories for amusement.[1]

But fairy tales are not the only form in which ancient myths persist. Myths have played their prominent part in the history of religion for the reason that they embody the conception of the tangible supernatural in a vivid and dramatic way. To this personalization and socialization of the supernatural men have continued to cling up to the present time; the mass of men demand not only the presence of the supernatural as protection and guidance, but also the realization of it in objective form. This objectiveness was useful and necessary in early times, and the demand for it remains in periods of advanced civilization. In the reigning religions of the world at the present day myths continue to hold their place and to exercise their influence,[2] the more that in the course of time they become fused with the constantly advancing ethical and spiritual thought of the communities in which they exist. The tendency appears to be to minimize, under the influence of general enlightenment, the crude supernatural parts of such combinations, to exalt the moral and spiritual, and to allegorize or rationalize the rest. But along with such process of rationalization the mythical form is maintained and continues to be a powerful element in the general structure of religious opinion and life.

[1] Confucianism, if it can be called a religion, is an exception.

[2] See the bibliographies in Johnson's *Universal Cyclopædia*, article " Fairy-lore," and *La Grande Encyclopédie*, article " Fée " ; Maury, *Croyances et légendes du moyen âge*, new ed.; Hartland, *The Science of Fairy-tales*.

CHAPTER VIII

MAGIC AND DIVINATION

882. The regulation of relations with the superhuman world has been attempted by means of friendly social intercourse with supernatural Powers, and by studying their methods of procedure with a view to applying these methods and thereby gaining beneficial results. Friendly social intercourse is practical religion in the higher sense of that term. The application and use of superhuman procedures takes two lines of action: the powers of superhuman agents may be appropriated and used independently of them, or the object may be simply to discover their will in order to be guided by it. The first of these lines is magic, the second is divination. While the two have in common the frank and independent employment of the supernatural for the bettering of human life, their conceptions and modes of procedure differ in certain respects, and they may be considered separately.

Magic [1]

883. The perils and problems of savage life, more acute in certain directions than those that confront the civilized man, demand constant vigilance, careful investigation, and prompt action. So far as familiar and tangible enemies (beasts and men) are concerned, common sense has devised methods of defense, and ordinary prudence has suggested means of providing against excessive heat or cold and of procuring food. But there are dangers and

[1] Tylor, *Primitive Culture*, Index, s.v. *Magic*; Frazer, *Golden Bough*, 2d ed., Index, do.; id., *Early History of the Kingship*, Index, do.; Hobhouse, *Morals in Evolution*, Index, do.; Westermarck, *Origin and Development of the Moral Ideas*, Index, do.; S. Reinach, *Orpheus*, Index, do.; Hubert and Mauss, in *Année sociologique*, vii; Marett, *Threshold of Religion*; articles "Magie" in *La Grande Encyclopédie* and "Magic" in *Encyclopædia Britannica*, 11th ed.; article "Magia" in Daremberg and Saglio, *Dictionnaire des antiquités grecques et romaines*.

ills that in the savage view cannot be referred to such sources, but must be held to be caused by intangible, invisible forces in the world, against which it is man's business to guard himself. He must learn what they are and how to thwart or use them as circumstances may require. They could be studied only in their deeds, and this study involves man in the investigation of the law of cause and effect. The only visible bond between phenomena is that of sequence, and on sequence the savage bases his science of causes — that which precedes is cause, that which follows is effect. The agencies he recognizes are spirits, gods, the force resident in things (mana), and human beings who are able to use this force.

884. But belief in such agencies would be useless to man unless he also believed that he could somehow determine their actions, and belief in the possibility of determining these appears to have come to him through his theory of natural law. The reasoning of savages on this point has not been recorded by them, but the character of their known procedures leads us to suppose that they have a sense of a law governing the actions of superhuman Powers. Being conscious that they themselves are governed by law, they may naturally in imagination transfer this order of things to the whole invisible world; spirits, gods, and the mana-power, it is assumed, work on lines similar to those followed by man, only with superhuman breadth and force. The task before the originators of society was to discover these modes of procedure in order to act in accordance with them. The discovery was made gradually by observation, and there grew up thus in process of time a science of supernatural procedure which is the basis of the practice of magic.

This science does not necessarily regard the superhuman power as purposely antagonistic to man. Rather its native attitude appears to have been conceived of as one of indifference (as nature is now regarded as careless of man); it was and is thought of as a force to be guarded against and utilized by available means, which, of course, were and are such as are proper to an undeveloped stage of social growth.

885. Magic is a science of sequences, but only of sequences supposed not to be explicable from ordinary experience. When the savage puts his hand into the fire or receives a spear-thrust in his body he recognizes visible and familiar causes of pain, and accepts the situation as a fact of life, calling for no further explanation. But when the pain comes from no familiar tangible source he is driven to seek a different sort of source. A cause there must be, and this cause, though superhuman, must follow definite methods — it must have the will to act, and it must have knowledge and skill to carry out its designs. To discover its methods man must observe the processes of nature and imitate them, and must at the same time have in mind familiar human modes of action. The savage scientific explanation of mysterious facts is that superhuman Powers are intellectually akin to human beings; the question of motive in such Powers (except in the case of developed gods) seems not to be considered. The basis of magical procedure is imitation of nature and of man. This principle is supplemented by the conception of the unity of the world, a feeling at first vague, that all things have the same nature and are bound together in a cosmos; animals and men, trees, stones and waters, and fragments of all these are parts of one great whole, and each feels, so to speak, what is done to or by one of the others. This feeling, derived from observation and reflection, is not formulated, but is influential in the construction of the unconscious philosophy of the savage.

886. The methods of man's magical procedure follow these principles; they are as various as the sequences that savage man thinks he observes.[1] Many of them are suggested by natural phenomena. Since rain was observed to fall from the sky, it was held that in time of drought it might be obtained by casting water into the air and letting it fall, or by dipping a stone in water and letting it drip; in general, by any process in which water falls on the ground. The wind might be raised by ejecting air from the mouth (as by whistling). Or ordinary human actions might be imitated: a stick thrown or pointed toward an enemy, it was

---

[1] Examples are cited in the works mentioned above.

believed, would cause a spear to enter his body ;[1] a hostile glance of the eye, indicating desire to inflict injury, might carry ill luck.[2] In such cases the fundamental conceptions are the sympathy that comes from unity and the activity of the pervasive mana. These conceptions are visible in procedures in which action on a part of the human body, or on an image or picture of it, was supposed to reach the body itself. The possession of a piece of the bone, skin, hair, or nail of a man might enable one who had knowledge of superhuman laws and processes to affect the man with sickness or even to cause his death. Contact of objects naturally suggests their unity, but the sympathy between them was not held to be dependent on contact ; a man's bone remained a part of him, however far it might be separated from him. A dead body did not lose its virtues ; the qualities of a dead warrior might be acquired by eating his flesh. The mysterious unity of things seems to have resided, in savage thought, in the omnipresent mana, a force independent of human limitations. Not that there was a definite theory on the subject, but something of this sort seems to be assumed in the ideas and usages of many low tribes.[3]

On the other hand, a magical effect may be set aside by magic. A sick man, believing his sickness to be the work of a magician (the usual savage theory of the cause of bodily ills), sends for another magician to counteract the evil work ; and a magician, failing to cure his patient, ascribes his failure to the machinations of a powerful rival. In all such cases the theory and the methods are the same ; the magic that cures is not different in principle (though it may differ in details) from the magic that kills.

887. The facts observed by practicers of magic probably contributed to the collections of material that furnished the starting-point

---

[1] On the view that many quasi-magical acts are spontaneous reactions of the man to his environment see I. King, *Development of Religion*, chap. vii. According to this view the thought suggests the act. The warrior, thinking of his enemy, instinctively makes the motion of hurling something at him (as a modern man shakes his fist at an absent foe), and such an act, a part of the excitation to combat, is believed to be efficacious.

[2] Westermarck, *Origin and Development of the Moral Ideas*, s.v. *The Evil Eye*.

[3] On mana see above, § 231 ff. Though the theory of mana was necessarily vague, the thing itself was quite definite.

for the scientific study of physical phenomena. The interest in the facts arose at first simply from their relation to magical procedure — it was from them that certain laws of supernatural action were learned, and men thus got control of this action. Magic is essentially a directive or coercive procedure and differs in this respect from fully formed religion, which is essentially submissive and obedient.

888. It is true that coercion of divine beings appears in well-developed religions. A Babylonian goddess (Nana) was carried off by the Elamites to their land that she might there do duty as divine protector; restored to her proper home 1635 years later, she resumed her old functions.[1] The Egyptians are said by Plutarch to have slain their divine animals if these failed to avert or remove calamity.[2] Prometheus and certain Homeric heroes are victorious over gods. In some savage tribes divine kings are put to death if they fail to do what is expected of them. A god was sometimes chained or confined in his temple to prevent his voluntary or constrained departure. A recusant deity was sometimes taunted or insulted by his disappointed worshipers.[3] There is, however, a difference between the two sets of coercive acts. The force used by developed religion is physical, that employed in magic is psychological and logical. When a god is chained or carried off, it is only his body that is controlled — he is left to his own thoughts, or it is assumed that he will be friendly to his enforced locus. Magic brings the supernatural Power under the dominion of law against which his nature is powerless. Religion, even when it employs force, recognizes the protective function of the deity; magic is without such acknowledgment, without emotion or worship. While it has, on one side, a profounder conception of cosmic force than appears in early religion, it is, on the social side, vastly inferior to the latter, to which it has necessarily yielded in the course of human progress. Nevertheless, if religion in the broadest sense includes all means of bringing man into helpful relations with the supernatural world, then magic is a form of religion.

---

[1] Jastrow, *Religion of Babylonia and Assyria*, p. 85.　　[2] *Isis and Osiris*, 73.
[3] Frazer, *Golden Bough*, 2d ed., i, 154 ff.

889. The much-discussed question whether magic was the earliest form of religion is not susceptible of a definite answer for the reason that we have no account of man's earliest conceptions of his relations with the world of invisible forces. There is some reason to hold, as is remarked above,[1] that in the lowest stage of life known to us men were logically indifferent spectators of the world, but in general stood in awe of phenomena, so that fear was their prevailing feeling. It may be surmised that this feeling would engender a sense of antagonism to such superhuman Powers as came to be conceived of, on which would naturally follow a desire to get control of them. Yet it is impossible to say at what stage of social development the necessity would be felt of establishing friendly relations with the Powers. The two lines of effort may have begun and gone on side by side, the two springing from the same utilitarian impulse, but each independent of the other — a coexistence that actually appears in many tribes ; finally the coercive effort tends to yield to the kindly influences of organized society. There is no ground for calling magic a " disease of religion." The presumption, from the general law of progress, is that, when there is a chronological difference, the socially lower precedes the socially higher. Religion and magic come to be mutually antagonistic, except in cases where religious authorities adopt magical procedures, giving them a theistic and socially useful coloring. Magic has been a natural, if not a necessary, step in the religious organization of society.[2]

890. Since religion and magic have in common the purpose to establish relations with extrahuman Powers the dividing line between the two is in some cases not easily fixed — the same procedure may be held to belong in the one category or the other, according as it invokes or does not invoke the aid of a god in friendly and submissive fashion. We may thus be carried back to a time when a sharp distinction between the two did not exist, as there was a time when such a distinction is not visible between " gods " (friendly divine members of the human community) and " demons " (unfriendly outside beings), both classes being regarded simply as agents affecting human life. Even when some fairly good

[1] § 6 f. [2] Cf. Lord Avebury, *Marriage, Totemism, and Religion*, p. 135.

form of organization has been reached it is often hard to say to which class a particular figure belongs. The Hawaiian Pele (the " goddess " of the great and dangerous volcano) is often vindictive, and then differs little or not at all from a demon that sends sickness and death.[1] The Babylonians gave the same name (*shedu*) to a class of demons proper and to the divine or half-divine winged beings (to which, apparently, the Hebrew cherubs are allied) that guarded the entrances to temples, sacred gardens, and palaces.[2] The Navaho beings called *yei* and *anaye* seem to hover on the border line between the divine and the demonic classes.[3] The difference between the two seems to be merely that the one class (the gods) has been adopted (for reasons not originally ethical) into the human community, while the other has not received such adoption.[4] In such a case a given figure may easily pass from one class into the other. According to the Thompson River folk-lore the sun was once a cannibal but became beneficent.[5] The early Christians converted the Græco-Roman gods (*daimonia*) into " demons." [6] There being this fluid relation between supernatural beings, it is not strange that such a relation should exist between procedures intended to act on them.[7]

891. Magic, as we have seen, is based on the observation of sequences, and before the development of reflection and the acquisition of a knowledge of natural law the disposition of human beings is to regard all sequences as exhibiting the relation of cause and effect. A typical example is that of the anchor driven ashore, a piece of which was broken off by a man who died soon after; the conclusion was that the anchor caused his death and therefore was divine, and accordingly it received religious worship.[8] In the course

---

[1] Alexander, *Short History of the Hawaiian People.*
[2] Jastrow, *Religion of Babylonia and Assyria*, p. 263.
[3] Matthews, *Navaho Legends*, p. 36.
[4] Cf. W. R. Smith, *Religion of the Semites*, lecture iii.
[5] Teit, *Thompson River Indians*, p. 53 f.   [6] 1 Cor. x, 20 f.
[7] Certain ceremonies of the higher religions produce effects that must be regarded as magical.
[8] Lubbock, *Origin of Civilization*, p. 188. Similar logic appears in the story of the origin of Goodwin Sands, told by Bishop Latimer (in a sermon preached before Edward VI). An old man, being asked what he thought was the cause of the Sands,

of ages thousands of such sequences must have been observed, and these, handed down from one generation to another, would shape themselves into a handbook of magic. They would, however, be constantly reëxamined and sifted under the guidance of wider experience and a better acquaintance with natural causes, and this process, carried on by experts, would give rise to the science of magic as we find it among lower tribes.

Magic, like religion, is a social product. The two, as is remarked above, may coexist in the same community. But when a State religion is established to which all citizens are expected to conform, the pursuit of magic assumes the aspect of departure from, and hostility to, the tribal or national cult. It is then under the ban, and can be carried on only in secret [1] (as is the case with prohibited religions also). Secrecy of practice is not of the essence of magic; among the Australian Arunta, for example, magical ceremonies constitute the publicly recognized business of the community acting through its accredited representatives; the partial exclusion of women and uninitiated boys from these ceremonies (and from political councils) is due mainly to the desire of the elders to keep the power in their own hands. The State religion may sometimes be forced by public opinion to adopt particular magical procedures.

892. It was natural that the specific study of sequences and laws should fall into the hands of special persons and classes of men. The human agent in the discovery of laws is the magician (sorcerer, shaman), who, since he was generally a physician also, sometimes received the name of " medicine man." As the office of chief arose for the direction of social culture and political affairs, so the office of magician arose naturally for the direction of supernatural relations. He may have been the earliest religious teacher and guide.[2] He knows the will and nature of the supernatural Powers and is therefore a necessity to men. He is specifically in charge of all that relates to the control of these Powers.

replied that he had lived near there, man and boy, fourscore years, and before the neighboring steeple was built there was no Sands, and therefore his opinion was that the steeple was the cause of the Sands.

1 So among the old Hebrews, according to 1 Sam. xxviii, 9. For Rome cf. Fowler, *Religious Experience of the Roman People*, lecture iii.   2 Cf. above, § 889.

893. In the course of time there arises a differentiation of functions, and, when religion becomes friendly, the office of priest is created. The priest, like the magician, understands the will of the gods, but his procedure is intended simply to propitiate them or to discover their will in particular cases.[1] He is a development out of the magician in so far as friendly religion is a development out of magical religion.[2] The prophet also, in the rôle in which he appears among the Greeks, is a development out of the old magician; he knows the will of the gods and is thus able to predict events. This is the character of the old Hebrew seer; the Hebrew prophet, originally a seer, assumed in the course of time a quite different character — he became a preacher of ethical religion.

894. The office of magician, once established, became subject to all the rules that govern official persons in barbarous, half-civilized, and civilized societies. Of the way in which the position was attained in the earliest times we have no information, but in relatively low tribes it appears that it is attained in various ways. There is sometimes a suggestion of vocation in a dream or a vision.[3] Among some tribes a candidate for the office has to undergo a process of education, that is, of training in the signs by which the presence of superhuman Powers is recognizable and of the way of dealing with disease and other evils.[4] It is not unusual that the candidate is required to submit to a test, sometimes of physical endurance (as is required also in the case of the young warrior), but chiefly of susceptibility to supernatural influences and capacity of insight, and of the conduct of magical operations.[5] Generally in the lower tribes the office comes by free choice of the individual, or by choice of the body of magicians, without regard to the social position of the man. In West Africa,

---

[1] In some cases the priest is a magician (Grey, *Polynesian Mythology*, p. 114 ff.) — he acts as the mouthpiece of a god, and in sympathy with the god. Cf. Westermarck, *Origin and Development of the Moral Ideas*, ii, 658. On a connection between the magician and the poet see Goldziher, in *Proceedings of the Tenth International Congress of Orientalists*.   [2] Cf. above, § 889.

[3] Dixon, *The Northern Maidu*, p. 267 f.; id., *The Shasta*, 471 ff.

[4] Ellis, *Tshi*, p. 120.

[5] Dixon, *The Shasta*, loc. cit.; Miss Fletcher, *Indian Ceremonies*, p. 280.

says Miss Kingsley, everybody keeps a familiar spirit or two for magical purposes; this is unlawful only when the spirit is harmful.[1]

895. In somewhat more advanced societies the office falls into the hands of families and descends from father to son, in which case the younger man is instructed by the older in the secrets of the profession.[2] In some higher religions magical performances are in the hands of certain clans or tribes. In most of these cases women as well as men may be masters of the art. In the more advanced systems it is often the case that it is especially women who are considered adepts; so it was in Babylonia;[3] in the Old Testament Saul seeks the woman of Endor;[4] Thessalian witches were famous;[5] women who tie magical knots are provided against in the Koran by a special form of prayer;[6] in Europe, medieval and later, the practicers of magic have generally been women.

896. The grounds for the ascription of magical superiority to women — whether from their supposed greater susceptibility to demoniac influence, or for some other reason — are not clear. In the lowest tribes sorcerers are commonly men[7] — the profession is an influential and honored one, and naturally falls into the hands of leading men; the magician is often the most powerful man in the community.

897. Reputation for magical power appears sometimes to attach to a tribe or other body of persons as the representatives of a religion which is adopted by a lower community. Possibly this is the explanation of the rôle ascribed at an early period to the Mazdean Magi.[8] The Magi (apparently Median of origin) formed the priestly tribe of the Mazdean religion, and we do not know that they played originally any part as sorcerers. But it seems

---

[1] M. Kingsley, *Studies*, p. 136.   [2] Grey, *Polynesian Mythology*, p. 278.

[3] Jastrow, *Religion of Babylonia and Assyria*, p. 267 f.   [4] 1 Sam. xxviii.

[5] Apuleius, *Metamorphoses*, bk. ii f.   [6] Sura cxiii.

[7] Women, however, are sometimes shamans in such tribes, as in the California Shasta (while in the neighboring Maidu they are commonly men). See Dixon, *The Shasta*, p. 471; *The Northern Maidu*, p. 267 f.

[8] Tiele, *Elements of the Science of Religion*, ii, 140; cf. Spiegel, *Eranische Alterthumskunde*, iii, 564 f., 587 f.; Jackson, in Geiger and Kuhn's *Grundriss der iranischen Philologie*, ii, 630, 671, 692.

that they were so considered in Greece as early as the fifth century B.C.,[1] and after the Moslem conquest of Persia and the suppression of Zoroastrianism a fire-worshiper or Magian is especially a representative of magic.[2] On the other hand, it sometimes happens among adjoining tribes that the lower become the special practitioners of magic,[3] which is then considered to be a mysterious art, alien to the official religion, and therefore proper to the ministers of the old mysterious cults.

898. The power exercised by the magician extends over the whole world of men and things, and is generally considered to be practically without limit. He guards men against diseases, noxious beasts, and all other forms of injury; he destroys one's enemies and guards one against plots of enemies, including other magicians; he is able to induce or destroy love, to give physical strength, to inflict disease, to kill, and to restore to life; he ascends to heaven or descends into the world below; he is able to coerce the gods themselves; in fact, he does everything that a god is commonly supposed to do — the tendency was to identify the magician and the god.[4] Such identification is natural or necessary in early faiths, inasmuch as it was held that there was no difference of nature between men and gods. A god was as a rule the stronger. But how gods arose and how they gained their superior strength was not clear, and it might thus easily happen that a man should acquire powers equal to those of divine beings.[5]

---

[1] Sophocles, *Œdipus Tyrannus*, 387; Euripides, *Orestes*, 1498. Hence the term 'magic' as the designation of a certain form of procedure.

[2] So in the *Thousand and One Nights*, passim.

[3] Tylor, *Primitive Culture*, i, 113 ff.; Castrén, *Finnische Mythologie*, pp. 186 ff., 229; Skeat, *Malay Magic*, p. 162; Rivers, *The Todas*, p. 263; Crooke, *Popular Religion and Folklore of Northern India*, ii, 283 ff. For modern usages see Wuttke, *Der deutsche Volksaberglaube der Gegenwart*, 2d ed., pp. 131, 241.

[4] A magician, as a man of special social prominence and of extraordinary power over the forces of the world, becomes, in some cases, the political head of his community (as a priest sometimes has a like position). Where the divinization of men is practiced, the magician may be recognized as a god. But no general rule can be laid down. The office of king had its own political development, and a god was the natural product of the reflection of a community. The elevation of the magician to high political or ecclesiastical position was dependent on peculiar circumstances and may be called sporadic. Cf. Frazer, *Early History of the Kingship*, p. 107 ff. and lecture v.

[5] Cf. Frazer, *Golden Bough*, 2d ed., Index, s.v. *Kings*.

899. The methods employed by the magician to effect his purpose are various. In early times it is usual for him to fall into an ecstatic state ; by drinking intoxicating liquors, by violent movements, or by contemplation he gets out of himself and comes into ·relations with the mysterious potencies. In such a condition he acts as his imagination suggests.[1] But in the organized forms of magic long experience has devised various means of producing results beyond the power of ordinary men. Certain objects are magically charged with supernatural power (charms), and these worn on the person guard the possessor against malign influences. Various formulas are employed which are supposed to coerce the Powers ; these are sometimes names of ordinary objects regarded as sacred, the name of some plant or animal.[2] Names of divine persons have special potency. The name of a god was supposed to carry with it his power, and the utterance of his name secured all that he could secure ; thus, in the early Christian times the tetragrammaton YHWH (Yahweh) had absolute power against demons.

900. Similar efficacy attached to sacred compositions, prayers,[3] and the like. The Mazdean petition, Honover (Ahuna-Vairya), was so employed, and in Christian circles even the Lord's Prayer. Charms or incantations often took rhythmical form — verses, couplets, or quatrains were widely used. All such methods were the product of ages of experience.[4] They were handed down from generation to generation, often in families or classes of magicians, were modified or enlarged from time to time, and thus came at last to form a literature.

901. In the great civilized religions magical practice gradually assumed a tone somewhat different from that of the earliest times. It continued to be coercive toward evil Powers, but in regard to

---

[1] See Lord Avebury, *Marriage, Totemism, and Religion*, chap. iv.

[2] The plant or animal may be a totem, but its magical power is not derived from its totemic character. Magical potency may dwell in nontotemic objects ; in magical ceremonies connected with totems (as in Australia) it is the ceremony rather than the totem that is efficacious. Cf. Marett, *Threshold of Religion*, p. 22 f.

[3] Cf. Marett, " From spell to prayer," in his *Threshold of Religion*, p. 33 ff.

[4] Cf. J. H. King, *The Supernatural*, Index, s.v. *Charm* ; Tylor, *Primitive Culture*, ii, 148 ; article " Charms and Amulets " in Hastings, *Encyclopædia of Religion and Ethics*.

the good Powers it assumed rather to discover their modes of action. It was not anti-religious; it remained alongside of the official religious systems in friendly relations. It relied on the assistance of the good gods and not on that of the demons. There was good magic and bad magic, white magic and black magic, as these came to be called. A procedure of white magic can thus, from the point of view of religion, hardly be distinguished from prayer to a deity. The difference between the two appears to be that the magic produces abnormal or violent effects, which experience taught could not reasonably be expected from the deity. It is the old crude science brought (as the lesser divine Powers were brought) into a relation of subordination to the chief god of the community.

902. Elaborate magical systems are found in some of the ancient national religions. In India the Atharva-Veda, though it contains a mass of crude old material, is nevertheless recognized as one of the sacred books, standing by the side of the Rig-Veda, though of less authority and significance than that. The Atharvan was originally a priest of fire, but in this work he becomes simply a magician; the immense number of magical procedures in the book provided for all emergencies of life.[1] The Babylonian magical formulas also go back to an early time, but they were preserved by the priests and recognized as a legitimate element in the religious practice.[2] The old Egyptian stories introduce a number of magical proceedings, and the formulas have been preserved in treatises.[3] Of the earliest periods of the Mazdean religion we have unfortunately no records; in the time of the decadence of the national religion, especially in the Thousand and One Nights, the fire-worshiper or Magian is commonly a wicked magician, as was natural since he belonged to a faith hostile to Islam, and the practicer of good magic is generally a Moslem.[4] The early Greeks and Romans appear not

---

[1] Eng. tr. by Bloomfield, in *Sacred Books of the East*.

[2] L. W. King, *Babylonian Magic and Sorcery*.

[3] *Records of the Past*, first series, vols. ii, vi; Griffith, article " Egyptian Literature" in *Library of the World's Best Literature*; Maspero, *Dawn of Civilization*, p. 212 ff.; Breasted, *History of Egypt*, Index, s.v. *Magic*.

[4] Cf. Macdonald, *Religious Attitude and Life in Islam*, Index, s.v. *Magic*.

to have been greatly interested in magical practices, though these existed.[1] But a great outburst of magic occurred in the Græco-Roman world in the first and second centuries of our era, the magician being, however, generally not Greek or Roman, but of an inferior alien race.[2] Among the old Hebrews we have no details of magical procedure except in the invocation of the dead;[3] this procedure was denounced by the prophets as hostile to the worship of the national god, but it continued among the people a long time.[4] The practice of magic existed abundantly among the early peoples of Europe, the Teutons, and others. The primacy, however, in magic belongs to the Finns and Lapps, alien races regarded as inferior in civilization.

903. The hold of magic on the minds of men is shown by the fact that it has persisted up to the present day. Its basis is a belief in occult powers and the conviction that man may attain to mastery over them. Certain forms of this belief, called theosophical, are held by many at the present day; it is supposed that men are capable of transcending the ordinary limitations of humanity. In general, however, the whole system of magic yielded gradually to the organized religions, the essence of which was a friendly and rational relation with the deity. Religion has organized itself in accord with the general organization of human social systems. It has seen the necessity of getting rid of force, of depending on humane feeling, cultivating simply friendly relations, attempting a unity of work, a coöperation of divine and human forces. All this has worked against magic. In addition to these tendencies the constantly growing belief in the domination of natural forces

1 Daremberg and Saglio, *Dictionnaire des antiquités grecques et romaines*, article "Magia"; cf. articles "Medeia" and "Kirke" in Roscher's *Lexikon*.

2 Apuleius, *Metamorphoses*; Gibbon, *Decline and Fall of the Roman Empire*, ii, 535 ff.; Friedländer, *Roman Life and Manners under the Early Empire* (Eng. tr.), i, 260 f.; Fowler, *The Religious Experience of the Roman People*, p. 57 ff.; cf. Cumont, *Astrology and Religion among the Greeks and Romans*, Index, s.v. *Magic*.

3 1 Sam. xxviii; Isa. viii, 19.

4 In the later Judaism Solomon is the great master of magic; see the story of the Queen of Sheba in the Second Esther Targum; Baring-Gould, *Legends of Old Testament Characters*. For the Arabian legends of Solomon (borrowed from the Jews) see *Koran*, sura xxxviii; *History of Bilkis, Queen of Sheba*, compiled from various Arabic sources, in Socin's *Arabic Grammar* (Eng. tr., 1885).

has made it impossible in civilized societies to accept the powers called magical.[1]

904. To sum up: magic is a means of securing superhuman results by adopting the methods of the superhuman Powers.[2] It may be coeval with religion proper or may have preceded it in human religious organization. In any case it has been, up to the present day, the rival of religion, though more and more driven to take a secondary place. It has collected physical facts which have served as a basis for the study of physical science and have indirectly furthered the cause of religion by leading men to recognize natural law and also by necessitating a distinction between theistic and other superhuman results.[3] In the absence of distinct religious systems it has been a bond of social union, and to that extent has been a civilizing influence. On the other hand, it has fostered belief in a false science of sequences and thus helped to introduce confusion into thought and the conduct of life. The aim of religion has been, and is, to banish magic from the world.[4]

DIVINATION

905. Divination is the science that seeks to discover the will of the supernatural Powers by means of the observation of phenomena. Men desire to learn the causes of present and past misfortunes and the story of the future, that they may know at any moment what is the best course to pursue. The underlying supposition is that these things are indicated by the appearances and movements of the various objects of the world. It is in these phenomena that the purposes of superhuman forces become visible to man; the gods, it is held, cannot but so reveal themselves (for they produce·

---

[1] Lecky, *History of the Rise and Influence of the Spirit of Rationalism in Europe*; Westermarck, *Origin and Development of the Moral Ideas*, Index, s.vv. *Magic* and *Witches*.

[2] These Powers, including mana, may all be called " divine " as distinguished from the purely " human."

[3] A superhuman phenomenon, if produced by a deity, is called a " miracle," and is held to be beneficent; if produced by a nontheistic process, it is called " magical," and is looked at doubtfully.

[4] Cf. Westermarck, *Origin and Development of the Moral Ideas*, ii, 696; Hobhouse, *Morals in Evolution*, Index, s.v. *Magic and Morals*.

all phenomena), and man's task is to discover the laws of phenomenal revelation. The question of the motive in this revelation is not distinctly raised, but it is taken for granted that the Powers are willing to help man by guiding his uncertain footsteps; their attitude is so far friendly — they belong in feeling to the human community.[1]

Divination has in common with magic the assumption of the unity of the world and its control by law, and the search for divine activity in the facts of life. But the two differ essentially in their aims. Divination seeks to learn the divine will in order to be guided; magic studies divine action in order to imitate it and accomplish divine results. Divination is an inquirer, and its virtue is obedience; magic is an investigator, and its virtue is achievement. Both are self-seeking, but divination is the more reverent and allies itself more easily with religion. But both tend to become corrupt and decadent, and their rôles are determined from time to time by the conditions of the communities in which they are found.[2]

906. The organization of divination resembles that of magic in several respects. It comes to have its special functionaries, into whose hands all its authority falls. The divinatory power (like the magical) comes to a man sometimes as a gift of nature (that is, of a god) or in some mysterious external way, sometimes as a result of a course of training in which the significance of the various signs is learned. It is sometimes a property of a clan or a family and descends from father to son, always, however, under the condition of instruction of the young by the old. The diviner, like the magician, sometimes performs various ceremonies for the purpose of bringing himself into relation with the gods, and his utterances are frequently given in an ecstatic condition. In this condition he is said in some instances (as among the Todas[3]) to speak a language not his own, with which in his ordinary state of mind he is

---

[1] Ultimately, in early religious theory, all objects are divine or abodes or incarnations of divine beings and capable of independent action; sometimes, doubtless, the recognition of the natural character of a thing (as of courage and other qualities in animals) coalesces with the belief in its guiding power.

[2] Cf. article " Magia " in Daremberg and Saglio, *Dictionnaire des antiquités grecques et romaines*, p. 1496.   [3] Rivers, *The Todas*, p. 254.

unacquainted, or to utter words that are not understood either by himself or by others. Ecstasy means possession by the deity; the interpretation of the diviner's words, which, in the ecstatic condition, are the words of a spirit or a god, is sometimes left to the bystanders; or, if unintelligible to them, must be recovered by the seer himself when he returns to his normal condition.

907. The highest development of ecstasy is found in the prophet proper. Originally the prophet was a foreteller and acted under the inspiration of a god, a divine seizure that was allied to madness. The ravings of the savage shaman[1] are repeated in the ravings of Cassandra and in the excited utterances and bodily exhaustion of the early Hebrew prophets.[2] A nobler use of ecstasy is exhibited in the youth of Byblos, who rescued an unfortunate Egyptian envoy from insult and secured him honorable treatment.[3] The more advanced thought tended to abandon the abnormal state of the diviner and make him simply a recipient of divine knowledge by the favor of a god — the gods came to choose thoughtful men instead of beasts as their intermediaries.[4] The Hebrew prophets whose utterances have been preserved, from Amos onward, are men of insight, essentially critics of the national life, and moral watchmen; but features of the old conception of divinatory power continue for some time to attach to them.[5]

908. The differentiation of functions between magician, diviner, and priest appears to have taken place at a comparatively early period, though it is probable that in the earliest times all these characters might be united in a single person. As soon as an organized religion is established the priest acquires his specific function as intermediator between men and gods, often, however, retaining the power of discovering the will of the deity.[6] Magic, as we have seen, tends to become an unsocial and hostile thing,

---

[1] Cf. article "Bantu" in Hastings, *Encyclopædia of Religion and Ethics*, p. 358.

[2] 1 Sam. x, 5; xix, 24.

[3] Breasted, *History of Egypt*, p. 513 f The envoy not only failed to procure cedar for the sacred barge of Amon but was ordered by the prince to leave the city; the youth intervened successfully (ca. 1100 B.C.).

[4] So Teiresias (*Odyssey*, x, 492 ff.; *Œdipus Tyrannus*, 92) and Samuel (1 Sam. ix).

[5] Mic. i, 8; cf. 2 Kings iii, 15 (music as a preliminary condition of inspiration).

[6] As among the Hebrews, the Greeks, and other ancient peoples.

and the magician is in later times punished or discountenanced by public opinion. The diviner, on the other hand, has generally retained possession of his public for the reason that he is in sympathy with the gods of the community and his work is held to be wholly friendly. In all stages of religious development, except the very highest, he has been recognized by public opinion and by law as a part of the religious constitution of society and has often attained great civil and political power.[1] Among civilized peoples he comes to be a man of learning, acquainted with many things besides the mere signs of the will of the gods.

909. Divinatory signs may be grouped in various classes according as they belong to the outer world or to men's inward experiences, and according as they present themselves without or with preparation by man. Outward signs in ordinary occurrences which, so far as human initiative is concerned, are accidental may be called, for convenience, "omens." Uncommon occurrences may be called, if they appear in the forms of men and animals, "prodigies," and if they are seen in the physical world, "portents." These designations are arbitrary, and sometimes two or more of them may be appropriate for the same event. Inward signs are dreams, revelations in the ecstatic state, and prophetic inspirations.[2] We may begin with divination from the observation of external objects, and consider first such as are accidental (omens, prodigies, portents).

910. Omens, prodigies, and portents are to be regarded as the product of ages of experience. The observations of early men seem to them to show that certain appearances are followed by certain events, and the details of experience, handed down and interpreted by successive generations, are in the course of time sifted, systematized, and formulated. In savage and half-civilized communities divinatory signs are usually simple, drawn from appearances of familiar objects and occurrences. They become more complicated in civilized times — they are mingled with elaborate

---

[1] Formerly, says Cicero (*De Divinatione*, i, 16), almost nothing of moment, or even in private affairs, was undertaken without an augury.

[2] For a tabulation of omens and other signs and of forms of divinatory procedure see article " Divination " in *La Grande Encyclopédie.*

astrological ideas. Divination becomes a science for the practice of which a technical education is required. Belief in omens and other signs survives among the highest civilized peoples long after the conceptions on which they rest have been abandoned. The origin of signs among savage peoples may often be traced with more or less probability; in the case of such as survive in periods of high culture the origin is necessarily obscured by the lapse of time and can be surmised only by comparison with earlier conceptions.

The belief in such signs may be traced over a great part of the world. It is found among the ancient Egyptians, Babylonians, Assyrians, Hindus, Chinese, Hebrews, Greeks, Romans, Arabians, and at a later time among the Celtic, Slavic, and Teutonic peoples.[1] At the present day it occurs most highly developed in Polynesia, Northern Africa, Southern India, and Central Asia; it is relatively unimportant in Western and Central Africa, North America, South America, and Australia. One difference between divination and magic thus appears to be that the latter is vigorous in savage communities that pay little attention to the former. Further collections of facts may require a modification of this statement; but, in general, it would seem that an organization of signs, demanding, as it does, orderly reflection on phenomena, is proper to communities that have advanced beyond the hunting and nomadic stages. For the rest, there are few objects or occurrences that have not been

---

[1] Cicero, *De Divinatione*, i, 1–4; Diodorus Siculus, i, 70, 81; Maspero, *Dawn of Civilization*, p. 216 ff.; Steindorff, *Religion of the Ancient Egyptians*, p. 113 ff. (cf. Gen. xliv, 5, 15, which may point to an Egyptian custom of divination by cup); Jastrow, *Religion Babyloniens und Assyriens*, and *Aspects of Religious Belief and Practice in Babylonia and Assyria*; Hopkins, *Religions of India*, pp. 256, 328; De Groot, *Religious System of China*, i, 103 ff.; iii, chap. xii; Buckley, in Saussaye's *Lehrbuch der Religionsgeschichte*, 2d ed. (China); articles "Divination" in *Encyclopædia Biblica*, Hastings's *Dictionary of the Bible*, and *Jewish Encyclopedia*; Bouché-Leclercq, *Histoire de la divination dans .'antiquité*; articles "Divinatio" and "Haruspices" in Daremberg and Saglio, *Dictionnaire des antiquités grecques et romaines*; Gardner and Jevons, *Greek Antiquities*, chap. vii; Stengel and Oehmichen, *Die griechischen Sakralaltertümer*; Wissowa, *Religion der Römer*, p. 450 ff.; Fowler, *Religious Experience of the Roman People*, lecture xiii; Wellhausen, *Reste arabischen Heidentumes*, pp. 126 ff., 148 ff.; article "Celts" in Hastings, *Encyclopædia of Religion and Ethics*; Hastings, op. cit., ii, 54 ff.; Saussaye, *Religion of the Teutons*, Index, s.v. *Divination*.

regarded at some time by some people as indications of divine will in respect to present, past, or future events.

911. A fair illustration of the early belief in omens is afforded by the divinatory system that prevails in Samoa and the neighboring group of islands.[1] It appears that all omens are derived either from the movements of animals that are regarded as incarnations of deities,[2] or from phenomena that are held to be produced immediately by deities. The flight of owls, bats, or rails, according to its direction, indicates the result of a battle or a war; the howling of a dog is a sign of coming misfortune; if a centipede crawls on the top of a mat it is a good omen, if on the bottom of a mat it is bad; it is unfortunate when a lizard crosses one's path; if a basket be found turned upside down in a road, this is a sign of evil; the way in which sacred stones fall to the ground is an indication of the future. The animals mentioned above (and there are many other such) are all regarded as incarnations of deities. So as to portents: loud thunder, taken to be the voice of the great god Tangaloa, is a good sign; the significance of lightning (which also is sent by the god) depends upon the direction taken by the flash. An eclipse is regarded as a presage of death. A similar system of interpretation of signs is found elsewhere. The Masai and the Nandi draw omens from the movements of birds.[3] In Ashantiland the cry of the owl means death.[4] When in Australia the track of an insect is believed to point toward the abode of the sorcerer by whom a man has been done to death, the conception is probably the same. The modern Afghans hold that a high wind that continues three days is a sign that a murder has been committed.[5] Examples from Brazil, Borneo, New Zealand, Old Calabar and Tatarland are given by Tylor.[6] In the early Hebrew history

---

[1] Turner, *Samoa*, Index, s.v. *Omens*.

[2] These animals were originally themselves divine, and therefore, by their own knowledge, capable of indicating the course of events; cf. § 905, note.

[3] Hollis, *The Masai*, p. 323 f.; id., *The Nandi*, p. 79.   [4] Ellis, *Tshi*, p. 203.

[5] Conolly, *Journey to the North of India*, 2d ed., 1838, ii, 137 ff.

[6] Tylor, *Primitive Culture*, i, 78, etc. For South Africa cf. Callaway, *The Amazulu*, Index, s.vv. *Omens, Divination, Diviners*; Kidd, *The Essential Kafir*, Index, s.v. *Divining*; article " Bantu " in Hastings, *Encyclopædia of Religion and Ethics*, p. 362.

it appears that a rustling in trees was looked on as a sign of divine intervention.[1]

912. In ancient Babylonia and Assyria an elaborate system of interpretation of ordinary occurrences prevailed — the movements and appearances of various species of birds, of bulls, of dogs of all colors are noted, with minute interpretations.[2] The Greeks recognized omens in the acts of various animals, especially in the flight and cries of birds; so important were these last that the words for 'bird' came to be employed for 'omens from birds' and even simply for 'omens';[3] Aristophanes, laughing at the Athenians, declares that they called every mantic sign 'bird'.[4] Skepticism, however, appears in Hector's passionate rejection of the signs of birds and his declaration that the best omen is to fight for one's country.[5] A similar mantic prominence of birds appears in ancient Rome where the terms for the observation of birds (*auspicium, augurium*) came to signify 'omens' in general. The preëminence thus accorded to birds was due perhaps to the fact that they move in a region above the earth, the larger species (οἰωνός) seeking the sky near the abode of the gods, as well as to the frequency and variety of their actions.[6] The feeling of direct contact with the deity appears in the significance attached to the movements of a sacrificial animal: if it approached the altar willingly, this, showing accord with the deity, was a good omen, and unwillingness was a bad omen.[7] Among the later Romans the entrance of a strange black dog into a house, the falling of a snake through the opening in the roof, the crowing of a hen were unfavorable signs which prevented the immediate undertaking of

---

[1] 2 Sam. v, 24.

[2] Jastrow, *Religion of Babylonia and Assyria* (Eng. and Ger. edd.), in which references to the original documents are given.

[3] ὄρνις, οἰωνός. *Iliad*, ii, 859; xii, 237; xxiv, 219; Hesiod, *Works and Days*, 826; cf. Bouché-Leclercq, *Histoire de la divination dans l'antiquité*, i, 127 ff.

[4] *Birds*, 715 ff.   [5] *Iliad*, xii, 243.

[6] In Borneo, which has an elaborate scheme of omens from birds, prayer is sometimes addressed to them. Furness, *Home Life of the Borneo Head-hunters*, Index, s.v. *Omen*; Haddon, *Head-hunters*, p. 344.

[7] The sacrificial animal was regarded as divine, and its movements had the significance of divine counsels.

any new affair;[1] these were all unusual and therefore uncanny occurrences. Some of the animals that furnish omens are totems, and in such cases the totemic significance coalesces with that of the omen; the animal that appears to the young Sioux candidate as his manitu has both characters — it is the sign of divine acceptance and the embodiment of the divine patron.[2]

913. Prodigies connected with the birth of children are numerous. The complete or incomplete character of the infant's body, various marks and colors, and the number produced at a birth have been carefully noted by many peoples. The birth of twins seems to have been more commonly regarded in savage and half-civilized communities either as a presage of misfortune (as being unusual and mysterious) or as a sign of conjugal unfaithfulness (as indicating two fathers, one of whom might be a god). Interpretations of births are given in Babylonian records.[3] Everywhere monstrous births, misshapen forms, and abnormal colors in the bodies of men and beasts have been regarded as indications of divine displeasure.

914. That the stars early attracted the attention of man is shown by the fact that constellations are recognized in some lower tribes — for example, in the New Hebrides Islands, among the Todas, the Masai, the Nandi, and elsewhere.[4] Since all heavenly bodies were regarded originally as divine, and later as controlled by divine beings, sometimes also as the abodes of the dead or as the souls of the dead, it was natural that astral movements should be looked on as giving signs of the will of the gods. Astronomy appears to have been pursued in the first instance not from interest in the natural laws governing the movements of sun, moon, and stars, but from belief in their divinatory significance. How far this study was carried on all over the ancient world we have no means of knowing; but, as far as

---

[1] Terence, *Phormio*, IV, iv, 25 ff.

[2] Frazer, *Totemism and Exogamy*, ii, 137; Tylor, *Primitive Culture*, i, 119 f.; Miss Fletcher, *Indian Ceremonies*, p. 278 ff.

[3] Jastrow, *Religion of Babylonia and Assyria*, p. 384 ff.

[4] Turner, *Samoa*, p. 319; Rivers, *The Todas*, p. 593; Hollis, *The Nandi*, p. 100, and *The Masai*, p. 275 ff.

the records go, it was the Babylonians that first reduced astral divination to the form of a science,[1] and it is probable that from them it spread over Western Asia and India, and perhaps into Europe. Babylonian and Assyrian documents contain many accurate statements of the appearances of heavenly bodies; and in the third or second century B.C., as we learn from the Book of Daniel, the term ' Chaldean ' was synonymous with ' magician.' While astronomy was pursued by the Egyptians with great success, whereby they made a notable construction of the calendar, they seem not to have cultivated astrology, though they associated certain stars with certain gods and with lucky or unlucky days.[2]

915. Of all divinatory methods astrology has played the greatest rôle in human history, and is still believed in and studied by not a few persons. It derived its prominence originally, no doubt, from the splendor and mystery of the sidereal heavens; the identification (by the Babylonians) of certain planets with certain deities gave it more definite shape. It was necessarily a learned pursuit, and, falling naturally into the hands of priestly bodies, was developed by them in accordance with the needs of the situation. Rules of interpretation were established that became more and more specific. In the early period of astrology it was concerning matters of public interest that information was sought — crops, wars, and the fortunes of the king as the head of the nation.[3] At a later time, but before the beginning of our era, in accordance with the growth of ethical individualism, the stars were interrogated for the destinies of private individuals;[4] the aspect of the heavens at the moment of birth, the horoscope, announced the fate of the nascent man.[5]

In the hands of the Chaldeans astrology remained exclusively or largely a science of omens. An advance toward a higher conception, however, was made by their identification of certain planets

---

[1] On the exaggerated range and importance ascribed by some modern writers to early conceptions of the divinatory function of heavenly bodies see above, §§ 826, 866 ff.   [2] Erman, *Handbook of Egyptian Religion*, pp. 163, 180.

[3] Jastrow, *Aspects of Religious Belief and Practice in Babylonia and Assyria*, p. 240 ff.; R. F. Harper, *Assyrian and Babylonian Literature*, p. 451 ff.

[4] Persius, vi, 18.   [5] Cicero, *De Divinatione*, ii, 42 ff.

with certain gods,[1] whereby the regularity and certainty of movement of the astral world were carried over to the world of divine
Powers. When, in the centuries just preceding and following the
beginning of our era, Chaldean astrology was adopted by the
Greeks and Romans, it was organized by them in accordance
with their philosophy, and it entered into alliance with all the
higher religious tendencies of the period. In the unchangeable-
ness of stellar movements the Stoics saw a principle substantially
identical with their doctrine of fate. Along various lines (in
Judaism and Christianity, and in the mysteries of Mithra and
Isis) men were moving toward the conception of a single supreme
ruler of the world, and astrology fell into line with this movement.
The starry universe was held to be the controller of human life,
worthy of worship, and able to call forth emotion. Thus astrology
became a religion [2] — it was adopted by learned and unlearned,
its ethical and spiritual quality being determined by the character
and thought of the various groups that professed it. For some
centuries it was a religious power in the world; as a religious
system it gave way gradually to more definite constructions, but
it survived as a science long after it had ceased to be believed in
as a life-giving faith.

The persistence of faith in it as a science is an additional illustration of men's demand for visible signs of the intervention of
the deity in human affairs; [3] as often as certain supposed embodiments of the supernatural are discarded, others are taken up.

---

[1] The largest planet was brought into connection with the chief god of Babylon,
Marduk; the bright star of morning and evening with Ishtar; the red planet with
Nergal, god of war, and the others with Ninib and Nebo respectively. The Romans
changed these names into those of their corresponding deities, Jupiter, Venus, Mars,
Saturn, and Mercury.

[2] Cumont, *Les religions orientales dans le paganisme romain*, chap. vii, and Eng.
tr., *The Oriental Religions in Roman Paganism*; id., *Astrology and Religion among
the Greeks and Romans*; Bouché-Leclercq, *L'astrologie grecque* and *Histoire de la
divination dans l'antiquité*.

[3] Medieval belief in astral power is embodied in the English word 'influence,'
properly the inflow from the stars (so in Milton's *L'Allegro*, 121 f., "ladies whose
bright eyes rain influence"). An astrologer was often attached to a royal court or
to the household of some great person, his duty being to keep his patron informed
as to the future.

The earlier philosophical views of the relation of the heavenly bodies to human life are now generally abandoned, and such belief in this relation as now exists has no scientific basis, but is founded on vague desire.

In savage and in civilized times eclipses, comets, the appearance of a new star, and earthquakes have been regarded as indications of the attitude of the deity — sometimes favorable, sometimes unfavorable.

916. The words and actions of men and their normal peculiarities of bodily form have furnished comparatively few divinatory signs, the reason being, probably, that in early times animals and other nonhuman things arrested the attention of observers more forcibly, while in later times such acts and forms were more readily explained from natural conditions and laws. The palpitation of the eye, which seems sometimes to uneducated man to be produced by an external force, has been taken as a presage of misfortune. A burning sensation in the ear is still believed by some persons to be a sign that one is being talked about; in early stages of culture the sensation was regarded as a warning sent by the guardian spirit or some other superhuman being. Sneezing was once looked on as a happy omen : when Telemachus gave a resounding sneeze Penelope interpreted it as a sign that news of his father was at hand.[1] An act performed without ulterior purpose may be taken to symbolize some sort of fortune. When the Calif Omar sent an embassy to the Persian King Yezdegird summoning him to embrace Islam, the angry king commanded that a clod of earth should be brought and that the ambassadors should bear it out of the city, which they accordingly did; and this act was taken both by Arabs and by Persians as a presage of Moslem victory — the invaders had a portion of Persian soil.[2] An element of magic, however, may have entered into this conviction; the bit of soil was supposed, perhaps, to

---

[1] *Odyssey*, xvii, 541 ff. The fear of a sneeze (which must be followed by some form of ' God bless you!') belongs in a different category; the danger is that a hurtful spirit may enter the sneezer's body, or that his soul may depart.

[2] Muir, *The Caliphate*, p. 112.

carry with it the whole land. A chance word has often been seized on as an indication of the future, or a proper name taken as a presage.

917. The belief in the sacredness or divinity of the human body has led to the search for divinatory signs in its parts. But it is only the hand that has been extensively employed in this way. The hand has offered itself as most available for divination, partly, perhaps, because of the variety and importance of its functions, partly because of the variety of lines it shows and the ease with which it may be examined. Chiromancy, or palmistry, has been developed into a science and has maintained itself to the present day; but it has largely lost its divinatory significance and has become a study of character, which is supposed to be indicated by the lines of the hand. In its divinatory rôle it has often been connected with astrology.

918. The preceding examples deal with occurrences that present themselves without human initiation. In certain cases the materials for divination are arranged by men themselves. In such methods there is always an appeal to the deity, a demand that a god shall intervene and indicate his will under the conditions prepared by men, the assumption being that the god has prepared the event or thing in question, and that, when properly approached, he will be disposed to give his worshipers the assistance desired. The casting of lots and similar random procedures have been common methods of divination the world over. The African Kafir diviner detects criminals by the fall of small objects used as dice. The Ashanti discover future events by the figures formed when palm wine is thrown on the ground, and from the nature of the num-bers, whether even or odd, when one lets fall a handful of nuts. In a dispute the Yoruban priest holds in his hand a number of grass stalks, one of which is bent, and the person who draws the bent stalk is adjudged to be in fault.[1] The Hebrews had the official use of objects called " urim and thummim " (terms whose meaning is unknown to us), which were probably small cubes, to

[1] Hastings, *Encyclopædia of Religion and Ethics*, ii, 362; Ellis, *Tshi*, p. 202; id., *Yoruba*, p. 97; cf. Hollis, *The Masai*, p. 324.

each of which was somehow attached an answer " yes " or " no," or the name of a person. Thus, when David inquired whether he was to attack the Philistines, the answer seems to have been " yes." [1] When it was a question who had violated the taboo announced by Saul, the urim and thummim first decided that it was not the people but the royal family; and then, as between Saul and Jonathan, that it was the latter who was guilty.[2] According to the Book of Ezekiel the Chaldean King Nebuchadrezzar drew lots by arrows to determine what road he should take in a campaign.[3] The old Arabs employed a species of divination by arrows, which, when thrown down, by their position indicated the will of the gods; and in the division of the flesh of a beast slaughtered by a clan or group, the portions to be assigned to various persons were determined by the drawing of arrows.[4] Divination by lot was also largely employed by the Greeks and the Romans.[5] The method called " sortes vergilianae " is still in vogue; it was and is a custom among pious persons, Christian or Moslem, to learn the course that they are to take in an emergency by opening a Bible or a copy of the Koran at random and accepting the first words on which the eye falls as an indication of the divine will, the deity being supposed to direct the eye.[6]

919. One of the commonest and most important methods of divination in antiquity was the examination of the entrails of animals (haruspication). Of this system there are a few examples among savage peoples,[7] but it has attained special significance only among the great civilized nations and especially among the Babylonians, the Etruscans, and the Greeks and Romans. The slaughtered animal was generally held to be itself sacred or divine,

---

[1] 1 Sam. xxiii, 2.   [2] 1 Sam. xiv, 38–42 (see the Septuagint text).
[3] Ezek. xxi, 21 [26].   [4] *Moallakat of Imru'l-Kais*, ver. 22.
[5] Bouché-Leclercq, *Histoire de la divination dans l'antiquité*, i, 195 ff.; iv, 153, 159; Augustine, *Confessions*, iv, 5 : de paginis poetae cujuspiam longe aliud canentis atque intendentis ; if, says Augustine's friend, an apposite verse so appears, it is not wonderful that something bearing on one's affairs should issue from the human soul by some higher instinct, though the soul does not know what goes on within it.
[6] Cf. Comparetti, *Virgilio nel medio evo*, i, 64 f. (Eng. tr., p. 47 f.).
[7] As the Masai (Hollis, *The Masai*, p. 324).

and, as it was offered to the deity, it was a natural belief that the god would indicate his will by the character of the inward parts, which were supposed to be particularly connected with the life of the animal. Of these animal parts the liver was regarded as the most important. The liver was for the Babylonians the special seat of thought, whether from its position or its size or from some other consideration we have no means of knowing. The explanation of the form and appearance of the liver became itself a separate science, and this science was developed with extraordinary minuteness by the Babylonians. The whole structure of the liver, together with the gall, bladder, and the ducts, was analyzed, and to every part, every line, and every difference of appearance a separate significance was assigned. Thus hepatoscopy, demanding long training and influencing political action (and, doubtless, calling for ingenuity and tact in interpretations), assumed great importance in Babylonia and Assyria; and it was hardly less important among the Etruscans, the Greeks, and the Romans.[1] It is held by some scholars that Babylonia was the original home of the developed science, whence it passed into Greece and Italy.[2] It may be recognized in Babylonia in the third millennium B.C., and there is no improbability in the supposition that Babylonian influence was felt in Asia Minor and Eastern Europe; but, in view of the number of possibly independent centers of culture in this region in ancient times and the paucity of data, the question may be left open.

920. Other parts of the animal bodies also were employed in divination. Tylor[3] mentions the examination of the bones of the porcupine among North American Indians, the color giving indications as to the success of hunting expeditions. The shoulder blade, when put into the fire, showed by splits in it various kinds of fortune. The heart was of less significance in ancient thought than the liver, it being of less size, and its function in the circulation

---

[1] Bouché-Leclercq, *Histoire de la divination dans l'antiquité*; Daremberg and Saglio, *Dictionnaire des antiquités grecques et romaines*, s.v. *Haruspices*; Fowler, *The Religious Experience of the Roman People*, Index, s.v. *Haruspices*.

[2] M. Jastrow, "The Liver in Antiquity" (*University of Pennsylvania Medical Bulletin*, 1908) and *Religion Babyloniens und Assyriens*. [3] *Primitive Culture*, i, 124.

of the blood not being known. The brain also did not come, until a comparatively late period, to be regarded as the seat of the intellect.[1]

921. From these external signs we may now pass to consider divinatory facts derived from men's inward experience.

Dreams. The importance attached all over the world to dreams as presages is a familiar fact. It would appear that among savage peoples a dream is regarded as representing an historical fact, the actual perception of an occurrence or a situation. It is believed that the mysterious inward thing, the soul, endowed with peculiar power, is capable, during sleep, of leaving the body and wandering to and fro;[2] why, then, in its journeys, should it not be able to see the plans of friends and enemies, and in general to observe the course of events? We do not know the nature of savage logic in dealing with these visions of the night, but some such line of reasoning as this, it seems probable, is in their minds. The soul, they hold, is an entity, possessing intellectual powers like those of the ordinary living man — it sees certain things, and its knowledge becomes the possession of the man when he awakes. Thus the soul in dreams is a watchman, on the lookout for what may help or harm the man. Perhaps there is, even in low tribes, a vague feeling that it has extraordinary powers of perception; whether such a feeling, if it exists, is connected with a belief that, during sleep, the soul is freed from the limitations of the everyday corporeal man we are not able with our present data to say.[3] Savages often follow the suggestions made in dreams [4] (particularly when they are vivid) and are confirmed in their faith by occasional fulfillments of predictions; the mind, working during sleep on the observations made by day, may sometimes fall on situations that afterwards really appear, and a few such realizations are sufficient to establish a rule or creed.

---

[1] See above, § 28. The skull is employed as a means of divination (Haddon, *Head-hunters*, p. 91 ff.).   [2] See above, § 24.

[3] Cf. Roscher, *Lexikon*, article "Oneiros," col. 904.

[4] J. H. King, *The Supernatural*, i, 168 ff.; Tylor, *Primitive Culture*, i, 121 ff., 440 f.; Howitt, *Native Tribes of South-East Australia*, p. 436; Mrs. K. Langloh Parker, *The Euahlayi Tribe*, pp. 28, 83 f.

922. This naïve conception of dreams as products of the soul's perception of realities survives to a greater or less extent among higher tribes and nations, but finally gives way, when some sort of theistic construction is reached, to the view that they are sent immediately by deities. An approach to this view appears in North America when, for example, a Pawnee Indian sees in a dream some being who gives him important information, though in the folk-tales nothing is said of the source of the dream.[1] A step in advance appears in the belief of the Ashanti, according to which the existence of a tutelary family deity is indicated in a dream;[2] it is, however, not clear whether or not they hold that the tutelary deity has himself suggested the dream. In the higher religions a dream is often sent by a patron deity as a prediction or for guidance in a coming emergency. Doubtless it was only in the case of specially distinct dreams and such as related to important matters that attention was paid to them — the deity intervened only in affairs that called for his special direction. Examples are numerous in the history of the great nations of antiquity. The Egyptian King Merneptah in a time of great danger had a dream in which the god Ptah appeared to him and bade him banish fear;[3] and the Hebrew Yahweh is represented as having sent dreams to a king of Egypt (probably in the interests of the Hebrews) to warn him of a coming famine.[4] The Assyrian Ashurbanipal was favored with special communications from Ishtar, and the god Ashur in a dream ordered Gyges, King of Lydia, to submit to the Assyrian king.[5] In some documents of the Pentateuch Yahweh regularly announces his will in dreams to both Hebrews and non-Hebrews;[6] and a Hebrew writer of a later time (the third or second century B.C.) represents the God of Israel as giving Nebuchadrezzar an outline of the history of the rise and fall of the kingdoms of Western Asia and Greece.[7] A god might employ a dream for a less worthy purpose: Zeus sends a dream to Agamemnon to mislead him and thus direct the issue of the

---

[1] Dorsey, *The Skidi Pawnee*, Index, s.v. *Dreams*.
[3] Breasted, *History of Egypt*, p. 468, and see p. 558.
[5] Jastrow, *Religion of Babylonia and Assyria*, p. 349 f.
[6] Gen. xx, 3; xxviii, 12; xxxi, 11; xxxvii, 5.

[2] Ellis, *Tshi*, p. 90.
[4] Gen. xl f.
[7] Dan. ii, iv.

war.[1] So important for life did the Greeks conceive the dream to be that, as it would seem, they personified it.[2]

Incubation. Divine direction by dreams was not always left to chance. The custom arose of sleeping near a shrine (*engkoimesis,* incubation) where, doubtless, after appropriate ritual preparation the god was expected to signify his will in a dream (his generally friendly feeling was assumed and the dream would be of the nature of an answer to prayer). This was one of the means employed by Saul when he desired to learn what would be the issue of the impending battle with the ·Philistines.[3] In Greece, and later in Italy, the most famous shrine of incubation was that of Asklepios (Aesculapius), which was widely resorted to and came to exert a good moral influence.[4] The renown of the shrine was doubtless increased by the fact that Asklepios was a god of healing.[5]

923. As a dream was often obscure the services of a trained interpreter became necessary in order that the dream might be effective. The interpreters were magicians, priests, or sages [6] — men in intimate association with deities and acquainted with their modes and vehicles of revelation ;[7] dreams thus became equivalent to oracular responses. An interpreter would become famous in proportion to the number of fulfillments of his interpretations, and his god would share in the glory of his renown.[8] Of the particular conditions through which certain men and certain shrines attained special fame we have few details.

[1] *Iliad,* ii, 1 ff. So Yahweh, by a lying spirit, sends Ahab to his death (1 Kings, xxii, 19 ff.) and deceives the prophet, who misleads the people (Ezek. xiv, 9). The theory of these ancient writers was that a deity, like an earthly king, had a right to use any means to gain his ends.   [2] Cf. article " Oneiros " in Roscher's *Lexikon.*

[3] 1 Sam. xxviii, 6. The other means used, it is said, were the urim (urim and thummim) and prophets. These all failing, the king had recourse to necromancy.

[4] See article "Asklepios " in Roscher's *Lexikon.*

[5] See the description in Pater's *Marius the Epicurean.*

[6] A god might send a dream to a seer for the benefit of some other person. So Ishtar spoke to Assurbanipal through the dream of a seer (George Smith, *History of Assurbanipal,* p. 123 f.).

[7] Jastrow, *Religion Babyloniens und Assyriens* ; Dan. ii, 2 ff. ; Deut. xiii, 1 ; Gardner and Jevons, *Greek Antiquities,* p. 258 ; Aust, *Religion der Römer,* Index, s.v. *Traum, Traumdeutung* ; Roscher, *Lexikon,* article " Oneiros."

[8] So it was in the case of magicians and prophets generally; cf. Ezek. xxxix, 21 ; Isa. xliii, 9.

Oneiromancy, in unorganized form, was studied in very early periods of religious life. It shared in the general advance of thought, and in the course of time a traditional science of the explanation of dreams arose. There were records of experiences, particularly of notable fulfillments, and it became possible to make lists of dreams with interpretations;[1] these were written down and passed on from generation to generation, increasing in volume as they went. Such manuals have played no inconsiderable part in the life of the people.[2]

924. *Ordeals.* Divination has played an important part in civil life as a means of determining the guilt or innocence of an accused person. From very early times ordeals of various sorts have been devised for securing a judicial opinion when ordinary means of investigation have failed. One of the simplest methods is to require an accused person to swear that he is innocent, the belief being that the god will avenge false swearing with immediate and visible punishment.[3] This method is employed by the Ashanti:[4] the accused is required to drink a certain decoction; if he is made sick by it this is proof of his innocence;[5] and if there be a question between two men, and one after drinking is made sick, the other is regarded as guilty, and executed. On the Lower Congo the accused swallows a pill made of a bark said to be poisonous; if he soon vomits it he is declared innocent, if not, he is adjudged guilty.[6] A similar procedure was employed in Samoa:[7] standing in the presence of representatives of the village god, the suspected person laying his hand on the object wishes that if he is guilty he may speedily die. Among the Hill people of Ceylon also this custom exists. Ordeals in Loango are described by Purchas.[8]

---

[1] Jastrow, *Religion of Babylonia and Assyria*, p. 404, and German ed., ii, Index.

[2] Dream-books exist at the present day. Those who believe in the predictive power of dreams regard them as messages from God or as products of telepathy.

[3] The Nandi invoke a skull as divine witness (Hollis, *The Nandi*, p. 76 f.).

[4] Ellis, *Tshi*, chap. xviii.

[5] Apparently because he is thus shown to be unsupported by any evil spirit.

[6] Frobenius, *Childhood of Man*, p. 190 ff.   [7] Turner, *Samoa*, p. 184.

[8] Purchas, *Pilgrimage*, ed. Ravenstein, pp. 56 f., 59 f.

925. Among the ancient nations the earliest example of an ordeal occurs in the code of Hammurabi (about 2000 B.C.). Here the accused is thrown into the sacred water, and if not drowned is declared innocent; he is protected by the deity.[1] The same principle appears in the old Hebrew ordeal: when a woman was accused of unfaithfulness to her husband the accused was made to drink sacred water; if she was innocent no bad consequences followed; if she was guilty she died.[2] In India, where various tests by fire, water, and food have been and are employed, the decision is sometimes as in the Hebrew procedure; sometimes (when the accused is thrown into the water) the principle (found elsewhere abundantly) is recognized that it is the innocent person that suffers and the guilty that is uninjured.[3] The ordeal as a civil process continued in Europe until the Middle Ages. In the submersion in water of a woman suspected of being a witch the principle of decision was the same as is now practiced in Ashantiland and India — if the woman was drowned it was a sign that she was innocent, but if she rose unharmed from the water she was adjudged guilty and was put to death.[4]

926. The imprecation is similar to the ordeal. A man invokes the curse of the deity on his enemy, and it is supposed that such curse will bring its punishment.[5] A curse was regarded as an objective thing, which reached its object quite independently of guilt or innocence.[6] In Morocco a conditional curse is pronounced and is supposed to become effective if the wrong complained of is not righted.[7] These ordeals and imprecations were sometimes effective in fixing guilt; the dread of incurring the wrath of the deity sometimes forced a guilty person to confess, or his dread of

---

1 " Code of Hammurabi " (§§ 2, 132), by C. H. W. Johns, in Hastings's *Dictionary of the Bible*, extra volume.   2 Numb. v.   3 Hopkins, *Religions of India*, p. 275 ff.

4 She was rejected by the sacred water; cf. W. R. Smith, *Religion of the Semites*, 2d ed., p. 179; Tylor, *Primitive Culture*, i, 140. Cf. Ellis, *Yoruba*, p. 190 f.; id., *Tshi*, pp. 198, 201.   5 Turner, *Samoa*, p. 184.

6 Similarly, a blessing once uttered remains effective and cannot be recalled; so in the story of Isaac blessing Jacob and Esau, Gen. xxvii.

7 Westermarck, "' L-'âr " in *Anthropological Essays presented to Tylor*; cf. his *Origin and Development of the Moral Ideas*, Index, s.v. *Curses*.

the punishment produced signs of guilt. On the other hand, it is probable that just as often innocent persons were convicted and punished through such tests.

With all such systems of signs may be compared the Chinese quasi-science called Fung-Shui ('Wind and Water'), which determines proper sites for graves and for temples and other buildings by observations of the influences of the sky (moisture, warmth, wind, thunder), of waters and hills, and of the earth, and by the study of various magical combinations. Thus, it is held, it is possible in important undertakings to obtain the favor and support of the good Powers of the world. The site of a grave, affecting the future of the dead, is of especial significance, and the Fung-Shui interpreters, regularly trained men, levy what contributions they please from surviving relatives, sometimes purposely prolonging their investigations at a ruinous cost to the family of the deceased.[1] The system sprang from the Chinese conception of heaven and earth as the controlling Powers of the world ; but, neglecting the higher side of this conception, it has sunk into a fraudulent trade.[2]

927. *Oracles.* As men went to the tents or palaces of chiefs or kings for guidance in ordinary matters, so they went to the dwelling places of superhuman Powers for direction in matters that were beyond human ken. Such appeal to divine or quasi-divine beings began early in religious history. In Borneo and the islands of Torres Straits the abodes of skulls are places from which responses are obtained ;[3] speaking heads are found there and elsewhere. The Sunthals of West Bengal have the ghost of a specially revered ancestor as a dispenser of superhuman knowledge.[4] When local gods arose every local shrine, it is probable,

---

[1] Hence the opposition (now disappearing) to lines of railway and telegraph, which were supposed to interfere with the happy influences of rivers and hills and other natural features.

[2] De Groot, *Religious System of China* and *Development of Religion in China*; and his article " Die Chinesen " in Saussaye, *Lehrbuch der Religionsgeschichte*. See above, § 747 ff.

[3] Haddon, *Head-hunters*, pp. 42, 182 f. ; on the sacredness of the head see Frazer, *Golden Bough*, 2d ed., i, 362 ff. ; Frobenius, *Childhood of Man*, chap. xiii.

[4] Hopkins, *Religions of India*, p. 532.

contained an oracle.[1] The shrines of the great gods naturally acquired special prominence, their oracles were consulted by kings and other leaders on affairs of importance, and thus came to exert a great influence on the course of events.[2] The stars also, though they had no earthly habitations, were consulted through their interpreters. Such astrological oracles, as used by men like Posidonius, the teacher of Cicero, might be morally inspiring; but when, at a later time, the consultation of heavenly bodies fell into the hands of wandering "Chaldeans" (who might be of any nation) it became a system of charlatanry, and thus morally debasing.[3]

The greater nations of antiquity differed considerably among themselves in regard to the part played in their lives by oracles. In general, the organization of oracular shrines grew in proportion to the rise of manlike gods — deities whose relation to men was socially intimate. In Egypt such shrines were not of prime importance;[4] the functions of the gods were mainly governmental — the most human of them, Osiris, became an ethical judge rather than a personal friend. The pre-Mohammedan Arabs did not create great gods, and their resort to local divinities was commonly in order to ask whether or not a proposed course of action was desirable; the answer was "yes" or "no."[5] The famous warrior and poet, Imru'l-Kais, desiring to go to war to avenge his father's death, received at a shrine three times a negative answer, whereupon, hurling abusive epithets at the god, he exclaimed, "If it were your father, you would not say 'no.'" Such independence was probably rare; most men would have accepted the divine decision. The answer of the Hebrew oracle was, as among the Arabs, "yes" or "no" (by urim and thummim) — the gods were remote, and the oracle, whose minister was a priest, gradually

1 So when Rebecca wished to obtain information about her children, soon to be born, it is said simply that she went to inquire of Yahweh (Gen. xxv, 22), as if there was, as a matter of course, a shrine in the neighborhood.

2 Bouché-Leclercq, *Histoire de la divination dans l'antiquité*, ii, 250 ff.; iii.

3 Cumont, *Les religions orientales dans le paganisme romain*, Eng. tr., *The Oriental Religions in Roman Paganism*, pp. 105, 124 f., 168.

4 Cf. Steindorff, *Religion of the Ancient Egyptians*, p. 113 f.

5 Wellhausen, *Reste arabischen Heidentumes*, p. 126 ff.

yielded to the prophet, the human interpreter of the deity.[1] The Philistines appear to have had well-organized oracles; when King Ahaziah was sick he sent to inquire of Baalzebub, god of Ekron, whether or not he should recover.[2] Many Babylonian and Assyrian deities gave oracular responses;[3] it is not known whether the shrines were resorted to by the people at large, and their importance was probably diminished by the great rôle played by the priestly interpretation of omens, whereby the will of the gods was held to be clearly revealed. The Romans under the republic were practically independent of oracles at shrines: in household affairs they had a family god for every department and every situation, and for State matters they found the Sibylline oracles sufficient.[4] Later, with the widening of the horizon of religion, the resort to Greek and other oracular shrines became general — a departure from the old Roman constitution.[5] The greatest development of oracular service took place in Greece. The Greek gods, with their anthropomorphically emotional characters, entered intimately and sympathetically into human life, communal and individual. The great shrines of Zeus at Dodona and Apollo at Delphi were centers of Hellenistic religious life, and there were others of less importance.[6] Zeus, as head of the pantheon, naturally took a distinguished place as patron of oracles; and Apollo's relation to music and inspiration may account in part for the preëminence of his oracular shrine. In many cases, however, the grounds of the choice of a particular deity as oracle-giver escape us.

[1] i Sam. xiv, 36 ff.; xxiii, 2; xxx, 7 f.; Isa. lxv, 1; Ezek. xxxiii, 30 ff.

[2] 2 Kings, i, 2. The prophet Elijah, who was a zealous Yahwist, was very angry with the king for applying to a foreign deity; but evidently the Philistine shrine enjoyed a greater reputation than any in Israel.

[3] Jastrow, *Religion of Babylonia and Assyria*, Index, s.v. *Oracles*.

[4] Cf. Aust, *Religion der Römer*, Index, s.v. *Orakel*; see below, § 933 ff.

[5] Friedländer, *Roman Life and Manners under the Early Empire* (Eng. tr.), p. 3, 129 ff.; Fowler, *Religious Experience of the Roman People*, p. 339.

[6] Cicero, *De Divinatione*, i, 34, 37 f.; Plutarch, *De Pythiae Oraculis* and *De Defectu Oraculorum*; Gardner and Jevons, *Greek Antiquities*, Index, s.v. *Oracles*; Bouché-Leclercq, *Histoire de la divination dans l'antiquité*, Index, and Stengel and Oehmichen, *Die griechischen Sakralaltertümer*, Index; *Encyclopædia Britannica*, 11th ed., article "Oracle."

The human demand for divine guidance long maintained the influence of oracles everywhere, and it is not improbable that in general they furthered what was good religiously and socially. They were bonds of union between communities, and their authoritative rôle would naturally force on them a certain sense of responsibility. As to the character of the mouthpieces of the gods and the material on which they based their answers to questions we have not the means of forming a definite opinion. There can be little doubt that the official persons were sometimes sincere in the belief that they were inspired — such is the testimony of observers for both savage and civilized communities — and many modern instances bear out this view. On the other hand, there is reason to suppose that pretense and fraud often crept into the administration of the oracles. When the questions were known beforehand the responses may have been based on information that came from various quarters and on insight into the particular situation about which the inquiry was made. When the questions were not known beforehand we are in the dark as to the source of the answers. Sometimes, doubtless, they were happy or unhappy guesses; sometimes they were enigmatical or ambiguous in form, so that they could be made to agree with the events that actually occurred. In most cases the authorities would know how to explain the issue in such a way as to maintain the credit of the oracle. The best-known and the most impressive of the utterers of oracles is the priestess of Apollo at Delphi, the Pythia. She occupied a commanding position in the Hellenic world (and beyond it), such as was enjoyed by few persons of the time.[1] She was invested with special sanctity as the dispenser of divine guidance to the Western world (to nations and individuals). It was required of her that she be morally and ceremonially pure, and she had to undergo a special preparation for the delivery of her message. The manner of her revelation did not differ from that of similar officials in noncivilized communities — she spoke in a condition of ecstasy; she is the best

---

[1] On the position of women in ancient religion cf. Farnell's article in *Archiv für Religionswissenschaft*, 1904.

representative of the intimate union of the diviner and a great god, a union that tended to give dignity and wisdom as well as authority to the oracular utterance.[1] She was, thus, in the best position for exerting a good influence on the world of her time. How far the oracles of Apollo and other deities furthered the best interests of religion it may be difficult to say — the data for an exact answer are lacking. Socially they were useful in maintaining a certain unity among peoples, and they may sometimes have upheld justice and given judicious advice, but they were always exposed to the temptation of fraud.

Necromancy. While in ancient times the dead were everywhere placated by gifts and were sometimes worshiped, the consultation of them for guidance seems to have been relatively infrequent. The attitude of existing lower tribes toward ghosts varies in different places,[2] but the predominant feeling seems to be fear; these tribes have not accomplished that social union between themselves and the departed without which, as it appears, the living do not feel free to apply to the latter for information concerning things past, present, and future.[3] Savage and half-civilized peoples depend for such information on divination by means of common phenomena (omens) and on the offices of magicians and soothsayers, and references in published reports to necromantic usages among them are rare and vague. But among civilized peoples also application to the dead is not as frequent as might be expected; there is still fear of ghosts, and the part assigned in early times to spirits in the administration of human life has been given over to gods — family divinities and the great oracular deities supply the information that men need. There are few signs of dependence on necromancy in China, India, Persia, and Rome. The Babylonian mythical hero Gilgamesh procures (through the aid of an Underworld god) an interview with his dead friend Eabani in order to learn the nature of the life below;[4] this story

---

[1] Gruppe, *Griechische Mythologie*, pp. 102, 105 ; Farnell, *Cults of the Greek States*, iv, 187 ff.   [2] See above, §§ 362, 366.

[3] See article " Ancestor-worship " and articles on lower tribes in Hastings, *Encyclopædia of Religion and Ethics*.

[4] Jastrow, *Religion of Babylonia and Assyria*, p. 511.

points, perhaps, to necromantic usages, but in the extant literature there are no details of such usages. Application to the dead is certified for the old Hebrews not only by the story of Saul's consultation of Samuel (which, though a folk-story, may be taken to prove a popular custom) but by a prophetic passage condemning the practice.[1] Teraphim were employed, probably, for divination, but there is no proof that they were connected with necromancy.[2] After the sixth century B.C. we hear nothing of consultation of the dead by the pre-Christian Jews. Among the Greeks also such consultation seems not to have enjoyed a high degree of favor. There were oracles of the dead (of heroes and others), but these were inferior in importance to the oracles of the great gods[3] and gradually ceased to be resorted to. Where the practice of incubation existed, answers to inquiries were sometimes, doubtless, held to come from the dead, but more commonly it was a god that supplied the desired information.

The stages in the history of necromantic practice follow the lines of growth of psychical and theistic beliefs. There was first the era of spirits when men were doubtful of the friendliness of ghosts, and held it safer in general to trust to soothsayers for guidance in life. Then, when the gods took distinct shape, they largely displaced ghosts as dispensers of knowledge of the future, and these latter, standing outside of and in rivalry with the circle of State deities, could be approached only in secret — necromancy became illicit and its influence was crippled. And when, finally, in the earlier centuries of our era, the old gods disappeared, the rise of monotheistic belief was accompanied by a transformation of the conception of the future of the soul; it was to be no longer the inert earthly thing of the old theories but instinct with a high life that fitted it to be the companion of divine beings and the sharer of their knowledge and their ideals.[4] This conception

---

[1] 1 Sam. xxviii; Isa. viii, 19.

[2] Ezek. xxi, 26 [21] (King Nebuchadrezzar divines by teraphim).

[3] Bouché-Leclercq, *Histoire de la divination dans l'antiquité*, iii, 363 ff.; Daremberg and Saglio, *Dictionnaire des antiquités grecques et romaines*, article " Divination," p. 308.

[4] 1 Cor. xv, 49; 2 Cor. v, 8; Cumont, *Astrology and Religion among the Greeks and Romans*, lecture vi.

led to the belief in the possibility of a nonmagical friendly intercourse with the departed, who, it was assumed, would be willing
to impart their knowledge to their brethren on earth. Saints have
thus been appealed to, and it has been attempted in recent times
to enter into communication with departed kin and other friends.

928. The office of diviner, though it has always been an influential one, has followed in its development the general course
of social organization, becoming more and more specialized and
defined. In the simplest religions the positions of magician and
diviner are frequently united in one person. In Greenland the
Angekok, acting as the interpreter or mouthpiece of a supernatural being from whom men learn how they may be fortunate,
foretells the condition of the weather and the fortunes of fishing.[1]
A similar combination of the offices is found among the Ainu,
and apparently among the Cakchiquels, among whom the divining
function is said to have related particularly to war.[2]

929. There was, however, as is remarked above, a tendency
to invest the priest with the function of divination. The Arabian
kahin was a soothsayer, the Hebrew *kohen* was a priest.[3] The
Yorubans have a special god of divination whose priest is the
soothsayer of the community. In Ashantiland priests and priestesses, who are exceedingly influential and powerful, owe a great
deal of their importance to their ability to explain signs and
omens, especially to discover guilt and to foretell events.[4] In the
elaborate divinatory ceremonies of the Ahoms of Southeastern
Asia, the conductors, who are highly considered in the community, are priests; these people are partly Hinduized, but probably
retain much of their ancient religious forms.[5] A noteworthy
specialization of functions is found among the Todas of Southern
India, who distinguish the diviner from the magician, the prophet,
and the dairyman. The diviner is inspired by a god, gives his

---

[1] Cranz, *Greenland*, i, 192 ff.; Rink, *Danish Greenland*, p. 142 f.

[2] Brinton, *Cakchiquels*, p. 47.

[3] Cf. Nöldeke, article "Arabs (Ancient)" in Hastings, *Encyclopædia of Religion
and Ethics*, i, 667, 671.   [4] Ellis, *Yoruba*, p. 56 ff.; id., *Tshi*, p. 124 ff.

[5] P. R. Gurden, article "Ahoms" in Hastings, *Encyclopædia of Religion and
Ethics*.

utterances in an ecstatic state, and for the most part limits himself to the explanation of the origin of misfortunes.[1] It would be
a matter of interest to trace, if it were possible, a history of this
specialization, but the early fortunes of the Toda religion are
without records and can only be surmised. In ancient Gaul
the diviner, it is said, was distinguished from the priest and the
prophet.[2] Where divination is the duty of the priestly body,
there is sometimes a differentiation within this body, some persons devoting themselves specifically to soothsaying; so among
the Babylonians, where this function was most important.[8]

930. Among the old Hebrews the soothsaying function is
connected not only with priests but also with prophets.[4] The
priest was the official diviner, employing the urim and thummim.
Prophets and dreamers are mentioned together as persons of the
same class and as sometimes employing their arts for purposes
contrary to the national religion; various classes of diviners are
mentioned as existing among the Israelites in the seventh century B.C., but the distinctions between them are not given.[5] From
a statement in Isaiah ii, 6, it may perhaps be inferred that some
form of divination was imported into Israel in the eighth century
or earlier from the more developed Philistines and from the countries east of the Jordan;[6] and the passage just referred to in Deu-
teronomy probably reveals Assyrian influence. While the Egyptian
documents have much to say of magic, they give little information
with regard to the existence of a class of diviners; but it appears,
according to a Hebrew writer,[7] that the art of divination might
belong to any prominent person — Joseph is represented as divining from a cup.

931. The greatest development of the office of the diviner in
ancient times was found among the Greeks and Romans.[8] The

---

[1] Rivers, *The Todas*, p. 249 ff.

[2] A. Bertrand, *La religion des Gaulois*, pp. 257, 259, 263.

[8] Jastrow, *Religion of Babylonia and Assyria*, p. 341.

[4] On Hebrew divination see articles " Divination " in Hastings, *Dictionary of the
Bible*, and in the *Encyclopædia Biblica*.　　　[5] Deut. xiii, 1; xviii, 10.

[6] The Hebrew text is doubtful, and its meaning is not clear; cf. Gray, "The Book
of Isaiah," in *The International Critical Commentary*.　　　[7] Gen. xliv, 5.

[8] Cf. Bouché-Leclercq, *Histoire de la divination dans l'antiquité*, ii, 1 ff., 62 ff.

Greek word *mantis* appears to have been a general term for any person, male or female, who hád the power of perceiving the will of the gods. The early distinction between the *mantis* and the *prophetes* is not clear. Plato, indeed, distinguishes sharply between the two terms :[1] the *mantis*, he says, while in an ecstatic state cannot understand his own utterances, and it is, therefore, the custom to appoint a *prophetes* who shall interpret for him ; some persons, he adds, give the name *mantis* to this interpreter, but he is only a *prophetes*. We find, however, that the terms are frequently used interchangeably ; thus the Pythia is called both *mantis* and *prophetis*. Whatever may have been the original sense of these terms, the office of diviner in Greece was in the main separate from that of priest. It is found attached to families and was hereditary. It was recognized by the State from an early time and became more and more influential. According to Xenophon Socrates believed in and approved divination.[2] Plato held that it was a gift of the gods, and that official persons so gifted were to be held in high esteem.

932. In Rome, in accordance with the genius of the nation, sooth-saying was at a comparatively early period organized and taken in charge by the State. There were colleges of augurs,[3] standing in various relations to political and social life, having their heads (chief augurs) — thus in their organization similar to the priesthood, but standing quite apart from this. The same sort of organization was established in the Etruscan office of *haruspex*[4] when this was introduced into Rome. The members of these colleges were at first Etruscans and, as such, looked down on ; but gradually Roman youth of good family and education were trained for the duty, and in the time of the Emperor Claudius the social difference between augurs and haruspices seems to have been almost eliminated.[5]

---

[1] *Timæus*, 72.

[2] Xenophon, *Memorabilia*, i, 3, 4 : τὰ ὑπὸ τῶν θεῶν σημαινόμενα.

[3] Originally diviners from the flight of birds, but the area of their divinatory functions was gradually extended. See Wissowa, *Religion der Römer*, p. 450 ff. ; Fowler, *Religious Experience of the Roman People*, lecture xiii.

[4] Charged with the interpretation of the entrails of sacrificed animals, and also of lightning and portents.   [5] Wissowa, op. cit., p. 474.

933. Sibyls. In the old Græco-Roman world inspired women played a great rôle.[1] The belief in such personages goes back to the old conception of the possession of human beings by a supernatural being, which, as we have seen, was common in early forms of religion. This idea assumed various shapes in Greece, and in the course of time the inspired women were connected with various deities. In the Dionysus cult the orgiastic rites (in which women took a chief part) seem to have grown up from old agricultural ceremonies in which the spirit or god of vegetation was invoked to give his aid. Such ceremonies naturally coalesced here as elsewhere with the license of popular festivities. The legends connected with the Dionysus cult introduced savage features into the rites, as, for example, in the story of Pentheus.[2] But whatever may have been the case in Thrace, whence the cult came to Greece, it was not so in historical times in Greece, where the celebrations were controlled by the State. These exhibit then only the natural frenzy of excited crowds without the element of divination.

934. The development of the rôle of women as representatives of deities is illustrated by the character of the priestesses of oracular shrines.[3] These, like the Dionysiac devotees, are seized and possessed by the god, and speak in a state of frenzy. But their frenzy is controlled by civilized conditions. It exists only as a preparation for divination; it is the movement of the god in them laboring to express himself, and his expression is couched in intelligible human language. The priestess is a part of an organized and humanized cult and, as such, represents to a certain extent the ideas of a civilized society. The Dionysiac woman yields to an excess of animal excitement, without thought for society; the priestess feels herself responsible to society. A similar progress in civilized feeling appears among the old Hebrews; the incoherency of the earlier prophets[4] gives way to the thoughtful discourses of the ethical

---

[1] Cf. above, § 895 f.

[2] This story (connected with Thebes) appears to represent some sort of protest against the Dionysiac cult when it was first brought to Greece ; cf. Roscher, *Lexikon*, article " Pentheus."   [3] Cf. above, § 927.   [4] 1 Sam. xix, 24 ; cf. Mic. i, 8 ff.

leaders.[1] The manner and the expression of revelation always conform to existing social usages.

935. Of a still different character is the figure of the Sibyl, created by the Greeks and adopted by the Romans.[2] She, too, is possessed by a god and sometimes, at least, raves in ecstasy; but she does not officiate at a shrine and is not controlled by any official body. She dwells in a cave or a grotto, has her life in the open air, and gives her answers on the leaves of the forest. She represents the divine voices that are heard by early men everywhere in the world; in the myth, when she displeases Apollo she is condemned to fade finally, after a long life, into a voice.[3] She is not, like the Pythia, an actual human being — she is never seen except in legends and myths. She is a creature of Greek imagination, the embodiment of all the divine suggestions that come to man from the mysterious sounds around him.

936. The historical origin of the fully developed figure of the Sibyl is obscure.[4] In the literature she appears first in the sixth century B.C. along with the Pythia, but she was then thought of as well established and ancient. She is not mentioned by Homer or Hesiod, but their silence is not proof positive that the conception of the character did not exist in their time; they may have had no occasion to mention her, or the figure may have been so vague and unimportant as not to call for special mention. For such a figure it is natural to assume a long development, the beginnings of which are, of course, enveloped in obscurity. However this may be, the Sibyl appears to have received full form under the religious impulse of post-Homeric times, under conditions the details of which are not known to us.

937. In the scant notices of the figure that have been preserved the indications are that there was originally only one Sibyl — she was the mythical embodiment of divine revelation, as the muse was the embodiment of intellectual inspiration. At a

---

1 Their "visions" sometimes show literary art (Ezek. xl ff.; Zech. i–viii).
2 Roscher, *Lexikon*, article "Sibylla."
3 That is, she was not to be tolerated as a rival of the great oracular god.
4 Cf. Wissowa, *Religion der Römer*, pp. 239, 462 ff.

later time many sibyls came into being; Varro reckons ten and other authors give other numbers. Apparently a process of local differentiation went on; when the idea of the revealer was once established and the historical beginnings of the figure were unknown, many a place would be ambitious to have so noble a figure domiciled in its midst. One line of tradition referred the original Sibyl to the Ionian Erythræ, and when the Sibylline Books were burned in the year 83 B.C., it was to Erythræ that the Romans sent to make a new collection of oracles. Whatever the original home of the figure, one of the most famous of the Sibyls was she of Cumæ.[1] She was regarded as being very old, and she was probably a permanent diviner of that place. It was from Cumæ, according to the legend, that the Sibylline Books came to Rome. The story of how they were first offered to King Tarquinius Priscus, who refused to pay the price, how three of them were destroyed and then three more, and how finally the required price was paid for the remaining three, points to a belief that the material of the oracles had once been larger than that which came to Rome. There is also the assertion that the utterances of the Sibyl were at that time recorded in books. This fact suggests that oracular responses had long been known at Cumæ, and that some persons, of whose character and functions we know nothing, had from time to time written them down, so that a handbook of divination had come into existence.

938. In whatever manner the oracles were first brought to Rome it is certain that they were accepted by the Romans in all good faith, and they came to play a very important part in the conduct of public affairs. They were placed in the temple of Jupiter Capitolinus under the charge of two men (*duumviri*), and later a college was established for their guardianship. They were used in Rome especially for guidance in national calamities: when the existence of the city was threatened by the victorious career of Hannibal, it was the Sibyl who prescribed the importation of the worship of the Phrygian Great Mother. It is certain that the books were manipulated by political and religious leaders for their

---

[1] Bouché-Leclercq, *Histoire de la divination dans l'antiquité,* ii, Index, s.v. *Cumes.*

own purposes, old dicta being recast and new ones inserted as occasion required ;[1] but probably this procedure was unknown to the people — it does not appear that it affected their faith. Even Augustine speaks of the theurgi as dæmones, and cites a passage from the Erythræan Sibyl as a prediction of Christ.[2]

939. To the poetical books which have come down to us under the name of Jewish Sibylline Oracles no value attaches for the history of the Sibyl except so far as they are an indication of the hold that the conception kept on men's minds.[3] They are a product of the passion for apocalyptic writing that prevailed among the Jews and Christians in Palestine and Alexandria, from the second century B.C. into the third century of our era. The fame of the Græco-Roman Sibyl was widespread, and to the Jews and Christians of that time it seemed proper that she should be made to predict the history of Judaism and Christianity ; possibly it was believed that such a prophetess must have spoken of this history. Naturally the Jewish Sibyl has a Biblical genealogy — she is the daughter of Noah.

940. Her utterances, given in heavy Greek hexameters, have been preserved for us in a great mass of ill-arranged fragments, with many repetitions, indicating them as the work of various authors. What we have is clearly only a part of what was produced, but the nature of the whole body of pseudo-predictions is easily understood from the material that has been preserved. They follow the history down to the author's time, giving it sometimes an enigmatical form, and the future is described in vague phrases that embody the guesses or hopes of the writer. It seems certain that all of the existent material of these oracles is from Jewish and Christian hands. Even when Greek mythical stories are introduced, as in the euhemeristic description of the origin of the

---

[1] Wissowa, *Religion der Römer*, p. 463; Fowler, *Religious Experience of the Roman People*, p. 339.

[2] Augustine, *De Civitate Dei*, x, 27 (in connection with Vergil's verses, *Eclogues*, iv, 13 f.) ; xxviii, 23 (the initial letters in *Sibylline Oracles*, viii, 268–309, giving a title of Christ). So Eusebius, in his report of the Oration of Constantine, xviii ; cf. Lactantius, *Divinae Institutiones*, lib. i, cap. vi.

[3] *Oracula Sibyllina*, ed. Alexandre (Greek text, with Latin tr.) ; ed. Friedlieb (Greek text, with German tr. and additions by Volkmann) ; ed. Rzack (critical Greek text); Terry, *The Sibylline Oracles* (Eng. tr., blank verse).

Greek dynasties of gods in the third book, the whole is conceived under the forms of Jewish or Christian thought. The Sibyllines are quoted by Josephus and by many Christian writers from Justin Martyr to Augustine and Jerome and later. They give a picture of certain Jewish and Christian ideas of the period and of the opinions held concerning certain political events, but otherwise have no historical value. An illustration of the fact that the belief in them as real inspired prediction continued to a late time is found in the hymn *Dies Irae*, in which the Sibyl is cited along with David as a prophet of the last judgment. The whole history of the figure is a remarkable illustration of the power of a written record, held to be a divine revelation, to impress men's minds and control their beliefs and actions.

941. While divination has played a great part in the religious history of the world, it has rarely brought about important political or religious results.[1] The exceptions are the great Greek oracles of Dodona and Delphi and the Roman Sibylline Books ; to these last, as is observed above, the Roman people owed the introduction of some important religious cults. But for ordinary procedures priests and other officiators everywhere were disposed to give favorable responses, especially to the questions of prominent men ; and military and other political enterprises were usually in such form that they could not conveniently be modified in accordance with unfavorable omens — the omen had to be favorable. There were exceptions, but this was the general rule. The science of divination, however, did good service in fostering the observation of natural phenomena, and especially in the development of astronomy and anatomy. In connection with these observations it called into being bodies of men — corporations that in process of time became centers of general culture.

942. On the ethical side it may be doubted whether divination has been an advantage to society. It has produced much deceit,

---

[1] On the attitude of early Greek philosophers (Pythagoras, Democritus, Empedocles, Thales, Xenophanes) toward divination, and the relation of the latter to the idea of divine providence, see Bouché-Leclercq, *Histoire de la divination dans l'antiquité*, i, 29 ff.

unconscious and conscious. Whether diviners believed or did not believe in their science, the result was bad. If they did not believe, they fostered a system of deceit. Whether there was real belief or not, the practice of divination encouraged false methods and turned men's minds away from immediate appeals to the deity, and in general from a spiritual conception of religion. On the other hand, it helped to maintain the external apparatus of religion, which for ancient life was an important thing. Like all great institutions its effects have been partly good, partly bad. It belongs to a lower stage of human thought and tends to disappear gradually before enlightenment.

CHAPTER IX

THE HIGHER THEISTIC DEVELOPMENT

943. The preceding survey of early religious customs and institutions discloses a recognizable unity in diversity. Everywhere we find the same classes of sacred objects and the same methods of approaching them. Whether the supernatural Powers are conceived of as animals or as plants or as what we call inanimate things, or, in more advanced thought, as ghosts or spirits or gods, they are held to be factors in human life, are regarded with awe, are dreaded and avoided, or are welcomed as helpers, and in any case are propitiated by gifts and other marks of respect. The potency inherent in things is the object of observation, its laws are studied, and it is used for purposes of life. The diversities in the form of ceremonies, in the conception of the characters of the Powers, and in the general tone and coloring of worship arise from economic and cultural differences, and are as numerous as the tribes of men; the unity of cults is a result of the psychological unity of the human race — the religious needs of men in all stages of culture are the same; there is nothing in the highest religious systems that is not found in germ in the lowest.

944. The earliest expression of religious feeling, as is pointed out above,[1] is in the form of ceremonies. But ceremonies tend to group themselves round the persons of divine beings. Gods, as the controllers of human fortunes here and hereafter, naturally become the centers of religious thought. Their characters and functions reflect the ideals of their worshipers, and all ritualistic and other usages and all doctrines concerning the relations between gods and men and, in general, all ideas concerning the physical and moral constitution of the world attach themselves perforce to

[1] See Chapter iii.

the divine embodiments of these ideals. Thus, in one sense, the history of the gods is the history of religion. From the earliest times up to the present the efforts of men have been directed toward defining the divine Powers that have been supposed to stand behind all phenomena. The problem of harmonizing diverse divine activities has always been a serious one, and its solution has been sought in various ways. Gods have been locally limited, every one to his own human tribe, district, or nation; or, when they dwell together and their spheres of influence are larger, they have been given free scope of action, and the resulting contradictions in human affairs have been accepted as a part of the mysterious nature of things; or order has been sought in simplification — headship has been ascribed to some one deity, and the relation between him and the subordinate divinities has been somehow explained or has been left unexplained. The process of simplification has gone steadily on with the result that the great religious systems of the world fall into groups distinguished from one another by their conceptions of the divine government of the world, whether as pluralistic or as unitary. The development of these different conceptions may be traced here in outline, though the absence of exact data and the variety and complexity of the formative influences (economic, philosophical, political, and other) necessarily make it difficult or impossible to account satisfactorily for all details. The groups to be considered are polytheism, dualism, and monotheism, to which may be added brief mention of systems that do not recognize a personal divine ruler of the world.

POLYTHEISM

945. The first stage in the final theistic history of the world up to the present day, polytheism, appears in all the great civilized nations. The great polytheistic systems have much in common: for example, protection of civil order and morality by a god; prominence of the god of a ruling tribe or family or of a great city; disposition to embody certain general facts, as war, love, learning, in divine figures; tendency to make some god universal. On the other hand, they differ among themselves in certain regards : in the degree of specialization and differentiation of divine functions, and in the stress that they lay on the various departments of human life. Their agreements and disagreements seem to be in some cases independent of racial relations and climatic conditions ; their roots lie so far back in history that we have no means of tracing their genesis and development.

946. The Egyptian and the Semitic peoples were parts of the same original stock,[1] and their systems of social and political organization were substantially identical — the government in its developed form was monarchical, but tribal and other locally isolated forms of organization maintained themselves to a certain extent — and their literary and artistic outputs do not differ materially. We might, then, expect their religions to be in the main identical. In fact they agree in having a relative meagerness of theistic differentiation, but in some important points they are far apart. The Semites were indifferent to the future life, the Egyptians constructed it elaborately (in this point taking precedence among the ancients) ; the Semites were averse to divinizing human beings, for the Egyptians kings were divine. In this last point Egypt resembles China, but in other respects is at a world-wide remove from it. Other peoples thought of their gods as having relations with beasts ; the Egyptians alone, among civilized nations, worshiped the living animal.[2] Some Greek writers regarded Egypt as the religious mother of Greece, but Hellenic cults show little resemblance to Egyptian.

947. The Hebrews had the general Semitic theistic and cultic scheme, but in their capacity (in their higher development) to content themselves with one deity, and in their elaboration of ritualistic forms and institutions, were more closely akin to the Aryan Persians than to any Semitic community, and borrowed freely from them. The resemblance between the two cults, however, was confined to these two points ; in other respects they were very different.

948. The linguistic identity of the Indo-European peoples does not carry with it theologic identity. The theistic scheme of India

---

[1] Cf. Barton, *Semitic Origins*, chap. i.
[2] Cf. Breasted, *Religion and Thought in Ancient Egypt*.

is more nearly allied, in the disposition to grant equality of significance to all gods, to the Egyptian and Semitic than to the Persian and the Greek, yet the tone and color of the Hindu deities do not resemble the tone and color of the Egyptian and Babylonian divinities.

. Even between Greece and Rome the religious differences are great. Greece stands alone in its artistic creation of divine forms. Rome rather resembles the Hebrews in its sobriety of theistic creations, and particularly is like the Chinese in the purpose to make religion subservient to the interests of the family and the State ; Roman religion, like Chinese, might be described as a body of public and private ceremonies to which gods were attached.[1] The Roman gods, however, are much more definite figures than the Chinese ; the latter are either unimportant folk-gods or powers of nature.

949. The contrast between Mexico, with its considerable number of departmental gods, some of them savage, and Peru, whose quasi-monotheistic system is relatively mild, is striking. But the origin of these two peoples (who perhaps are made up of different sets of tribes) is involved in obscurity, and it is uncertain whether or not we should expect a greater resemblance between their cults.

950. The differentiation in the theistic scheme of the Teutons, especially the Scandinavians, is noteworthy. Several of their deities, particularly Wodan (Odin), Thor, and Loki, are well-developed persons, and these and some others do not differ materially in character from the earlier corresponding Hindu and Greek gods. A comparison between the Teutonic figures and the Celtic and Slavic would be pertinent if we knew more of the character of these last ; but the information about them is slight.[2]

951. The extent of the anthropomorphization of gods in any system may be measured by the richness and refinement of its mythology. When the gods live apart from men, being conceived

---

[1] Fowler, *Religious Experience of the Roman People*, chaps. i, xvi.

[2] Bertrand, *La religion des Gaulois* ; Rhys, *Celtic Heathendom*; Usener, *Götternamen*; articles " Celts " and " Aryan Religion " in Hastings, *Encyclopædia of Religion and Ethics*.

of mainly as transcendent Powers, or when they are not fully developed men, there is little room for the play of social emotions and for the creation of biographies of individual deities. It is the humanized god that has emotional life, and it is in this mythical life that the religious feeling of the worshiper is expressed with greatest fullness of detail.

952. The development of mythology through all its gradations of fullness and fineness can be traced in the religious systems of the world.[1] Where there is no recognizable worship there is, of course, no mythology. This is the case in Australia, in Pygmy lands, in Tierra del Fuego, in parts of New Guinea, and perhaps elsewhere.[2] Scarcely above these are parts of Central and Southern Africa, the countries of the Bantu, the Hottentots, and the Bushmen.[3] A feeble mythological invention appears among the Zulus, whose conception of gods is indistinct;[4] and the Masai and the Nandi, who are somewhat farther advanced in the construction of deities, show mythopœic imagination in a single case only (the famous myth of the embrace of the earth and the sky), and this is perhaps borrowed.[5] Along with these we may place the Todas whose theogonic conceptions appear to have been cramped by their buffalo cult, and their mythical material is small and vague.[6]

953. A somewhat higher stage of mythopoetic development is represented by peoples of Oceania and North America. The myths are still prevailingly cosmologic and sociologic, but the beginning of biographical sketches of supernatural Powers is visible. The Melanesian Qat and the Polynesian Maui are on the border line between culture-heroes and gods, but they are real persons, and their adventures, while they describe origins, are also descriptions of character. Hawaii and Borneo have departmental gods and

---

[1] Cf. the sketch given above, Chapter vii ; Tylor, *Primitive Culture* ; Frazer, *Golden Bough*, 2d ed., passim.

[2] Spencer and Gillen, *Native Tribes of Central Australia*, and *Northern Tribes of Central Australia* ; Howitt, *Native Tribes of South-East Australia* ; Quatrefages, *The Pygmies* ; Hyades and Deniker, *Mission scientifique du cap Horn* ; Seligmann, *The Melanesians of British New Guinea*.

[3] Fritsch, *Die Eingeborenen Süd-Afrika's* ; article " Bantu " in Hastings, *Encyclopædia of Religion and Ethics*. [4] Callaway, *The Amazulu*. [5] See above, § 837.
[6] Rivers, *The Todas*.

a body of stories about them.[1] Certain tribes of Redmen have not only divine genealogical systems but also narratives resembling the Melanesian in character, the line between myth proper and folk-lore being often hard to trace.[2] The stories fall into more or less well-defined groups, and of the Coyote and, less definitely, of certain other personages biographies might be written.

954. The half-civilized peoples of Madagascar, West Africa (Dahomi, Ashanti, Yoruba), the Malay Peninsula, and Southern India (Khonds) have more coherent figures and stories of divine personages.[3] Here something like living human beings appear, though there is crudeness in the portraiture, and the interest is chiefly in the history of origins. The Malayan and Khond figures are especially noteworthy, but are not free from the suspicion of influence from higher religions.

955. True literary mythology is found only in civilized peoples, and among these a gradation is recognizable. We have first the stage of culture represented by the Japanese, the Finns, the Mexicans, and the Peruvians, with fairly well-developed gods, who have emotions and histories. In this group Japan takes the lowest place;[4] it is chiefly in the figures regarded as deified men that definiteness of character and human warmth are found. Japanese theogony was depressed by the interest of the people in family and State organization; the gods, though civilized, are vague personalities. The Finnish literary mythical material, given in the Kalevala, has a highly humanized coloring and is worked up into a coherent story; the social system revealed in the myths is superior in many regards to that of the Redmen, but the theistic scheme is crude.[5]

---

[1] Codrington, *The Melanesians*; W. Ellis, *Polynesian Researches*; Williams and Calvert, *Fiji*; Turner, *Samoa*; Krämer, *Die Samoa-Inseln*; Taylor, *New Zealand*; H. Ling Roth, *The Natives of Sarawak and British North Borneo.*

[2] Brinton, *The Lenâpé*; Matthews, *Navaho Legends*; Dorsey, *Traditions of the Skidi Pawnee*; Teit, *Thompson River Indians*; Boas, *The Kwakiutl*; Dixon, *The Northern Maidu* and *The Shasta*; *Journal of American Folklore*, passim.

[3] Van Gennep, *Tabou et totémisme à Madagascar*; A. B. Ellis, *Ewe, Tshi, Yoruba*; Skeat, *Malay Magic*; Skeat and Blagden, *Pagan Races of the Malay Peninsula*; Hopkins, *Religions of India.*

[4] Aston, *Shinto*; Knox, *Development of Religion in Japan.*

[5] *The Kalevala*; Castrén, *Finnische Mythologie.*

The few Mexican myths that have come down to us (probably only the remains out of a large mass) show reflection and portray human experiences.[1] Both in Mexico and in Peru the Spanish conquest appears to have destroyed no little material that, if preserved, would have illustrated the mythical constructions of these lands. In Peru, further, it may be that the monotheistic tinge of the State religion had the effect of banishing subordinate deities and the stories connected with them. For whatever reason little is known of its mythical material, but the little that is known shows a certain degree of refinement. South America, excluding Peru, has no mythical constructions of interest.[2]

956. Of the great religions the Chinese may be passed by in the present sketch; its form leaves no place for mythology; its virtual monotheism excludes lesser supernatural figures as actors in the drama of human life.[3]

957. The Persian cosmogonic myths are merely statements of great facts without biographical features. In the hands of late writers they shaded into legendary accounts of the origin of the kingdom, and the whole was colored by the developed Mazdaism. We thus have theological constructions rather than true myths.[4] The few mythical stories that have survived play an insignificant part in the religious system — a sort of result that is to be expected whenever a substantially definite monotheistic conception has been reached.

958. Egypt produced a couple of myths of great interest.[5] The story of Ra's anger with men, and his act of wholesale destruction, belongs in the group of myths (in which flood stories and others are included) the motif of which is antagonism between gods and men. The conception of such antagonism seems to go back to the

---

[1] Prescott, *Conquest of Mexico* and *Conquest of Peru*; Winsor, *Narrative and Critical History of America*; Brinton, *American Hero-Myths*, Index; Lang, *Myth, Ritual, and Religion*, Index, s.vv. *Mexican Divine Myths* and *Peruvian Myths*.

[2] Ehrenreich, *Mythen und Legenden der südamericanischen Urvölker*.

[3] De Groot, *Religious System of China*.

[4] The *Avesta*; Spiegel, *Eranische Alterthumskunde*, vol. ii, bk. iv, chaps. i, ii; De Harlez, *Avesta*, Introduction, p. lxxxiv ff.; *The Shahnameh*.

[5] Maspero, *Dawn of Civilization*, p. 155 ff.; Steindorff, *Religion of the Ancient Egyptians*, p. 106 ff.

early opinion that all misfortunes were caused by supernatural beings; in civilized times some great calamity would be singled out as a special result of divine anger, and imagination would construct a history of the event, why the god was angry, and how he was appeased. What particular occurrence this Egyptian story refers to is unknown.

The Osiris myth has better literary form and more cultic significance.[1] The slaying of Osiris by Set, Isis's search for the body of her husband, and the rôle of the young Horus as avenger of his father make a coherent history. Osiris had the singular fortune of being the most widely popular god in Egypt, the hero of a romantic episode, and the ethical judge of men in the Underworld. The motif of the myth is the cosmic struggle between life and death; the actors are made real persons, and the story is instinct with human interest. No great cultic association like the Eleusinian mysteries was created in connection with it, but the echo of the conception appears in the great rôle later assigned to Isis.

959. All Semitic myths of which we have records are cosmogonic or sociologic or, in some late forms, theological constructions. It is Babylonia that has furnished the greater part of the material, perhaps all of it.[2] The stories preserved give little or no portraiture of divine persons — it is always cosmic phenomena that are described, and gods and heroes are introduced simply as actors. The purpose in the two cosmogonic poems — to explain the reduction of the world to order and the existing constitution of earth and sky — is one that is found everywhere in ancient systems of thought. The Gilgamesh epic, a collection of popular usages and tales without definite unity, is contaminated with legend; Gilgamesh is now a god, now a national hero; at the end, however, there is a bit of speculation concerning the future state of men. Ishtar's descent to the Underworld is a pure nature myth; Ishtar and the goddess of the Underworld are real persons, yet merely attachments to the

---

[1] Plutarch, *Isis and Osiris*; Steindorff, op. cit., Index, s.vv. *Isis* and *Osiris*; Roscher, *Lexikon*, articles "Isis," "Usire."

[2] R. F. Harper, *Assyrian and Babylonian Literature*; Jastrow, *Aspects of Religious Belief and Practice in Babylonia and Assyria*, Index, s.v. *Myths*.

fact. The seizure of the tablets of fate from Bel by the storm-god Zu represents some natural phenomenon (perhaps the reign of winter), possibly, also, a transference of headship from one deity to another. The story of Adapa is in part an explanation of how men came to lose immortality. There is, thus, in these myths a fairly full history of the origin of the large facts of human life, with little interest in the personalities of the divine actors.

Hebrew mythical material is in general identical with Babylonian; its Old Testament form has been more or less revised by late monotheistic editors. The two cosmogonies in Genesis, the flood story, and the dragon of chaos (a late figure in the Old Testament [1]) are merely descriptions of cosmic or local facts. The dispersion at Babel (not now found in Babylonian records, but paralleled elsewhere) deals with a sociological fact of great interest for the Hebrews, marking them off, as it did, from all other peoples.[2] The heroes of the early time[3] belong to folk-lore, probably a mixture of myth and legend. The explanation of various human experiences in the Eden story[4] appears to be of Hebrew origination; it is, however, rather a late theological theory than a myth. The Syrian and Palestinian Tammuz (Adonis) myth is identical in general form with the Babylonian myth of Tammuz and Ishtar.[5]

960. The Indo-European mythical material shows an advance over the Egyptian and Semitic in distinctness and fullness of life corresponding to the distincter individuality of the Indo-European divine personages. These are not mere powers in the world, more or less identified with natural forces and phenomena, nor a collection of deities substantially identical in character and functions; they have grown into persons, differing, indeed, in the degree of individualization, but all pronounced personalities.

---

[1] Job xxvi, 12 ; Ps. lxxxix, 11 [10] ; Isa. li, 9.   [2] Deut. xxxii, 8 f.
[3] Gen. iv, 17 ff. ; v, vi, 4 ; Ezek. xxxii, 27 (revised text).
[4] Gen. iii, 14 ff. On the loss of immortality see above, § 834.
[5] On the ceremony of mourning for Tammuz (Ezek. viii, 14) see Jastrow, *Religion of Babylonia and Assyria*, p. 574 ff.; Pseudo-Lucian, *De Syria Dea*. In Babylonia the ceremony appears to have been an official lament for the loss of vegetation (the women mourners being attached to the temple) ; in Syria (Hierapolis) it took on orgiastic elements (perhaps an importation from Asia Minor). The women of Ezek. viii were attached, probably, to the service of the temple.

961. Hindu myths, though less numerous and less highly elaborated than the Greek, still reflect fairly well the characters of certain divinities, especially Indra, Agni, the Açvins, the Maruts, and some others.[1] Indra, particularly, is portrayed in detail, so that he is as distinct a person as Ares or Mars. Krishna and other figures in the epics live human lives with all human virtues and vices.

962. The full literary form of the myth is found only in Greece. As Zeus, Apollo, Athene, Aphrodite, and others are well-defined personalities, each with certain intellectual and moral characteristics and with a unity of development, so the stories about them recount adventures and acts that form biographical unities; and, as these stories are of diverse nature, some reflecting barbarous periods, others marked by refinement, they exhibit, when brought together and arranged in order of moral or intellectual excellence or according to their geographical or ethnical origin, not only the history of the gods, but also the development of Greek religious feeling. Being the embodiment of human experiences, they lend themselves readily to processes of allegorizing and spiritualizing.[2]

963. Roman gods, homely figures, occupied with agriculture and affairs of State, have no adventures and no biographies. The practical Roman mind was concerned with the domestic functions of divine beings, and the Roman genius was not of a sort to conceive gods as individuals leading lives filled with human passions. Myths do not figure in the Roman religious scheme except as they are borrowed from Greece or from some other land.

964. Teutonic mythology is largely cosmogonic or cosmologic, not without shrewd portraitures and attractive episodes, but never reaching the point of artistic roundness and grace.[3] The adventures of Odin, Thor, Loki, and other divine persons reflect for the most part the daring and savagery of the viking age, though there are

---

[1] Barth, *Religions of India*; Hopkins, *Religions of India*; Macdonell, *Vedic Mythology*; Lang, *Myth, Ritual, and Religion*, Index.

[2] This is true of all mythical and legendary creations of the thought of communities, but in an especial degree of the Greek.

[3] Saussaye, *Religion of the Teutons*, Index, s.v. *Myths*; he distinguishes between the earlier and the later stories; R. M. Meyer, *Altgermanische Religionsgeschichte*, chaps. iii, iv.

kindly features and an occasional touch of humor.[1] Loki in some stories is a genuine villain, and the death of Balder is a real tragedy. The great cosmogonic and eschatological myths are conceived in grandiose style. The struggle between gods and giants is in its basis the widespread nature myth of the conflict of seasons. The overthrow of the old divine government (the Twilight of the Gods) and the rise of a new order appear to have a Christian coloring, but the belief that the world is to be destroyed may be old Teutonic.[2]

The history of theistic movements in civilized peoples shows that the effectiveness of a polytheistic system as a framework of religious life is in proportion to the extent of its anthropomorphization of deities, that is, it is in proportion to their humanization that gods enter into intimate association with human experiences. On the other hand, it is true that the tendency toward a unitary conception of the divine government of the world is in inverse proportion to such humanization; the more definitely aloof from men the gods have stood (as among the Hebrews and the Persians), the easier it has been for the people to attach themselves to a single deity as all-sufficient. The Romans form no exception to this general rule, for though, while they did not create great anthropomorphic deities, there was yet no native Roman movement toward monolatry, the place of such deities in worship was taken by a multitude of minor divine patrons who presided over all the details of private and public life and satisfied the demand for divine guidance.

While polytheism has assumed various forms, differing from one another in elaboration of deities and in general cultural character, it has had, as a system, a distinctly marked place in human experience.

965. *General rôle of polytheism.* Polytheism has played a great rôle in the religious history of the world. Representing in general a thoughtful protest against the earlier shapeless mass of spirits, it expressed more definitely the belief in the intellectual and moral divine control of all things. It flourished at a time when there was no general demand in human thought for coöperation in

---

[1] Folk-lore and legend mingle with the myths.
[2] See R. M. Meyer, op. cit., p. 444 ff.

supernatural Powers. The sense of variety in the world was predominant, corresponding to the absence of coöperation among the tribes and nations of the world; the apparently isolated character of natural phenomena and the independence of the nations, each of the others, seemed to men to demand a number of separate divine agencies. These were all made to accord with the external and internal condition of their worshipers and met the demands of life in that they represented redemption, salvation, and, in general, all blessings. They were not offensive ethically to the people for the reason that they embodied the ethical conceptions and usages of their time. Thus they furnished the framework for religious feeling — they secured the union of divine and human in life, brought the divine, indeed, into most intimate contact with the human, and so supplied the material for the expression of pious feeling. When the gods were represented by idols, these tended to become merely the symbols and reminders of their divine originals. The elastic character of this theistic system permitted the widest variety of cults, with the possibility of bringing any new social tendency or idea into immediate connection with a divine patron, so that human life became religious with a degree of intelligence and intensity that has perhaps not existed under any other system.

966. The great civilizations of the ancient world arose and were developed under polytheism — many noble human characters and customs and institutions were created under the dominance of this system in Babylonia, Egypt, Greece, Rome, and elsewhere — that is to say, human instincts and aspirations developed freely under a theistic organization that satisfied in general the intellectual and moral needs of the time. The different polytheistic cults of the world differed considerably in intellectual and moral value. These differences pertain to the diversity of characteristics among the nations of the world and are to be studied in connection with the histories of the various peoples. Here it is sufficient to note the general position which polytheism has occupied in the whole religious development of the world.[1]

---

[1] Even in great modern religions nominally monotheistic a virtual polytheism continues to exist.

967. At a relatively early time, however, dissatisfaction arose with the discordances of the polytheistic conception. It raised many problems and failed to account for many phenomena, and efforts were made to systematize and simplify the conceptions of the divine government of the world. These efforts took the shape of dualism, monotheism, pantheism, Buddhism, Confucianism, and later tended to regard the supernatural in the world as Ultimate Force or as Moral Ideal. These tendencies may be examined in the order just given.

DUALISM

968. In all the religious systems so far considered the existence of human suffering is assumed. The sole object of religious practices, in all cults except the highest, has been to secure extrahuman or superhuman aid and comfort in the ills of life. There has been the conviction, for the most part implicit, that man is not in harmony with his surroundings. We have now to consider those systems of religious thought in which the existence of this disharmony is more or less distinctly announced and the effort is made to discover its source.

The conception of two sets of Powers in the world, one helpful and the other harmful, is suggested by human experience and by the larger observation of natural phenomena, and it is found all over the world, among low communities as well as high, perhaps in all tribes of men.[1] Possibly there are some low groups, such as the Fuegians and the African Pygmies in which the conception does not exist; but as the religious ideas of these low groups are yet imperfectly understood, we cannot say what their position on this point is. In general, for the lower tribes the world is peopled by spirits, which are the ghosts of the departed or the embodiment of natural forces, and the feeling has been that these are sometimes friendly, sometimes unfriendly.[2] In some cases the hurtful spirits stand in contrast with a god who may be a strict ruler

---

[1] See above, § 683 ff.

[2] This conception survives in the great polytheistic cults, and may be recognized in the later religions of redemption.

and somewhat indifferent to men, but not hostile; in other cases there is a simple division of spirits into two classes, the friendly and the unfriendly,[1] and in the higher forms of savage life there may be two such classes of deities.[2] The double feeling of man respecting the attitude of ghosts toward living human beings is referred to above.[3]

969. In certain higher forms of savage and half-civilized life we find the conception of a definite contrast between the two sets of Powers. The Hottentots are said to believe in two opposed supernatural beings, the struggle between them ending to the advantage of the one who is beneficent toward men.[4] The Masai have two powerful beings, one accounted good, the other bad; the difference between them is not ethical, but represents only the relation of their acts to man's well-being.[5] The Malays have a very elaborate system of good and evil spirits, but the system is colored by foreign influences.[6] For the Ainu snakes are an embodiment of merely physical evil, and other Powers are the dispensers of physical well-being.[7] The Arab jinn represent the unwholesome and antagonistic conditions of nature, stand opposed to the gods, and are without ethical motives.[8] Even the Andamanese, one of the lowest of human communities, have a division of Powers into one who is friendly and two who are unfriendly.[9] In all these cases we have to recognize simply the expression of the perception of two sets of physical agencies in the world. It is easy to exaggerate the

---

[1] Compare the Brazilian Tapuyas (Botocudos); see article "Brazil" in Hastings, *Encyclopædia of Religion and Ethics*.

[2] For West Africa cf. A. B. Ellis, *Yoruba*, p. 87; *Tshi*, chaps. iii–viii; *Ewe*, chaps. iii–v.

[3] § 365 ff. On this attitude see the reports of the religions of particular peoples and the summaries of such reports in dictionaries and encyclopedias, and in such works as Steinmetz, *Ethnologische Studien zur ersten Entwicklung der Strafe*; Westermarck, *Origin and Development of the Moral Ideas*; also articles in the *Journal of the Anthropological Institute*, the reports of the American Bureau of Ethnology, and similar publications. [4] Theoph. Hahn, *Tsuni-Goam*, p. 38.

[5] Hollis, *The Masai*, p. 264 f. [6] Skeat, *Malay Magic*, pp. 93 ff., 320 ff.

[7] Batchelor, *The Ainu*, pp. 195 f., 200.

[8] Wellhausen, *Reste arabischen Heidentumes*, p. 135 ff.; W. R. Smith, *Religion of the Semites*, Index, s.v. *Jinn*.

[9] R. C. Temple, article "Andamans" in Hastings, *Encyclopædia of Religion and Ethics*.

nature of these contrasts and to represent certain low tribes as possessing general divine embodiments of good and evil.

970. Such a conception has been attributed to the American Redmen,[1] but on insufficient grounds. The most careful recent investigations of the religious ideas of the Creeks, the Lenâpé, the Pawnees, and the Californian Shasta (four typical communities) fail to discover anything that can be called a real dualistic conception.[2] Dorsey mentions a Pawnee myth of the introduction of death into the world by a member of the heavenly council of gods who felt himself slighted; but this isolated story does not prove the existence of a general dualistic scheme — the act in question has parallels in savage systems that recognize various unfriendly Powers.[3] The reports we have of two definite morally antagonistic deities in Redmen tribes resolve themselves on examination into misconceptions or exaggerations on the part of the reporters; or, so far as the antagonism really exists, it is due to Christian influence. The Iroquois dualistic system as described by Chief Cusic (in 1825) — two brothers, Good Mind and Bad Mind, the former the creator of all things good, the latter the creator of all things bad — appears in the version of Brébeuf (in 1636) as a simple nature myth, the two deities in question being somewhat more definite forms of the friendly and unfriendly spirits met with in all lower communities.[4] In like manner Winslow's two opposed Powers of the New England Algonkins turn out not to be morally antagonistic to each other, in fact, according to Brinton, not antagonistic at all.[5] These facts warn us to treat with caution the vague

---

[1] For example, by Waitz, *Anthropologie*, iii, pp. 182 f., 330, 334 f.; Waitz expresses doubt (p. 345) as to the correctness of certain accounts of the religious ideas of the Oregon tribes.

[2] Gatschet, *Migration Legend of the Creeks*, p. 215 f.; Brinton, *The Lenâpé*, p. 67 f.; Dorsey, *The Skidi Pawnee*, p. xviii f.; Dixon, *The Shasta*, p. 491 ff.

[3] On methods of accounting for the existence of death in the world see above, § 834.

[4] Brébeuf's account is given in *Relation des Jésuites dans la nouvelle France*, 1635, p. 34; 1636, p. 100; cf. the edition of the *Relation* by R. G. Thwaites, viii, 116 ff.; x, 126 f. Brébeuf appears to have followed Sagard, *Canada* (see Troas ed., p. 452 ff.). The story is discussed by Brinton, in *Myths of the New World*, 3d ed., p. 79 ff., and his criticism is adopted by Tylor, *Primitive Culture*, 3d ed., ii, 322.

[5] Brinton, op. cit., p. 77.

statements of early travelers respecting dualistic views supposed to be held by tribes in North America and South America.[1]

971. In West Africa the Ashanti embody the sources of physical misfortune in several deities, who are malignant but do not stand in opposition to the friendly gods. A preliminary step to the conception of a god of misfortunes is the assignment of a sort of headship to one of a mass of unfriendly or hurtful spirits — such a crude organization is natural in a community in which there is a fairly developed form of social organization, and the head spirit easily grows into a god. A simple headship over hurtful spirits appears to be found in the Ainu system, though this latter is in general not well developed.[2]

972. A definite antagonism of good and bad Powers is found in the religion of the non-Aryan Khonds of Orissa: the earth-goddess Tari, the creature but the opponent of the sun-god Bella Pennu, introduced sin and death into the world and contested (and, according to one native account, still contests) with her creator the control of life. This explanation of the origin of death is a higher form of stories that occur abundantly in savage lore, with the important difference that in these death comes by accident, but here by malicious purpose. It is not clear whether or not the characters of Tari and Bella Pennu are conceived of ethically. The weapons (comets, winds, mountains) employed by the two deities indicate that the basis of the representation is a nature myth. Advanced eschatological thought appears in the opinion, held by some natives, that the good god was victorious in the contest.[3]

973. In the great ancient religions, with the exception of Zoroastrianism, no dualistic scheme appears. An Egyptian god may be angry, as, for example, Ra, who in a fit of resentment causes men to be slain but soon repents; and Set, the enemy of Osiris, a nature god, seemed at one time to be on the way to become an embodiment of evil, but the Egyptian cult rejected this idea and

---

[1] Cf. Tylor, *Primitive Culture*, ii, 324 ff.; article "Algonquins" in Hastings, *Encyclopædia of Religion and Ethics*, pp. 320, 323.

[2] Batchelor, *The Ainu*, and his article in Hastings, op. cit.

[3] Hopkins, *Religions of India*, p. 528 ff. The influence of Brahmanism is possible here; but cf. Hopkins, op. cit., p. 530, note 3.

Set gradually disappeared.[1] The Babylonian cosmogonic myth, in which Tiamat is the enemy of the gods of order, has no cultic significance; the great mass of demonic beings was not organized into a kingdom of evil, and the Underworld deities, nature gods, while subject to ordinary human passions, are not hostile to the gods of heaven and earth. The Hebrews adopted the Babylonian cosmogonic myth,[2] but it became a mere literary attachment to the conception of the supreme god Yahweh, and was otherwise ineffective.

974. The same thing is true of certain cosmogonic myths of the Greeks, such as the war of the Titans against Zeus and similar episodes. Ate and the Erinyes are embodiments of man's own evil nature or represent the punishment that overtakes guilt, but they do not represent a formal opposition to goodness nor are they organized into a definite body.[3] The Roman Furies are practically identical in function with the Erinyes. In the old Teutonic religion the only figure who approaches essential badness is Loki; but he, though at times malignant and treacherous (as a human chieftain might be), remains a recognized member of the assembly of gods. As a nature god he may represent the elements of darkness and unhappiness in life, just as the various evil spirits in the world do, but he never approaches the position of an independent creator of evil.[4] The Celtic deities Llew and Dylan are said to stand over against each other and to represent good and bad tendencies and elements of life; but they are not very distinct and are probably nothing more than somewhat developed local deities.[5] In the Chinese

---

[1] Maspero, *Dawn of Civilization*, pp. 172, 202 ; Breasted, *History of Egypt*, p. 571 ; Steindorff, *Religion of the Ancient Egyptians*, p. 67 ff.

[2] This myth may have trickled down to them (through the Canaanites or in some other way) in subdued form — it appears, perhaps, in the serpent of Gen. iii ; but it seems to have been adopted in full form at a later time, apparently in or after the sixth century B.C.

[3] Rohde, *Psyche*, Index, s.v. *Erinyen* ; articles "Ate," "Erinys," in Roscher's *Lexikon*.

[4] On the diverse elements in Loki's character, and on his diabolification, see Saussaye, *Religion of the Teutons*, p. 259 ff.; R. M. Meyer, *Altgermanische Religionsgeschichte*, p. 335 ff. (Loki as fire-god developed out of a fire-demon).

[5] Hastings, *Encyclopædia of Religion and Ethics*, article "Celts," p. 289. On the anthropinizing or the distinctly euhemerizing treatment of these two personages see Rhys, *Celtic Folklore*, Index, s.vv.

and Japanese cults there is no indication of a conflict; evil spirits there are in abundance, but no cosmic antagonism.

975. In India the cosmogonic myths are to be interpreted in the same way as those mentioned above. Soma and Indra, as slayers of the demon Vritya, represent order as against disorder, but Vritya never had cultic significance; he appears only as a bodily demonstration of the power of the great gods. The asuras are not essentially different from the harmful spirits of savages, though it is true that they come into conflict with the friendly gods. Rahu, who causes eclipses by swallowing the sun, is only a nature deity of great might. In the Mahabharata there are powerful demons, and the Çivaite cult includes the worship of dread beings, but such worship only reflects the fear of the unfriendly elements of physical nature.[1] Nor do we find in the persons of Durga, Kali, and the Yakshas, unpleasantly savage as these are, a conception of evil as an organized force directed against the good gods; they are rather the embodiment of evil human dispositions. The underground demons are punishers of sin, but not themselves morally evil. There is, it is true, in the Hindu religious scheme the general antithesis of light and darkness, which are connected with right and wrong — an antithesis that appears abundantly in other religious systems;[2] but the powers of darkness are not organized against the powers of light, and there is no complete dualism, though we have here, perhaps, the starting-point for such a conception.

976. While thus a vague sense of duality has existed all over the world, and in certain cases, as it seems, there were vague attempts at organization, it is only in Zoroastrianism that the decisive step has been taken. We have to recognize in this system a distinct movement towards a unitary conception of the world; but the sense of difference in human experiences was so great in the mind of the creators of the system that they were led to a unification in two divisions.[3] The origin of the movement lies far back

---

[1] Hopkins, *Religions of India*, pp. 367, 377, 414.   [2] See above, § 857.

[3] It has been suggested that climatic conditions (sharp contrasts of storm and calm, with consequent strain and peace in life) led to this dual arrangement. But we

at a time when there were no records of thought and social movements, and it is impossible now to say definitely what were the original elements of the cult. We may surmise that there was an Indo-Iranian conception of a general contrast between light and darkness, and that this was the starting-point or the basis of the developed Iranian theological system. The old Indic and the old Iranian religions seem to have been independent developments from a common original mass of material; but we do not know what determined the differences in the two developments. The constructions were the work, doubtless, of successions of reformers, but the details of these long-continued efforts have not come down to us.[1] The essential point is that the evil mass in the world was conceived of as a unity by the Iranians and assigned a head, Angro Mainyu. This name does not occur in the Achæmenian inscriptions, but it is mentioned in the Gathas and by Aristotle,[2] so that it appears to belong to an early stratum of the Iranian religion. The present state of the world is regarded as the result of a constant series of antagonisms between the two creators, Spenta Mainyu (Ahura Mazda) and Angro Mainyu, these being attended each by a circle of helpers. A polytheistic interpretation of the helpers is avoided by making them abstractions (though with a tendency toward personification), the representatives of various features or elements in the government of the world or in the experiences of men.[3]

977. A strictly dualistic system recognizes only two Powers in the world. The Avestan religion, however, admits other deities besides Ahura Mazda and Angro Mainyu; Mitra, Anahita, and others are objects of worship. The ancient national faiths, that is, were not content with a simple division of things between two divine beings. An approach to such a view was made by Judaism,

do not know that there were specially strong contrasts of weather in the Iranian home, and there is no mention of such a situation in the early documents, in which the complaint is of inroads of predatory bands from the steppe.

[1] See above, § 742 ff.   [2] According to Diogenes Laertius, Proem, viii.

[3] To designate the unfriendly supernatural Powers two terms meaning 'divine beings' were available, 'asuras' and 'divas' (daevas); the Hindus chose the former, the Iranians the latter. Cf. Darmesteter, *Ormazd et Ahriman*, p. 268 ff.; Macdonell, *Vedic Mythology*, p. 156 ff.

which, partly under Persian influence, produced the figure of the Satan, a quasi-independent being hostile to the Supreme Deity.[1] Christianity, adopting this conception from Judaism, elaborated it into the person of the Devil, the veritable head of a kingdom of evil, called in the New Testament " the god of this age."[2] Though doomed to final defeat, as Ahriman in the Avesta is doomed, the Devil in the orthodox Christian system is practically omnipresent and is powerful enough to defeat the plans of God in many cases. In modern enlightened Christian feeling, however, he has become little more than a name. Though he is credited in theory with suggesting evil and alluring men to sin, this dogma has small force in the better minds against the strong conviction of individual freedom and responsibility. Current Christianity, in its highest forms, is theoretically, but not really, dualistic. The Satan is taken more seriously by Islam, which has adopted the conception from Christianity and Judaism.[3] For the ordinary Moslem he belongs in the category of evil spirits and is as real as one of the jinn; he may be cursed and stoned and driven away,[4] but he does not affect the Moslem belief in the oneness of God.

978. From the conquest of Persia by Alexander to the fall of the Parthian dynasty (a period of over five hundred years) little is known of the history of Mazdaism beyond the fact that it seems to have been adopted by the Parthians in a debased form; but about the time of the Persian revival under the Sassanians (226 A.D.) it passed the bounds of its native land and made its way into the Roman Empire in the shape of Manichæism, a mixture of dualistic and Christian Gnostic conceptions. That Manichæism had a certain

---

[1] Zech. iii; Job i, ii; 1 Chron. xxi, 1, contrasted with 2 Sam. xxiv, 1; Enoch xl, 7; liii, 3, etc.; Secrets of Enoch (Slavonic Enoch), xxix, 4, 5; xxxi, 3, 4. The word Satan means 'adversary,' and, as legal adversary, 'accuser.' The germ of the conception is to be sought in the apparatus of spirits controlled by Yahweh, and sometimes employed by him as agents to harm men (1 Kings xxii, 19–23). The idea of an accusing spirit seems to have arisen from the necessity of explaining the misfortunes of the nation (Zech. iii); it was expanded under native and foreign influences.

[2] 2 Cor. iv, 4.   [3] *Koran*, vii, 10 ff.

[4] So in the ceremonies of the pilgrimage to Mecca and in common life. The "satans" have in part coalesced with the jinn; see Lane's *Arabian Nights*, " Notes to the Introduction," note 21.

force is shown by the fact that it attracted such a man as Augustine, and its survival for several centuries in spite of persecutions attests its vitality. It may be doubted whether its attractiveness lay so much in its dualism as in its gnosticism, though the former element maintained itself in some minor Christian sects. However this may be, it gradually faded away, leaving no lasting impression; it was a form of faith not suited to the peoples who professed Christianity.[1]

979. The modern philosophic proposals to recognize two deities instead of one are as yet too vague to call for discussion. Dualism, though it accounts in some fashion for the twofold character of human experiences, raises as many problems as it solves; in particular it finds itself confronted apparently by a physical and psychological unity in the world which it is hard to explain on the hypothesis of conflicting supernatural Powers.[2] On the moral side the record of dualistic schemes is in general good. The ethical standard of Mazdaism is high, and the ethical practice of Mazdean communities hardly differs from that of other prominent modern religious bodies. Though the Manichæans were accused of immoral practices, it does not appear that Mani himself or any prominent disciple of his announced or favored or permitted such practices.

MONOTHEISM

980. The preceding survey has shown that the theory of dualism has not proved in general acceptable to men. It was adopted by one people only, and even by them not in complete form, and its character as a national cult was destroyed by the Moslem conquest of Persia in the seventh century. The Zoroastrian system was indeed carried by a body of emigrants to India and has since been professed by the Parsis there; but it has been converted by them into a practical monotheistic cult, so that a consistent dualism now exists nowhere in the world. The thought of the great civilized nations has turned rather to a unitary view of the divine government of the world.

[1] Herzog-Hauck, *Real-Encyklopädie*, s.v. " Mani u. Manichäismus."
[2] On a lack of unity in the world see W. James, *A Pluralistic Universe.*

981. The history of the movement which has elevated mono-theism to the highest place among the civilized cults extends over the whole period of man's life on the earth. It is pointed out above[1] that very generally in low tribes a local supernatural personage is invested with great power: he is creator, ruler, and guardian of mo'rals; where a tolerably definite civil and political organization exists he has virtually the position and performs the functions of the tribal chief, only with vastly greater powers and privileges; where there is no such organization he is simply a vaguely con-ceived, mysterious man who has control of the elements and of human fortunes, and punishes violations of tribal custom. Such a personage is, however, at best only the highest among many super-natural Powers. It is immaterial whether we regard such a figure as developed from a spirit or as the direct product of religious imagination. He is always crudely anthropomorphic and, notwith-standing his primacy, is limited in power by his own nature, by other supernatural Powers, and by men. Frequently, also, he tends to become otiose and virtually loses his supremacy;[2] that is to say, in the increased complexity of social life a god who was once suf-ficient for the needs of a simpler organization has to give way to a number of Powers which are regarded as the controllers of special departments of life. Such an otiose form may sometimes indicate a succession of divine quasi-dynasties, somewhat as in the Greek sequence of Ouranos, Kronos, Zeus. Handed down from a former generation, he becomes dim and is neglected. That he is not wor-shiped is a result of the fact that other divine beings, standing nearer to existing human interests, have come to the front.

982. The theory has been held in the past, and is still held, that monotheism was the primitive form of religion and that the wor-ship of many spirits or many gods is a corruption of primitive thought due to man's intellectual feebleness or to his moral de-pravity. It is urged that such a monotheistic system was the natural one for unsophisticated man. The view has been widely held also that it was the result of a primitive divine revelation to

[1] § 643.
[2] So the Zulu Unkulunkulu, the Fiji Ndengei, the Virginia Ahone, and others.

men. It is obvious that neither of these opinions is susceptible of proof on a priori grounds; the question can be settled only by a survey of the phenomena known to us. When the facts are clearly stated, it is then allowable to deduce from them such conclusions as may seem legitimate.

983. As a matter of fact, it does not appear that real monotheistic belief exists or has existed among savage and half-civilized communities of whose history we have any knowledge. Where a certain supernatural being is described by observers as " the god " or " the supreme god " of a tribe, it turns out on inquiry that he is at most, as is remarked above, a very prominent divine figure, perhaps the most prominent, but never standing alone and never invested with those physical, intellectual, and moral capacities that are necessary for a complete monotheistic faith.

984. While, however, this conclusion is generally admitted for the majority of cases,[1] it has been held, and is still held, that there are found in savage cults certain " self-existent, eternal, moral " beings who satisfy all the conditions of a monotheistic faith. Among the examples cited are the American gods described by Strachey and Winslow as supreme in power and ethically good.[2] But, even in the curt and vague accounts of these early observers (who were not in position to get accurate notions of Indian beliefs), it appears that there were many gods, the supposed supreme deity being simply the most prominent in the regions known to the first settlers. The " Great Spirit " of the Jesuit missionaries is found, in like manner, to be one of many supernatural patrons, locally important but not absolute in power.[3] The Zulu Unkulunkulu is revered by the natives as a very great being, morally good according to the standards of the people, but he is of uncertain origin and is valueless in the existing cult.[4] The much-discussed Australian figures, Baiame, Bunjil, and Daramulun, appear not to differ essentially

[1] Compare Lang's sketch of the gods of the lower races in *Myth, Ritual, and Religion*, chap. xii f., and *Making of Religion*, preface and chaps. xii–xiv.

[2] Strachey, *Historie of Travaile into Virginia Britannica* (1612), p. 98 f. and chap. vii ; Winslow, *Relation* (1624), printed in Young's *Chronicles of the Pilgrim Fathers*, see chap. xxiii.   [3] Cf. Tylor, *Primitive Culture*, ii, 324, 339.

[4] Callaway, *The Amazulu*, p. 1 ff.

from those just mentioned. The reports of the natives who have been questioned on the subject are often vague and sometimes mutually contradictory, and exact biographical details of these divine personages are lacking; but careful recent observers are of opinion that they are nothing more than supernatural headmen, having such power as tribal chiefs or headmen possess, and credited in different regions with different moral qualities.[1]

985. In the systems of many other low tribes there are quasi-divine beings who are credited with great power and are revered without being thought of as eternal or as standing alone in the government of the world. A specially interesting example is the Andaman Puluga, a sort of creator who receives no worship; his abode is a mountain or the sky, and he seems to have been originally a local supernatural figure who is traditionally respected but is no longer thought of as an efficient patron.[2] The mysterious Ndengei of Fiji is judge of the dead, but one of many gods and not all-powerful.[3] In many tribes there is no one great divine figure; the control of things is divided among hosts of spirits and gods. This is the case with the Ainu, the Maoris, the Greenlanders, the Kwakiutl of Northwest America,[4] and is probably the rule in most of the lower communities.

The terms 'self-existent' and 'eternal' are not found in savage vocabularies and seem to have no representatives in savage thought. Savage cosmology carries the history of the world back to a certain point and stops when there is no familiar hypothesis of genesis.[5] As a rule spirits (as distinguished from ghosts) are not thought of as having a creator; they are a part of the system of things and are not supposed to need explanation, and so it seems to be with simple clan gods. Nor is there any reason, in savage theory, why

---

[1] Howitt, *Native Tribes of South-East Australia*, Index (cf. Spencer and Gillen, *Northern Tribes of Central Australia*, p. 492); cf. Thomas, *Natives of Australia*, chap. xiii, and article "Australia" in Hastings, *Encyclopædia of Religion and Ethics*.

[2] Temple, article "Andamans" in Hastings, *Encyclopædia of Religion and Ethics*.

[3] Williams and Calvert, *Fiji*, chap. vii.

[4] Batchelor, *The Ainu*, chap. xvii; Taylor, *New Zealand*, chaps. v-vii; Rink, *Danish Greenland*, p. 204 ff.; Boas, *The Kwakiutl*, chap. vi.

[5] The confusion incident to savage theogonic reflection is illustrated by Zulu attempts to explain Unkulunkulu (Callaway, loc. cit.).

gods or spirits should die; death is an accident for human beings. not an essential feature of their constitution; but such an accident is not usually supposed to occur in the case of gods. What takes the place of the conception of 'eternal' in savage thought is an existence that is supposed to continue for the reason that its cessation does not come into consideration. As to creation, there is no need, in a low community, to suppose more than one originator of the world, and cosmogonic theory may stop at that point, though this is not an invariable rule. The title "father" for persons of distinction, human or divine, is found among many undeveloped peoples, and a headman or patron may be called, by a natural extension of thought, "all-father," a title that is not essentially different in signification from the simple "father," and does not carry with it the refined sense of later times. The question of savage monotheism need present no difficulty if the conditions are clearly defined.[1] It is true that there is in some cases a monarchical conception of the divine control of a clan or a tribe, and that this simple system is followed by a more or less elaborate theology. In both civil and religious systems the increasing complexity of social life has called forth correspondingly complex organizations, but this movement away from simplicity does not denote falling off in civil and religious purity and wisdom. A true monotheism has never arisen except as a criticism of polytheism.

986. It is obvious that the popular cults of the great nations of antiquity were far removed from monotheism. The Egyptians, the Babylonians and the Assyrians, the Phœnicians, the Hebrews, the Arabs, the Hindus, the Greeks and the Romans, down to a late period, worshiped a multitude of gods and were not disturbed by any feeling of lack of unity in the divine government of the world. The proof that such was the case among the ancient Hebrews down to the sixth century B.C. is found in the Old Testament writings: the historical books from the entrance of the Hebrew tribes into Canaan down to the destruction of Jerusalem by the Chaldeans

---

[1] Lang, in the works cited in the preceding paragraph, is right in his contention that the clan god is not always derived from a spirit; but the coloring he gives to the character of this sort of god is not in accordance with known facts.

and the prophetical writings of the eighth, seventh, and sixth centuries represent the people generally as addicted to the worship of a great number of gods. In Persia also, since the Mazdean system recognized a considerable number of deities, it cannot be doubted that the people were polytheistic, not to speak of the probability that there were survivals of a lower form of religion which preceded Mazdaism. In the modern nations of the east of Asia, China and Japan, the popular worship is anything but monotheistic: in China the local spirits play a very great part in the life of the people, and in Japan the old gods are still objects of worship. It may be added that among the masses in some nominally Christian countries, particularly among the peasants of Southern Europe, the old polytheism continues in the form of the worship of saints and the Madonna.

987. While the popular cults in the civilized world have held somewhat pertinaciously to pluralistic views, there has been a general tendency in advanced circles everywhere toward a unitary conception of the government of the world. As this tendency has been general it must be referred to the general progress of thought, the demand of the human mind for unity or simplicity. The particular lines of the movement have varied among different peoples according to the peculiarities of their culture, and the unitary feeling has varied in its degree of definiteness. In some cases the political predominance of a city or region has secured preëminence for its deity, or national attachment to the national god has elevated him above all other gods; where a people has cultivated poetry or philosophy, the idealizing thought of the one or the scientific analysis of the other has led in the same direction.

988. First, then, we may note the disposition to give substantial absoluteness to some one god, the choice of the deity being determined by the political condition as is suggested above, or by local attachments, or possibly by other conditions which do not appear in the meager records of early times. Examples of this form of thought are found in several of the great nations of antiquity. The hymns to the Egyptian gods Ra, Amon, Amon-Ra, Osiris, and the Nile describe these deities as universal in attributes and in power.

At the moment the poet conceives of the god whom he celebrates as practically the only one — if Ra does everything, there is no need of any other deity. At another moment, however, the same poet may celebrate Osiris with equal enthusiasm — these high gods are interchangeable. The suggestion from such fluid conceptions of the divine persons is that the real thought in the mind of the poet was the supremacy of some divine power which is incorporated now in one familiar divine name, now in another. It does not, however, quite reach the point of well-defined monotheism, for these gods remain distinct, sometimes with separate functions and duties.

989. But this mode of conceiving of the supernatural Power would naturally pave the way for monotheism, and it is not surprising that very early in Egypt a definite monotheistic view was developed. King Amenophis IV, or to give him the name that he adopted in conformity with his later cult, Khuen-Aten, made a deliberate attempt to elevate the sun-god Aten to the position of sole ruler and object of worship. Though the nature of his belief in this deity is not stated in the documents with the fullness and precision that we should desire, it seems clear, from the fact that he ordered the destruction of the shrines of the other deities in the land, that he regarded the worship of this one god as sufficient. The movement was not a successful one in so far as the national religion was concerned — it lasted only during his lifetime and that of his son, and then a counter-revolution swept Aten away and reinstated the Theban Amon in all his former dignity and powers — but its very existence is a testimony to the direction of thought of educated minds in Egypt about the year 1400 B.C. The Aten revolution appears to have been distinctively Egyptian — there is no trace of foreign influence in its construction. It has been suggested that Amenophis got his idea from Semites of Western Asia or particularly from the Hebrews. But neither the Hebrews nor any other Semitic people of that period were monotheistic, nor do we find in Egyptian history at the time such social intercourse as might produce a violent upturning of the religious usage. We can only suppose that Amenophis was a religious genius who put into definite shape a conception that was in the air, and by the force of his enthusiasm made it for the moment effective. Such geniuses have arisen from time to time in the world, and though the revolution of this Egyptian king may seem to us to have sprung up with abnormal abruptness, it is more reasonable to suppose that the way had been prepared for it in Egyptian thought. He was a man born out of due time; but it cannot be said that his attempt was without influence on succeeding generations.

990. Passing now to the oldest Semitic civilizations, we find in Babylonia and Assyria many local deities, one or another of whom comes to the front under the hegemony of some city or state. Here we are met by the fact already referred to that the gods are interchangeable — it is practically a matter of indifference whether one deity or another is elevated to headship. In the great empires the gods of the capital cities naturally became preëminent; so Marduk in Babylonia and Ashur in Assyria. The royal inscriptions speak of these gods as if they were all-powerful and all-controlling. In both countries the goddess Ishtar appears as the supreme director of affairs, and other deities are similarly honored. What might have been the issue if the later Babylonian kingdom had continued for a long time it is impossible to say, but the impression made by the words of the devout king Nebuchadrezzar II (605–562 B.C.) is that he would have been content with Marduk as the one object of worship. Babylonia produced no such radical reformer as the Egyptian Amenophis — there is no formulation of monotheism; but the general tone of the Babylonian religion of the sixth century is not very different from that of the Hebrew religion of the same time.

991. The religious point of view of the Vedas belongs in the same category with the early Egyptian. Varuna, Agni, and Indra appear in the hymns, each in his turn, as supreme. The rôle of Varuna seems to be practically identical with that of the Iranian Ahura, but unlike the latter he does not succeed in expelling his brother divinities. This difference of development between the Hindu and the Iranian people we cannot hope to explain. India moved not toward monotheism, but toward pantheism. But the

Vedic hymns prove the existence of a certain sense of oneness in the world, held by the poets, though not by the mass of the people, and destined to issue in a very remarkable religious system.

992. It has been by a very different line that China has reached its unitary conception of the world. The details of the movement are obscure, but its general course is clear.[1] As with many other peoples it is the objects of nature to which Chinese worship is mainly paid, but the Chinese mind, impressed by the power of these objects, is content to rest in them in their visible form; no proper names are attached to them, and they have a more or less vague personality which varies in definiteness at different times and with different persons. The theistic system is a reflection of the social system. The eminently practical Chinese mind lays the chief stress on the earthly life: in the common everyday life the family is the unit; but the general course of affairs is controlled by the great natural Powers of earth and sky, whence arise the two great divisions of Chinese worship. The State is a larger family in which the duke or emperor or other chief political officer occupies the same position that is occupied by the father in the smaller social circle; the government is patriarchal, with gradations which correspond to those of the family. Life, it is held, is controlled by the heavenly bodies, by the mountains and rivers of the earth, and by deceased members of families. To these the people sacrifice, the principal part being taken by the civil heads of the larger and smaller constituent parts of the empire; there is thus no place for priests. As the emperor (or other head of the State) is supreme on earth, so Heaven and Earth, Sun and Moon occupy the highest positions in the divine hierarchy, and ancestors are influential and entitled to worship according to the rank of the families they represent.[2] From an early time, long before Confucius, the headship of the divine Powers, it would seem, was assigned to Heaven — not the physical sky, but, at least in the thinking circles of the

---

[1] See above, § 746 ff.

[2] It is not probable that the recent abolition of the office of emperor (supposing the present revolutionary movement to maintain itself) will affect the essence of the existing cult.

nation, the Power therein residing. Thus arose the conception
of an imperial divine government in which Heaven, though it does
not stand alone, is recognized as supreme. The larger theistic
conception is embodied in the annual sacrifices conducted by the
emperor,[1] especially at the winter and summer solstices when sacrifices are offered to Heaven and Earth, Sun and Moon, the Four
Quarters and the mountains and rivers of the empire and to his
ancestors, whose worship includes the interests of the whole State.
Thus with a vast number of objects of worship (spirits of all departments of life, and a few gods proper) the Chinese religion has
attained and maintained a general unitary conception of the
divine government of the world.[2]

993. Some resemblance to the Chinese system appears in the
religion of Peru, so far as this can be understood from the accounts
that have come down to us.[3] The supreme position given to the
Sun in Peru and to the Inca as child of the Sun is parallel to the
supremacy of Heaven in China and the headship of the emperor
as the son of Heaven. The Peruvian cult appears not to have
reached the distinctness of the Chinese. There were, in fact, in
Peru a considerable number of tolerably well-formed divinities
along with a vast crowd of spirits. Yet it appears that the sun
was regarded, at least by the Inca and his circle, as supreme ruler
of the world. The Sun, as god, has no proper name in Peru, as
in China Heaven, as god, has no proper name. In both countries,
it would seem, the imagination of the people was overpowered by
the spectacle of the majesty of a great natural object. The two
religions differ in their ritual development: while the Inca, like
the Chinese emperor, was the religious head of the nation, the
Peruvians created an elaborate system of worship, with temples
and ministrants, which is wanting in China.[4] The remarkable
character of the Peruvian system makes it all the more regrettable

---

[1] In place of the emperor some high official personage will doubtless be de-
puted to conduct the national sacrifices.

[2] De Groot, *Religious System of China, Religion of the Chinese,* and *Development
of Religion in China.*

[3] Prescott, *Conquest of Peru*; Spence, *Mythologies of Ancient Mexico and Peru.*

[4] An approach to such a system appears in the later cult of Confucius.

that the data available do not enable us to trace its growth from the simplest beginnings.

994. Still another line of theistic development is furnished by the Hebrew system. The Hebrews are remarkable among ancient peoples as having had, so far as our information goes, only one national god. This god they brought with them into Canaan from the wilderness over which they appear to have roamed with their flocks for a period and under conditions not definitely known to us. Arrived in Canaan, the masses were attracted by the local Canaanite deities (whose worship represented a higher civilization than that of the nomadic Hebrews), and later, in the seventh century B.C., a great part of the people of the little kingdom of Judah adopted the Assyrian astral cult; but a group of Israelites had always remained faithful to the national deity Yahweh (Jehovah) and vigorously opposed all foreign worship. It was naturally the more thoughtful and ethically better-developed part of the community that took this uncompromising position, and their spokesmen, the writing prophets whose discourses are preserved in the Old Testament, became preachers of morality as well as champions of the sole worship of Yahweh. It does not appear that they denied the existence of other gods, but they regarded their own god as superior to all others in power, standing in a peculiarly close relation to his people and bound to them by peculiarly intimate ties.

995. This attachment to one deity proved to be the dominant sentiment of the nation. As time went on and the people were sifted by the Assyrian and Babylonian deportations, the higher moral feeling of the best men attached itself more and more definitely to the national god. Thus was established a monolatry which was practically monotheism, though a theory of absolute monotheism was never formulated by the pre-Christian Jews. It must be added, as is remarked above, that, from the third or second century B.C. on, the somewhat undefined range of activity attributed to Satan produced a sort of dualism, yet without impairing the practically unitary conception of the divine government of the world.[1] The course of their national fortunes and the

[1] See § 977.

remarkable power of self-contained persistence of the Jews brought about a segregation of the people and, finally, their organization into a community governed by a law held to be divinely revealed. This capacity of social religious organization was the distinctive characteristic of the Jewish people and, supported by their unitary theistic system and a high moral code, gave the example of popular monotheism which, through the medium of Christianity, finally imposed itself upon the Roman world.

996. In the ancient world the most thorough investigation of the theistic problem was made by the Greeks, whose leading thinkers, like the Hebrews, moved steadily toward a unitary conception of the divine power, but, unlike the Hebrews, did not succeed in impressing their views on the people at large. What the theistic conception in the pre-Homeric times was we are unable to say definitely, but presumably in every separate community there was a local deity who had practically the direction of affairs. In process of time, through conditions not known to us, Zeus came to be recognized throughout the Hellenic world as the principal delty. In the Homeric poems and in Hesiod we find a political or governmental organization of the gods which followed the lines of the social organization of the times. As Agamemnon is the head chief over a group of local chiefs, so Zeus, though not absolutely supreme, is a divine king, the head over a considerable number of deities who have their own preferences and plans, and in ordinary matters go their own way and are not interfered with so long as they mind their own business; but at critical points Zeus, like Agamemnon, intervenes, and then no god disputes his decisions.

997. This conception of the divine government appears, therefore, to rest on the Greek demand for political organization; the world was thought of as divided into various departments which had to be brought into a unity by the ascription of a quasi-supreme authority to some one personage. Necessarily, however, larger intellectual and ethical ideas were incorporated in this political view. Though the popular anthropomorphic conceptions of the deities appear throughout the Homeric poems (the gods being sometimes morally low as well as limited in knowledge and power), yet on the other hand they are said to know everything. To Zeus in particular lofty qualities are ascribed; he is the father of men and their savior and the patron of justice. How it came about that these two sorts of conceptions of a supreme deity are mingled in the poems is a question that need not be discussed here; a similar mingling of contradictory ideas is found in the Old Testament, in which the unmoral god of the people stands alongside of the highly developed ethical Yahweh of the great prophets.

998. In Homer and Hesiod, however, the conception of headship is complicated by the introduction of the idea of fate. In the Iliad Zeus is sometimes ignorant of the future and has to employ the scales of destiny, and in Hesiod appear the three Fates who control the lives of men independently of the gods. The conception of a controlling fate may be regarded as an effort to reach an absolutely unitary view of the world. Above all the divine powers that regulate affairs, after the manner of the government by a king with his attendant chieftains and officers, there is a sense of a dim and undefined power of unknown origin, mysterious, absolute, universal. The question whether this conception was a reflection of a sense of the controlling power resident in the universe itself, or merely an endeavor to rise above the variations of anthropomorphic deities, is important from the point of view of the genesis of ideas, but its decision will not affect the fact just stated.[1] Obviously in the Homeric world there appears this general conviction that men and gods are bound together in unity and that some force or power controls all things.[2]

999. This sense of the governmental unity is further developed by the later great poets who infused into it higher and more definite moral elements. The polytheistic view continues; to the thinkers of the time there was no more difficulty in conceiving of a single headship along with many deities of particular functions than was felt by Hebrew prophets who recognized the existence of foreign

---

[1] So later, for example, in Plato, necessity appears as something limiting the deity. See below, § 1001. Cf. Cicero, *De Fato.*

[2] Cf. the Chinese conception of the supreme order of the world. Possibly this goes back to the general savage conception of mana.

deities, with Yahweh as a superior god, or by the modern Christian world with its apparatus of angels, saints, and demons alongside of the supreme God. For Pindar Zeus is lord of all things and is far removed from the moral impurities of the popular conception. Æschylus represents him as supreme and in general as just, though not wholly free from human weaknesses. A real unity of the world is set forth by Sophocles: there is a divinely ordered control by immutable law, and the will of Zeus is unquestioned. The unitary conception is found also in Euripides notwithstanding his skeptical attitude toward the current mythology. The sense of symmetry potent in the poets forced them to this unitary conception of government, and the natural progress of ethical feeling led them to ascribe the highest ethical qualities to the deities.

1000. Similar motives appear in the speculations of the Greek philosophers: Greek philosophy in seeking to discover the essential nature of the world moved definitely toward the conception of its unity — so, for example, as early as the sixth century, in Xenophanes and Parmenides. The conception of a supreme spiritual ruler of the world appears in Heraclitus and Anaxagoras (fifth century). To these and other Greek thinkers the unity of the world and the dominance of mind or spirit appeared to be necessary assumptions. The most definite expression of these conceptions is found in Plato and Aristotle. According to Plato (in the Timæus) God, the eternal Father, created the world (for nothing can be created without a cause), brought order out of disorder and made the universe to be most fair and good, so that it became a rational living soul, the one only-begotten universe, created the gods and the sons of the gods, and framed the soul to be the ruler of the body. Aristotle, in simpler phrase, represents the ground of the world as self-sufficient Mind, an eternal Power ($\delta \acute{\nu} \nu a \mu \iota s$), from which all action or actuality ($\acute{\epsilon} \nu \acute{\epsilon} \rho \gamma \epsilon \iota a$) proceeds.[1]

1001. There are certain apparent limitations, it is true, to this conception of unity. Both Plato and Aristotle recognize the existence of a host of subordinate deities (created but immortal) to whom

[1] *Metaphysics*, ix, 8; xii, 6 f.

is assigned a share, by direction of the supreme God, in the creation of things; yet essentially these deities are nothing more than agents or intermediaries of the divine activity, and may be compared to the natural laws and agents of modern theism and, more exactly, to the Hebrew angels through whom, according to the Old Testament, God governed the world. Plato has also a somewhat vague notion of a something in the nature of the material of the world that limits or constrains the divine creative power — a " necessity " that forces the deity to do not the absolutely best but the best possible. Perhaps this is a philosophical formulation of the old " fate," perhaps Plato is merely trying to account for certain supposed inconcinnities and inadequacies in the world. He is not quite consistent with himself, since he represents the creation of the universe as resulting from the fact that necessity yielded to the persuasion of mind, which thus became supreme.[1] In spite of this vagueness his view is unitary, and the unitary conception is continued by the Stoics, its best Stoic expression being found in the famous hymn of Cleanthes to Zeus : " Nothing occurs on earth apart from thee " and " We are thy offspring." [2]

1002. In the last centuries before the beginning of our era the Jews, partly under Persian and Greek influence, clarified their theistic view, attaining a practically pure monotheism, only retaining their apparatus of angels and demons. This theistic scheme passed over in complete form to early Christianity, in which, however, greater prominence was given to the chief demon, the Satan ; his larger rôle arose from the fact that he was brought into sharp antagonism with the Christ, the head of the kingdom of God. When Christianity was adopted by the Græco-Roman world, the doctrine of the Trinity was worked out and formulated in accordance with Greek and Roman philosophic thought, but was held not to impair the monotheistic view since the three Persons were regarded as being in substance one. Islam adopted the Jewish

---

[1] *Timæus*, 47 f.

[2] Stobæus, *Eclogæ*, ed. Wachsmuth, lib. i, cap. i, no. 12 ; Pearson, *Fragments of Zeno and Cleanthes* ; Eng. tr. in Arnold, *Roman Stoicism*, p. 85 ff. The quotation in Acts xvii, 28, may be from Cleanthes or from Aratus. On the Græco-Roman Stoicism and the relation between it and Christianity see Arnold, op. cit.

form of monotheism, with its Satan and angels, retaining also the old Arabian apparatus of demonic beings (the jinn).

1003. A certain tendency to a practically unitary view is discernible in the cults of Isis and Mithra, which were widely diffused in the Roman Empire.[1] In both these cults the main interest of the worshipers was centered in a single deity, though other deities were recognized. The unifying impulse was devotional, not philosophic.

So far as a unitary conception of the divine governmnt of the world existed it must be referred to the spirit of the age which had outgrown the old crude polytheism. Such modern monotheistic movements as the Brahma-Samaj and the Parsi in India, the Babist in Persia, and the reformed Shinto in Japan owe much to European influence, though doubtless some part of them is the outcome of natural progress in intellectual and moral conceptions.

PANTHEISTIC AND NONTHEISTIC SYSTEMS

1004. The systems of theistic thought considered above all make a sharp separation between God and the world. Plato and Aristotle regarded mind or spirit as a force that dominated matter. The Persian, Hebrew, and Christian theologies conceive of the deity as transcendent, standing outside of and above the world and entering into communication with it either by direct revelation or through intermediaries. To certain thinkers of ancient times this dualistic conception presented difficulties — an absolute unity was held to be incompatible with such separation between the world and God. The precise nature of the reflections by which the earliest philosophers reached this conclusion is not clearly set forth, but it may be surmised that in general there were two lines of thought that led to this inference: first, a metaphysical conception of unity as something that was demanded by the sense of perfectness in the world; and, secondly, observation of facts that appeared to characterize the world as a unit. Among several different peoples, and apparently in each independently, the idea

---

[1] Apuleius, *Metamorphoses*, bk. xi; Roscher, *Lexikon*, article "Isis"; Cumont, *Mysteries of Mithra*; id., *Astrology and Religion among the Greeks and Romans*, Index, s.vv. *Isis and Serapis* and *Mithra*.

arose that the divine manifests itself in the world of phenomena and is recognizable only therein. Such a view appears in India in the Vedanta philosophy, and in Greece a little later it is more or less involved in Orphic theories and in the systems of several philosophers. The tendency to deify nature appears even in writers who do not wholly exclude gods from their schemes of the world — in the sayings of Heraclitus, for example: " All things are one," " From all comes one, and from one comes all." A similar view is attributed to Xenophanes by Aristotle,[1] and traces of such a conception appear in Euripides.[2] For the modern forms of pantheism, in Spinoza and other philosophers, reference must be made to the histories of philosophy.

1005. Pantheism has never commended itself to the masses of men. It is definitely theistic, but the view that the divine power is visible only in phenomena and is to be identified practically with the world is one that men in general find difficult to comprehend. The demand is for a deity with whom one may enter into personal relations — the simple conception of a god who dwells apart satisfies the religious instincts of the majority of men. The ethical questions arising from pantheism seem to them perplexing: how can man be morally responsible when it is the deity who thinks and acts in him? and how can he have any sense of loyalty to a deity whom he cannot distinguish from himself? Nor do men generally demand so absolute a unity as is represented by pantheism. Such questions as those relating to the eternity of matter, the possibility of the existence of an immaterial being, and the mode in which such a being, if it exists, could act on matter, have not seemed practical to the majority of men. Man demands a method of worship, and pantheism does not permit organized worship. For these reasons it has remained a sentiment of philosophers, though it has not been without effect in modifying popular conceptions of the deity: the conception of the immanence of God in the world (held in many Christian orthodox circles), when carried to its legitimate consequences, it is often hard to distinguish from pantheism.

---

[1] *Metaphysics*, i, 5: " The one is god."
[2] So in Goethe, Wordsworth, and other modern poets.

1006. *Nontheistic systems.* A further attempt to secure a complete unity of the world appears in those systems of thought which regard the world as self-sufficient and, therefore, dispense with extramundane agency. These start either from the point of view of man and human life or from contemplation of the world. In China the sense of the sole importance of the moral life and the impossibility of knowing anything beyond mundane life led Confucius practically to ignore divine agency. He did not deny the existence of Powers outside of men, but he declined to speak of them, regarding them as of no practical importance. This sort of agnosticism appears in Greece as early as the fifth century B.C., when Protagoras's view that " man is the measure of all things " makes extrahuman Powers superfluous. Epicurus reached a similar practical atheism apparently from a scientific view of the construction of the world. According to him there are gods, but they are otiose — living a life of happy ease, they are to be thought of as a pleasant phenomenon in the world, but ineffective as regards human fortunes, and men may go their ways certain that if they obey the laws of the world the gods will not interfere with them.

1007. The Sankhya philosophy of India dispenses completely with gods, holding that the primordial stuff is eternal, but it also holds that souls have a separate existence and are eternal. Thus a species of dualism emerges. Buddhism goes a step further, ignoring the soul as well as gods. It is agnostic in that, admitting the world to have a cause, it holds that it is impossible to know this cause. Its practical aim — to get rid of suffering by getting rid of desire, and thus to pass into a blissful state of existence in which apparently there is to be no effort as there is to be no pain — has enabled it to establish a vigorous organization, a sort of church, in which the undefined universe takes the place of a personal god, and character takes the place of soul, this character (Karma) passing from one being to another without the assumption of identity in the beings thus united in destiny.[1]

[1] In certain regions, especially in Tibet and Japan, Buddhism coalesces with popular nature-cults and shamanistic systems, and loses its nontheistic character.

1008. In Greece pure materialism (similar in essence to the Sankhya) took the shape of the assumption of an original and eternal mass of atoms whence have come all forms of being (so Democritus in the fifth century B.C.), and this conception was adopted by Epicurus and expounded at length by Lucretius.[1] The necessary qualities and movements being attributed to the atoms, the conclusion was that nothing else was required in order to explain the world. With this may be compared the view of Empedocles (fifth century) that love and hate (in modern phrase, attraction and repulsion) are the creative forces of the world. The simplicity of this scheme has commended it to many minds in modern as in ancient times. Man, it is said, can know nothing outside of phenomena, and, so far as regards the origin of things, it is as easy to conceive of an eternal self-existent mass of matter as of an eternal self-existent deity. The nobler part of man, it is held, is not thereby surrendered — reason and all high ethical and spiritual ideals have grown naturally out of the primordial mass. In such systems there is often the hypothesis of an original force or life resident in matter, and this force or life, being credited with all that has issued from it, may be regarded as having the elements of personality, and in that case becomes practically a deity. Such a deistic materialism approaches pantheism nearly.

General Survey of the Theistic Development

1009. The theistic conceptions of men have followed the general line of social development. All systems and shades of thought are faithfully reflected in the various ideas that men have formed for themselves of the gods. Human nature is the highest thing known to men, and their conception of supernatural forces has been based on ideals derived from experience. The sphere of divine activity has been determined for men by their systems of physical science; the moral character of the gods is a reflection of human ethical conceptions; the internal activity of the deity in man's mind is defined by man's spiritual experience.

[1] Cf. Santayana, " Lucretius," in his *Three Philosophical Poets.*

1010. From the earliest times the extent to which the gods were supposed to intervene in human affairs has been fixed by scientific observation, by the knowledge of natural law — the gods have been called on to intervene only when it was necessary because ordinary powers failed. When finally the conception is reached that all nature is governed by natural law, the theistic view assumes that the deity works through ordinary natural means, and the supposition of particular interventions is rejected by the mass of scientific thinkers. It was natural in early times to suppose that reward and punishment were administered by the deity in this world in accordance with the principles of right, that the good prospered and the bad failed; but this view has vanished before observation, and, by those who demand an exact accordance between conduct and fortunes, the final compensations of life have been relegated to the other world.

1011. The belief in miracles, however, has never completely vanished from the world. A miracle is an intervention by the deity whereby a natural law is set aside. No a priori reasoning can ever prove or disprove the possibility of miracles — such proof or disproof would involve complete knowledge of the universe or of the divine power in the universe, and this is impossible for man. The indisposition to accept a miracle has arisen from the conviction that the demand for interventions that set aside the natural order is a reflection on the wisdom of the Creator's arrangement of the world, and further from long-continued observation of the dominance of natural law, and, when appeal is made to alleged miraculous occurrences, from the arbitrary way in which, according to the reports, these have been introduced. In the records of peoples we find that miracles increase in number and magnitude in proportion as we go back to dim times without exact historical documents. They appear, it is held, in connection usually with insignificant affairs while the really great affairs in later times are left without miraculous elements.[1] The history of the world, so historical

---

[1] The great exception is the resurrection of Jesus, regarded in the New Testament and by the mass of orthodox Christians as an historical fact, and one of infinite significance for the salvation of the world.

science holds, receives a satisfactory explanation from the character of the general laws of human nature, and the principle of parsimony demands that no unnecessary elements of action be introduced into affairs. The exclusion of miracles from the world does not exclude divine agency and government; it only defines the latter as being in accordance with man's observation of natural law.

1012. Philosophy constructs the constitution of the deity and the relation of divine elements to the world. Whether the deity stands outside of the world or within it, whether the divine power is unitary or dual or plural, or whether there is any need to assume a power outside of physical nature — these are the questions that are discussed by philosophy, whose conclusions sometimes favor a religious view of the world, sometimes oppose it. Few persons are able to follow elaborate philosophic lines of thought — the majority of men accept the simple doctrine of a personal god who is generally supposed to stand outside of the world. The controlling consideration here is that everything must have a cause — a line of reasoning in accordance with common sense, but not always, in its crude form, regarded by philosophers as decisive.

1013. The moral character of a deity is always in accordance with the moral ideas of his worshipers. Religions have sometimes been divided into the ethical and the nonethical; but so far as the character of the deity is concerned no such division holds, for there never has been a supernatural Power that has not reflected the moral ideas of its time and place. A cannibal god is not only natural in a cannibal society, but he represents moral ideals, namely, the attempt to acquire strength by absorbing the physical substance of men. The deity who deceives or is vindictive arises in a society in which deceit and vindictiveness are regarded as virtues. The pictures of what we regard as immoralities in the deity as given in the Iliad and in the Old Testament were not regarded as immoral by the writers. The progress in the characterization of the deity has been not by the introduction of an ethical element, but by the purification and elevation of the already existing ethical element.[1]

[1] An emotional element possessing moral force may exist in any religion; cf. below, §§ 1167, 1192, 1199.

CHAPTER X

SOCIAL DEVELOPMENT OF RELIGION

1014. Religion is social because man is a social animal. This does not exclude individual religion — in fact religion must have begun with individuals, as is the case with all social movements. Morality, indeed, understood as a system of conduct among human beings, could not exist except in a society which included at least two persons; but if we could imagine a quite isolated rational being, he might be religious if, as is perfectly possible, he conceived himself as standing in relation with some supernatural being or beings. This question, however, is not a practical one — there is no evidence of such isolation, and no probability that there ever has been a time when man was not social.

1015. It is generally agreed that men lived at first in small detached groups, gradually forming tribes and nations, and finally effecting a social fusion of nations. Religious worship has followed these changes. Religion is simply one line of social growth existing along with others, science, philosophy, art; all these, as is remarked above,[1] go on together, each influencing and influenced by the others. Human life has always been unitary — no one part can be severed from the others; it is a serious error, impairing the accuracy of the conception of religion, to regard it as something apart from the rest of human life.

1016. The external history of religion, then, is the history of social growth in the line of religious organization; that is, it has been determined by religious outward needs in accordance with the growth of ideas. In the consideration of this history we have to note a growth in ritual, in devotional practices, and in the organization of religious usages, first in tribal or national communities and then in religious communities transcending national and racial boundaries.

[1] § 13 ff.

EXTERNAL WORSHIP

1017. We assume a human society recognizing some supernatural or extrahuman object or force that is regarded as powerful and as standing in some sort of effective relation with human life. It is possible that societies exist that do not recognize any such object or force or, recognizing them, do not employ any means of entering into relation with them. Such cases, if they exist (and their existence has not been fully established), we may pass by with the remark that the absence of worship need be taken to show only that ritual has been a slow growth.

Our information regarding the least-developed communities indicates that with them religion, when it exists, is an affair of custom, of tradition and usage, handed down during a period the history of which we have no means of knowing. Worship as it first appears consists of ceremonies, generally, perhaps always, regarded as having objective effectiveness.[1] The ritual act itself, in the earliest systems, is powerful, in a sort magical, but tends to lose this character and take on the forms of ordinary human intercourse.

1018. The precise ways in which extrahuman Powers were first approached by men it is not possible now to determine — these procedures lie far back in a dim prehistoric time. Coming down to our first knowledge of religious man it may be assumed that the superhuman Powers recognized by him were of varying sorts: a quasi-impersonal energy which, however, must probably be ascribed ultimately to a personal being; animals; ghosts; spirits resident in objects; anthropomorphic beings. With all these it was necessary to establish relations, and while the methods employed varied slightly according to the nature of the object of worship, the fundamental cultic principle appears to have been the same for all. Several different methods of approaching the Powers appear in the material known to us, and these may be mentioned without attempting exact chronological arrangement.

1019. One of the earliest methods of establishing a relation with the Powers is by certain processes — acts or words. The most

[1] See above, Chapter iii.

definite example of a mere process is that found among the Central Australians, the nature of which, however, is not yet well understood. They perform ceremonies intended to procure a supply of food. It is not quite clear whether these ceremonies are merely imitations of animals and other things involved, or whether they contain some recognition of a superhuman Power. In the former case they are magical, not religious in the full sense of the term. But if they involve a belief in some force or power with which man may enter into relation, however dim and undefined this conception may be, then they must be regarded as belonging definitely in the sphere of religion. A certain direct effect is in many cases supposed to issue from ritualistic acts, a belief that is doubtless a survival of the old conception of mana.[1]

1020. In many cases efficacy is attached by savages to singing — the word " sing " is used as equivalent to " exert power in a superhuman way." It is not the musical part of this procedure that is effective — the singing is simply the natural tendency of early man — the power lies in the words which may be regarded as charms. A charm is primarily a form of words which has power to produce certain results with or without the intervention of the gods.[2] In the form of an invocation of a deity the charm belongs to a comparatively late stage of religion; but where its power lies wholly in its words, it involves merely some dim sense of relation, not necessarily religious. Obviously the idea of law underlies all such procedures, but the law may be a sort of natural law and the charm will then not be religious. Religious charms are to be sharply distinguished from prayers; a prayer is a simple request, a charm is an instrument of force.[3] The history of the growth of savage charms it is impossible for us to recover; it can only be supposed that they have grown up through a vast period of time and have been constructed out of various signs and experiences of all sorts that appeared to connect certain words with certain results. There is no evidence that they came originally or usually from

---

[1] See above, §§ 128, 131, 231 ff.
[2] Cf. article " Charms and Amulets " in Hastings, *Encyclopædia of Religion and Ethics.*   [3] Cf. Marett, *Threshold of Religion*, p. 77 ff.

prayers that had lost their petitionary character, petrified prayers, so to speak, of which there remained only the supposition that they could gain their ends, though bits of prayers, taken merely as words, are sometimes supposed to have such potency. Charms and prayers are found side by side in early stages of religion; the former tend to decrease, the latter to increase. Charms are allied to amulets, exorcism, and to magic in general.[1]

1021. Certain processes and words are supposed to have power to summon the dead and to gain from them a knowledge of the future. This is a case of coercion by magical means. Nonmagical coercion belongs to a relatively late period in religious history and may be passed over at this point. It is not in itself incompatible with religion; a god is subject to caprice and ill humor, and may have to be controlled, and we know that coercion of the gods has been practiced by many peoples, with the full sanction of the religious authorities.[2] But coercive procedures do not accord with the general line of social development. The natural tendency is to make friends with the gods, and coercive methods have died out with the growth of society.

1022. The methods of establishing friendly relations with the supernatural Powers are the same as those which are employed to approach human rulers, namely, by gifts and by messengers or intermediaries.

Gifts. The custom of offering gifts to the dead is universal.[3] Among low tribes and in highly civilized peoples (the Egyptians and others) things are placed by the grave which it is supposed the spirits of the dead will need. Food and drink are supplied, and animals and human beings are slain and left to serve as ministers to the ghosts in the other world. Possibly these provisions for the dead are sometimes suggested by sentiments of affection, but more commonly the object in making the provision appears to be to secure the favor of the deceased: ghosts were powerful for

---

[1] Examples are found in J. H. King, *The Supernatural*, Index, s.v.; Tylor, *Primitive Culture*, Index, s.v.; L. T. Hobhouse, *Morals in Evolution*, Index, s.v.; and see the references in these works.   [2] See above, § 3.

[3] Spencer, *Principles of Sociology*, i, 280 ff.; Westermarck, *Origin and Development of the Moral Ideas*, ii, 550 al.

good or for evil — they were numerous, always hovering round the living, and the main point was to gain their good will. For a similar reason such gifts were made to spirits and to gods. It was a common custom to leave useful articles by sacred trees and stones, or to cast them into rivers or into the sea. The food and drink provided was always that in ordinary use among the worshipers : grain, salt, oil, wine, to which were often added cooking and other utensils. It was common also to offer the flesh of animals, as, for example, among the Eskimo, the American Indians (the Pawnees and others), the Bantu, the Limbus, and the Todas of Southern India.[1] It was supposed that the god, when he was in need of food, sometimes used means to stimulate his worshipers on earth to make him an offering.

1023. Since it was obvious that the food set forth for the spirit or deity remained untouched, it was held that the gods consumed only the soul of the food. This conception, which is found in very early times, was natural to those who held that every object, even pots and pans, had its soul. The ascending smoke carried with it the essence of the food to spirits and deities — they smelled the fragrance and were satisfied.[2] The visible material part of the offering, thus left untouched by the god, was often divided among his worshipers, and generally it furnished a welcome meal. These communal feasts are found in various parts of the world, among the Ainu of the Japan Archipelago, the American Indians, and others.[3] They were social and economical functions. It was desirable that the good food not consumed by the deity should be utilized for the benefit of his worshipers. There was also the

---

[1] Dorsey, *Skidi Pawnee*, p. 341 ; article "Bantu" in Hastings, *Encyclopædia of Religion and Ethics*, ii, 359 ; Rivers, *The Todas*, p. 393 ; Tylor, *Primitive Culture*, ii, 392 ; Westermarck, op. cit., ii, 518 al.

[2] Tylor, op. cit., ii, 385, 395 al. ; Gen. viii, 21.

[3] Batchelor, *The Ainu* ; Miss Fletcher, *Indian Ceremonies* ; Hollis, *The Nandi*, p. 12 ; Hopkins, *Religions of India*, pp. 449 ff., 528 : Saussaye, *Religion of the Teutons*, pp. 373, 383 ; R. M. Meyer, *Altgermanische Religionsgeschichte*, pp. 416, 419 ff. ; N. W. Thomas, article "Animals" in Hastings, *Encyclopædia of Religion and Ethics*. Cf., for the Hebrews, W. R. Smith, *Religion of the Semites*, 2d ed., p. 217 ff. ; for the Greeks, Gardner and Jevons, *Greek Antiquities*, p. 245 f. ; Miss Harrison, *Prolegomena to the Study of Greek Religion*, chap. x.

natural desire and custom of eating with friends. To this was added the belief that the bodies of such animals possessed powers which the worshiper might acquire by eating. The powers and qualities of the animal were both natural and sacred, or divine. The devotion of the dog, the courage and physical power of the bear, the cleverness of the fox — all such natural powers might be assimilated by the worshiper; and since the animal was itself sacred, its body, taken into the human body, communicated a certain special capacity. Thus the virtue of the communal feast was twofold: it placated the supernatural Power, and it procured for the worshiper a satisfactory meal and probably also an infusion of superhuman power. The favor of the deity was gained simply by the presents offered him; in these early times there is no indication of the belief that there was a recognized sacramental sharing of sacred food by the gods and their worshipers.

1024. *Messengers.* The supernatural Power was sometimes approached by a messenger who was instructed to ask a favor. The messenger was an animal regarded as sacred, akin to men and to gods, and therefore fitted · to be an intermediary. Examples of such a method of approaching a deity are found among the Ainu, in Borneo, and among the North American Indians. The Ainu, before slaying the bear who is to serve as messenger, deliver to him an elaborate address in which he is implored to represent to his divine kinsfolk above how well he has been treated on earth and thus gain their favor; he is also invited to return to earth that he may be again captured and slain. His flesh is eaten by the worshipers, and his head is set up as an object of worship. Thus, he is after death a divine Power and a portion of his own flesh is offered to his head, but this is simply to gain his good will, and there is no suggestion of a joint feast of gods and men.[1] Somewhat like this is the procedure in Borneo, where on special occasions when some particular favor is desired, a pig is dispatched with a special message to the gods.[2] In America the sacred turtle, regarded as a brother to the tribe and affectionately reverenced by his human brethren, is dispatched with tears to the other world to

[1] Batchelor, *The Ainu.*   [2] A. C. Haddon, *Head-hunters*, p. 353 ff.

join his kinsmen there and be an ambassador and friend.[1] A similar conception is to be found perhaps in the great Vedic animal
sacrifice in which the victim was likewise made ready by ceremonies
to go to the heavenly court and there stand as the friend of the
worshipers.[2]

1025. In all these cases there was a certain identification of the
victim with men on the one side and gods on the other. This is
simply a part of the general belief in the kinship existing between
all forms of being. Early men in choosing animal gifts for the
gods, or an animal as messenger to them, could not go astray, for
all animals were sacred. The effective means of procuring the
favor of the supernatural Powers is always a friendly gift or a
friendly messenger. When animals lost their religious prestige,
their ambassadorial function gave way to the mediatorial function
of gods and men.

Incense, tobacco, and other such things that were burned before
the deity are also to be regarded as food, though in the course of
time, when the recollection of this primitive character was lost, a
conventional significance was attached to the act of burning. A
more refined period demanded more refined food for the gods,
such as ambrosia and nectar, but these also were finally given up.

1026. Food was conveyed to the gods either by simply laying
it down at some sacred place (where it was devoured by beasts,
but more generally taken by official ministers of the god), or by
burning it.[3] In the body of the victim the blood came to play the
most important part as an expiatory force. Early observation, as
is pointed out above,[4] showed that the life was in the blood, and
so a principle of economy naturally suggested that it would be sufficient to offer the blood to the deity, though this was generally
supplemented by some choice portion of the flesh. Thus, the

---

[1] F. H. Cushing, " My Adventures in Zuñi " in *The Century Magazine* for May,
1883.

[2] Cf. Hubert and Mauss, "Essai sur le sacrifice" in *Année sociologique*, ii
(1898).

[3] A more socially refined conception appears in the lectisternium, in which the
gods sit at table with their human friends. Cf. Wissowa, *Religion der Römer*, p. 355 ff.;
Fowler, *Religious Experience of the Roman People*, Index, s.v.   [4] § 23.

opinion arose that blood had a special expiatory power, and this conception remained to a late period.[1] But the expiatory power rested finally on the fact that the blood was a gift of food to the gods. The gift was most effective, apparently, when the whole of the animal was burned, since thus the greatest honor was shown the deity and the most ample satisfaction of his bodily needs was furnished. The holocaust proper appears in religious history at a comparatively late stage, but the essence of it is found in all early procedures in which the whole of any object is given to the deity.

1027. *Human sacrifice.* That taste for human flesh on the part of men is not unnatural is shown by the prevalence of cannibal customs in many parts of the world. When such customs existed, it was natural that the flesh of human beings should be offered to the supernatural Powers.

The slaying of human beings at the graves of deceased clansmen or friends has prevailed extensively, though apparently not among the lowest tribes; it represents a certain degree of reflection or intensity; it is found in the midway period when religious customs were fairly well organized and when manners were not yet refined. Not every slaughter at a grave, however, is an act of religious offering to the dead. It is sometimes prompted by the spirit of revenge, to ease the mind of the slayer, or perhaps by desire to do honor to the deceased — doubtless there was a sentiment of piety toward the dead.

1028. The slaughter of slaves and wives to be the attendants of the deceased in the other world is of the nature of an offering — it is intended to procure the good will of the ghost. The self-immolation of widows and other dependents was in some cases a selfish act. It was supposed that the persons thus offering themselves up would procure certain advantages in the other world, while at the same time they would there minister to the manes of their husbands or lords.

As there was no practical difference between ghosts and spirits or gods in respect of power and influence in human life, the offering of human beings to these last came as a matter of course.

[1] For the worshiper the blood had strengthening power.

Their bodily appetites were the same as those of men — they were fond of human flesh. Wherever it was necessary to invoke their special aid this sort of offering was presented: for the success of crops; to insure the stability of houses and bridges[1]; to avert or remove calamities, such as pestilence and defeat in battle.

1029. While in the simpler societies human sacrifice was simply an offering of food to the Powers, in later times it came to be conceived of as the devotion of an object to the deity, and thus as a sign of obedience and dependence. The offering of firstborn children was a recognition of the fact that the god was the giver of children as of crops. The sacrifice of the dearest object, it was supposed, would soften the heart of the deity. In some cases the person who was supposed to be the occasion or source of misfortune was offered up. In general, human sacrifice followed the lines of all other sacrifices and disappeared when it became repugnant to humane and refined feelings.

1030. The testimonies to its existence are so numerous that we may suppose it to have been universal among men.[2] There is a trace of its early existence in Egypt.[3] In the Semitic region it is known to have been practiced by the Phœnicians, Carthaginians, Moabites, Hebrews, Arameans, and some Arabs.[4] There is no evidence of the practice in Babylonia; an indication of its existence in Assyria is possibly found in an Old Testament passage.[5] Its existence in early times in India is held to be implied in the Rig-Veda.[6] It appears in the Brahmanic period also: a man (who had to be a Brahman or a Warrior) was bought, allowed liberty and the satisfaction of all his desires (except that sexual intercourse was forbidden) for one year, and then ceremonially slain.[7] It is only recently that the sacrifice of children in the New Year festival

[1] 1 Kings, xvi, 34; article "Bridge" in Hastings, *Encyclopædia of Religion and Ethics.*

[2] Cf. Westermarck, *Origin and Development of the Moral Ideas,* Index, s.v. *Human Sacrifice.* [3] Breasted, *History of Egypt,* pp. 325, 411, 478.

[4] Pietschmann, *Phönizier,* p. 167; Tylor, *Primitive Culture,* ii, 403; 2 Kings, iii, 27; Exod. xiii; i, 13; Nöldeke, article "Arabs (Ancient)" in Hastings, *Encyclopædia of Religion and Ethics.* [5] 2 Kings, xvii, 31. [6] *Rig-Veda,* x, 18, 8; viii, 51, 2.

[7] *Sánkhayan Srauta Sutra,* xvi, 10–14; Weber, *Indische Streifen,* i, 65; Hopkins, *Religions of India,* pp. 196, 198.

at the mouth of the Ganges has been abolished ; and it is doubtful whether, in spite of the efforts of the British Government, it has been completely put down among the wild tribes, as the Gonds and the Khonds.[1] The records of China, from the eighth century B.C. onward are said to prove the existence of human sacrifice.[2] Among the ancient Scandinavians and Germans it was frequent.[3] In more recent times the practice is known either to exist or to have existed in Polynesia (Fiji, Samoa), Melanesia (Florida Islands), Borneo (formerly),[4] and North America (the Iroquois, the Natchez, the Florida peninsula, and the Southwest coast).[5] Nowhere does it appear on so large a scale as in Mexico ; and it existed also in Peru.[6] In Africa it was practiced to a frightful extent in Ashantiland and Dahomiland and more guardedly in Yoruba.[7]

1031. Its gradual disappearance (a result of increasing refinement of feeling) was marked by the substitution of other things for human victims or of aliens for tribesmen. In early times indeed it seems to have been slaves and captives taken in war that were commonly sacrificed. In more civilized times the blood of a tribesman, as more precious than other blood, was regarded as being more acceptable to the deity, and it was then a sign of advance when aliens were substituted for tribesmen. Lower animals were sacrificed in place of men : in India, where the recently sown fields had been fertilized with human blood, it became the practice to kill a chicken instead of a human being; and so in the story of Abraham (Gen. xxii) a ram is substituted for the human being.[8] Elsewhere

---

1 Hopkins, op. cit., p. 526 ff. Cf. also the practice of the thugs, which has now been put a stop to by the British Government.

2 De Groot, in Saussaye, *Lehrbuch der Religionsgeschichte*, 2d ed., p. 77 f.

3 Saussaye, *Religion of the Teutons*, Index, s.v.

4 Williams, *Fiji*; Turner, *Samoa*; Codrington, *The Melanesians*.

5 Waitz-Gerland, *Anthropologie der Naturvölker*, Index; J. G. Müller, *Geschichte der amerikanischen Urreligionen*, Index; Gatschet, *Migration Legend of the Creeks*, p. 36.

6 Payne, *The New World, Called America*. In Mexico the victim was surrounded with luxuries (including wives) and treated as a god for one year and then sacrificed (Frazer, *Golden Bough*, 1st ed., ii, 218 ff. ; 2d ed., ii, 342 f.).

7 A. B. Ellis, *Tshi*, *Ewe*, and *Yoruba*.

8 For such substitutions in Greece see Gardner and Jevons, *Greek Antiquities*, p. 243 f.

paste images are offered to the deity as representing men; an interesting development is found in Yoruba, where the proposed victim, instead of being sacrificed, becomes the protector of the sacrificer; that is, he is regarded as substantially divine, as he would have been had he been sacrificed.[1]

1032. Along with gifts, which formed perhaps the earliest method of conciliating divine beings, we find in very early times a number of procedures in honor of the deity, and intended in a general way to procure divine favor. Among these procedures dances and processions are prominent. The dance, as is observed above,[2] is simply the transference to religious rites of a common social act. It is, however, often supposed to have been communicated supernaturally, and in some cases it attains a high religious significance by its association with stories of divine persons. This organized symbolic dance has been developed to the greatest extent among certain North American Indian tribes.[3] Here every actor and every act represents a personage or procedure in a myth, and thus the dance embodies religious conceptions. This sort of symbolism has been adopted also in some sections of the Christian church, where it is no doubt effective in many cases as an element of external worship.

1033. While human sacrifice continued to a comparatively late period, it was the ordinary sort of sacrifice that constituted the main part of the ancient religious bond of society.[4] In the course of time the apparatus of sacrifice was elaborated — altars, temples, priests came into existence, and an immense organization was built up. Sacrifices played a part in all the affairs of life, took on various special shapes, and received different names. They were all placatory — in every case the object was to bring men into friendly relations with the god. They were *expiatory* when they were designed to secure forgiveness for offenses, whether by bloody or by unbloody offerings, or by anything that it was supposed would

---

[1] Ellis, *Yoruba*. [2] § 106 ff.

[3] Alice Fletcher, *Indian Ceremonies*; *Journal of American Folklore*, vol. iv (1891), no. 15, and vol. xvii (1904), no. 64; *Reports of the Bureau of Ethnology*, vol. xiv, p. 701.

[4] Cf. Tylor, *Primitive Culture*, Index, s.v. *Sacrifice*, and Westermarck, *Origin and Development of the Moral Ideas*, Index, s.v. *Sacrifice*.

secure the favor of the deity. They were performed when it was desired to procure some special benefit, for on such occasions it was necessary that the deity should be well disposed toward the supplicant; such *supplicatory* or *impetratory* sacrifices have been among the most common — they touch the ordinary interests of life, the main function of religious exercises in ancient times being to procure blessings for the worshiper. These blessings secured, it was necessary to give thanks for them — *eucharistic* sacrifices formed a part of the regular worship among all civilized peoples. When the crops came in, it was felt to be proper to offer a portion, the first fruits, to the deity, as among the Hebrews and many others, and, this custom once established, the feeling naturally arose that to partake of the fruits of the earth before the deity had received his part would be an impious proceeding likely to call down on the clan or tribe the wrath of the god. When a gift was made to a temple, since it was desirable that the deity should accept it in a friendly spirit, a sacrifice was proper. In the numerous cases in which some person or some object was to be consecrated to the deity a sacrifice was necessary in order to secure his good will; the ordination of temple-ministers, or the initiation of the young into the tribe, demanded some *consecrative* sacrifice. And, on the other hand, there was equal necessity for a sacrifice, a *deconsecrative* or *liberative* ceremony, when the relation of consecration was to be terminated (as in the case of the Hebrew Nazirite) or when a person was to be relieved from a taboo — in this latter case the ceremony of cleansing and of sacrificing was intended to secure the approval of the deity in whose name and in whose interest the taboo had been imposed.

1034. Sacrifices might be individual or communal, occasional or periodical. The early organization of society into clans made the communal sacrifice the more prominent [1] — the clan was the social unit, the interests of the individual were identical with those of the clan, and there was rarely occasion for a man to make a special demand on the deity for his individual benefit. Such occasions did, however, arise, and there was no difficulty in an individual's making a request

---

[1] Cf. Wissowa, *Religion der Römer*, p. 338 f.

of the tribal god provided it was not contrary to the interests of the tribe. If the petitioner went to some god or supernatural Power other than the tribal god, this was an offense against tribal life.

1035. The great communal sacrifices were periodical. They were determined by great turning-points in the seasons or by agricultural interests. Sowing time; when the crops became ripe; harvest time; midsummer and midwinter — such events were naturally occasions for the common approach of the members of the tribe to the tribal deity. The same thing is true of military expeditions, which were held to be of high importance for the life of the tribe. War was, as W. R. Smith calls it, a " holy function," [1] and its success was supposed (and is now often supposed) to depend on the supernatural aid of the deity. The particular method of conducting the ceremonies in such cases varied with the place and time, but the purpose of the worshiper and the general methods of proceeding are the same among all peoples and at all times. Occasions connected with the individual, such as birth, initiation, marriage, death, and burial, are also affairs of the family or clan, and the same rule applies to sacrifices on such occasions as to the great communal periodical offerings.

1036. It was inevitable that the ritual, that is, the specific mode of procedure, should receive a great development in the course of history. As colleges of priests were established, ceremonial elaborateness would become natural, and precise methods of proceeding would be handed down from generation to generation. Thus in many cases the worshiper had to be prepared by purificatory and other ceremonies, and the priest had to submit to certain rules before he could undertake the sacrifice. The victim was selected according to certain prescriptions: it had to be of a certain age or sex, of a certain color, generally free from impurities and defects, and sometimes it was necessary that it should show itself willing to be sacrificed.[2] These details do not at all affect the essence of the

---

[1] *Religion of the Semites*, 2d ed., p. 455.

[2] Lev. i–iv, viii, xvi, xxi; Numb. xix; Hopkins, *Religions of India*, p. 197 ff.; Gardner and Jevons, *Greek Antiquities*, Index, s.v. *Priests and Sacrifices*; Lippert, *Geschichte des Priesterthums*.

sacrifice. They are all the result of the ordinary human tendency to organization, to precise determination of particulars, and while certain general features are easily understood (those, for example, relating to the perfectness of the victim) others are the result of considerations which are unknown to us. It would be a mistake to seek for the origin of sacrifice in such ritualistic details.

THEORIES OF THE ORIGIN OF SACRIFICE

1037. Up to a very recent time the institution of sacrifice was generally accepted either as a natural human custom, due to reverence for the gods, or as of divine prescription. In very early documents, as, for example, in the Iliad and in certain parts of the Old Testament, it is assumed that the material of sacrifice is the food of the gods — a fact of interest in the discussion of the origin of sacrifice, never, however, in ancient times formulated as a theory. In the Græco-Roman and later Jewish periods sacrifices seem to have been conceived of in a general way as a mark of respect to the deity and fell more and more into disuse as the ethical feeling became distincter. In the New Testament there is a trace of the view that the victim is a substitute for the offerer: in the Epistle to the Hebrews it is said that the blood of bulls and goats could never effect the remission of sin — a nobler victim was necessary.[1] A similar conception is found in the later Greek and Roman literature, but there is still no distinct theory. In the third century of our era Porphyry, who was greatly interested in religious matters and, doubtless, represents a considerable body of thoughtful current opinion, says simply that sacrifices are offered to do honor to a deity or to give thanks or to procure favors.[2] The early Christian writers make no attempt to explain the origin of the custom, nor do we find any such attempt in the European philosophy of the seventeenth and eighteenth centuries. It was not until the spirit of historical inquiry had entered the sphere of religious investigation that the question as to the historical beginning and the significance of sacrifice was fairly put.

---

[1] Heb. x, 3.　　　　[2] *De Abstinentia*, ii, 24.

1038. In discussions of this question a distinction is sometimes made between bloody and unbloody offerings — they are supposed to differ in placatory or expiatory virtue, and one or the other of them is held to precede in order of time. The facts seem, however, not to warrant this distinction. Everywhere the two sorts of offering have equal power to please and placate the deity; the special prominence that may be given to the one or the other is due to peculiar social conditions that do not affect the essential nature of the rite.[1] As to precedence of one or the other in time the available data offer nothing definite beyond the fact that choice between them is determined by the circumstances of a community — the material of an offering is whatever (food or other thing) seems natural and appropriate in a particular place and at a particular time, and this may vary, of course, in the same community at different stages of culture.

1039. Current theories of the origin and significance of sacrifice divide themselves into two general groups, the one laying stress on the idea of gift, the other on the idea of union with the deity. Both go back ultimately to the same conception, the conviction, namely, that man's best good can be secured only by the help of the supernatural Powers; but they approach the subject from different points of view and differ in their treatment of the rationale of the ritual.

1040. The conception of an offering as a gift to a deity is found in very early times and is common in low tribes. In Greece the word for "gift," as offering, occurs from Homer on, and in Latin is frequent, and such a term is employed in Sanscrit. The common Hebrew term for sacrifice (*minḥa*) has the same sense; it is used for both bloody and unbloody offerings, though from the time of Ezekiel (sixth century B.C.) onward it became a technical term for cereal offerings.[2] The details of savage custom are given by Tylor,[3] who proposes as the scheme of chronological development "gift, homage, abnegation." This order, which is doubtless real, embodies and depends on growth in social organization and in the

---

[1] See below, § 1045 ff.   [2] Gen. iv, 3, 4 ; Lev. ii, al.
[3] *Primitive Culture*, ii, 375 ff. ; cf. Spencer, *Principles of Sociology*, i, 280 ff.

consequent growth in depth and refinement of religious feeling. The object of a gift is to procure favor and protection ; homage involves the recognition of the deity as overlord, and, in the higher stages of thought, as worthy of reverence — always, however, with the sense of dependence and the desire for benefits ; abnegation is the devotion of one's possessions and, ultimately, of one's self ; this idea sometimes assumes a low form, as if the deity were pleased with human loss and suffering, or as if human enjoyment were antireligious,[1] sometimes approaches the conception of the unity of the worshiper with the object of worship.[2]

1041. A special form of the gift-theory, with a peculiar coloring, is that which holds that some object is substituted for the worshiper who has fallen under the displeasure of the deity and is in danger of punishment. This conception, however, is found only in the most advanced religions. The cases in which an animal is substituted for a human victim [3] are of a different character — they are humane reinterpretations of old customs. In early popular religion the only examples of a deity's deliberately inflicting on innocent persons the punishment of another's wrongdoing are connected with the old conception of tribal and national solidarity — Œdipus, Achan, David, and others, by their crimes, bring misfortune on their peoples ; when the guilty have received their punishment the innocent are relieved. A real vicarious suffering is not found in these cases or in any ancient sacrificial ritual — the victim is not supposed to bear the sin of the sacrificant.[4] It is only in comparatively late theological constructions that vicarious atonement occurs. Some Jewish thinkers were driven to such a theory by the problem of national misfortune. The pious and faithful part of the nation, the " Servant of Yahweh," had shared in its grievous sufferings, and, as the faithful did not deserve this punishment, the conclusion was drawn that they suffered for the

---

[1] So often in ascetic practices.   [2] So, for example, in the *Imitatio Christi*.

[3] Euripides, *Iphigeneia in Aulis*, 1581 ff. (Iphigeneia) ; Gen. xxii (Isaac) ; and similar procedures in Hesiod, *Theogony*, 535 ff. ; Ovid, *Fasti*, iii, 339 ff. ; *Aitareya Brahmana*, ii, 8 ; *Çatapatha Brahmana*, i, 2, 3, 5.

[4] The expulsion of sin or evil in the person of a beast or a human being is a totally different conception. See above, § 143.

iniquities of the body of the people; [1] their suffering, however, was to end in victory and prosperity. In this conception the theory of solidarity is obvious, but it differs from the old tribal theory in that the suffering of the innocent brings salvation to the whole mass. In the prophetic picture there is no explanation of how this result was to be brought, about — there is no mention of a moral influence of the few on the many — only there is the implication that the nation, taught by suffering, would in future be faithful to the worship of the national deity. It does not appear wherein the ethical and religious significance of the unmerited suffering of the pious consisted; apparently the object of the writer is merely to account for this suffering and to encourage his countrymen. In another passage,[2] suffering is represented as having in itself expiatory power; the view in this case is that a just deity must punish sin, forgives, however, when the punishment has been borne.

1042. The view that the efficacy of sacrifice is due to the fact that it brings about a *union between the deity and the worshiper* has been construed in several different ways according as the stress is laid on one or another of the elements of the rite. One theory represents atonement, the reconciliation of god and man, as effected by the physical act of sharing the flesh of a sacred animal; another finds it in the death of an animal made sacred and converted into an intermediary by a series of ceremonies; a third holds that union with the divine is secured by whatever is pleasing to the deity.

1043. *Reconciliation through a communal meal.* Meals in which the worshipers partook of the flesh of a sacred animal (in which sometimes the dead animal itself shared) have probably been celebrated from an immemorial antiquity. Examples of such customs among savages are given above.[3] A familiar instance of a communal meal in civilized society is the Roman festival in which the shades of the ancestors of the clan were honored (the *sacra gentilicia*) — a solemn declaration of the unity of the clan-life.[4] A more definite

---

1 Isa. liii.   2 Isa. xl, 2.   8 Cf. §§ 128, 217 ff., 1023.
4 Other examples are given in Fowler, *Roman Festivals*, pp. 81 (shepherd sacrifice), 96 (Feriæ Latinæ), 194 (at the temple of Hercules), and cf. his *Religious Experience of the Roman People*, Index, s.v. *Meals, Sacrificial.*

act of social communion with a deity seems to be recognizable in the repasts spread in connection with the Eleusinian mysteries, which appear, however, to have been merely a social attachment to the mysteries proper.[1] In the feasts of the Mithraic initiates, in which mythological symbolism is prominent, a more spiritual element becomes visible: the participant absorbs something of the nature of the god — power to overcome evil, with hope of immortality.[2]

1044. In the ancient records of these ceremonies there is no theory of the means by which man comes into friendly relations with the deity. The meal is an act of friendly intercourse — it doubtless involves the ancient belief that those who eat together thus absorb a common life and are bound together by a strong tie. In the earliest and simplest instances the feeling apparently is that the communion is between the human participants — the divine animal is honored as a brother; but, even when, as among the Ainu,[3] he receives a part of the food, the tie that binds him to them rests on the fact of original kinship rather than on the communal eating. Later the view that the god was pleased and placated by the nourishment offered him assumed more definite form;[4] but it is doubtful whether on such occasions man was regarded as the guest of the deity.[5]

1045. However this may be, it is the effect of the food on the god that has been made by W. Robertson Smith the basis of an elaborate theory of sacrifice;[6] his view is that the assimilation of the flesh and blood of the kindred divine animal strengthens the deity's sense of kinship with his worshipers, and thus, promoting a kindly feeling in him, leads him to pardon men's offenses and grant them his protection. Smith's argument is mainly devoted to

---

[1] Foucart, *Des associations religieuses chez les Grecs*. For the Isis ceremony cf. Apuleius, *Metamorphoses*, xi, 24 f.

[2] Cumont, *The Mysteries of Mithra* (Eng. tr.), p. 160. On the magical element in mysteries cf. De Jong, *Das antike Mysterienwesen*, chap. vi.

[3] See above, § 1024.   [4] *Iliad*, i, 66 f.; *Odyssey*, x, 518 ff.; Gen. viii, 21.

[5] So Wellhausen, *Prolegomena to the History of Israel* (Eng. tr.), p. 62. In the Roman *sacra gentilicia* it was rather the divinized ancestors who were the guests — they were entertained by the living.

[6] In his article "Sacrifice" in *Encyclopædia Britannica* (1886) and his *Religion of the Semites* (new ed., 1894).

illustrating the ancient conception of blood-kinship between gods, men, and beasts. He assumes that sacrifice is the offering of food to the deity (the blood of the animal, as the seat of life, coming naturally to be the most important part of the offering), the sacredness of the victim, and the idea of communion, and further that the victim is a totem — the existence of totemism in the Semitic area, he holds, though not susceptible of rigid proof, is made practically certain by the wide diffusion of the totemic conception elsewhere.[1] As evidence that the effective thing in sacrifice is the sharing of sacred flesh and blood, he adduces a great number of offerings (such as the shedding one's own blood and the offering of one's hair) in which there is no death of a victim, and no idea of penal satisfaction of the deity. In the Israelite ritual he lays special stress on the common clan-sacrifice (the *zebaḥ*) in which a part of the victim is given to the god and a part is consumed by the worshiper; this he contrasts with offerings that are given wholly to the god, and, leaving aside piacula and holocausts, this distinction he makes correspond to that between animal and vegetable offerings, the latter, he holds, being originally not conciliatory. Thus, he concludes, the expiatory power lies in the sharing of animal flesh. Here the theory is confronted by the holocaust and the piaculum, expiatory sacrifices in which there is no communal eating. Smith meets this difficulty by suggesting that these two sorts of sacrifice belong to a relatively late period, when, in the progress of society, the original conception had become dim. As time went on, he says, the belief in kinship with animals grew fainter. Sacrificial meals became merely occasions of feasting, and at the same time the establishment of kingly government familiarized men with the idea of tribute — so sacrifice came to be regarded as a gift and the victim was wholly burnt (holocaust); the same result was reached when the feeling arose that the victim was too sacred to be eaten — it must be otherwise disposed of (piaculum). The piacula he refers to times of special distress, when

---

[1] The assumption that the victim is a totem is not necessary to his argument, which rests on the sacredness (that is, the divinity) of the victim — a fact universally admitted.

recourse was had to the sacrifice of ancient sacred animals, old totems (Hebrew: "unclean" animals), supposed to have special potency.[1] It is true that in the course of time certain old conceptions grew dim, but this does not set aside the fact that expiatory power was supposed to attach to animal sacrifices in which there was no communal eating; though some of these were late, they doubtless retained the old idea of the nature of the efficacy of sacrifice.

1046. In Smith's theory there is confusion between the two ideas of communion and expiation or placation. All the facts adduced by him go to show only that the earliest form of animal sacrifice took the form of communal eating; and in such repasts as in the savage feasts on the bodies of warriors and others, the prominent consideration seems to have been the assimilation of the qualities of the thing consumed — in this case a divine animal. There is not a word of proof of the view that the placation of the deity was due to his assimilation of kindred flesh and blood. Such a view is not expressed in any ancient document or tradition, and, on the other hand, placation by gifts of food (animal or vegetable) and other things appears in all accounts of early ritual. Even in the sacramental meals of later times, Eleusinian, Christian, and Mithraic, there is no trace of the theory under consideration. In the "Teaching of the Twelve Apostles" (ix f.) the conception of the eucharistic meal is simply symbolical. The origin of the Australian custom[2] (in which the food brought in by a clan is not eaten till the old men have first tasted it) is obscure; but there is no hint that the food was supposed to be shared by a supernatural being.[3] Piacula arose under the influence of a deep sense of individual relation to the deity, and sometimes in connection with voluntary associations in which a special sanctity was held to accrue to the initiates through the medium of a cult in which special sacrifices were prominent. It was natural that peculiarly

---

[1] Isa. lxv, lxvi.

[2] Spencer and Gillen, *Native Tribes of Central Australia*; id., *Native Tribes of Northern Australia*.

[3] On this point and on Smith's theory in general see the exposition of the theory by Jevons, *Introduction to the History of Religion*, chap. xii.

solemn or dreadful offerings should be made to the deity in times of great distress; the placating efficacy in such cases seems to have been due to the pleasure taken by the deity in the proof of devotion given by the worshipers. In general, the communal meal lost its early significance as time went on, and came at last to be celebrated merely as a traditional mark of respect to the deity, or as a social function; the belief in its efficacy, however (and sometimes belief in its magical power), survived into a relatively late period.

1047. In one point, the death of the god, J. G. Frazer, while accepting Smith's theory in general, diverges from his view. Smith regards the death of the god as having been originally the sacrificial death of the divine totem animal, with which later the god was identified. Frazer [1] (here following Mannhardt [2]) finds its origin in the death of the vegetation-spirit (the decay of vegetation), which was and is celebrated in many places in Europe, and furnishes an explanation of the myths of Adonis, Attis, Osiris, Dionysus, Demeter and Proserpine, and Lityerses. This explanation is adopted and expanded by Hubert and Mauss. [3] So far as the mere fact of the sacrifice of a divine being is concerned it might be accounted for by either of these theories; but the numerous points of connection between the deities in question and the ancient ideas concerning the death of vegetation make the view of Mannhardt and Frazer the more probable. The kernel of the original custom is not expiation but celebration or worship; the myths are dramatic developments of the simple old idea. Frazer suggests that the spirit or god, supposed to be enfeebled by age, was slain by the worshipers in order that a more vigorous successor might infuse new life into the world — an explanation that is possible but cannot be considered as established or as probable. [4] However this may be, it was at a relatively late period that the conception of communion was introduced into ceremonies connected with the death of a deity. Originally the grain, identified

1 *The Dying God* (part iii of 3d ed. of *The Golden Bough*).
2 *Wald- und Feldkulte*, 2d ed., ii, 273 ff.   3 *L'année sociologique*, ii, 115 ff.
4 Frazer, *The Dying God*, chap. ii, § 2.

with the god, was eaten in order to acquire his strength;[1] such seems to be the purpose in the Mexican ceremonies in which paste images of the deity were eaten by all the people. With the growth of moral and spiritual conceptions of worship such communal eating came naturally to be connected with a sense of union of soul with the deity, as we find in the higher religions, but still without the feeling that reconciliation and unity were effected through the absorption, by god and man, of the same sacred food.

1048. In some forms of Christianity the sacramental eating is brought into connection with the atoning death of a divine person, but this latter conception came independently by a different line of thought. Its basis is the idea of redemption, which is an element in all sacrifice proper. And, as the death of the divine victim is held to rescue the worshiper from punishment for ill doing, the conclusion is natural that the former stands in the place of the latter. In the higher forms of thought such substitution could only be voluntary on the part of the victim. Traces of the self-sacrifice of a god have been sought in such myths as the stories of the self-immolation of Dido and Odin; but the form and origin of these myths are obscure [2] — all that can be said of them in this connection is that they seem not to contain expiatory conceptions.[3] The higher conception of a divine self-sacrifice is a late historical development under the influence of convictions of the moral majesty of God and the sinfulness of sin.

1049. *Union with the divine through a sanctified victim.* The conception of sacrifice as bringing about a union of the divine and the human is reached in a different way from that of Smith by MM. Hubert and Mauss, and receives in their hands a peculiar coloring.[4] They hold that the numerous forms of sacrifice cannot be reduced to " the unity of a single arbitrarily chosen principle " ; and in view of the paucity of accurate accounts of early ritual (in

---

[1] Cf. Frazer, *Adonis Attis Osiris* (part iv of 3d ed. of *The Golden Bough*) ; 2d ed. of *The Golden Bough*, ii, 365 f.

[2] Article " Dido " in Roscher's *Lexikon* ; Saussaye, *Religion of the Teutons*, p. 231.

[3] For the view that Odin's self-sacrifice is merely an imitation of the reception into the Odin-cult see Meyer, *Altgermanische Religionsgeschichte*, p. 241.

[4] *L'année sociologique*, ii.

which they include the Greek and the Roman) they reject the "genealogical" (that is, the evolutionary) method, and devote themselves to an analysis of the two ancient rituals, the Hindu and the Hebrew, that are known in detail and with exactness. They thus arrive at the formula: " Sacrifice is a religious act which, by the consecration of a victim, modifies the state of the moral person who performs it, or of certain objects in which this person is interested." The procedure in sacrifice, they say, consists in establishing a communication between the sacred world and the profane world by the intermediation of a victim, that is, of a thing that is destroyed in the course of the ceremony; it thus serves a variety of purposes, and is dealt with in many ways: the flesh is offered to hostile spirits or to friendly deities, and is eaten in part by worshipers or by priests; the ceremony is employed in imprecations, divination, vows, and is redemptive by the substitution of the victim for the offender; the soul of the beast is sent to join its kin in heaven and maintain the perpetuity of its race; all sacrifices produce either sacralization or desacralization — both offerer and victim must be prepared (for the victim is not, as Smith holds, sacred by nature, but is made sacred by the sacrifice), and, the ceremony over, the person must be freed from his sanctity (as in the removal of a taboo); all sacrifice is an act of abnegation, but the abnegation is useful and egoistic, except in the case of the sacrifice of a god.

1050. The essay of MM. Hubert and Mauss is rather a description of the mode of procedure in Hindu sacrifice than an . explanation of the source of its power. A victim, it is said, sanctified by the act of sacrifice, effects communication between the two worlds, but we are not told wherein consists this sanctifying and harmonizing efficacy. The rituals chosen for analysis are the product of many centuries of development and embody the conceptions of theological reflection; it does not appear why they should be preferred, as sources of information concerning the essential nature of sacrifice, to the simple rites of undeveloped communities. The authors of the essay, though they deny the possibility of finding a single explicative principle chosen arbitrarily, themselves announce a principle, which, however, amounts simply to the statement that sacrifice is placatory. In thus ascribing the virtue of the ceremony to the act itself it is possible that they may have been influenced by the Brahmanic conception that sacrifice had power in itself to control the gods and to secure all blessings for men; it was credited by them with magical efficacy, and the efficacy depended on performing the act with minutest accuracy in details — the slightest error in a word might vitiate the whole proceeding.[1] The developed Hindu system thus embodied in learned form the magical idea that is found in many early procedures, and in some other cults of civilized communities. So far as regards the variety of functions assigned by MM. Hubert and Mauss to sacrifice, they may all be explained as efforts to propitiate supernatural Powers; and the obligation on priests and worshipers to purify themselves by ablutions and otherwise arises from a sense of the sacredness of the sacrificial act, which is itself derived from the feeling that the sacredness of supernatural beings communicates itself to whatever is connected with them. The view that the victim is not in itself sacred is contradicted by all the phenomena of early religion. Though the essay of MM. Hubert and Mauss formulates no definition of the ultimate efficient cause in sacrifice, passing remarks appear to indicate that they look on the offering as a gift to superhuman Powers, and that their object is to show under what conditions and circumstances it is to be presented.

1051. *Sacrifice as the expression of desire for union with the Infinite.* Professor C. P. Tiele, dissatisfied with existing theories of the significance of sacrifice, contents himself with a general statement.[2] After pointing out that the material of sacrifice in any community is derived from the food of the community, he passes in review briefly the theories of Tylor (gifts to deities), Spencer (veneration of deceased ancestors), and Robertson Smith; all these, though he thinks it would be presumptuous to condemn them hastily, he finds insufficient, most of them, he says, confining

---

[1] *Yajur-Veda*, passim; *Çatapatha Brahmana*, i, 3, 6, 8; ii, 6, 2; Hopkins, *Religions of India*, p. 188 al.; Bloomfield, *Religion of the Veda*, pp. 31 ff., 215.
[2] *Elements of the Science of Religion* (Gifford Lectures), ii, 144 ff.

themselves to a single kind of offering, whereas every kind should be taken into account, gifts presented, objects and persons consecrated, victims slain with or without repasts, possessions and pleasures renounced, acts of fasting and abstinence, every kind of religious self-denial or self-sacrifice. The question being whether one and the same religious need is to be recognized in all the varieties, he finds the root of sacrificial observances in the yearning of the believer for abiding communion with the supernatural Power to which he feels himself akin, the longing of finite man to become one with the Infinity above him.

1052. Tiele here has in mind the highest form of the religious consciousness, which he carries back to the beginnings of religious thought. He is justified in so doing in so far as all later developments must be supposed to exist in germinal form at the outset of rational life ; but such a conception tells us nothing of the historical origin of customs. The idea of the relation between the finite and the infinite is not recognizable in early thought ; to trace the history of such an institution as sacrifice we desire to know in what sort of feeling it originated, and we may then follow its progress to its highest definition. All the details mentioned by Tiele are included under the head of gift except acts of abstinence and self-sacrifice, and these last belong properly not to what is technically known as " sacrifice," but to man's endeavor to bring himself into ethical harmony with an ethical deity. With equal right prayer and all moral conduct might here be included ; Tiele thinks of " sacrifice " as embracing the whole religious life. In the earliest known cults the " yearning for union with the Infinite " takes the form of desire to enter into friendly relations with superhuman Powers by gifts, in order to derive benefit from them ; when old forms have been outgrown the conviction arises that what is well-pleasing to God is the presentation of the whole self, as a " living sacrifice," in service in accordance with reason (Rom. xii, 1).

1053. The various theories of the origin and efficacy of sacrifice (omitting the ambassadorial conception) are thus reducible to three types : it is regarded as a gift, as a substitution, or as an act securing union (physical or spiritual) with the divine. These have all maintained themselves, in one form or another, up to the present day. The old ritual slaughter of an animal and the presentation of vegetables and other things have, indeed, vanished. The movement of thought against animal sacrifice began in the Western world (among the Greeks and the Hebrews) probably as early as the fourth century B.C.[1] In Greece the formulation of philosophic thought and the rise of individualism in religion (embodied, for example, in the great Mysteries) brought larger and more spiritual ideas into prominence. Rational law and inward impulse took the place, in the higher circles, of ritual offerings. The object of law, says Plato, is the encouragement of virtue of all kinds and the securing of the highest happiness; but, he holds, there is something higher than law: the good Athenian is above other men, for he is the only man who is freely and genuinely good by inspiration of nature, and is not manufactured by law.[2] The Mysteries assumed that every man, with suitable inward preparation, was fitted to enter into a spiritual union with the deity. The later Jews showed equal devotion to their law, held to be divinely given, laying the stress on the moral side;[3] jurists became more important than priests, and the synagogue (representing individual worship) more influential than the temple-ritual. In certain psalms[4] sacrifice is flatly declared not to be acceptable to God; this attitude had been taken by the earlier prophets,[5] but is emphasized in the psalms in the face of the later opinion that the sacrificial ritual was of divine ordination (so in Exodus, Leviticus, Numbers). In the Gospels the sacrificial ritual is practically ignored. In India the Brahmanic and Buddhistic movements toward rational conceptions of religion showed themselves as early as the sixth century B.C. Thus, over a great part of the civilized world intellectual and moral progress took the form of protest against the old idea of sacrifice.

1054. Yet old customs are long-lived, and the ancient theories, as is remarked above, still have a certain power. The crudest of them — that the deity may be propitiated by gifts — shows itself

---

[1] Plato (*Laws*, iii, 716) says that a bad man gets no benefit from sacrifice.
[2] *Laws*, i, 631, 642.　　[3] Ps. xix, 7 ff.; cxix.　　[4] Ps. xl, 7; l, 8–15; li, 18 f., al.
[5] Amos, v, 21 ff.; Isa. i, 11 ff.; Mic. vi, 6 ff.; Jer. vii, 21 ff.

in the belief that ill-doing máy be atoned for by the support of charitable and religious institutions — by the building of churches and hospitals, by the maintenance of religious worship, and by aid to the poor. Society has benefited largely by this belief, especially jn medieval Europe and to some extent in Buddhistic and Moslem communities; it has formed a transition to higher conceptions, by which it has now been in great measure replaced. The same thing is true of ascetic observances. The idea of sacrificial substitution, which has been prominent in organized Christianity from an early period (though it has no support in the teaching of Jesus), might seem to be prejudicial to religion for the reason that it tends to depress the sense of individual responsibility by relegating the reconciliation with the deity to an external agency — and such has often been its effect; but this unhappy result has been more and more modified, partly by the natural human instinct of moral responsibility and the ethical standard of the Christian Scriptures, partly by the feeling of gratitude and devotion that has been called forth by the recognition of unmerited blessing The third theuiy of sacrifice, according to which its essence is union with the divine, has passed gradually from the sphere of ritual to that of moral culture. In mystical systems, Christian and Moslem, it has lent itself sometimes to immorality, sometimes to a stagnant, egoistic, and antisocial quietism; but in the main it has tended to avoid or abandon mechanical and mystical features, and confine itself to the conception of sympathetic and intelligent coöperation with what may be regarded as the divine activities of the world.

1055. *Further external apparatus of religion.* Along with the growth of sacrifice there has been a natural development of everything that was necessary to give permanent form to public worship — ritual, priests, temples, idols, and whatever was connected with the later church organizations.

Ritual

Apart from magical procedures the earliest known public religious worship consisted simply in the offering of an animal, a vegetable, a fluid, or other object to a superhuman being, the offering being performed by any prominent person and without elaborate ceremonies. Inevitably, however, as the social organization grew more complex and the conception of sanctity more definite, the ceremonial procedure became more elaborate. The selection and the handling of the victim came to be objects of anxious care, and the details increased in importance as they increased in number. It was believed that minute accuracy in every ritual act was necessary for the success of the offering. Various elements doubtless entered into this belief : often a magical power was attributed to the act of sacrifice ; and there was a feeling, it may be surmised, that the deity was exacting in the matter of ceremonies — these were marks of respect, such as was paid to human potentates, and well-defined court rituals (on which the religious ritual was probably based) appear in early forms of society. Thus ritual tended to become the predominant element in worship, serving first the interests of unity and order in religion, and later always in danger of becoming a mechanical and religiously degrading influence.

1056. In most savage and half-civilized communities sacrifice is a simple affair, and the details of the ceremonies of worship are rarely reported by travelers and other observers.[1] An exception exists in the case of the Todas of Southern India, who have elaborate ceremonies connected with the milking of buffaloes.[2] The ordinary buffaloes of a village are cared for by some prominent man (never by a woman), who is sometimes a sacred person and while carrying on his operations performs devotional acts (prayer and so forth), but without a fixed ritual. A higher degree of sanctity attaches to the institution called *ti*, which comprises a herd of buffaloes belonging to a clan and provided with dairies and grazing-grounds ; each dairy has appropriate buildings, and the *ti* is presided over by a sort of priest called a *palol*. The migration of the buffaloes from one grazing-ground to another is conducted as a sacred function. In the case of an ordinary herd the procession

---

[1] See Ellis, *Ewe* (Dahomi), *Tshi* (Ashanti), *Yoruba*; Miss Kingsley, *Travels*; Codrington, *The Melanesians*; Turner, *Samoa*; articles " Andeans," " Bantu," " Bengal," " Brazil," al., in Hastings, *Encyclopædia of Religion and Ethics*.
[2] Rivers, *The Todas*, chaps. vi, xi, xiii.

of animals is accompanied by a religious official who carries the dairy implements; on reaching the destination the new dairy is purified, the sun is saluted, and prayer is offered. In a *ti* migration the procedure is more elaborate: the milking of the buffaloes is accompanied by prayers for the older and the younger members of the herd, and every act of the *palol* is regulated by law. The same thing is true of the animal sacrifices: the slaughter of the victim and the disposal of the various parts are accomplished in accordance with definite rules that are handed down orally from one generation to another. The Todas are a non-Aryan people, hardly to be called half-civilized: if the buffalo-ritual is native with them, the natural inference will be that the custom is ancient. Rivers adduces a considerable number of similarities between Toda institutions and those of the Malabar coast (such as polyandry and other marriage institutions), and this agreement, as far as it goes, may point to a common culture throughout a part of Southern India;[1] the early history of these tribes is, however, obscure. It is possible that the Todas have borrowed some customs from the Hindus. They have certainly adopted some Hindu gods, and Rivers suspects Hindu influence in their recognition of omens and lucky and unlucky days, in certain of their magical procedures, and in their use of pigments and ashes in some sacred ceremonies. There seems, however, to be no proof that the buffalo-ritual has been borrowed from the Hindus. On this question, which is of importance as bearing on the early history of ritual, it is to be hoped that further information will be got.

1057. Various nonsacrificial rituals (dances and so forth) are referred to above.[2] Magical processes should be here included so far as they involve a recognition of superhuman agents; they are then to be regarded as religious. Definite magical ritual is found in many of the lower tribes, and there are ceremonies in which a shaman is the conductor — these are governed by fixed customs as to dress, posture, acts, and words.[3] They differ from magical

---

[1] Cf. also Crooke's *Popular Religion and Folklore of Northern India*, in which similar customs are mentioned.   [2] Chapter iii.

[3] Dixon, *The Northern Maidu* and *The Shasta*. For Korea see H. G. Underwood, *Religions of Eastern Asia*.

processes in that they are assemblies of the people, religious because there is communication with spirits. In the Californian tribes and others they become occasions of merrymaking; a peculiar feature of these gatherings among the Maidu and other tribes is the presence of a clown who mimics the acts and words of the dancers and performs knavish tricks; the origin of this feature of the dances is not clear. In all such ceremonies the tendency to regulate the details of religious performances is apparent, and such regulation is found in so many parts of the world that it may be regarded with probability as universal.

1058. For the ancient national religions we have the fullest details in the case of the Hindus and the Hebrews. The Hindu sacrificial ritual is described by MM. Hubert and Mauss;[1] the Hebrew procedure is given in the later sections of the Pentateuch.[2] The Egyptian ritual also appears to have been elaborate, including much music.[3] These show methods similar to those described above, and probably the same general modes of procedure were followed in Babylonia and Persia, though of the ritual in these countries only slight notices have been handed down.[4] The great Chinese Imperial sacrifices are described by H. Blodget.[5]

1059. These national systems exhibit a gradual quiet enlargement of the ritual resulting from increasing specialization in the conception of sin and forgiveness and in the functions of religious officials. A different sort of development appears in the rites of the cults that sprang up on the ruins of the old faiths — Greek Mysteries, Mithraism, Isisism, Christianity. These were all redemptive religions, highly individualistic and intense, efforts to infuse into old forms the ideas concerning moral purity, union with the deity, immortality, and future salvation that had arisen

---

[1] *L'année sociologique*, ii; see above, § 1049.

[2] Exodus, Leviticus, Numbers. A single early detail is mentioned in 1 Sam. ii, 13 ff. For the later Jewish ceremonial see article " Sacrifice " in *Encyclopædia Biblica*.

[3] Mariette, *Abydos*; Maspero, *Dawn of Civilization* (Eng. tr.), p. 121 ff.; Erman, *Handbook of Egyptian Religion*, pp. 46–49, 122, 179 f. (reports of Herodotus).

[4] For Babylonia see Jastrow, *Religion of Babylonia and Assyria*, Index, s.v. *Rituals*; for Mazdean, De Harlez, *Avesta*, Introduction, pp. clxvi, clxx.

[5] *Journal of the American Oriental Society*, xx, 58 ff.; cf. De Groot, in Saussaye, *Lehrbuch der Religionsgeschichte*, p. 60 ff.

in the Græco-Roman world by the natural growth of thought and the intermingling of the various existing schemes of religious life. They are all marked by a tendency toward elaborate organization, a sharp differentiation from the national cults, and purificatory and other ceremonies of initiation. The differentiation was most definite in Christianity, the ritual was most highly developed in the other movements. In the Greek public Mysteries [1] and in those of Mithra [2] there were (besides ablutions) the old communal meals, processions, striking dramatic performances, and brilliant effects of light and music, and in Mithraism trials of courage for the neophyte after the manner of the old savage initiations. The ceremonies in the Isis cult were less sensational, more quiet and dignified.[3] In all these cults there was symbolism, and the moral teaching was of a lofty character.

1060. Christian ritual was at first simple,[4] but rapidly grew in elaborateness. The liturgy and the eucharistic ceremonies were expanded into great proportions, and came to be the essence of worship. This movement went on throughout Christendom (with variations here and there) up to the rise of Protestantism, and after that time continued in the Greek and Roman Churches. Protestantism, in its recoil from certain doctrines of the Church of Rome, threw off much of its ceremonial, which in the minds of the people was associated with the rejected dogmas. Since the separation, however, especially in the last hundred years, the violent antagonism having largely quieted down, there has been in some Protestant bodies a slow but steady movement in the direction of ritualistic expansion; procedures that three centuries ago would have called forth earnest protest are now accepted and interpreted in accordance with Protestant ideas. Doubtless the temperament of a people has something to do with the amount of ceremonial it favors in religious service.

1061. The history of ritual thus shows that it tends to grow in elaborateness and importance as social forms become more

---

[1] Foucart, *Associations religieuses chez les Grecs*; Jevons, *Introduction to History of Religion*, chap. xxiii; De Jong, *Das antike Mysterienwesen*, p. 18 ff.
[2] Cumont, *Mysteries of Mithra*.   [3] Apuleius, *Metamorphoses*, chap. xi.
[4] 1 Cor. xi, 20 ff.; xiv (cf. Acts ii, 46); *Teaching of the Twelve Apostles*, chap. ix f.

elaborate and important — the mode of approaching the deity imitates the mode of approaching human dignitaries, postures are borrowed from current etiquette.[1] Form was especially sought after under the old monarchies, Egyptian and Assyrian.[2] The exaggerated Oriental court etiquette, introduced into Roman life as early as the time of Diocletian, was maintained and developed under the Byzantine emperors.[3] These usages may have affected the growth of the Greek and Roman Church liturgies.[4] In modern China, under the imperial government, divine worship was substantially identical in form with the worship of the emperor. In some cases it may be doubtful in which direction the borrowing has been.

The expansion of liturgical forms has often been accompanied by the effort to interpret them symbolically. Intelligent reflection has led to the conviction that forms without religious meaning are valueless, and it has been easy, after ceremonies were established, to attach spiritual definitions to their details. This relieves their materialism, and gives a certain realness and force to religious feeling.

PRIESTS [5]

1062. A priest is a person commissioned by the community or its head to conduct the sacrificial service and related services connected with shrines. Such a person differs in two respects from the religious official of the simplest times, the magician (shaman, or medicine man): the latter acts in his own name and by his own authority, and the methods he employs are magical — they are based on the belief that the supernatural Powers are subject to law and may be controlled by one who knows this law; the priest

---

[1] So, for instance, postures in prayer, such as kneeling, bowing, standing.

[2] The *Amarna Letters*; *Records of Ancient Egypt*, ed. Breasted; cuneiform inscriptions. The Egyptian king, however, was regarded as divine.

[3] Gibbon, chaps. xiii (Diocletian), xl, year 532; cf. descriptions in Scott's *Count Robert of Paris*.

[4] Daniel, *Codex Liturgicus*; articles "Liturgie" and "Messe" in Herzog-Hauck, *Real-Encyklopädie*; articles "Liturgy" and "Liturgical Books" in Smith and Cheatham, *Dictionary of Christian Antiquities*.

[5] Cf. J. Lippert, *Allgemeine Geschichte des Priesterthums*; Westermarck, *Origin and Development of the Moral Ideas*, Index, s.v. *Priests*.

acts in the name and by the authority of the community, and his methods are dictated by the friendly social relation existing between the community and the Powers. He differs, further, from those religious ministrants (chiefs of clans, fathers of families, and other prominent men) who acted by virtue of their social or political positions in that his functions are solely religious and are in that regard distinct from his civil position. He represents a differentiation of functions in an orderly nonmagical religious society. Such an office can arise only under a tolerably well-organized civil government and a fairly well-defined sacrificial ritual. It is doubtless a slow growth, and there may be, in a community, a period of transition from one grade of religious ministers to another when the distinction between the priest and the magician or between the priest and the headman is hardly recognizable; the distinction comes, however, to be well marked, and then indicates an important turning-point in religious history. It may be, also, that at certain times under certain circumstances the civil ruler may have priestly functions or the priest may exercise civil authority; but these exceptional cases do not affect the specific character of the sacerdotal office.

1063. The priest is a sacred person, and is affected by all the conditions pertaining to the conception of "sacred." In early times he has to be guarded against contamination by impure or common (profane) things, and care has to be taken that his quality of sacredness be not injuriously communicated to other persons or to any object.[1] The parts of his person, such as hair and nail-parings, must not be touched by common folk. The dress worn by him when performing his sacred duties must be changed when he comes out to mix with the people. He must keep his body clean, and the food that he may or may not eat is determined by custom or by law. His sexual relations are defined — sometimes he is forbidden to marry or to approach a woman, sometimes the prohibition extends only to marriage with a certain sort of woman

---

[1] On priestly taboos see Frazer, *Golden Bough*, 2d ed., Index, s.v.; these are often of the same sort as royal taboos. See above, § 595 ff. For Hebrew priestly taboos see Ezek. xliv, Lev. xxi f.

(a foreigner, a widow, or a harlot). In some cases he is forbidden to engage in warfare or to shed human blood;[1] the ground of this prohibition was physical, not moral.[2]

1064. Similar rules in regard to food, marriage, chastity applied to priestesses.[3] Women were often, in ancient times, the ministrants in the shrines of female deities — there was a certain propriety in this arrangement; they were, however, in some cases attached to the service of male deities.[4] Their duties were in general of a secondary character: they rarely, if ever, offered sacrifice;[5] they were often in charge of the temple-music; the function of soothsaying or of the interpretation of oracular sayings was sometimes assigned them. On the other hand, female ministrants in temples, who were closely connected with temple duties, were sometimes considered as wives of the god, and in some cases had sexual relations with priests and worshipers, and became public prostitutes.[6] This custom does not exist among the lowest tribes, and it attained its largest development in some of the great civilized cults. It seems not to have existed in Egypt.[7] The consecrated maidens described in the Code of Hammurabi appear to have been chaste and respected ;[8] the relation between these and the harlots of the early Ishtar cult is not clear. A distinction may be made between priestesses proper and maidens (hierodules) consecrated to such a deity as Aphrodite Pandemos ; Solon's erection of a temple to this goddess, which he supplied with women, may have been an attempt to control the cult of the hetæræ. The thousand hierodules at Corinth[9] were probably

---

[1] Westermarck, *Origin and Development of the Moral Ideas*, i, 348, 381.
[2] Not all these conditions were to be found in any one community.
[3] Westermarck, op. cit., ii, 406 ff.   [4] Pausanias, ii, 33, 3.
[5] For a possible case see Wilkinson, *The Ancient Egyptians*, 1st ed., i, 317.
[6] Ellis, *Ewe*, p. 141 ; Ward, *History, Literature and Religion of the Hindoos*, ii, 134 : Jastrow, *Religion of Babylonia and Assyria*, p. 660 ; Hos. iv, 14 ; Deut. xxiii, 17 f. (prohibition) ; Gen. xxxviii, 14 ff.
[7] Erman, *Handbook of Egyptian Religion*, pp. 72, 221, is disposed to reject the statement of Strabo (xvii, i, 46) that there was libertinage at Thebes. Cf. Wilkinson, *The Ancient Egyptians*, Index, s.v. *Priestesses.*
[8] C. H. W. Johns, article " Code of Hammurabi" in Hastings, *Dictionary of the Bible*, extra volume; D. G. Lyon, "The Consecrated Women of the Hammurabi Code" in *Studies in the History of Religions presented to C. H. Toy.*   [9] Strabo, p. 378.

not priestesses, and the same thing may be surmised to be true of the women devoted to the Semitic prototype of Aphrodite, the Syrian Ashtart (Astarte), and to the Babylonian Ishtar.[1]

1065. The origin of temple prostitution is not clear. In many cases (in Greece, Rome, Mexico, Peru, and elsewhere) the consecrated women were required to be virgins and to remain chaste — this higher conception is obviously the natural one in a civilized community in which the purity of wives and daughters is strictly guarded. The old idea that sexual union was defiling may have originated or strengthened the demand for chastity. The institution of the lower class of women does not seem to have originated in a society in which this regard for purity is lacking, for the hierodulic class is rarely if ever found in existing societies of this sort. The origin of the class is not to be sought in a low valuation of woman, nor, on the other hand, is it to be found in a desire to secure fruitfulness; fruitfulness is generally secured by offerings to the gods, and though the belief has doubtless existed that it could be secured by commerce with a supernatural being,[2] there is no trace of this belief in the accounts of the lives of the hierodules; the benefit would be restricted also to a small number of women. Probably the custom was developed gradually and, like other such customs, had its ground in simple needs. Women were required for the menial work of shrines.[3] Once established in service, they would acquire a certain sanctity and power by their relation to sacred things, and at the same time would, as unattached, be sought by men. Their privileges and license would grow with time — they would become an organized body, and would seek to increase their power. In the course of time current religious ideas, low or high, would attach to them. They would be supposed to be in the confidence of the deity, able to interpret his will, and endowed with the power of cursing or blessing.[4] With the growth of refinement they would be thought of as servants

---

[1] Roscher, *Lexikon*, article " Aphrodite," col. 401. Cf. the practice mentioned in 1 Sam. ii, 22.   [2] Curtiss, *Primitive Semitic Religion To-day*.

[3] See, for example, 1 Sam. ii, 22.

[4] For a description of their privileges and power in Ashanti see Ellis, *Tshi*, p. 121 ff.

of the deity, belonging to him and to no other, and might be described, as in fact they are sometimes described, as his wives. The title "wife" would be compatible with purity in the higher religious systems, but in the lower systems would be connected with license.

1066. *Theories of the origin of religious prostitution.* The license just referred to is a part of a widespread custom of the prostitution of sacred persons, of which various explanations have been offered.[1] The existence of the custom is attested for the larger part of the ancient civilized and half-civilized world, and for many more recent peoples. In old Babylonia, Canaan, Syria, Phœnicia, Asia Minor, Armenia, Greece, and now in West Africa and India, we find officially appointed "sacred" women a part of whose religious duty it was or is to offer themselves to men.[2] The service in ancient times was not regarded as degrading; on the contrary, maidens of the noblest families were sometimes so dedicated, and the rôle of devotee might be continued in a family for generations.[3] Such service was sometimes a necessary preliminary to marriage. This seems to be the case in the custom reported by Herodotus[4] that every native Babylonian woman had, once in her life, to sit in the temple of Mylitta (Ishtar) and wait till a piece of money was thrown into her lap by a stranger, to whom she must then submit herself — this duty to the goddess accomplished, she lived chastely. In Byblos a woman who refused to sacrifice her hair to Ashtart on a certain festival day had to yield herself to a stranger.[5]

Official male prostitutes also there were in some ancient cults; but information about such persons is scanty, and they seem not

---

[1] License in festivals and mystical or symbolic marriages are excluded as not being official consecration of a class of persons.

[2] Examples are given in Westermarck, *Origin and Development of the Moral Ideas*, ii, 443 ff.; Frazer, *Adonis Attis Osiris*, chap. iv; Seligmann, *Der böse Blick und Verwandtes*, ii, 190 ff.; and see above, § 384 ff.

[3] Inscription of Tralles; see Ramsay, *Cities and Bishoprics of Phrygia*, i, 94 ff.; Farnell, *Cults of the Greek States*, ii, 636.

[4] Herodotus, i, 199. The correctness of Herodotus's statement has been doubted; but, though the procedure is singular, it is not wholly out of keeping with known Babylonian customs. It must be remembered, however, that Herodotus wrote long after the fall of the Babylonian empire, when foreign influence was possible. See also *Epistle of Jeremias*, v. 43.   [5] Pseudo-Lucian, *De Syria Dea*, chap. vi.

to have been numerous.[1] The most definitely named case is that of the Hebrew official class called *kedeshim*, that is, persons devoted to the service of the deity and therefore sacred[2] (as it is said in Zech. xiv, 20 ff., that bells on horses and temple-vessels shall be sacred to Yahweh). These, together with the female devotees, *kedeshot* (" prostitutes "), are denounced as abhorrent to Yahweh; both were features in the ritual of the Jerusalem temple of the seventh century B.C. and apparently earlier.[3] The female devotee is called a " harlot " and the male a " dog " (*kalb*). The original religious sense of the latter term is uncertain. In the Old Testament it occurs, in this sense, only in the passage cited above. In a Phœnician inscription of Larnaca (in Cyprus)[4] the plural of the word designates a class of attendants in a temple of Ashtart, and there are proper names in which the term is an element (and therefore an honorable title). It is not improbable that it meant originally simply a devotee or minister of a god in a temple,[5] the bad sense having been attached to it in the Old Testament from the license sometimes practiced by such ministers.

The sentiment of chastity is a product of the highest civilization. In many savage and half-civilized tribes the obligation on a woman to keep herself pure is not fully recognized, and in the case of married women the opposition to unfaithfulness sometimes springs from the view that it is a violation of the husband's right of property in the wife. In some ancient civilized communities a god's right to a woman seems to have been taken for granted.[6] Ordinary prostitution seems to have existed in the world,

---

[1] Homosexual practices do not belong here (Westermarck, op. cit., chap. xliii). The intercourse of priests with sacred and other women is likewise excluded.

[2] Deut. xxiii, 18 [17] f., " sodomite."

[3] 1 Kings, xiv, 24 (tenth century), where the *kedeshim* seem to be described as a Canaanite institution. Cf. Deut. xxii, 5.

[4] *Corpus Inscriptionum Semiticarum*, part i, i, 86, B 10.

[5] With allusion, perhaps, to the dog's faithfulness to his master. In the *Amarna Letters* a Canaanite governor calls himself the " dog " (*kalbu*) of his Egyptian overlord. Cf. W. R. Smith, *Religion of the Semites*, 2d ed., p 292, n. 2. For examples of the sanctity of the dog see article " Animals " in Hastings, *Encyclopædia of Religion and Ethics*, p. 512.

[6] Cf. Frazer, *Adonis Attis Osiris*, p. 71 f., and the curious story told in Josephus, *Antiquities*, xviii, 3.

in all grades of civilization, from the earliest times. This attitude toward the custom being so widespread, it is not strange that it has established itself in religious organizations.

Two types of organized religious prostitution have to be considered:[1] there is the Babylonian (Mylitta) type, in which every woman must thus yield herself before marriage; and there is the attachment of a company of official public women to a temple permanently or for a considerable time. The explanations that have been offered of these institutions fall into two classes, one tracing their origin to some nonreligious custom, the other regarding them as originally religious (these classes are, however, not necessarily mutually exclusive).

Secular explanations. It has been held that all such customs go back to a period of sexual promiscuity,[2] which has been modified in the course of ages. It is doubtful whether such a period ever existed,[3] but it is certain that prenuptial license has been common, and this laxity may have prepared the way for organized prostitution. More particularly, reference is made to puberty defloration ceremonies, when the girl is handed over to certain men no one of whom can, by tribal rule, be her husband — that is, before marriage she becomes sexually the property of the tribe through its regularly appointed representatives, and is thus prepared for membership; then, it is added, at a later period, when religious service has been established, the girl is given over or devoted not to the tribe but to the tribal god, in whose shrine she must submit to defloration, in accordance with rules fixed from time to time. The act thus becomes religious — it is a recognition of the sovereignty of the deity, and procures divine favor. Such may be a possible explanation of the procedure in the temple of Mylitta and at Byblos.[4] But the meaning of the condition imposed at these places, namely, that the man

---

[1] The Lydian method by which girls earned their dowries (Herodotus, i, 93) is economic, and had, apparently, no connection with religion.

[2] See above, § 180. Cf. Ramsay, *Cities and Bishoprics of Phrygia*, 1, 94 ff.

[3] Westermarck, *History of Human Marriage*, chap. iii ff.

[4] At Byblos the prostitution of the woman was required only in case she refused to offer her hair to the goddess. This offering was probably originally a substitute for the offering of her virginity, but there is no evidence that the latter was of the nature of a sacrifice.

to whom the woman yields herself must be a stranger, is not clear. It is hardly probable that an outsider was called on to perform what was regarded as a dangerous duty — a stranger would not be likely to undertake what a tribesman feared to do.[1] Nor is the power of a stranger to confer benefits so well established that we can regard his presence as intended to bring a blessing to the girl.[2] More to the point, in one respect, is the conjecture that we have here an attenuated survival of the exogamic rule — the girl must marry out of her social group;[3] the old social organization having disappeared, the " stranger " takes the place of the original functionary, and the deity the place of the clan. This explanation has much in its favor ; but, as it is hardly possible to establish an historical connection between the older and the later custom, it cannot be said to be certain, and the origin of the " stranger-feature " remains obscure.

Religious explanation. Sacred prostitution is supposed by many writers to have sprung from the cult of the goddess who represented the productive power of the earth[4] (Mother Earth, the Great Mother). While such a figure is found in many of the lower tribes, it is only among civilized peoples, and particularly in Western Asia, that the cult acquired great importance. By the side of the female figure there sometimes stands a male representative of fertility (Tammuz by the side of Ishtar, Attis by the side of Kybele) who is regarded as the husband or the lover of the goddess, but occupies a subordinate position. In early times the goddess is represented as choosing her consorts at will, but this is merely an attribution to her of a common custom of the period. All deities, male and female, might be and were appealed to for increase of crops and children, but a Mother goddess would naturally be

---

[1] Farnell, in *Archiv für Religionswissenschaft*, vii, 88 (see above, §§ 182, 594, and cf. Crawley, *Mystic Rose*, p. 322). Farnell does not mention this suggestion in his *Greece and Babylon*, p. 269 ff.

[2] Westermarck, *Origin and Development of the Moral Ideas*, ii, 446 ; cf. Frazer, *Golden Bough*, 2d ed., Index, s.vv. *Stranger, Strangers.*

[3] Cumont, *Les religions orientales dans le paganisme romain* (Eng. tr., *Oriental Religions in Roman Paganism*, p. 247 f.) ; cf. Hartland, in *Anthropological Essays presented to Tylor*, p. 201 f.

[4] On this cult see Mannhardt, *Baumkultus* and *Antike Wald- und Feldkulte.*

looked on as especially potent in this regard. Prayer would be addressed to her, and that, with offerings, would be sufficient to secure her aid; simply as patroness of fertility she would not demand prostitution of her female worshipers — some special ground must be assumed for this custom, and it is held that, as fertility was produced by the union of the goddess with her consort or her lovers, this union must be imitated by the women who sought a blessing from her.[1] The probability of such a ground for sacred prostitution is not obvious. There are communities of temple-courtesans (in West Africa and India) where such an idea does not exist. If the license was in imitation of the goddess, this feature of her character requires explanation, and the natural explanation is that such a figure is a product of a time of license. In the ancient world it was only in Asia Minor and the adjacent Semitic territory that religious orgies and debauchery existed — they seem to have been an inheritance from a savage age. Or, if the prostitution is explained as a magical means of obtaining children,[2] this also would go back to a religiously crude period. Magical rites, many and of various sorts, have been performed by women desiring offspring — imitations and simulations.[3] But the giving up of the body is not imitation or simulation — it is the procreative act itself.

Organized official sacred prostitution must be regarded as the outcome of a long period of development. License, starting at a time when sexual passion was strong and continence was not recognized as a duty or as desirable, found entrance into various social and religious customs and institutions, accommodating itself in different places and periods to current ideas of propriety. Appropriated by organized religion, it discarded here and there its more bestial features, adopted more refined religious conceptions, its scope was gradually reduced, and finally it vanished from religious usage. The objections urged to such a process of growth are not conclusive.[4] Explanations of communities of temple-courtesans

[1] Mannhardt, *Antike Wald- und Feldkulte*, ii, 284; Frazer, *Adonis Attis Osiris*, p. 33 ff.   [2] Cf. Hartland, op. cit., p. 199.   [3] Hartland, *Primitive Paternity*, chap. ii.   [4] Frazer, *Adonis Attis Osiris*, p. 50 ff.

and male prostitutes and of customs affecting individual women are suggested above.[1] Many influences, doubtless, contributed to the final shaping of the institution, and we can hardly hope to account satisfactorily for all details; but the known facts point to an emergence from savage conditions and a gradual modification under the influence of ideas of morality and refinement.

1067. *Organization and influence of the priesthood.* In accordance with the law of natural human growth the priests in most of the greater religions came to form an organized body, hierarchical grades were established, many privileges were granted them, and they exercised great influence over the people and in the government. In Egypt they were exempt from taxes and had a public allowance of food; the temples at the capitals, Memphis and Thebes, became enormously wealthy; the priests exercised judicial functions (but under the control of the king); they cultivated astronomy and arithmetic, and controlled the general religious life of the people; as early as the thirteenth century B.C. they had attained a political power with which the kings had to reckon, and still earlier (ca. 1400 B.C.) the Theban priests were able to overthrow the religious reformation introduced by Amenhotep IV; the departments of sacerdotal functions were multiplied, and the high priest of the Theban Amon, whose office became hereditary, controlled the religious organization of the whole land, set himself up as a rival of the Pharaoh in dignity, and finally became the head of a sacerdotal theocracy.[2]

1068. While the Babylonian and Assyrian priesthoods were not so highly organized as the Egyptian, and never attained great political power, they were nevertheless very influential. Astronomy and astrology, the interpretation of omens and portents, the science of magic and exorcisms, the direction of the religious life of kings and people were in the hands of the priests; the great temples were rich, there were various classes of temple-ministers, all well cared for, and the chief priest of an important shrine was a person

---

[1] Cf. Nilsson, *Griechische Feste.*
[2] Maspero, *Dawn of Civilization*; Erman, *Handbook of Egyptian Religion*, Index, s.v.; Breasted, *History of Egypt*, Index, s.v.

of great dignity and power. The interpretation of sacrificial phenomena was made into a science by the priests, and, passing from them to Greece and Italy, exerted a definite influence on the religious life of the whole Western world.[1]

1069. The process of organizing the Hebrew priesthood began under David and Solomon, at first, under Solomon (who favored the Zadok family), affecting only the Jerusalem temple. In the Northern kingdom (established about 930 B.C.) there seems to have been a similar arrangement. As long as the old royal governments lasted (the Northern kingdom fell in the year 722 B.C., the Southern in 586) the priests were controlled by the kings. On the building of the Second Temple (516) and the reorganization of the Judean community they became, under Persian rule, independent of the civil government and finally, in the persons of the highpriests, the civil heads of the Palestinian Jews. The Maccabean uprising resulted in the establishment of the Asmonean priest-dynasty, in which the offices of civil ruler and religious leader were united. After the fall of this dynasty (37 B.C.) the priestly party (the Sadducees, that is, the Zadokites), forming an aristocracy, conservative of ritual and other older religious customs and ideas, was engaged in a constant struggle with the democratic party (the Pharisees), which was hospitable to the new religious ideas (resurrection, immortality, legalism). The latter party was favored by the people, and with the destruction of the temple (70 A.D.) the priests disappeared from history. From the beginning they appear to have been not only religious ministrants and guides but also civil judges ; their great work was the formulation of the religious law, as it appears in the Pentateuch, and it is probable that the shrines (especially that of Jerusalem) were centers of general literary activity. The national development turned, however, from sacerdotalism to legalism — the later religious leaders were not priests but doctors of law (Scribes and Pharisees).

1070. In India the priests formed the highest caste, were the authors of the sacred books (which they alone had the right to expound), conducted the most elaborate sacrificial ceremonies that

---

[1] Jastrow, *Religion of Babylonia and Assyria*, Index, s.v.

man has invented, and by ascetic observances, as was believed, sometimes became more powerful than the gods.[1] Ritual propriety was a dominant idea in India, and the influence of the priesthood on the religious life of the people was correspondingly great. Priests did not attempt to interfere in the civil government, but their religious instruction may sometimes have affected the policy of civil rulers. On the other hand, the Hindu priesthood, by its poetical productions and its metaphysical constructions, has become a permanent influence in the world.

1071. The early (pre-Zoroastrian) history of the Mazdean priesthood is obscure. In the Avestan system, however, a great rôle is assigned the priests, as is evident from the vast number of regulations concerning ceremonial purity, of which they had charge.[2] It does not appear that the early sacerdotal organization was elaborate or strict. There were various classes of ministrants at every shrine, but they differed apparently rather in the nature of their functions than in rank.

1072. The Greek priestly class had the democratic tone of the Greek people.[3] There was little general organization: every priest was attached to a particular deity except the Athenian King Archon, who had charge of certain public religious ceremonies. The mutual independence of the Greek States made the creation of a Hellenic sacerdotal head impossible. In Sparta the priestly prerogatives of the king were long maintained; usually, however, there was a separation of civil and religious functions. Generally in Greece priests were chosen by lot, or were elected by the priestly bodies or by the people, or were appointed by kings or generals. They were usually taken from good families, were held in honor, and were housed and fed at the public expense (their food came largely from sacrificial offerings). It was required that they should be citizens of the place where they officiated, and should be pure in body and of good conduct. They seem to have been simply citizens

---

[1] Barth, *Religions of India*, Index, s.v.; Hopkins, *Religions of India*, Index, s.v.

[2] Spiegel, *Eranische Alterthumskunde*, vol. III, bk. vi.

[3] O. Gruppe, *Griechische Mythologie*, Index, s.v. *Priester*; Gardner and Jevons, *Greek Antiquities*, Index, s.v.; Farnell, *Cults of the Greek States*, passim.

set apart to conduct religious ceremonies, and their influence on the general life was probably less than that of civil officers, poets, and philosophers. Greek educated thought moved at a relatively early period from the conventional religious forms toward philosophical conceptions of the relation between the divine and the human.[1]

1073. The minute details of the Roman ritual might seem to give great importance to priests;[2] and the flamens (the ministers of particular deities) were of course indispensable in certain sacrifices. But the organization of Roman society was not favorable to the development of specifically sacerdotal influence. Religion was a department of State and family government. For the manifold events of family life there were appropriate deities whose worship was conducted by the father of the family. The title *rex* (like the Greek *basileus*), in some cases given to priests, was a survival from the time when kings performed priestly functions. Later the consul was sometimes the conductor of public religious ceremonies. There was hardly a religious office, except that of the flamen, that might not be filled by a civilian. In the Augustan revival membership in the College of the Arval Brothers was sought by distinguished citizens. It was thought desirable that the Pontifex Maximus, the most influential of the priests, should be a jurist; and the office was held by such men as Julius Cæsar and Augustus. The increase of temples and priests by Augustus did not materially change the religious condition. The adoption of foreign cults was accompanied by ideas that did not belong to the Roman religion proper. In general, if we except the augurs, who represent the lowest form of the sacerdotal office, the priest was relatively uninfluential in Rome.[3]

1074. The minimum of priestly influence is found in the national religion of China, in which there is no priestly class proper.[4]   In

---

[1] This remark applies to the oracles as well as to the ordinary temple-service.

[2] Cf. Wissowa, *Religion der Römer*, Index, s.v. *Pontifex, Pontifices*; Fowler, *Roman Festivals*, s.v. *Pontifices*; Saussaye, *Lehrbuch der Religionsgeschichte*, 2d ed. (Roman religion).

[3] On the other hand, the Romans have given us such fundamental terms as ' religion,' ' superstition,' ' cult,' ' piety,' ' devotion,' all theocratic and individual.

[4] De Groot, *Religious System of China* : Legge, *Religion of China* : Doolittle, *Social Life of the Chinese*.

the worship of ancestors, which satisfies the daily religious needs of the people, every householder and every civil official is a ministrant. The great annual sacrifices to the heavenly bodies have been conducted till recently by the emperor in person.[1] Public religion is, in the strictest sense, a function of the State. Society, according to the Chinese view, is competent to manage relations with the supernatural Powers — it needs no special class of intermediaries. This thoroughgoing conception of civic autonomy in religion connects itself with the supreme stress laid on conduct in the Confucian system, which represents the final Chinese ideal of life :[2] man constructs his own moral life, and extrahuman Powers, while they may grant physical goods, are chiefly valued as incidents in the good social life. The great speculative systems of thought, Confucianism and Taoism, gradually gave rise to definite sacerdotal cults; but the priests of the Confucian temples serve mainly to keep before the people the teaching of the Master, and the Taoist priests have become largely practicers of magic and charlatans. Chinese religious practice remains essentially nonsacerdotal.

1075. The Peruvian cult presents a remarkable example of a finely organized hierarchy closely related to the civil government.[3] The priests were chosen from the leading families; the highpriest was second in dignity to the Inca only. The functions of the priests were strictly religious; and as the masses of the people were devoted to the worship of local deities and natural objects, it seems probable that the sacerdotal influence was merely that which belonged to their supervision of the State religion. Details on this point are lacking.

Priests played a more prominent part in Mexico, entering, as they did, more into the life of the people.[4] On the one hand, the

---

[1] Some high official will, doubtless, now take the emperor's place.

[2] This seems to remain true notwithstanding the present movement in China toward the adoption of Western methods of education. De Groot's estimate of Chinese religion (in op. cit.) is less favorable.

[3] Garcilasso de la Vega, *Royal Commentaries of the Yncas*, ed. C. R. Markham, part i, bk. ii, chap. ix; Prescott, *Peru*, vol. i, chap. iii; Payne, *New World, called America*, Index; A. Réville, *Native Religions of Mexico and Peru*, Index.

[4] Sahagun, *Historia General de las Cosas de Nueva España*, Eng. tr. by Markham; Payne, op. cit.; Réville, op. cit.

numerous human sacrifices, of which the priests had complete control, kept the terrible aspect of religion constantly before the mind of the public; and, on the other hand, the milder side of the cult (for the Mexican religion was composite) brought the priests into intimate relations with adults and children. As the priests, apart from their monstrous sacrificial functions, appear to have been intelligent and humane, it is not unlikely that their general moral influence was good.

1076. The influence of the priesthood on religion (and on civilization so far as religion has been an element of civilization) has been of a mixed character. On the one hand, while not the sole representative of the idea of the divine government of the world (for soothsayers and prophets equally represented this idea), it has stood for friendly everyday intercourse between man and the deity, and has so far tended to bring about an equable and natural development of the ordinary religious life; it was involved in the sacerdotal functions that the deity might be placated by proper ceremonies, whence it followed that the priest, who knew the nature of these ceremonies, was a benefactor, and, more generally, that man had his salvation in his own hands. The business of the priest was to maintain the outward forms of religion, to order and elaborate the ritual, to organize the whole cultus.[1] This was a work that required time and the coöperation of many minds. Priests were, in fact, naturally drawn together by a common aim and common interests — with rare exceptions they lived in groups, formed societies and colleges, had their traditions of policy, gathered wealth.[2] For this reason they were in general opposed to social changes — they were a conservative element in society, and in this regard were the friends of peace.

1077. On another side they did good work; they were to some extent the guardians of morals. In ancient popular life ethics was not separated from religion — religion adopted in general the best

---

[1] In the political and social disorders in Judea in the seventh and sixth centuries B.C. the priesthood was, probably, influential in maintaining and transmitting the purer worship of Yahweh, and thus establishing a starting-point for the later development.

[2] Cf. Breasted, *Religion and Thought in Ancient Egypt*, lecture x.

moral ideas of its time and place and undertook to enforce obedience to the moral law by divine sanctions. Priests announced, interpreted, and administered the law, which was at once religious and ethical; they were teachers and judges, and this function of theirs was of prime importance, particularly where good systems of popular education did not exist. Further, as a leisured class they often turned to literary occupations; examples of their literary work are found in India (poetry and philosophy), Babylonia (the history of Berossus), Palestine (Old Testament Psalter, the works of Josephus). They offered a place of rest in the midst of the continual warfare of ancient times.

1078. On the other hand, the priesthood has been generally conservative of the bad as well as of the good. It has maintained customs and ideas that had ceased to be effective and true, and in order to preserve them it has resorted to forced interpretations and has invented accounts of their origin. It has thus in many cases been obscurantive and mendacious. It has tended to make the essence of religion consist in outward observances, and has not infrequently degraded the placation of the deity to a matter of bargaining — it has sold salvation for money. Priests have not always escaped the danger that threatens all such corporations — that of sacrificing public interests to the interests of the order. They have drifted naturally toward tyranny — the enormous power put into their hands of regulating men's relations with the deity has led to the attempt to regulate men's general thought, though in most of the great religions their power in this regard has been partly controlled by the civil authority and by the general intelligence of the community. When they have not been controlled, they have often succumbed to the temptations that beset wealth; they have fallen into habits of luxury and debauchery.

1079. In a word the history of the priesthood has been like that of all bodies of men invested with more or less arbitrary power. Its rôle has varied greatly in different places and at different times. It has numbered in its ranks good men and bad, and has favored sometimes righteous, sometimes unrighteous, causes. It is not possible to define its influence on religion further than to say that it has been a natural element of the organization of religion, taking its form and coloring from the various communities in which it has existed, embodying current ideas and thus acting as a uniting and guiding force at a time when higher forces were lacking. It has formed a transitional stage in the advance of religious thought toward better conceptions of the relation of man to the deity.

1080. Islam has no priesthood, as it has no provision for atonement for sin except by the righteous conduct of the individual; its cultic officials are preachers or leaders of prayer (imams) in the mosque worship, and jurists or scholars (ulamas) who interpret the Koran. Judaism has had no priests since the destruction of the Second Temple (70 A.D.); its synagogue services are conducted by men trained in the study of the Bible or the Talmud (rabbis). In Christianity the conception of a sacrificial ministrant has been retained in those churches (the Greek and the Roman) which regard the eucharistic ceremony as a sacrifice. In the West the "presbyter" (such is the New Testament term), the head of the congregation, took over the function of the old priest as conductor of religious worship, and the word assumed the form "priest" in the Latin and Teutonic languages. Among Protestants it is employed only in the Church of England, in which, however, for the most part it has not the signification of ' sacrificer.'

WORSHIP

1081. *Places of worship.* The simplest form of early worship is the presentation of an offering to the dead or to some extrahuman object of reverence. Such objects were held to exist in all the world, in the sky, in rocks, streams, woods, caves, hills and mountains, and beneath the surface of the earth; but it was chiefly in places of human resort that their presence was expected. On some natural object or at some spot regarded as sacred, particularly where, it was believed, a spirit or deity had manifested himself (in some remarkable natural phenomenon, or in some piece of good fortune or ill fortune), the worshiper would place his offering. Sometimes it was left to be disposed of by the deity or spirit or dead person at his pleasure. When the offering was an animal, the blood, as food, was often applied to the grave or to the stone or other object connected with a superhuman Power. In the course of time, it may be supposed, it would be found convenient to erect a table or some other structure on which an animal could be slain. Such a structure would be an altar. At first simple, a heap of stones, a pile of dirt, a rough slab, it was gradually enlarged and ornamented,[1] and itself, by association, became sacred.

1082. Places where the presence of the divine was recognized were sacred. In them worship was paid to the deity, and in the course of time they were marked off and guarded against profane use. At first, however, they were merely spots on hills or in groves, by streams or in the open country, needing no marks or watches, for they were known to all and were protected by the reverence of the people.[2] When the land came to be more thickly populated and religion was better organized, such places were inclosed and committed to the care of official persons. Well-known examples are the Greek *temenos* and the Arabian *haram*.[3] Taboos and privileges attached themselves to such inclosures. Precautions had to be taken on entering them ; the shoes, for example, were removed, lest they should absorb the odor of sanctity and thus become unfit for everyday use. The spaces thus set apart were sometimes of considerable extent (as was and is the case at Mecca); within them no war could be waged and no fugitive seized. Sometimes they owed their sacredness to the buildings to which they were attached.

1083. The necessity for a house of worship arose very early.[4] Where there was an image or a symbol of a god, or where the

---

1 So Ezekiel's altar (probably a copy of that in the Jerusalem temple-court), over 16 feet high, with a base 27 feet square (Ezek. xliii, 13 ff.). The Olympian altar was 22 feet high and 125 feet in circumference. Cf. W. R. Smith, *Religion of the Semites*, 2d ed., pp. 202, 341, 377 ff. On the general subject see article "Altar" in Hastings, *Encyclopædia of Religion and Ethics*.

2 So in Australia (Spencer and Gillen, *Native Tribes of Central Australia*, Index, and *Native Tribes of Northern Australia*, Index), Samoa (Turner), Canaan (Genesis, Judges, passim), Greece (Gardner and Jevons, *Greek Antiquities*, p. 173), etc.

8 Gardner and Jevons, op. cit., Index, s.v. τέμενος, *Temple*; Wellhausen, *Reste arabischen Heidentumes*, Index; W. R. Smith, op. cit., Index, s.v. *Temples*. There is perhaps a hint of such a place in Ex. iii, 5.

4 K. F. Hermann, *Gottesdienstliche Alterthümer der Griechen*, § 18; Jevons, *Introduction to the History of Religion*, 1st ed., p. 137.

apparatus of sacrifice or of other ritual practice was considerable, buildings were required for the protection of these objects and perhaps for the convenience of the ministrants. The development of buildings followed the course of all such arrangements — at first rude, they became gradually elaborate and costly. In many savage tribes and in the earliest period of civilized peoples (Egyptians, Hebrews, al.) a hut, constructed like those of the people and therefore of a very simple character, houses the image or other representative of the god. With the progress of artistic feeling and skill abodes of men grow into palaces and abodes of deities into temples. It is on the temples that the greatest labor has been expended, partly because they are the work of the whole community, partly because it has been believed that the favor of the deity would be gained by making his dwelling-place magnificent.[1] The essential fact in a temple — its definition — is (in the lower cults) and was (in the great ancient cults) that it is or was the home of a god, the specific place of approach to him, with the possibility of face-to-face intercourse and a greater probability of gaining the blessings desired. This local conception of the deity continued after larger ideas had arisen,[2] and is to be found at the present day in some Christian circles.

1084. Temples have tended to grow not only in beauty and magnificence but also in elaborateness of interior arrangements and of connected structures. Anciently they were specifically places of sacrifice — the abodes of gods to whom sacrifice was offered — and this function generally determined their interior form. Sometimes they contained a single room in which stood an image and an altar; this was the simplest architectural embodiment of the idea of divine sacredness. But the progress of ritual forms was accompanied by the notion of grades of sanctity, and a special sanctity was indicated by a special room, an adytum, an inner or most holy shrine;[3] where, as was often the case, gradations in priestly rank existed, only the highest priest could enter the adytum.

---

[1] Cf. article " Architecture " in Hastings, *Encyclopædia of Religion and Ethics*.
[2] Ps. xlii, 3 [2] ; lxxxiv, 3 [2].
[3] So in Egypt, Palestine, Greece, and probably in Babylonia and Assyria.

For the implements of service and for the priests there were buildings attached to the temple. The people gathered in courts adjoining the sacred structure; where ritual exactness was carried very far (as in Ezekiel's plan and in Herod's temple), there were gradations in the courts also.[1] Usually an altar stood in one of the courts. The sacredness of the sanctuary communicated itself to the vessels and other implements of the sacrificial service.

1085. Temples, like sacred inclosures and altars, were often asylums, and doubtless in many cases served to protect innocent persons. The privilege, however, was often abused, and it became necessary in Greece and Rome to restrain it.[2]

1086. As a factor in the development of art the temple has been important. It has called forth the best architectural skill of man, and the statues that often adorned sacred buildings have stimulated sculpture. It does not appear that symbolism entered into the idea of ancient temples.[3] The Babylonian and Assyrian zikkurat (or ziggurat) was a staged structure (resembling in this regard the Egyptian pyramid), supposed by many scholars to be an imitation of the mountains whence the predecessors of the Semites in Babylonia came, and on which they worshiped;[4] if this be so, there is no attempt at pointing upward to the abode of the gods. Nor is there any trace elsewhere in the ancient world of a symbolic significance attached to temples beyond the distinction of place, referred to above, between the sacred and the profane and between different degrees of sacredness. The form of temples appears to have been determined by imitation of early nonreligious usage or by considerations of convenience;[5] the ziggurat may have been suggested by a high place, the adytum by a cave, but most temples were probably copies of ordinary

---

[1] In Herod's temple: the Court of the Gentiles, the Court of Women, the Court of Israel (Nowack, *Lehrbuch der hebräischen Archäologie*, ii, 76 ff.).

[2] Pauly-Wissowa, *Real-Encyclopädie der classischen Altertumswissenschaft*; article " Asylum " in *Jewish Encyclopedia*. The right of asylum goes back to very early forms of society in all parts of the world; many examples are cited by Westermarck, *Origin and Development of the Moral Ideas*, Index, s.v. *Asylums*.

[3] Cf. above, § 121.   [4] Jastrow, *Religion of Babylonia and Assyria*, chap. xxvi.

[5] On the supposed difference of symbolism between Greek and Gothic temples (churches) see Ruskin, *Seven Lamps of Architecture*.

human dwellings or civic buildings (as in late Latin, basilica is used in the sense of 'cathedral'). As abodes of priests temples were the centers of all priestly activities in the development of ritual and literature. Being strong and well guarded they were often used by kings as treasure-houses; but they were stripped of their wealth by native kings in times of need, and were freely plundered by conquerors.

1087. *Forms of worship.* The ancient forms of divine worship, as is remarked above,[1] follow in a general way the modes of approaching human potentates. Ceremonies of worship reached a high degree of elaboration in the great religions, Egyptian, Babylonian-Assyrian, Hebrew, Hindu, Greek, Roman.[2] The central fact was the presentation of the offering, and with this came to be connected prayers and hymns, ceremonies of purification, vows, imprecations, exorcisms, oracles; the festivals also were religious functions. Prayer is spoken of below.[3] Hymns sometimes consisted of or contained petitions, more generally were laudations of the power and benefactions of a deity. For poetical charm the first place is to be assigned to the Egyptian, Hebrew, and Hindu hymns. The religious ideas expressed in such compositions varied with time and place, but they show a general tendency toward a monolatrous or henotheistic point of view and toward higher ethical and spiritual feeling. Many of the Egyptian hymns seem to be substantially monotheistic, and the same thing is true of the Babylonian, the Assyrian, and the Vedic. The Babylonian hymns so far recovered (belonging in their present form mostly to the seventh century B.C.) are chiefly penitential[4] and show a close resemblance to some Hebrew psalms. In the Veda traces of philosophical thought, pantheistic and other, are not lacking. The poems of the Old Testament Psalter vary greatly in breadth and

---

[1] §§ 15, 120, note 3.

[2] For details see Erman, *Handbook of Egyptian Religion*, p. 45 f.; Jastrow, op. cit., p. 658 ff.; articles "Ritual" and "Sacrifice" in *Encyclopædia Biblica*; Bloomfield, *Religion of the Veda*, p. 213 f.; Hopkins, *Religions of India*, p. 124; *L'Année sociologique*, ii.   [3] § 1199.

[4] Some hymns to Tammuz are lamentations for dying vegetation and petitions for its resuscitation.

elevation of thought — some, dealing generally with national affairs (occasionally with individual experiences), are narrow and ethically low ; others show exalted conceptions of the deity and fine moral feeling. The Avestan ritual is concerned largely with physical details, but is not lacking in a good ethical standard ; the Gathas, particularly, though not free from national coloring, give a noteworthy picture of the government of the world according to moral law. Of Greek ritual hymns we have few remains, and these are of no great interest.

1088. Everywhere the temple-hymns, as is natural, deal chiefly with the desires and hopes of the worshiper, and often do not rise above mere egoism. Their object is to secure blessing, and the blessing is often, perhaps generally, of a nonmoral character — wealth, children, triumph over enemies. Desire for moral purity appears in some Hebrew hymns, and perhaps in some Babylonian. Of the modes of presenting liturgical poems to the deity we have few details. In the Second Temple at Jerusalem there were choruses of ministrants (Levites), and some of the titles of the psalms contain what seem to be names of musical instruments and melodies ; but of this temple-music nothing further is known than that it was sometimes sung antiphonally, but without harmony.[1] In some parts of Greece boys were trained to render hymns musically in the daily service and on special occasions. The general character of old Greek music is indicated in the Delphian hymn to Apollo discovered in 1893 ;[2] the melody is simple but impressive — there is no harmony.

1089. The temple-music doubtless tended to heighten devotional feeling among the worshipers, and possibly a similar popular effect was produced by the festivals that were common in the ancient world. Here the whole population took part, there were religious ceremonies, and the consciousness of the presence of the deity was made more distinct not only by visible and tangible representations, but often also by the fact that these occasions were

---

[1] 1 Chron. xvi; commentaries on the Psalms; works on Hebrew archæology (Nowack, Benzinger) ; articles in Biblical dictionaries and encyclopedias.

[2] *Revue des études grecques*, 1894. On savage songs and music see above, § 106.

connected in current myths and legends with histories of gods and ancient national experiences. Processions and pilgrimages brought the people to sacred places to which stories were attached, and the religious life became a series of object lessons. The Greek and Roman calendars contain a great number of feast days, each assigned to some god.[1] The Hebrews at a comparatively early date (eighth or ninth century B.C.) connected their great festivals with remote national events;[2] examples of festivals attached to recent historical events are Purim,[3] the Feast of Dedication established in commemoration of the rededication of the temple by Judas Maccabæus (December, 165 B.C.) after the Syrian profanation,[4] and the "Day of Nicanor" commemorating the victory of Judas over that general (March, 161 B.C.).[5] In the Hindu festivals (New Year's Day and during the spring months) stories of gods formed a prominent feature.[6] The Greek Genesia, the season of mourning for the dead, came to be connected with the victory of Marathon.[7]

All such celebrations tend to become seasons of merrymaking, and the religious element in them then receives less and less attention.[8] This remark holds of the festivals that Christianity took over from the old religions, adapting them to the new conditions.[9] Such occasions lose their distinctive religious significance in proportion as the events they commemorate recede into the past and become less and less distinct. It is in very early times, when they are thought of as representing realities, that they are religiously effective; in later times they give way to more reflective forms of devotion.

1090. Vows, blessings, and curses may be considered to belong to worship in the regard that they contain petitions to the deity; the curse or the blessing, however, sometimes rested on a baldly

---

[1] Pauly-Wissowa, *Real-Encyclopädie der classischen Altertumswissenschaft*; Fowler, *Roman Festivals*.
[2] Passover with the departure from Egypt; Sukkot (Tabernacles) with the march through the wilderness; later, Weeks (Pentecost) with the revelation of the law at Sinai.   [3] Book of Esther.   [4] 1 Macc. v, 47 ff.   [5] 1 Macc. vii, 49.
[6] H. H. Wilson, *Religious Sects of the Hindus*; Monier-Williams, *Hinduism*, Index.   [7] Gardner and Jevons, *Greek Antiquities*, p. 289.
[8] They sometimes degenerate into coarseness or immorality.
[9] Christmas, New Year's Day, May Day, Midsummer, All Souls, and others.

objective conception of the power of words, sometimes was held to be magical: once uttered, the word, beneficent or maleficent, went to its object, person or thing, did its work, and could not be recalled; its effect could be set aside only by an utterance in the opposite direction.[1] A magician, by the power resident in him, could fix a curse or a blessing on man or thing. An exorcism, also, might be effected by magic or by invoking the aid of a deity; an evil spirit is a supernatural Power and has to be considered — one does not worship such a being, but one may employ religious means to circumvent him. Bad magic may be overcome by good magic, and a deity, hostile and maleficent under certain circumstances, may be placated by offerings. It is not always easy to draw the line between worship proper and modes of defense against injurious Powers. But in general true worship implies friendly relations between human and superhuman persons.

1091. *Idols.* From an early time men have desired to have visible representatives of the supernatural. So long as natural objects, trees, stones, mountains, were regarded as themselves divine or as the abodes of spirits, so long as a loose social organization and the absence of definite family life led men to spend their lives in the open air, there was no need of artificial forms of the Powers. Such a need arose inevitably, however, under more advanced social conditions. Exactly at what stage men began to make images it is hardly possible to say, — the process was begun at different stages in different regions, — but it appears that in general it was synchronous with some fairly good form of social organization. Yet, where such forms exist, there are differences in the use of images. These are found — to take the lower peoples — in Melanesia and the Northern Pacific Ocean, in the northern part of South America, in North America apparently only among the Eastern Redmen (as the Lenâpé or Delawares),[2] and on the western coast of .Africa

---

[1] The protest in Prov. xxvi, 2, against this whole conception shows that it existed among the Jews down to a late time.

[2] Totemic poles, with carved figures of animals, are found in Northwest America (Boas, *The Kwakiutl*; Swanton, in *Journal of American Folklore*, xviii, 108 ff.) and in South Nigeria (Partridge, *Cross River Natives*, p. 219) ; but these figures are rather tribal or clan symbols than idols.

(Ashanti, Dahomi, Yoruba). Where the cult of beasts (whether totemic or not) is a living one, idolatry does not find a place; it, is only when communities have begun to be agricultural that they have artificial forms of gods; that is, idolatry comes in with the stage of culture connected with the agricultural life.[1]

The development in the form of images is familiar. The rude and, to modern eyes, grotesque idols of the lower peoples gradually pass into the more finished forms of the civilized nations.[2] Really artistic forms, however, were produced only by some Semites (Babylonians and Assyrians) and in the Hellenic and Græco-Roman worlds. In Central America, Mexico, and Peru images are anthropomorphic but lacking in symmetry and grace. Hindu idols are often composite and grotesque, sometimes (especially images of Buddha) highly impressive.

1092. The Hebrews appear to have had no anthropomorphic images of their national deity. Down to a late period there was a cult of household gods,[3] and of these, probably, there were images in private houses and in shrines, whether anthropomorphic or not is uncertain. In Solomon's temple (and in Ezekiel's proposed plan) figures of cherubs (originally divine beings) stood on the walls of the main room and guarded the ark in the adytum; they were winged creatures, the forms derived immediately from Phœnicia, ultimately from Babylonia; they appear only in the great public cult, probably did not enter into the religious life of the people at large, and there is no evidence that they ever received divine worship.[4] The Hebrews had no plastic art of their own, seem to have had small disposition in their earlier history to make images, and later such forms were excluded by the antagonism of the prophets to foreign cults and by refined ideas of the deity.[5] The absence

---

[1] The situation in Egypt was exceptional; after the idolatrous stage had been reached the old worship of the living animal survived.

[2] Aniconic representations of deities in civilized communities (like the stone representing the Ephesian great goddess) are survivals from the old cult of natural objects.   [3] Teraphim, 1 Sam. xix, 13 al.

[4] In the literature they are guardians of sacred places (Gen. iii, 24) and throne-bearers of the deity (Ezek. i, 26; Ps. xviii, 11 [10]).

[5] The numerous images mentioned in the Old Testament as worshiped by the Israelites appear to have been borrowed from neighboring peoples. The origin of

of images in the Zoroastrian cult may be accounted for in a similar way — from early lack of artistic impulse and later elevated conceptions. In China there are images in household worship, but none in the great imperial religious ceremonies.[1] Though the Koran does not expressly forbid the cult of images, yet, as the old Arabian cults denounced by the prophet were all idolatrous, images were identified with false religion (polytheism) and have been avoided by the Moslems, whose strict monotheism left no place for them.

1093. Images were credited in half-civilized times with a certain personality, were flogged or destroyed when they failed to do what was expected of them, or were bound in order to prevent their going away.[2] In such cases the conception of the power of these objects was probably a confused one; though they were known to be inanimate pieces of wood or stone or other material, it was believed that they were inhabited by spirits or deities, and it was held that in some undefined way the power of the divine agent was transferred to its physical incasement — the two were practically identified. This sort of conception soon passed away and was succeeded by a symbolical interpretation. Whatever the ultimate origin of the Egyptian, Babylonian, and Hindu divine and semidivine forms (which are sometimes monstrous),[3] it is probable that for the more thoughtful worshipers they represented divine powers and functions. Uncouth shapes may be softened or transformed by familiarity, and by association with higher ideas — things in themselves repulsive may become vehicles of devotion.[4] In all religious worship objects associated with pious acts acquire sanctity and beauty.

the bull figures worshiped at Bethel and Dan is obscure, but they appear to represent the amalgamation of an old bull-cult with the cult of Yahweh.

[1] Possibly the civilization of China was in earliest times identical with or similar to that Central Asiatic civilization out of which Mazdaism seems to have sprung. Cf. R. Pumpelly, in *Explorations in Turkestan* (expedition of 1904), i, pp. xxiv, 7, chap. iv f.

[2] The same feeling appears in the treatment of images of saints by some European peasants.

[3] For Egyptian forms see Rawlinson, *History of Ancient Egypt*, vol. i; Maspero, *Dawn of Civilization*; for Semitic, Ohnefalsch-Richter, *Kypros, the Bible, and Homer*; for Indian, Lefmann, "Geschichte des alten Indiens" in Oncken's *Allgemeine Geschichte*.

[4] Even the Hindu women's linga-cult is said to be sometimes morally innocent.

1094. That idolatry in ancient times was not a wholly bad feature of worship is shown by the excellence of the great religions in which it was practiced. Its general function was to make the deity more real to the worshiper, to make the latter more sharply conscious of the divine presence, to fix the attention, and so far to further a real communion. On the other hand, it tended to produce a low physical conception of the divine person, and to distract the mind of the worshiper from the ethical side of worship. Its moral effect was dependent on the man's character and thought. When the image was regarded as the symbol of an ethically good Power, it was a reënforcement of pure religious feeling; when it was regarded as in itself a source of physical benefit, it was a degrading influence. This difference of effect exists in those Christian bodies that include images and pictures of the deity and of saints in their apparatus of worship.

CHURCHES

1095. The history of the social organization of religion is the history of the growth of churches — voluntary associations for worship; it is toward the Church that society has hitherto moved.[1] Every ancient community may be said to be an incipient church in the sense that it contains the germs of the later ecclesiastical development. But this later form exists in such communities only in germ — the most ancient worship was communal, an affair of clan, tribe, or State. Men were born into their religious faith and could no more change it, or think of changing it, than they could change, or think of changing, their language or any other inheritance. It was inevitable, however, that there should be a growth of individualism — instinct impelled men to think for themselves in religion as in all other things. Religion was a part of the general social movement, affected by all other parts of that movement. Independence of thought led to social aggregations, the members of which were drawn together by similarity of ideas and

---

[1] A church is here taken to be a voluntary religious body that holds out to its members the hope of redemption and salvation through association with a divine person or a cosmic power.

aspirations. This is the familiar history of social movements, and that in religion such movements have been continuous will be evident from a brief statement of the historical facts.

1096. *Savage secret societies.* These societies are referred to above;[1] here we have only to notice their germinal ecclesiastical character. They represent a partial break-up of tribal communal worship by assigning special duties and granting special privileges to certain initiated persons. Totemic groups are sometimes (as in Central Australia) charged with specific functions in the tribal life; but membership in such groups is a matter of birth, and they everywhere tend to give way to secret societies. These latter often have charge of certain religious rites, and from their secret proceedings and from a knowledge of their secret lore the rest of the tribe are excluded.

The extent to which religious organization and influence have been carried is illustrated by the history of the Polynesian Areoi, the most remarkable of such fraternities.[2] The Areoi created 'mysteries,' with an elaborate ritual whose effectiveness was dependent on absolute accuracy in words; its members were chosen without regard to tribal position and entered of their own free will; it was a voluntary association and made its own religious laws. It was restricted (as all such associations are) by the necessity of paying regard to existing customs, but within such limits it was independent of the tribe, and its members were held to be entitled to special honors and enjoyments in this life and the next (a crude conception of salvation). It was essentially a church, and other societies, in Polynesia, Africa, and North America, approached this position more or less nearly. They all tended to become tyrannical — their social influence enabled them to impose their authority on the tribe, and they did not hesitate to employ violence in asserting their rights.[3] To foreign influence they were naturally hostile, since this generally diminished their power. Founded as they are on savage ideas they have disappeared, or are disappearing, before foreign civilizations. In their best

---

[1] § 530 f.   [2] W. Ellis, *Polynesian Researches*, vol. i, chap. ix.
[3] H. Webster, *Primitive Secret Societies*, chap. vii.

form they doubtless gave a certain unity to communities and were thus an element of order.

1097. *Greek mysteries.* In Greece dissatisfaction with the current cults expressed itself in various ways, largely through poets and philosophers, who asserted themselves, indeed, individually, but showed no power of organization. The task of organizing religious opinion fell to that new direction of thought (vaguely called " Orphic " [1]) which, while it gave prominence to spiritual ideas and moral ideals, introduced a lively emotional element into worship. In the Eleusinian and other mysteries this element was both external (dramatic representations, songs, processions, ceremonies of initiation) and internal (the hope of salvation). Without breaking with the popular religious forms the mysteries constructed their own forms, chose their members, and created a religious *imperium in imperio.* They were voluntary associations for worship, ignored distinctions of social rank, had great ideas and impressive rituals — apparently all the elements necessary to the establishment of churches or of a national church. Yet they faded gradually away, and perished finally without leaving any definite impression, as it seemed, on Greece or the world without.[2]

1098. The reasons of their failure are not far to seek. They did not reach the Hellenic mind for the reason that they were of foreign origin and much in them was opposed to the genius of the Hellenic religion. Even the Pythagorean reform movement of Southern Italy, with its strenuous moral culture of the individual, seems to have had a foreign (Asiatic) coloring. It was, indeed, at one with the better Greek thought of the time (sixth century B.C. and later) in its elevated conception of the deity and of worship, but with this it combined ascetic observances and, apparently, mystical ideas; it established what may be called a church, which had a great vogue in Southern Italy for several centuries but did not, as an organization, penetrate into Greece. It attracted some thoughtful men, but was too calm and restrained for the masses.[3]

---

[1] For a large definition of the term see S. Reinach, *Orpheus* (Eng. tr.), p. v.
[2] For a possible influence see below, § 1101.
[3] See the histories of philosophy of Ueberweg, Windelband, Meyer, Zeller.

1099. It was different with the Dionysiac cult, whose wildness made it popular; of foreign origin, it was in time partly Hellenized and in Athens took its place in the regular national worship; some of its foreign features were taken up in the mysteries. These latter, with their enthusiasm and their half-barbaric ceremonies, excited the contempt of most of the educated class.[1] These cults were Asiatic — not Semitic — but probably a product of a non-Hellenic population of Asia Minor (Phrygia and other regions), developed during a period the history of which is obscure.

1100. The Semites seem to have produced no mysteries — there is no record of such cults in Babylonia, Syria, Phœnicia, the Hebrew territory, or Arabia; Semitic religion was objective, simple, nonmystical.[2] The Syrian cult of Tammuz (Adonis), which was adopted by Hebrews in the sixth century B.C. (Ezek. viii, 14), was an old folk-ceremony, not a mystery; it is allied to the Attis ceremonies of Asia Minor and to the mourning ceremony mentioned in Judges xi, 40 (mourning for a dead deity, but there referred to Jephthah's daughter).

1101. The Greek mysteries, then, derived their orgiastic side partly from Thrace, partly from Asia Minor. They chiefly attracted the lower classes and particularly slaves, for they offered individual independence in religion, freedom from the sense of social inferiority, and hope for the life to come. Thus they did not appeal to the Hellenic spirit, and did not, as organizations, survive the political decadence of the Greek States. But it is probable that their effects survived in the recognition of the possibility of religious worship apart from the traditional cults, and, more generally, in contributing to the establishment of the principle

---

[1] See the reference in the *Republic* (ii, 364 f.) to the mendicant prophets with their formulas for expiation of sin and salvation from future punishment, and Demosthenes's derisive description of Æschines as mystagogue (*De Corona*, 313).

[2] It is not clear that the peculiar cults described in Isa. lxv, 3–5; lxvi, 3 f., are of Semitic origin. Their history, however, is obscure — they are not referred to elsewhere in Jewish literature. In part they are, like the cults mentioned in Ezek. viii, 10, the adoption of the sacred animals of neighboring peoples; Isa. lxv, 5 seems to point to a close voluntary association with a ceremony of initiation, but nothing proves that the association was of Semitic origin. For a different view see W. R. Smith, *Religion of the Semites*, 2d ed., p. 357 ff.

of individualism in religion. An historical connection between the Greek mysteries and the later individualistic cults is, indeed, not probable. Cumont believes that Mithraism did not imitate the organization of the Greek secret societies.[1] The New Testament use of the term 'mystery' in the sense of 'esoteric doctrine'[2] may have come from the Asian cult; the Mithraic worship was practiced in Tarsus, the native city of the Apostle Paul, in the first century of our era. However this may be, it seems probable that the conception of a church existed in the Græco-Roman world before the beginning of our era, and that its existence was due in part to the Greek mysteries, whose members were scattered throughout the empire of Alexander.

1102. The *philosophical systems* that arose in Asia and Europe concurrently with the Greek mysteries did not found ecclesiastical organizations. The disciples of philosophers formed schools, and the adherents of each school constituted a group the members of which were united one with another by the bond of a common intellectual aim and a common conception of life and of the world; and there was also a scientific union between the various groups, the fundamental methods of investigation and lines of thought being the same everywhere. But the object of thought was the discovery of truth by human reason, not the quest of salvation by worship of the divine. The emotional element essential to the formation of a church was wanting, and where philosophical systems adopted devotional forms these were not the creation of philosophy but were borrowed from current cults. They sought happiness, but not through religious ritual. They did not always formally discard or condemn existing cults, but they ignored them as means of salvation; they sometimes recognized traditional gods and forms of worship, but interpreted them in accordance with their own ideas.

1103. In India the Upanishads practically abolished the national pantheon and the old Brahmanic ritual — knowledge, they taught, was the key to bliss, and the knowledge was not that of the Veda,

---

[1] *The Mysteries of Mithra* (Eng. tr.), p. 29.
[2] 1 Cor. ii, 7; Mk. iv, 11 al.

it came by reflection; emancipation from earthly bonds, absorption into the Infinite, was the goal of effort, but the effort was individualistic and led to no devotional organization. Ascetic observances, as a means of attaining perfection, were an inheritance from popular Brahmanism.[1] In China Taoism, originally a system of thought (based on the conception of all-controlling order) that appealed only to a certain class of philosophic minds, became a religion by borrowing crude ideas and sensational methods from a debased form of Buddhism and other sources.[2] Confucius steadily declined to teach anything about divine worship; Confucianism remained merely an ethical system, dealing only with the present life, until its founder, with disregard of his teaching, was divinized.

1104. Many of the Greek philosophers, from Socrates and Plato on, were definitely (some of them warmly) religious, but their religion was chiefly valued as an aid to ethical life, and it did not respond to the demand for communal worship. The Platonic and Stoic conceptions of the deity were pure, but they remained individualistic — salvation was the creation of the man himself. The noble hymn of Cleanthes to Zeus [3] and the fine religious morality of Marcus Aurelius led to no church organization. The attempted combination of Platonism and Judaism by Philo was equally resultless. Neo-Platonism also, though it had enthusiasm and some sense of brotherhood, showed itself unable to produce a church. Plotinus, indeed, proposed to the Emperor Gallienus the establishment in Campania of a city of philosophers, a Platonopolis, in which the ideal life should be lived, but the proposal came to nothing.[4] The Neo-Platonic union with the deity was too vague a conception to bring about communal worship, and the deity had no definite rôle in securing the salvation of men.

1105. Thus, in the period beginning about the sixth century B.C. and extending into the Christian era, all over the civilized world

---

[1] Barth, *Religions of India*, p. 76 ff.; Hopkins, *Religions of India*, p. 216 ff.; cf. Bloomfield, *Religion of the Veda*, p. 282 ff.

[2] " Die Chinesen," in Saussaye, *Lehrbuch der Religionsgeschichte*; R. K. Douglas, *Confucianism and Taoism*; De Groot, *Religion of the Chinese*; cf. H. G. Underwood, *Religions of Eastern Asia*. [3] Stobæus, *Eclogues*, i, 30.

[4] Porphyry, *Vita Plotini*, cap. 3.

attempts were being made to reconstruct life by ethical and philosophical systems, by ascetic observances, and by mysteries. These attempts bear witness to the prevailing sense of the insufficiency of current schemes of life. They differ according to differences of place and time, but agree in the search after something better; this better thing was always ethical and in most cases religious. Their failure to construct effective organizations was due to the deficiencies pointed out above.

1106. *Buddhism and Jainism.* The first churches produced by civilized men arose in India in the sixth century B.C. out of the bosom of Brahmanism, whose failure to establish a church was due in part to its dependence on philosophical speculation. Of the protests against the Brahmanic orthodoxy the most important were Buddhism and Jainism.[1] Buddhism discarded philosophy and asceticism, and came forward with a plan of salvation that was intelligible to all.[2] Disciples gathered about the Master and he became the object of enthusiastic devotion. All complete churches have owed their origin each to a single founder; this is due to the fact that the insight and constructive genius of the founder have chosen out of the mass of the existing thought those broad principles that the times demanded and have presented them in incisive form and with freshness and enthusiasm.[3] Buddha's followers quickly formed themselves into associations, the entrance into which was by free choice. As his doctrine of salvation was nontheistic, so his church was nontheistic, but not therefore nonreligious. The ecclesiastical organization was simple, but effective. The original Buddhism has been degraded, especially in Tibet, China, and Korea, but the church form remains everywhere more or less recognizable.[4]

[1] Hopkins, *Religions of India*, chap. xii f.; Rhys Davids, *Buddhism*; Barth, *Religions of India*; Oldenberg, *Buddha*.

[2] The problem of life is stated to be how to get rid of desire, which is the source of all suffering; the Buddhist answer is that desire is eliminated by moral living, for which knowledge is necessary. So the Socratic school based virtue and happiness on knowledge. Cf. also the Biblical book of Proverbs.

[3] It does not follow that every founder of a religion will establish a church; other things than the person of the founder, such as the nature of his teaching and the character of his social milieu, enter into the problem.

[4] On current proposed reforms of Buddhism in Japan see Underwood, *Religions of Eastern Asia*, p. 222 ff.

1107. Jainism, while differing from its contemporary, Buddhism, in its metaphysical dualism and its asceticism, agreed with it practically in its method of salvation from the ills of life. It established a nontheistic church which has had experiences (polytheistic and other) like those of Buddhism. Historically it is less important than the latter; it still has a considerable following, but it has never passed out of India. Apparently its local features, metaphysical and ascetic, have impeded its progress — it lacks the simplicity of Buddhism.

1108. *Judaism.* Judaism stands on the border line — it was a cult that approached the position of a church, yet failed to reach it. Its line of movement differed *in toto* from those described above. It had no philosophy, no asceticism, no secret societies, and it did not rely on its ethical code. It was essentially religious, in theory a theocracy, in form a national cult. The steps by which the old polytheistic Israelite nation passed into the monotheistic Judaism can be traced historically, but the impulse to the movement was a part of the genius of the people and cannot be further explained. The leaders of the small body of people that gathered at Jerusalem in the sixth century, after the break-up of the year 586, were animated by a patriotic devotion to the national deity; without political autonomy, merely a province of the Persian empire, the sole interests possible for the people were racial and religious, and these isolated them from the neighboring peoples. Those who remained in Babylonia (where they were prosperous and comfortable) were similarly isolated, devoted themselves to their own development, and their religious attitude was the same as that of the Palestinian community. Distance from the temple led to gatherings in various places for worship (synagogues).

The Jews thus became a nation organized under religious law, with an institution devoted to voluntary communal worship, and offering salvation, at first for this life only, but later (from the second century B.C. onward) for the future life also — these were elements of a church. But in two points this cult fell short of the complete church idea: the business of a church is wholly and solely religious, and the Jewish nation was organized not only for religion, but also for commerce, politics, and war ;[1] and the synagogue and the temple-service were not free to all the world — only Jews and proselytes [2] might take part in them. Any religious body, it is true, may properly define the conditions of entrance into it; but here the restriction was national — the synagogal cult, individualistic and simply devotional as it purported to be, was a part of the national system, and its membership depended almost exclusively on the accident of birth. Proselytes, indeed, formed an exception — they came in of their own choice — but they were numerically not important and did not affect the general character of the cult.[3] The Jews came as near the ideal of a voluntary religious association as was then possible under the hampering conditions of a racial organization and peculiar national customs. Their genius for the organization of public religion appears in the fact that the form of communal worship devised by them was adopted by Christianity and Islam, and in its general outline still exists in the Christian and Moslem worlds.

1109. *Zoroastrianism* resembled Judaism in its later practical monotheism and its elaborate ritual, but was more isolated and less advanced in the formation of assemblies for voluntary worship. Its pre-Sassanian period produced no church, only a national cult, which was adopted by the Parthians and others in debased form, but otherwise did not attract outsiders. On a sect that arose in Persia in Sassanian times see below.[4]

1110. *Christianity.* The teaching of Jesus was directed toward a purification of the existing cult, the elimination of mechanical views, and the emphasizing of spiritual and ethical ideals.[5] There

---

[1] The two last of these functions ceased on the destruction of Jerusalem by the Romans (70 A.D.), the first remained.

[2] Proselytes arose mostly from the general liberal tendency of the times (from about the second century B.C. and on), sometimes from lower impulses, sometimes they were made by force. See articles in Cheyne, *Encyclopædia Biblica* ; Hastings, *Dictionary of the Bible* ; and *Jewish Encyclopedia.*

[3] They were virtually identified with the Jewish people. On the early form of voluntary devotion to a foreign deity see W. R. Smith, *Religion of the Semites,* 2d ed., p. 75 ff.   [4] § 1115.

[5] On attempts to discover forms of Christianity before Jesus see W. B. Smith, *Der vorchristliche Jesus,* and *Ecce Deus* ; M. Friedländer, *Synagoge und Kirche.*

is no indication that he purposed founding a separate organization.[1] But, after his death, his disciples were drawn together by their relation to him, particularly when the new congregation became predominantly Græco-Roman. For its administration the synagogue was the model — from it were taken the titles and functions of some of its officers and the method of conducting public service.[2] But the new ekklesia, the church, followed its own lines and speedily created a new cult. Its fundamental conception was salvation in the future through Jesus of Nazareth, the Christ. In the beginning it was thoroughly individualistic and voluntary. It had no connection with the State, was not a *religio licita* ; its adherents joined it solely out of preference for its doctrines ; its activity was wholly religious. But this ideal constitution of a church was not long maintained. The introduction of infant baptism (toward the end of the second century) and the adoption of Christianity as the religion of the State by Constantine went far to make membership in the Church an accident of birth or of political position ; in this regard Imperial and Medieval Christianity did not differ from the old national religions — it was a religion but not a church. At the present day in the greater part of Christendom one's ecclesiastical position is inherited precisely as the ancient clansman inherited his special cult.[3] The word "church" has largely lost its early signification of voluntary religious association, and has come to mean any Christian organization, or, by further extension, any religious body.

1111. The secularization of the Church, the failure to discriminate between its function and that of the State, is an inheritance from

---

[1] The two passages in the Gospels (Matt. xvi, 18 ; xviii, 17) in which the word "church" occurs appear clearly, on exegetical grounds, to be scribal insertions of the later period.

[2] " Elder " and " apostle " are Jewish titles, and the reading of the Scriptures, prayer, and exhortation formed part of the synagogal service ; see Schürer, *The Jewish People in the Time of Jesus Christ* (Eng. tr.), II, ii, 52 ff., and article " Apostle " in *Jewish Encyclopedia*. Other offices arose in the church out of the peculiar conditions ; the eucharistic meal appears to have been developed under non-Jewish influence.

[3] So far has the idea of the civil character of the Church been carried that in some places the keeper of a licensed brothel has been required to be a member of the State Church.

Roman Imperialism, which in its turn was derived from the primitive clan constitution of society in which the individual had no standing apart from the community. From the Roman Empire it passed to Medieval Europe, and it has survived in the Christian world by force of inertia. It is, however, not universal in Christendom (there are religious bodies in which individual freedom of choice is fully recognized), and in some cases where it exists formally or theoretically it is practically ignored. Notwithstanding departures from the ideal the services of the Church often represent voluntary worship; such worship, however, has been the rule in all religions from the earliest times to the present day and does not in itself distinguish Christianity from any other religion.

1112. The word " church " meant at first a local Christian congregation, but was enlarged so as to designate the whole body of Christians. In this body various tendencies of thought showed themselves from time to time, and new organizations were formed that constituted new churches in the sense that they had their own theological dogmas, ritual, and conditions of membership. Most of them had brief careers and offer nothing of interest for the history of the development of the church-idea. Gnosticism was a serious and noteworthy attempt to bridge over the gap between a good supreme God and an evil world, and was in form a church, but its philosophical and mystical sides had so much that was fanciful and grotesque or ethically dangerous that it did not commend itself to the mass, and soon ceased to exist as a separate organization, though its echoes long continued to be heard in certain Christian groups.[1]

1113. *Cults of Mithra and Isis.* The Mithraic communities were wholly voluntary associations, without distinctions of birth or social position, were recognized by the State, but received no pecuniary aid from it and had no official connection with it. Perhaps this independence helped to nourish the enthusiasm that carried Mithraism from one end of the Roman Empire to the other; a church appears to flourish most on the religious side

---

[1] Harnack, *Dogmengeschichte*; articles in Herzog-Hauck, *Real-Encyklopädie*, and *Jewish Encyclopedia*; Mansel, *The Gnostic Heresies*.

when it confines itself to religion. A more important fact was that Mithraism was a religion of redemption. It does not appear that there was any general organization of the Mithraic associations; each of these was local, probably small, had its own set of officers, and managed its own affairs.[1] It was thus free from some of the perils that beset Christianity. It is not improbable that some of its liturgical forms were adopted by the Christian Church, but it seems itself not to have borrowed from the latter. Its weakness was its semibarbarous ritual and its polytheism; it yielded of necessity to the simpler and loftier forms of Christianity.

1114. The cult of Isis, in spite of its ethically high character and its impressive ceremonies of initiation (as described by Apuleius[2]), did not give rise to associations like the Mithraic. It belongs to the mysteries, but had not their organization of meetings and ritual, had no brotherhoods (except those whose bond of union was devotion to this cult) and no general organization embracing the Empire. The reason for its failure in this regard appears to lie in its lack of definiteness in certain important points: it was in a sense monotheistic, since the goddess was called the supreme controller of the world of external nature and of men, but its monotheism was clouded by its connection with the old national cults and by current theological speculations — for Apuleius, it would seem, Isis was rather a name for a vague Power in nature than for a well-defined divine person, and particularly it offered no clear picture of the future and no clear hope of moral redemption, two things that were then necessary to the success of any system that aspired to supplant the popular faiths.[3] Such lacks as these appear in the cult of Sarapis also, which never developed the characteristics of a church.

1115. *Manichæism.* Of the religious movements that sprang from the contact of Christianity with the East Manichæism was the most important on account of its great vitality. It possessed all the elements of a church, voluntary membership, independence of the State (it was always persecuted by the State), and the claim

---

[1] Cumont, *Textes et monuments* and *The Mysteries of Mithra.*
[2] *Metamorphoses*, chap. xi.   [3] Cf. article " Isis " in Roscher's *Lexikon.*

to a divine revelation of salvation. Like Buddhism, Jainism, and Christianity, it owed its origin to a single founder. Its plan of organization and its ethical standards were good. Like Mithraism its basis was Persian (its rise was synchronous with the Sassanian revival of Mazdaism), but the two went different ways : the former laid stress on mystical ceremonies, the latter on moral and theological conceptions. The vogue that Manichæism enjoyed was due, apparently, to its eclectic character : adopting the Persian dualism, it modified and expounded this by a Gnostic doctrine of æons, which was intended to harmonize the goodness of God and the existence of evil, and it added the figure of the highest æon, Christ, the savior of men. On the other hand, its involved and fantastic machinery led to its downfall.

1116. Two theocratic bodies that failed to reach the full church form are *Islam* and the *Peruvian cult of the sun.* The Islamic constitution is based on a sacred book, its theology and its form of public worship are borrowed from Christianity and Judaism, its private worship is individualistic, and it offers paradise to the faithful. But Islam is in essence a State religion rather than a church. Its populations belong to it by descent ; its head is the Calif (now the Sultan of Turkey). Its diffusion, though due in certain cases to the superiority of its ideas and the simplicity of its customs,[1] has yet come largely (as in Egypt, Syria and Palestine, Persia, and North Africa) from social and political pressure — in some cases it has been adopted by whole nations at a blow ; Mohammed forced all the people of Arabia to accept it. Individual choice recedes into the background, except (as in Judaism) in the case of proselytes. Its conception of sin and salvation are largely external. It bears a great resemblance to the Judaism of the Hasmonean dynasty, a national cult with a priest-sovereign at its head.

Within Islam there have arisen organizations that imitate the form of a church in certain respects ; such were the Morabits (Almoravides) and the Mohads (Almohades),[2] whose bond of

[1] Cf. A. G. Leonard, *Islam, her Moral and Spiritual Value.*
[2] A. Müller, *Islam,* ii, 614 ff. ; Coppée, *Conquest of Spain* ; Dozy, *Histoire des musulmans en Espagne* ; Stanley Lane-Poole, *Story of the Moors in Spain.*

union was in part theological, and such are the great fraternities in Africa and Asia, which are devoted, among other things, to religious work, and have elaborate organizations and ceremonies of reception.[1] But these are all largely political and military. The Ismalic movement (from ca. 900 A.D. on), the central doctrine of which was the incarnation of God in certain men and finally in the Mahdi, was not Islamic and not Semitic; with a nominal acceptance of the Koran, it was in fact a mixture of Persian and Buddhistic ideas; from it came the Fatimide califate of Egypt, and from this (ca. 1000 A.D.) the Druse sect, which began as a church, but has become merely a local religion.[2]

1117. It was in Peru that the most thoroughgoing identification of religion with the State was effected.[3] In the old national religions the individual followed the custom of his country; in Peru the State, in the person of the Inca, determined every person's religious position and duties. If Islam resembles Maccabean Judaism, the Peruvian organization resembled some forms of Medieval Christianity. The Inca was a Pope, only with more power than the Christian Pope, since he acted on every individual. The general ethical standard was good, in spite of some survivals of savagery, but there was a complete negation of individual freedom in religion.[4]

1118. *Modern Hindu sects.* The vast multiplication of sects in India is an indication of activity of religious thought;[5] the movement has been in general toward the formation of voluntary associations, though with many variations and modifications. The reform sects, while they may be considered as developments out of the old systems, Vedic, Çivaic, Vishnuic (Krishnaic), have been

---

[1] Of these fraternities the largest and most powerful is the Senussi of North Africa, a splendidly organized body with a central administration clothed with absolute authority; see Depont and Coppolani, *Les confréries religieuses musulmanes.*

[2] S. de Sacy, *Exposé de la religion des Druses*; J. Wortabet, *Researches into the Religions of Syria*; C. H. Churchill, *Ten Years' Residence in Mt. Lebanon.*

[3] Cf. Dr. Thomas Arnold's ideal, the identification of Church and State (A. P. Stanley, *Life and Correspondence of Thomas Arnold*).

[4] Payne, *History of the New World called America*; Markham, *Rites and Laws of the Incas*; Prescott, *Conquest of Peru*, bk. i, chap. iii.

[5] On India's fertility in the production of religions cf. Bloomfield, *Religion of the Veda*, p. 2 ff.

affected by foreign influence, Mohammedan or Christian. Of the organizations influenced by Islam (followers of Kabir and Dadu) several have produced societies that for a time had the form of a church, with voluntary membership and a plan of salvation; but it has been hard for them to overcome the national tendencies to idolatry and to deification of founder or teacher. The Sikhs, beginning (in the fifteenth century) as a purely religious body, became, by the eighteenth century, a powerful political and military organization. Along with theological reform these sects have been constantly in danger of reverting more or less closely to the old national type, and their church form has been only feebly effective.

1119. The case has been different with the movements induced by contact with Christian forms of belief. The organizations founded or carried on by Rammohun Roy[1] (early part of the eighteenth century) and later by Chunder Sen,[2] Mozoomdar, and others are churches in the full sense of the word, and, notwithstanding occasional individual lapses into old Hindu ideas, have so far maintained this character; but they are not wholly native creations, and it remains to be seen what their outcome will be.[8]

1120. *Babism and Bahaism*,[4] the transformation of Babism effected by Bahâu'llah, is a church in all essential points, though its organization consists merely in the devotion of its adherents to the teaching and the person of its founder; it has no clergy, no religious ceremonial, no public prayers, no connection with any civil government, but its dogma is well-defined and it offers eternal salvation to its adherents. Its chief source of inspiration is the belief that its founder was an incarnation of God, the Manifestation

---

[1] This organization was first called the " Brahma-Samaj " (the Church of Brahma), later the " Adi-Samaj " (the First Church).   [2] The Brahma-Samaj.

[8] There are other theistic bodies in India. The Arya-Samaj (Aryan Church) derives its doctrines (monotheism and other) from the Veda (necessarily by a forced interpretation) ; it is a sort of protest against foreign (Christian) influence. See articles " Arya Samaj " and " Brahma Samaj " in Hastings, *Encyclopædia of Religion and Ethics*.

[4] Gobineau, *Les religions et les philosophies dans l'Asie centrale* ; R. G. Browne, *The Episode of the Bab* and *The New History of the Bab* ; article " Bab, Babis " in Hastings, op. cit. ; article " Bahaism " in the *Nouveau Larousse, Supplément* ; *Some Answered Questions*, translated by Laura C. Burney (exposition of the doctrine by the son of the Bahaist founder).

of God announced by his forerunner, the Bab (the "Gate" to God and truth). That its lack of official ministers and public communal religious services is no bar to its effectiveness is shown by the favor it has met with not only in Persia and other parts of Asia but also in Europe and America. Possibly its success is due in part to its eclectic character and its claim to universality (it seeks to embrace and unite Buddhism, Hinduism, Zoroastrianism, Judaism, and Christianity) as well as to the simplicity of its dogma (theism and immortality) and its admirable humanitarian spirit.[1]

MONACHISM

1121. An effective outgrowth from the church is the monastic system, which is an *ecclesia in ecclesia*, emphasizing and extending certain features of the parent organization.[2] It sprang from a dualistic conception, the assumption of a relation of incompatibility or antagonism between God and the world — a feeling whose germ appears in savage life (in taboos and other forms). It has assumed definite shape only in the higher religions and not in all of these — it is foreign to Semitic, Persian, Chinese, and Greek[3] peoples. Austerity there has been and abstention from certain things but not with the aim of ministering to spiritual life.[4]

1122. The birthplace of monachism proper was India. In the Brahmanic scheme the highest sanctity and the most brilliant prospects attached to the man who forsook the life of men and devoted himself to solitary meditation in the forest.[5] The seclusion was individual — the man was an eremite. The organization into communities was made by Buddha[6] and, apparently contemporaneously, by Mahavira, the founder of Jainism. It is this organization that

---

[1] Babism is fairly well represented in Persia at the present day; see R. G. Browne.

[2] Cf. articles in Herzog-Hauck, *Real-Encyklopädie*; McClintock and Strong, *Biblical Cyclopædia*; *New Schaff-Herzog Encyclopædia of Religious Knowledge*.

[3] On the community founded by Pythagoras see the histories of philosophy; it appears to have embodied a suggestion of monastic life, but its origin is uncertain.

[4] The Hebrew Nazirite vow, for example, was merely a consecration of a part of the body to the deity with the observance of old nomadic customs of food and dwellings.   [5] Hopkins, *Religions of India*, Index, s.v. *Monks*.

[6] Rhys Davids, *Buddhism*, chap. vi.

has made the institution a power in religious history. Buddha's associations were open to all, without distinction of social position or sex. From India monachism passed into all the lands that were occupied by Buddhism.

1123. In Egypt under the Ptolemies there arose a sort of monastic life : after the cult of Sarapis was established men wishing to devote themselves to religious meditation would go to the Sarapeum and shut themselves up in cells.[1] It is, however, not clear that there was an organization or any sort of communal life in connection with these gatherings. There is no evidence of foreign influence beyond a possible suggestion from the fact that Sarapis was a foreign deity and his cult may have imported foreign ideas into Egypt; but he was completely domiciled in his new abode, was identified by the Greeks with their Zeus and by the Egyptians (by a popular etymology) with their Osir-Apis; there was nothing foreign in his cult, and the claim, sometimes made, for Buddhistic influence (through embassies sent by Asoka to Greek kings) has no definite historical foundation.[2] Possibly Greek (Pythagorean) influence is to be recognized,[3] but it cannot be considered strange that a practice of this sort should arise independently in Egypt at a time when a practical monolatry with a good ethical conception of the deity might dispose some men to solitary reflection.

1124. The Egyptian Therapeutae, the " Servants " of God, described by Philo,[4] resemble these Sarapis monks in certain respects, particularly in their habit of contemplation. Their kernel, however, was Jewish — they had the Jewish Scriptures and observed the seventh day of the week. On this Jewish substratum was imposed Greek thought; they adopted the Alexandrian allegorizing interpretation of the Scriptures, and Philo includes them in that group of persons who found it desirable to withdraw from the common

---

[1] Cf. H. Weingarten, *Ursprung des Mönchthums*, cited with approval by Meyer, *Geschichte des Alten Aegyptens*, p. 401; cf. Lehmann-Haupt, in Roscher's *Lexikon*, article " Sarapis," col. 362 ff.

[2] Cf. Hopkins, *Religions of India*, chap. xix; J. Estlin Carpenter, " Buddhist and Christian Parallels " in *Studies in the History of Religions presented to C. H. Toy*.

[3] Against this view see Breasted, *History of Egypt*, p. 578 ff.

[4] *De Vita Contemplativa*; see the edition of F. C. Conybeare. The work is probably to be considered genuine.

life of men in order to cultivate philosophical and ethical thought. Six days they lived each by himself; on the seventh day they came together for a religious service. Women as well as men were admitted into the association, but the place of general meeting had two divisions, one for men, the other for women. The date of the rise of the sect is uncertain, but it must probably be put in the Ptolemaic period. Their monastic organization must be referred to some current practice, Greek or Egyptian, or to a blending of various lines; the details of their history are too sparse to build on with definiteness.

1125. The similar sect of the Essenes, or Essaei, which was confined to Palestine, is better known.[1] The Jewish features in their system are: acceptance of the Jewish Scriptures, observance of the Sabbath, recognition of the temple by sending unbloody offerings, regard for ceremonial purity. Non-Jewish features are: rejection of marriage, trade and (according to Philo) animal sacrifice, turning to the sun in prayer (or, according to Josephus, praying to the sun), the teaching that the soul, when set free from the body, passes, if good, to a delightful region across the ocean, and, if bad, to a dark den of ceaseless punishment. Foreign influence in these latter practices and beliefs is obvious, but its precise source is uncertain. There are suggestions of Pythagoreanism and possibly of Zoroastrianism;[2] it can only be said that various ideas were in the air of Palestine, and that the Essene formulation was effected under conditions and at a time not known to us.[3] The monastic constitution was clearly of foreign (non-Jewish) origin. Essenism seems not to have affected the Jewish religious ideas of the time. Jesus, though he may have taken from it the prohibition of swearing and possibly one or two other points, was in the main and on all important points (except ethical teaching, which was largely common property) the reverse of what Essenism stood for.

---

[1] Philo, *Quod omnis probus liber*; Pliny, *Historia Naturalis*, v, 17; Josephus, *Antiquities*, xviii, 1, and *War*, ii, 8; Schürer, *The Jewish People in the Time of Jesus Christ* (Eng. tr.), II, ii, 188 ff. (and the bibliography there given); articles in Cheyne, *Encyclopædia Biblica*, and Hastings, *Dictionary of the Bible*.

[2] From the geographical and historical conditions a Pythagorean origin (perhaps indirect) seems the more probable.

[3] The earliest appearance of an Essene is in the latter part of the second century B.C. (Josephus, *Antiquities*, xiii, 11, § 2).

1126. Christian monachism, which appeared first in eremitic form (second century) and later in organized communal form, may have been an independent creation of Christian piety; but it is also possible that it was suggested by the traditions of its birthplace, Egypt;[1] definite data on this point are lacking. Whatever its origin, it speedily overran the Christian world, in which it has maintained itself up to the present day.[2]

1127. Monachism has rendered valuable aid to Buddhism and Christianity by training men and women, laity and clergy, who were devoted to the forms of religion represented by these organizations. It has done a higher service by establishing communities that have often been beacon lights, representing, particularly in times of popular ignorance, ideals of conduct. Such communities have often been homes of beneficence and learning. They have, on the other hand, injured religion by severing it from ordinary life. By assuming that the secluded life was holier than that of the world they have tended to put a stigma of unholiness on the latter. Buddhism taught that only the monk could attain the highest sanctity and receive the highest reward, and such has generally been the teaching in those forms of Christianity in which monachism exists. Monasteries and convents, further, have in many cases become rich in this world's goods — a favorite form of devotion has been to build and endow or aid such communities (often with the belief that this atoned for sin); with wealth has come worldlymindedness and corruption of morals. Numerous examples of such decadence occur in Buddhistic and Christian history. There are, however, many examples of holy monastic living. It is true in general of these institutions, as of all others, that when moral supervision of them is exercised by society the possibilities of moral decline are greatly diminished; in an enlightened age they may be assumed to be generally exemplary. Their specifically useful rôle in the development of religion, as refuges in times of turbulence and centers of charity and thought, belongs to an imperfectly organized form of society; with the growth of enlightenment they tend to disappear.

---

[1] Roscher, *Lexikon*, article "Sarapis," col. 362 f.
[2] See references given above in § 1121, note.

SACRED BOOKS

1128. All churches and all bodies approaching nearly the church-form have writings that embody their beliefs and are regarded as sacred. Such sacred Scriptures necessarily grow up with the organ-izations to which they belong, since these latter originate in literary periods and claim divine authorship. Great religious communities naturally produce a large number of such books, and at some time it becomes necessary (from the growth of heresies or rivals) to sift the whole mass and decide which works are to be considered to have permanent divine authority; the process of sifting is performed in each case by its community under the guidance of leading men, and the result is a canon of sacred Scriptures. Such canons are found in Buddhism, Judaism, Zoroastrianism, Christianity, and Islam, and in minor bodies like the Essenes, Mormons, and others, but not among the Chinese, Greeks, and Romans; Brahmanism occupies a middle ground — it regards the Veda and the accessory books as entitled to great reverence, but has never drawn the line between sacred and nonsacred writings so sharply as has been done in the group named above.

1129. While the general method of fixing the canons has been the same everywhere, the details of the process have differed in different lands. In India the canon of Southern Buddhism (acknowledged formerly in India and now in Ceylon, Burma, and Siam) was settled in a series of councils coming down to the middle of the third century B.C. or later (several centuries after the death of Buddha), the object being to define the faith against heresies; probably the reports of the Master's discourses (he left no writings) were examined, and those declared authentic were brought together, but the date of the final settlement of the canon is not certain, and the sacred books were not reduced to writing till the first century B.C. The canon of Northern Buddhism (accepted in Tibet, Mongolia, Manchuria, China, Japan) is less definite and was fixed later.[1]

1130. The development of the Jewish canon extended over a long period, and its history in outline is well known. While the

---

[1] Rhys Davids, *Buddhism*; R. S. Copleston, *Buddhism*.

discourses of the prophets were regarded with respect as giving divine revelations, there is no record of the recognition of an authoritative book before the fifth century B.C., when a sacred law was proclaimed by Nehemiah and Ezra.[1] Even then there seems to have been no definite collection of writings. The Law was the national religious constitution, and in process of time prophetic books and others came to be regarded with reverence. The translator of Ben-Sira (Ecclesiasticus) into Greek (132 B.C.) mentions three groups of national books (the law, the prophets, and "other writings"), but does not speak of them as divinely inspired. But the intimate contact with the Greek world, and especially the Maccabean struggle, deepened the Palestinian Jewish reverence for the national literature. A process of sifting and defining, at first unofficial, began, and this work naturally passed, with the growth of legal learning, into the hands of leading doctors of law. Early in the first century of our era public opinion in Palestine had taken shape; the standard established was a local national one — books illustrating the national history and teachings, and written in Hebrew, were accepted (so, for example, the book of Esther, which is nonreligious but national), others (as the Wisdom of Solomon) were rejected. For various reasons certain books (Ezekiel, Proverbs, Ecclesiastes, Song of Songs) remained doubtful. After the destruction of Jerusalem the increasing literary feeling, the establishment of rabbinical schools, and the necessity of defining the Jewish position against growing Christianity and other heresies led to definite action[2] — in the Synod of Jamnia (about 100 A.D.) the Palestinian canon, after hot debates, was finally settled in the form in which the Hebrew Old Testament now appears. Alexandrian Judaism had a different standard and accepted, in addition to the Palestinian collection, a group of books (the Apocrypha) that the Palestinians rejected. Certain other books (as the various Enoch apocalypses) were not accepted by either

---

[1] Ezekiel, early in the sixth century, and Haggai and Zechariah in the latter part of the century, show no consciousness of the existence of authoritative writings.

[2] Cf. G. F. Moore, "The Definition of the Jewish Canon and the Repudiation of Christian Scriptures" in *Essays in Modern Theology and Related Subjects . . . Testimonial to C. A. Briggs.*

Jewish body, though they were highly esteemed. Both canons were slow growths of national feeling — books were chosen that accorded with prevailing ideas; but it is now impossible to recover all the critical views that determined the results.[1]

1131. Young Christianity, at first a Jewish body, naturally adopted the Jewish canons, but in the course of a century produced a considerable normative literature of its own. The Christian canon was settled much in the same way as the Jewish. There was doubt about certain books, there were differences of opinion in different quarters, the growth of heresies called for the establishment of a definite standard, and a final decision was reached in the West and announced toward the end of the fifth century by Pope Gelasius; in the East the action was less definite, but the conclusion was about the same. The books of the Alexandrian canon that were rejected by the Palestinians were largely used by early Christian writers, by whom some of them are constantly cited as sacred Scripture, for they were found in the Greek translation of the Old Testament (the Septuagint), which was the Old Testament text used by Christians. So great was their popularity that Jerome was led, against his judgment, to include them in his translation (the Latin Vulgate), and by the Council of Trent (1546) they were indorsed as deuterocanonical, and are still so regarded in the Roman Church. In the Greek Church they were accepted as canonical in the beginning and up to the early part of the nineteenth century, but are now, it would seem, looked on only as useful for the instruction of catechumens.[2] By Protestants their canonical authority is generally denied, though up to the early part of the nineteenth century they were commonly printed in editions of the Bible; the Articles of the Church of England characterize them as instructive but not of authority for doctrine, and lessons from them now appear in the Lectionary of the Church.[3]

---

[1] G. Wildeboer, *Het Onstaan van den Kanon des Ouden Verbonds*; H. E. Ryle, *Canon of the Old Testament*; articles "Canon" in *Encyclopædia Biblica*, "Bible Canon" in *Jewish Encyclopedia*, "Kanon des Alten Testaments" in Herzog-Hauck, *Real-Encyklopädie*. [2] See the *Longer Catechism of Philaret*, 1839.
[3] T. Zahn, *Geschichte des neutestamentlichen Kanons*; E. C. Moore, *The New Testament in the Christian Church*; article "Canon" in *Encyclopædia Biblica*.

1132. The history of the collection of the Zoroastrian sacred books is involved in obscurity. A late tradition was that many such writings were destroyed by Alexander. This points to a belief that the existing writings were later than the fall of the old Persian empire. When a beginning was made of committing Zoroastrian material to writing is uncertain. In the first century of our era Pliny had heard of verses ascribed to Zoroaster,[1] and, as Mazdean books were in existence at the rise of the Sassanian dynasty, the probability seems to be that the reduction to writing had then been going on for a considerable time — how long it is impossible to say. The material grew with the development of the people and was ascribed to Zoroaster [2] (as the Jews ascribed their legal material to Moses). An official collection of sacred writings was made in the fourth century of our era — the exact extent of this collection and the principle that governed its formation are not clear. It may be surmised that the appearance of strange teachings, such as that of Mani, and the spread of Christianity eastward, forced on the leaders the task of defining the orthodox faith.[3] In making their collection they would naturally take only such writings as were in accord with the spirit of the religion of their time. Thus they established (in the fourth century) a body of sacred writings; it does not follow that no additions were later made to the canon — how far it is represented in the present Avesta it may be difficult to say.

1133. The history of the Islamic canon is simple. The Koran enjoys the distinction of being the only sacred canon produced by one man. There never was any question of its sacredness, and there has been hardly any question of its content. Mohammed's discourses were taken down by his followers in his lifetime, were put into shape just after his death, the collection was revised a few years later (under the Calif Othman), has since been universally accepted in the Moslem world as the authoritative divinely given standard of religious truth, and there is no reason to doubt

---

[1] *Historia Naturalis*, xxx, chap. i, § 2.

[2] The question whether any of this material went back to Zoroaster must here be left undecided.   [3] Spiegel, *Eranische Alterthumskunde*, iii, 778 ff.

that it contains substantially all the teaching of the Prophet and only his teaching. The scribe Zayd, who acted as editor, may have altered or inserted a word here and there, but he would not have dared to change the thought. The traditions of extra-Koranic sayings ascribed to Mohammed (the *hadith*), so far as they may be supposed to be genuine utterances of his (most of them are spurious), do not add anything to his doctrine.[1]

1134. As to the influence of sacred books on religion, it is obvious, in the first place, that they are always formulations of the ideas of the places and times in which they originate, and that they vary in tone and in importance accordingly. It is true, however, that the canonical collections of the great religions, having arisen in enlightened circles, all have, along with local (social, mythological, eschatological) features, generally high ethical and spiritually religious standards. For this reason they have always been, as religious and ethical guides and sources of inspiration, important factors in the development of civilization as well as in the life of the churches. Their teachings, generally representing the ideas of gifted men formulated under the pressure of great religious enthusiasm, have perpetuated high standards, holding them up in times of decadence and corruption and clouded moral vision.

1135. A specially noteworthy point in their influence is their rôle of household monitors and comforters. As religious manuals, invested with divine authority, they have found their way into families and other small and intimate circles, have been children's textbooks and parents' guides, and thus have entered in an extraordinary way into individual life. They have reached wider circles through expositions and discourses held in connection with stated religious services. They have been used as textbooks in schools, and in general have been the most widely read books in the world. They have thus been unifying forces, each in its special community.

Their influence, further, has not been confined to purely religious life. Being regarded as containing the final truth, they have been objects of study and occasions of the development of learning. The

[1] Nöldeke, *Sketches from Eastern History* (Eng. tr.), p. 25 ff.

necessity of explaining their use of words and grammatical constructions, their historical and geographical statements and views, their pictures and theories of social life, their psychology and philosophy, their theistic and eschatological ideas, have led to investigations of all these subjects. Early Moslem science sprang from the study of the Koran, and the later Moslem discussions of freewill, immortality and other points were called forth by Koranic statements. The philosophical writings of Maimonides, produced under Greek influence (through Moslem translations of Aristotle), were directed to the elucidation of Old Testament ideas. The contributions of modern Christians, Jews, Moslems, and Parsis to knowledge, sacred books being the occasions, are numerous and important.

1136. Along with these beneficent influences there have been others less praiseworthy. As any sacred book belongs to a particular age, it inevitably, in the course of time, falls into disaccord with later ideas on certain points. When this happens there are always some persons who, failing to discriminate between the local and transitory and the permanent, unjustly reject the book *in toto*; others, making a distinction, take it as a literary product, accept what they think valuable, and treat the rest as an imperfect product of the past. Those who accept the book as divinely inspired and therefore, as they think, infallible either maintain literally all its statements (cosmological, historical, eschatological, and other) or else undertake to interpret certain of them in accordance with current views. When such interpretation is forced, it becomes intellectually and morally an evil — it accustoms the religious public to logical distortions, and it nourishes a disingenuousness that easily becomes immoral. The belief that a sacred book is final authority often results in limitation of freedom of thought — certain things are excluded from discussion. The instinctive demand for freedom asserts itself, however, in various ways: sometimes, as described above, a desired sense is obtained by violence; sometimes a religious body that is regarded by its adherents as authoritative interpreter changes its decision, in accord with the spirit of a new age, and grants liberty where it had previously refused it. The treatment of sacred books follows the phases of general culture.

The dogmatic statements of these books are condensed into creeds, which become organic law.[1] They express each the interpretation put by a given church on the words of its sacred Scriptures. The interpretations are the outcome of historical processes, the final result of which is a formulation of the ideas of its time; where the same sacred book is accepted by several churches, there may be several different creeds based on the one book — that is, churches and creeds alike are subject to the variations of human opinion that result from differences of temperament, social surroundings, and general culture. Creeds are convenient and effective manuals. They may be made to change their meaning by processes of interpretation; elasticity in a creed is favorable to permanence — it is thereby able to adapt itself to changing conditions — and the degree of elasticity depends largely on the persons who are its authorized expounders, that is, on the area of public opinion that these persons represent.

1137. *General influence of churches.* All organized religion has been a potent factor in human life. In savage and half-civilized communities it enters into every detail of life, since, in the absence of knowledge of natural law, everything that happens is ascribed to supernatural agency. In the old national cults, in which other departments of thought (art, commerce, science, philosophy) became prominent, religion was somewhat isolated — it received a particular representation in sacrifices, festivals, and other observances; but such ceremonies were so numerous, and so many ancient customs survived, that it still played a conspicuous part in daily life.[2] In the period in which churches arose there was a still greater specialization of the activities of life, and this specialization has become more pronounced in modern times, in which from various causes the tendency is to mass religious observances

---

[1] A creed usually contains also an affirmation of the authority of the book on which it is based. Some religious bodies do not regard any book as absolutely authoritative, and their creeds are merely expressions of their independent religious beliefs.

[2] So among the Egyptians, Hebrews, Hindus, Greeks, Romans, and others.

in certain days and seasons and leave the rest of the time free. This apparent banishment of religion from everyday affairs does not, however, signify diminution of interest in religion itself — partly it is an economic arrangement, the assignment of a definite time to every particular duty, but mainly it is the result of a better conception of what religion means, the feeling that, being an inward experience, it is less dependent on external occasions.

1138. Churches, as is remarked above, differ from the old national religions mainly in the emphasis they lay on individualism and on the idea of redemption. They represent a profounder conception of the ethical relation between man and God, or, as in Buddhism, between man and the ideal of perfection in the universe. They foster religion by holding public services and by the production of devotional works ; they advance learning by supplying men of leisure ; socially they are in general a conservative force, with the good and bad effects of conservatism. But their special function is to treat man as a spiritual being having immediate personal relations with the deity. Charitable and educational work (ethical and other) and social gatherings they share with other organizations, and they are incompetent in themselves to deal with economic and other scientific questions. That wherein they stand apart from other organizations is the emotional element they introduce into man's attitude toward the universe. According to this point of view man regards himself not merely as a part of the world but as bound to its author by ties of gratitude and affection. This sentiment may be independent of all scientific theories, may be shared by the learned and the unlearned ; it is thus a great unifying force, and gives to life the glow of enthusiasm with the repose of trust.

1139. The temptations to which churches are exposed are those that are touched on above, and they may be briefly summed up here. There is the tendency to an excessive elaboration of the externals of religion, ritual, and dogma. Something of these is doubtless necessary in churches as in all human organizations, but they may easily be carried so far as to obscure the essential things. The history of all churches exhibits this tendency. There are protests from time to time, revolts against formalities and speculations, and then frequently in the new organizations the old movement is resumed. For our own times a distinction may perhaps be made : while there seems to be a steady general increase of ritual, there is in many quarters a disposition to minimize or curtail dogma.

1140. However this may be, a more important tendency in churches is toward the claim to absolute authority in religious matters. This tendency is universal in bodies that hold to the infallibility of certain sacred books. It is obvious that absolute authority in an organized body and individual freedom are mutually incompatible,[1] and that all that makes for freedom makes against the church influence in this direction. Finally, when churches enter into administrative alliance with the civil authorities, or assume civil and political power, they to that extent abdicate their spiritual rights and abandon their true function.

UNIVERSAL RELIGIONS

1141. So far only particular religions, belonging to particular peoples or regions, have been considered. In recent years the question has been much discussed whether any of these may be called universal. A universal religion may be defined either as one that has been accepted by all peoples, or as one whose doctrines are such that it may be so accepted. The term is frequently used loosely to describe a religion that has passed definitely beyond its birthplace and has been adopted by different nations or districts. Obviously, if we take the stricter definition, the question at issue can be decided only by an appeal to facts. Whether or not a given religion has actually been universally accepted can be determined from statistics, and the question whether it is fitted to be generally adopted must be answered by a similar appeal. It may be held, and is held, of various religions that their standards are so high and their schemes of worship and conceptions of salvation so obviously suited to human nature that they cannot fail to be

---

[1] Cf. Sabatier, *Authority in Religion* (Eng. tr.), and the bibliography therein given.

adopted when they are known; but such are the diversities of human thought that this consideration cannot be regarded as decisive — a religious system that seems to one set of men to be perfect may appear to others to be unsatisfactory,[1] and it is only by trial that it can be determined how far it is capable of conquering new territory. The test of actual diffusion, then, must be applied to those religions for which the claim to universality has been made — these are Buddhism, Judaism, Christianity, Zoroastrianism, and Islam.[2]

1142. Buddhism has had a history full of vicissitudes.[3] Beginning in Northern India as an Aryan faith, in the course of a few centuries it overran a great part of the peninsula, then began to decline, gradually lost its hold on the people, partly, it is said, by reason of the corruption of its morals, chiefly, doubtless, because it was not suited to the character of the Hindu people, and finally, in the twelfth century of our era, left its native land, to which it has never returned. Meantime it had established itself firmly in Ceylon and later in Burma and Siam and had been carried to China (not long after the beginning of our era), whence it passed to Korea, Central Asia, Japan, and adjacent islands, and as early as the sixth century gained a footing in Tibet. It has maintained its conquests outside of India to the present day, except that it has been driven out of a considerable part of Central Asia by Mohammedanism; in China and Japan it exists alongside of the native cults, its relations with which are friendly. It presents the curious spectacle of a religion, originally Hindu Aryan, that now finds a home exclusively (with one exception, Ceylon) among non-Aryan peoples; but among these peoples it has generally been degraded by the infusion of low native elements, and has discarded its original essence. By reason of its negative attitude toward life it has found no favor as a system with Western Indo-Europeans, Persians, and Semites, except that it gave a coloring to certain Persian sects (the

[1] The contention that a given religion must triumph because it is divine and its triumph is divinely predicted introduces a discussion that cannot be gone into here, where the object is to consider existing facts.

[2] Babism (or Bahaism) also claims to be universal, but its origin is so recent that this claim cannot be tested. [3] Rhys Davids, *Buddhism*.

Ismailic) and has perhaps influenced Bahaism.[1] As far as present appearances go there is no probability of its gaining general acceptance.

1143. Judaism is too much encumbered with peculiar national usages to commend itself to non-Jews. There was a time just before and just after the beginning of our era when a considerable number of persons resorted to it for escape from the confusion of current religious systems, and since that time there have been conversions here and there; but these have been too few to affect the general character of religion in any community. Even to Reform Judaism, which has discarded Talmudic usages and does not differ doctrinally from certain forms of Christianity, there clings a racial tone that tends to isolate it, and it does not seem that this isolation is likely to cease soon.

1144. Christianity, beginning as a Jewish movement, speedily became Græco-Roman, and in this form took possession of the whole of Western Asia (except Jewish districts and parts of Arabia), Greece, Italy, Egypt, and the northern coast of Africa, and was adopted, under Byzantine and Roman influence, by the Celtic, Slavonic, and Teutonic tribes. Most of its Asiatic and all of its African territory except Abessinia was taken from it by Mohammedanism in the seventh century, but small bodies of Christians remained in Armenia, Mesopotamia, Syria, and Egypt. With this exception it has since been the religion only of the Western Indo-Europeans and of a few half-civilized peoples who have been Christianized either by missionaries (the Karens of Burma, a part of the Telugus of Southeastern India and others) or by contact with Westerners (Philippine Islands, tribes of North America and South America) or by both these agencies (the Hawaiian Islands). Local peculiarities have been largely banished from its usages but not from its dogma. It is, apparently, its dogma (in the orthodox form) that has prevented its acceptance by most Semites, by the

---

[1] It has been professed by a few persons in Europe and America, but the so-called "theosophy" is not Buddhism. On supposed points of contact between the New Testament and Buddhism cf. C. F. Aiken, *The Dhamma of Gotama the Buddha and the Gospel of Jesus the Christ.*

peoples of Central and Eastern Asia, and by many undeveloped tribes of Africa and Oceania.

1145. Zoroastrianism has never advanced to any important extent beyond the boundaries of its native land. It has never recovered from the crushing blow dealt it by Mohammedanism in the seventh century, and is now professed by hardly more than 100,000 persons (mostly in Bombay).

1146. Islam is now the religion of the Turkish empire (except the Christian groups in Europe, Syria, Mesopotamia, and Armenia), Persia, Egypt (except the Copts), and the North African coast, and has a large following in Central Asia, China, India, the Malay peninsula, the Malay Archipelago, the Sudan, and a considerable representation on the east and west coasts of Africa. Its spread, as is remarked above, has been effected sometimes by force, but oftener by social pressure and through traders and missionaries. Decadent Christianity in Palestine, Syria, and Egypt readily yielded to it; Persian Zoroastrianism made some effort to maintain itself but succumbed to the combination of military pressure and the prospect of civil advancement and peace; after the fall of Constantinople conversions of Christians in Europe were numerous, and the Moslem conquests in India were followed by a considerable accession of Hindus to the Islamic faith. At the present time it appears to be advancing only among the half-civilized tribes of Central Africa, but it maintains its position against Buddhism and Christianity.[1]

1147. There is, thus, now no religion that, so far as extent of diffusion is concerned, can be called universal. Omitting the Jewish and Parsi groups, the Brahmanic and other religions of India, and the Chinese Confucian cult, three great religions have divided the world among them, Buddhism taking Eastern Asia, Islam Western Asia and Northern Africa, and Christianity Europe and America. It is sometimes suggested that the religion of the leaders of civilization, the Christian nations, must become the faith of the world. But, even if we may look forward to a time when social fusion, under the control of the present Christian nations, shall have brought about substantial unity of religious thought in the world,

[1] T. W. Arnold, *The Preaching of Islam.*

it is impossible now to predict what the nature of that thought will be, since Christianity has undergone and is now undergoing change, and may in the far future assume a different form from that of to-day; fundamentals may remain, but opinions differ even now as to what are fundamentals.

1148. *Classification of religions.* A word may be added on proposed classifications of religions.[1] Certain resemblances and differences between religions are obvious, and groups may be made, geographical, ritualistic, theologic, or soteriological, but it is difficult to find a principle of classification that shall bring out the essential characteristic or characteristics of every religion and yet distinctly mark every one off from all others. All have much in common, and the elements in all are so mixed that divisions necessarily cross one another. Every religion is the product of some one community and represents its peculiar view of human life in its relation to the supernatural; there may be borrowings and fusions, but the final outcome is shaped by the thought of the people to whom the religion specifically belongs.[2] The differences between various religions are the differences of thought between the communities involved, and the differences and the resemblances are often curious and sometimes defy explanation.

1149. Leaving aside ritual, which, so far as it is a merely external form of approach to the deity, does not touch the essence of religion, the following points may be said to be common to all religions: (1) The sense of a supernatural control of life, and the conviction that the supernatural Power must be placated or obeyed.[3] (2) The belief that religion deals with and controls the whole of life; this belief is pronounced among savages, who know nothing of natural law, and is regarded as essential in more advanced communities, in which, from the religious point of view, law, physical

---

[1] See Tiele, article " Religion " in *Encyclopædia Britannica*, 9th ed., and cf. his *Elements of the Science of Religion*, i, 28 ff.; R. de la Grasserie, *Des religions comparées au point de vue sociologique*; M. Jastrow, *The Study of Religion*, pp. 58 ff.; article " Religion " in *Encyclopædia Britannica*, 11th ed.

[2] Cases of adoption of alien cults bodily are here of course excluded; in such cases the cults are to be referred to the creators and not to the borrowers.

[3] In some forms of Brahmanism, in Buddhism, and in some modern systems this Power is impersonal or undefined.

or mental, is taken to be an expression of the will of the deity. (3) The creation of divine personalities [1] (representing popular ideals), and movements toward a unitary view of the divine control of the world. (4) An ethical element in the conception of the character of the supernatural Power and the modes of pleasing this Power. The ethical side of religion corresponds to the general ethical standard of the people — in savages it is low, but it exists. (5) The conception of salvation as the goal of religious faith and service; the salvation looked for is at first physical, is gradually moralized, and ultimately takes the form of spiritual union with the deity. These are the essential elements of religion; they all exist in crude form in the lowest strata of society, and are purified in the course of social growth.

1150. A classification naturally suggested by this enumeration of fundamentals would be one based on grades of general culture, savage, half-civilized, and civilized; but such a classification would not take account of the differences of character in the members of the higher grades. These differ from one another in the conception of the ultimate Power of the world and of the nature of salvation and the mode of attaining it, and in other less important points. They are so highly composite in structure that their interrelations are complicated, and those that are brought together by one critical canon may be separated by another. Buddhism is allied on one side (the ignoring of deity) to Confucianism and Epicureanism, on another side (the hope of moral salvation) to Christianity. Zoroastrianism touches the Veda in its theistic construction, and is remarkably like Judaism in its organization. Christianity is Jewish on one side and Græco-Roman on another. Islam has Christian and Jewish conceptions attached to the old-Semitic view of life.

1151. A distinction of importance is that between national religions and those founded each by a single man (Buddhism, Christianity, Islam).[2] This distinction may be pressed too far — all religions have great men who have given new directions to

---

[1] On Gautama's attitude toward divine beings cf. Rhys Davids, *Buddhism*, p. 87 f.; Hopkins, *Religions of India*, p. 333 f.

[2] W. D. Whitney, *Princeton Review*, May, 1881.

thought, and no religion can be said to be wholly the creation of an individual man, since all, as is pointed out above, are outcomes of the ideas of communities.[1] The distinction in question is not a satisfactory basis for a general classification since it fails to note the theological differences between the various religions. Nevertheless, it embodies a significant fact: in the course of the history of the world the three religions above-named have come to divide the civilized world among them, that is, they have been selected as best responding to the religious needs of men. No one of them is universal, but the three together practically include the civilized world.[2] They are modified in various ways by their adherents, but they have not been superseded. They have grown beyond the ideas of their founders, but these latter nevertheless occupy a unique position. Moses and Zoroaster are dim figures whose work it is impossible to define, but the teachings of Buddha and Jesus, though they left no writings, are known with substantial accuracy, and Mohammed has expressed himself in a book. The persons of the three founders are the objects of a devotion not given to other leaders. These things justify us in putting Buddhism, Christianity, and Mohammedanism in a class by themselves, of which the distinguishing note is the discarding of local national ideas and usages. These last are not wholly given up, but they are less prominent than in Judaism and Zoroastrianism. It is to the insight of the individual founders that this relative freedom from local features is due. This characteristic does not necessarily carry with it superiority in ethical and general religious conceptions.

A different line of cleavage is indicated by the designation " religions of redemption." In one sense all religions come under this head,[3] for all have for their object the freeing man from the ills of life. In a higher sense the term ' redemption ' means deliverance

---

[1] Kuenen, *National Religions and Universal Religions* (Hibbert Lectures, 1882) ; Tiele, *Elements of the Science of Religion*, i, 43 ff. ; Jastrow, *Study of Religion*, p. 89 ff.

[2] Confucian China and Shintoist Japan are excluded ; but in both these countries Buddhism is widespread. Pure Confucianism is not a religion, and the old Shinto is no longer believed in by educated Japanese.

[3] Cf. Tiele, *Elements of the Science of Religion*, Index, s.v.

from the power of sin and from its punishment, particularly in the world to come. This meaning appears in definite form in Buddhism and Christianity, and somewhat less distinctly in Mithraism and the later Judaism; in the Old Testament religion and Islam it is not clearly stated. As it appears in germinal form in the lower cults, its development may be traced up to its culmination in the systems in which man is freed from moral taint through the agency of an individual savior or in accordance with a cosmic ethical law.

1152. Unity exists among the lowest and among the highest religious systems. Among savage and half-civilized cults there are no important differences — they all have the same ideas respecting the nature and functions of supernatural Powers and the ways of approaching them.[1] In the higher cults a process of differentiation goes on for a certain time while each is developing its special characteristics, and then a counter-movement sets in — they all tend to come together by suppressing local features and emphasizing general ideas.[2] Thus at the present day there are groups of Buddhists, Zoroastrians, Jews, Christians, and Moslems that, without abandoning their several faiths, find themselves in substantial accord on some essential points. The unity of savages is the uniformity of undeveloped thought; the later unity rests on discrimination between fundamentals and accessories.

1153. Tabulated classifications of religions, it would seem, must be arbitrary and misleading — they give undue prominence to some one religious fact, they maim the individuality of cults, and they obscure the relations between certain cults by putting these into different divisions. The true relations between the various religious systems may be brought out by comparisons. In this way individuality and unitary character may be preserved in every case, while the agreements and disagreements may be made clear by referring them to general principles of religious development.

---

1 Myths, it may be remarked, are not confined to the uncivilized and the old national cults; they are found in all great religious systems.

2 See, in this connection, the account of the faith of the philosopher Sallustius, the Emperor Julian's friend, by Professor Gilbert Murray, " A Pagan Creed," in the *English Review* for December, 1909. The term 'pagan' now has a connotation that is singularly out of accord with the character of a man like Sallustius.

CHAPTER XI

SCIENTIFIC AND ETHICAL ELEMENTS IN RELIGIOUS SYSTEMS

1154. It is remarked above [1] that the sphere of religion is wholly distinct from that of science (including philosophy and art) and from that of constructive ethics (the determination of rules of conduct), while it is true that the three, being coexistent and original departments of human nature, must influence one another, and must tend to coalesce and be fused into a unitary conception of life. This process goes on in different degrees in different times and places, sometimes one department of thought getting the upper hand and sometimes another, but we cannot suppose that it ever ceases entirely. The relation between religion and its two companions may become clear from a brief survey of the facts given by historical records, this term being used to include all trustworthy sources of information.

THE SCIENTIFIC ELEMENT

1155. Man is bound by his constitution to inquire into the nature of things, to seek for the facts of the world, including the human soul. This search is made by both religion and science, but their procedures are somewhat different. Religion demands only the fact of an ultimate moral ground of the world; science observes all phenomena and endeavors to connect and organize them by a thread of natural causation or invariable sequence; religion looks behind phenomena to what it regards as its source. This source is reached by some process of reasoning, either by acceptance, on grounds held to be satisfactory, of a divine revelation, or by inference from the facts of the world (as the presence

[1] § 14 f.

573

of design or of moral order); but, when it is reached, all other facts of science are treated as irrelevant. If, then, science confines itself to the observation of sequences, the relation between the two cannot be one of permanent hostility, since their material is not the same. They clash when an old nonreligious belief, adopted by religion, is confronted by an antagonistic scientific discovery; the first result is a protest, but the mind demands harmony, and religion always ends by accepting a well-attested scientific conclusion,[1] and bringing it into harmony with its fundamental beliefs.

1156. Certain phases in the relations between religion and science may be distinguished, but an earlier or cruder phase may continue to exist alongside of a later and higher one. There is first the time when science based on a recognition of natural laws does not exist. The existing science is then one of imagination, the fanciful application of crude observations to the explanation of all phenomena. The *verae causae* are supernatural agencies — science and religion are one. Explanations of phenomena take the form of what we call myths, what the people of the time regard as true histories. There is no place for the conception of miracle; the supernatural agents are all-powerful, one thing is no harder than another, nothing is strange or inexplicable. There is a crude conception of the unity of God and the world.

1157. The period of the rise and decline of the great national religions and the rise of monotheistic cults (along with which may be included Confucianism and Buddhism) is characterized by a great development of philosophy (in China, India, and Greece) and a beginning of scientific research properly so called (especially in astronomy, physics, medicine, and chemistry, in Greece and by the Moslems of Persia). There is a revolt against the older conception of unity. Deities are highly personalized, stand outside of the world, and intervene in human affairs at crises. It is the age of miracles — supernatural Powers, by reason of their intimate social relations with their respective communities, are expected to come to their

---

[1] Examples are the Copernican and Newtonian theories; the magnitude of the stellar universe; Biblical criticism; the theories of evolution and the conservation of energy.

aid in all important matters, and, for most persons, there is no difficulty in holding that they are able to change the course of nature, which is not regarded as being absolutely fixed. In certain philosophical circles, however, this view is rejected, and nature, with its laws, is conceived of as a separate and independent existence, accompanied or not by gods. Science begins to define the nature of deities, and to limit the sphere of their practical activities — this is a precursor of the fall of the old divinities. The old myths are retained, but they are purified, humanized, and allegorized, and in some cases applied to new persons and events, according to changes in religious construction.

1158. The next phase is the recognition by science of the absolute domination of natural law in the world of phenomena. Religion, when it accepts this view, holds fast to the belief in the ultimate personal moral Force, and conceives of this Force as working and expressing and manifesting itself only in phenomena in accordance with natural law — that is, this law is regarded as the expression of the divine will. Science is thus given liberty to investigate phenomena to the fullest extent, and religion is freed from the incumbrance of physical, psychological, and metaphysical theories; the spheres of the two are sharply defined and kept separate. Such a conception is held to differ from " naturalism " or " materialism " in that it recognizes a Power distinct from matter — to differ from what has been called " humanism " (which makes man the sole power in the world), or from positivism (which regards man as the only worthy object of worship), in that it ascribes to the will and activity of divine spirit the high position of humanity as the center and explanation of the life of the world — to differ from pantheism in that for it God is a personal being who enters into relations with a free humanity — and to differ from agnosticism in that it holds that God may be known from his works.

1159. Whatever difficulties may attach to this conception are regarded by its adherents as not insuperable. In all religious systems except Buddhism and Positivism the personality of the ultimate ground of the world is looked on as a necessary datum. In the view under consideration it is held that God exists for the world in which he expresses himself, as the world exists for him, its source and end. The world, with all its parts and incidents, is conceived of as a sacred thing, consecrated to God, and ever striving to realize him in itself, and itself in him. Under the guidance of exacter scientific thought the old crude idea of the unity of the divine and the world is thus transformed into the idea of a unity of will and work. In this conception there is no place for myths, and no need is felt for miracles : histories of the external world and of human society are held to rest on observation of facts, and generally the possibility of miracles is not denied, but they are regarded as unnecessary and improbable — they are thought unnecessary because the conception of the divine character and the religious life are not supposed to be dependent on them, and they are thought improbable because they are held to be not supported by experience. This is the attitude of those persons who accept the conclusions of science; there is, however, great difference of opinion in the religious world on this point.[1]

1160. Certain scientific and philosophical positions discard religion as a department of human life. When it is held that man knows nothing and can know nothing but phenomena, or when, if something is assumed behind phenomena, it is regarded as too vague to enter into personal relations with men, religion as a force in life becomes impossible. In these cases the two conceptions must stand side by side as enemies till one or the other is proved, to the satisfaction of men, to be untenable. Meanwhile it appears that one result of scientific investigations has been to delimitate religion by making it clear that, while it belongs as an influence to all life, it cannot include scientific theories as a part of its content — a result that cannot be otherwise than favorable to its development.

THE ETHICAL ELEMENT

1161. Conduct has always been associated with religion. Supernatural Powers have been regarded as members of the tribe or other society, divine headmen part of whose function it is to see

[1] The general religious attitude may be the same whether the world be regarded as monistic or as pluralistic.

that the existing customs are observed, these customs being ethical as well as ritual. Even in such low tribes as the Fuegians and the Australians the anger of some Power is supposed to follow violation of law. Instructions to initiates often include moral relations.[1] The connection of morals with religion in the more advanced peoples is close. In this regard a distinction is to be made between the creation and the adoption and treatment of ethical ideals.

1162. Ethical codes are never created by religion but are always adopted by it from current usages and ideas.[2] Rules respecting the protection of life, property, and the family are found everywhere — they arise out of natural social relations, even the simplest, and grow in definiteness and refinement with the advance of society, so that things at one period lawful, and accepted by religious authorities, are at a later period prohibited.[3] Kindness to one's fellows is common in the lowest tribes, and in higher civilizations is formulated as a golden rule (Confucius, Book of Tobit, New Testament, and virtually the Egyptian Ptahhotep, the Old Testament Book of Proverbs, Buddha). Truthfulness, fidelity, and justice have been generally recognized as things to be approved — roughly defined and aimed at in rude communities, more exactly defined and more clearly held up as ideals in higher communities. All these virtues are taken up more or less definitely into religious codes.

1163. Less praiseworthy customs and ideas also have been indorsed by religious law. Where sexual license prevails it is made a feature in religious ritual and other ceremonies after it has become a part of social usage and law. It is true that it is generally at first naïve, and, being not illegal, is not a violation of rights and not immoral in the sense in which a refined age regards it.[4]

---

[1] See above, § 172.
[2] Cf. L. T. Hobhouse, *Morals in Evolution*, part ii, chaps. v–vii.
[3] An example is the Old-Hebrew usage respecting marriage with a half-sister or with a wife (not one's mother) of a father. Up to about the seventh century B.C. such marriages were lawful (Gen. xx, 12; 2 Sam. xiii, 13; xvi, 22); later they were forbidden (Ezek. xxii, 10 f.; Lev. xviii, 11). Maspero (in the *Annuaire de l'école des hautes études*, 1896) points out that in Egypt marriage between uterine brothers and sisters in the royal family was not only legal but a sacred duty, its object being to maintain the purity of the divine blood. [4] See above, §§ 107, 180, 219.

But it tends, even among savages, to become socially bad, and, when it survives into times of higher standards, is a corrupting influence. In this bad form it was sanctioned by religious authorities in Canaan (even at one time among the Hebrews),[1] Greece, and Syria, and exists to-day in India as an accompaniment of religious worship. The records of religious cruelty are familiar. Wholesale slaughter, persecution, torture have been abundantly practiced in the name of religion.[2] Many social institutions (such as slavery and polygamy) countenanced by a given age have been adopted in the religious codes of the age. These examples illustrate the fact that religion does not undertake to fix the details of ethical conduct — its rôle is something different. This statement applies to the institution of taboo, as is remarked above [3] — its ritual rules are not moral, and its moral rules are adopted from social usage. It was influential in the organization of society, but not in the way of adding anything to the moral code. In modern economic and other social questions that have an ethical side the details are left to science; religion contents itself with insisting on moral principles as having divine authority, and these principles, as moral, are already recognized by society.

1164. Discrepancy between codes and conduct has always existed — few religious persons live up to the standards that they regard as authoritative. This failure concerns not the sincerity of the religious society in setting up its standard, but the conditions regulating actual conduct.

A natural consequence of the coexistence of religion and ethics in human life has been that each has influenced the other. Advance in the purity and clearness of social ethical ideals has had the effect of modifying not only religious codes but also religious dogmas. The old belief (founded on the conception of social solidarity) that

---

[1] Amos ii, 7; Hos. iv, 14.

[2] The Old Testament command to exterminate the Canaanites (Deut. vii, 2; xxv, 19; Josh. vi–xi) is not historical, that is, was not given at the time stated or at any other time. The Israelites, in fact, settled down among the Canaanites and intermarried with them, and at the time when the passages just cited were written (seventh century and later) there were no such alien tribes in Canaan. But these passages show how a current barbarous custom of war could be regarded by religious leaders as pleasing to God.   [3] See § 630 ff.

a family, tribe, or nation was punished by the deity for the sin of one of its members vanished before the recognition of individual responsibility. The doctrines of eternal punishment and vicarious expiatory suffering are now rejected by some religious bodies and circles as unjust. When they are maintained, it is on the ground that they are not unjust — the appeal is to an ethical principle. Apart from the fact of maintenance or rejection, the tendency is to try all doctrines by moral standards. If they are rejected and yet stand, or seem to stand, in sacred books, then either the statements of the books are interpreted in accordance with the moral standards, or the ethical authority of the books is set aside.

1165. The influence of religion on ethics has been in the way not of modifying codes but of enforcing existing ideas and customs and giving an impulse to moral life. It has commonly furnished supernatural sanctions — rewards and punishments in this life or in the other. How far this conception has been effective in restraining men from actual ill-doing, in furthering good conduct, and in developing inward loyalty to the right, may be a question. To answer this question would require such a collection of facts as has never been made and perhaps cannot be made. We can see that the belief in divine rewards and punishments has sometimes been a real power, sometimes seems to have no effect. The character of the sanctions varies with the growth of refinement, advancing from the crude savage and later ideas of physical pains and pleasures to the conception of moral degradation or salvation. The recognition of rewards and punishments for one's self as incentives to good living is not regarded as immoral if they are not made the chief motive — the prevailing view is that it is legitimate to look for results of action, that, however, devotion to right must always be independent of results that affect only the actor. Whatever the general effect of belief in supernatural sanctions, it must be concluded that the existence of morality in the world is not dependent on this belief. The common social motives for practicing justice and kindness are so strong and so persistent that these virtues must always retain a certain supremacy apart from men's religious creeds. The term 'supernatural' is used above in the more usual sense of 'opposed to natural,' but, according to one religious point of view, all things are the direct work of God, so that there is no difference between 'natural' and 'supernatural,' and the real sanctions of morality are all the conditions of life, external and internal.[1]

1166. The most important elements that religion (though only in its highest form) has introduced into ethics are a grandiose conception of the basis and nature of the moral life, and a tone of tenderness in the attitude toward the deity and toward men. The moral code it regards as the will of God, conscience as the voice of God, morality as obedience to God, all activity as a coworking with God. Nobility is given to the good life by making it a part of the eternal divine purpose of the world. The conception of human life as an essential factor in the constitution and history of the world is common to religion and philosophy, but religion adds the warmth of personal relation with the divine head of the world. Into the philosophical and ethical view of the unity of humanity religion infuses reverence and affection for the individual as being not merely one of the component parts of the mass but a creature of God, the object of his loving care, capable of redemption and union with God. Here again, while there is no addition to the content of the ethical code, there is added intensity of feeling, which may be a spur to action.

1167. In the sphere of religion, as in all spheres of human activity, ideas and tendencies are embodied in human personalities by whom they are defined, illustrated, and enforced — not only in founders of religious systems and other great leaders of thought, but in lesser everyday persons who commend religion, each to his limited circle, by purity of life. The special ethical figures contributed to history by religion are those of the martyr and the saint. The martyr is one who bears witness passively to what he regards as truth at the cost of his life ; he thus differs from the hero, who is a man of action. The martyr spirit is found elsewhere than in religious history, but it is in this latter that it has played its special ethical rôle — divergencies from established faiths always excite

[1] So, for example, Butler's *Analogy*.

peculiarly sharp hostility. When it is pure loyalty to convictions of truth, it is an ethical force of great moment — a permanent inspiration.[1] It is less valuable when it springs from the hope of personal advantage, when a controlling consideration is the belief that one goes directly from the stake (as Moslem warriors believed they went from death in battle) to celestial happiness. There arose at times (for example, in the Decian and Diocletian persecutions of the third century, and in Cordova in the ninth century, when there was no persecution) a fanatical desire for the honors of martyrdom that had to be checked by the Church leaders.

1168. The saint is related to the virtuous man as holiness to virtue. The difference between them is one not of ethical practice but of motive and sentiment — holiness is virtue consecrated to the deity. The saint, like the martyr, is often an ethical power. When the title is given officially as an ecclesiastical honor, it may or may not carry with it moral excellence. In Brahmanism, Buddhism, Judaism, Christianity, and Islam saintship has sometimes been contaminated with physical and ritual ideas and practices, and so far ceases to have ethical value.[2]

1169. The evil influence of the religious point of view on ethical life has been of the general nature already referred to : [3] embalming and sanctifying outgrown and injurious social institutions ; substituting form for spirit ; encouraging asceticism ; drawing sharp lines of demarcation between men on the basis of religious opinions, and so far creating an antisocial spirit.

1170. The development of the sense of obligation to do right (conscience) is due to so many different influences that it is hard to say exactly what part any one of these has taken in the process. But obviously religion has been an important factor in the result

---

[1] It is an exaggeration to say (as has been said) that the sentiment of the sacred obligation of opinion was first formulated or created in the world by the early Christian martyrs — before their time Socrates, Jews in the Antiochian persecution, and probably others, had embodied this sentiment — but the Christian devotion helped to make it a generally recognized ethical principle.

[2] Hopkins, *Religions of India*, Index, s.v. *Yoga* ; Bloomfield, *Religion of the Veda*, Index, s.v. *Baksheesh* ; article "Saint and Saintliness" in *Jewish Encyclopedia* ; Christian hagiologies ; Goldziher, *Muhammedanische Studien* ; C. Trumelet, *Les saints de l'Islam*.　　　　[3] See above, § 1163.

so far reached. By its distinct connection of the favor of the deity with conduct it has tended to fix attention on the latter and to strengthen the feeling that righteousness is the sovereign thing. Though such regard for right-doing is at first mainly egoistic, it easily becomes an ideal, reverenced for its own sake, and more powerful because it is identified with a person and colored by the sentiments of gratitude and love that religion calls forth. Religion, especially in the earlier forms of society, though not only in them, has been a pedagogue to lead men to the acknowledgment of the supremacy of the moral law. It differs from other such guides in the tone of mingled humility and enthusiasm that it gives to this fealty.

1171. As to the existence of moral evil in the world, religion can only regard it as the work of supernatural Powers. In the savage period the question does not come up — moral evil is taken as a part of the nature of things and is not curiously inquired into. In later times it is ascribed to some malevolent spirit or deity who is either independent of the supreme deity (as in certain half-civilized tribes) or is tolerated by him (Angro Mainyu, Satan), or to a subordinate employed by him (lies put into the mouths of prophets by a deity),[1] or to a quite separate divine Power, not necessarily malevolent (as in some philosophical theories). Religion may adopt some philosophical explanation — as that evil is only failure to reach the good, or only the lower step to which we look back from a greater height, or an inevitable accompaniment of a scheme of life characterized by struggle and intended to recognize the freedom of the will and to develop moral autonomy — but, from its own resources it can only say that it is a thing inexplicable by man, belonging to a divine plan that the devout soul accepts as right because God has ordained it.

1172. The theory of man's native incapacity to do right (total depravity), held by some religious bodies, is ·antimoral since it denies human freedom. The attempt to modify it by the supposition of divine impartation of moral power is inadequate unless such power is held to be given to every person, and this amounts to an

---

[1] Ezek. xiv, 9.

indirect affirmation of freedom and denial of moral impotency. The theory is, however, practically innocuous, being rejected or ignored by the universal consciousness of freedom.

1173. To the questions, raised by philosophy, whether the world is essentially good or bad and whether life is worth living, theistic religion gives a simple answer: a perfect God implies a perfect universe; this answer is germinal and confused in early religion, and is definitely stated only in the higher systems. The great theistic sacred books, Jewish, Christian, Mazdean, and Moslem, all teach that though there are present limitations and sufferings, there is to be a happy issue for the faithful out of all distresses, and the Buddhistic view, though nontheistic, is essentially the same as this; as for other persons, they are sometimes included in a final restoration, when moral evil is to disappear, sometimes are excluded from the happy outcome, but in both cases the scheme of the world is regarded as good. Leaving out of view the question as to the exact interpretation of the facts of life, this optimism is ethically useful as giving cheerfulness and enthusiasm to moral life, with power of enduring ills through the conviction of the ultimate triumph of the right. It may pass into a stolid dogmatic ignoring or denial of the existence of evil, and then tends to become inhuman and therefore ethically bad.[1] It is, however, commonly saved from such an unfortunate result by common sense and the instinct of sympathy. And it is so general a conception and its goal is so remote that it cannot be a strong and permanent moral force for most persons — immediate experiences are as a rule more powerful than remote expectations. But, so far as it is a living faith, religious optimism is in the main a healthy ethical factor in life.

---

1 It is this sort of insensate optimism that Voltaire ridicules in *Candide* — a just and useful protest against a superficial view of life.

SELECTED LIST OF BOOKS OF REFERENCE

ENCYCLOPÆDIAS AND DICTIONARIES

Encyclopædia Britannica (9th ed., Edinburgh; 11th ed., Cambridge, England, and New York).

La Grande Encyclopédie (Paris, 1886–1902).

Le Nouveau Larousse (Paris, 1898–1904).

Johnson's Universal Cyclopædia (New York, 1893–1895).

The New International Encyclopædia (New York, 1905).

Encyclopædia of Religion and Ethics (Edinburgh, 1908–).

LICHTENBERGER. Encyclopédie des sciences religieuses (Paris, 1877–1882).

ROSCHER. Ausführliches Lexikon der griechischen und römischen Mythologie (Leipzig, 1884–).

DAREMBERG ET SAGLIO. Dictionnaire des antiquités grecques et romaines (Paris, 1873–1884).

PAULY-WISSOWA. Real-Encyclopädie der classischen Altertumswissenschaft (new ed., Stuttgart, 1904).

GEIGER AND KUHN. Grundriss der iranischen Philologie (Strassburg, 1895–1904).

Jewish Encyclopedia (New York and London, 1901–1906).

Encyclopædia Biblica (London and New York, 1899–1903).

HASTINGS. Dictionary of the Bible (Edinburgh, 1900–1904).

HUGHES. Dictionary of Islam (London, 1896).

Encyclopædia of Islam (Leiden) (in course of publication).

HERZOG-HAUCK. Real-Encyclopädie für protestantische Theologie und Kirche (Leipzig, 1895–1909).

HAMBURGER. Realencyclopädie des Judenthums (2d ed., Leipzig, 1896).

The Catholic Encyclopedia (New York, 1907–1911).

SMITH AND CHEETHAM. Dictionary of Christian Antiquities (London, 1875).

McCLINTOCK AND STRONG. Cyclopædia of Biblical, Theological and Ecclesiastical Literature (New York, 1868–1881).

MEUSEL. Kirchliches Handlexikon (Leipzig, 1887–1902).

WETZER AND WELTE. Kirchenlexikon (Freiburg im Breisgau, 1882–1903).

PERIODICALS

Revue de l'histoire des religions (Paris).
Archiv für Religionswissenschaft (Leipzig).
Le Muséon et La Revue des religions (Louvain, 1882–   )
Journal asiatique (Paris).
Journal of the Royal Asiatic Society (London).
Journal of the Ceylon Branch of the Royal Asiatic Society (Colombo).
Journal of the Straits Branch of the Royal Asiatic Society (Singapore).
Journal of the China Branch of the Royal Asiatic Society (Hongkong).
Journal of the Asiatic Society of Bengal (Calcutta).
Journal of the Indian Archipelago and Eastern Asia (Singapore).
De indische Gids (Amsterdam).
The Indian Antiquary (Bombay).
Transactions of the Royal Society of Edinburgh.
Zeitschrift der deutschen morgenländischen Gesellschaft (Leipzig).
Wiener Zeitschrift für die Kunde des Morgenlandes.
Mittheilungen der vorderasiatischen Gesellschaft and Der alte Orient (Leipzig).
Mitteilungen der deutschen Orient-Gesellschaft (Berlin).
Transactions of the Asiatic Society of Japan (Yokohama).
Journal of the American Oriental Society (New Haven).
Zeitschrift für die Mythologie (Göttingen).
Journal of the Anthropological Institute (London).
Transactions of the Ethnological Society (London).
Man (anthropological monthly) (London).
Annals of Archæology and Anthropology (Liverpool Institute of Archæology).
Archæological Review (London).
Transactions of the Royal Society of Canada (Ottawa, Montreal, and London).
Transactions of the Society of Biblical Archæology (London).
L'Anthropologie (Paris).
Revue internationale de sociologie (Paris).
Annales du Musée Guimet (Paris).
L'Année sociologique (Paris).
Zeitschrift für Ethnologie (Berlin).
Archiv für Anthropologie (Braunschweig).
Archäologische Gesellschaft (Berlin).
Archiv für slavische Philologie (Berlin, 1876–   ).
Jahreshefte des oesterreichischen archäologischen Instituts (Vienna).
Mitteilungen der anthropologischen Gesellschaft in Wien.
Anthropos, Ephemeris internationalis ethnologica et linguistica (Salzburg, 1906–   ).
Archivio per l'Antropologia e la Etnologia (Florence).

Internationales Archiv für Ethnologie (Leiden).
'Εφημερὶς 'Αρχαιολογικὴ (Athens).
American Journal of Archæology (New York and London).
Transactions of the American Ethnological Society (New York).
The Anthropologist (Washington).
American Antiquarian Society (Worcester, Mass.).
Reports of the National Museum (Washington).
Reports of the Bureau of Ethnology (Washington).
Reports of the Smithsonian Institution (Washington).
University of California Publications in American Archæology and Ethnology (Berkeley).
Revue des questions historiques (Paris).
Revue égyptologique (Paris).
Zeitschrift für aegyptische Sprache und Altertumswissenschaft (Leipzig).
Revue sémitique (Paris).
Revue du monde musulman (Paris).
American Journal of Semitic Languages and Literatures (Chicago).
Revue d'Assyriologie (Paris).
Zeitschrift für Assyriologie und verwandte Gebiete (Leipzig).
Beiträge zur Assyriologie und semitischen Sprachwissenschaft (Leipzig).
Revue des études grecques (Paris, 1888-   ).
Journal of Hellenic Studies (London).
Revue des études juives (Paris).
Folklore (London).
Folklore Journal (London).
Revue des traditions populaires (Paris).
Mélusine (mythology and popular traditions) (Paris).
Zeitschrift des Vereins für Volkskunde (Berlin).
Ons Volksleven (Tijdschrift voor Taal-Volks- en Oudheidkunde) (Brecht).
Revue Celtique (Paris).
Celtic Review (Edinburgh).
Mittheilungen der Gesellschaft für jüdische Volkskunde (Breslau).
Archivio per lo studio delle tradizioni popolari (Palermo).
International Journal of Ethics (Philadelphia and London).
Hibbert Journal (London).

WORKS ON THE NATURE OF RELIGION

PLATO. Phædo; Phædrus; Republic.
HUME, DAVID. Natural History of Religion (vol. ii of Green and Grose's ed. of Hume's Essays, London, 1882); Dialogues concerning Natural Religion (ibid.).
KANT, IMMANUEL. Religion innerhalb der Grenzen der blossen Vernunft (Königsberg, 1793; in new ed. of his Works, Berlin, 1912).

HEGEL, G. W. F. Philosophie der Religion (Berlin, 1832; new ed., Leiden, 1890; Eng. tr., London, 1895) (cf. John Caird's Philosophy of Religion, London, 1876).

BURNOUF, E. La science des religions (3d ed., Paris, 1876; Eng. tr., London, 1888).

ARNOLD, MATTHEW. Literature and Dogma (London and New York, 1873).

PFLEIDERER, O. Religionsphilosophie auf geschichtlicher Grundlage (3d ed., Berlin, 1896); Eng. tr., The Philosophy of Religion on the Basis of its History (London, 1886); Philosophy and Development of Religion (Edinburgh, 1899); Evolution and Theology, and Other Essays (Eng. tr., London and New York, 1900); Religion und Religionen (Munich, 1906); Eng. tr., Religion and Historic Faiths (New York, 1907).

GHEYN, J. VAN DEN. La science des religions (Lyon, 1886).

HARTMANN, E. VON. Religionsphilosophie (Leipzig, 1888).

MARTINEAU, J. A Study of Religion (London, 1888).

BENDER, W. Das Wesen der Religion (4th ed., Bonn, 1888).

DEUSSEN, P. Allgemeine Geschichte der Philosophie, mit besonderer Berücksichtigung der Religionen (Leipzig, 1894; new ed., 1899–1911).

JASTROW, MORRIS, JR. The Study of Religion (London and New York, 1901).

EVERETT, C. C. The Psychological Elements of Religion (New York and London, 1902); Theism and the Christian Faith (New York and London, 1909).

JAMES, WILLIAM. The Will to Believe, and Other Essays (London and New York, 1897); Varieties of Religious Experience (London and New York, 1902); Pragmatism (London and New York, 1907); A Pluralistic Universe (New York, 1909).

ROYCE, JOSIAH. Religious Aspects of Philosophy (Boston, 1886); The World and the Individual (London and New York, 1900–1901); The Sources of Religious Insight (New York, 1912).

CAIRD, E. Evolution of Religion (London and New York, 1893).

LA GRASSERIE, RAOUL DE. De la psychologie des religions (Paris, 1899).

BOUSSET, W. What is Religion? (Eng. tr., New York and London, 1907).

HÖFFDING, H. Philosophy of Religion (Eng. tr., London and New York, 1906).

PERRY, R. B. The Approach to Philosophy, chaps. iii, iv, vii (New York, 1905).

SANTAYANA, G. Reason in Religion (vol. iii of his Life of Reason) (New York, 1905).

KING, IRVING. Development of Religion (New York, 1910).

LEUBA, J. H. A Psychological Study of Religion (New York, 1912).

KANT, IMMANUEL. Kritik der praktischen Vernunft (4th ed., Riga, 1797), and see his Collected Works (Berlin, 1912–   ).

MARTINEAU, JAMES. The Relations between Ethics and Religion (London, 1881).

GUYAU, J. M. Esquisse d'une morale sans obligation ni sanction (Paris, 1885; 4th ed., 1896; Eng. tr., London, 1898); L'irreligion de l'avenir (Paris, 1887).

PALMER, G. H. The Field of Ethics (Boston, 1901).

OTTO, R. Naturalism and Religion (Eng. tr., London and New York, 1909).

GENERAL DESCRIPTIVE WORKS

CICERO. De Fato and De Natura Deorum.

BROSSES, C. DE. Du culte des dieux fétiches (Paris or Geneva, 1760).

DUPUIS, C. F. Origine de tous les cultes, ou religion universelle (Paris, 1794; new ed., 1870).

MEINERS, C. Allgemeine kritische Geschichte der Religion (Hannover, 1806–1807).

WAITZ, T. Anthropologie der Naturvölker (Leipzig, 1859–1872).

BASTIAN, A. Beiträge zur vergleichenden Psychologie (Berlin, 1868).

MÜLLER, FR. MAX. Introduction to the Science of Religion (2d ed., London, 1880); Natural Religion (London, 1890); Physical Religion (London, 1891); Anthropological Religion (London, 1892); Theosophy, or Psychological Religion (London, 1893).

SPENCER, H. Descriptive Sociology (London, 1873–1881); Principles of Sociology (London, 1879–1896); vol. i (on religious phenomena) (New York, 1882).

LIPPERT, J. Religionen der europäischen Culturvölker (Berlin, 1881); Allgemeine Geschichte des Priesterthums (Berlin, 1883).

RÉVILLE, A. Prolégomènes de l'histoire des religions (Paris, 1881; Eng. tr., London, 1884); Les religions des peuples non-civilisés (Paris, 1883).

KUENEN, A. National Religions and Universal Religions (London, 1882).

CLARKE, J. F. Ten Great Religions (Boston, 1883; popular ed., 1899).

D'ALVIELLA, GOBLET. Introduction à l'histoire générale des religions (Brussels, 1887); Origin and Growth of the Conception of God (London, 1892); Croyances, rites, institutions (Paris, 1911).

LA SAUSSAYE, P. D. CHANTEPIE DE. Lehrbuch der Religionsgeschichte (Freiburg, 1887–1888; Eng. tr. of vol. i, London, 1892; 2d ed., 1897).

TYLOR, E. B. Researches into the Early History of Mankind (London, 1878); Primitive Culture (3d ed., London, 1891 and 1903).

The Hibbert Lectures (London and New York, 1878–1894).

The Gifford Lectures (London and New York, 1890–   ).

USENER, H. Religionsgeschichtliche Untersuchungen (Bonn, 1889); Götternamen (Bonn, 1896).

FRAZER, J. G. The Golden Bough (London, 1890; 3d ed., 1906–1911); Early History of the Kingship (London, 1905).

KING, J. H. The Supernatural (London, 1892).

Article " Fetishism " in Hastings's Encyclopædia of Religion and Ethics.

TRUMBULL, H. C. The Blood-Covenant (New York, 1893); The Threshold-Covenant (New York, 1896).

MARILLIER, L. La survivance de l'âme et l'idée de justice chez les peuples non-civilisés (Paris, 1894); L'originé des dieux [criticism of Grant Allen's Evolution of the Idea of God] (Paris, 1899).

STEINMETZ, S. R. Ethnologische Studien zur ersten Entwicklung der Strafe (Leiden and Leipzig, 1894).

TIELE, C. P. Geschichte der Religion im Alterthum bis auf Alexander den Grossen (Germ. tr., Gotha, 1895; ed. Gehrich, Gotha, 1896–1903).

MENZIES, A. History of Religion (London and New York, 1895; New York, 1906).

Religious Systems of the World (London, 1896; new ed., 1902).

CARPENTER, J. E. Place of Christianity among the Religions of the World (London, 1904).

Orientalische Religionen (in Die Kultur der Gegenwart) (Berlin and Leipzig, 1906).

BLOOMFIELD, M. The Symbolic Gods (in Studies in Honor of B. L. Gildersleeve) (Baltimore, 1902).

JEVONS, F. B. Introduction to the History of Religion (London, 1896; 2d ed., 1902); Introduction to the Study of Comparative Religion (New York, 1908); The Idea of God in Early Religions (Cambridge, England, 1910).

JOHNSON, SAMUEL. Oriental Religions and their Relation to Universal Religion (1872–1885; Boston, 1897).

WHITE, A. D. Warfare of Science with Theology in Christendom (New York, 1897).

DURKHEIM, E. Définition des phénomènes religieux (in *L'Année sociologique*, ii) (Paris, 1897–1898).

ALLEN, GRANT. Evolution of the Idea of God (London and New York, 1897).

TIELE, C. P. Elements of the Science of Religion (Edinburgh and London, 1897–1899).

BRINTON, D. G. Religions of Primitive Peoples (New York and London, 1897).

RATZEL, F. History of Mankind (Eng. tr., London, 1898).

LANG, A. Custom and Myth (London, 1884); Myth, Ritual and Religion (2d ed., 1899); The Making of Religion (2d ed., London, 1900).

ANDREE, R. Die Flutsagen (Braunschweig, 1891).

USENER, H. Die Sintfluthsagen (Bonn, 1899).

WOODS, F. H. Article " Flood " (in Hastings's Dictionary of the Bible) (Edinburgh and New York, 1900).

SUTHERLAND, A. The Origin and Growth of the Moral Instinct (London and New York, 1898).

LA GRASSERIE, RAOUL DE. Des religions comparées au point de vue socio-logique (Paris, 1899).

INGRAM, J. K. Outline of the History of Religion (London, 1900).

LORD AVEBURY (Sir John Lubbock). Prehistoric Times (6th ed., London, ·1900).

HIRN, Y. Origins of Art (London, 1900).

ELLIS, HAVELOCK. Studies in the Psychology of Sex (London, 1900; and Philadelphia, 1904–1910).

MORRIS, MISS M. The Economic Study of Religion (in *Journal of the American Oriental Society*, xxiv) (New Haven, 1903).

REINACH, S. Cultes, mythes et religions (Paris, 1905–1908).

HOPKINS, E. W. The Universality of Religion (in *Journal of the American Oriental Society*, xxv) (New Haven, 1904).

JORDAN, L. H. Comparative Religion, its Genesis and Growth (Edinburgh, 1905).

DIETERICH, A. Mutter Erde, ein Versuch über Volksreligion (Leipzig and Berlin, 1905).

FARNELL, L. R. Evolution of Religion (London and New York, 1905).

DULAURE, J. A. Des divinités génératrices (2d ed., Paris, 1905).

REITZENSTEIN, R. Hellenistische Wundererzählungen (Leipzig, 1906).

CUMONT, F. Les religions orientales dans le paganisme romain (Paris, 1907 ; Eng. tr., Chicago, 1911).

HAMILTON, MARY. Incubation (London, 1906).

HOBHOUSE, L. T. Morals in Evolution (London and New York, 1906).

Article "Art" in Encyclopædia of Religion and Ethics (Edinburgh and New York, 1908).

PERROT AND CHIPIEZ. Histoire de l'art dans l'antiquité (Paris, 1882–1911 ; Eng. tr., London and New York, 1883–1890).

MEYER, EDOUARD. Geschichte des Altertums (2d ed., Stuttgart and Berlin, 1907–1909).

WESTERMARCK, E. Origin and Development of the Moral Ideas (London, 1908).

PREUSS, K. T. Ursprung der Religion und Kunst.

WEBSTER, H. Primitive Secret Societies (New York, 1908); Rest-Days: a Sociological Study (reprinted from *University Studies*) (Lincoln, Nebraska, 1911).

CONDER, C. R. The Rise of Man (London and New York, 1908).

PLOSS, H. H. Das Kind (Stuttgart, 1876); Das Weib, ed. M. Bartels (Leipzig, 1902).

HARTLAND, E. S. Primitive Paternity (London, 1909).

FRAZER, J. G. Psyche's Task [influence of superstition on the growth of institutions] (London, 1909).

REINACH, S. Orpheus (Paris, 1909; Eng. tr., revised by the author, London and New York, 1909).

FROBENIUS, L. Childhood of Man (Eng. tr., London and Philadelphia, 1909).

THOMAS, W. I. Source-Book for Social Origins (Chicago and London, 1909).
MARETT, R. R. The Threshold of Religion (London [1909]).
SELIGMANN, S. Der böse Blick und Verwandtes (Berlin, 1910).
ELWORTHY, F. T. Article " Evil Eye " (in Hastings's Encyclopædia of Religion and Ethics).
BOEHMER, J. Religions-Urkunden der Völker (Leipzig).
Article "Cosmogony and Cosmology" in Encyclopædia of Religion and Ethics (Oxford, 1912).
CRAWLEY, A. E. Articles " Cursing and Blessing," " Dress," and " Eating the God," ibid.
Articles " Dwarfs and Pygmies," " Dualism," " Fate," " Calendar," " Feasting," " Fasting," " Festivals and Fasts," ibid.
SCHNEIDER, H. Religion und Philosophie (Leipzig, 1912).
CARPENTER, J. ESTLIN. Comparative Religion (London and New York, 1913 (?)).

WORKS ON TOTEMISM AND EXOGAMY

MORGAN, L. H. Ancient Society (London, 187).
SPENCER, H. Principles of Sociology, i, § 171 ff. (London and New York, 1882).
HAHN, ED. Die Haustiere (Leipzig, 1896); Demeter und Baubo (Lübeck, 1897).
TYLOR, E. B. Remarks on Totemism, *Journal of the Anthropological Institute* (1899).
PIKLER AND SOMLÓ. Ursprung des Totemismus (Berlin, 1900).
HARTLAND, E. S. Totemism and Some Recent Discoveries, *Folklore* (1900).
DURKHEIM, E. La prohibition de l'inceste et ses origines, *L'Année sociologique*, i (Paris, 1896–1897); Sur le totémisme, *L'Année sociologique*, v (1900–1901).
ZAPLETAL, V. Totemismus und die Religion Israels (Freiburg (Swiss), 1901).
HILL-TOUT, C. Origin of Totemism among the Aborigines of British Columbia, *Transactions of the Royal Society of Canada* (2d Series, 1901–1902 and 1903–1904).
SMITH, W. R. Kinship and Marriage in Early Arabia (2d ed., London, 1903) (criticized by Nöldeke in *Zeitschrift der deutschen morgenländischen Gesellschaft*, 1886).
LANG, A. Social Origins (London, 1903); Secret of the Totem (London, 1905); Australian Problems (in Anthropological Essays presented to Tylor) (Oxford, 1907).
JEVONS, F. B. Introduction to the History of Religion (2d ed., London, 1902).
MARILLIER, L. La place du totémisme dans l'évolution religieuse [criticism of Jevons], *Revue de l'histoire des religions*, xxxvi, xxxvii (Paris, 1897–1898); article " Totem " (in La Grande Encyclopédie) (Paris, 1886–1902).

WUNDT, W. Mythus und Religion (in his Völkerpsychologie, Leipzig, 1908–1910).
CRAWLEY, A. E. Exogamy and the Mating of Cousins (in Essays presented to Tylor, Oxford, 1907).
RIVERS, W. H. H. On the Origin of the Classificatory System of Relationships (in Essays presented to Tylor, 1907).
THOMAS, N. W. La survivance du culte totémique . . . dans le pays de Galles, *Revue de l'histoire des religions*, xxxviii (Paris); Origin of Exogamy (in Essays presented to Tylor, Oxford, 1907).
GOMME, G. L. Totemism in Britain, *Archæological Review* (London, 1889).
GOLDENWEISER, A. A. Totemism, an Analytical Study, *Journal of American Folklore* (Boston and New York, 1910).
FRAZER, J. G. Totemism and Exogamy (London, 1910).

WORKS ON TABOO

FRAZER, J. G. Article "Taboo" (in Encyclopædia Britannica, 9th ed.).
CRAWLEY, A. E. Mystic Rose (London, 1902); Exogamy and the Mating of Cousins (in Essays presented to Tylor, Oxford, 1907).
GENNEP, A. VAN. Tabou et totémisme à Madagascar (Paris, 1904).
HODSON, T. C. The Genna amongst the Tribes of Assam, *Journal of the Anthropological Institute*, xxxvi (London, 1906).
MARILLIER, L. Article "Tabou" (in La Grande Encyclopédie) (Paris).
TYLOR, E. B. Early History of Mankind, p. 129 ff. (3d ed., London, 1878).
FRAZER, J. G. Lectures on the Early History of the Kingship [holds that taboo is a negative magic] (London, 1905); Taboo and the Perils of the Soul (part ii of 3d ed. of the Golden Bough) (London, 1911).
MARETT, R. R. Is Taboo a Negative Magic? (in Essays presented to Tylor) (Oxford, 1907) [reply to Frazer].
THOMAS, N. W. Article "Taboo" (in Encyclopædia Britannica, 11th ed.).
GAIT, E. A. Article "Caste" (in Encyclopædia of Religion and Ethics) (Edinburgh and New York, 1911).
TAYLOR, R. New Zealand (London, 1870).
ALEXANDER, W. D. Brief History of the Hawaiian People (New York, 1892).

The Hebrew Sabbath as a Taboo Day

TOY, C. H. The Earliest Form of the Hebrew Sabbath, *Journal of Biblical Literature* (Boston, 1899).
DRIVER, S. R. Article "Sabbath" (in Hastings's Dictionary of the Bible) (Edinburgh and New York, 1902).
PINCHES, T. G. Sapattu, the Babylonian Sabbath, *Proceedings of the Society of Biblical Archæology* (London, 1904).

ZIMMERN, H. Comments on Pinches's article, *Zeitschrift der deutschen morgenländischen Gesellschaft* (Leipzig, 1904).

MEINHOLD, J. Sabbat und Woche in Alten Testament (Göttingen, 1905).

WEBSTER, H. Rest Days: a Sociological Study, *University Studies* (Lincoln, Nebraska, 1911).

ON MAGIC

Articles in La Grande Encyclopédie (Paris); Encyclopædia Britannica (London, 11th ed.); Daremberg and Saglio, Dictionnaire des antiquités grecques et romaines (Paris).

TYLOR, E. B. Researches into the Early History of Mankind, p. 129 (3d ed., London, 1878); Primitive Culture, Index, s.v. (3d ed., London, 1891).

KING, J. H. The Supernatural, bk. ii, chap. iii f. (London, 1892).

DAVIES, T. WITTON. Magic, Divination, and Demonology (London, 1898).

TIELE, C. P. Elements of the Science of Religion, Index, s.v. (Edinburgh and London, 1899).

JEVONS, F. B. Introduction to the History of Religion, Index, s.v. (London, 1896; 2d ed., 1902).

LANG, A. Magic and Religion (London, 1901).

HOBHOUSE, L. T. Morals in Evolution, Index, s.v. (London and New York, 1906).

HADDON, A. C. Magic and Fetishism (London, 1906).

WESTERMARCK, E. Origin and Development of the Moral Ideas, Index, s.v. (London, 1908).

HUBERT AND MAUSS. In *L'Année sociologique*, vii (Paris, 1902–1903).

REINACH, S. Orpheus, Index, s.v. (Paris, 1909 ; Eng. tr., London and New York, 1909).

FRAZER, J. G. Early History of the Kingship, Index, s.v. (London, 1905).

MARETT, R. R. Is Taboo a Negative Magic? (in Anthropological Essays presented to E. B. Tylor) (Oxford, 1907).

HARRISON, MISS J. E. Chap. iv of her Themis (Cambridge, England, 1912).

Egypt

ERMAN, A. Life in Ancient Egypt (Eng. tr., London, 1894).

BUDGE, E. A WALLIS. Egyptian Magic (London, 1899).

WIEDEMANN, A. Magie und Zauberei im alten Aegypten (Leipzig, 1905).

BREASTED, J. H. History of Egypt, Index, s.v. (New York, 1905).

Babylonia and Assyria

KING, L. W. Babylonian Magic and Sorcery (London, 1896).

JASTROW, M. Religion of Babylonia and Assyria (Boston, 1898); Religion Babyloniens und Assyriens (Giessen, 1906–).

FOSSEY, CH. La magie assyrienne (Paris, 1902).

Jewish

Articles in Encyclopædia Biblica (London and New York); Hastings's, Dictionary of the Bible (Edinburgh and London); Jewish Encyclopedia (New York and London).
SCHÜRER, E. Geschichte des jüdischen Volkes im Zeitalter Jesu Christi (3d ed., Leipzig, 1901 ; Eng. tr., History of the Jewish People in the Time of Jesus Christ, Index, s.v. (New York, 1891).
BLAU, L. Das alt-jüdische Zauberwesen (Strassburg, 1898).

Arabia and Modern Egypt

WELLHAUSEN, J. Reste arabischen Heidentumes, Index, s.v. (Berlin, 1897).
LANE, E. W. The Thousand and One Nights, Index (London, 1883).

Finnish

CASTRÉN, M. A. Finnische Mythologie (Germ. tr., St. Petersburg, 1853).

India

BLOOMFIELD, M. Eng. tr. of the Atharva-Veda (in Sacred Books of the East) (Oxford).
HOPKINS, E. W. Religions of India, Index, s.v. (Boston and London, 1895).

Greek

HARRISON, MISS J. E. Themis, a Study of the Social Origins of Greek Religion (Cambridge, England, 1912).

Roman

APULEIUS. Metamorphoses.
FRIEDLÄNDER, L. Darstellungen aus der Sittengeschichte Roms (8th ed., Leipzig, 1910); Eng. tr., Roman Life and Manners under the Early Empire, Index (London and New York, ca. 1903).
WISSOWA, G. Religion und Kultus der Römer (München, 1902).
FOWLER, W. W. Religious Experience of the Roman People, Index (London, 1911).

Teutonic

LA SAUSSAYE, P. D. CHANTEPIE DE. Religion of the Teutons, Index, s.v. (Boston and London, 1902).

Noncivilized Peoples

ELLIS, A. B. Tshi (London, 1887) ; Ewe (London, 1890); Yoruba (London, 1894).
CODRINGTON, R. H. The Melanesians, Index, s.v. (Oxford, 1891).
SPENCER AND GILLEN. Native Tribes of Central Australia (London, 1899) ; Northern Tribes of Central Australia [the Intichiuma ceremonies] (London, 1904).
HOWITT, A. W. Native Tribes of South-East Australia (London, 1904).

HOLLIS, A. C. The Masai, Index (Oxford, 1905); The Nandi, Index (Oxford, 1909).

WESTERMARCK, E. L'âr, or the Transference of Conditional Curses in Morocco (in Essays presented to Tylor) (Oxford, 1907).

SELIGMANN, C. G. Melanesians of British New Guinea, Index (Cambridge, England, 1910).

BROWN, G. Melanesians and Polynesians, Index (London, 1910).

DIXON, R. B. The Northern Maidu (New York, 1905); The Shasta (New York, 1907).

SKEAT, W. W. Malay Magic (London, 1900).

RIVERS, W. H. H. The Todas (London, 1906).

CROOKE, W. Popular Religion and Folklore of Northern India, Index (London, 1896).

TEIT, J. Traditions of the Thompson River Indians of British Columbia, Index (Boston and New York, 1898).

BELL, H. H. J. Obeah: Witchcraft in the West Indies (2d ed., London, 1893).

ON DIVINATION

La Grande Encyclopédie (Paris), article "Divination."

Encyclopædia Britannica (11th ed.), articles "Divination" and "Oracle."

Encyclopædia Biblica (London and New York), article "Divination."

Hastings's Dictionary of the Bible (Edinburgh and New York), articles "Divination" and "Soothsaying."

Jewish Encyclopedia (New York and London), articles "Divination," "Astrology," "Necromancy."

CICERO. De Divinatione.

PLUTARCH. De Pythiae Oraculis; De Defectu Oraculorum.

MANILIUS. Astronomica (ed. Theod. Breiter, Leipzig, 1907–1908).

FIRMICUS MATERNUS. Matheseos Libri viii (ed. Pruckner, Basel, 1551); bks. i–iv and bk. v, proem (ed. Kroll and Skutch, Leipzig, 1897).

TYLOR, E. B. Primitive Culture, Index (London, 1891).

KING, J. H. The Supernatural (London, 1892).

ERMAN, A. Handbook of Egyptian Religion (Eng. tr., London, 1907).

JASTROW, M., JR. Religion of Babylonia and Assyria (Boston and London, 1898; and the German ed., Giessen, 1906–   ); Aspects of Religious Belief and Practice in Babylonia and Assyria (New York and London, 1911).

HOPKINS, E. W. Religions of India, pp. 256, 328 (Boston and London, 1895).

STENGEL AND OEMICHEN. Die griechischen Sakralaltertümer (Munich, 1890).

BOUCHÉ-LECLERCQ. Histoire de la divination dans l'antiquité (Paris, 1879–1882); L'astrologie grecque (Paris, 1899).

DAREMBERG AND SAGLIO. Dictionnaire des antiquités grecques et romaines, articles "Divinatio" and "Haruspices" (Paris, 1873-1884).
FARNELL, L. R. Cults of the Greek States, iv, 179 ff. (Oxford, 1896-1909) (Oracles); Greece and Babylon, Index, s.v. (Edinburgh, 1911).
GARDNER AND JEVONS. Greek Antiquities (London, 1895).
WISSOWA, G. Religion und Kultus der Römer (München, 1902).
FOWLER, W. W. Religious Experience of the Roman People (London, 1911).
Article "Sibylla" (by Buchholz in Roscher's Lexikon).
CUMONT, FR. Astrology and Religion among the Greeks and Romans (New York and London, 1912).
WELLHAUSEN, J. Reste arabischen Heidentumes (Berlin, 1897).
Article "Celts" in Hastings's Encyclopædia of Religion and Ethics (Edinburgh and New York, 1911).
LA SAUSSAYE, P. D. CHANTEPIE DE. Religion of the Teutons, Index (Boston and London, 1902).
GROOT, J. J. M. DE. Religious System of China (Leiden, 1892-1907).
Articles "Ancestor-worship," "Ahoms," "Bantu" in Hastings's Encyclopædia of Religion and Ethics.
TURNER, G. Samoa, Index (London, 1884).
FURNESS, W. H. 3d. Home Life of Borneo Head-hunters (Philadelphia, 1902).
RIVERS, W. H. H. The Todas, Index (London, 1906).
THURSTON, E. Omens and Superstitions of Southern India (London, 1912).
ELLIS, A. B. Tshi (London, 1887).
CALLAWAY, H. Religious System of the Amazulu (Natal, 1868-1870).
Article "Dreams and Sleep" in Hastings's Encyclopædia of Religion and Ethics.

ON FOLKLORE

See periodicals mentioned above, p. 587.
FRAZER, J. G. Golden Bough (3d ed., London, 1911).
KEIGHTLY, T. Fairy Mythology (2d ed., London, 1850).
MACCULLOCH, J. A. Article "Fairy" (in Hastings's Encyclopædia of Religion and Ethics).
MANNHARDT, J. W. E. Wald- und Feldkulte (Berlin, 1877).
History of the Æsopic Fable (in Caxton's Æsop, ed. Jos. Jacob) (London, 1889).
JACOBS, J. Migration of Fables (Introduction to his Fables of Pilpay) (London, 1888); Fables of Æsop (London, 1894).
HARTLAND, E. S. Science of Fairy Tales (London, 1891); Folk-lore, what is it? (London, 1897); Mythology and Folktales (London, 1900).
GOMME, G. L. Ethnology in Folklore (London, 1892); Folklore as an Historical Science (London, 1908).

GENNEP, A. VAN. La formation des légendes (Paris, 1910).
Bibliotheca Diabolica (New York, 1874).
CARUS, P. History of the Devil and of the Idea of Evil (Chicago, 1900).

Oceania

BATCHELOR, J. The Ainu and their Folklore (London, 1901).
SEIDENAGEL, C. W. Language spoken by the Bontoc-Igorot [of Luzon] (Chicago, 1909).
EMERSON, N. B. Unwritten Literature of Hawaii (Washington, 1909).

America

BOAS, F. Dissemination of Tales among the Natives of North America, *Journal of American Folklore*, iv (Boston, 1891); Indianische Sagen von der nordpacifischen Küste Nord-Amerikas (Berlin, 1895).
DORSEY, G. A. The Dwamish Indian Spirit Boat, *Bulletin of Philadelphia Free Museum of Science and Art* (1902).

Egypt

MASPERO, G. Les contes populaires de l'Égypte ancienne (Paris, 1882).
WIEDEMANN, A. Altägyptische Sagen und Märchen (Leipzig, 1906).

Asia

BENFEY, TH. The Pantschatantra (Leipzig, 1859); Introduction to Bickell's ed. of the Kalilag and Damnag (Leipzig, 1876).
KEITH-FALCONER, F. G. N. Eng. tr. of Wright's ed. of the Late Syriac Kalilah and Dimnah (Cambridge, England, 1885).
CROOKE, W. Popular Religion and Folklore of Northern India, Westminster (London, 1896).
THURSTON, EDGAR. Omens and Superstitions of Southern India (London, 1912).
The Jesup North Pacific Expedition (New York and Leiden, 1900–　).
BOGORAS, W. The Folklore of North-Eastern Asia as compared with that of North-Western America, *American Anthropologist* (Washington, 1902).
COSQUIN, E. Origine et propagation des contes populaires européens (in his Contes populaires de la Lorraine) (Paris, 1886); Le lait de la mère et le coffre flottant (reprint from *Revue de questions historiques*) (Paris, 1908); Le prologue-cadre des Mille et Une Nuits, les légendes perses et le livre d'Esther (Paris, 1909).

Africa

THEAL, G. M. Kaffir Folklore (London [1872]).
BLEEK, W. H. I. Specimens of Bushman Folklore (Eng. tr., London, 1911).
RIVERS, W. H. H. The Todas, Index, s.vv. *Folklore*, *Mythology* (London and New York, 1906).
HOLLIS, A. C. The Masai, Index (Oxford, 1905); The Nandi, Index (Oxford, 1909).

Europe

GRIMM, W. Die deutsche Heldensage (1829; 3d ed., Göttingen, 1889).
WUTTKE, A. Der deutsche Volksaberglaube der Gegenwart (3d ed., Berlin, 1900).
RHYS, J. Celtic Folklore (Oxford, 1901).
CAMPBELL, J. F. Popular Tales of the West Highlands and Heroic Gaelic Ballads (1872; new ed., Edinburgh, 1890–1893).
BRAND, J. Popular Antiquities of Great Britain (new ed., London, 1905).
SÉBILLOT, P. Le folklore de France (Paris, 1904–1907).
MAURY, L. F. A. Croyances et légendes du moyen âge (new ed., Paris, 1896).
GELDART, E. M. Folklore of Modern Greece (London, 1884).
KRAUSS, F. S. Volksglaube und religiöser Brauch der Südslaven (Vienna, 1885; Münster, 1890).
KNOWLSON, T. S. Origin of Popular Superstitions (London, 1910).
WLISLOCKI, H. VON. Volksglaube und religiöser Brauch der Zigeuner (Münster i. W., 1891); Volksglaube und religiöser Brauch der Magyaren (Münster i. W., 1893).

ON MYTHOLOGY

General

Articles in Encyclopædia Britannica (11th ed.) and La Grande Encyclopédie (Paris).
MÜLLER, K. O. Prolegomena zu einer wissenschaftlichen Mythologie (Göttingen, 1825).
MÜLLER, F. MAX. Comparative Mythology (1856; in vol. ii of Chips from a German Workshop, London, 1858; New York, 1869).
BRÉAL, M. Mélanges de mythologie et de linguistique (Paris, 1877).
PFLEIDERER, O. Religionsphilosophie auf geschichtlicher Grundlage (3d ed., Berlin, 1896; Eng. tr., London, 1886).
TYLOR, E. B. Early History of Mankind (London, 1878); Primitive Culture (3d. ed., London, 1891).
VIGNIOLI, T. Myth and Science (London, 1882).
LA SAUSSAYE, P. D. CHANTEPIE DE. Lehrbuch der Religionsgeschichte (1st ed., Freiburg, 1887–1889); Eng. tr. of vol. i (London and New York 1891).
LANG, A. Myth, Ritual and Religion (2d ed., London, 1899); Custom and Myth (London, 1901).
GARDNER, P. Origins of Myth (Oxford, 1896).
TIELE, C. P. De Oorsprong van myth en godsdienst, *Theologisch Tijdschrift*, iv (Amsterdam and Leiden); Elements of the Science of Religion, Index, s.vv. *Mythology, Myths* (Edinburgh and London, 1897–1899).
JEVONS, F. B. Introduction to the History of Religion (2d ed., London, 1902).

RÉVILLE, J. De la complexité des mythes et des légendes, *Revue de l'histoire des religions*, xiii (Paris).

JASTROW, M. Study of Religion (London and New York, 1901).

SCHULTZ, H. Old Testament Theology, Introduction (Eng. tr. of 4th Germ. ed., Edinburgh, 1892).

Articles " Demons and Spirits," " Earth, Earth-gods " in Hastings's Encyclopædia of Religion and Ethics.

Special

TAYLOR, R. New Zealand (London, 1870).

BÜLOW, W. Die samoansche Schöpfungssaga, *Internationales Archiv für Ethnologie*, xii (Leiden).

BASTIAN, A. Die samoanische Schöpfungssage (Berlin, 1894).

ALEXANDER, W. D. Brief History of the Hawaiian People (New York, 1892).

TURNER, G. Samoa (London, 1884).

BRINTON, D. G. American Hero-Myths (Philadelphia, 1882) ; Myths of the New World (New York, 1896).

EHRENREICH, P. Mythen und Legenden der südamerikanischen Urvölker (Berlin, 1905).

CASTRÉN, M. A. Finnische Mythologie (Germ. tr., St. Petersburg, 1853).

COX, G. W. Mythology of Aryan Nations (London, 1887).

MEYER, E. H. Germanische Mythologie (Berlin, 1891).

GRUPPE, O. Griechische Mythologie (München, 1897–1906).

JASTROW, M. Religion of Babylonia and Assyria (Boston and London, 1898).

MUIR, JOHN. Original Sanskrit Texts (London and Edinburgh, 1858–1870).

HOPKINS, E. W. Religions of India (Boston and London, 1895).

MACDONELL, A. A. Vedic Mythology (Strassburg, 1897).

FARNELL, L. R. Cults of the Greek States (Oxford, 1896–1909).

GRIMM, J. Deutsche Mythologie (4th ed., Berlin, 1875–1878) ; Eng. tr., Teutonic Mythology (London, 1888).

LA SAUSSAYE, P. D. CHANTEPIE DE. Religion of the Teutons, Index (Boston and London, 1902).

CAMPBELL, J. F. The Celtic Dragon-Myth (Edinburgh, 1911).

Articles " Celts," " Cuchulainn Cycle," " Feinn Cycle " in Hastings's Encyclopædia of Religion and Ethics.

COLLIGNON, M. Manual of Mythology in Relation to Greek Art (translated and enlarged by Jane E. Harrison) (London, 1899).

Article " Female Principle" in Hastings's Encyclopædia of Religion and Ethics.

CURTIN, J. Myths of the Modocs (Boston, 1912).

Article " Animal " [on cults of animals, plants, stones, waters] in La Grande Encyclopédie, section iv, " Mythology " (Paris).

THOMAS, N. W. Article "Animals" (in Hastings's Encyclopædia of Religion and Ethics); Article "Animal-Worship" (in Encyclopædia Britannica, 11th ed.).

TYLOR, E. B. Primitive Culture, Index, s.vv. *Stock- and Stone-Worship*, *Mountain, River-Worship* (London, 1891).

COOKE, S. A. Article "Tree-Worship" (in Encyclopædia Britannica, 11th ed.).

American Bureau of Ethnology, *16th Annual Report* (Washington). .

SMITH, W. R. Religion of the Semites, lecture v (new ed., London, 1894).

ERMAN, A. Handbook of Egyptian Religion, Index (Eng. tr., London, 1907).

STEINDORFF, G. Religion of the Ancient Egyptians (New York and London, 1905).

JASTROW, M., JR. Religion of Babylonia and Assyria, pp. 662 f., 688 f. (Boston, 1898).

GARSTANG, J. Land of the Hittites, Index (London, 1910).

HOPKINS, E. W. Mythological Aspects of Trees and Mountains in the Great Epic, *Journal of the American Oriental Society* (September, 1910); The Sacred Rivers of India (in Studies presented to C. H. Toy) (New York, 1912).

GUBERNATIS, A. DE. Zoological Mythology (London, 1872); La mythologie des plantes (Paris, 1878–1882).

FERGUSSON, JAMES. Tree- and Serpent-Worship (2d ed., London, 1873).

CROOKE, W. Popular Religion and Folklore of Northern India (London, 1896).

HOS AND MCDOUGALL. Relation between Man and Animals in Sarawak, *Journal of the Anthropological Institute*, xxxi (London).

ELLIS, A. B. Ewe, pp. 49 f., 98 (London, 1890).

BOETTICHER, K. Baumkultus der Hellenen und Römer (Berlin, 1856).

GRUPPE, O. Die griechischen Culte und Mythen (Leipzig, 1887).

OVERBECK, J. Das Cultusobject bei den Griechen in seinen ältesten Gestaltungen, *Berichte der sächsischen Gesellschaft der Wissenchaften*, p. 121 ff. (1864).

OHNEFALSCH-RICHTER, M. Kypros, the Bible and Homer (London, 1893).

WELLHAUSEN, J. Reste arabischen Heidentumes, Index (Berlin, 1897).

HUGHES, T. P. Dictionary of Islam, Index, s.v. *Kaaba* (2d ed., London, 1896).

LA SAUSSAYE, P. D. CHANTEPIE DE. Religion of the Teutons, Index, s.v. *Tree-Worship* (Boston and London, 1902).

MANNHARDT, W. Baumkultus der Germanen und ihrer Nachbarstämme (Berlin, 1875).

FRAZER, J. G. Golden Bough, Index, s.v. *Tree-Worship* (London, 1907); Adonis Attis Osiris, Index, s.vv. *Animals, Water*, and p. 158 (London, 1907).

Articles "Asherah" and "Pillar" in Hastings's Dictionary of the Bible.

Articles " Asherah " and " Massebah " in Encyclopædia Biblica.
TRUMBULL, H. C. Threshold Covenant, p. 228 (New York, 1896).
HARTLAND, E. S. Primitive Paternity, Index, s.v. *Trees* (London, 1910).
PHILPOT, MRS. J. H. The Sacred Tree, or the Tree in Religion and Myth (London, 1897).

WORKS ON PARTICULAR RELIGIONS

Egyptian

PLUTARCH, Isis and Osiris.
RAWLINSON, G. History of Ancient Egypt (London and New York, 1881).
TIELE, C. P. History of the Egyptian Religion (Eng. tr., Boston, 1882).
LE PAGE RENOUF, P. Religion of Ancient Egypt (London, 1884).
BRUGSCH, H. Religion und Mythologie der alten Aegypter (1884).
MEYER, ED. Geschichte des alten Aegyptens (Berlin, 1887).
MASPERO, G. Études de mythologie et d'archéologie égyptiennes (Paris, 1893); The Dawn of Civilization (Eng. tr., London, 1896).
MÜLLER, W. MAX. Asien und Europa (Leipzig, 1893); Article "Egypt" (in Encyclopædia Biblica).
WIEDEMANN, K. A. Religion of the Ancient Egyptians (London, 1897); Egyptian Doctrine of Immortality (London, 1895); Religion of Egypt (in Hastings's Dictionary of the Bible, vol. v) (1904).
PETRIE, W. M. F. Religion and Conscience in Ancient Egypt (London, 1898); Article " Egyptian Religion " (in Hastings's Encyclopædia of Religion and Ethics).
STEINDORFF, G. Religion of the Ancient Egyptians (New York and London, 1905).
ERMAN, A. Aegypten und aegyptisches Leben im Altertum (1887); Eng. tr., Life in Ancient Egypt (London, 1894); Handbook of Egyptian Religion (Eng. tr., London, 1907).
BREASTED, J. H. History of Egypt from the Earliest Times to the Persian Conquest (New York, 1905); Development of Religion and Thought in Ancient Egypt (New York, 1912).
CUMONT, F. The Religion of Egypt (Eng. tr., in *The Open Court*, Chicago, September, 1910).
REITZENSTEIN, R. Poimandres (Leipzig, 1904).
FOUCART, G. Article " Dualism (Egyptian) " (in Hastings's Encyclopædia of Religion and Ethics).

General Semitic

BAUDISSIN, W. W. Studien zur semitischen Religionsgeschichte (Leipzig, 1876–1878).
HALÉVY, J. Mélanges de critique et d'histoire relatifs aux peuples sémitiques (Paris, 1883).
BAETHGEN, FR. Beiträge zur semitischen Religionsgeschichte (Berlin, 1888).

NÖLDEKE, TH. Sketches from Eastern History (Eng. tr., London and Edinburgh, 1892).

MÜLLER, W. MAX. Asien und Europa (Leipzig, 1893).

SMITH, W. R. Religion of the Semites (2d ed., London, 1894); Kinship and Marriage in Early Arabia (2d ed., London, 1903).

BARTON, G. A. A Sketch of Semitic Origins (New York and London, 1902).

CURTISS, S. I. Primitive Semitic Religion To-day (London, 1902).

LAGRANGE, M. J. Études sur les religions sémitiques (2d ed., Paris, 1905).

Arabian

SALE, G. Preliminary Discourse to Translation of the Koran (1734; new ed., London, 1857) (and in Wherry's Commentary on the Quran, London, 1882).

SPRENGER, A. Das Leben und die Lehre des Mohammeds (Berlin, 1861–1865).

SYED, AHMED. Essays on the Life of Mohammed and Subjects Subsidiary thereto (London, 1870).

AMEER, ALI. Life and Teachings of Mohammed, or the Spirit of Islam (London, 1873); Islam (London, 1897).

TASSY, GARCIN DE. L'Islamisme d'après le Coran (Paris, 1874).

KREMER, A. VON. Kulturgeschichte des Oriento untei den Chalifen (Vienna, 1875–1877).

SMITH, R. B. Mohammed and Mohammedanism (New York, 1875).

GOLDZIHER, I. Muhammedanische Studien (Halle, 1889–1890).

MUIR, SIR WILLIAM. Mahomet and Islam (London, Religious Tract Society; New York, ca. 1894).

CASTRIES, LE COMTE HENRY DE. L'Islam (Paris, 1896).

WELLHAUSEN, J. Reste arabischen Heidentumes (Berlin, 1897).

SMITH, H. P. The Bible and Islam (New York, 1897).

KLEIN, F. A. The Religion of Islam (London, 1906).

LEONARD, A. G. Islam, her Moral and Spiritual Value (London, 1909).

MACDONALD, D. B. Religious Attitude and Life in Islam (Chicago, 1909); Aspects of Islam (New York, 1911).

MARGOLIOUTH, D. S. Article "Mahomet" (in Encyclopædia Britannica, 11th ed.).

THATCHER, G. W. Article "Mahommedan Religion," ibid.

NÖLDEKE, TH. Article "Arabs (Ancient)" in Encyclopædia of Religion and Ethics.

REES, J. D. The Muhammadans (in Epochs of Indian History) (London and New York, 1894).

LANE, E. W. Notes to his Thousand and One Nights (ed. E. S. Poole, London, 1883).

HARTMANN, M. Article "Islam in China" (announced to appear in Encyclopædia of Islam).

MEYER, EDOUARD. Der Ursprung des Islams und die ersten Offenbarungen Mohammeds (excursus in his Ursprung und Geschichte der Mormonen, p. 62 ff.) (Halle a. S., 1912).
TOY, C. H. Mohammed and the Islam of the Koran, *Harvard Theological Review* (Cambridge, Mass., 1912).
GARNETT, LUCY M. J. Mysticism and Magic in Turkey (London, 1912).

Babylonian-Assyrian

JENSEN, P. Die Kosmologie der Babylonier (Strassburg, 1890).
TIELE, C. P. Babylonisch-assyrische Geschichte (Gotha, 1886); Die Religion in Babylonien und Assyrien (in his Geschichte der Religion im Alterthum) (new ed., Gotha, 1896–1903).
JEREMIAS, FRIEDR. Die Babylonier und Assyrier (in Saussaye's Lehrbuch der Religionsgeschichte) (2d ed., Freiburg, 1897).
KING, L. W. Babylonian Religion and Mythology (London, 1899).
JEREMIAS, ALFRED. Die babylonisch-assyrischen Vorstellungen vom Leben nach dem Tode (Leipzig, 1897); Das Alte Testament im Lichte des alten Orients (2d ed., Leipzig, 1906; Eng. tr., London and New York, 1911).
JASTROW, M., JR. Religion of Babylonia and Assyria (Boston, 1898; Germ. ed., Giessen, 1904–   ); Religion of Babylonia and Assyria (in Hastings's Dictionary of the Bible, vol. v) (Edinburgh and New York, 1904); Aspects of Religious Belief and Practice in Babylonia and Assyria (New York and London, 1911).
HARPER, R. F. Assyrian and Babylonian Literature (New York, 1901).
DELITZSCH, FRIEDR. Babel und Bibel (Leipzig, 1902; and Stuttgart, 1903; new ed., Stuttgart, 1905); Eng. tr., ed. C. H. W. Johns (London, 1903); Eng. tr. by McCormack and Carruth [with German criticisms and the author's replies] (Chicago, 1903).
ROGERS, R. W. Religion of Babylonia and Assyria, especially in its Relations to Israel (New York, 1908).
DHORME, P. La religion assyro-babylonienne (Paris, 1910).
ZIMMERN, H. Article "Babylonians and Assyrians" (in Encyclopædia of Religion and Ethics).
LANGDON, S. H. Sumerian and Babylonian Psalms (New York and Paris, 1909); Babylonian Eschatology (in Essays offered to C. A. Briggs, New York, 1911).
TOY, C. H. Panbabylonianism, *Harvard Theological Review* (Cambridge, Mass., 1910).
Articles on Marduk, Nebo, Oannes, etc., in Roscher's Lexikon.

Mandean

NÖLDEKE, TH. Mandäische Grammatik, Einleitung (Halle, 1875).
BRANDT, A. J. H. W. Die mandäische Religion (Leipzig, 1889).
KESSLER, K. Article "Mandäer" (in Herzog-Hauck's Real-Encyklopädie).
GOTTHEIL, R. J. H. Article "Mandæans" (in Johnson's Universal Cyclopædia).

Yezidi

IBN HALLIKAN. Wafayât al-Áyân (Biographical Dictionary) (ed. F. Wüstenfeld, Göttingen, 1835–1840); Eng. tr. by MacGuckin de Slane (Paris and London, 1842–1871).

LAYARD, SIR A. H. Nineveh and its Remains (2d ed., London, 1849; new ed., New York, 1853); Discoveries among the Ruins of Nineveh and Babylon (London, 1853).

BADGER, G. P. Nestorians and their Rituals (London, 1852).

SIOUFFI, N. In *Journal asiatique* (Paris, 1882 and 1885).

MENANT, J. Les Yezidiz, *Annales du Musée Guimet* (Paris, 1892).

PARRY, O. H. Six Months in a Syrian Monastery (London, 1895).

HUART, CLÉMENT. History of Arabic Literature, p. 272 f. (London and New York, 1903).

JACKSON, A. V. W. In *Journal of the American Oriental Society*, vol. xxv, p. 178 ff. (1904); Sketch in his Persia, Past and Present (New York, 1906).

Article "Yesidis" in New International Encyclopædia (New York, 1905).

LIDZBARSKI, M. In *Zeitschrift der deutschen morgenländischen Gesellschaft*, vol. li (Leipzig).

JOSEPH, ISYA. Yezidi Texts (reprinted from *American Journal of Semitic Languages and Literatures*) (Chicago, 1909).

Hebrew, Edomite, Phœnician, Aramean, etc.

KUENEN, A. Religion of Israel to the Fall of the Jewish State (Leipzig, 1873–1874; Eng. tr., London, 1874); The Prophets and Prophecy in Israel (Eng. tr., London, 1877).

SCHULTZ, H. Old Testament Theology (Eng. tr. of 4th Germ. ed., Edinburgh, 1892).

SCHWALLY, F. Das Leben nach dem Tode nach den Vorstellungen des alten Israel und Judentums (Giessen, 1892).

MONTEFIORE, C. G. Religion of the Ancient Hebrews (London, 1892).

DILLON, E. J. The Sceptics of the Old Testament (London, 1895).

GUNKEL, H. Schöpfung und Chaos in Urzeit und Endzeit (Göttingen, 1895).

MARTI, K. Geschichte der israelitischen Religion (3d ed., Strassburg, 1897); Religion des Alten Testaments (Tübingen, 1906; Eng. tr., London, 1907).

CHEYNE, T. K. Jewish Religious Life after the Exile (New York and London, 1898).

BUDDE, K. Religion of Israel to the Exile (New York and London, 1899).

SMEND, R. Alttestamentliche Religionsgeschichte (Leipzig, 1899).

KAUTZSCH, E. Religion of Israel (in Hastings's Dictionary of the Bible, vol. v) (Edinburgh and New York, 1904).

KENT, C. F. History of the Hebrew People (New York, 1896–1899).

MANN, NEWTON. The Evolution of a Great Literature (2d ed., Boston, 1906).

ADDIS, W. E.   Hebrew Religion to the Establishment of Judaism under Ezra (London and New York, 1906).

WELLHAUSEN, J.   Israelitisch-jüdische Religion (in Kultur der Gegenwart) (Berlin and Leipzig, 1909).

LOISY, A.   La religion d'Israël (2d ed., revised and enlarged, Ceffonds, chez l'auteur, 1908); Eng. tr., The Religion of Israel (London and New York, (190).

WALLIS, LOUIS.   The Sociological Study of the Bible (Chicago, 1912).

MITCHELL, H. G.   Ethics of the Old Testament (Chicago, 1912).

BENZIGER, I.   Hebräische Archäologie (2d ed., Tübingen, 1907).

NOWACK, W.   Lehrbuch der hebräischen Archäologie (Leipzig, 1894).

WACE, W.   The Apocrypha (Eng. tr., in Speaker's Commentary) (London, 1888).

SCHÜRER, E.   Geschichte des jüdischen Volkes im Zeitalter Jesu Christi (3d and 4th edd., Leipzig, 1898–1907); Eng. tr. of 2d. ed., History of the Jewish People in the Time of Jesus Christ (New York, 1891).

BÜCHLER, A.   Die Priester und der Cultus im letzten Jahrzehnt des jerusalemischen Tempels (Vienna, 1895).

BOUSSET, W.   Die Religion des Judentums im neutestamentlichen Zeitalter (Berlin, 1903).

RIGGS, J. S.   History of the Jewish People during the Maccabean and Roman Periods (New York, 1910).

HOLLMANN, G.   The Jewish Religion in the Time of Jesus (Eng. tr., London, 1909).

GRAETZ, H.   History of the Jews (Eng. tr., Philadelphia, 1891–1895).

GROSSMAN, L.   Judaism and the Science of Religion (New York and London, 1889).

SUFFRIN, A. E.   Article " Dualism (Jewish) " (in Hastings's Encyclopædia of Religion and Ethics).

WEBER, F.   Jüdische Theologie (2d. ed., Leipzig, 1897).

LAZARUS, M.   Ethics of Judaism (Eng. tr., Philadelphia, 1900–   ).

PHILIPSON, D.   The Reform Movement in Judaism (New York and London, 1907).

OESTERLEY, W. O. E., AND BOX, G. H.   Religion and Worship of the Synagogue (New York, 1907).

BLISS, F. J.   The Religions of Modern Syria and Palestine (New York, 1912).

JOSEPH, M.   Judaism as Creed and Life (London and New York, 1910).

PHILO OF BYBLOS.   Greek tr. of Sanchuniathon (text, Greek and Latin, in K. Müller's Fragmenta Historicorum Graecorum) (Paris, 1848).

CORY, I. P.   Ancient Fragments of the Phœnician . . . and Other Writers (London, 1876).

GUTSCHMID, A. VON.   Kleine Schriften (Leipzig, 1890).

RAWLINSON, G.   History of Phœnicia (London, 1889).

PIETSCHMANN, R.   Geschichte der Phoenizier (Berlin, 1889).

BAUDISSIN, W. VON. Adonis und Esmun (Berlin, 1911).
MÜLLER, W. MAX. Remarks on the Carthaginian Deity, *Journal of the American Oriental Society*, vol. xxxii (December, 1912).
Articles "Edomites" and "Syrians" (announced) in Hastings's Encyclopædia of Religion and Ethics.
ALEXANDRE, CHARLES. Oracula Sibyllina (Greek text with Latin tr.) (Paris, 1841, new ed., 1869).
FRIEDLIEB, J. H. Oracula Sibyllina (Greek text with German tr.) (Leipzig, 1852).
RZACH, A. Oracula Sibyllina (critical Greek text) (Vienna, 1891).
TERRY, M. S. The Sibylline Oracles (translated from the Greek) (New York, 1890).

Asia Minor

PSEUDO-LUCIAN. De Syria Dea.
MEYER, EDOUARD. Geschichte des Altertums, vol. i, part ii (2d ed., Stuttgart and Berlin, 1909).
PERROT AND CHIPIEZ. History of Art in Sardinia . . . and Asia Minor (Eng. tr., 1890).
MESSERSCHMIDT, L. Corpus Inscriptionum Hettiticarum, *Mitteilungen der vorderasiatischen Gesellschaft* (Leipzig, 1900); The Ancient Hittites, *Smithsonian Institution, Annual Reports* (1893, 1894).
RAMSAY, SIR WILLIAM. Historical Geography of Asia Minor (in supplementary papers of the *Royal Geographical Society*, iv) (London, 1890); articles in *Journal of Royal Asiatic Society*, xv.
WINCKLER, H. In *Mitteilungen der deutschen Orient-Gesellschaft* (Berlin, 1907).
HOGARTH, D. G. Article "Hittites" (in Encyclopædia Britannica, 11th ed.).
GARSTANG, J. Land of the Hittites (London, 1910).
WARD, W. H. The Greek and the Hittite Gods (in Essays presented to C. A. Briggs, New York, 1911); Asianic Influence in Greek Mythology (in Studies presented to C. H. Toy, New York, 1912).
ROSCHER. Lexikon, article "Kybele."

Mithraism

CUMONT, FRANZ. Textes et monuments figurés relatifs aux mystères de Mithra (Brussels, 1899); Mystères de Mithra (2d ed., Paris, 1902; Eng. tr., Chicago, 1903); Astrology and Religion among the Greeks and Romans (New York and London, 1912); article "Mithras" in Roscher's Lexikon.

Indian (Vedic, Brahmanic, Modern)

WARD, W. A View of the History, Literature and Mythology of the Hindoos (London, 1822).
WILSON, H. H. Sketch of the Religious Sects of the Hindus (in Asiatic Researches, 1828–1832) (republished, London, 1861).

MACPHERSON, S. C. Religious Opinions and Observances of the Khonds, *Journal of the Royal Asiatic Society* (London, 1842 and 1852).

BURNOUF, EMILE. Essais sur le Véda (Paris, 1863).

COLEBROOKE, H. T. Essays (new ed., London, 1873).

BERGAIGNE, A. La religion védique (Paris, 1878–1883).

MÜLLER, F. MAX. Religions of India (London, 1878).

ZIMMER, H. Altindisches Leben (Berlin, 1879).

LEFMANN, S. Geschichte des alten Indiens (Berlin, 1880).

BARTH, A. Religions of India (Eng. tr., London, 1882).

DEUSSEN, P. Das System des Vedanta (Leipzig, 1883); Eng. tr., The system of the Vedanta (Chicago, 1912).

WILKINS, W. J. Modern Hinduism (London, 1887).

LE BON, G. Les civilisations de l'Inde (Paris, 1887).

LANMAN, C. R. Beginnings of Hindu Pantheism (Cambridge, Mass., 1890).

MONIER-WILLIAMS, SIR MONIER. Hinduism (London, 1890); Brahmanism and Hinduism (4th ed., London, 1891); Indian Wisdom (London, 1893).

GARBE, R. Die Samkhya Philosophie (Cambridge, Mass., and Boston, 1895); Beiträge zur indischen Kulturgeschichte (Berlin, 1903); Akbar, Emperor of India, *The Monist*, (Chicago, April, 1909).

OLDENBERG, H. Religion des Veda (Berlin, 1894).

MACDONELL, A. A. Vedic Mythology (Strassburg, 1897).

HILLEBRANDT, A. Vedische Mythologie (Breslau, 1891–1902).

BLOOMFIELD, M. Religion of the Veda (New York and London, 1908).

HOPKINS, E. W. Religions of India (Boston, 1895); The Great Epic of India (New York, 1901); India Old and New (New York, 1901).

DUBOIS, J. A. Hindu Manners, Customs and Ceremonies (tr. from the author's later French manuscript, by H. K. Beauchamp) (Oxford, 1897).

DUTT, R. C. Civilization of India (London, 1900).

EGGELING, H. J. Article "Hinduism" (in Encyclopædia Britannica, 11th ed.) (London).

BEVERIDGE, H. Article "Akbar" (in Encyclopædia of Religion and Ethics) (Edinburgh and New York).

GRIERSON, G. A. Article "Bhakti-Marga," ibid.

PRIDHAM, C. An Account of Ceylon [the Veddas] (London, 1849).

CROOKE, W. Popular Religion and Folk-Lore of Northern India (London, 1896); article "Bengal" in Encyclopædia of Religion and Ethics; article "Dravidians (North India)," ibid.

FRAZER, R. W. Article "Dravidians (South India)," ibid.

ROBERTSON, SIR G. SCOTT. The Kafirs of the Hindu Kush (London, 1896).

RIVERS, W. H. H. The Todas (London, 1906).

HODSON, T. C. The Naga Tribes of Manipur (London, 1911).

Buddhism

BURNOUF, EMILE. Introduction à l'histoire du bouddhisme indien (Paris, 1844); Le lotus de la bonne loi (tr. of the Saddharma-Pundarika) (Paris, 1852).

Huc, Abbé. Travels in Tartary, Thibet and China (1844–1846; Eng. tr., Chicago, 1898).

Hardy, R. Spence. Eastern Monachism (London, 1850); Manual of Buddhism in its Modern Development (2d ed., London, 1860).

Davids, T. W. Rhys. Some Points in the History of Indian Buddhism (London, 1881); Buddhism (London, 1882); Buddhist India (London, 1903); Buddhism, its History and Literature (2d ed., New York and London, 1907).

Oldenberg, H. Buddha, his Life, his Doctrine, his Order (Eng. tr., London, 1882).

Kern, H. The Lotus of the True Law (tr. of the Saddharma-Pundarika), vol. xxi of Sacred Books of the East (Oxford, 1884).

Monier-Williams, Sir Monier. Buddhism (London, 1890).

Hardy, Edmund. Der Buddhismus (Münster, 1890).

Copleston, R. S. Buddhism Primitive and Present in Magadha and in Ceylon (London, 1892).

Barth, A. Religions of India (Eng. tr., London, 1882).

Hopkins, E. W. Religions of India (Boston and London, 1895); India Old and New (New York, 1901).

Warren, H. C. Buddhism in Translations (Cambridge, Mass., 1896).

De la Vallée Poussin. Buddhisme et religions de l'Inde (Brussels, 1910).

Waddell, L. A. Buddhism in Tibet, or Lamaism (London, 1895).

Grünwedel, A. Lamaismus (in Kultur der Gegenwart, Die orientalischen Religionen) (Berlin, 1906).

Rockhill, W. W. Life of the Buddha and the Early History of his Order [from Tibetan works] (London, 1907).

Beal, Samuel. Buddhism in China (London, 1884).

De Groot, J. J. M. On Mahayana (in his Religion of the Chinese) (New York, 1910).

Hackmann, H. Der Buddhismus (Halle a. S., 1905–1906); Eng. tr., Buddhism as a Religion (London, 1909).

Oltramare, P. Histoire des idées théosophiques dans l'Inde, Annales du Musée Guimet, v (Paris, 1906).

Cowell, Müller and Takakusu. Tr. of Buddhist Mahâyâna sûtras (including the Buddha-Karita of Asvaghosha), vol. xlix of Sacred Books of the East (Oxford, 1894).

Articles (announced) on Hinayana and Mahayana in Encyclopædia of Religion and Ethics.

Suzuki, T. Eng. tr. of Asvaghosha's Discourse on the Awakening of Faith (Chicago, 1900); Outlines of Mahâyâna Buddhism (London, 1907).

Aung, S. Z., and Mrs. Rhys Davids. Compendium of Philosophy (London, 1910).

Haas, H. Article " Amida Buddha unsere Zuflucht," Religions-Urkunden der Völker (Leipzig, 1910).

RICHARD, T. The New Testament of Higher Buddhism (Edinburgh, 1910); Eng. tr. of Asvaghosha's Discourse on the Awakening of Faith (Shanghai, 1907).

ANESAKI, M. Article "Docetism (Buddhist)" (in Encyclopædia of Religion and Ethics).

LLOYD, A. The Creed of Half Japan, Sketches of Japanese Buddhism (New York, 1912).

AIKEN, C. F. The Dhamma of Gotama the Buddha and the Gospel of Jesus the Christ (Boston, 1900) (with bibliography).

EDMUNDS, A. J. Buddhist and Christian Gospels (4th ed., Philadelphia, 1908–1909).

Jainism

JACOBI, H. Ğaina-sutras, vol. xxii of Sacred Books of the East (Oxford, 1884).

HOPKINS, E. W. Religions of India (Boston and London, 1895), and the bibliography there given.

Sikhs

TRUMPP, ERNST. Religion der Sikhs (Leipzig, 1881); The Adi Granth (Eng. tr., London, 1907).

HOPKINS, E. W. Religions of India, pp. 510 ff., 591 (Boston, 1895).

MACAULIFFE, M. A. The Sikh Religion (Oxford, 1909).

BLOOMFIELD, M. The Sikh Religion (in Studies in the History of Religions presented to C. H. Toy) (New York, 1912).

Gypsies

WLISLOCKI, H. VON. Volksglaube und religiöser Brauch der Zigeuner (Münster, Westphalia, 1891).

BURTON, SIR R. F. The Jew, the Gypsy, and El Islam (Chicago and New York, 1898).

GASTER, MOSES. Article "Gipsies" (with bibliography) (in Encyclopædia Britannica, 11th ed.).

Article "Gypsies" in New International Encyclopædia.

Ethnologische Mitteilungen (Berlin, 1892).

Malay Peninsula and Assam

SKEAT, W. W. Malay Magic (London, 1900).

SKEAT, W. W., AND BLAGDEN, C. O. Pagan Races of the Malay Peninsula (London, 1906).

HODSON, T. C. Genna amongst the Tribes of Assam, *Journal of the Anthropological Institute*, (London, 1905).

GAIT, E. A. History of Assam (Calcutta, 1906).

ANDERSON, J. D. Article "Assam" (in Encyclopædia of Religion and Ethics).

Indo-Chinese Peninsula

CABATON, A. Article " Annam " (in Encyclopædia of Religion and Ethics).

Persian

WINDISCHMANN, F. Zoroastrische Studien (Berlin, 1863).
SPIEGEL, FR. Eranische Alterthumskunde (Leipzig, 1871–1878).
HARLEZ, C. DE. Introduction to his French Translation of the Avesta (Paris, 1881).
HAUG, M. Essays on the Parsis (3d ed., London, 1884).
JUSTI, F. Geschichte des alten Persiens, p. 67 ff. (Berlin, 1879).
GEIGER, W. Civilization of the Eastern Iranians in Ancient Times (Eng. tr., London, 1885-1886).
DARMESTETER, J. Le Zend-Avesta (Paris, 1892–1893).
JACKSON, A. V. Williams, Die iranische Religion (in Geiger and Kuhn's *Grundriss der iranischen Philologie*) (Strassburg, 1896–1904); Zoroaster (New York and London, 1899); Persia, Past and Present (New York, 1906); article "Avesta" (in Encyclopædia of Religion and Ethics); Religion of the Achæmenian Kings (according to the inscriptions), *Journal of the American Oriental Society*, xxi (New Haven, 1901).
BROWNE, E. G. Literary History of Persia, p. 95 ff. (London, 1902).
GELDNER, K. F. Avestalitteratur, *Grundriss der iranischen Philologie*, ii; Eng. tr., in Studies in honor of Sanjana (Strassburg, 1904).
SANJANA. Zarathushtra and Zarathushtrianism in the Avesta (Leipzig, 1906).
MENANT, D. Zoroaster d'après la tradition parsie, *Annales du Musée Guimet*, vol. xxx (Paris).
MILLS, L. H. Zarathushtra (Zoroaster), Philo, the Achæmenids and Israel (Chicago, 1906); articles (on Asha and Vohumanah) in *Journal of the American Oriental Society*, xx, xxi (New Haven, 1899–1901).
GRAY, L. H. In *Archiv für Religionswissenschaft*, vii, 345 (Leipzig, 1904).
CASARTELLI, L. C. Philosophy of the Mazdayasnian Religion under the Sassanids (Eng. tr., Bombay, 1889); article " Dualism, Iranian " (in Hastings's Encyclopædia of Religion and Ethics).
MOORE, G. F. Zoroastrianism, *Harvard Theological Review*, vol. v. (Cambridge, Mass., 1912).
DARMESTETER AND MILLS. Eng. tr. of the Avesta (in Sacred Books of the East) (Oxford, 1879–   ).
CUMONT, FR. Article " Mithras " (in Roscher's Lexikon).

Manichæism

BEAUSOBRE, ISAAC DE. Histoire critique de Manichée et du manichéisme (Paris, 1734–1735).
FLÜGEL, G. Mani, seine Lehre und seine Schriften (from the *Fihrist*) (Leipzig, 1862).

KESSLER, K. Mani (Berlin, 1889 and 1903); article "Mani und die Mani-chäer" (in Herzog-Hauck's Real-Encyklopädie) (Leipzig, 1903).
KUGENER AND CUMONT. Recherches sur le manichéisme (Brussels, 1908 ff.).

Druses

SACY, SILVESTRE DE. Exposé de la religion des Druses (Paris, 1838).
CHURCHILL, C. H. Ten Years' Residence in Mount Lebanon (London, 1853).
WORTABET, J. Researches into the Religions of Syria (London, 1860).
GUYS, H. La théogonie des Druses (Paris, 1863).
HERZOG-HAUCK. Real-Encyklopädie, Index, s.v. *Drusen.*
HOGARTH, D. G., AND BELL, GERTRUDE L. Article "Druses" (in Encyclo-pædia Britannica, 11th ed.).

Babism and Bahaism

COMTE DE GOBINEAU. Les religions et les philosophies dans l'Asie Cen-trale (Paris, 1866).
BROWNE, E. G. The Episode of the Bab: a Traveller's Narrative, vol. i Persian text, vol. ii Eng. tr. (Cambridge, England, 1891); New History of the Bab (Eng. tr., Cambridge, England, 1893).
PHELPS, M. H. Life and Teaching of Abbas Effendi [son of the founder, Behåu'llah] — Religion of the Babis and Behais (New York, 1903).
BURNEY, LAURA C. Some Answered Questions [statement of Bahaist be-liefs by Abbas Efendi] (London, 1908).

Armenian

SAYCE, A. H. Article "Armenia (Vannic)" (in Encyclopædia of Religion and Ethics).
ANANIKIAN, M. H. Article "Armenia (Zoroastrian)," ibid.

Ægean

PERROT AND CHIPIEZ. La Grèce primitive (in their Histoire de l'art) (Paris, 1895).
EVANS, A. J. Mycenæan Tree and Pillar Cult (London and New York, 1901); Scripta Minoa [written documents of Minoan Crete] (Oxford, 1909–   ).
Articles in *Journal of Hellenic Studies* and *Annals of the British School at Athens.*
HOGARTH, D. G. Article "Ægean Religion" (in Encyclopædia of Religion and Ethics).

Greek

AUGUSTINE. De Civitate Dei.
WELCKER, F. G. Griechische Götterlehre (Göttingen, 1857–1863).
HERMANN, K. F. Lehrbuch der gottesdienstlichen Alterthümer der Griechen (Heidelberg, 1858).

GLADSTONE, W. E. Juventus Mundi, the Gods and Men of the Heroic Age (London, 1869).
BOETTICHER, C. Baumkultus der Hellenen und Römer (Berlin, 1856).
GRUPPE, O. Die griechischen Culte und Mythen (Leipzig, 1887); Griechische Mythologie (München, 1897–1906).
STENGEL AND OEHMICHEN. Die griechischen Sakralaltertümer (München, 1890).
DYER, LOUIS. Studies of the Gods in Greece (London, 1891).
CAIRD, E. Evolution of Religion, lecture v (London and New York, 1893).
GARDNER AND JEVONS. Greek Antiquities (London, 1895).
MOMMSEN, A. Feste der Stadt Athen (new ed., Leipzig, 1898).
DICKINSON, G. LOWES. The Greek View of Life (2d ed., London, 1898).
FARNELL, L. R. Cults of the Greek States (Oxford, 1896–1909); The Place of the 'Sondergötter' in Greek Polytheism (in Anthropological Essays presented to E. B. Tylor) (Oxford, 1907); Greece and Babylon (Edinburgh, 1911); Higher Aspects of Greek Religion (London, 1912).
ROHDE, E. Psyche, 1894 (3d issue, Leipzig, 1903).
HARRISON, MISS J. E. Prolegomena to the Study of Greek Religion (Cambridge, Eng., 1903); Themis, a Study of the Social Origins of Greek Religion (Cambridge, England, 1912).
HATCH, E. Influence of Greek Ideas and Usages upon the Christian Church (London, 1904).
SEYMOUR, T. D. Life in the Homeric Age (New York and London, 1907).
ADAM, JAMES. The Religious Teachers of Greece (Edinburgh, 1908).
PFISTER, F. Reliquien-Cult im Altertum (Giessen, 1909).
FOUCART, P. Des associations religieuses chez les Grecs (Paris, 1873); Les grands mystères d'Eleusis (Paris, 1900).
JEVONS, F. B. Introduction to the History of Religion (2d ed., London, 1902), chap. xxiii f.
JONG, K. H. E. DE. Das antike Mysterienwesen (Leiden, 1909).
FAIRBANKS, A. Handbook of Greek Religion (New York, 1910).
REIZENSTEIN, R. Hellenistische Mysterienreligion (Leipzig and Berlin, 1910).
Article "Dionysos" in Roscher's Lexikon.
Articles "Mystery" and "Orpheus" in Encyclopædia Britannica 11th ed.
Article "Mystery" in New International Encyclopædia.
BEVAN, E. R. Article "Deification (Greek and Roman)" (in Encyclopædia of Religion and Ethics) (Edinburgh and New York, 1912).
LEHMANN-HAUPT, C. F. Article "Sarapis" (in Roscher's Lexikon).
MAHAFFY, J. P. History of Egypt under the Ptolemaic Dynasty, p. 56 ff. (London, 1889).
STEINDORFF, G. Religion of the Ancient Egyptians, p. 72 f. (New York and London, 1905).
PLUTARCH. Isis and Osiris.

PREUSCHEN, E. Mönchtum und Sarapiskult (Giessen, 1903).

APULEIUS. Cult of Isis (in his Metamorphoses, bk. xi).

DREXLER, W. Article "Isis" (in Roscher's Lexikon).

Religious Relations between Greece and India

SCHRÖDER, L. VON. Pythagoras und die Inder (Leipzig, 1884).

WEBER, A. Die Griechen in Indien, *Literarisches Centralblatt* (1884).

GARBE, R. Connexion between Indian and Greek Philosophy, *The Monist* (July, 1894).

HOPKINS, E. W. Religions of India, chap. xix (Boston and London, 1895).

PRINGLE-PATTISON, A. S. Article "Pythagoras" (in Encyclopædia Britannica, 11th ed.).

Histories of Philosophy, on Pythagoras.

Roman

VARRO, M. T. Res Rusticae (Leipzig, 1889); Res Divinae (from Augustine's De Civitate Dei) (Leipzig, 1896); De Lingua Latina (Leipzig, 1910).

ARNOBIUS. Disputationes adversus Gentes (or Nationes) (Latin text, Vienna, 1875; Eng. tr., New York, 1888).

SERVIUS. Commentary on Vergil (Leipzig, 1881–1887).

MACROBIUS. Saturnalia (Fr. tr., Paris, 1883).

AUGUSTINE. De Civitate Dei.

MOMMSEN, TH. Römische Geschichte (new ed., Berlin, 1856–1887; Eng. tr., London and New York, 1870, 1894, 1903).

ZELLER, E. Religion und Philosophie bei den Römern (in his Beiträge und Abhandlungen) (Berlin, 1872).

BOISSIER G. La religion romaine d'Auguste aux Antonins (2d ed., Paris, 1878).

RENAN, E. Influence of the Institutions, Thought and Culture of Rome on Christianity (London, 1880).

PRELLER-JORDAN. Römische Mythologie (Berlin, 1881–1883).

AUST, E. Religion der Römer (Münster, Westphalia, 1899).

WISSOWA, G. Religion und Kultus der Römer (Munich, 1902).

FOWLER, W. W. Roman Festivals of the Period of the Republic (London, 1899); Social Life at Rome in the Age of Cicero (New York, 1910); Religious Experience of the Roman People (London, 1911).

FRIEDLÄNDER, L. Sittengeschichte Roms (8th ed., Leipzig, 1910); Eng. tr. of 7th ed., Roman Life and Manners under the Early Empire (London and New York [19–]).

GLOVER, T. R. Conflict of Religions in the Early Roman Empire (2d ed., London, 1909).

GRUPPE, G. Kulturgeschichte der römischen Kaiserzeit (München, 1903–1904).

CARTER, J. B. Religion of Numa (London, 1906); The Religious Life of Ancient Rome (Boston and New York, 1911).

REINACH, S. Orpheus [a general history of religions], chap. iii (Paris, 1909; Eng. tr., revised by the author, London and New York, 1909).

ARNOLD, E. V. Roman Stoicism (Cambridge, England, 1911).

Etruscan

HERBIG, G. Article "Etruscan Religion" (in Hastings's Encyclopædia of Religion and Ethics).

Celtic

RHYS, J. Celtic Heathendom (London, 1886).

BERTRAND, A. Religion des Gaulois (2d ed., Paris, 1891).

IHM, M. Der Mütter- oder Matronenkultus und seine Denkmäler, *Bonner Jahrbücher* (1887).

MacCULLOCH J. A. Religion of the Ancient Celts (Edinburgh, 1911); article "Celts" (in Encyclopædia of Religion and Ethics); article "Druids," ibid.

GRUFFYDD, W. J. Welsh Literature (in article "Celt" in Encyclopædia Britannica, 11th ed.).

QUIGGIN, E. C. Article "Celtic Languages and Literature," ibid.

ROBINSON, F. N. Article "Deae Matres" (in Encyclopædia of Religion and Ethics).

Revue Celtique (Paris).

Celtic Review, Edinburgh.

Teutonic

GRIMM, J. Deutsche Mythologie (Berlin, 1835; 4th ed., 1875–1878); Kleinere Schriften (Berlin, 1864–1890).

MÜLLENHOFF, K. Deutsche Altertumskunde (Berlin, 1870–1892).

BUGGE, S. Studier over de nordiske Gude- og Heltesagns oprindelse (1880); Germ. tr., Studien über die Entstehung der nordischen Götter- und Heldensagen (Munich, 1889).

GRUPPE, O. Griechische Culte und Mythen in ihren Beziehungen zu den orientalischen Religionen, Index (Leipzig, 1887).

MOGK, E. Germanische Mythologie (in Paul's Grundriss der germanischen Philologie) (2d ed., Strassburg, 1898).

MEYER, E. H. Germanische Mythologie (Berlin, 1891).

GUMMERE, F. B. Article "Teutonic (or Germanic) Mythology" (in Johnson's Universal Cyclopædia); Germanic Origins (New York, 1892).

LA SAUSSAYE, P. D. CHANTEPIE DE. Religion of the Teutons (with bibliography) (Boston and London, 1902).

CHADWICK, H. M. Article "Teutonic Peoples," p. 683 ff. (in Encyclopædia Britannica, 11th ed.).

MANNHARDT, W. Baumcultus der Germanen und ihrer Nachbarstämme (Berlin, 1875); Antike Wald- und Feldkulte aus nordeuropäischen

Uberlieferungen erläutert (Berlin, 1877); Mythologische Forschungen, *Quellen und Forschungen* (1884).
JÓNSSON, F. Article " The Eddas " (in Hastings's Encyclopædia of Religion and Ethics).
VIGFUSSON, G., AND POWELL, F. YORK. Corpus Poeticum Boreale (Old Norse Poetry, Scaldic and Eddic) (Oxford, 188?).
THORPE, B. Metrical Translation of the Edda (London, 1866).

Slavic

Archiv für slavische Philologie (Berlin, 1876–   ).
MANNS, E. H. Article " Slavs," p. 230 (in Encyclopædia Britannica, 11th. ed.).
USENER, H. Götternamen (Bonn, 1896).
KRAUSS, F. S. Slavische Folkforschungen (Leipzig, 1908).
MONE, F. J. Geschichte des Heidenthums in nördlichen Europa (Leipzig, 1836).

Central and Northern Asia

RATZEL, F. History of Mankind (Eng. tr., London, 1896–1898).
FEATHERMAN, A. Races of Mankind, iv (London, 1881–1891).
PUMPELLY, R. Explorations in Turkestan (Prehistoric Civilizations of Anau) (Washington, 1908).
VÁMBÉRY, A. Die primitive Cultur des turko-tatarischen Volkes (Leipzig, 1879).
HUC, E. R. Travels in Tartary, Tibet, and China (Eng. tr., London, 1859).
KEANE, A. H. Asia (London, 1896–1906); article " Asia " (in Encyclopædia of Religion and Ethics).
KING, L. W. History of Sumer and Akkad, Appendix (New York, 1910).
MOUHOT, H. Travels in the Central Parts of Indo-China (London, 1864).
CROSS, E. B. The Karens, *Journal of the American Oriental Society*, iv (New York, 1854).
KLEMENTZ, DEMETRIUS. Article " Buriats " (in Encyclopædia of Religion and Ethics).
WASILJEV, J. Heidnische Gebräuche, Aberglaube und Religion der Wotyaken (Helsingfors, 1902).
JOCHELSON, W. The Koryak (in Jesup North Pacific Expedition, vi) (New York).
BOGORAS, W. The Chukchee, ibid.
WRIGHT, J. H., editor. History of All Nations, vol. ii, Central and Eastern Asia in Antiquity (by F. Justi, F. W. Williams, M. Jastrow, Jr., and A. V. W. Jackson) (Philadelphia and New York, 1902 and 1905).
WLISLOCKI, H. VON. Volksglaube und religiöser Brauch der Magyaren (Münster, Westphalia, 1893).
CASTRÉN, M. A. Finnische Mythologie (Germ. tr., St. Petersburg, 1853).

Acta Societatis Scientiarum Fennicæ (Helsingfors).
COMPARETTI, D. Il Kalevala, o la poesia tradizionale dei Finni (Rome, 1891).
CRAWFORD, J. M. Eng. tr. of the Kalevala (New York, 1888).
KIRBY, W. F. Eng. tr. of the Kalevala (London, 1898).

Japan

GRIFFIS, W. E. The Religions of Japan (London, 1895).
ASTON, W. G. Shinto (London, 1907).
KNOX, G. W. Development of Religion in Japan (New York and London, 1907).
LONGFORD, J. H. Story of Old Japan (London, 1910).
BRINKLEY, F. In article " Japan " (in Encyclopædia Britannica, 11th ed., p. 222 ff.).
BATCHELOR, J. The Ainu and their Folklore (London, 1901); article "Ainus" (in Encyclopædia of Religion and Ethics).
HOWARD, B. D. Life with the Trans-Siberian Savages (London, 1893).

China and Korea

DOUGLAS, R. K. Confucianism and Taouism (London, 1889).
LEGGE, JAMES. Religions of China (London, 1880); articles "Confucius" and " Lâo-Tsze " (in Encyclopædia Britannica, 11th ed.); Texts of Taoism (in Sacred Books of the East, vol. xl).
DE GROOT, J. J. M. Religious System of China (Leiden, 1892–1907); Religion of the Chinese (New York, 1910); Religion in China: Universism, a Key to the Study of Taoism and Confucianism (New York and London, 1912).
GILES, H. A. Articles "Religions of Ancient China," "China" (in Encyclopædia Britannica, 11th ed.).
GRIFFIS, W. E. Corea, the Hermit Nation (New York, 1901).
LONGFORD, J. H. Story of Korea (New York, 1911).
HOWARTH, O. J. R. Article " Korea " (in Encyclopædia Britannica, 11th ed.).
UNDERWOOD, H. G. Religions of Eastern Asia (New York, 1910).
PARKER, E. H. Studies in Chinese Religion (London, 1910).
CHAVANNES, E. Mémoires historiques, vol. i, Introduction to tr. of the Tao-Teh-King (Paris, 1895).
DVORAK, R. China's Religionen, No. 2 (Münster, 1903).
HEYSINGOR, J. W. The Light of China (metrical version of the Tao-Teh-King) (Philadelphia, 1903).

Oceania

RATZEL, F. History of Mankind (Eng. tr., London, 1896–1898).
FRAZER, J. G. Totemism and Exogamy, Index (London, 1910); The Belief in Immortality and the Worship of the Dead (the Gifford Lectures, 1911–1912) (London and New York).

BASTIAN A. Inselgruppen in Oceania (Berlin, 1883).
KEANE, A. H. Article "Australasia" (in Encyclopædia of Religion and Ethics).

Polynesia

MARINER, W. Tonga Islands (London, 1817).
GREY, G. Polynesian Mythology (Auckland, 1885).
ELLIS, W.· Polynesian Researches (London, 1859); Tour around Hawaii (London, 1829).
JARVES, J. J. History of the Hawaiian Islands (Honolulu, 1872).
BASTIAN, A. Zur Kenntniss Hawaiis (Berlin, 1883).
ALEXANDER, W. D. Brief History of the Hawaiian People (London, 1892).
ACHELIS, THOS. Ueber Mythologie und Cultus von Hawaii, 1895 (reprint from Ausland, 1893).
TAYLOR, R. New Zealand and its Inhabitants (London, 1870).
GILL, W. Myths and Songs of the South Pacific (London, 1876).
TURNER, G. Samoa (London, 1884).
KRÄMER, A. Hawaii, Ostmikronesien und Samoa (Stuttgart, 1906).
TREGEAR, E. The Maori race (Wanganui, New Zealand, 1904).
SHORTLAND, E. Traditions and Superstitions of the New Zealanders (London, 1854).
BÄSSLER, A. Südsee Bilder (Berlin, 1895); Neue Südsee Bilder (Berlin, 1900).

Melanesia

WILLIAMS, J., AND CALVERT, J. Fiji and the Fijians (London, 1870).
CODRINGTON, R. H. The Melanesians (Oxford, 1891).
SELIGMANN, C. G. The Melanesians of British New Guinea (Cambridge, England, 1910).
BROWN, GEORGE. Melanesians and Polynesians (London and New York, 1910).
FURNESS, W. H., 3d. The Island of Stone-Money (Uap of the Carolines), (Philadelphia and London, 1910).

Australia and Tasmania

SPENCER, B., AND GILLEN, J. Native Tribes of Central Australia (London, 1899); Northern Tribes of Central Australia (London, 1904).
HOWITT, A. W. Native Tribes of South-East Australia (London, 1904).
PARKER, MRS. K. L. The Euahlayi Tribe (London, 1905).
GENNEP, A. v. Mythes et légendes d'Australie (Paris, 1906).
THOMAS, N. W. Native Tribes of Australia (London, 1907); article "Australia" (in Encyclopædia of Religion and Ethics).
TYLOR, E. B. On the Tasmanians as Representatives of Palæolithic Man, *Journal of the Anthropological Institute*, xxiii.

Malay Archipelago and the Philippines

MARSDEN, W. History of Sumatra (London, 1811).
BOCK, C. Head-hunters of Borneo (London, 1881).

MAN, E. H. The Aboriginal Inhabitants of the Andaman Islands, *Journal of the Anthropological Institute*, xii (London, 1885).
WALLACE, A. R. The Malay Archipelago (London, 1890).
WILKEN, G. A. Het shamanisme bij de volken van den Indischen Archipel ('S-Hage, 1887).
KRUIJT, A. C. Het animisme in den indischen Archipel ('S-Gravenhage, 1906).
SARASIN, P. AND F. Die Weddas von Ceylon und die umgebenden Völkerschaften (Wiesbaden, 1893).
ROTH, H. L. The Natives of Sarawak and British North Borneo (London, 1896).
HADDON, A. C. Head-hunters, Black, White and Brown (London, 1901).
FURNESS, W. H., 3d. Home-life of Borneo Head-hunters (Philadelphia, 1902).
MORRIS, MISS M. Harvest Gods of the Land Dyaks of Borneo, *Journal of the American Oriental Society* (July, 1905).
HURGRONYE, C. SNOUCK. The Achehnese (London, 1906).
WARNECK, J. Die Religion der Batak (in J. Böhmer's Religionsurkunden der Völker, Abth. iv, Bd. i) (Leipzig, 1909).
Reports of the Bureau of Ethnology of the Philippine Government.
Journal of American Folklore.
Philippine Journal of Science, Manila.
Bureau of American Ethnology.
BLUMENTRITT, F. Diccionario mitologico de Philippinas (2d ed., Madrid, 1895).
BEYER, H. O., AND BARTON, R. F. An Ifugao Burial Ceremony (reprint from *Philippine Journal of Science*) (1911).

NORTH AMERICA

Relation des Jésuites de la Nouvelle France [17th century] (edited, with Eng. tr., by R. G. Thwaites, Cleveland, 1901).
PARKMAN, F. The Jesuits in North America in the Seventeenth Century (London, 1867).
WILLIAMS, ROGER. Key into the Language of America (London, 1643).
HODGE, F. W. Handbook of American Indians North of Mexico (Washington, 1907-1910).
Journal of American Folklore (Boston and New York).
SMITH, JOHN. General History of Virginia (London, 1627; new issue, 1907).
STRACHEY, W. Historie of Travaile into Virginia Britannia (1618; ed. R. H. Major, London, 1849).
HENDERSON, S. R. The Government and Religion of the Virginia Indians, *Johns Hopkins University Studies in History and Political Science*, xiii (Baltimore).
MÜLLER, J. G. Geschichte der amerikanischen Urreligionen (Basel, 1867).

SCHOOLCRAFT, H. R. Indian Tribes of the United States (Philadelphia, 1851–1860).

BANCROFT, H. H. Native Races of the Pacific States of North America (New York, 1875–1876).

WINSOR, J. Narrative and Critical History of America (Boston, 1889).

PAYNE, E. J. History of the New World, called America (Oxford, 1899).

CUSHING, F. H. My Adventures in Zuñi, Century Magazine (New York, May, 1883).

FLETCHER, ALICE. Indian Ceremonies (from the Sixteenth Report of the Peabody Museum of American Archæology and Ethnology (Cambridge, Mass., 1883) (Salem, Mass., 1884).

GATSCHET, A. S. A Migration Legend of the Creek Indians (Philadelphia, 1884).

BRINTON, D. G. The Lenâpé and their Legends (Philadelphia, 1885).

FEWKES, J. W. The Winter Solstice Ceremony at Walpi (reprinted from the American Anthropologist, xi) (Washington, 1898).

MATTHEWS, W. Navaho Legends (Boston and New York, 1897).

BOAS, F. The Indians of British Columbia (reprinted from Report of the British Association, 1889) (London); The Kwakiutl (Washington, 1897).

TEIT, J. Traditions of the Thompson River Indians of British Columbia (Boston and New York, 1898).

MORICE, A. G. Notes . . . on the Western Dénés, Transactions of the Canadian Institute (1894).

WILL, G. F., AND SPINDEN, H. J. The Mandans [of North Dakota], (Peabody Museum, Cambridge, Mass., 1906).

HILL-TOUT, C. British North America (the Far West) (London, 1907).

DIXON, R. B. The Northern Maidu [of California], Bulletin of American Museum of Natural History, vol. xvii (New York, 1905); The Shasta (California), ibid. (New York, 1907); The Chimariko Indians, University of California Publications in American Archæology and Ethnology (Berkeley, 1910).

CRANZ, D. History of Greenland (London, 1820).

RINK, H. J. Tales and Traditions of the Eskimo (Edinburgh and London, 1875); The Eskimo Tribes (Copenhagen and London, 1887).

BOAS, F. The Central Eskimo, Reports of the Bureau of Ethnology, 1884–1885 (Washington, 1888).

RASMUSSEN, KNUD. People of the Polar North (London, 1908).

RADIN, P., AND GRAY, L. H. Article "Eskimos" (in Hastings's Encyclopædia of Religion and Ethics).

Mormonism

RILEY, I. W. The Founder of Mormonism, a Psychological Study of Joseph Smith (New York, 1902).

LINN, W. A. The Story of the Mormons . . . to the Year 1901 (New York, 1902).

MEYER, EDOUARD. Ursprung und Geschichte der Mormonen (Halle a. S., 1912).

Mexico

SAHAGUN, F. B. DE. Historia general de las cosas de Nueva España (Mexico, 1829–1830, and Fr. tr.).

ACOSTA, J. DE. Historia de las Indias (Eng. tr., C. R. Markham, London, ' 1880).

HERRERA, A. DE. Historia de las Indias Ocidentales (Eng. tr., London, 1825–1826).

SELER, E. Altmexikanische Studien, *Publications of Berlin Museum für Völkerkunde*, vi (1899); Gesammelte Abhandlungen zur amerikanischen Sprach- und Alterthumskunde (Berlin, 1902–1909).

PRESCOTT, W. H. Conquest of Mexico (Boston, 1843).

RÉVILLE, A. Native Religions of Mexico and Peru (London, 1884).

SPENCE, L. Mythologies of Ancient Mexico and Peru (London, 1907).

PREUSS, K. T. Die Feuergötter als Ausgangspunkt zum Verständniss der mexikanischen Religion, *Mitteilungen der* [Wiener] *anthropologischen Gesellschaft* (1903).

NUTALL, ZELIA. A Penitential Rite of the Ancient Mexicans, *Archæological and Ethnological Papers of the Peabody Museum, Harvard University* (Cambridge, Mass., 1904).

TOY, C. H. Mexican Human Sacrifice, *Journal of American Folklore* (Boston and New York, 1905).

CENTRAL AMERICA

BRINTON, D. G. The Names of the Gods in the Kiche Myths of Central America, *Proceedings of the American Philosophical Society* (Philadelphia, 1881); The Annals of the Cakchiquels (Philadelphia, 1885); Nagualism, a Study in Native American Folklore and History (Philadelphia, 1894).

SCHELLHAS, P. Representations of Deities of the Maya Mss. (Eng. tr. of 2d ed. in *Papers of the Peabody Museum, Harvard University*) (Cambridge, Mass., 1904).

TOZZER, A. M. Comparative Study of the Mayas and Lacandones [of Yucatan] (New York and London, 1907).

Porto Rico

FEWKES, J. W. Aborigines of Porto Rico (in *Reports of the Bureau of Ethnology*, xxv) (Washington).

SOUTH AMERICA

LA VEGA, GARCILASO DE. Comentarios reales de los Incas (1609; Eng. tr., ed. C. R. Markham, Rites and Laws of the Yncas) (London, 1870).

PRESCOTT, W. H. Conquest of Peru (Boston, 1847).

BERNAU, J. H. Missionary Labors in British Guiana (London, 1847).
IM THURN, F. Among the Indians of Guiana (London, 1883).
RÉVILLE and SPENCE. See under ' Mexico.'
HYADES, P., AND DENIKER, J. Mission scientifique du Cap Horn (Paris, 1882–1883, 1891–   ).
VON DEN STEINEN, K. Unter den Naturvölkern Zentral-Brasiliens (Berlin, 1894).
BÄSSLER, A. Altperuanische Kunst (1902).
EHRENREICH, P. Mýthen und Legenden der südamerikanischen Urvölker (Berlin, 1905).
FARABEE, W. C. Some Customs of the [Peruvian] Machegongos (reprinted from Proceedings of the American Antiquarian Society) (Worcester, 1909).

AFRICA

WAITZ-GARLAND. Anthropologie der Naturvölker (Leipzig, 1859–1872).
ELLIS, W. History of Madagascar (London, 1838).
FRITSCH, G. Die Eingeborenen Süd-Afrika's (Breslau, 1872).
HAHN, TH. Tsuni-Goam, the Supreme Being of the Khoi-Khoi (London, 1881).
MACDONALD, D. Africana (London, 1882).
MACDONALD, J. Manners, Customs, Superstitions and Religions of South-African Tribes, Journal of the Anthropological Institute, xix, xx (London); East Central African Customs, ibid., xxii (London, 1893).
CALLAWAY, H. Religious System of the Amazulu (Natal, 1868–1870).
ELLIS, A. B. The Tshi-speaking Peoples of the Gold Coast of West Africa (London, 1887); The Ewe-speaking Peoples of the Slave Coast of West Africa (London, 1890); The Yoruba-speaking Peoples of the Slave Coast of West Africa (London, 1894).
SCHNEIDER, W. Religion der afrikanischen Naturvölker (Münster, Westphalia, 1891).
HANOTEAU, A., AND LETOURNEAUX, A. La Kabylie (2d ed., Paris, 1893).
WESTERMARCK, E. Nature of the Arab Ğinn, Journal of the Anthropological Institute (London, 1900); L'âr, or the Transference of Conditional Curses in Morocco (in Anthropological Essays presented to E. B. Tylor) (Oxford, 1907).
KINGSLEY, MARY. Travels in West Africa (London, 1897); West African Studies (London, 1901).
THEAL, G. M. Records of South-Eastern Africa (London, 1898–1900); History and Ethnography of South Africa (London, 1907–1910).
QUATREFAGES, A. DE. The Pygmies (Eng. tr., New York, 1895).
JOHNSTON, H. The Pygmies of the Great Congo Forest, Smithsonian Institution Reports, 1902 (Washington).
SCHMIDT, W. Stellung der Pygmäenvölker in der Entwicklungsgeschichte des Menschen (Stuttgart, 1910).

MAC-RITCHIE, D. Article "Dwarfs and Pygmies" (in Hastings's Encyclopædia of Religion and Ethics).

FROBENIUS, L. Ursprung der afrikanischen Kulturen (1898; Eng. tr. in *Smithsonian Institution Reports*, 1898, Washington).

HINDE, S. L., AND MRS. HILDEGARDE. The Last of the Masai (London, 1901).

HOLLIS, A. C. The Masai (Oxford, 1905); The Nandi (Oxford, 1909).

NASSAU, R. H. Fetichism in West Africa (London, 1904).

KIDD, D. The Essential Kafir (London, 1904).

JOHNSTON, H. The Uganda Protectorate (London, 1904).

PARTRIDGE, C. Cross River Natives (London, 1905).

ROSCOE, J. Manners and Customs of the Baganda, *Journal of the Anthropological Institute*, xxxi, xxxii (London); The Bahima, ibid, xxxvii (London).

BRUN, P. Croyances et pratiques religieuses des Malinkés fétichistes, *Anthropos*, ii (Salzburg, 1907).

LEONARD, A. G. The Lower Niger and its Tribes (London, 1906).

MILLIGAN, R. H. The Fetish Folk of West Africa (New York, 1912).

INDEX

(The Arabic figures refer to paragraphs)